AFGHANISTAN RISING

Afghanistan Rising

Islamic Law and Statecraft between the Ottoman and British Empires

FAIZ AHMED

HARVARD UNIVERSITY PRESS
Cambridge, Massachusetts
London, England
2017

Second printing

Library of Congress Cataloging-in-Publication Data

Names: Ahmed, Faiz, 1980– author.
Title: Afghanistan rising : Islamic law and statecraft between the Ottoman and British empires / Faiz Ahmed.
Description: Cambridge, Massachusetts : Harvard University Press, 2017. | Includes bibliographical references and index.
Identifiers: LCCN 2017014627 | ISBN 9780674971943 (alk. paper)
Subjects: LCSH: Law—Afghanistan—History. | Islamic law—Afghanistan—History. | Constitutional history—Afghanistan. | Afghanistan—Politics and government. | Afghanistan—Relations—Turkey. | Turkey—Relations—Afghanistan. | Afghanistan—Relations—India. | India—Relations—Afghanistan.
Classification: LCC KNF68 .A366 2017 | DDC 349.581— dc23
LC record available at https://lccn.loc.gov/2017014627

For all daughters and sons of Afghanistan.

And the world.

CONTENTS

MAPS AND ILLUSTRATIONS

MAPS

FIGURES

NOTE ON TRANSLITERATION AND USAGE

This book draws on sources in Afghan Persian (also known as Dari or Kabuli Persian), Arabic, Ottoman Turkish, Pashto, and Urdu, and utilizes up to four calendars as methods of dating. The following standards are adopted to balance orthographic and chronological consistency with an appreciation for the pluralism at the heart of the subject matter.

Translation and Transliteration

Words found in the Merriam-Webster Dictionary (e.g., amir, effendi, Kandahar, pasha, ulema) are not translated or transliterated. Barring those exceptions, Ottoman Turkish words are transliterated to republican Turkish following the *International Journal of Middle East Studies* (*IJMES*) (hence Abdülmecid, not ʿAbd al-Majid). Dari, Pashto, and Urdu words are transliterated according to Persian usage following *IJMES*, with two exceptions: first, preserving the common Dari pronunciation of و as *w*, and not *v* (hence Wali, not Vali); second, retaining the common Anglicized spellings of Pashtun suffixes as *-zai* (hence Barakzai, not Barakzaʾi or Barakzay) as well as the names of Indian authors who published in English (hence Abdul Ghani Khan, not ʿAbd al-Ghani Khan). Southern / Kandahari dialect of Pashto has been preferred over eastern / Peshawari "Pakhto." In all other cases the default transliteration system is Arabic following *IJMES*. The following pronunciation guide is provided for readers' reference.

Long Vowels in Arabic, Dari / Persian, Pashto, and Urdu

ā	a, as in *basket*
ī	ee, as in *tree*
ū	oo, as in *zoo*

Distinctive Turkish Letters

c	j, as in *jasmine*
ç	ch, as in *charity*
ğ	unvocalized; lengthens preceding vowel
ı	u, as in *up* (upper case: I)
İ	upper case of the letter *i*
ö	as the German *ö*, or as *eu* in the French word *deux*
ş	sh, as in *shine*
ü	as the German *ü*, or as *u* in the French word *tu*

Calendars

Historical records and manuscripts cited in this book employ one or more of the following calendars as chronological techniques: Gregorian (CE), Hijri, Ottoman Rumi, and Persian Jalali. The Hijri calendar is the Islamic lunar calendar dating to the migration (*Hijra*) of the Prophet from Mecca to Medina in 622 CE. Traditionally, Hijri months begin and end based on confirmed local sightings of the new crescent moon with the naked eye, hence leaving room for minor variation between locales of great distance before the advent of modern telecommunications. The Ottoman Rumi calendar (also known as Maliye, or fiscal calendar) is solar-based and derived from the Roman Julian dating system, but with a start date from the Hijra. Persian Jalali is the official solar calendar of Afghanistan and Iran, also with a start date from the Hijra.

For precision and consistency, Gregorian dates are used by default, whereas Hijri (h), Rumi (r), and Jalali (j) dates are followed by their equivalent Gregorian date or approximate Gregorian year range, as in the following examples:

(1294h Ş 20 / 1877 08 29)
(1330r / 1914–1915)
(1302j Mizan 24 / 1923 10 17)

For the Persian Jalali calendar, Afghan Dari month names have been used in place of their Iranian equivalents.

AFGHANISTAN RISING

Introduction

ON MAY 17, 1929, an intrepid high school student in Los Angeles, California, sat at his desk, pulled out a sheet of paper and pencil, and began his homework. A particularly daunting class project had been weighing on his shoulders, and time to procrastinate was running out. His assignment: to find primary source material on the state of law and government in Afghanistan. At a loss with where to begin, the young Edison Ostrom was aware the British Raj had a thorny relationship with the Forbidden Kingdom, as Afghanistan had been infamously known in English novels and newspapers since Victorian times. So he decided to press his case with the British Embassy in Washington, D.C. Edison's handwritten letter, still legible in faded pencil lead, was forthright in its request: "Our class here in school has been studying Asia but has been unable to get any up to date material on Afghanistan," Ostrom confessed. "Would you please inform me what the present form of government is." Before affixing his signature, Edison could not resist scribbling a final query at the letter's close: whether London would confirm rumors that famed British superspy T. E. Lawrence was involved in covert operations against the Kabul government from the tribal zone of northwestern India, as he had been over a decade earlier against the Ottomans in Arabia.

Two months later, Edison received a response, but from a source much closer to the action than he expected: Simla, northern India, the summer capital of the British Raj. In a formal reply from the Foreign and Political Department of the government of India, veteran Raj official Sir James Glasgow Acheson first lauded the youth's initiative—"the enterprise displayed in which undoubtedly deserves encouragement"—but regretted to inform him that "there is unfortunately no generally recognized central Government in Afghanistan, which is in a state of civil war." As for the purported role of Colonel Lawrence in the Afghan tumult, Sir Acheson was resolute and dismissive: "These rumours, which were partly due to anti-British propaganda and partly to sensationalism pure and simple are absolutely without any foundation of any kind."[1]

The student from Los Angeles had received an answer, but reasonable minds could differ as to its educational value. Though not exactly inaccurate, the transoceanic letter exchange was noticeably silent on Afghanistan's more positive and instructive achievements in recent years, including its independence from Britain in 1919 and the promulgation of its first constitution in 1923, among other milestones in law, governance, and diplomacy in that decade alone. Instead, one student's search for reliable material on the country yielded an ahistorical portrait bereft of context—just another day of mayhem in Afghanistan, so it would seem. In the end, perhaps a fixation on motifs of war, chaos, and regime change by the questioner and questioned here is not so remarkable. Nearly a century later, after all, when it comes to Afghanistan many a writer and reader continue to be drawn to the same themes.

Challenging conventional narratives of Afghanistan as a perennial war zone, and the rule of law as a secular-liberal monopoly, this book presents an account of the first Muslim-majority country to gain independence, codify its own laws, and ratify a constitution after the fall of the Ottoman Empire. If Afghanistan seems an unexpected candidate for this distinction, it is because historical approaches to Afghan law and governance before the Soviet invasion of 1979 remain few and far between. Based on archival research in six countries, the book uncovers the lost history behind the rise of Afghanistan as a sovereign nation amid empires, the makers of its first constitution from Constantinople to Kandahar, and the hurdles they overcame in crafting a modern state within the interpretive traditions of Islamic law and ethics, or shariʿa, *and* international norms of legality.

Far from being a landlocked wilderness or remote frontier, roughly a century ago Kabul was a virtual seaport for itinerant scholars and statesmen shuttling between the Ottoman and British imperial domains. Tracing the country's long-standing but oft-ignored scholarly and educational ties to Istanbul, Damascus, and Baghdad, as well as Greater Delhi and Lahore, this book explains how the court of Kabul became both a laboratory and launchpad for diverse visions of modern Muslim reform at the turn of the twentieth century.

"Does Afghanistan Even Have a Legal History?"

Brazen as it appears, this question was unapologetically posed to the author by a foreign news correspondent during an interview one morning in Kabul. The reporter should not be blamed. Nearly a century after high school student Edison Ostrom's inquiry on the state of law and government in Afghanistan for a class project, one would still be hard-pressed to locate a scholarly monograph on Afghan legal history.[2] While droves of journalists, novelists, and foreign policy strategists have been writing about Afghanistan since the Soviet invasion of 1979, the vast majority of literature on the country has focused on the past four decades of serial conflict. The result: a nigh erasure of "antebellum" Afghanistan's past to all but academic specialists, dilettantes, and the increasingly small number of survivors old enough to remember less tumultuous times.

To be sure, scholarly silence on Afghan legal and constitutional history is neither new nor entirely a result of recent turmoil. In 1900, the law graduate of Christ's College, Cambridge, and Indian Muslim barrister of London Sultan Mohammad Khan authored one of the first legal studies of the country in English, *The Constitution and Laws of Afghanistan.* This was a formidable scholarly venture, and from the outset Khan lamented the paucity of sources: "I may mention here that the absence of books on Afghan law to quote from as my authorities has rendered mine a very difficult task," he confessed in the work's preface. "In searching the libraries of the University of Cambridge and the British Museum, all the books of reference on Afghanistan which I have been able to find were either on history, travels, or war, and none specially on law."[3] As late as the 1970s, even foundational documents like the country's first constitution (1923) were practically impossible to find, with a rare surviving copy being fortuitously discovered in a Kabul booksellers' bazaar, for example.[4]

This regretful state of affairs has meant lost histories and lost opportunities—most of all for Afghans, but not exclusively so. Due to Afghanistan's distinguishing characteristics in the greater Islamicate world, as multiple observers have noted, rediscovering its legal heritage has implications for understanding the modern development of Islamic law and constitutionalism at large. "Unlike most of the other Islamic and non-Western countries, Afghanistan never came under the political and juridical dominance of an European power," noted international lawyer Robert Hager in his 1975 primer, *Forward of Laws of Afghanistan.* "Because the law of Afghanistan is, thus, for the most part, either the traditional Islamic law or an indigenous product, it is a system somewhat unique in the world," the United Nations Development Programme (UNDP) consultant declared in a rare Western commentary on Afghan laws published on the eve of communist rule in the country. "These materials," that is to say, Afghan state legislation before the coup d'état of April 1978 and ensuing Soviet occupation, "therefore may be interesting from a comparative perspective as materials for study of the indigenous growth and development of an Islamic legal system," Hager concluded. Forty years later, this book accepts one UNDP lawyer's call to scholarly action in Afghanistan, quickly forgotten as it was amid more burning concerns taking hold of the country and that development agency's work ever since.[5]

What follows in the chapters to come is more than a story of law and legal history in the strict sense of the terms, however, because the work also has some other goals in mind. Exacerbating the scholarly chasm in Afghan legal and constitutional history is a deeper problem in how the country's past has come to be framed in academic and public discourse. Of particular concern here is a predilection for academic works on Afghanistan to be situated in one of three regions or area studies fields—namely, the Middle East, South Asia, or Central Asia—with the peculiar result that Afghanistan is rarely awarded fully fledged membership in any of the three. (Highly emblematic here is the tendency in maps of the Middle East, South Asia, and Central Asia to exclude or only partially include Afghanistan in its eastern, western, or southern-most extremities respectively, and rarely with its full territory intact.) Beyond the cartographic violence inflicted on Afghanistan and its people owing to their location at the juncture of three constructed regions, the long-term impact of trisecting the country has been to marginalize Afghans to the periphery of regional histories, while presuming the impaired nature of their national home. Though countless merchants, pilgrims, scholars, and other itinerants seldom experienced such boundaries in practice, area studies continue to demarcate the study not only of Afghanistan but also of the Ottoman and British empires according to the established borders of professional associations or geographic and linguistic expertise.[6]

Transgressing such regional divides, this book approaches modern Afghanistan's legal and constitutional heritage from a multiregional perspective by examining the contributions of a diverse cast of political actors in Kabul—Ottoman Turks, Arabs, and Indians, but most of all, Afghans—from the last quarter of the nineteenth century to the first quarter of the twentieth. Paradoxically, the transnational dimensions at the heart of this work emerged from a prototypically national question: What are the historical roots of Afghanistan's independence as a sovereign state and constitutional monarchy? In pursuit of this inquiry the book trains its eye on the critical half century between the country's transition from a British protectorate in the late 1870s to an independent nation-state under the late Muhammadzai king Aman Allah Khan in the 1920s. Extant historiography credits Aman Allah with winning Afghanistan's independence from Britain, securing the country's international recognition as a fully sovereign state, and promulgating an extraordinary body of legal literature, the *Nizamnamihha-yi Amaniyyih* ("Aman Allah Codes" in Persian and Pashto). Totaling over seventy originally crafted statutes, the Aman Allah Codes comprised the most ambitious legislative campaign in Afghanistan's history. As a state-building project the latter included a spectacular range of laws and manuals spanning the gamut of modern governance: from a census bureau, identification cards, and passports to education, land registration, and taxation; and from the training of a civil service and national army to animal rights. Among Aman Allah's reforms were the opening of public schools for girls, the introduction of legal protections for minorities, the banning of slavery, and the drafting of statutes criminalizing the overburdening of pack animals.[7] The most prominent text of all, however, was the Qanun-i Asasi (Basic Code) of 1923, the country's first written constitution.

That these achievements occurred during the early reign of the reformist king Aman Allah is known to scholars of Afghanistan's modern history. What has not been acknowledged, however, is how this remarkable project of legal modernism and statecraft in the 1920s emerged not as a transplant by colonial administrations or European codes, or as an imitation of Kemalist secularism, but from a deeper history of Pan-Islamic—or more precisely, *interislamic*—linkages beginning shortly after the first Ottoman mission to Afghanistan in 1877. This mission included a confluence of Ottoman Turkish jurists, Afghan clerics, and Indian bureaucrats who converged in Kabul to market their legal and administrative expertise to one of the early twentieth century's only fully sovereign Muslim states. While casting a bright light on the Afghans who remain center-stage of this story, *Afghanistan Rising* does not approach the country's history in a vacuum, disconnected from legal currents or constitutional movements in neighboring lands. Nor will one find support for conventional tropes of Afghanistan as the "buffer state par excellence," a purported no-man's-land existing only to placate the rivalries of colonial powers, whether in the nineteenth or twentieth centuries.[8]

By opting out of many routine frameworks where Afghan history and governance is concerned, this book proposes a new series of questions: What role did transnational (or transregional) Muslim networks play in the making of modern Afghanistan's early legal and constitutional history? What original projects and innovative solutions came out of the experiments in autonomous Muslim governance during the successive reigns of the Afghan Muhammadzai amirs ʿAbd al-Rahman Khan (r. 1880–1901), Habib Allah Khan (r. 1901–1919), and Aman Allah Khan (r. 1919–1929)? Did these monarchs and their advisors simply reproduce European models of law and expertise, or did they contribute something uniquely Islamic that expanded the horizons of legality for Muslim governments and international norms at large? If the latter, what approaches, methodologies, and tensions were most prominent in formulating their visions of the shariʿa in a modern state? Put together, how did Afghans, Ottomans, and Indian Muslims interpret and apply Islamic law and statecraft in the virtual laboratory of a rising independent Afghanistan?

As a historical undertaking, the labor for this book began with asking what light Afghan, Ottoman Turkish, and British Indian archives could shed on these questions. By unearthing a genealogy of Afghanistan's first constitution and its first comprehensive promulgation of nation-state law, the outcome addresses a gap in scholarly literature on Afghan legal history, but also "interislamic" legal networks between the Ottoman Empire and British India in Afghanistan as they evolved over the late nineteenth and early twentieth centuries. Recent years have seen historians of international law and sovereignty in the age of empire advance the study of Ottoman extraterritoriality in global directions, pushing scholars to rethink questions of imperial citizenship as not simply a one- or two-sided story of European capitulations and Turkish response in the eastern Mediterranean.[9] Rather, scholars have begun to explore the myriad possibilities for contestation, negotiation, and movement for subjects of diverse status and stripe—Christians, Jews, or Muslims; nationalists, socialists, or Pan-Islamists, to name a few—in a multipolar and increasingly interconnected late imperial world. This book contributes to the growing body of literature on extraterritoriality and imperial citizenship by highlighting the mobility and activities of Afghan, Ottoman, and Indian Muslim statesmen in Afghanistan as the latter transitioned from a semiautonomous protectorate of Britain to a fully sovereign nation-state.

Here the study problematizes literature on the modern Middle East that silences the non-Ottoman periphery as stagnant backwaters or passive objects caught between the colonial rivalry of Britain and Russia. By examining the Afghan court's patronage of scholarly and bureaucratic networks from Constantinople to Kandahar, and from Damascus to Delhi, it argues that this unique constitutional project can be reduced neither to European mimicry and obeisance nor to an identity politics of Pan-Islam triggered at the behest of the Sublime Porte. In this manner, the book aims to lift the study of Afghanistan from the confines of the Great Game, Cold War, or more recent literature on failed states. Instead, readers are invited to rediscover Afghanistan with a different past—when Kabul represented a burgeoning model of Islamic legal modernism, constitutional monarchy, and independent state building during an age of waning empires and rising nation-states.

Reconstructing Afghan Pasts: Archives to Actors

The research behind this book was grounded in work at five principal places: the National Archives of Afghanistan in Kabul, the Prime Ministry Ottoman Archives in Istanbul, the archives of the Turkish Republic and Red Crescent Society in Ankara, the National Archives of India in Delhi, and the India Office Records in London. Beyond hosting these world-class repositories, all of the aforesaid cities play critical roles in the book's central plot. Drawing on manuscripts, maps, and government records in Ottoman Turkish, Dari, Arabic, Urdu, English, and French, the first half of the book traces the burgeoning tripartite ties between Ottomans, Afghans, and Indian Muslims from the Sublime Porte's first diplomatic mission to Kabul in 1877 to the eve of the Great War. In the process, the book highlights the intersecting legal and administrative worlds of the late Ottoman Empire, British Raj, and then semiautonomous amirate of Afghanistan.

Afghan ties to neighboring states and regions will not come as a surprise to specialists in medieval and early modern India, Iran, or Central Asia. Far less is known, however, about this landlocked country's links to the eastern Mediterranean. Ask even an avid observer of global politics about international linkages between cities like Kabul, Kandahar, and Peshawar to the greater Middle East, and the response will almost certainly be the so-called Arab Afghans—a network of predominantly Saudi, Egyptian, and Algerian Islamists recruited to fight in Afghanistan in the 1980s (later evolving into the terrorist organization al-Qaeda following Soviet withdrawal from the country and the first US invasion of Iraq). Over a century before Osama bin Laden and Aymen al-Zawahiri were born, however, Afghanistan and the Ottoman-ruled lands of Greater Syria, Arabia, and North Africa were as intimately connected, but by a very different set of actors and themes: sufis, scholars, and royal families working in tandem with Muslim jurists, constitutionalists, and administrators to build an independent state within recognized borders and the nascent international legal system.

There were long-standing connections between Afghans and the Ottoman lands well before the late nineteenth century, but this book argues that the nature and intensity of these relations changed dramatically due to a re-regionalization of Muslim-majority societies and minority communities after the Russo-Ottoman War (1877–1878). The emergence of a new "interislamic region" between Istanbul, Kabul, Lahore, and Delhi, among other locales, therefore had a great deal to do with geopolitics, and the triangular vortex of the British, Ottoman, and Russian imperial rivalries in particular. (It was an Anglo-Ottoman alliance against Russian expansion in Asia, for example, that formed the background of the first Ottoman mission to Kabul in 1877—the subject of Chapter 1.) The formation of new interislamic currents and circuits had roots beyond interimperial geopolitics, however. Increased mobility facilitated by new infrastructure, transportation, and communication grids created new portals for enhanced Muslim-to-Muslim interaction across imperial and early national lines. At the same time, a growing racialization of Muslims within European empires, and the extension of this racially discriminatory approach to existing Muslim dynasties, including to the Ottoman Empire as the so-called Sick Man of Europe and Afghanistan as the Forbidden Kingdom, not only made inter-Muslim visions of exchange and solidarity a theoretical project and imagined identity but also furthered historical processes of exchanging expertise in modern law and state building. In that process, as the first half of the book shows, Kabul at the turn of the twentieth century became akin to a port city, harboring Muslim scholars, diplomats, and administrators from as far as Baghdad, Damascus, and Istanbul in the west, and Lahore, Deoband, and Lucknow in the east. Yet the connective tissue bridging these locales was not unbridled jihadist militancy but modern articulations of Islamic law, state building, and constitutional monarchy operating within an evolving international system at large.

The second half of the book turns to the convergence of three simultaneous developments of profound impact in the twentieth-century greater Middle East: the collapse of the Ottoman Empire after World War I, Afghanistan's independence from Britain in 1919, and the Indian Khilafat movement (1919–1924). Amid this dramatic backdrop of revolutionary politics and anticolonial coalitions, the book draws attention to an untold juridical story: the collaboration between Afghan scholars, Ottoman lawyers, and Indian technocrats who converged in Kabul to market their expertise to one of the world's only fully sovereign Muslim-majority countries—Afghanistan during the reign of Amir Aman Allah Khan. The hallmark of Islamic legal modernists in Afghanistan was a fierce resistance to transplanting European legal codes, instead opting for a synthesis of Afghan-Muslim jurisprudential heritage—particularly of the Hanafi school of Islamic law—with the presumed requirements of modern statehood, legality, and governance.[10] By paying close attention to the question of originality, heritage, and provenance in Afghan state legislation, Aman Allah's lawmakers combined jurisprudential continuity and innovation at the same time. Ultimately, the book argues, it was the synergistic fusion of these diverse visions of modern Islamic law and statecraft in Kabul that produced Afghanistan's first constitution and the twentieth century's first Muslim-majority nation-state.

This account presents a rare opportunity to understand the complexity and dynamism of Afghanistan's legal history during a formative interval in the country's not too distant past. Because most works on nineteenth- and early twentieth-century Afghanistan are based on British or Russian diplomatic records, or on the observations of other European representatives in Kabul, internal perspectives on Afghan royal courts have been elusive in the historiography.[11] As much as this is a book about Afghans and Afghanistan, however, it is also about a broader transnational world of Muslim scholars, jurists, administrators, and other professionals from the waning years of the Ottoman Tanzimat reforms (1839–1876) to the ruptures of World War I. By virtue of their having been hired by Afghan governments, the study follows a diverse array of Muslim experts as they contributed to forming a cosmopolitan court of policy makers in Kabul. Tracing the personalities and politics behind the formative state-building campaigns of Afghan Muhammadzai amirs ʿAbd al-Rahman Khan, Habib Allah Khan, and Aman Allah Khan in particular, the book uncovers the contested visions of Islam and modernity at the heart of a struggle to constitute Afghanistan as a nation and state.

Deprovincializing Afghanistan

Four major themes comprise the connective tissue of this book. The first is a centering of Afghanistan from its conventional treatment as a peripheral backwater, the Forbidden Kingdom of Middle East and South Asian studies, but also Islamic legal studies. Rather than treating the country in isolation, however, this is also a book about the making of a modern interislamic region commonly (but inaccurately) conflated today as "the Muslim world." The book traces how, just at the time of Eurocentric globalization and a scramble for African and Asiatic colonies, the barriers between Ottomans, Afghans, and the Muslims of British India were becoming fewer and more porous than ever before.

There were certainly myriad forms of ties between the regions covered in this book before the period of study, from mercantile networks and nomadic circuits to sufi orders, pilgrims, and marriages between Ottoman, Mughal, and Afghan royalty.[12] Nor should the deep roots and long arc of Turco-Persianate court cultures from medieval Baghdad and Samarqand to early modern Delhi or Lucknow be forgotten. But a major theme of this work is that the "Muslim world" as such emerges as a political region in the late nineteenth century. Before then, Muslim populations were too scattered and divided among competing small-scale principalities, or embedded within states and empires in which other religions were as large or even dominant, to constitute a global region or geopolitical player as such. Paradoxically, the era of European imperial hegemony in Eurasia coincided with, and produced, stronger interislamic connections; the latter processes intensified through profound demographic shifts within the Ottoman, Russian, and Austro-Hungarian empires in the late nineteenth to early twentieth centuries.[13] The book highlights how intellectual, political, and juridical ties between a modern "Balkans-to-Bengal" complex were not merely imagined or Orientalist constructions, but were anchored in actual interstate exchanges between royal courts and a nineteenth-century version of today's NGOs and social media outlets combined: Muslim philanthropic and cultural societies known as *anjumans*.[14] This study focuses on how juridical exchanges linking Muslim scholars and administrators in Istanbul, Kabul, and Greater Delhi emerged through the crucible of European imperial hegemony and through the independent dynastic and state-building projects of the Muhammadzai amirate of Afghanistan, with important consequences for this new region as a whole.

In approaching these problems, this book employs a conceptual framework influenced by legal anthropologist Laura Nader's user theory of law and sociologist Pierre Bourdieu's concept of a juridical field. Rather than viewing law as an autonomous body of texts or rules deduced by authorized experts in the sterile environs of a courtroom, judge's chambers, or scholar's den, this book treats law as an inherently political arena, a field of power relations where rival groups clash over competing interests, beliefs, and visions of the good society. Here, dynastic rulers and military commanders, avant-garde intellectuals and religio-legists, but most of all ordinary people, prosecute, defend, negotiate, and ultimately shape "the law" vis-à-vis practices of learning, professional habitus, mediation, and everyday living. It is the interaction between these multiple sites of authority and dispute resolution that together form a society's juridical field.[15]

There comes the question when Afghanistan is concerned, however, of whether one can talk of a juridical field in the singular. In relation to this problem, the book also draws from historian Christopher Tomlins's notion of multiple legalities to highlight the challenges and novelties of legal history in so-called frontier or borderland settings. As Tomlins has argued with regard to colonial North America, English law digests of the seventeenth and eighteenth centuries represented not so much theoretical solutions to abstract jurisprudential quandaries, but how expanding empires and states endeavored to homogenize, uniformize, and consolidate juridical authority amid environments of extreme legal pluralism. Simply put, it was in such frontier settings where the law code signified, above all else, a "struggle to transform strangeness into familiarity and to fix authority on the outcome, so that henceforth that outcome would prevail and no other."[16] These observations are far from exclusive to England's colonies in the New World. From the beginning of the nineteenth century until the mid-twentieth century, Britain's Indian Empire adopted similar approaches in governing its northwestern and predominantly Pashtun territories bordering Afghanistan in the form of the Frontier Crimes Regulation.[17] Better known as the Murderous Outrages Act in Raj parlance, this special enactment of laws exclusively for British India's Federally Administered Tribal Areas zone (later Pakistan's FATA) represented European attempts, as in North America, "to colonize the landscape—to give it system, regularity, purpose, familiarity."[18]

From the legal manuals of ʿAbd al-Rahman in the 1880s to the *niẓāmnāmihs* (codes, regulations, or ordinances) of Aman Allah in the 1920s, the Afghan legislation examined in this book presents important parallels and contrasts with the British Raj's Frontier Crimes Regulation. First issued between 1867 and 1877, the latter was designed to exclude frontier tribes from the British Indian state judiciary, nonetheless managing them through notions of fixed "traditions."[19] It is thus important to remember that projects of legality, including drafting constitutions and codes, do not necessarily signify liberal, democratic, or other kinds of participatory politics as much as the drive to reconstitute society in a more legible mold to a centralizing state.

Equally important is a recognition that the juridical fields of different states and societies—in this case the Ottoman Empire, Afghanistan, and British India—are not pure, autonomous, or self-contained units, but are mutually constituted and enriched by overlap, entanglement, even intertwining. Here, I adapt comparative law scholar Annelise Riles's analysis of the network "inside out" to emphasize not the ruptures of colonialism in many Muslim states and communities in this period—devastating as they were—but the often overlooked continuities of institutionalizing sacred knowledge in the modern social and legal history of Islam. As much as the eighteenth to twentieth centuries witnessed the dwindling or destruction of once powerful Muslim dynasties from the Balkans to Bengal, this work highlights how Muslim populations and even some surviving royal courts continued to revere the ulema for their knowledge of Islamic law. As authoritative interpreters of the shariʿa, the ulema and their students continued to learn and teach as they continued to be revered and patronized within particular Muslim societies and borders, including Ottoman Turkey, British India, and the amirate of Afghanistan. But as evolving scholarly networks, they also became a key means for the circulation of new Islamic juridical models across them.[20]

Applying these frameworks to our subject, the result is that a book about law and expertise in Afghanistan connects to a much wider world of contacts, collisions, and exchange, in particular between the Ottoman and British empires. This is a story of geopolitics; but it is also a story of steamships, railroads, and telegraph lines, as well as one of new and improved postal services, printing presses, and bookbinding. It is a story of the racialization of Muslims under European imperialism, when the "oriental despotism" of the Ottoman Empire, as the Sick Man of Europe, and Afghanistan, as the Forbidden Kingdom, was proclaimed by colonial powers (and Orientalist scholars) but also contested, internalized, and even reasserted by many Ottomans, Afghans, and Indian Muslims themselves in making their own cases for reform.

Here, the deprovincialization of Afghanistan from Middle East and South Asia studies also extends to the interdisciplinary and increasingly global field of Islamic legal studies. Academic literature on Islam, state building, and constitutionalism in the modern Middle East has been largely dominated by a handful of cases: by Ottoman Turkey and Qajar Persia in the nineteenth century; by Saudi Arabia, Egypt, and the Islamic Republics of Pakistan and Iran in the twentieth, among other populous Muslim-majority nation-states from North and West Africa to Southeast Asia. More broadly, scholarship on Muslim modernism, whether in its intellectual or political manifestations, has tended to focus on the Arab world, the Indian subcontinent, Turkey, Iran, or the Malay Archipelago—again understandably so, as they contain the largest Muslim populations in the modern world.[21]

Afghanistan, however, also had a role—a distinctive role—as a conduit for dialogues and debates between Muslim sovereigns, scholars, and administrators from the Ottoman Empire to British India as they struggled to craft states and societies that met the challenges of domestic governance, resisting European imperialism, and navigating inter-Muslim political rivalries alike. Between the last quarter of the nineteenth century and the first quarter of the twentieth, the book argues, these various struggles of contestation and negotiation gelled into a matrix of legal engineering in the newly independent state of Afghanistan. In this way, the study centers Kabul as a crucial player not only in the political history of modern Pan-Islam but also in the evolution of Islamic legal modernism as an ideology in the late nineteenth to early twentieth centuries. This is also a corrective to a heavy emphasis on tribal and customary law approaches to the legal history of Afghanistan, overlooking the juridical heritage of the Afghan state and the administrative architecture it bequeathed to Kabul regimes over a century before the Soviet invasion.[22] To grasp the full extent of Afghanistan's contributions in this regard, more needs to be said about the juridical aspects of Pan-Islam in the modern world.

Demilitarizing Pan-Islamism

A second theme of this book is an emphasis on the legal and administrative dimensions of interislamic networks that cross imperial and national borders. From the "jihadist state" of Sayyid Ahmad of Rai Bareilly in early nineteenth-century British India, to the so-called Islamic State of Iraq and the Levant in the twenty-first, Euro-American scholarship on modern Muslim movements that transcend political boundaries has devoted a considerable amount of attention to militants, apocalyptic ideologues, and other confrontational figures of a millenarian, Mahdist, or other radical ilk. As a result, Pan-Islamism has tended to be equated with anti-Western, fundamentalist ideologies, and a scourge of violence bent on overthrowing governments and annexing territory ad infinitum.

This is in no small part a reflection of current political malaise and anxieties in and outside Muslim-majority contexts.

By highlighting the internal diversity and disagreements (if not outright hostility) between various Islamist camps and nonstate actors today, academic work on Pan-Islamism has contributed much to undermining the constructed binary of an Islamic world versus a Judeo-Christian West that still dominates multiple contemporary ideologies—and to recognizing the modern political roots of these narratives.[23] These important contributions notwithstanding, without a deeper historical context for Pan-Islamic case studies within recognized states in the international system—such as the late Ottoman Empire and Afghanistan—readers are often left with an impression of transnational Islam as a tinderbox of belligerent factions with a single raison d'être: grandiose visions of world domination, a totalitarian implementation of shariʿa, and political unification under a restored caliphate.

Eschewing overly militaristic approaches to the study of Muslim transnational networks, the book invests closer attention to the legal and jurisprudential dimensions of modern Pan-Islam that preceded its more radical manifestations by nearly a century. By focusing on juridical connections between influential Muslim scholars and administrators of the late Ottoman Empire, Afghanistan, and the British Raj, the book locates crucial spaces for exchange and debate across three very different kinds of modern states: the late Ottoman Empire, British India, and Afghanistan. The first, even as it faced territorial losses and economic challenges within, was still the greatest Muslim power in the world and possessor of the caliphate; the second was the richest and most populous British colony and home to the largest Muslim population in the world; the third proved to be one of the biggest thorns in Britain's Asian empire and the first independent Muslim nation-state after the fall of the Ottomans. By tracking the intersections, and divergences, between legal actors in these states at a transformative historical juncture, the book highlights a spectrum of approaches to law and statecraft subsumed within Muslim interpretations of the shariʿa.

This is not an account of a puritanical, insular, or monolithic Islam or "Muslim world view" in Afghanistan framed in juxtaposition against an equally imagined West. There is a role for ideological fault lines—not between believers and nonbelievers, but between Muslim rulers and the Muslims they ruled, each promoting different interpretations of the shariʿa. It argues that Afghan monarchs—enlisting the support of Ottoman and Indian technocrats, but also leading Afghan jurists from Kabul and Kandahar—espoused a complex and dynamic approach to the intersection of law, religion, and governance at the turn of the twentieth century, an approach that can best be described as Islamic legal modernism. The latter is defined as a state-making project to centralize power through the codification and constitutionalization of Islamic jurisprudence (*fiqh*) by Muslim jurists, as opposed to importing, translating, or otherwise transplanting European civil law. At the same time, this narrative of Afghan modernization at the turn of the twentieth century is not a simplistic binary of progressive, modernizing secularists battling retrograde "mullahs and tribals," but is a more complex story of madrasa-trained jurists opting to ally with administrators, bureaucrats, and monarchs in Kabul to promote a stronger modern Islamic state. Refusing to grant their opponents the moral, ethical, or legal advantage, the Muhammadzai amirs in Kabul crafted a "rule of shari'a" discourse of their own to counter more locally made versions such as those espoused in the Indo-Afghan frontier or in Deobandi madrasas.[24]

From another angle, one of the most striking dimensions of the Islamic legal modernism and state-building campaigns of the Muhammadzai amirs was their aversion to certain fundamentalist approaches to Islamic law associated with the founders of the modern *salafiyya* movement, including the dubiously Afghan Jamal al-Din Afghani (d. 1897) and his renowned Egyptian and Syrian pupils, Muhammad 'Abduh (d. 1905) and Rashid Rida (d. 1935). "Salafists" or "Salafis," as they are often labeled, forsake adherence to one school of law (madhab), yet continue to attract the bulk of scholarly attention when it comes to Islamic modernism—in its legal dimensions, or any other domain.[25] In contrast to Salafi ideologues gaining ground in other Sunni Muslim-majority societies like Egypt, Algeria, and Arabia at this time, Afghanistan's model of modern reform stressed continuity rather than rupture with the predominant Hanafi jurisprudential traditions of the country. Far from Salafi iconoclasts, Afghan jurists and their Ottoman and Indian advisors working with them remained faithful to a single school of Islamic jurisprudence—the Hanafi madhab—reflecting the normative and historically cumulative approach to Islamic knowledge known as *taqlīd*, or deference to scholarly precedent.[26] In other words, although they opposed the transplantation of European civil law in Afghanistan, the Muhammadzai amirs shunned puritanical campaigns to discover an "original" or "authentic" Islam of the seventh and eighth centuries, stripped of the voluminous commentary and gloss literature of the historical Sunni madhabs. Judging from the texts they produced, neither did Afghan jurists endorse a skeptical approach to classical conceptions of jurisprudence by calling for a new methodology to interpret Islamic theology, exegesis, or law, nor is there the slightest indication they were uncomfortable with sufism as a popular form of Islamic expression in Afghanistan.[27] Rather, from the 1880s to the early 1920s the authors of the Afghan legislation—a majority of whom were Afghan clerics—worked to extend the living precepts of the Hanafi school of law to the new challenges of modern governance. As such, scholarly literature on Islamic modernism, with its focus on the *salafiyya* generation and their global interlocutors during the previous century and a half, has overlooked an important episode, arena, and cast of actors. In spite of the undoubtedly profound impact of thinkers such as Muhammad ʿAbduh and Rashid Rida, few modernists of the Salafi persuasion ever wielded political power or implemented state policies in the way the Muhammadzai amirs and their Hanafi jurists did in Afghanistan.

At the same time, Hanafi legal modernism in Kabul emerged at a transitional moment worldwide, amid the fall of empires and the rise of new discourses of territorial nationalism, constitutionalism, and international law.[28] Modern Afghanistan and its distinctive history of Islamic law, statecraft, and diplomacy have yet to be included in these high-stakes discussions. Historiography on Afghanistan has been so colored by emphases on religious extremism, terrorism, and civil war as to imply these maladies were somehow endemic to Afghan culture, while the hackneyed alternating tropes of romanticized freedom fighter and demonized terrorist both caricature Afghans as prone to violence, irrationality, and recalcitrance.[29] These themes have manifested in works on the late Muhammadzai amirs as well. For the nineteenth century, with a few exceptions, historiographical attention has largely focused on the brutal repression of the "Iron Amir" ʿAbd al-Rahman Khan, overlooking the administrative achievements of his amirate and of earlier Afghan monarchs.[30] Similarly with ʿAbd al-Rahman's son, Habib Allah, the short-lived German expedition to Kabul in the middle of World War I has captured far more scholarly attention than the schools, hospitals, or bureaucratic improvements built with Ottoman and Indian assistance during his nearly two decades in power.[31]

Most of all, however, the historiographical attraction to war, violence, and disorder in Afghanistan studies surfaces especially strongly in the controversial reign of Aman Allah, also known as the Amani era. Works on the latter have by and large been more interested in Aman Allah's dramatic overthrow from tribal revolts in 1929 than in the considerable administrative and constitutional legacy he built during the first half of his reign.[32] This omission is all the more surprising given the paucity of cases of modern state-building projects by independent Muslim rulers at the time, as opposed to the largely colonized North Africa, Middle East, and South Asia following World War I.

By uncovering a deeper history of scholarly and administrative networks linking Ottoman Turkey, British India, and Afghanistan since the Sublime Porte's first mission to Kabul in 1877, this book highlights the exchange of multiple modernist legal interpretations and political governance models within a semi-contiguous region during the era of imperial globalization. Although the book focuses on Afghanistan as a conduit and repository of legal modernism and statecraft during the formative era of interislamic globalism, it also shows how Afghanistan was not an exception during this process. Here, the book highlights the significance of a set of ideas circulating between the interislamic region from the Balkans and Arab world to India and Central Asia. It seems Istanbul set a model for various Muslim dynasties and polities—not only in larger semiautonomous states like Egypt, Persia, and Afghanistan but also in smaller princely states and principalities such as Johor, Zanzibar, Bhopal, and Hyderabad. There are even similarities here to the persistence of the Chinese model in Vietnam and Korea until the third quarter of the nineteenth century, and to the emergence of a Japanese model in the early twentieth century.[33] Attention to models of good governance and legal reform within a particular region—in this case between Istanbul and Kabul—invites us to rethink our notions of modernization and Westernization centered on Eurocentric experiences and epistemes.

Historicizing the Islamic Nation-State

One of the most striking features of the successive reigns of amirs ʿAbd al-Rahman, Habib Allah, and Aman Allah is that they each represented sustained enterprises to synthesize Afghanistan's predominantly Islamic jurisprudential traditions with a project of modern state building—albeit with important differences between them. With the help of Afghan clerics and of Ottoman and Indian bureaucrats, the legislation they drafted and implemented signaled a bold experiment: an attempt by Muslim jurists to develop an Islamic theory of the modern nation-state in a noncolonial context through a process that cannot be dismissed as European imitation on the one hand, or as "playing footloose" with the shariʿa on the other. To presume so would be to ignore the very real struggles of Afghan, Turkish, and Indian Muslim jurists to render the modern state and its custodians subject to the greater moral community—that is, under Islam's rule of law.[34]

To proceed responsibly with this inquiry, however, some words are in store concerning its conceptual vocabulary. In light of intensifying academic debates (to say nothing of the political) on the meanings of such fraught terms as "shariʿa law," "Islamic state," "the Islamic tradition," or even more fundamentally, the "Islamic," a clarification of terminology is in order. Following theorist of religion Talal Asad and philosopher Alasdair MacIntyre, but also now countless academic scholars of Islam for whom the ensuing observation is a platitude, this study approaches the Islamic religio-legal tradition, or shariʿa, not as a fixed code or timeless corpus of medieval edicts.[35] Having said what it is not, the most accurate definition of Islamic law used in this work would be a set of historically evolving texts, arguments, and practices from which Muslim scholars (ulema), and specifically the jurists (*fuqahāʾ*), base their reasoned evaluations of human choices to be in the eyes of God.[36] As a number of academic scholars of the shariʿa have emphasized, in spite of its sacred connotations Islamic law is therefore a quintessentially human endeavor because built in to Muslim legists' attempts to interpret the divine will is a recognition that said jurists do not command divine knowledge themselves and therefore can and do get it wrong.[37]

As scholars of the shariʿa will also emphasize, however, recognition of human fallibility is in tension with another facet of the human condition: the fact that people, whether subjects or governors, must inevitably make decisions about the structure and direction of their lives and societies. People do so through a combination of choices—alongside many more nonchoices accompanied by varying strategies of contestation, negotiation, and acquiescence—but act they must. Often those decisions are made in reference to a higher authority, be it a powerful or revered figure, sacred text, political ideology, or other reified source bearing ultimate legislative authority. For many Muslims, at the core of Islam is a recognition that the ultimate source of epistemic authority is God's guidance, as manifest in the Qurʾan and collections of traditions attributed to the Prophet.

Historically speaking, because Islam's final and most important prophet exercised political power toward the end of his life (like the ancient Jewish prophets but unlike Jesus Christ), and because his successors established large governments and empires in the name of their religion (like the Holy Roman Empire but unlike Jewish communities of the Diaspora), Muslim legacies of synthesizing law and politics within the ambit of their religion have at times seemed strange or even threatening to adherents of fellow Abrahamic faiths. But it is within the aforesaid epistemology, and political history, that the ulema and historic schools of Islamic law derived their epistemic and religio-legal authority to teach, advise, and, sometimes, legislate.[38]

It is also within that epistemic framework and historical context that this book's use of the term Islamic must be understood. As a modifying adjective, "Islamic" in this book connotes not a fixed set of doctrines and rules, nor a uniform corpus of positive law, but simply put, a human *aspiration*. More precisely, it is the aspiration of Muslims to engage the challenges of the time in a manner they believe to be pleasing to God, by adhering to teachings found in the Qur'an, Prophetic example, and interpretive principles of law, ethics, and devotional practice based on these sources. It is that aspiration, and not simply naked power and authoritarianism cloaked in religious garb, that at least in part motivated Afghan, Ottoman, and Indian Muslims to make certain kinds of decisions concerning the questions of law and governance they faced as modern state builders in turn-of-the-twentieth-century Afghanistan. We can be confident of this because of the surviving texts they left—historical documents from Kabul, Istanbul, and Delhi, among other locales, which drove the research behind this book. The latter texts were explicit in claiming inspiration and precedent from the Qur'an, Prophetic example, and historic schools of thought associated with the religion of Islam (especially the Hanafi school of jurisprudence), as they crafted the first internationally recognized Muslim-majority nation-state after the fall of the Ottomans.

Far from a foil to modernity, then, or a prescriptive statement on Muslim orthodoxy, "Islamic" in this book connotes that which was lived, debated, and shaped by modern Muslims at the turn of the twentieth century; more specifically, by those residing, writing, and traveling within the adjoining territories of the late Ottoman Empire, Persia, Afghanistan, and India, but also other key sites within Britain's global empire at the time, including Egypt, Yemen, South Africa, and the metropole itself. Above all this is a book about what it meant for a group of Afghan, Ottoman, and Indian Muslims in Kabul to apply the aspirational Islamic to their struggle for a modern state in a rising independent Afghanistan.[39]

These subtle definitions and approaches notwithstanding, there is little question that the quest for an Islamic state has produced abhorrent results in the late twentieth and twenty-first centuries, including in Afghanistan. But as political theorist Saba Mahmood reminds us, this should not blind readers to the fact secular-liberal governments have produced their own share of spectacular failures (and arguably much more devastating and wide-reaching) in the same centuries.[40] Equally instructive are the thoughtful arguments of legal scholars Wael Hallaq and Abdullahi An-Naʿim concerning the implausibility, or oxymoron rather, of an Islamic state today, for reasons having to do less with Islam or Muslims than with the empirical realities of modern states.[41] There is also little historical evidence to suggest that an Islamic state must follow the likes of today's rogue Islamist statelets like Boko Haram, al-Shabab, or the so-called Islamic State—vigilante, sectarian, pugnacious, and opposed to Islam's traditionalist schools of law, sufism, and the international state system all at once. The early modern world's greatest Sunni Muslim states—the Ottomans in the eastern Mediterranean and the Mughals in India—both endorsed the Hanafi school of law in their internal governance and liberally patronized sufi orders, including the upkeep of mausoleums, *dergahs, tekkes,* and *zawiyes.* They also engaged in trade with, hosted envoys from, and even allied politically with Christian Europeans or Indian Hindus—often against neighboring Muslim states or populations (including Afghans, for example, in the case of the Mughals). In the case of the Ottoman caliphate, until the late nineteenth century the House of Osman had some of its strongest allies in England, from the Houses of Tudor to Hanover.[42] Throughout its history and until the First World War, the Sublime Porte enjoyed friendly relations and commercial ties with a host of European monarchies and states, at times forging military alliances with Britain, France, the Netherlands, the Papacy and Kingdom of Naples, not only its later World War I ally Germany.

But one need not dwell on the Ottomans and Mughals, or on the early modern period, to glean such examples of Islamic states thriving within a wider international state system. The first example of an Islamic nation-state in the twentieth century, Afghanistan, shows just as much. Keeping in mind the conceptual vocabulary presented here, a closer examination of the Afghan Muhammadzai monarchy's campaign for independence and internal governance presents us with one of the first and most remarkable Islamic state projects of modern times. Here, independent Muslim policy makers struggled to navigate the competing tensions of colonial encroachment on their borders and internal dissent by those opposed to centralizing regimes within. The only other fully sovereign Muslim-majority states in the region—Kemalist Turkey, Pahlavi Iran, Hashemite Hejaz, Oman, and northern Yemen—either formally marginalized the shariʿa as a source of law, imported European codes to constitute the new state's laws, or cannot be said to have developed a comprehensive body of statutory law that substantially reflects an Islamic theory of the nation-state. Far from seeing the shariʿa as "dead" after colonialism, and its custodians as passive spectators of their own marginalization, Muslim jurists and administrators are presented here as skilled agents who struggled—and negotiated—to carve a space of autochthonous legal production that has gone unnoticed. Here, it must be emphasized, the architects of the Afghan state-building campaigns pursued their goals by engaging the challenges of modern state building from within an Islamic legal tradition. It thereby provides a juridical example of what political theorist Dilip Gaonkar has termed "creative adaptation," whereby "a people 'make' themselves modern, as opposed to being 'made' modern by alien and impersonal forces, and where they give themselves an identity and a destiny."[43]

To be sure, the late Muhammadzai amirs of Afghanistan were not the first Muslim monarchs to pursue a modern state-building campaign with an emphatic commitment to upholding the shariʿa. The Ottoman Civil Code and Constitution of 1876, and arguably several of the Tanzimat reforms before them, represent the most famous precedents of Islamic legal modernism by a dynamic consortium of ulema, lawyers, and bureaucrats working in tandem under the aegis of a centralizing state.[44] Earlier, seventeenth-century Mughal emperor Aurangzeb ʿAlamgir (r. 1658–1707) commissioned the *Fatawa-yi ʿAlamgiri*, an eponymous collection of authoritative opinions from the Hanafi school of Islamic jurisprudence that the emperor sought to be applied in his courts, and which some historians have even called a proto-modern "code" of Islamic civil law.[45] An early-modern tour de force, the compilation reflected a two-prong ambition to streamline administration of the empire and Islamicize state institutions to facilitate the centralization of power in Delhi—consistent imperatives at work in later projects of Islamic legal modernism in the nineteenth and twentieth centuries, including the Ottoman Tanzimat and Afghan Aman Allah Codes.

Other literatures we might include in the genre of Islamic legal modernist projects are the memoranda of the Tunisian jurist and one-time Ottoman grand vizier Khayr al-Din Pasha (1820–1890) on the codification of shariʿa in North Africa, the Cairene lawyer Muhammad Qadri Pasha's code of personal status law (1875), and the civil law codes of Egyptian jurist ʿAbd al-Razzaq Sanhuri (1895–1971), later adopted by several post-Ottoman and postcolonial Arab states. Drawing substantively but also selectively from classical manuals of *fiqh* while also exercising innovative scholarly expertise in their own right, the authors of these legal manuals, codes, and indeed constitutions challenge the notion of a "Shariʿa-Siyāsa Divide" and "Closing of the Gates of Ijtihād," a pair of once predominant theses in Western studies of Islamic law attributed to the influential German-British Islamicist Joseph Schacht (1902–1969).[46] Put another way, these codes and constitutions become especially important for seeing modern Muslim jurists as embodying a resilient, living, and evolving tradition rather than a fossilized or obscurantist class, agents of Western imperialism, or apologists for oppressive postcolonial regimes.[47]

Viewed in historical context, Islamic legal modernism emerged not against nor in isolation from but in engagement with social and political developments across the region, as more loosely governed empires and patrimonial regimes of the seventeenth and eighteenth centuries were replaced by highly centralized administrative nation-states of the nineteenth to twentieth centuries. The latter, in the Middle East as elsewhere, brought new political discourses, including constitutionalism, citizenship, and the laws of nations, but also disciplinary and surveillance tools such as passports, identity cards, and the codification of law.[48] This book argues Afghanistan was at the forefront of such processes among Muslim states in the late nineteenth and early twentieth centuries. What is more, by the time of its independence in 1919 and through the 1920s, Afghanistan pursued these goals not in isolation, but in conversation—and collaboration—with neighboring Muslim populaces and the international community, earning it rare recognition as one of the only fully sovereign Muslim-majority nation-states in the world.

It is hoped these aspects of the book will stimulate further academic work not only on Afghanistan but also on the articulation and practice of Islamic law in the modern world. The people and places at the heart of this book provide real, lived examples of a diverse group of modern Muslims engaging in the challenges of modern state building, European colonialism, and the vested interests of political and economic forces within their societies, be they scholars, foreign militaries, or domestic militias contesting state centralization campaigns. The intersection of geopolitics, the Islamic legal tradition, and competing ideologies of Muslim modernism all contributed to the development of these historical processes in Afghanistan, with important lessons for scores of Islamic nation-states that were born after it.

Modernizing Muslim Monarchy

The fourth and final theme, overlapping but also distinct from the idea of an Islamic nation-state, is the emergence of a modern theory of Muslim kingship under the late Muhammadzai amirs of Afghanistan. Concerning this aspect of political theology in the Afghan experience, the book illustrates how from the 1870s to the 1920s the Muhammadzais experimented with novel forms of sovereignty to assert their legitimacy internationally and domestically, while establishing Afghanistan's autonomy as an autonomous amirate, and ultimately, independent country under a constitutional monarchy. The latter was the first model of modern Muslim kingship to be designed and implemented in a fully sovereign nation-state after the fall of the Ottomans.

The story of Afghanistan here is of a Muslim dynasty establishing the legitimacy of its hereditary line while claiming to rule in the name of Islam and the delimited territory of a nation—a project distinct from earlier modalities of Muslim kingship, caliphate, or imamate in premodern contexts.[49] The Muhammadzai dynasty and supporting political elites read the global situation and developed a notion of modern kingship accordingly. In retrospect, this was an extraordinary achievement for the Muslim kingship project—and not only because it preceded better-known examples in the region by several decades, nor must we limit our comparison to Muslim states. Two other nations richer in resources and further advanced in diplomatic recognition in the late nineteenth century—the kingdoms of Hawai'i and Korea—lost their sovereignty as Afghanistan gained it. That Afghans succeeded in their drive for independence did have something to do with their geopolitical position and other contingent factors. Yet, beyond these contingent factors, the Muhammadzai kings asserted the spiritual and material sovereignty of their nation with various diplomatic and legal steps that included ties to the Ottoman Empire and other transnational networks, including Indian Muslim educational institutions. The result was the crafting of a constitution that fulfilled both the domestic demands and international "standards of civilization." The Afghan monarchs also managed to receive the support of different segments of their society while promulgating legal and political reforms to strengthen the central state. In the process they remade Afghanistan into a pivotal state both in broader Muslim political imagination and in the newly designed international order in the early 1920s.

Though boldly declaring their allegiance to the shari'a, the Islamic state-building projects of 'Abd al-Rahman, Habib Allah, and Aman Allah were grounded in notions of territorial nationalism and dynastic succession. All three rulers signed treaties with the British Empire delimiting Afghan territory—and in the case of Aman Allah, with most major Western powers including Britain, France, Germany, Italy, and the Soviet Union. None of the Muhammadzai amirs pursued grandiose notions of a caliphate, either recognizing Ottoman claims to the office, or, in the case of Aman Allah, actually declining to accept offers to replace the deposed Ottoman caliph-sultan in Istanbul. This was, hence, not a project of global conquest or neo-caliphatism, but one of resurrecting notions of a Muslim amir, shah, or other kind of monarch (but not caliph) who was responsible for a specific, demarcated territory at peace with its neighbors. It therefore represented an adaptation of medieval notions of the just Muslim king to the context of the modern, territorial nation-state. In Afghanistan, that model of kingship did not die out until the early 1970s, despite the rise of republicanism in postcolonial Asia, Africa, and other parts of the Global South / Third World. In some Muslim-majority societies, the ideal of a just or benevolent king who could unite multiethnic and fragmented societies therefore remained powerful in spite of competing political projects and visions.

The legitimacy of Muslim monarchs became more challenging in an era of Young Turks, Young Afghans, and politicized citizenries. As with the Young Ottomans' 1876 Constitution and its restoration under the Young Turks in 1908, the 1923 Constitution of Afghanistan illustrates a case when older notions of kingship could be synthesized with newer notions of legality, legitimacy, and sovereignty. And yet, in light of observations that all of the major Arab Spring uprisings were in republics (barring the exceptional sectarian case of Bahrain), the theory, history, and resilience of modern Muslim kingship deserves attention. This part of the book should be relevant to anyone concerned with the notion of an Islamic state or the relevance of shariʿa to modern modalities of sovereignty, statecraft, and governance. Today, these debates are filtered through the ideologies of a relatively tiny group of extremists—be they of the radical Islamist or Islamophobic variety—or textual Orientalism, and they miss the historical experience of Muslim kingship as in the cases of Kabul, Istanbul, Tehran, Fès, and Cairo, among other locales, in the nineteenth and twentieth centuries. This book tells a story of Islamic law and statecraft through the Afghan prism, but it is also a story linked to other centers of modern Muslim thought in a circulatory network of interislamic exchanges. It therefore offers a new interpretation of Muslim-majority societies against the conventional Western modernity versus traditional Islam binary, suggesting that there was a model of Islamic law and statecraft in Afghanistan over a century ago that was modern but not necessarily Eurocentric. Unearthing the sociolegal history behind the making of a sovereign constitutional monarchy, Islamic state, and member of the international community of nations all at once, this work should challenge us to reflect on both the achievements and the lost possibilities of Afghan modernity.

The Arc of the Book

While 1747 is conventionally treated as the birth of the Afghan state in most national accounts, Chapter 1 considers the country's emergence within a broader constellation of "interislamic" relations between the Ottoman Empire, Persia, the Uzbek khanates, and India. From the fifteenth-century Ottoman-Portuguese wars in the Indian Ocean to history's only Ottoman-Afghan war in the borderlands of Mesopotamia, the chapter offers a concise prehistory of relations between Afghans, Turks, Iranians, and Indian Muslims during the early modern period and what some historians have termed proto-Afghanistan. It then proceeds to the emergence of Afghanistan as a new imperial dynasty arising from the ashes of the Mughal and Safavid empires in India and Iran respectively. The core of Chapter 1 is devoted to the Ottoman Empire's first official mission to Afghanistan in the summer of 1877. In spite of the unprecedented nature of the mission, little is known about the envoy's background or the consequences of his expedition for Afghanistan. The chapter provides a biographical window into Şirvanizade Ahmed Hulusi Effendi's career in the Ottoman legal bureaucracy before he arrived in Kabul, followed by a discussion of the envoy's meetings with Afghan statesmen and scholars. It then takes up the hitherto unexplored question of the legal dimensions of Hulusi's visit, including connections between reform projects taking place in the Ottoman Empire and Afghanistan over the next two decades. In particular, we consider not just the relations but the exchanges between the centralizing governments of Sultan Abdülhamid II in Istanbul and the "Iron Amir" of Afghanistan, ʿAbd al-Rahman Khan, revising historiographical assumptions that the British and Russians were the sole experts in the court of Kabul.

Chapter 2 takes up the landmark shifts within Afghanistan's domestic and foreign policies following the death of ʿAbd al-Rahman, beginning with the amnesty offered to Afghan exiles following the ascent of his son, Habib Allah, to the Kabul throne. It then follows the far-reaching impact of the return of Afghan expatriates from two profoundly important intellectual and professional streams connecting Kabul with the greater Islamicate world: Ottoman Turkey from the west, and British India from the east. The chapter traces the activities and contributions of the "Ottoman Afghan" journalist Mahmud Tarzi, who returned to Kabul after nearly two decades of exile in Baghdad, Istanbul, and Damascus; and the Yahya Khel clan of Nadir Khan, who returned to Afghanistan from northern India. These influential individuals did not return to Kabul by themselves, but each attracted a band of experts from both empires to trail behind them. Utilizing archival records from Istanbul, Delhi, London, and Kabul, the chapter illustrates how dual streams of Ottoman and Indian professionals included an enterprising and impressive array of engineers, journalists, and military officers—as well as physicians, teachers, and lawyers. Sundry in trade and nationality, these multinational experts competed for the patronage and attention of the new amir in Kabul. The only apparent threads tying the members of the commission together were a common religious identity of Islam and a commitment to building a strong, centralized, and independent state of Afghanistan under the leadership of their patrons in the Muhammadzai court.

In light of the high numbers from the Ottoman Empire and British India in particular, the chapter describes the beginning of an Indo-Ottoman rivalry in Kabul, each faction representing differing styles of technical expertise, cultural norms, and at times, political loyalties. It also traces the role of Habib Allah's ambivalent role to both sides, admiring the Ottoman caliph in Istanbul and "sultanis" of Kabul on the one hand, while courting British patronage on the other. The chapter closes with an examination of Mahmud Sami Bey, an Ottoman Arab colonel from Baghdad who had arrived in Kabul during this period. Mahmud Sami is credited with establishing Kabul's Maktab-i Harbiyyih (Turkish: Mekteb-i Harbiye), a military school for Afghan princes and other elites modeled on similar academies established in major Ottoman cities during the Hamidian era. Beyond providing modern military training akin to Mahmud Sami's own in his native Iraq, Afghanistan's Harbiye became a brewing ground for underground political parties and secret societies including, most famously, the Young Afghans who sowed the seeds of a constitutional movement in Habib Allah's kingdom on the eve of the Great War.

Chapter 3 addresses the outbreak of World War I and its impact on the Kabul court. When a European conflict spiraled into the Great War, and with the Ottomans joining the Central Powers, Habib Allah found himself caught between two drifting boats. On one side was the Ottoman sultan and caliph of the world's Muslims; on the other, the British Raj, Afghanistan's patron state since the 1893 Durand Agreement. Initially, the amir played his cards skillfully, maintaining Afghanistan's neutrality amid the most devastating war in history as the world knew it. Matters soon became grave for Habib Allah, however, when successive waves of Indian revolutionaries began congregating in Kabul to organize support for the Ottoman jihad. Politically neutral and geographically central, Kabul became an ideal gathering point for a lethal combination of Ottoman military officers, Afghan volunteers, and Deobandi clerics, generating visions for a Pax Islamica more ambitious than even those provoked by the 1857 Indian Rebellion. Ultimately, Habib Allah's decision to remain neutral was interpreted as a betrayal of the close links the Porte had nurtured with Muslims of Afghanistan since the first Ottoman mission to Kabul and through the first decade of his own reign. Here, however, the historiographical tendency to render the Turco-German mission to Kabul as a failure elides the dramatic consequences of bringing Ottoman, Afghan, and Indian Muslim networks into closer contact than ever before. In the end, Habib Allah paid the ultimate price for his unpopular stance with the British. His mysterious assassination in the early hours of February 20, 1919, led to the coronation of his son Aman Allah, a staunchly pro-Turkish and constitutionalist prince.

Chapter 4 begins with watershed events and policies following Aman Allah's succession as the new amir of Afghanistan. Less than six months after his ascent to the Kabul throne, Aman Allah had secured independence from Britain following the Third Anglo-Afghan War, and with it, the world eyed one of its only independent and fully sovereign Muslim-majority states. The chapter then turns to the historical conditions leading to an unprecedented nexus of late Ottoman, Indian, and Afghan political actors in Kabul, beginning with post-Armistice Turkey and Afghanistan fighting simultaneous wars of independence, and the Indian Khilafat movement emerging in full steam. As with previous episodes of Indo-Ottoman Pan-Islamism, the focal point of this tripartite nexus was again Kabul, but with very different results. What followed Afghanistan's independence in the summer of 1919 were two very different migrations to Kabul originating from, once again, Turkey and India. The former included a high-profile group of Ottoman Turkish officials fleeing Allied-occupied Istanbul; the latter constituted one of the most remarkable mass mobilizations in South Asian history. In an uncanny foreshadowing of the trauma and dislocations of Partition a quarter-century later, an estimated sixty thousand Indian Muslims, mostly poor farmers of the Punjab, Sindh, and NWFP, migrated to Afghanistan in the Hijrat movement of 1920–1921.

Although historians of the early Turkish republic, modern Afghanistan, and the late British Raj have tended to focus on each of these national struggles in isolation, few have examined the intersection of all three movements in Kabul during Aman Allah's early reign. For Aman Allah and his newly sovereign government, the fluid years of 1919 to 1923 presented opportunities for a mutual meeting of minds with both the Turkish national resistance in Anatolia and the Indian Khilafatists. As for the latter, like the amir himself, the Khilafatists were unwavering in their support for the Turkish national resistance and the Ottoman caliphate, which in their minds were still one and the same cause. As a monarch in his mid-twenties, Aman Allah was anxious to bolster both his international credentials and domestic legitimacy in the aftermath of his father's murder.

Among his first strategic moves in this regard was seeking to expand his sphere of influence on both sides of the Durand Line, especially areas inhabited by Pakhtun tribes. As for the Hijrat, he fanned the flames of Pan-Islamic fervor in the subcontinent to his favor, and used the migration of tens of thousands of Indian Muslims as a bargaining chip to secure bonus gains in negotiating treaties with the British. By historicizing the conditions that led to new alliances between Turkish, Indian, and Afghan actors in Kabul, the chapter lays the foundation for understanding the subsequent legal and constitutional milestones achieved in those pivotal early years of Afghanistan's history as an independent state.

Chapter 5 examines the postbellum confluence of a multinational corps of lawyers, technocrats, and officers in Kabul who, despite their relatively brief tenure, contributed to a landmark juridical accomplishment in Afghanistan: the country's first constitution and the over seventy auxiliary Aman Allah Codes that laid the legal and administrative groundwork for the newly independent state. The chapter focuses on the extraordinary confluence of Ottomans, Indians, and Afghans who served on the constitutional commission assembled by Aman Allah. It provides biographical sketches of the key individuals who served on the commission, their background and training, and professional histories they brought to the Afghan lawmaking project. Here, the premium placed by Aman Allah Khan on promoting an Islamic legal modernist vision for the Afghan state emerges from the very composition of the drafting committee—an eclectic group of jurists and politicians that included liberal bureaucrats from the palace administration, conservative clerics linked to Deobandi madrasas in India, Young Afghan constitutional activists, Pashtun notables of the influential Muhammadzai tribe, and Ottoman legal advisors. Among the latter was Osman Bedri Bey—an Istanbul attorney who Aman Allah appointed as the constitutional commission's director. The chapter also provides an overview of Afghanistan's first constitution—along with its over seventy supplementary *niẓāmnāmih* law codes—as a product and legacy of this remarkable Indo-Ottoman juridical nexus. Reviewing the charter's outstanding features, it argues that by means of clearly enunciated, carefully crafted shariʿa-compliant articles, Aman Allah pursued the ever-elusive goal of constituting Afghanistan in a manner conducive to administration by a centralized, territorial nation-state. Here, we arrive at a most decisive intervention of the book: far from being latecomers to Muslim modernity, Afghanistan's 1923 Constitution and supplemental Aman Allah Codes should be considered as one of the twentieth century's first projects of Islamic state making, for two reasons. First, it signified a "modernized" shariʿa, a sacred law instrumentalized to fulfill the prerogatives of sovereign power—maintaining civil order, supervising officials, and adjudicating between subjects, markets, and property disputes. Second, unlike his reformist strongmen Mustafa Kemal Atatürk in Turkey and Riza Shah Pahlavi in Iran, Aman Allah's distinctive approach empowered him to pursue his state-building goals while hoisting the populist banner of establishing an Islamic state in Afghanistan. As Aman Allah sought to propel progressive but top-down social change in Afghanistan through law, I argue, a closer examination of select codes and the jurists who authored them reveals a simultaneous attempt to establish the codification project as a legitimate interpretation of shari'a in light of modern conditions and in tune with international norms of legality.

Chapter 6 provides a postscript to the remarkable story of Afghanistan's first constitution and the Indo-Ottoman-Afghan network that produced it. The chapter reflects on how the "life of the law" behind the first constitution of Afghanistan does not end in 1923, nor was it ever limited to Afghanistan to begin with. The chapter focuses on the tumultuous events in Turkey and Afghanistan between 1924 and 1929, a short period but with profoundly consequential events for both countries and the interislamic region, including the abolition of the Ottoman caliphate, the establishment of a secular Turkish republic, and the fall of Aman Allah Khan. It then discusses what happened to the Indo-Ottoman constitutional commission and the government of Aman Allah, developments that are completely intertwined with the formation of an ultra-secular-nationalist Kemalist republic in Turkey, and the collapse of the Khilafat movement in India in 1923–1924. The chapter also reflects on the long-term legacies of the rise and fall of one of the most controversial leaders in twentieth-century Middle East history. By focusing on emerging debates and transformations at the time rather than on Aman Allah's failures, one can appreciate the complexity of Afghanistan's legal history at a defining moment of internal peace and stability in the country. Readers will also see important precedents and ramifications for the constitutional and codification projects in subsequent Arab and Muslim-majority states, including the calls for restoring the shari'a that would become a rallying call for both Islamist regimes and ballot-based parties from Tunisia to Malaysia over the course of the twentieth century.

The Conclusion reflects on the role "interislamic" juridical networks have played in the making of the modern Afghan state, from the Iron Amir's centralization campaign to the country's first constitution during the reign of his grandson, Aman Allah. It emphasizes how through and in Afghanistan Muslims rose against European assertions of inferiority, backwardness, and *kadijustiz* to establish and legally equip one of the modern world's first Islamic nation-states. It also contrasts the legacy of these achievements with Afghanistan's fraught history in more recent decades. A major goal of this book, therefore, is to address an important lacuna not only in the study of Afghanistan but of the evolution of Islamic law and statecraft during a transformative era across "the region," however the latter may be defined. On a broader level, it seeks to cultivate more transnational and dynamic approaches to histories of constitutionalism, state building, and rule-of-law discourse, not only in Islamicate and Muslim-majority countries but in our world at large.

All too often marginalized to the periphery of empires, superpowers, and now area studies, Afghanistan was in fact an early testing ground for what it meant to be a modern Muslim monarchy, Islamic state, and member of the international community all at once in the early twentieth century. As this book goes to press, it is unclear to what extent the chronic themes of state failure, civil war, and terrorist attacks will continue to define global images of Afghanistan. They have represented the lion's share of journalism and scholarship on the country for the past four decades, and for the entirety of the author's life to date, stacked as they are atop earlier caricatures of a so-called Forbidden Kingdom since Victorian times. As Afghans across their country and beyond continue to struggle and survive, fight and negotiate, and hope and pray for a just and lasting peace in their homeland, this book sets its eyes on more humble goals. If *Afghanistan Rising* inspires students and scholars to discover the life of the law behind the ink of constitutions, across political borders, and in less-recognized milieus, then it will have already fulfilled its purpose.

ONE

An Ottoman Scholar in Victorian Kabul

The First Ottoman Mission to Afghanistan

IN THE EARLY hours of August 9, 1877, British naval authorities off the Indian coast of Bombay identified an unusual ship on the horizon. Though scores of vessels carrying transcontinental passengers, commercial cargo, and military supplies routinely entered Bombay's bustling seaport, from the beginning there were signs this steamer was different. As port authorities briskly prepared for the seacraft's imminent landfall and anchoring, a company of British officers surrounded the pier, scanning for disturbances on shore. At last the ship made contact with the dock, grinding to a screeching halt. Disembarking, the passengers were immediately escorted to a smaller boat waiting nearby, which whisked them away to an agreed-upon location down the harbor: the Ottoman Imperial Consulate of Bombay.[1]

The attempts by British authorities at Bombay to cloak the arrival of an Ottoman delegation in a veil of secrecy proved to be in vain. Within hours of their landing, accounts from the Ottoman consulate describe ecstatic, chanting crowds—presumed to be made up of the city's Muslims—overflowing into the streets and generating an atmosphere of glee and pandemonium. The hero's welcome in Bombay was far from over, however. When the visitors from Istanbul expressed a desire to attend Friday prayers in a local mosque the next day, to the astonishment of the Turks—and their British hosts—by midday there were an estimated sixty thousand people already gathered in and around the mosque.[2] As one member of the mission wrote in his travel diary, "Because of the crowd we were nearly suffocated."[3] Blindsided by this explosive display of pro-Ottoman sentiment so far from the sultan's domains, and right under their own watch, British authorities arranged for the visitors' immediate departure from the city. The decision must have appeared particularly abrupt given the delegation's voyage from Yemen and the Horn of Africa only a day earlier, Egypt a week prior, and Istanbul itself three weeks before that. With this pomp and circumstance—albeit not the kind either Turkish or British officials had in mind—the Ottoman delegation resumed its journey and mission at hand: an appointment with the amir of Afghanistan in Kabul.[4]

PAN-ISLAMISM, A TERM of markedly European origin, has no equivalent in Arabic, Persian, or Ottoman Turkish, entering the latter languages as a modern loan word. There is evidence to suggest the term was coined by the British Foreign Office in the mid-1870s, with continental equivalents *Panislamisme, Pan-Islamismus,* and *Pan-islamismo* surfacing in rival colonial lexicons at roughly the same time.[5] By the early twentieth century, European administrators from Algiers to Aceh were regularly using the word to describe—or imagine—the specter of colonized Muslim subjects making common cause across territorial and geographic boundaries from Mali to the Malay Archipelago.[6] One source of European apprehension over mobile Muslims was the prospect of new technologies being harnessed against them. Newer, faster, and cheaper modes of transportation and communication, including transcontinental steamships, railroads, and the telegraph, carried Muslim travelers across the Mediterranean and Indian Ocean waterways—as well as across the landlocked hinterlands of northern India, the Russian steppe, and Afghanistan—while bringing their relatives and communities back home into closer and more regular contact than before.

Few could know this better than the legions of intelligence officers administering Queen Victoria's global empire. From the late nineteenth century into the first decades of the twentieth, British officials in consular stations and military garrisons employed the same technologies—and a good deal more—to surveil mobile Muslims crossing political and geographic boundaries in increasing numbers and frequency. In the case of India, Her Majesty's richest and most populous colony, internal records of the British Raj's security apparatus reveal a special interest in travelers shuttling between the territories of the Ottoman Empire and the subcontinent. Partly because they were still anxious after the 1857 Sepoy Rebellion, partly because they were growing suspicious over Turkish intentions in the region, British officials suspected many of these travelers to be agents of the Sublime Porte or to be part of more locally inspired campaigns to bolster Ottoman influence beyond the sultan's domains and on the international stage.

A century and a half after the British Foreign Office coined the term, Pan-Islamism continues to be a subject of intense scrutiny, governmental or otherwise. Scholars have endeavored to explain the genesis of borderless movements that fuse modern religious revivalism with anticolonial politics in especially potent combinations.[7] Prevailing historical interpretations rightly identify a considerable spike in Pan-Islamic activity with the eastern policies of Sultan Abdülhamid II (r. 1876–1909), including the latter's outreach to Muslim minorities from the northern Caucasus to China. Intellectual histories of Pan-Islamism focus on the incendiary writings of the itinerant ideologue and founder of the modern Salafist movement, Jamal al-Din al-Afghani (d. 1897), among earlier revivalist thinkers of the Arab world and the Indian subcontinent in particular.[8] In either its political or ideological iterations, Pan-Islamism is presented as a stridently anti-Western movement born out of European imperial hegemony in the eighteenth and nineteenth centuries.

By emphasizing conflict or confrontation with the West, however, the prevailing treatment of Pan-Islamism has overshadowed more subtle internal processes and connections linking mobile Muslim populations across geographic and political boundaries. Among these processes was the surge in scholars, students, and journalists—bringing texts, ideas, and debates—as they traversed between the Ottoman and British empires with increasing regularity, from the locomotive and steamship age to the first automobiles and airplanes. Eschewing the predominantly militaristic emphasis to the study of modern Pan-Islam, this chapter invests closer attention to the legal and jurisprudential dimensions of Muslim transnational networks between the Ottoman Empire, Afghanistan, and British India in particular. By focusing on scholars, jurists, and other literate elites who traveled to Kabul between the last quarter of the nineteenth century to the first quarter of the twentieth, this book proposes Afghanistan as a crucial site for the study of modern Pan-Islamic networks, but of a very different nature.

The case of the Ottoman Empire and Afghanistan—two Muslim monarchies and states in friendly contact but who never joined forces in combat against another power—presents such an opportunity for exploring "juridical Pan-Islam" in action. In the eighteenth century, the Hotaki (1709–1738) and Durrani (1747–1823) dynasties, a pair of Afghan empires that emerged from the ashes of Mughal India and Safavid Persia, initiated contact with the Sublime Porte in 1725 and 1761 respectively. Afghan outreach to the Ottomans in the eighteenth century appears to have borne little fruit, however, apart from an exchange of letters between the royal courts of Istanbul and Kandahar that produced more suspicion than friendship, and even history's only Ottoman-Afghan war, in 1726.[9]

Though never as powerful or commanding as extensive a territory as its Hotaki and Durrani predecessors, Afghanistan's subsequent Muhammadzai dynasty (1826–1929; also known as the Barakzai dynasty) garnered more attention from the Sublime Porte. Without controlling territories contiguous to the Ottomans, the Muhammadzai amirs of Afghanistan strengthened ties with the sultans of Istanbul beginning in the late nineteenth century. As leaders of a fellow Sunni state nestled in the strategic borderlands between Iran, India, and Bukhara, like the Ottomans the Muhammadzais patronized the Hanafi school of Islamic law in their governance, bolstering the Kabul court's claims to be legitimate Muslim sovereigns, upholding justice and social order as embodied in the shariʿa, in exchange for obedience from their subjects. While both Afghanistan and the Ottoman Empire shared doctrinal affinities as Sunni states of the Hanafi order, resemblances fade when considering the distinct contexts of a relatively centralized, multireligious Ottoman state straddling three continents, versus a loose confederacy of predominantly Pashtun tribes headed by royal dynasties in Kandahar and Kabul. Yet precisely because their social and political contexts differ so starkly, exploring instances of encounter and exchange between the late Ottoman Empire and Afghanistan promises valuable insights into the extent of shared processes of juridical Pan-Islam during a pivotal era of transformation across the region.

Complicating bilateral relations between the Sublime Porte and amirs of Afghanistan was a legal technicality of great consequence: Afghanistan's status as a British protectorate since 1879, which subjected Afghanistan's foreign affairs to the British Raj's control. What is more, it rendered the already porous border between Afghanistan and India that much more contested. Few images could capture the intersection—and tensions—of this arrangement better than the dramatic arrival of Ahmed Hulusi Effendi, the first Ottoman envoy to Kabul, at the bustling British Indian seaport of Bombay in late summer of 1877. Before continuing our account of the Turkish envoy's mission to Afghanistan via India, it would be useful to offer a historical context for "tripartite" relations between Muslims of all three states.

Turks, Afghans, and Hindustanis

The earliest recorded ties between Ottoman Turks, Afghans, and Muslims of the Indian subcontinent date to the late fifteenth century. In 1481–1482, Sultan Mehmed II, the conqueror of Constantinople, and Beyazıd II, his successor, corresponded with Bahmani kings Muhammad Shah III and Mahmud Shah of India's southern Deccan plateau. As both Mughal and Ottoman historians have shown, early Indo-Ottoman contacts consisted primarily of the exchange of letters and gifts, with no evidence of political or military alliances being concluded at this time.[10] Such diplomatic courtesies, it should be remembered, were not limited to Ottoman relations with Muslim rulers or principalities.[11]

Roughly a century later, maritime conflict with the Portuguese drove the Ottomans into a series of short-lived alliances with Muslim potentates along the southern Malabar coast. The rise of Portuguese power in Africa and the Indian Ocean had seriously threatened Ottoman seaborne trade connecting ports from Constantinople to Alexandria and from Aden to Bombay.[12] Hajj routes for Indian pilgrims seeking to reach Hejaz were also disrupted by Portuguese intervention on the high seas. Istanbul's response was swift and decisive. In 1531, with the goal of curbing Iberian expansion and keeping the hajj routes open, Sultan Süleiman I dispatched an Ottoman fleet of two thousand men to Gujarat, making landfall at Diu on the Malabar coast. Preventing a Portuguese attack, the Ottoman success raised the confidence of Indian Muslims in the Turkish sultan, whose prestige consequently soared, for a time. Subsequent Ottoman expeditions to India followed—those of Hadim Süleyman Pasha in 1538 and Piri Reis in 1551, but neither resulted in a permanent Ottoman presence in the subcontinent.[13] Even the memory of this rather dramatic incident in early modern Pan-Islamism seems to have been forgotten by all but a handful of academics and local tourism dilettantes. Furthermore, in light of the Ottoman-Portuguese rivalry in the Indian Ocean region, and the long-standing presence of thriving Muslim communities and commercial networks along India's southern coast, these historical episodes of inter-Muslim entente hardly indicate a Pan-Islamic agenda; rather, they reflect the myriad contingent imperatives characteristic of any state pursuing its geostrategic interests.

Ottoman communication with Indian rulers increased substantially after the founding of the Mughal dynasty of India by the Timurid chieftain Zahir al-Din Babur (1483–1530) in 1526. Establishing a preliminary capital in Kabul, over the sixteenth and seventeenth centuries Babur's descendants consolidated Mughal power across the Indian plains to found a vast empire stretching from Kandahar to Bengal and from Delhi to the Deccan plateau, constituting the world's penultimate Sunni Muslim power in the early modern period. In spite of this prominence, early references to the Mughals in Ottoman sources dating to the first half of the sixteenth century suggest that court-to-court links were not established until the reign of Mughal emperor Jahangir (r. 1605–1627).[14]

Recorded contacts between Ottomans and Afghans arise considerably later, and much less frequently. This is hardly surprising. With over five times the territory and many more times the population, India features much more prominently in Ottoman foreign policy in Asia than Afghanistan or the Bukharan khanates. There were also important, more strategic benefits to be gained: the Indian subcontinent boasted some of the richest agricultural basins as well as maritime ports and overland trade routes in the world as they knew it. Manuscripts produced from Ottoman correspondence with and intelligence reports about Hindustani shahs, amirs, and princes, especially along the subcontinent's coastal regions, far outnumber those of their Afghan counterparts in the Asian interior.[15] Documents in the Ottoman central archives in Istanbul do contain scattered references to Afghans traveling in the sultan's domains, mostly from the nineteenth century. Mainly pilgrims, scholars, and sufi mendicants, the latter Afghans are usually grouped together in documents on "foreign Muslims" traveling in the Ottoman lands, including Moroccans, Algerians, Tunisians, and Uzbeks.[16] On the other hand, interimperial relations between the Afghan kings and the House of Osman present a more complicated case given the historical conditions under which Afghanistan emerged as an autonomous territory and state.

Afghans before Afghanistan

Over two thousand years before most histories mark the emergence of Afghanistan as an independent state in the eighteenth century, ancestors of today's Afghans were part and parcel of a rich and varied sociocultural landscape between Mesopotamia and Bengal, which include some of the oldest continuously inhabited regions in the world. Archaeologists have cited evidence of agricultural settlements in the region surrounding today's Kandahar as early as 5000 BC, and prehistoric clues of human activity for many millennia earlier.[17] Historians have detected written references to diverse peoples inhabiting the mountainous expanses and fertile valleys between the eastern provinces of the ancient Persian Achaemenid Empire (550–350 BC) and the Indus River, a region known to the Greco-Romans as Ariana. The birthplace of Zoroastrianism and home to some of humanity's earliest civilizations, including the greatest Buddhist kingdoms in history, Ariana grew especially notable for its city-states that emerged in the lush valleys, rolling hills, and irrigated flatlands between the Hindu Kush mountain range and the Amu Darya River, an area the ancient Greeks also knew as Bactria, Pactiya, or Paktha. Little can be generalized about the ancient "Pakhtans," who spoke a variant of Indo-European languages, other than they included early ancestors of today's Pashtuns of Afghanistan—also known as Pakhtuns and Pathans in Pakistan and India—terms synonymous with the Persian word *Āfghān* since at least the third century CE.[18]

Contrary to common lore, Afghans were never a self-contained, closed, or immutable community, fixed to the rugged, mountainous territory it is known as today, and juxtaposed against outside invaders and influences from time immemorial. Neither can they be stereotyped as recalcitrant hill peoples bent on rebellion against central authority. The early Pashtuns comprised not only pastoral nomads and mountaineers but also settled agricultural communities, urban merchants, and even a few powerful but short-lived imperial dynasties.[19] While pastoral groups of Pakthan heritage continued to migrate and settle in territories from the eastern frontiers of Alexander's Greco-Macedonian empire in the pre-Islamic fourth century BC, to the first Arab-Islamic conquests of Khorasan in the seventh century CE and founding of the Turco-Persian Delhi Sultanate (1206–1526), Pashtun dynasties ruled substantial portions of northern India in the settled Lodi (1451–1526) and Suri (1540–1557) kingdoms.[20] As late as the eighteenth century a Pashtun dominion flourished in the Rohilkhand region of north India, hence the origin of the term "Rohillas" for Pashtuns in India. At its height, as many as five thousand scholars were said to be supported by its ruler Hafiz al-Mulk and other patrons.[21]

The earliest instances of Ottoman-Afghan diplomatic contact date to the mid-sixteenth century. In 1544 the first Ottoman-Afghan alliance against Safavid Iran was proposed when Shir Shah Suri (1486–1545), founder of the second major Pashtun dynasty in India, dispatched an envoy to Istanbul proposing a joint Ottoman-Afghan assault on Persia, with apparent anti-Shiʿi overtones. The plans for a joint Sunni attack on Iran fell apart, however, upon Shir Shah Suri's death in 1545.[22] Apart from this relatively isolated case of early modern Ottoman-Afghan entente, however, records discussing Afghans in the Sublime Porte's central archives do not surface until well into the eighteenth century.[23] The historical presence of Pashtun kingdoms in northern India notwithstanding, extant Ottoman government documents and travel literature do not consistently employ the term "Afghanistan" to signify a distinct territory or state until the late eighteenth century. Rather, when speaking of Afghans, Ottoman records for this period refer either to travelers and pilgrims within the Ottoman domains or to nomadic tribes (*kabileler*) inhabiting the region triangulated between Iran, India, and Bukhara—a nondemarcated zone Shah Mahmoud Hanifi has aptly termed Proto-Afghanistan.[24]

As for the Safavid and Mughal courts, both Turco-Persianate dynasties drew on Afghan tribal levies to augment their armies and employed individual Afghans as mercenaries. The more independently minded, such as the Pashtun warrior-poet Khushal Khan Khattak (1613–1689), revolted against their Mughal overlords by taking to the mountainous precipices between the Sulaiman, Pamir, and Hindu Kush ranges—today's Federally Administered Tribal Areas (FATA) and Khyber Pakhtunkhwa of Pakistan—engaging in sustained guerrilla warfare against the shahs of Delhi. In this sense, from the sixteenth through seventeenth centuries, the Afghans' fate was entangled with imperial competitions between the three Turco-Mongolian "Gunpowder Empires" of the Ottomans, Safavids, and Mughals, but hardly in a uniform or predictable fashion.[25] In the meantime, caught between the expansionist rivalries of Persia and India in particular, the possibility of a unified and autonomous Afghanistan remained elusive until conditions on the ground shifted dramatically in Delhi and Isfahan, beginning in the early eighteenth century.

Ahmad Shah Durrani, Greater Afghanistan, and the Ottoman Caliphate

Conventional histories of Afghanistan mark the emergence of an independent Afghan state with the ascent of Ahmad Khan Abdali (1722–1772), an able Pashtun commander in the Iranian Afsharid imperial bodyguard. In 1747, the twenty-five-year-old Ahmad Khan seized on the vacuum created by the assassination of his patron and Afsharid king Nadir Shah—itself following the early eighteenth-century collapse of the once mighty Mughal Empire to the east and Safavid Persia to the west—to establish an imperial dynasty of his own with a capital based in Kandahar. Following a humble coronation that has since been mythologized as Afghanistan's protonational Loya Jirga (Great Assembly), the young chieftain was anointed king of the Afghans and renamed Ahmad Shah Durrani (following the sobriquet, Durr-i Durran, or "Pearl of Pearls").[26]

With a new title and enlarged army, Ahmad Shah Durrani galvanized his predominantly Pashtun troops, but also contingents of Tajik, Uzbek, and Qizilbash forces, for a lightning campaign of conquest into Iran, Central Asia, and India. The result was a vast empire stretching from Khorasan to Kashmir and from the Oxus to the Arabian Sea, capturing some of the wealthiest cities in the greater Islamicate world. By the time of his demise a quarter century later, the former Afsharid bodyguard had founded an expansive Afghan empire that comprised virtually all of today's Afghanistan and Pakistan, in addition to territories of today's Iran, India, Tajikistan, Turkmenistan, and Uzbekistan—including Mashhad, Lahore, Kashmir, and Delhi.[27]

Despite his remarkable successes on the battlefield and his emerging as one of the most powerful Muslim kings in the world, Ahmad Shah struggled to gain recognition from the Ottoman sultans in Istanbul. The latter were still the world's greatest Muslim power even following a spate of territorial losses to neighboring empires, especially Russia. Shortly after his stunning victory over Marathi forces at the Battle of Panipat (January 14, 1761), the Durrani king reached out in correspondence to Ottoman sultan Mustafa III (r. 1757–1773). Addressing the sultan on equal terms as *birādar* (brother), Ahmad Shah elaborated on his accession to a new Afghan throne, his victories in Persia, and glorious expeditions to India.[28] Notably, he also acknowledged the Ottoman sultans as rightful possessors of the caliphate, continuing an Afghan tradition established by Ahmad Shah's Hotaki predecessors in the 1720s. Seeking to gather momentum for an Ottoman-Afghan Sunni entente, the Afghan king also expressed regret that he was not able to embark on a large-scale attack on their Shiʿi rivals in Persia, subtly implying he expected such action from the caliph and leader of all Sunni Muslims himself.[29]

It seems Ahmad Shah's letter did not made an impression. No Ottoman-Afghan entente materialized; there was no joint attack on Iran; and there was not even an investiture of Ottoman recognition on the Afghan court. Perhaps the causes lay in lingering suspicions from the Ottoman-Hotaki skirmish earlier that century, or perhaps the Ottomans simply found the letter pretentious.

For the greater regional legitimacy Ahmad Shah anxiously sought as founder of a new great Muslim empire in Asia, he would have to seek it elsewhere—expanding his conquests further into Khorasan in the west and Punjab in the east. The latter campaign went as far as to capture Delhi upon the overtures of prominent Indian ulema lamenting the decline of Mughal power, including the city's renowned eighteenth-century scholar, Shah Wali Allah (1703–1762).[30] To the north, Ahmad Shah sealed Afghan hegemony over the Uzbek khanates of Central Asia, including the historic city of Balkh. It was around this time that the Uzbek-Manghit dynast of Bukhara, Shah Murad, presented the Durrani ruler with a *khirqih sharīf*, a sacred cloak of the Prophet long guarded by the Bukharans, and held under cherished guardianship by the Dahpidi Naqshabandi sufis of Faizabad.[31]

Even as the Durranis launched a remarkable campaign to preeminence in the eastern Islamicate world, Ottoman disregard for the Afghans tells us another story: the unsullied confidence, and indeed supremacy, of the Ottomans as the world's greatest Muslim power. The grand conquest of Constantinople by Sultan Mehmed II (r. 1451–1481) in 1453 would seem to tell us just as much. But in the eyes of other Muslim powers, later Ottoman sultans had even more glory to showcase. In 1517, Sultan Selim I (r. 1512–1520) catapulted the Porte's Pan-Islamic credentials to unequaled levels following his triumph over the Mamluks and resulting annexation of Greater Syria, Egypt, and Hejaz. Following their decisive victory over the Safavids at the Battle of Chaldiran three years earlier, the Ottomans had also established sovereignty over the Shiʿi shrine cities of Najaf, Karbalaʾ, Kazimayn, and Samarra, sealing the House of Osman's distinction as custodians of Islam's holiest sites par excellence.[32] For the remainder of their existence, the Ottomans were preeminent among Muslim powers, resulting in eagerly sought-after recognition from independent Muslim rulers as far as Central Asia, Indonesia, and Afghanistan—all lands where no Ottoman army had ever set foot.

Although we have few sources documenting official contacts between Afghan rulers and the Ottomans before the nineteenth century, the annual hajj offered a premier venue for contact and interaction between Muslims across political boundaries. It also provided Muslim rulers with a partly neutral space to negotiate alliances of political, economic, and other strategic value, and Afghans were no exception in this regard. In the early eighteenth century, Mir Wais Khan Hotak (1673–1715), founder of the Hotaki Afghan dynasty, traveled to Mecca hoping to obtain the support of leading Ottoman ulema to endorse his rebellion against the Safavid governor of Kandahar. Emboldened by a fatwa in his favor, Mir Wais returned to Persia and succeeded in rousing a confederation of Afghan tribes to march on Safavid-controlled Kandahar. The result was not only an Afghan conquest of Kandahar but also the collapse of the Safavid Empire and sacking of Isfahan by his son Mahmud in 1722.[33] Although the Hotakis' success was short-lived, the role of even indirect Ottoman support was not lost on subsequent rulers based in Kandahar and Kabul, including the founder of the next great Afghan empire, Ahmad Shah Durrani.[34]

Enter the British and Russians

For at least two reasons, the Afghans' stunning victory over the Marathan forces at Panipat in 1761 would prove to be among the most consequential battles in the history of Asia. To begin with, it neutralized one of the most powerful confederations in India, creating a political vacuum that would soon be filled by a new power. Second, the Durrani emperor's fateful decision to retire to Kandahar rather than establish a new capital in Lahore or Delhi and campaign further east prevented a clash with another rising force in the subcontinent, a highly militarized joint-stock corporation known as the British East India Company. Backed by British ships and firepower, the East India Company proceeded to accumulate taxes, territory, and political dominion over local Indian principalities and completed a virtual conquest of Bengal in 1793.

Over the next half century, the East India Company continued to uphold the legal fiction of merely tax collecting for the sovereign Mughal emperor at Delhi. But as the latter withered under virtual house arrest in the Red Fort, the joint-stock company flourished into a de facto empire. As the Raj grew into Britain's richest and most populous colony, the English Crown's historic rival in Asia was meanwhile cultivating designs of its own. In a series of devastating wars lasting from 1804 to 1813 and from 1826 to 1828, an emboldened Russian Empire under the late Romanov tsars conquered the entire Caucasus region formerly ruled by Persia, including present-day Dagestan, Georgia, Armenia, and Azerbaijan, and strengthened its presence in the new Qajar court of Tehran. St. Petersburg exploited its influence with the Qajars to progress plans to make the Caspian a Russian lake, linking the Caucasus with Turkistan through Khorasan. In this way, Afghanistan in the nineteenth century would again be encircled by two powerful empires but of a very different color: the British Raj to the east and south, and tsarist Russia to the west and north. The interimperial strategic rivalry in Central Asia, coined by British Indian intelligence officer Arthur Conolly (1807–1842) as the Great Game, also popularized Afghanistan as a Forbidden Kingdom of swashbuckling adventures in many a Victorian consciousness through the works of English novelists Rudyard Kipling and Arthur Conan Doyle, among others.[35] Ahmad Shah's successors would eventually cede significant portions of the Durrani Empire's frontiers to these very same rivals, although the subsequent Muhammadzai dynasty succeeded in preserving an internationally recognized territory known as Afghanistan.

In the nineteenth century, Afghanistan was not the only sovereign Muslim power that found itself caught between imperial rivalries on its borders and, increasingly, within its own domains. In spite of the Sublime Porte's global prestige among Muslims due to its custodianship of the hajj and caliphate since the sixteenth century, earlier Ottoman dominance in the Mediterranean and Indian Ocean was not to last. By the mid-eighteenth century, the maritime and inland expansion of European joint-stock companies, armies, and colonial administrations across Africa and Asia had transformed how sultans, shahs, and amirs viewed themselves, and each other, vis-à-vis non-Muslim powers. Never before had navies, armies, and merchants from the Eurasian continent presented such a stark military and economic threat to Muslim imperial courts, including the Sublime Porte in Istanbul. In what became known as the Eastern Question, over the course of the late eighteenth to early twentieth centuries, the Ottoman Empire became subject to a series of interimperial contestations between the major European powers, especially Britain, France, Russia, and Austria-Hungary.

To some observers it might seem natural that in the face of such an overwhelming European threat, Muslim powers would be encouraged to join together in defensive alliances. As developments in the nineteenth and twentieth centuries would reveal, however, in practice European colonialism divided subject populations, and the increasingly few Muslim sovereigns who resisted them, as much as it unified them.[36] Amir Dost Muhammad Khan's refusal to join the great 1857 Indian Rebellion, and the Ottoman sultan's overt criticism of the rebels, for example, caution us to be wary of essentialist notions of political Islam that presuppose a perennial jihad of Muslim states against non-Muslim powers, such as between Ottomans or Afghans and the British Empire in the Victorian age. Understanding the roots of Pan-Islamic ententes lay, then, not in the realm of abstract ideology but in the historically specific and contingent political contexts within which modern Muslim powers from Istanbul to Kabul

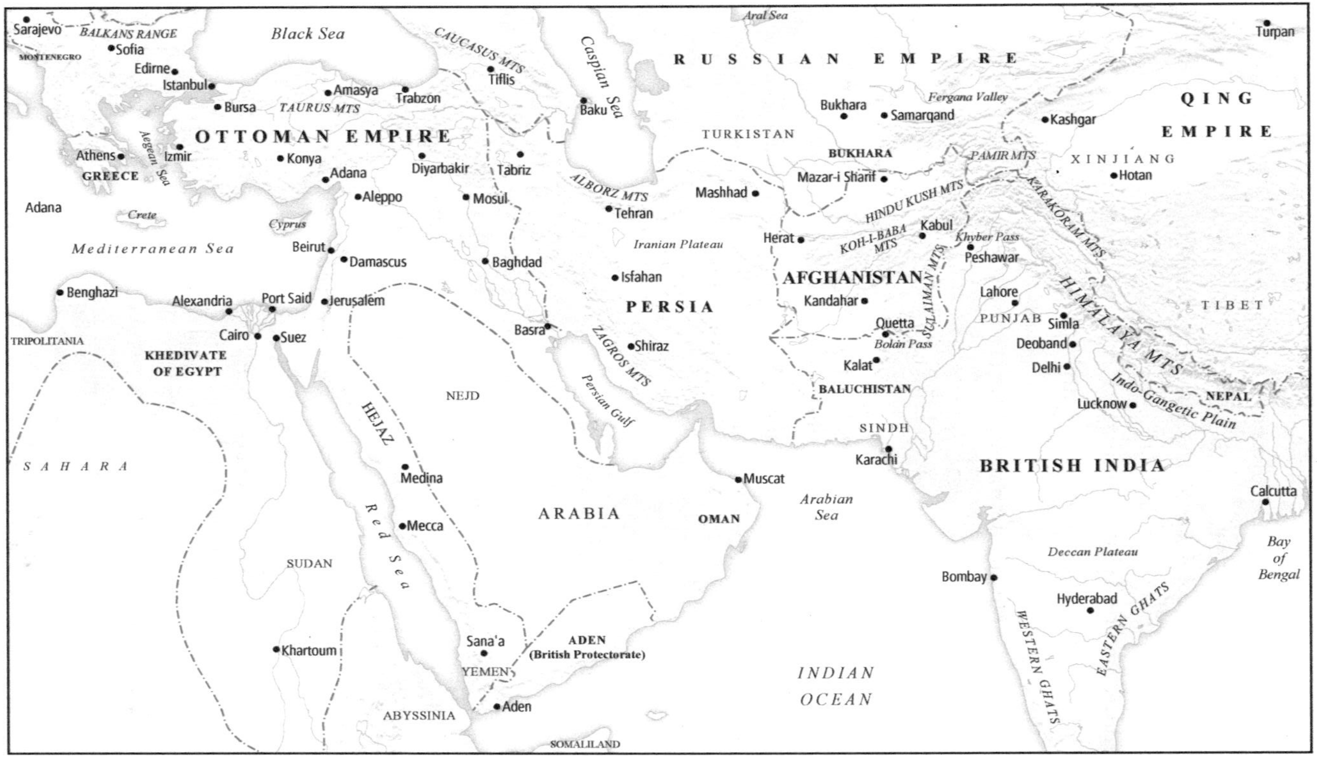

MAP 1. The Ottoman Empire, Afghanistan, and British India, early 1877

found it in their interest to build stronger ties with each other, while pursuing independent geostrategic imperatives on their own terms.

Both the Great Game and Eastern Question were Eurocentric paradigms that disregarded the agency of Ottomans, Afghans, and Indian Muslims, reducing them to captive subjects of British or Russian imperial rivalries. Such paradigms endured well into the twentieth century. Hence an American political scientist writes in 1982, "The classical notion of Afghanistan as a buffer state consisted principally in the maintenance of a shaking balance, which engaged the entire statecraft of the Afghan government, between the two great powers in the region: Britain and Russia."[37] Such frameworks underestimate the efforts of Muslim sovereigns—in the Ottoman Empire and Qajar Iran in particular—to contest both British and Russian colonial encroachment in the region, while pursuing realpolitik objectives peculiar to their respective courts. It is precisely because it faced interimperial competition, rather than because it was ideologically committed to Pan-Islamism, that the Porte decided to send an official delegation to strategically located Kabul (see Map 1), and to an Afghan amir who prepared to host them.

An Ottoman Gaze to the East

Though evidence of correspondence between the Ottomans and various Muslim rulers of India dates to the mid-fifteenth century, the Sublime Porte did not establish permanent diplomatic sanctuaries in the subcontinent until 1849. The royal firman authorizing the appointments of liaisons to Calcutta and Bombay specified their duties as "executing the affairs of the merchants and our people" and "consulting their interest and ensuring the respect of property and honour."[38] Officially, at least, there was little reason to surmise anything more than regular diplomatic protocols were at play between the Ottoman and British empires, friendly powers as they were for most of the nineteenth century. As for Muslims of British India, following the termination of the Mughal sultanate in 1857 political ties with the Ottomans largely rested on individual outreach with the semiautonomous rulers of princely states, such as the Begum of Bhopal or Nizam of Hyderabad, none of whom had embassies in Constantinople.

Within two years of his ascent to the throne, however, a new sultan in Istanbul, Abdülhamid II (r. 1876–1909), was already reconfiguring the Porte's foreign policy to reflect a more robust engagement with the Muslims of Asia. Primary evidence of this shift is reflected in the swell of Ottoman intelligence gathering on the internal affairs of Iran, Afghanistan, India, and eastern Turkistan (Central Asia) during the last two decades of the nineteenth century.[39] This documentary surge can be partially attributed to enhanced print and paper technologies. But given the more regular correspondence between the Porte and Indian Muslims during the Hamidian era, including the establishment of an Ottoman consulate at Bombay, to attribute the increase in reporting to enhanced print technologies alone misses the substantive boost in perceived geostrategic value of these regions to the Porte. While Ottoman state records during the last quarter of the nineteenth century indicate that the Porte was taking a deeper interest in Asian affairs, a simultaneous recorded increase in private letters, telegrams, and even delegations of Indians and Afghans to Istanbul inform us the relationship was not a one-way road. In the late nineteenth century, more Afghans and Indian Muslims were exploiting the enhanced mobility that steamships and railroads provided to travel—and emigrate—to Ottoman lands. Such movements often attracted the attention of British surveillance. It was not uncommon for the British agency at Istanbul to report in routine intelligence exchanges with the Raj's foreign department, for example, that a visiting Indian had "taken a house in Constantinople" where he "sees a good deal of the Turkish notables and of the Mussulman population of the city."[40]

By the late nineteenth century, Indian Muslim notables were also known to bypass official diplomatic channels in their outreach to the Porte by forming a number of transnational Muslim associations (*anjumans* in Persian and Urdu). Founded as cultural and philanthropic societies to connect expatriate communities in Europe with their ancestral homes in the subcontinent, Indian anjumans also served another purpose: to bolster ties with the Ottoman sultan-caliph in Istanbul. Whether in Lahore or Liverpool, the activities of these organizations were not unidirectional; some anjumans founded in England made their way back to India. A British Indian intelligence briefing from 1880, for example, describes the founding of a branch of the London Islamic Society in Calcutta, Bengal, where weekly meetings were held in a prominent notable's home and communications were drafted for correspondence with the Ottoman government.[41]

Private correspondence not only provided the Porte with valuable intelligence but also helped link Ottoman officialdom with local Muslim notables and populations who did not reside in the sultan's domains. In addition to the activities of anjumans, Abdülhamid was keen to employ even more long-standing links between the predominant Naqshabandi and Qaderi sufi orders of India, Afghanistan, and Central Asia with counterparts in Ottoman-governed Mesopotamia,

FIGURE I.1. Pro-Ottoman proclamation of Qaderi sufis of Baghdad to Muslims of India and Afghanistan, 1876. *Left to right:* Arabic original; Urdu translation; Persian translation. Prime Ministry Ottoman Archives, Istanbul, Turkey (Y.PRK.HR 1.16).

Syria, Anatolia, and as far as the Balkans.[42] The role of the Qaderi Naqibs of Baghdad as particularly well-placed intermediaries between the Sublime Porte and Indian and Afghan Muslims was amply displayed in the lead-up to the same war. In December 1876, representatives of the Naqibs in Baghdad transmitted a fatwa in Arabic, with accompanying Urdu and Persian translations, to India and Afghanistan in support of the looming Ottoman conflict with Russia (see Figure 1.1).[43]

As Ottoman intelligence reports noted later that year, the Naqibs' fatwa was received enthusiastically by local religious figures in the Indo-Afghan frontier, including the Akhund of Swat. The latter preached to a large gathering after Friday prayers in December 1876 that the last great Muslim power was in danger and it was incumbent upon the believers of India, Arabia, and Afghanistan to join in the Ottoman jihad against Russia by means of arms or financial subscription.[44] From the reverse geographic direction, in late summer 1877, scholars of northern India's influential seminary, the Dar al-ʿUlum at Deoband, delivered an ardently composed and elegantly ornamented letter to Abdülhamid expressing their desire for stronger ties (see Figure 1.2).[45]

Beyond the material support local anjumans and sufi orders in India and Afghanistan provided to the Ottomans, the Porte's access to these grassroots contacts and sources of information also supplemented regular reports from Ottoman consulates abroad, providing Turkish officials with a window into myriad aspects of community life, politics, and economies of Muslims, from Balkh to Bengal, Kashgar to Kandahar, and Bukhara to Bombay. Conversely, special lodging was endowed for Central Asian pilgrims in Istanbul with thorough knowledge of the Porte, such as the Uzbek and Afghan dervish lodges of Üsküdar, located in near proximity on the Asian side of the city (see Figure 1.3).[46] In addition to the aforesaid institutions we must also consider the role of Ottoman interest or even patronage of Muslim religious and educational sites in the Indian subcontinent, such as the Muhammadan Anglo-Oriental College at Aligarh and Osmania University of Hyderabad.[47]

Put in historical context, then, the Sublime Porte's ties with Indian Muslims and Afghans constituted neither a significant nor sustained factor in Ottoman geopolitics until the Hamidian period.[48] Having consolidated a grip on power following his defeat of the constitutionalists and annulment of the 1876 Kanun-ı Esasi itself, Abdülhamid reached out to Indian Muslims and Afghans in an attempt to identify and consolidate political assets outside the empire. During the last two decades of the nineteenth century, the sultan-caliph grew increasingly

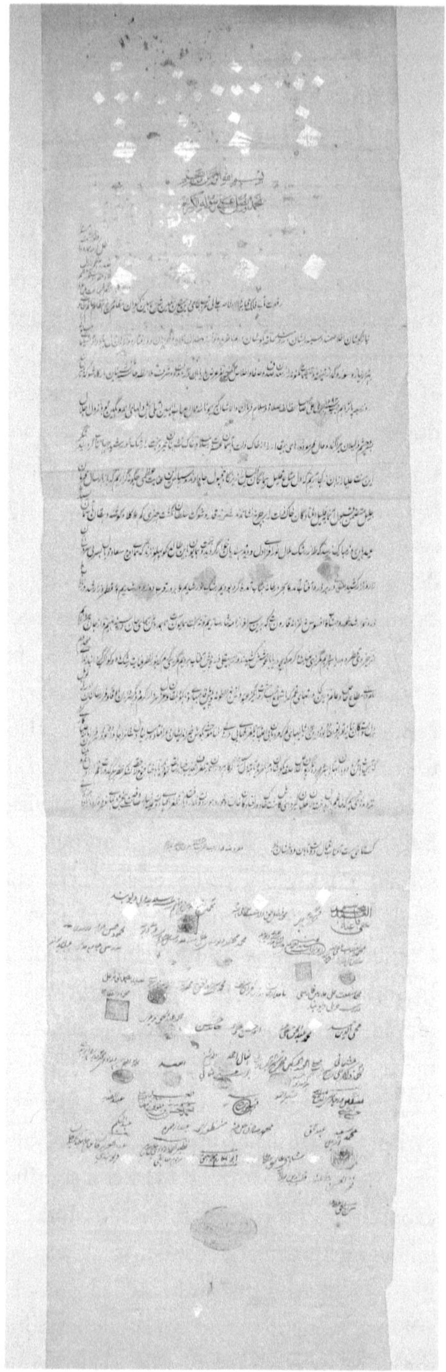

FIGURE I.2.
Letter from Indian scholars of Dar al-ʿUlum Deoband seminary to Sultan Abdülhamid II during the first Ottoman mission to Afghanistan, 1877. Prime Ministry Ottoman Archives, Istanbul, Turkey (Y.A. HUS 159/14).

FIGURE 1.3. Uzbek *tekke* (dervish lodge), Üsküdar, Istanbul. Also in the vicinity are historic Afghan and Indian dervish lodges. Author photograph.

adept at employing Pan-Islamic rhetoric and policy for political and diplomatic gain.[49] That these overtures came in the midst of a catastrophic spate of territorial, demographic, and economic losses in the Russo-Ottoman War (1877–1878), the French occupation of Tunisia (1881), and the British occupation of Egypt a year later, to say nothing of the Treaty of Berlin and broader European scramble for colonies in Africa and Asia, must be kept in mind.[50] Seeking to bolster the Porte's international clout with Russia and Britain in particular, it is in this historical context of international imperial competition, rather than an a priori religious orientation of Abdülhamid II's psychology, that we can locate late Ottoman efforts to reach out more assertively to Muslims in the east.[51] It is also for these reasons that following the outbreak of war with tsarist Russia in the spring of 1877, Sultan Abdülhamid dispatched a special envoy to Kabul with a tangible goal in mind: to convince the Afghan amir, Shir ʿAli Khan, to join forces with the Ottomans against St. Petersburg. Together, so the plan went, the Ottomans and Afghans would open a devastating third front against the

Russian Empire in the latter's Achilles' heel: the Turkic, Muslim-majority regions of Central Asia.

In light of the high stakes of the mission, Abdülhamid II took a personal interest in selecting a qualified envoy to represent the sultan-caliph in the Kabul court. When he opted for a distinguished Islamic scholar and jurist over a seasoned statesman from the Porte's diplomatic corps, for some it was an unexpected choice. British Raj officials in particular, including some who were facilitating the Ottoman delegation's passage through Indian territory, were surprised a more senior official from the Ottoman foreign service was not chosen for the job.[52] Initial responses from British officialdom notwithstanding, the choice of Ahmed Hulusi Effendi as the first official Ottoman envoy to Afghanistan is significant for other reasons, reasons that have received insufficient attention.[53]

Şirvanizade Seyyid Ahmed Hulusi Effendi was born in the first half of the nineteenth century in Amasya, a provincial town in northeastern Anatolia famous for its apple orchards and as a former governorate of Ottoman princes.[54] The son of Şirvani İsmail Effendi, a local judge with a venerated ancestry hailing to the Prophet, Hulusi Effendi's notable background is also evident in him being a brother of the one-time grand vizier, Şirvanizade Mehmed Rüşdü Pasha (1828–1874).[55] Ottoman and British sources before the mission offer complimentary portraits of the man, an indication of his respected stature in Istanbul during the late Tanzimat and early Hamidian eras. Independent accounts from the capital, Egypt, Diyarbkir, and Delhi—all places he would visit between 1877 and 1878—describe Hulusi as an erudite, devout, and well-regarded *ʿālim*, or religious scholar. "Well spoken of" by both the Porte and Palace, he enjoyed a distinguished rank in the uppermost echelons of the empire's Islamic scholarly class.[56]

After completing his formal studies, Hulusi rapidly scaled the ranks of the Ottoman judiciary, beginning with his 1849 appointment as qadi (judge) to the Aydos district of Istanbul. In May 1867, after serving in a number of similar judicial posts, he was promoted to judge of Istanbul's prominent Galata district. The next year he was transferred to a judgeship in the sacred precincts of Mecca, by all accounts a promotion. Soon thereafter, he reached the apex of the Ottoman judiciary with his appointment as *kazasker* of Anatolia. Literally translating as "military judge" in Ottoman Turkish, the title more accurately corresponds to chief judge (or justice), and was among the most prominent juridical positions in the empire after the sheikh ül-Islam and kazasker of Rumelia.[57] In the same year, Hulusi was recognized by the sultan with an honorary medal for outstanding judicial service to the state.[58]

Hulusi's most prestigious appointment, in a fluid Ottoman juridical field undergoing considerable transformation, was still to come, however. In 1869, the powerful administrator-jurist, president of the Council of Judicial Ordinances, and later minister of justice, Ahmed Cevdet Pasha (1822–1895), personally selected Hulusi to be one of the fifteen jurists to participate in the compilation of the landmark Mecelle-i Ahkam-ı 'Adliye, otherwise known as the Ottoman Civil Code.[59] It would not be an exaggeration to describe the Mecelle as the most famous codification of Islamic law in modern history. The sixteen-volume text, containing 1,851 articles, continues to be well regarded and studied by legal professionals and colleges of law throughout the Islamicate world, in both Hanafi jurisdictions and otherwise.[60] Hulusi's role in compiling the Mecelle was not marginal. Serving on the drafting committee from the launch of the project in 1869 until its completion in 1876, he participated in the preparation of all sixteen volumes of the code save the sixth and eighth. His role in compiling the thirteenth book on admissions (*Kitabü'l-İkrar*) has been described as especially preponderant.[61]

Far from being a neutral bystander in emergent debates about the codification of Islamic jurisprudence (*fiqh*), Hulusi's participation in the drafting of the Mecelle highlights the influential role he played in one of the most important Islamic legal reforms of the nineteenth century. Having served for over a decade in the uppermost echelons of the Ottoman judiciary, Hulusi's remarkable career was about to take another turn in the years following his service on the Mecelle committee, but in a direction few could have expected.

The 1877–1878 Ottoman Mission to Kabul

In the late summer of 1877, the Sublime Porte dispatched its first official diplomatic mission to Afghanistan.[62] At the helm of an entourage of Turkish scribes, cartographers, and statesmen was Ahmed Hulusi Effendi. Traveling initially by sea, the delegation sojourned briefly in Alexandria, Egypt, where they were hosted by Khedive Ismail. Reboarding at Port Said, the travelers continued southward through the Suez Canal before stopping briefly at the British-controlled port of Aden. By early August, Hulusi and his delegation had sailed past the Horn of Africa and through the Arabian Sea, making landfall at the bustling south Indian seaport of Bombay on August 9.[63]

On August 11, hardly a day after their rapturous reception, Hulusi and his colleagues had already departed from the city under British escort.[64] Likely still weary from their sea journey, the group proceeded to follow their British hosts through the Indian interior, moving through obscure provincial towns with the goal of reaching the Khyber Pass in under a week. This was a brisk pace, and revealed no shortage of anxiety on the British Indian government's part. Though officially acquiescing to the mission in light of the shared Anglo-Ottoman goal of curbing Russian expansion in Asia, behind the scenes British correspondence reveals a deep sense of misgiving. With memory of the 1857 Rebellion still very much alive in Calcutta and London, British officials remained on high alert as to the potentially volatile effects of the Ottoman delegation's presence on India's Muslim populations. So vigilant were Raj officers responsible for overseeing the foreign delegation's passage that officers escorting the Turks were under strict orders to stay clear of all "Mussulman concentrations," and to be vigilant for any signs of "firebrands," "mutineers," and "intrigue."

For precisely these reasons, even before the Ottoman delegation had stepped foot on Indian soil, the British secretary of state to the government of India penned a memo to Calcutta earlier that summer with the following warning: "I need hardly call your attention to the probability that, if the envoy is permitted to remain in any of the towns where a powerful Mussulman population exists, popular demonstrations will result, which may involve hazard to the public peace as well as be likely to give a false impression of the intentions of Her Majesty's Government." The secretary was keen to instruct the Indian government to leave no stone unturned in preparing for the arrival of Hulusi Effendi and his colleagues. "Your Excellency will best avoid this danger," he further advised, "by arranging that the envoy should rest at places where the Mussulman element is not predominant in the population."[65] In early August, these instructions were repeated in the government of India's orders to those responsible for the envoy's imminent arrival at Bombay and passage through the Indian interior. "Every care was to be exercised, consistent with politeness, to render the Envoy's stay in Bombay, and other populous Mahomedan cities, as brief as possible, and His Excellency's journey through British territory quiet and unostentatious," the instructions from Calcutta emphasized.[66] In light of these warnings, the Turkish delegation's arrival created all the more embarrassment for Raj officials as they escorted the visitors through thronging crowds in Bombay. Keen not to repeat their mistakes, British escorts took every precaution on the remainder of the envoy's itinerary. After an arduous journey under the sweltering summer heat of Sindh and Punjab, Hulusi and his companions entered India's northwest frontier by early September. Shortly thereafter, the first Ottoman mission to Afghanistan crossed the Khyber Pass from Peshawar to Jalalabad, reaching Kabul on September 8, 1877.[67]

Both Ottoman and British sources describe the historic meeting between the Afghan amir, Shir ʿAli Khan, and the Ottoman envoy as a cordial exchange. "His Highness received me most amicably," Hulusi himself later described in an interview with British authorities, adding, "I was treated in Cabul with great respect."[68] Here the envoy was keen to emphasize that honors bestowed on the Turkish delegation were an expression of reverence for the Ottoman sultan by the very head of the Kabul court. "The Ameer commanded that due honor and courtesy should be extended to me," an order that appears to have been thoroughly heeded well beyond the capital and as far as the Indo-Afghan frontier.[69]

Reports by British informants embedded in the Kabul court state the meeting began with an offering of gifts on behalf of the Ottoman sultan, including a sacred hair from the Prophet's beard, a symbolic act of piety and fraternal solidarity reported to have "much pleased" the Afghan amir. After a meeting between Hulusi and the Afghan amir, British sources reveal a series of letters were also exchanged between the two Muslim sovereigns. The latter provided a channel for familiarizing the Afghan amir with recent developments in the Ottoman domains directly from the source.[70] Also significant are descriptions by British informants in Kabul at the time indicating that Hulusi was largely unrestricted in his movement in the capital, especially during the latter stages of the delegation's stay in Kabul. Subsequent correspondence between Hulusi and the Porte, as well as declassified British intelligence records on the mission, indicate that the envoy also met with leading members of the Afghan ulema in Shir ʿAli's royal administration.[71] In contrast to the general confinement and suspicion nineteenth-century foreign visitors to Afghanistan were often subjected to, available evidence indicates that by the end of his stay in Kabul, Hulusi was granted virtual carte blanche to meet with Afghan scholars, courtiers, and other elites.[72]

These aspects of the Ottoman envoy's sojourn in Afghanistan raise an important question that has hitherto been given insufficient attention: To what extent did Hulusi share with Afghan statesmen and scholars his novel perspectives on the modern administration of Islamic law, including his considerable experience in the Ottoman juridical field, not least of which involved contributions to the landmark Mecelle codification project?[73] We know that conversations between Hulusi and Afghan scholars took place immediately following his seven-year participation in the most renowned codification of Islamic law in modern history. By emphasizing the overt political dimensions of the Ottomans' first mission to

Afghanistan—namely, the spectacular prospect of a Pan-Islamic jihad uniting Kabul and Istanbul in an alliance against Russia—historians have overlooked less obvious but potentially more long-lasting exchanges in the realms of law and administration. More specifically, in light of Hulusi's groundbreaking meetings with the Afghan amir and ulema of Kabul, it seems probable that the topic of the Ottoman Tanzimat reforms, the Mecelle, the Ottoman Constitution of 1876, and other watershed (if not controversial) judicial projects in the sultan's domains would have surfaced in the meetings between these two groups of Muslim scholars and statesmen, who clearly much respected each other. Might Hulusi's intermingling with the notables of Kabul have contributed to new kinds of conversations in Afghanistan's royal court, including the codification of Hanafi jurisprudence, Islamic constitutionalism, and the role of the shariʿa in a modern state?

That the earliest recorded projects for the codification of Hanafi *fiqh* in Afghanistan began almost immediately after the Ottoman mission to Kabul, and within a decade of the Mecelle's completion, lends some support to this theory.[74] For more concrete signs of Ottoman influence on the late nineteenth-century Afghan court, however, we must turn to the aftermath of the Porte's 1877–1878 mission to Kabul. By October 1877, even though the Ottoman delegation had been given a warm reception and showered with an embarrassment of honors, it became clear that the Afghan amir was unwilling to commit to the sultan's invitation for a joint attack on Russia. Following a final cordial exchange, Hulusi and his entourage departed Kabul for Istanbul. Although Shir ʿAli had declined Abdülhamid's offer to join hands in combat against Russia, it is in the years immediately following the Ottoman mission to Kabul when internal Afghan developments give us even more reason to consider the possibilities and kinds of exchanges between the Sublime Porte and the Muhammadzai amirs of Kabul in the last two decades of the nineteenth century.

After the Mission: From the Second Anglo-Afghan War to the Iron Amir

In late autumn 1878, for the second time in the nineteenth century, a British army invaded Afghanistan. As casus belli, London cited Russian infiltration of the Kabul court, coupled with their lingering disappointment over Shir ʿAli's unwillingness to confront St. Petersburg's expansion into Central Asia.[75] The Raj government had already amassed Indian troops in the strategic border town of

Quetta as early as 1876. In the months that followed, the Raj's imperial army won a series of decisive battles against a disorganized and splintered Afghan resistance in the northwest borderlands of India and southern Afghanistan. By 1879, Shir ʿAli, the monarch who had warmly received the first Ottoman envoy to Afghanistan just over a year earlier, abdicated amid the imminent occupation of Kabul by British forces. In 1880, following a brief internecine power struggle, a new amir assumed the Muhammadzai throne in Kabul. ʿAbd al-Rahman Khan (r. 1880–1901) proceeded to launch the most ambitious modern state-building project in Afghanistan's history. Over the course of two decades, ʿAbd al-Rahman brutally consolidated his writ over the then-recognized territory of Afghanistan through a relentless process of internal imperialism, or series of domestic military conquests that included the violent repression of over one hundred tribal rebellions, earning him the sobriquet Iron Amir.[76]

Scholars of modern Afghan history generally agree that ʿAbd al-Rahman's was the first Kabul government to establish central authority over an internationally demarcated and recognized territory.[77] It was during ʿAbd al-Rahman's reign that Afghanistan's international borders were established and ratified by treaty. At the center of the Iron Amir's state-building campaign was a proto-national army drawn from a combination of tribal levies and newly introduced modes of conscription—but that is not all. ʿAbd al-Rahman's military strength explains how he crushed rebellions and conquered new provinces, but it fails to tell us how he held them. It was during ʿAbd al-Rahman's reign that the first countrywide codifications of law were promulgated, albeit designed for a rudimentary network of state courts established only in the country's major cities. Distinct from the expansive imperial forays into India, Iran, and Central Asia of his early modern forebears, Mirwais Hotaki and Ahmad Shah Durrani, ʿAbd al-Rahman's success was an internal struggle for sovereignty and legitimacy over a bounded territory between the British, Russian, and Qajar Iranian empires.

It is, however, also important not to overstate the innovative aspects or unprecedented nature of ʿAbd al-Rahman's strategies of modern statecraft and governance of Afghanistan.[78] Among the rare sources from this period, in a Western language at least, are the books and notes of Scottish statesman and historian Mountstuart Elphinstone (1779–1859). In 1808, Elphinstone was appointed as the first British envoy to the Durrani court in Kabul. In his classic travelogue of early nineteenth-century Afghanistan, the envoy provided the following description of law in the "Kingdom of Cabul," as the British Raj referred to the ruling Afghan Durrani dynasty:

> [The] general law of the kingdom is that of Mahomet, which is adopted in civil actions in the Ooloosses [Afghan interior and nomadic tribes] also; but their peculiar code, and the only one applied in their *internal* administration of criminal justice, is the Pooshtoonwulle, or usage of the Afghauns; a rude system of customary law, founded on principles such a one would suppose to have prevailed before the institution of civil government.[79]

Though rife with Orientalist tropes of wild tribes and the arbitrary *kadijustiz* of Afghan mullahs, Elphinstone's commentary nevertheless provides a rare early nineteenth-century account of Afghan law and society: Islamic jurisprudential principles intertwining with highly localized social norms in Afghanistan before the onset of centralization campaigns later in the century. The blending of Islamic jurisprudence with local customary law, known as *ʿurf, ʿādat,* or *Pashtūnwalī,* has characterized Afghan law and society in the predominantly rural, nomadic, and predominantly but not exclusively Pashtun population of the country since Ahmad Shah established the Durrani Empire in 1747, and probably much earlier as well. This decentralized state of affairs was most significantly challenged by what could be described as a nineteenth-century Islamicization campaign by ʿAbd al-Rahman. Apart from scattered snapshots such as Elphinstone's diaries, however, no systematic study has been carried out on law and administration during the amirates preceding the Iron Amir. A major reason for this historiographical gap is the relative paucity of written sources in local languages, sources that could provide a window into social life before the more well-documented practices of ʿAbd al-Rahman's government. For this reason, histories of the Afghan state have often left readers with the impression that no legal system existed in the country before his reign.[80]

Undisputed among scholars is that by the mid-1890s, ʿAbd al-Rahman had established Afghanistan's national borders roughly as they are today. He did so through a series of agreements with the country's neighbors. Most prominent among these accords was the Durand Agreement (1893), which created one of the modern world's most porous and contentious borders in the so-called Durand Line.[81] The demarcation of Afghanistan's borders continued with the governments of Persia to the west and Bukhara (annexed by Russia between 1868 and 1873) to the north. Of all his territorial concessions, the Iron Amir compromised most with the British Raj. In exchange for internal sovereignty and Britain's not interfering in the domestic affairs of his kingdom, ʿAbd al-Rahman confirmed the Raj's control over the contested border cities of Peshawar and Quetta, relinquishing jurisdiction over the roughly half of the world's Pashtun population who lived east of the Durand Line. These heavy capitulations notwithstanding, the Iron Amir exploited the solidified borders and free rein within his amirate to bolster his government's authority over the newly defined territory of Afghanistan. By 1896, after a decade and a half of brutal repression and state-sanctioned terror, the Iron Amir had effectively brought all regions of Afghanistan under the mandate of his central authority in Kabul.[82]

Perhaps the most apt representation of the Iron Amir's consolidation of state authority over the territory of Afghanistan lies in the first recorded official government map of the country, published in Kabul in 1898. By including and labeling areas that had been autonomous regions of Afghanistan as provinces of the amir's kingdom, the map signaled the extension of uniform laws to the entirety of the territory and population. Beyond enhancing Kabul's ability to project power and influence, it also reflected material changes on the ground, including an expanded regime of taxes and conscription.[83] Illustrated with captions, the map was accompanied by a personal message from the amir, which was duly read out in town squares across Afghanistan. As David Edwards has observed, given that over ninety percent of the population was illiterate, it was the image on the document and any accompanying spoken practices associated with the map—such as public readings in mosques or conversations in teahouses—that mattered most.[84]

Taking our inquiry a step further, among the earliest recorded attempts to establish a countrywide division of provinces and districts in Afghanistan was the manual for governors, *Kitabchih-'i Hukumati* (The Book of Government), published during the middle of 'Abd al-Rahman's reign. The Book of Government is one of the first official government publications to fix the number of Afghan provinces at five—Kabul, Kandahar, Turkistan, Qataghan-and-Badakhshan, and Herat—a rudimentary division representing major ethnolinguistic and economic zones of the country still used today.[85] Notably, more detailed and accurate maps of Afghanistan's borders—composed in Ottoman Turkish, not Persian—emerge in the Sublime Porte's foreign ministry records at this time (see for example Figure 1.4).[86]

Although 'Abd al-Rahman had succeeded in demarcating the external boundaries of the country and in devising his own provincial demarcations on paper, in practice securing his government's control over everyday administration beyond Kabul proved more difficult. To consolidate his authority over the heterogeneous patchwork of urban, rural, and nomadic populations of the territory, 'Abd al-Rahman constructed a network of state-sponsored Islamic law codes and courts. These "shari'a courts" were part of a broader centralization campaign to

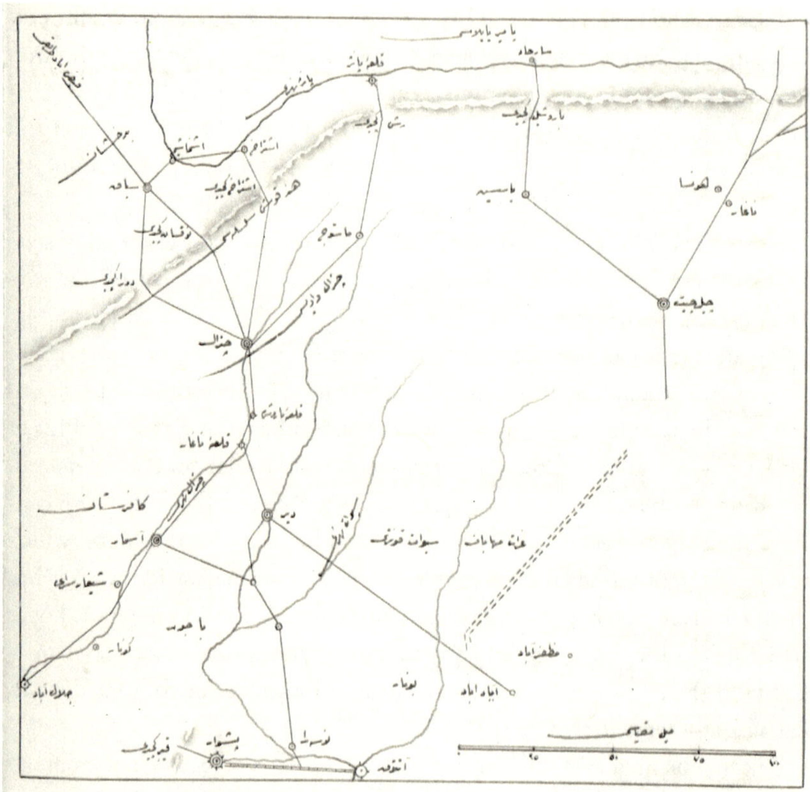

FIGURE 1.4. Ottoman cartographer's sketch of the Indo-Russo-Afghan borderlands, including Peshawar, Swat, Jalalabad, and southern Turkistan, 1892. Prime Ministry Ottoman Archives, Istanbul, Turkey (Y.PRK.TKM 26/7).

introduce greater government efficiency and control, while employing a discourse of upholding God's law. For ʿAbd al-Rahman, Islam was not just the religion of the vast majority of Afghans, but the fulcrum upon which he would simultaneously propel, impose, and negotiate his state centralization agenda.[87]

Without endorsing the brutality of his means, scholars agree that the Iron Amir achieved much of what he sought to achieve. For the first time, an Afghan ruler in Kabul succeeded in imposing a highly centralized and singular interpretation of the shariʿa (read: a streamlined codification of Hanafi *fiqh* by his authorized interpretation) as the supreme law of the land, over more localized and competing sociolegal norms that, in the eyes of his opponents at least, were certainly no less "Islamic." The Iron Amir could not achieve this through force alone, however. As much as he brought the sword, ʿAbd al-Rahman instrumentalized the ink of his scholars to produce legal discourses that stressed the imperative of civil order, strong leadership, and defense of the realm from attack. Believing his reign was the answer to those collective societal needs, ʿAbd al-Rahman employed the aforesaid discourses to canvas and extend his state-building program to areas of the country that, historically, had governed their own affairs, independent of Kabul. In light of these transformative policies he unleashed in the country, an important and unexplored question remains: What was his inspiration and model (or models) for reform?

A Tale of Two Cities—in Three Texts: Istanbul and Kabul in Tacit Exchange

During the two-decade reign of Amir ʿAbd al-Rahman (Figure 1.5), Ottoman-Afghan ties were never formalized to the degree of official relations. Kabul's diplomatic stasis with Istanbul was in line with the amir's treaty obligations since 1879, which relegated Afghanistan's foreign affairs under the exclusive jurisdiction of the British Raj. As other evidence shows, however, British restrictions on Afghan foreign affairs did not prevent ʿAbd al-Rahman from modeling many of his administrative measures on Ottoman state practices, even without official ties to the Porte.

Aside from the force of his army, the primary instrument of ʿAbd al-Rahman's centralization campaign took the shape of codifying Hanafi *fiqh* into bounded, user-friendly manuals for Afghan judges. These texts are some of the most important relics of the Iron Amir's reign, providing a window into Afghan internal governance policies at this time. Yet it is no accident that these documents coincided with ʿAbd al-Rahman's commissioning the publication of several works on Ottoman statecraft and administration, including new forms of judicial and bureaucratic organization found in the sultan-caliph's domains. More than parading coreligionist solidarity, ʿAbd al-Rahman aimed through these works to incorporate the latest advances in Ottoman administrative, judicial, and military reforms into existing patterns of Afghan domestic governance. Here, we focus on three of the most prominent works published by the Iron Amir's government press in Kabul, beginning in the early years of his reign.

The purpose of ʿAbd al-Rahman's manuals was to implement streamlined, transparent, and government-authorized law and procedure in a network of state

FIGURE 1.5. "Iron Amir" ʿAbd al-Rahman Khan (r. 1880–1901). Wellcome Library, London (L0020789) (CC BY 4.0).

courts established in major cities of the country. The background context of these texts, as described above, was to provide a key tool of judicial centralization that 'Abd al-Rahman could employ in his campaign to impose uniform rule in his kingdom. A representative example is *Asas al-Quzat* (Fundamental Rules for Judges), a legal manual compiled between 1885 and 1886 by the Hanafi jurist and scholar of Kandahar, Mawlawi Ahmad Jan Khan Alakozai.[88] The manual was designed for Afghan judges and other juridical personnel serving in 'Abd al-Rahman's newly established network of state-sponsored "shari'a courts." In some important structural and aesthetic respects, the manual is strikingly similar to the books comprising the Mecelle. With its vertical alignment of numbered articles, followed by a concise statement of the rule and only brief mention of its original jurisprudential source—almost always a canonical text of the Hanafi school of *fiqh*—the manual served to streamline the everyday administration of the state courts in a manner legible to a centralizing government (see Figure 1.6). In the process, *Asas al-Quzat* sought to replace the Kabul court's reliance on independent jurists, who were often trained outside the state-sponsored madrasa system, with loyal bureaucrats of the Iron Amir's state.[89]

As a late nineteenth-century "code" of civil procedure, *Asas al-Quzat* is also the first recorded attempt by the government of Afghanistan to extend a regularized judiciary over the whole country while establishing the Hanafi school of *fiqh* as the official law of the state. The contents of *Asas al-Quzat* are wide-ranging, from which opinions of the Hanafi school were to be determinative in a given type of case, to where and how far apart the parties were required to sit in court. Akin to the Ottoman Mecelle, *Asas al-Quzat* provided a means of consolidating and uniformizing law throughout the territories subject to Kabul's jurisdiction. Although the manual does not explicitly state a reliance on Ottoman models of law or administration, other texts produced by the Kabul government at this time did.

Evidence that Ottoman administrative practices inspired 'Abd al-Rahman's centralization program is even more marked in the Kabul government's publication of a work devoted exclusively to the administrative structures and practices of the Sublime Porte under Sultan Abdülhamid II. Between 1886 and 1887, less than a decade after Hulusi's visit to the Kabul court, 'Abd al-Rahman commissioned the publication of *Sarrishtih-'i Islamiyyih-'i Rum* (The Islamic Administration of the Ottoman Empire).[90] This text was intended to provide a prestigious Islamic model to 'Abd al-Rahman's governors of how to consolidate authority

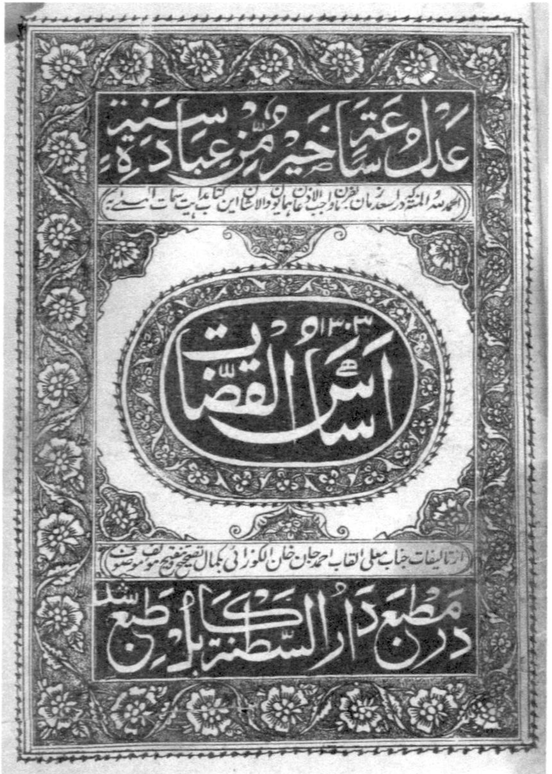

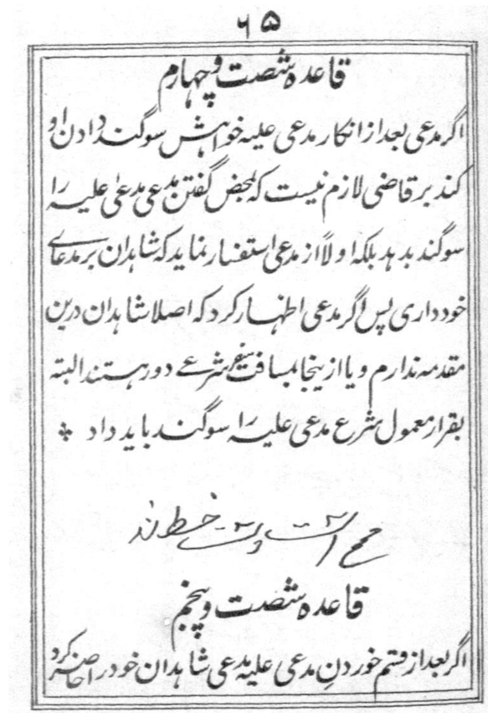

٦٥

قاعدهٔ شصت و چهارم

اگر مدعی بعد از انکار مدعی علیه خواهش سوگند دادن او
کند بر قاضی لازم نیست که بمحض گفتن مدعی مدعی علیه را
سوگند بدهد بلکه اولاً از مدعی استفسار نماید که شاهدان بر مدعای
خود داری پس اگر مدعی اظهار کرد که اصلاً شاهدان درین
مقدمه ندارم و یا از ینجا بمسافت شرعی دور هستند البته
بقرار معمول شرع مدعی علیه را سوگند باید داد ٭

قاعدهٔ شصت و پنجم

اگر بعد از قسم خوردن مدعی علیه مدعی شاهدان خود را حاضر کرد

FIGURE 1.6.
Asas al-Quzat (Fundamental Rules for Judges), Kabul, 1885/1886. *Left to right:* cover and sample page. Afghanistan Digital Library, Kabul/New York (adl10129).

over a heterogeneous population in order to establish domestic law and order and ward off external attacks (Figure 1.7). The work makes specific parallels between the multiethnic character of the Ottoman Empire and Afghanistan, as well as a shared sense of being encircled by hostile foes. In this context, the need for a powerful, disciplined, and professional army to protect the realm—and for increased taxes to finance it—emerge as a key pair of structural parallels in the Iron Amir's state-building campaign and that of the Porte's earlier nineteenth-century reforms.[91]

Addressing the various tribes and ethnic groups of Afghanistan as belonging to a single dominion, *Sarrishtih-ʾi Islamiyyih-ʾi Rum* envisions a unitary state in which all Afghans are equally subordinate to their lawful sovereign, the amir in Kabul. The work's opening lines address ʿAbd al-Rahman's subjects as Muslim believers and the people of Afghanistan—"be they Durrani or Ghilzai Pashtuns, Persian-speakers, Hazaras, or Turks."[92] Ostensibly a work on the Ottoman Empire, the parallels the work draws between the Muslim governments of Istanbul and Kabul tell us more about what the Iron Amir was seeking to achieve in Afghanistan under the rubric of "Islamic administration" than Ottoman law or society in the nineteenth century. In particular, the work justifies ʿAbd al-Rahman's reliance on the Turkish model for three reasons held to be common between both governments: the threat of external aggression by non-Muslim powers on an "Islamic" state; the ethnic diversity of Ottoman and Afghan subjects and the need for less division and greater unity as the "people of Islam" (*ahl-i Islam*); and the role of a professional army funded by internal taxation to both unite the population and defend the realm from attack.

A third major publication commissioned by ʿAbd al-Rahman on Ottoman state practice was a book, again ostensibly, about the Russo-Ottoman War (1877–1878).[93] We have already seen strong links between the Ottoman and Indo-Afghan frontiers through the communications and networks of sufi orders during the conflict with Russia, especially representatives of the Naqshabandi and Qaderi orders such as the Naqibs of Baghdad. While ʿAbd al-Rahman's Muhammadzai predecessor in Kabul, Shir ʿAli, had turned down Sultan Abdülhamid II's invitation to join forces against Russia, the Iron Amir was anxious to shore up ties with the Porte in less militaristic ways. Appearing to be a translation of an unacknowledged European work, *Kitab-i Jang-i Rum wa Rus* (The Russo-Ottoman War) again cites the Sublime Porte as an Islamic model for building a modern state amid the shared challenge of European imperial expansion across

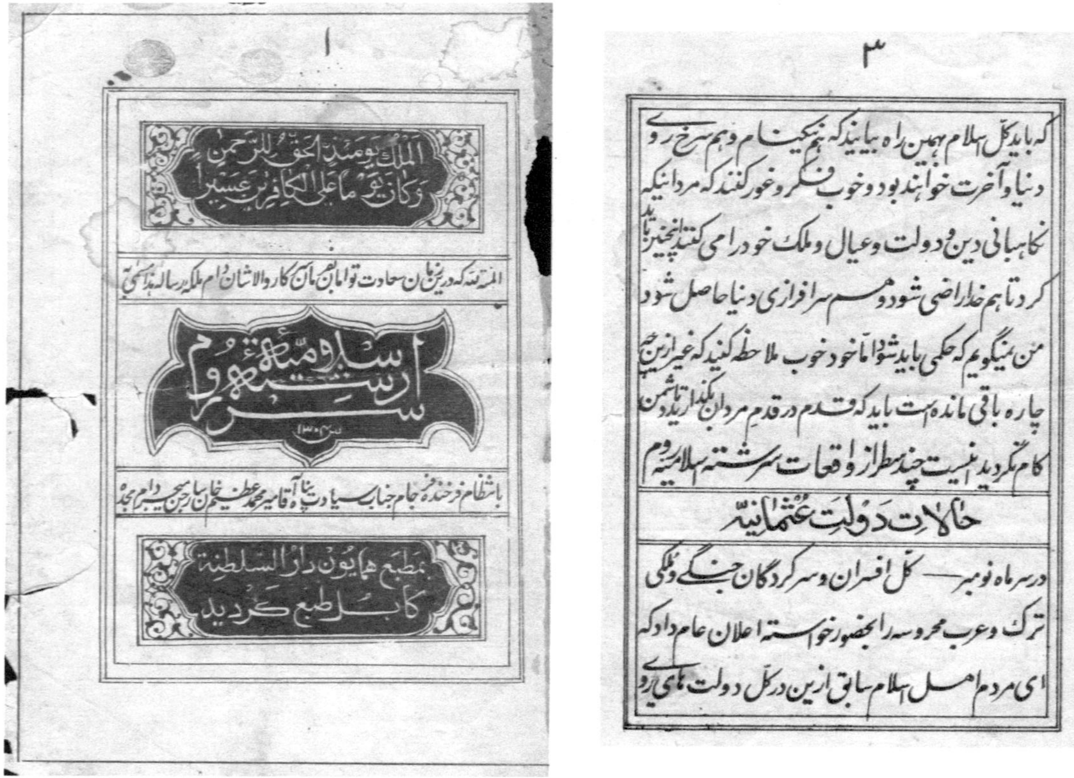

FIGURE I.7.
Sarrishtih-ʾi Islamiyyih-ʾi Rum (The Islamic Administration of the Ottoman Empire), Kabul, 1886 / 1887. *Left to right:* cover and sample page, "Conditions of the Ottoman State." Afghanistan Digital Library, Kabul / New York (adl10003).

the region (Figure 1.8). At the same time, the work contrasts the Afghan and Ottoman domains from British India, where Muslims are described as being deprived of the guardianship and guidance of a proper Islamic sovereign. Here, the central message of the work is to impress on Afghan subjects that they should be grateful for living under an independent Muslim ruler, and should be absolutely loyal to their king, not to lament the plight of Indian Muslims following the catastrophe of the 1857 Rebellion.

These three works were exclusively commissioned by ʿAbd al-Rahman and published by the Dar al-Saltanih government press at Kabul. All three cite the Ottomans not so much out of filial piety, and certainly not out of grandiose notions of combining territories under a single caliphate, but for specific administrative and juridical models of internal reform. The rhetorical purchase of espousing an Ottoman model of reform in Afghanistan—as opposed to British, Russian, or Iranian examples, for example—should not be underestimated. For ʿAbd al-Rahman and the Kabul court, associating with the House of Osman presented the added benefit of being connected with a venerated Sunni monarchy over five hundred years old, the domain of the caliphate and custodians of the Islam's holiest sites, and the greatest Muslim power in the world. As an ascendant king in Afghanistan, ʿAbd al-Rahman knew he could not rely on violence alone either to establish the legitimacy of his reign or to ensure the longevity of the Muhammadzai dynasty. Brutally repressive as he was with dissidents, the Iron Amir was not invincible. He well knew that he would have to increasingly rely on capable and trustworthy bureaucrats to administer the territories he conquered as much as on the loyal soldiers and commanders that had conquered them for him if his centralizing campaign were to succeed.

At the center of ʿAbd al-Rahman's attention in this regard was the Afghan scholarly establishment—a loosely organized but powerful association of ulema in Kabul, Kandahar, and other major cities of the country with long-standing ties to educational institutions, financial remittances, and grassroots sufi networks in the Indo-Afghan frontier and northern India, including the prominent Dar al-ʿUlum seminary at Deoband.[94] If only because he realized his own authority and state-building campaign ultimately hinged on their accepting him as a legitimate Muslim sovereign, even absolute rulers like ʿAbd al-Rahman were bound to consider the sensitivities and privileges, if not always the advice, of the Afghan ulema establishment. In this light, hoisting the Ottomans' "Islamic" model of reform provided the dual benefit of a blueprint for the amir's centralizing reforms that was still seen as deferential to the shariʿa and therefore legitimate.

FIGURE 1.8.
Kitab-i Jang-i Rum wa Rus (The Russo-Ottoman War), Kabul, 1890/1891. *Left to right:* cover and sample page. Afghanistan Digital Library, Kabul/New York (adl0208).

The latter was especially promising in light of Afghan reverence for the Ottoman sultan-caliph and his empire, a sentiment amply expressed during Hulusi's reception in Kabul.[95]

Although it cannot be assumed ʿAbd al-Rahman looked exclusively to the Ottomans to guide him in building a strong, centralized government, no longer can we presume he relied on British or Russian advisors or other European "officers for hire" as the impetus for his reforms. Nor can we assume this was a one-way road of interest, or exchange. Notably, ʿAbd al-Rahman's fascination with the Sublime Porte's military prowess and administrative expertise came at a time of increasing Ottoman attention, including of the cartographic variety, to the strategic Indo-Russo-Afghan borderlands.[96] Taken together, cases of Ottoman contact and exchange with the Afghan amirs in the late nineteenth century should revise notions of Afghanistan's modern history that rely too heavily on the dualistic paradigm of Great Game competition, where all too often British or Russian envoys are presumed to have been the only sources of expertise and foreign contact in the so-called Forbidden Kingdom of Kabul.

ʿAbd al-Rahman's enthusiasm for authoring and translating works on the Ottomans, and indeed for explicitly referring to the administrative and military practices of the Porte, might be contrasted with his relative silence about emulating British Indian models of law and governance. A revealing incident in the summer of 1895 provides a case in point. In July of that year, when the British agent in Kabul queried his superiors in Calcutta about offering the British Indian jail manual to ʿAbd al-Rahman for his perusal and possible benefit in administering law and order in his amirate, the government of India responded skeptically. In a memo W. J. Cunningham, Deputy Secretary to the Government of India, penned to the British agent at Kabul on July 18, 1893, Cunningham shared his reservations, and criticism, of the mere idea of presenting a Persian translation of the Raj's domestic governance literature to the amir: "His Highness may regard your action as an insidious attempt to interfere with his internal administration. I am to ask if you have considered your proposal from His point of view."[97] Acknowledging Cunningham's point, the agent rescinded his proposal.

British officials were well aware of the jealousy with which ʿAbd al-Rahman guarded the internal administration of his amirate—so much so that Raj officials were wary to even make suggestions about domestic Afghan affairs. In the meantime, the Iron Amir harbored no such reservations in proclaiming the Ottoman features of his own "Islamic" administration.

Amir ʿAbd Al-Rahman and Sultan Abdülhamid II: Two Models of Modern Muslim Kingship

Noncontiguous territories and diplomatic barriers between Istanbul and Kabul notwithstanding, there is evidence to suggest that the respect ʿAbd al-Rahman displayed to Sultan Abdülhamid II stemmed in no small part from the Afghan amir's belief in Ottoman claims to the caliphate. In a letter from the Indian National Archives dated January 10, 1883, Qadi ʿAbd al-Qadir Khan, a resident of Peshawar visiting Kabul, reported that the amir stated in private conversation that "I or the Sultan of Turkey must be considered to be the head of Islam," citing sectarian differences with Shiʿi Iran as the primary reason why the Qajars of Persia could never assume the position.[98] If true, these words illustrate the veneration with which ʿAbd al-Rahman held Abdülhamid II and the amir's view that together they constituted the premier Muslim sovereigns of the age.[99]

More than a case of idiosyncratic Turcophilism, ʿAbd al-Rahman's admiration for the sultan must also be viewed in the broader context of increased contact and exchange between the Ottoman and Afghan, but also Indian, scholarly fields.[100] It is during this same period, for example, that both Turkish and Afghan ulema were troubled by the resurgence of Wahhabi doctrines in the Arabian heartlands, and its spillover into the Indian subcontinent. Both Ottoman and Afghan rulers and their respective scholarly establishments found in Wahhabism a dangerous enemy. As an iconoclastic ideological and political movement, the Wahhabis challenged the authority of the four traditional schools of Sunni law, not to mention the House of Osman's claims on the caliphate.[101] After an Ottoman army led by Mehmed Ali Pasha, the governor of Egypt, crushed a Wahhabi insurrection in early nineteenth-century Hejaz, the movement retreated to its bastion in the central Arabian region of Nejd under the protection of Saudi tribal chieftains. Over time the movement was rehabilitated, resurging in alliance with the House of Saʿud in the nineteenth and early twentieth centuries, and launching a scourge of attacks on Ottoman state institutions, sufi shrines, Shiʿi Muslims, among other communities and practices held to be unorthodox in their view.[102]

Reflecting a shared ideological concern about the rise of Wahhabism, Ottoman ulema writing during the reigns of sultans Abdülaziz (r. 1861–1876) and Abdülhamid II, as well as Afghan scholars in ʿAbd al-Rahman's court, published vehement tracts against Wahhabi doctrine and practices. The extended treatise of theology and law *Taqwim al-Din* (Almanac of Religion) provides a case in point. The work's first edition was published in Kabul in the mid-1880s by the

Afghan scholars Mawlawis Mir Muhammad ʿAzim Khan and ʿAbd al-Razaq Dihlawi, with a second edition released in 1888. The final section of the book is devoted to a refutation of the Wahhabis.[103] Shorter proclamations were also published and circulated by ʿAbd al-Rahman's government, including one from 1888 condemning Wahhabi doctrines and distributed widely in Kandahar.[104] Around this time, the eminent Ottoman jurist-administrator and chief compiler of the Mecelle civil code Ahmed Cevdet Pasha (1822–1895) had published *Malumat-ı Nafia,* a stalwart defense of the Hanafi school of law with a scathing critique of Wahhabi ideas.[105] Beyond a shared mistrust of Wahhabism, the aforesaid Afghan and Ottoman works reflect a shared jurisprudential world rooted squarely in the Hanafi school of law, but also well-established notions of Sunni Muslim kingship that were not beholden to literalist interpretations requiring a single Islamic state, or the caliph to be of Qurayshi Arab descent.[106] In Istanbul and Kabul, predominantly Hanafi scholarly establishments endorsed the legitimacy of Ottoman sultan-caliphs and Muhammadzai amirs, respectively, to rule in what could be called an Islamicate "social contract" of sorts. The latter demanded obedience from Ottoman / Afghan subjects in exchange for the sultan / amir upholding the shariʿa as the law of the land and protecting the realm from foreign threats.

As with late Ottoman Turkey, important differences also separate the kind of state Afghanistan represented at this time from earlier Muslim dynasties and empires. In articulating a modern vision of governance committed to upholding the shariʿa, the Islamic state of ʿAbd al-Rahman was not an outward-looking struggle for conquest over neighboring India, Iran, or Turkistan (as with his Timurid, Durrani, or Hotaki predecessors, for example). By recognizing Ottoman claims to the office from a distance but maintaining his own autonomy as the independent leader of a Muslim kingdom, the Iron Amir was also not seeking an aggrandized global caliphate. To the contrary, for the vast majority of his reign ʿAbd al-Rahman accepted peace with the two greatest non-Muslim powers of the age—Britain and Russia—and with also the Shiʿi Qajars in Persia in exchange for their recognition of his sovereignty over a territorially defined area. Here, ʿAbd al-Rahman virtually single-handedly decided Afghanistan's borders in all cardinal directions in agreements with Britain, Russia, and Persia.

The story of Afghanistan here is of a Muslim dynasty establishing the legitimacy of its line while claiming to rule in the name of Islam and the territory of a nation. By holding the more modest ideal of a just Muslim king, sovereign over a limited territory, ʿAbd al-Rahman and his advisors read the global situation, and region, very carefully, developing a notion of modern kingship that fit accordingly. The result was an adaptation of late-antique and medieval notions of the just Muslim king to the context of a modern, territorial nation-state—a process that would continue under the reign of ʿAbd al-Rahman's son and heir, Habib Allah Khan (r. 1901–1919), and come to full fruition during the reign of his grandson, Aman Allah Khan (r. 1919–1929).

Archival records also reveal some continuity in private correspondence between the Istanbul and Kabul courts. Raising some eyebrows in the British Raj's foreign department, for example, was an 1896 intelligence briefing reporting that Abdülhamid II had conferred the honorific title of *Gazi Ziyaüddin* (Frontier Warrior and Light of the Faith) on ʿAbd al-Rahman. The report describes how ʿAbd al-Rahman, on hearing the bestowal of the title, "held great rejoicing and received *nazars* in memory of this honour."[107] Subsequent reports housed in the British Indian archives indicate that the Afghan amir not only received such a title but immediately vaunted it in official firmans and diplomatic correspondence. Later that year, for example, ʿAbd al-Rahman sent the viceroy of India a letter with the following words inscribed on the envelope: "From His Highness the Amir, Zia-ul-millat-wad-din, Independent King of the dominions of Afghanistan."[108] The prompt display of a title reported to have been granted by the Ottoman sultan on the Afghan amir would seem to indicate an even stronger relationship between the two sovereigns than has previously been assumed. It also reveals the amir's desire to inform the British of just that.

The role of affect in ostentatious displays of fraternal sentiment between two Muslim sovereigns cannot be discounted, but the driving force behind ʿAbd al-Rahman's turn to the Ottomans more likely stemmed from intensely pragmatic imperatives: warding off both Russian and British encroachment during the high tide of European empires and the Victorian age. To these external factors, we must add a crucial internal motivation: the need to cultivate legitimacy among Afghanistan's community of legal and religious scholars, especially the ulema of greater Kabul, Kandahar, Peshawar, and surrounding environs, including some of India's greatest cities: Lahore, Delhi, and Lucknow.[109]

The Kabul court's admiration for the Ottoman sultan must also be viewed in a broader context of increased contacts and exchange between the Afghan and Ottoman domains more generally. Though we do not see another mission the likes of the 1877–1878 delegation for the remainder of the nineteenth century, during the overlapping reigns of Abdülhamid II and ʿAbd al-Rahman, the flow of pilgrims, scholars, and other itinerants traveling between Ottoman domains—especially Mesopotamia and Hejaz—and Asia, including India, Bukhara, and Afghanistan, increased substantially.[110] The enhanced ability for Asiatic Muslims to travel and communicate across political boundaries—via the telegraph, transcontinental railroads, and steamships—significantly increased opportunities for contact and exchange, and Afghans were no exception. Although Afghanistan did not undergo the major import or construction of any of these new technologies on its soil at this time, through travel, correspondence, and periodical subscription Afghans were not at all strangers to them either.

Legacies of the First Ottoman Mission to Afghanistan

When Shir ʿAli respectfully declined an invitation from the Sublime Porte to join hands against a potential common Russian foe in late 1877, Hulusi knew his historic mission to Afghanistan had come to an end. For the next three decades, however, Abdülhamid II continued to train his eye on the subcontinent and Afghanistan as potential reservoirs of Ottoman muscle abroad. Hulusi's mission brought assets of immense potential value in any future conflict with Britain: the sympathy of coreligionists living in the prized jewel of Queen Victoria's global empire, India, and in one of the biggest thorns in the British Empire's side, Afghanistan. London and Calcutta were keen to keep the disparate seas of Pan-Islam from joining, but in the ensuing decades it would not be lost on the Porte, and many Indian Muslims as well as Afghans, that they would have to chart their own course of relations and establish venues for direct correspondence on their own terms.

Meanwhile, back at British Indian headquarters some of the very officials responsible for the Turkish delegation's passage through India, including the viceroy of India, Robert Bulwer-Lytton, and the ambassador at Constantinople, Sir Henry Austen Layard, regretted having allowed the mission to proceed in the first place. Sidestepping responsibility for the amir's decision, the disappointed officials faulted the Turks for the mission's "failure." They singled out Hulusi for blame, retracting earlier praise for the Ottoman scholar and labeling him a clergyman ill-suited for the post of ambassador. Raj officials overseeing the Ottoman transit to Kabul also heaped venom on Lal Shah, an Afghan-born Turkish translator who had accompanied the delegation, declaring him a traitor and "untrustworthy intriguer" who had poisoned the atmosphere in Kabul due to his anti-British views.[111] Both Layard and Bulwer-Lytton attributed the mission's failure to the selection of the envoy, stressing that "if he had been a diplomat rather than a 'mullah', the result would have been different."[112] In this way colonial administrators deflected responsibility by blaming the messengers for the unfavorable consequences of a mission they had facilitated, but the fruits of which were not to their liking. Perhaps the Queen's ministers would have been well advised to heed the Turkish adage, *elçiye zeval olmaz*—"an envoy cannot be blamed for his mission."

Having explored what Hulusi and the Ottoman delegation accomplished in their voyage to Kabul, it would be mistaken to brand it a failure. In addition to fomenting pro-Ottoman sentiments in strategic locations—including in two of India's greatest and most populous cities, Bombay and Delhi—the Ottomans had succeeded in sending an official emissary to Kabul where he was warmly received, hosted by courtiers, greeted by commoners, and bid a gracious farewell—accolades that representatives of few other world powers could claim. The failure narrative also elides a crucial, albeit long overlooked dimension to the Ottoman mission: the contributions Hulusi made to stimulating new kinds of conversations between Muslim scholars and administrators in the Ottoman Empire, Afghanistan, and British India in the late nineteenth century about what a modern Islamic legal system and state could mean. As an elite Ottoman Islamic jurist, judge, and member of the Mecelle codification commission, Hulusi probably discussed matters beyond political alliances and the impending war against the Russians to his landmark meeting with the Afghan amir and the ulema of Kabul. The meetings between Hulusi and Afghan scholars and administrators took place almost immediately following his seven-year participation in the most renowned codification of Islamic law in modern history, the Mecelle.[113] In light of this background, it is difficult to imagine that the topic of the Ottoman Civil Code, the Ottoman Constitution of 1876, and other momentous judicial projects taking place in the sultan's empire did not surface in conversations between Muslim scholars belonging to a transnational Islamic—and specifically Hanafi—juridical field. British sources lend some support to this theory. Although the Raj's intelligence reports on the mission were obsessed with the "failures" of the Ottoman mission to convince the Afghan amir to join the war against Anglo-Ottoman nemesis Russia, at least one British intelligence report goads us to consider an alternative form of Ottoman-Afghan entente achieved: the "many friends" Hulusi had made in Kabul.[114] Moreover, of this we can be certain: within a decade of the latter's mission, 'Abd al-Rahman's explicitly pro-Ottoman publications, coupled with the Sublime Porte's increased intelligence on Afghanistan, demonstrated that Kabul and Istanbul were growing ever closer.

At least one other major international development took place at ʿAbd al-Rahman's behest, a development that would bring Kabul and Istanbul even closer in the late nineteenth and early twentieth centuries, though it would have been hard to predict at the time. This was the amir's decision, based either on personal vendettas or on pure power politics, to expel two influential families from Afghanistan: the Yahya Khel (later known as the Musahiban) to India and the Tarzi family to the Ottoman Empire. As we explore later, the exiling of these families and their return to Kabul following ʿAbd al-Rahman's death would have profound consequences for Afghanistan's twentieth-century political, intellectual, and legal history.

And what became of Ahmed Hulusi Effendi, the illustrious Ottoman scholar, jurist, and ambassador extraordinaire whose arrival in Bombay caused such a commotion one summer's day in August 1877? Mehmed Süreyya Bey's *Sicill-i Osmani* (1890) notes that upon his return from Afghanistan, Hulusi served briefly as deputy governor in Diyarbakir before retiring to his hometown of Amasya off the Black Sea coast.[115] The documentary trail then largely goes cold, however, and we know little of Hulusi's activities thereafter. A communiqué in the Ottoman archives and the *Sicill-i Osmani* reports he passed away peacefully on January 17, 1889.[116] A hilltop mausoleum dedicated to Hulusi and his father still overlooks central Amasya and remains a site of visitation; the family's home is charitably endowed as a Qurʾanic school for children.

Like the renowned jurist-administrator Ahmed Cevdet Pasha, Ahmed Hulusi Effendi was a late Ottoman "transitional," who combined a traditional madrasa-training with a dynamic role in the Sublime Porte's post-Tanzimat bureaucracy and its most innovative projects of the age.[117] That Hulusi has received surprisingly little historical attention is remarkable, given the leading role he played in compiling the pathbreaking Ottoman Civil Code and given that he served as the Porte's first official envoy to Afghanistan. In retrospect, the Mecelle and the first Turkish mission to Kabul were some of the most ambitious and dynamic state projects—in domestic and foreign policy realms respectively—to be launched by the Ottomans in the nineteenth-century. What is more, the long-term juridical effects of Hulusi's mission to Kabul merge with a broader history of Ottoman experts arriving in Afghanistan in the early twentieth century. While Hulusi's retirement to the town of his birth brings to a close an epic journey and a dramatic chapter in the history of Ottoman relations with the Muslims of central and southern Asia, our primary story of Ottoman activity in Afghanistan has only just begun.

TWO

A Damascene Road Meets a Passage to India

Ottoman and Indian Experts in Afghanistan

ON OCTOBER 1, 1901, Afghanistan experienced its most peaceful transition of power of the twentieth century. With the demise of "Iron Amir" 'Abd al-Rahman Khan from natural causes, the latter's eldest son and designated heir, Habib Allah Khan (1872–1919), ascended the Kabul throne without contest. Two days after the amir's death, an audience of royal family members and courtiers assembled for a traditional recitation of the Qur'an in honor of the deceased. Seizing the opportunity to proclaim his accession to the Afghan throne, the new amir promised to uphold the legacies of law and order established by his late father.[1]

Having paid homage to the memory of his father, Habib Allah was nonetheless keen to depart from the Iron Amir's more austere precedents. Seeking to end the country's international isolation, he announced a series of measures designed to attract foreign experts for an array of infrastructure projects in the amirate, still officially a British protectorate at the time. Committed to a model of cautious and gradual reforms, beginning with the government's ill repute for repressing dissent, among the new amir's first edicts was issuing a general pardon to Afghans exiled during 'Abd al-Rahman's reign. Within months of Habib Allah's announcement, Afghan expatriates from British India in the east and the Ottoman Empire in the west began arriving in Kabul, some after two decades in foreign exile.[2] Beyond the symbolic gesture of amnesty to signal a new monarchical order in Afghanistan, Habib Allah had pragmatic motives in mind: to recruit sorely needed technocrats for a series of state-building measures in the administrative, educational, and military realms.

Within five years, Habib Allah had many of the men he needed. A diverse assortment of professionals, primarily from the Ottoman Empire and British India had arrived in his court to offer their services in a variety of fields, straddling both the civil and military branches of the amir's government. An incident from 1907 is illustrative. In January of that year, the annual *ʿĪd al-Aẓḥā* festivities held at the Kabul palace revealed a markedly more diverse guest list than usual. Rumors were rife that Habib Allah wished to introduce a distinguished group of foreign visitors. At the royal darbar celebration, the amir rose to welcome a group of newly arrived subjects of the Ottoman sultan in Istanbul, seated in honor not far from the king himself. A British informant embedded in the gathering reported the following excerpts from the royal address:

> These men have come for the sake of instructing my people. This is just as I send for Muhammadans from India for the same purpose. It makes no difference at all. Muhammadans of all the countries are the same to me. These men do not know Persian. I know the Turkish language, but it is different from the Turkish of Turkey itself. I saw these men this morning and talked to them for some time.[3]

Following these initial comments, Habib Allah again turned to his Ottoman guests and proceeded to question a member from the group in full audience of the court. After identifying the said individual's trade (land surveyor), the amir asked if he was proficient in sketching. When the man replied in the affirmative, Habib Allah asked if he had experience with the prismatic compass, the theodolite, or the level, three of the latest technological innovations in the field. The surveyor replied that he was skilled in all three instruments. It was an auspicious beginning for the Ottoman delegation's stay in Kabul, and the pro-Turkish camp of the amir's court in particular could not have been more pleased.[4]

THE HISTORY OF Ottoman ties to Afghanistan has been the subject of modest scholarly attention. Partly to blame are the boundaries of modern area studies which, combined with popular notions of Afghanistan as a landlocked, remote, and peripheral no-man's-land, have relegated the country beyond the purview of traditional Ottoman studies.[5] There are also some more straightforward historical reasons, however, including the relatively low numbers of Ottoman travelers and the short time within which the bulk of Ottoman emigration to Afghanistan occurred (c. 1901–1923)—relative to more long-standing Central Asian, Indian, and Iranian communities and influences in Afghanistan.[6]

These barriers notwithstanding, combining available sources in Ottoman, Afghan, and British Indian archives provides a remarkably rich view of the Sublime Porte's activities vis-à-vis Afghanistan and its demonstrably escalating interest in Afghans from ʿAbd al-Rahman's demise until the empire's dissolution in 1923. The picture that emerges is not a linear progression or bell-shaped curve of Ottoman subjects permanently resettling in Afghanistan but what could be described as three successive windows of opportunity that Ottoman subjects exploited by taking up employment in the Kabul court. The first window of Ottoman migrants, arriving between 1901 and 1914, emerged in the aftermath of the Iron Amir's death and the return of Afghan refugees to Kabul from exile in the Ottoman Empire. The second arose in the context of the Ottoman-German mission to Kabul in 1915 during World War I. The third and final wave, by far the most influential, arrived in the wake of simultaneous wars of independence in Afghanistan and Anatolia following World War I.

The first substantial episode of Ottoman migration to Afghanistan began after ʿAbd al-Rahman's demise in 1901. It included a mixed group of ethnic Turks and Arabs who founded the first Ottoman community in Kabul. While Ottoman subjects were not the only foreigners to visit Afghanistan at this time, judging by the positions they held in the Kabul court they constituted the most powerful group of foreigners in the Afghan capital. They were closely followed by Muslim migrants from the Indian subcontinent. Ottoman and Indian migration to Kabul should not be seen as completely separate tracks following independent courses, however, but were intertwined with political developments internal to Afghanistan, as well as the Ottoman and British domains. The history of Ottoman and Indian experts in Afghanistan at the turn of the twentieth century begins several decades earlier, with a consequential feud in the Afghan royal family.

An Afghan Exile in Ottoman Syria

In 1882, the patriarch of a prominent southern Pashtun clan descended from the Barakzai tribal confederation, and related to the Muhammadzai ruling family, fell into discord with Amir ʿAbd al-Rahman over the latter's brutality in suppressing a rebellion. Banished with his family from the realm, there was little to indicate at the time that the exile of Sardar Ghulam Muhammad Khan Tarzi (1830–1900) would be one of the Iron Amir's most consequential decisions for Afghanistan's relationship with the Ottoman Empire. The Tarzis initially relocated to the southern port city of Karachi, India. Choosing not to live under British rule, the patriarch Ghulam Muhammad Khan decided to emigrate with his family to Baghdad, an Ottoman province since the Porte's reconquest of Mesopotamia and decisive victory over Safavid Iran in 1638. When Sultan Abdülhamid II learned of the notable Afghan family's relocation to the Ottoman domains, he summoned them to Istanbul in 1885 and again the following year, where they were hosted in honor by the sultan himself. Ghulam Muhammad Khan and his family subsequently resettled in Damascus, where they received a regular stipend from the Porte.[7] According to Porte records, the stipend covered a plot of land, daily maintenance, and expenses for travel within the Ottoman domains.[8] Put in the context of the first Ottoman mission to Kabul just a few years earlier, ʿAbd al-Rahman's banishing the Tarzis from his kingdom and Abdülhamid II's resettling them as refugees in his domain proved to be two of the most consequential decisions for strengthening ties between Afghanistan and the Ottoman lands in the long term.

Of all the children of Ghulam Muhammad Khan, we know the most about his precocious son, Mahmud Tarzi (1865–1933).[9] Born in Ghazni, Afghanistan, the young Tarzi was allotted a special stipend to travel to Istanbul for education.[10] Spending his early years in the Ottoman metropolises of Baghdad, Istanbul, and Damascus, Mahmud would eventually become a critical link between Afghanistan and the Ottoman lands in more than one way, including functioning as an intermediary for the governing regimes in Istanbul and Kabul, *and* brewing constitutional movements in the Ottoman Empire and Afghanistan during the first two decades of the twentieth century.

By all accounts Mahmud Tarzi was an extraordinary personality, combining an inquisitive mind with polyglot abilities, and sheer determination. It was not long before opportunity came knocking. Ottoman authorities in Syria offered him employment in the local government of Damascus, beginning with a secretarial post in the Damascus police commissioner's office.[11] In 1891 he married Asma Resmiyya, the daughter of Shaykh Muhammad Salih al-Mossadiyya, a notable Damascene businessman and muezzin of the Ummayyad Mosque. Their marriage laid further roots for what appeared by all his accounts to be a permanent home in Syria.

As a bureaucrat in late Ottoman Damascus, the young Mahmud mastered Turkish and French, in addition to his primary languages of Persian, Pashto, and Urdu. He was particularly enthralled by poetry, philosophy, and modern literature, reading the original in several languages.[12] He translated several works from European languages into both Turkish and Persian, and mingled with scholars and literati of diverse political persuasions. The latter included some of the leading figures of a Muslim modernist renaissance burgeoning in Ottoman metropolises like Istanbul, Aleppo, and Damascus. In 1896, Mahmud Tarzi met the itinerant preacher and Pan-Islamic ideologue Jamal al-Din "al-Afghani" in Istanbul.[13] Above all, Tarzi was most influenced by the burgeoning reformist politics that came to be known as the Young Ottoman movement in major cities of the empire, laying the foundation for an even more popular and consequential amalgam of reformists better known as the Young Turks.[14] The latter's influence played an especially important role in shaping Tarzi's vision for Afghanistan, a place he does not appear to have forgotten while growing up in Syria. As Louis Dupree, Tarzi's first biographer in a European language, summarized, "Everything the dissident young Tarzi wanted to say about Afghanistan he said through the lips of the young Turk."[15]

One of the most remarkable and oft overlooked aspects of Mahmud Tarzi's exile in Syria was his continuing esteem in the eyes of the Hamidian regime in spite of his proximity to Young Turk dissidents. An internal Porte memorandum from 1893, for example, signed by the Ottoman grand vizier himself, describes the conferral of official honors on him for his services to the state.[16] At the same time, despite establishing firm roots in his new home of Damascus, Tarzi continued to maintain ties with Afghanistan. In 1897, for example, Tarzi sent a Persian translation of Ottoman bureaucrat Hasan Fehmi Pasha's treatise on international law, *Devletlerarası Hukuk,* to the Afghan amir.[17] These exchanges reflected a connection between Afghanistan and the Ottoman Empire over and above the bilateral governmental ties initiated in 1877. Given that Anglo-Afghan agreements since 1879 constrained Afghan amirs from carrying out official diplomacy with foreign powers other than the British Raj, the activities and correspondences of Afghan migrants to the Ottoman lands became all the more valuable.

Young Turks, Young Afghans

In a letter of February 1902, Habib Allah reassured the new patriarch that it was time for the Tarzi family to return home.[18] After paying cordial respects to the Ottoman sultan, the letter also granted Mahmud Tarzi and his family official amnesty, and earnestly invited them to return to Afghanistan, where Tarzi would be appointed chief of the court's translation bureau (Dar al-Tarjamih). When Tarzi received Habib Allah's letter, he had already spent two decades and the majority of his life in Damascus and Istanbul, likely making the invitation to uproot impracticable. Having attended schools, established a career, and raised a family in the Ottoman domains, it would not have been unusual for the new Tarzi family patriarch to politely decline the summons even of an Afghan king.

Defying expectations, Ottoman and British records indicate that Mahmud Tarzi responded enthusiastically to Habib Allah's letter.[19] By early May, hardly seven months after 'Abd al-Rahman's death, British and Ottoman sources reported Mahmud Tarzi's arrival at the port of Bombay via steamship. A week later, he was already in the Afghan capital. The short time between 'Abd al-Rahman's death and Tarzi's arrival in Kabul indicates that the Afghan exile prepared to travel to Afghanistan shortly after Habib Allah's invitation.[20] Returning to his homeland after two decades in exile, Mahmud Tarzi impressed on the new amir the need to recruit experts to Afghanistan to help build professional capacity for key projects in the administrative, educational, and military fields. As Habib Allah was already searching for professionals across a range of fields to provide crucially needed expertise for his state-building campaign, the timing was propitious.[21] With this goal in mind, Tarzi returned to Damascus not only to retrieve his family but to recruit Ottoman experts for employment in a number of important fields in Afghanistan.[22]

Mahmud Tarzi's initial attempts to recruit Ottoman experts to Kabul fell on sympathetic but largely unreceptive ears.[23] Undeterred by these early setbacks, he pressed on.[24] By the spring of 1904, Tarzi prepared to return to Kabul with signs that his recruiting efforts were bearing fruit. On April 4, 1904, Porte authorities issued a communiqué acknowledging, and permitting, the Tarzi family to relocate from Syria to Afghanistan.[25] Not long afterwards, the former Ottoman civil servant began his second journey back to Kabul, joined by his family.

Mahmud Tarzi's second and more lasting return to Kabul is significant to Afghanistan's modern history for more than its own sake. From this point on, a trail of Turkish experts followed behind him.[26] The arrival of Ottoman political exiles in Kabul in the early years of the twentieth century, after the Iron Amir's demise, had more than a coincidental relationship to the emergence of an underground constitutional society in Afghanistan around the same time.[27] Having resettled in Kabul, and exploiting his newfound status in the Kabul court, Tarzi forged contacts with likeminded segments of the royal family and educated elite, who were persuaded by the need for modernizing reforms along Ottoman lines, including the formation of more participatory modes of politics and governance. Tarzi's activities intersected with the underground activities of a more radical faction of Afghan, and some Indian, dissidents in Kabul—the Sirr-i Milli (National Secret)—who were devoted to establishing a constitutional government in the country.[28] The result was a loose association of intellectuals and bureaucrats coalesced in the capital known as the Young Afghans (Jawanan-i Afghan).[29] Inspired by a resurgence of constitutional activism in the Ottoman Empire and Iran, as well as by Pan-Asian political currents in the wake of Japan's historic naval victory over Russia in 1905, the Young Afghans were unified by a pair of national goals: constitutional government in Afghanistan and liberating the country from British suzerainty.[30]

Given the timing of constitutional developments unraveling within the Ottoman domains, and the arrival of Ottoman exiles like Ali Fehmi Bey and Mehmed Fazlı Effendi and other Young Turk associates in the Afghan capital, the Kabul association had more in common with the Young Turks than their name. Thanks to Tarzi's robust Ottoman connections and his newfound stature in the Afghan royal family—in 1912 his half-Syrian daughter Suraya Tarzi (1897–1968) and Habib Allah's youngest son, Aman Allah Khan (1892–1960), were married—it was not long before a Turcophile influence predominated among the Young Afghans and Kabul court alike. In addition to his royal connections, Tarzi utilized the influential Persian publication he edited and had helped found, *Siraj al-Akhbar,* to disseminate his message of Muslim renewal and unity from Istanbul to Delhi.[31] It is not surprising, therefore, given Tarzi's instrumental role in establishing an Ottoman camp in the Kabul court, that British intelligence documents from this period consistently describe him as a "pro-Turkish firebrand."[32]

To reduce the arrival of Ottomans in Afghanistan to the enterprise of a single returning exile—albeit an exceedingly prolific and influential one—would overlook additional sources of entente between the Ottoman Empire and Afghanistan before and during Tarzi's return. Other sources indicate that the idea of employing Ottoman experts was not simply Tarzi's brainchild. In late 1908, for example, British officers in Peshawar reported that the recruiting of "efficient Turks" for employment in Afghanistan, where they were to be given "posts of responsibility and trust," was originated by the amir's brother, Nasr Allah Khan, before being approved by Habib Allah himself.[33] The British agent's observations indicate that Turcophilic tendencies among Habib Allah's advisors were not limited to Tarzi, but enjoyed broader support among key members of the Kabul court, including the amir's own brother and powerful insider, Nasr Allah. "Nasrulla Khan prefers Turks to natives of India," the agent further noted, "and the Amir is inclined to share his views."[34]

The robust connections between the Young Turks and the Young Afghans notwithstanding, the Kabul court's internal dynamics were more complex than a simple transplant of Ottoman politics to Afghanistan would allow. To presume a direct, linear connection between the antimonarchical influence of the Young Turks in Kabul and the rise of the Young Afghans would miss a fundamental—and, to a certain degree, ironic—dimension of the Ottoman community in Kabul between 1901 and 1914: most of the Ottomans in Afghanistan, as advisors, bureaucrats, and officers, served an absolute monarch in Habib Allah. Despite the diplomatic risks of employing political dissidents against a fellow Muslim sovereign in his own court, in the years immediately after their arrival, and especially following the deposal of Sultan Abdülhamid II in 1908–1909, it appears the Turks of Kabul had Habib Allah's full confidence. Among the amir's personal medical staff were two Turkish doctors, one of whom served as the amir's own private physician. The same pair played an instrumental role in establishing the first state hospital in Kabul and a nascent ministry of public health in the country.[35] One of the most powerful men in Kabul at this time was an Ottoman colonel from Baghdad whom Habib Allah entrusted with training and educating a new class of Afghan cadets and officers. Ottoman engineers also played a leading role in launching some of the largest infrastructure projects the country had seen.

One way of reconciling the contradiction of Young Turk dissidents fleeing one absolute ruler in Istanbul only to serve another in Kabul is to understand these Ottoman subjects as simply visitors in a foreign land—some may have deemed it not their place to judge a monarch apart from their own, or interfere in a friendly country's internal policies. This assessment would overlook the complexity of the Ottomans in Kabul as a transnational community with fluid notions of imperial citizenship and pluralistic ideological commitments, however. The latter could incorporate Ottoman subject status and Young Turk constitutionalism, as well as Pan-Islamic, Pan-Turkic, and Pan-Asian political agendas at once. What is more likely, then, is Ottoman émigrés to Kabul at this time brought complex and evolving notions of their place in Afghanistan, notions that included ideals of strengthening a fellow Muslim realm against shared threats.

Any discussion of the Ottoman presence in Afghanistan during Habib Allah's era would also be incomplete without mention of the relevant international context within which the Afghan amir's modernization campaign was launched. On August 31, 1907, Britain and Russia signed the Anglo-Russian Convention in St. Petersburg. In this landmark agreement, an imperial meeting of minds between Britain and Russia seemed to temporarily resolve their century-old rivalry in Asia. Afghanistan was declared outside Russia's sphere of influence and therefore subject to Britain's jurisdiction, in exchange for Britain's recognizing a Russian sphere of influence over northern Iran. This agreement, in which neither the Afghan nor Persian government was consulted, created an uproar in Afghanistan and Iran, in the court and on the streets alike. In this dramatic twist to Anglo-Russian Great Game competition in Afghanistan, Habib Allah's quest for sovereignty and a strong Afghan state acquired added urgency. Together, these international factors pressured the amir to extend more vigorous invitations to the Ottoman Turks.

Examining the contributions of influential Ottoman subjects in Kabul under Habib Allah's reign reveals an episode insufficiently examined in scholarship on the late Ottoman Empire: the politics of Ottoman experts in other Muslim lands. Here, the combined efforts of Habiḅ Allah, the Young Afghans, and the Ottomans in Kabul reflect a keen search for models of good governance and state-building within a particular region, a search that invites us to rethink notions of modernization and Westernization centered on Eurocentric experiences. In relatively few but profoundly transformative years, the Ottomans in Kabul participated in strengthening Turco-Afghan ties in Kabul as the Ottoman Empire shook from the Young Turk Revolution (1907–1908), Italo-Turkish War (1911–1912), and Balkan Wars (1912–1913). Such notions were shaped by the crucible of their experiences in Kabul as much as by the tumultuous events unraveling in the Ottoman Empire.

The Naqibs of Baghdad, an Ottoman Arab Colonel, and the Mekteb-i Harbiye, Kabul

Among the most prominent "Turks" to settle in Afghanistan in the first quarter of the twentieth century was El-Seyyid Mahmud Sami Bey, an Ottoman Arab army officer of Baghdad. Sami's emigration to Kabul from Iraq in the early 1900s had its origins in familial ties between different branches of the notable *Naqib al-Ashraf* family of Baghdad. As descendants of the saintly founder of the Qaderi sufi order, Sayyid ʿAbd al-Qadir al-Gilani (1077–1166), the Naqibs of Baghdad were among the most influential Sunni religious figures of Ottoman Iraq, with strong connections to India and Central Asia, and even the royal House of Osman in Istanbul.[36] In the early 1880s, for example, the then Naqib of Baghdad, Shaykh Sayyid Sulayman, was known to travel to India and Afghanistan. Also in the 1880s, another member of the Naqibs of Baghdad, Shaykh Sayyid Hassan, traveled to Afghanistan and decided to settle in Kabul. British agents described Shaykh Hassan as being "in great favour with the Amir," receiving the support of ʿAbd al-Rahman until the latter's demise.[37] To patronize a prominent scholar and sufi shaykh of an eminent saintly family from the Ottoman domains was therefore a point of great prestige for the Afghan amir.[38]

Connections between the Naqibs of Baghdad and Kabul persisted and strengthened during the Habib Allah era. As early as 1902, British intelligence in Kabul reported that the Naqib of Baghdad served as the primary medium of communication between Constantinople and Kabul.[39] For this reason British intelligence wrote in an internal memorandum that "it is natural, therefore, to view with suspicion the visits of the Nakib's relations to India or Afghanistan."[40] So, when Mahmud Sami Bey—a nephew of the Naqib in Baghdad, and a colonel in the Ottoman army—arrived in Kabul in the early 1900s the reputation of his family preceded him. He was hence warmly received by Habib Allah on arriving in the Afghan capital. He was also monitored by British agents.

That Mahmud Sami was a predominant figure in the Ottoman community in early twentieth-century Kabul is evident in that internal correspondence of Ottoman, Afghan, and British governments frequently mentions him. From the mid-1900s until his demise in Afghanistan in 1930, Mahmud Sami was the subject of intelligence exchanges on Ottoman activity in Kabul by the British consul general at Baghdad, the British agent at Kabul, and the foreign secretary of the Government of India.[41] For over two decades, the colonel of Baghdad would go on to be one of the most prominent and prolific Ottomans in Kabul, even though the amir occasionally disciplined him for allegedly maltreating cadets.[42] Mahmud Sami began his service in Afghanistan under Habib Allah and in multiple capacities, including as a drill instructor, school administrator, and the author of multiple works on Ottoman military exercises. Most of all, Mahmud Sami is credited with leading the royal military academy for training Afghan officers that was established between 1904 and 1906.[43] Officially endowed by its Persian name Madrasih-ʾi Harbiyyih-ʾi Sirajiyyih, sometimes translated as the Royal Military College of Kabul, the college was also known by its Ottoman Turkish name, Mekteb-i Harbiye. Kabul's Harbiye was modeled on secondary schools for training officers established in major Ottoman cities during the Hamidian era, including the Mekteb-i ʿAnbar in Damascus and Mekteb-i Aşiret-i Hümayun (Imperial Tribal School) in Istanbul, but also their civil counterparts in the Imperial Sultani lycées, or *idadiyyes,* in other major provincial cities such as Baghdad and Beirut. The Hamidian schools began as elite academies for the sons of notable families of Syria and Arab tribes in Mesopotamia; but as they trained new kinds of officers and bureaucrats they also became breeding grounds for Young Turk dissidents, and for Turkish and Arab nationalist leaders for generations to come.[44]

Like its counterparts in the Ottoman domains, Kabul's Harbiye was initially designed to train both high and mid-rank officers for the capital and provinces, and began by instructing sons from notable families and influential tribes.[45] To the chagrin of some Indian-trained Afghan officers in the amir's service, it was through Kabul's Harbiye that Ottoman military practices began to overturn the Kabul court's historical preference for British Indian military practice.[46] It was also here that Mahmud Sami instructed children of the most elite families of Afghanistan, including Habib Allah's son and future amir, Prince Aman Allah Khan (1892–1960).[47] On the state of instruction in the school, one British informant was particularly struck by the remarkable display of discipline and order in spite of the young age of many of the students:

> On the day of *Jashan* the boys of the school came to pay their respects to the Amir. They behaved like disciplined soldiers. They were about seventy in number, all in full dress and carrying rifles. The youngest were seven or eight years old. They were carrying air guns. They have their separate band, who are also boys except three who are their instructors. Though it is yet a play, they make a very good show indeed.[48]

On the rise of Sami's career in Afghanistan, the diary of the British agent at Kabul in 1909 noted, "The influence of Mahmud Sami, the Turk, is increasing."[49] Of particular value to Habib Allah were the strides in education, including physical training, being made at the Ottoman-styled military academy. "The Amir has begun to consider him a useful man," the top British official in Afghanistan noted, pointing out the progress made at the Harbiye as especially noteworthy. "The military school had made a very good start and the credit is due to Colonel Mahmud Sami."[50]

Still yet, one of the most laudatory descriptions to be recorded of Mahmud Sami's activities in Kabul comes from an unexpected source: a British mineralogist briefly serving Habib Allah under the title "Dr. Saise." Following the conclusion of the latter's appointment in the amir's service, Saise agreed to an interview with the British political agent of Khyber, who was apparently anxious to learn more of the inner workings of the Kabul court. It remains one of the few extant sources by a European employee in Habib Allah's court. In addition to comments on the king's progressive orientation, Saise was particularly impressed by the state of education and training at the Mekteb-i Harbiye, citing the "excellence of the arrangements" at the school. It was here, the report continues, no less than eighty cadets emanating from Kabul's elite families were instructed in military subjects and trained in other "habits of discipline." Crucially, the report adds, all of this took place "under the supervision of a Turkish Colonel," Seyyid Mahmud Sami.[51]

Having earned a sterling reputation in the amir's service for his work at the Harbiye, Mahmud Sami's success in Kabul led to the arrival of even more Ottoman subjects in Kabul. According to one British source, Habib Allah specifically entreated Sami to recruit more officers and officials from the sultan's domains. "[A]ny Turk fit and qualified in work, suitable for the requirements of Afghanistan, will be taken into service if he would like to come," the amir was reported to have stated in no unclear terms to the Ottoman colonel.[52] In the decade between Tarzi and Mahmud Sami's arrival in Kabul from the early 1900s to the eve of World War I, a cadre of Ottoman officers skilled in various military and civilian trades made their way to Kabul. Limited as it was in numbers, the arrival of the sultan's subjects in the Afghan capital was greeted with anticipation and full salute by the amir. A diary entry of the British agent at Kabul from January 1908, for example, described the ceremonious noontime arrival of eight Ottoman officers at Kabul, where Habib Allah specifically arranged for his Turkish-speaking Uzbek cavalry regiment to line the roads and salute the Turks as a mark of honor but also familiar welcome.

Before long Mahmud Sami was not the only Ottoman officer to be training Afghan officers during Habib Allah's reign, and a critical mass of Ottoman officers had arrived to help launch the Harbiye and a range of other infrastructure, public works, and bureaucratic projects. As both Ottoman and British sources reveal, a Turkish delegation of officers was sent to the Afghan government to serve in an advisory capacity, arriving in Kabul via Russia and Iran in 1909–1910.[53] Among them was an Ottoman officer named Hasan Hüsnü Bey, who was said to be composing a textbook in Turkish containing rules and regulations for troops, including drilling exercises, with plans to translate the work into Persian. Copies of books and manuals authored by Mahmud Sami and Hüsnü Beys still rest in the Afghan archives, including children's grammar lessons, indicating plans to teach Ottoman Turkish to Afghan schoolchildren.[54] The same 1909 Raj dossier proceeds to explain the amir's order that, as a gesture of admiration for the Turks, drilling along British fashion would be replaced by *Sulṭānī* drill style—the latter being Kabuli vernacular for Ottoman subjects in Afghanistan at this time. Nor was the flow of Ottoman-Afghan military collaboration a one-way road. A pair of Ottoman archival documents from 1913 and 1914, for example, discuss the arrival of foreign volunteers in Adana (southern Anatolia) for training from places as diverse as Sudan, Bukhara, and Afghanistan.[55]

The work of Mahmud Sami and his supporting officers in laying the foundations of a national army in Afghanistan was far from the only legacy of Ottoman expatriates in Kabul at this time. As we shall see, "Sultani" influence in Afghanistan's military was complemented by wide-ranging Turkish influences in education, administration, and bureaucracy.

Ottoman Teachers, Journalists, and Physicians—and a New Civil Service in Kabul

Kabul's Mekteb-i Harbiye was not the only major educational initiative underway in the Afghan capital during Habib Allah's reign, nor was it the only one in which Ottomans made substantial contributions. In 1913, Prince ʿInayat Allah organized a professional conference on education in Kabul; out of a total of nine experts participating, three were Ottoman subjects, speaking to a considerable Turkish role in Habib Allah's educational plans.[56] The other significant educational legacy of Habib Allah's reign—the Madrasih-ʾi Habibiyyih (Turkish: Mekteb-i Habibiye), about which we will have more to say later—was founded by Indian Muslim teachers as a civilian counterpart to Kabul's Harbiye, but here, too, Ottoman instructors could be found on the faculty roster.[57]

Among the cohort of Ottoman advisors arriving in Afghanistan in the early years of Habib Allah's reign was a Young Turk exile, Mehmed Ali Fehmi. In late 1906, Fehmi accepted the invitation for Ottoman subjects to migrate to Kabul, where he was offered an advisorial position in Afghanistan's newly founded Ministry of Finance. Before his travel to Afghanistan in January of 1907, Fehmi pursued an eclectic career in law, education, and journalism, including positions as editor in the *Muvazene* magazine of Egypt, as caricaturist in another satirical newspaper in Cairo, and as law professor in Switzerland and Bulgaria.[58] Much of Fehmi's travels and activities out of the Ottoman domains had to do with his oppositional activities against the Hamidian regime. Indeed we know about his employment in Afghanistan partly because Ottoman records indicate the Hamidian government was carefully watching his activities far from Istanbul.[59]

Fehmi seems to have attracted special attention because of his demonstrated oratory skills and ability to recruit Turks to Afghanistan. For this reason the Sublime Porte was not the only government watching him and other Young Turks arriving in Afghanistan at this time. Fehmi also attracted the attention of British intelligence agents in Kabul. Concerning his activities in the Afghan capital, a British Indian intelligence report described Fehmi as "an expert who has offered his services to reorganize the revenue system and introduce schemes for improving the irrigation of the country."[60] The same document mentions Fehmi's promise to enlist "two or three experienced engineers" in the amir's service.

With an irony that was not lost on the Hamidian exile, Ali Fehmi's arrival in Kabul coincided with the watershed Young Turk Revolution of July 1908. Soon after his arrival in Kabul, Fehmi dispatched a telegram to the new Young Turk government in Istanbul, exhorting his compatriots to concurrently Pan-Islamic and Pan-Turkic agendas:

> O servants of the nation! Consider Turkistan deeply. Unite with the Turks of Russia, China, Afghanistan, and Persia, who are of the same religion and the same race as us. Let us establish firm political relations and friendly ties with the Chinese, the Russian, and the Afghan components of Turkistan.[61]

Ali Fehmi's remarks displayed the complex and multifaceted impetuses behind Ottoman outreach to Afghanistan at this time. Eliding the internal ethnic diversity of the country by stressing its Turkic components, nevertheless officials in both the Young Turk and Afghan governments viewed the Ottoman presence in Kabul as a positive development that promised not only a reinvigoration of fraternal ties but also a bulwark against the shared challenges of

European and Russian expansion on their borders. Fehmi's exhortations appear to have been well received. Limited though it was, in the months and years following Ali Fehmi's service in Afghanistan and return to Istanbul, an assortment of Ottoman technicians, teachers, politicians, military officers, and physicians continued to travel to Afghanistan to serve in the amir's court.

Among the Ottomans to journey to Afghanistan following invitations by Mahmud Tarzi, Mahmud Sami, and Ali Fehmi was a Turkish journalist and portraitist, Mehmed Fazlı Effendi. Shortly after the Young Turk Revolution restored the Ottoman Constitution and ushered in a reappearance of parliamentary politics in the empire, Mehmed Fazlı returned to Istanbul and published *Resimli Afgan Seyaheti* (An Illustrated Afghan Travelogue).[62] Although Fazlı's stay in Kabul was short-lived, his illustrated travel memoir offers one of the richest firsthand descriptions of the Ottoman community in Kabul, including what the foreign visitors found of interest during their sojourn in Afghanistan.

Also arriving in the same delegation as Mehmed Fazlı was a Turkish doctor who became Habib Allah's private physician. Unlike Mehmed Fazlı and Ali Fehmi, however, Dr. Munir İzzet Bey decided not to repatriate to the Ottoman domains when the Young Turk Revolution broke out. In light of the length of his stay and his proximity to the amir—and the breadth of initiatives launched under his authority—Dr. İzzet emerged as one of the most influential Ottomans in Habib Allah's court.

Dr. İzzet's rapport with Habib Allah appears to have transcended the personal trust embodied in his responsibility for the amir's physical health. Although the physician departed Kabul for a brief visit to Istanbul—possibly to relate information to the new Ottoman authorities—the fact that he returned to Kabul illustrated a commitment to fulfill his service to the amir and maintain continuity in Ottoman-Afghan relations.[63] It was under Dr. İzzet's watch that the first modern public hospitals and ministry of public health were established in Afghanistan. Among the medical staff led by İzzet was a strong Indian contingent, and together they established the first state hospital in Kabul in 1913.[64]

Attesting to İzzet's influence in the Afghan amir's court is a British intelligence report describing him as the preeminent Turk in Afghanistan. The British Indian informant takes particular note of the Turkish doctor's connections with the Ottoman government, including his role as a conduit of intelligence to the Porte on greater Asian affairs. As the report states in unequivocal terms:

> The most important personage in the Turkish community is (1) Dr. Munir Izzat. He goes to this country practically every year, ostensibly on leave, but really on duty, and brings full reports of the doings of Government in Turkey, for the information of His Majesty the Amir. He has many news-agents in Turkey who are paid through him, and keep the Afghan Government informed through him of what is taking place there. His chief mission is to create a sympathetic and brotherly feeling between the Turks and Afghans.[65]

Dr. İzzet would later serve as chief medical officer in Aman Allah's cabinet, along with chief civil physician Dr. Ahmed Fahim Bey, also an Ottoman Turk who arrived in Kabul during the Habib Allah era.[66] Like most of the Turks in Kabul at this time, both physicians engaged in diplomatic and political activities well beyond the call of their medical duties and their professional expertise, serving as representatives of an Ottoman government very much in flux.

"Efficient Turks": The Ottoman Community in Kabul before World War I

As early as 1904, the British agent at Kabul wrote to superior officers in India describing a noticeable increase in the arrival of Ottoman subjects in the city. Emphasizing the pronounced role said Turks seemed to be assuming as advisors in Habib Allah's government and reform program, the agent concluded,

> [T]he Amir has decided to take active steps for the education of his subjects on Turkish lines, and with this object in view he has been for some time past trying to induce Turks of the civil, military, and Ulema classes, respectively, to go and settle in Afghanistan in order to inculcate and diffuse Turkish principles and methods in administrative, military, and educational matters in that country.[67]

That the British agent's words were in 1904—years before the arrival of additional Ottoman subjects in Kabul—underscores the outsized impact the numerically small but influential community of Turks in Kabul were already having at this time. In no unclear terms, the British agent described the amir's recruitment policies as reflecting the amir's "marked preference for, and admiration of, the Sultan and his people."[68]

Far from mere fraternalist sentiments, pro-Turkish attitudes in Afghanistan were taking a concrete shape in the form of recruiting Ottoman experts for building modern administrative, educational, and military institutions in the country. The work of Mahmud Sami, Dr. İzzet, and Ali Fehmi, among the several unnamed who accompanied the aforesaid Ottoman subjects to Kabul, are instructive. The latter's arrival in Kabul did not just coincide, but directly resulted from the amir's coming to terms with a ubiquitous problem in his government: the shortage of adequately skilled professionals to implement his envisioned reforms. It is precisely with tackling this problem in mind that Habib Allah welcomed Mahmud Tarzi's plan of inviting Ottoman experts to Kabul to implement his desired reforms.

Contrary to the depictions of some concerned Raj officials in India's restive northwest frontier, Ottoman émigrés to Afghanistan at this time were not militant firebrands intent on stirring up revolt against the British. Most were professionals arriving in Kabul to share a specific and solicited form of expertise. Over and beyond the educational and public health projects launched by Mahmud Sami and Drs. İzzet and Ahmed Fahim, other examples of Ottoman-Afghan collaborations at this time of relative quiet were the constructive partnerships—quite literally—between Afghan municipal officials and Ottoman engineers. Among the latter were Turkish specialists employed in Afghan state machineries and mechanical factories. Ottoman engineers also played a role in launching some of Afghanistan's first large infrastructure projects, including a telephone line from Kabul to Jalalabad, an irrigation system linking the mountain springs of Paghman to the capital via a sophisticated piping system, and the country's first hydroelectric system, in 1910, which provided the capital with steady electricity.[69] Rıza Bey, a Turkish engineer, was put in charge of road improvements.[70]

Often the government projects launched by the Ottomans in Kabul synthesized a role for Afghans, Turks, Arabs, and Indian Muslims in varied fields, incorporating the expertise of diverse specialists. For example, Hilmi Pasha, who was charged with establishing Afghanistan's postal system, arrived in the country with an unnamed Turkish geologist who was appointed superintendent of mines in Afghanistan.[71] Over and above launching infrastructure improvements, delivering new technologies, and institutionalizing civil services associated with modern statehood, a crucial part of the responsibility of Ottomans in Kabul was to train Afghans for continuing and developing these large national projects on their own terms. In a Kabul printing house, for example, Ottoman technicians

Mehmed Hasan Effendi, Mehmed Nadir Effendi, and the aforementioned portraitist Mehmed Fazlı were entrusted with training at least five local apprentices.[72]

Facilitated by Tarzi's strong connections to the Ottoman realm, the amir's efforts yielded impressive results. In less than five years, Ottoman subjects of predominantly Turkish but also Arab background began arriving in Kabul in service of the amir. They went on to pioneer some of the most far-reaching military and civil reforms in the country's history up to that point.[73] The most common professions represented by Ottoman émigrés to Afghanistan during the Habib Allah era were mechanical and civil engineers and their associate technicians, followed by military officers, journalists, teachers, and physicians. Most were in receipt of salaries ranging from R500 to R1,200 Kabuli per month. Given the multifaceted and fluid qualities of this transnational community, it is difficult to generalize about the Turks in Kabul during the Habib Allah era. As highlighted above, however, combining Ottoman, British, Indian, and Afghan sources reveals a number of key individuals in influential positions of mostly Ottoman Turkish but also Ottoman Arab background in Kabul at this time.

That Habib Allah's "efficient Turks"—persons like Mahmud Sami, Ali Fehmi, Mehmed Fazlı, and Hilmi Pasha—emerged from a context of effective Ottoman educational, bureaucratic, and military reforms from the late Tanzimat to Hamidian eras must be emphasized. The latter included the Sublime Porte's massive restructuring of the Ottoman armed forces, legal-administrative institutions, and educational practices from a patrimonial system based on notables and elite families to a regimented, conscription-based military and bureaucracy trained in new civil schools and colleges. Taking nearly empire-wide roots during the Hamidian era, the long-standing impact of these institutional transformations shaped generations of the Arab world and Turkey for decades following the Ottoman collapse after World War I. Although the importance of the Hamidian reforms in remaking the empire have long been recognized by scholars, and even though valuable research has been carried out on the "new order" of schools and law courts in Syria, Iraq, and Yemen, as well as the imperial center of Istanbul, less attention has been given to the export of Hamidian institutions abroad to non-Ottoman lands such as Afghanistan. The latter represent, in effect, an Ottoman rule of experts and civilizing mission of their own.[74]

More broadly, Ottoman efforts in the nineteenth century to "strike back" at European military and economic ascendance in the eastern Mediterranean through a new vision of Ottomanism have been the subject of a rich scholarly literature. Central to these historiographical contributions has been not only a better understanding of the late Ottoman Empire's administrative and educational reforms championing centralization and equal citizenship, but the idea that Porte officials (and their subjects) were not passive spectators to European economic and political ascendance in the region—especially when occurring within Ottoman borders.[75] Examining the Porte's own bureaucratic reach across imperial borders challenges linear and one-dimensional narratives of a European scramble for empire.[76] Like the Iron Amir ʿAbd al-Rahman, Sultan Abdülhamid II also expanded his empire's extraterritorial influence in unintentional ways—through the very persons he forced into exile. The activities and contributions of Ottomans in Kabul like Mahmud Sami, Ali Fehmi, and Dr. İzzet underscore important international dimensions of Ottomanism abroad that have been given insufficient attention. It was through the latter's contributions that Afghanistan's most elite military and civilian educational institutions—the Harbiye and Habibiye colleges, respectively—were founded in Kabul at this time, with Ottoman instructors enjoying a substantial presence on the teaching roster. Beyond the institutions they established, the Turks of Kabul also played a role in disseminating attitudes of "Ottoman Orientalism" to fellow Muslim ruling elites intent on developing centralizing and civilizing campaigns of their own.

At the same time, these episodes highlight the agency of individual Hamidian dissidents in capitalizing on the opportunities exile could provide, bringing Afghanistan and the Ottoman Empire in closer contact even while they pursued their own aims and interests. This was most clear with the activities of dissident Young Turk journalists and the establishment of a new Ottoman Harbiye academy—not in the major Ottoman provinces of Aleppo, Mosul, or Baghdad, nor in the common destinations of exile in Europe, but in Kabul, Afghanistan.

The projects generated by Ottoman experts in Kabul under Habib Allah's aegis were wide-ranging, encompassing the military, educational, public health, civil engineering, and bureaucratic fields, as well as journalism and law.[77] Turkish journalists interacted with Kabul's premier publications, chief among them Mahmud Tarzi's *Siraj al-Akhbar*. In the realm of legal and administrative reforms, British sources indicate the arrival in 1912 of an Ottoman judicial officer in Afghanistan to serve in the amir's court.[78] From the diary of the British agent at Kabul for the week ending January 22, 1908, a report states that of the eight Turks who arrived on January 15, one was a lawyer "qualified in office routine," further described as "a barrister and is well up in law."[79] By and large, however, the greatest Ottoman contributions to Afghanistan in the field of law and administration would not take place until the reign of Aman Allah Khan, a period in which Turkish involvement in Afghanistan reached its zenith. At this time, the bulk of Ottoman contributions were in military training, medicine and public health, and big infrastructure projects.

As with the professions they represented, the Ottoman subjects who migrated to Afghanistan in this period did not belong to a single ideological stripe. Be they doctors, teachers, engineers, mechanics, or journalists, the Turks who came to Kabul also brought their own politics. When many of these Ottoman subjects arrived in Afghanistan from locales as diverse as Cairo, Damascus, and Europe, they did not check their political persuasions at the door, but rather engaged Afghan intellectuals and officials on their own terms. That many of the Turks who emigrated to Afghanistan in the early Habib Allah era were Ottoman exiles and likely active members of the revolutionary Young Turk party is evident in the response of Ottoman officials to queries on the subject by British consular officials.[80] For the Hamidian government's view on some of the Ottoman exiles who traveled to Afghanistan at this time, including Ali Fehmi, we might note the January 28, 1908, memorandum from Sir N. O'Conor, the British ambassador in Constantinople. The memo includes a summary of discussions between O'Conor, the Ottoman ambassador at Tehran, and the Ottoman grand vizier regarding an alleged Turkish "mission" in Afghanistan. In this report, O'Conor states,

> Upon my questioning the Grand Vizier on this subject yesterday, His Highness declared that there was absolutely no question of a Turkish mission, and that the Turks who have passed through Khorassan are most probably political suspects and exiles about whom the Porte has been inquiring for months past. The Porte learnt some time ago that Ali Fehmi, editor of the *Muazene,* a paper published at Philippopoli, and indulging in violent criticism of the existing régime in Turkey, had left for Geneva and subsequently proceeded to Cairo, with other Turkish political exiles, some of whom have been condemned to death by the Turkish Courts.[81]

In the interview that follows the report, the following Ottoman subjects are named as "fugitives from justice" in exile in Afghanistan: Ali Fehmi, editor of *Muazene,* described as "an outlaw"; Major Hussein, "a deserter from the Yemen"; Dr. Abdullah, "an outlaw"; Nejir; Ali Riza; Lieutenant Fazil Effendi, of the

Constantinople School of Medicine; and Reşid Effendi.[82] As evident in the grand vizier's distancing himself and the Hamidian government from these itinerant Turks, many of the Ottomans who came to Kabul in the early Habib Allah era were in fact exiles and dissidents who detested the Hamidian regime. Several were members of the Young Turk opposition, forced into self-exile due to their political activities.

Yet, other Ottomans arriving in Afghanistan at the turn of the twentieth century were not Young Turks in the least. At least one British Indian intelligence memorandum cites Ottoman expatriates en route to Afghanistan to have included "an ex-official of the old Turkish regime"—that is to say, of Abdülhamid II—and that the said Ottoman itinerant was "very bitter against the present constitution" and "proposes to deliver lectures in Arabic against the present [Young Turk] regime."[83] For these reasons the Ottoman community in Kabul cannot be generalized as a bastion of anti-Hamidian politics in Afghanistan. From Young Turk dissidents to Hamidian officials, then, the Ottomans of Kabul at this time were a heterogeneous group, representing diverse political stances and professional occupations, and at least two major Ottoman ethnicities (the majority being ethnic Turks, with at least one Ottoman Arab officer from Baghdad).

This diversity notwithstanding, we can draw a few conclusions about this transnational community. First, the Ottomans in Kabul constituted a pivotal means of bolstering Afghan-Ottoman ties and increasing the Porte's knowledge of greater Asian affairs, including along the restive Indian and Russian frontiers with Afghanistan. They were all, in that sense, "sultanis" and representatives of the Ottoman sultan-caliph, whether they endorsed Hamidian autocracy or not. Furthermore, due to the strong associations of the Ottoman state with the caliphate among the general public within Afghanistan and in the subcontinent, this is how they were most likely perceived by their Afghan and Indian counterparts in Kabul.

Second, although Ottoman subjects were variously motivated to migrate to Afghanistan, and cannot be generalized into a singular political or professional quid pro quo, British and Indian archives provide examples of how the attempts to bring Turks to Afghanistan were an expression of policy at the highest level of the Afghan government, and not a haphazard arrival of Turkish exiles, mercenaries, or adventurers seeking employment. From providing salaries, offices, and homes, to appointing Ottoman émigrés to leading roles in his reform program, Habib Allah had specific reasons for recruiting Ottoman experts over any other nationality. In this sense the Ottomans visiting Afghanistan were not casual travelers, but were specifically recruited, and even screened, for a range of responsibilities. Such scrutiny was evident in Habib Allah's personally interviewing Ottoman subjects upon their arrival in Kabul, similar to his public querying of the Turkish land surveyor described earlier. For example, British agents in the frontier reported in a November 1906 memorandum that a certain Cemil Effendi, "a Turk of Damascus," was found passing through Peshawar from Kabul en route to Bombay. The report describes a series of exchanges between the said Ottoman subject and the Kabul court, including direct conversations with Habib Allah himself and his brother Prince Nasr Allah Khan.[84]

> It has been ascertained that directly on his arrival in Kabul he had an interview with His Majesty and was granted 500 Kabuli. The Amir also directed his expenses to be defrayed from the State Treasury during his stay in Kabul . . . With the Amir's permission he visited Kohistani-i-Kabul, Chardehi and other places of interest. On his return from Logar, the Amir had again an interview with Jamil Effendi, and carried on a conversation in Turkish with the Amir . . . He has been told by the Amir not to disclose to anybody the grant made to him. This man is also said to be in receipt of pay from the Sultan of Turkey.[85]

As the concluding line suggests, British authorities in London and Calcutta were likely not to receive well the prospect of Ottoman Turks being on the payroll of both Abdülhamid II and the Afghan amir at a time when Britain was solely empowered by treaty to conduct Afghanistan's foreign affairs. Furthermore, British agents from Khorasan to Waziristan and within the Kabul court itself report that most Turks who came to Afghanistan arrived via Russia and Iran, entering via Herat, indicating not simply an overland route to Kabul but an Ottoman attempt to avoid British authorities.[86]

Still, as much as Raj officers were concerned by Ottoman influence in Afghanistan, they were far from powerless in these circumstances. The Raj still formally controlled Afghan foreign affairs, and as should be clear by now, embedded numerous agents in the Afghan court and Kabul public alike, providing a steady supply of intelligence from the highest echelons of Habib Allah's darbar to public disturbances in Kabul's markets. Furthermore, though not always in the British Raj's service, there was a long-standing Indian Muslim presence in the Kabul court, as reflected in the likes of the barrister Sultan Mohammad Khan and physician Dr. Abdul Ghani. Both men hailed from humble origins in the

Punjab, and both went on to study at the University of Cambridge, and to advise ʿAbd al-Rahman and Habib Allah in Kabul in a variety of roles. Above and beyond these prominent posts in the Kabul court, there were the more grassroots crossborder connections between Afghan and Indian students at Indian madrasas and colleges, especially the Dar al-ʿUlum seminary at Deoband and the Muhammadan Anglo-Oriental College at Aligarh (later Aligarh Muslim University).[87] Most of all, as the patron state and subsidizer of the Kabul court, Britain still wielded a powerful influence over the amir himself. This manifested most starkly in the amir's decision to take his only trip abroad of his reign: to British India in late 1906. Far from arising in a vacuum, the amir's tour of India emerged from a long history of Afghan rulers interacting with the British for at least a century. Over the course of his reign these long-standing historical factors, as well as the activities of Indian Muslims in Habib Allah's court, counterbalanced the influence of the Ottoman community in Kabul.

Countercurrents: The Musahiban and Indian Connections to the Kabul Court

Ottoman subjects were certainly not the first foreign Muslim subjects to be employed in the Afghan amir's court. Long-standing historical factors, including the geographic proximity of Afghanistan to India, the direction of trade routes, as well as linguistic and cultural familiarity between Afghanistan and India, contributed to Indian Muslims having a much older and larger presence in Kabul. As early as two millennia ago, imperial expansion by the Buddhist Mauryans and Kushans had connected the Indian subcontinent with most of the territory we call Afghanistan today. In the medieval to early modern periods, Hindustani merchants trafficked fine cloth, spices, and other goods through the Khyber and Bolan Passes or deserts of Sistan en route to the bustling markets of Central Asia or Iran, as did Afghans in India through a long history of settlement, horse trading, and even rule in India.[88] By the nineteenth century, British officials dispatched Indian Muslim translators, emissaries, and spies as an expanding East Indian Company sought to carve a "scientific frontier" out of the Pashtun hinterlands beyond Peshawar and Quetta, culminating in the First Anglo-Afghan War (1839–1842), where an imperial army made up of predominantly Indian sepoys marched on Kandahar, Ghazni, and Kabul, before retreating to Jalalabad with catastrophic results.[89] By the end of the Second Anglo-Afghan War (1878–1880), the British Raj had succeeded in installing a permanent Indian Muslim representative in the court of ʿAbd al-Rahman. It is during his reign and the reigns of his two successors, Habib Allah and Aman Allah, that Indian Muslim recruits began to form the largest community of foreigners in Afghanistan and the Kabul court. These recruits were particularly active in commerce, education, and record keeping. As historian Robert D. McChesney has observed, "Indian Muslims had long been an influential force in Afghanistan as educators, bureaucrats, and merchants and were an important line of communication between the highlands of Afghanistan and the northern Indian plain."[90]

To these historical trends we must add the considerable cultural and linguistic ties. Many formally educated Indian Muslims were still fluent in Persian, the late Mughal court's administrative language, and an increasing number of Afghans learned Urdu through commercial and educational ties or extended periods of living in India.[91] The prevalent use of Urdu as a lingua franca for Indian Muslims was not a far cry from Persian or many Afghans' native Pashto either.[92] Educationally, the establishment of institutions of higher learning by modern Muslim revivalist movements at Deoband (est. 1867) and Aligarh (est. 1875), where several Afghans studied and even some taught, reminds us that elite educational and juridical networks connected Afghans with Indian Muslims well before Ahmed Hulusi's visit to Kabul in 1877 and ʿAbd al-Rahman's turning to the Ottomans for administrative models during his reign.[93] Economically, Indian merchants enjoyed a long history of trade with Afghanistan and Central Asia.[94] Complimentary to all these connections were the interlaced networks of sufi tariqas connecting India and Afghanistan, as seen with the Mujaddadi family and Naqshabandi Hazrats of Shor Bazaar in Kabul, as well as with the Ottoman lands as seen with the Qaderi Naqibs of Baghdad.[95] Put together, these factors contributed to a consistently larger presence of Indians in Kabul compared to either the Ottoman Turks or Persians.

More specifically, Afghan amirs had long employed Indian Muslims, and per treaty agreements with the Raj, ʿAbd al-Rahman stipulated that the official British agent at Kabul be an Indian Muslim. Still, the appointment of Indian Muslims as teachers, doctors, and other professionals expanded considerably under Habib Allah's reign. By the time the Tarzi family had returned to Kabul after two decades in the Ottoman Empire, another prominent Afghan family abroad, descended from a rival branch of Barakzai Pashtuns, was also resettling in the Afghan capital after decades in foreign exile. Shortly before ʿAbd al-Rahman's death in 1901, the Yahya Khel family returned to their ancestral home, not from the Ottoman Empire, but from Afghanistan's neighbor to the east, British India. Reintegrated into the Kabul court, they eventually assumed the name of the "Musahiban," or royal companions, for their closeness to Amir Habib Allah.

The five Yahya Khel / Musahiban brothers—Muhammad ʿAziz, Nadir, Hashim, Shah Wali, and Shah Mahmud—had received an elite military training at the English-language Dehra Dun Hill Station School in India, roughly 300 kilometers north of Delhi.[96] Like Mahmud Tarzi, the Musahiban brothers spent the formative years of their youth in foreign exile, capitalizing on the educational and professional opportunities in other lands but maintaining a keen awareness of their Afghan notable roots. Also like the Tarzis, when the Musahiban clan returned to Kabul, they were embraced by a reformist amir who granted them leading positions in his court and eventually invited them into his closest circle of advisors. Habib Allah was eager not only to assimilate the returning exiles but also to benefit from the professional expertise they had accumulated from their time abroad.[97] Unlike the Tarzis, however, the powerful Musahiban represented political ties and a stream of expertise hailing not from Istanbul, Damascus, Baghdad, or other Ottoman domains, but from British India, sowing the seeds for an Indo-Ottoman rivalry at the Kabul court.

All five Musahiban brothers would have a profound influence in twentieth-century Afghan governments, but towering above the rest was a military general and future king of Afghanistan. Muhammad Nadir Khan (1883–1933), the grandson of prominent Barakzai chieftain Muhammad Yahya, was born in the north Indian hill station of Dehra Dun, home to the British Raj's exclusive military academy for officer training. Like Mahmud Tarzi's father, Muhammad Yahya had been banished to India following a dispute with the Iron Amir, but was finally pardoned shortly before ʿAbd al-Rahman's demise in 1901. The Musahiban's return therefore roughly coincided with Habib Allah's general amnesty for Afghan exiles on his coronation as the new amir of Afghanistan.[98]

Combining his elite British military training at Dehra Dun with his family's powerful standing in the Kabul court, by 1912 Nadir Khan was made lieutenant general (*naʾib-salar*) of the Afghan army. Two years later, on the eve of World War I, Habib Allah appointed Nadir Khan *Sipahsalar,* or general of all Afghan forces.[99] The Musahiban family emerges even more prominently in our story during Aman Allah's reign (1919–1929)—itself a prelude to Nadir assuming the Afghan throne in 1929—but even at this time, he and his brother counterbalanced Ottoman influence in the Afghan court. Just as Mahmud Tarzi's return from Damascus brought Ottoman experts, Nadir's return to Kabul coincided with the arrival of other Indian Muslims and Indian-educated Afghans. A major source of attraction for the latter were opportunities for employment at another school being built in the Afghan capital at this time.

Habibiye College and Modern Afghan Education

When Habib Allah assumed the reins of power in Kabul, he knew better than anyone that training a skilled bureaucracy was necessary to implement his goals. Whether it was implementing a modern taxation regime to fund his state-building campaign, or a unified network of courts to make the state the adjudicator between disputes, the reformist amir sought a new class of "native son" bureaucrats who commanded local languages and proficiency in the relevant administrative sciences. At the same time, Habib Allah was keen to avoid criticisms of having abandoned Muslim traditions or being a British puppet king, and it is in this context that recruiting Muslim experts from the Ottoman Empire—but also from India—comes into play.

Well before the arrival of Mahmud Tarzi and the first Ottoman recruits in Kabul, the practice of hiring Muslim graduates of Indian institutions like the Muhammadan Anglo-Oriental College at Aligarh, Islamia College at Lahore, and the Dar al-ʿUlum madrasa at Deoband was a common practice of Afghan amirs. By the time Ottoman experts first arrived in Kabul, at the invitation of Mahmud Tarzi, Habib Allah was already contemplating the establishment of Indian-modeled colleges and schools in his own kingdom. Together with a coterie of Indian advisors, most notably Abdul Ghani Khan, who had also served in the Iron Amir's court, in the years following his coronation Habib Allah launched one of the most important of his achievements: the Habibiye College in Kabul. Unlike its military counterpart, the Turkish-styled Mekteb-i Harbiye established by Mahmud Sami, the Habibiye largely owed its foundation to the work of Indian Muslims in Kabul. The most influential of them was the former principal of Islamia College of Lahore, Dr. Abdul Ghani Khan, who was later joined by his brother Chiragh al-Din and Husayn Khan Alighari, both schoolteachers from India. The project thereby reflected the amir's special esteem for Indian Muslims as educators.[100]

Most Afghan chronicles locate the seeds of Habibiye College with Amir Habib Allah's desire to educate his own children.[101] The project eventually grew into an institution of learning for the sons of Afghan notables in Kabul. In 1903, Habib Allah recruited five Indian Muslim professors from the Indian College at Lahore to found a college to educate the sons of the Afghan aristocracy. Soon the amir was contemplating a much bigger role for Indian teachers in Afghanistan. So vital was the state of education in Afghanistan to Habib Allah that he considered it both the ailment and the cure for the country's ills. In a 1906 speech delivered in full darbar with all ministers and courtiers present, the amir proclaimed the need to institute a new system of schooling and training for all government servants:

> I want to promote the condition of my country and better the state of my subjects; and this I cannot do without introducing in my land modern modes of education, science and arts. If anybody does not like this idea of mine, he ought to leave this durbar at once, because I cannot be pleased with such a person.[102]

Habib Allah often spoke about the need to improve the levels of education of his subjects across all ages, but he especially emphasized the role of secondary schools and colleges, which would graduate officials and officers to serve his government. One of Habib Allah's dream projects was to establish a modern university in Kabul to train skilled civil servants for state employment. "[E]ducation is the only path to service in the State," the amir was reported to have told his courtiers.[103]

While Habibiye College would eventually become one of Habib Allah's most celebrated achievements, the institution's early history was far from smooth. "The Habeebiya school was opened nearly three years ago," the amir lamented in 1906, "but now we observe its work retrogressing; it is the Government officers that are especially to blame."[104] The college's origins might be contested, but it is clear that within a few years of his coronation, Habib Allah was thoroughly dissatisfied with the state of Afghan schools, including his prized institution, the Habibiye.[105] Approaching the five-year mark of his rule, Habib Allah decided to reformulate his reform program to focus on building a new class of professionals to staff his bureaucracy. He appointed an Indian Muslim school principal from Lahore—Dr. Abdul Ghani Khan—as its new director, a move that caught the attention of newspapers in India. In October 1906, Indian newspaper *Mulk & Millut* wrote that Abdul Ghani, principal of the Islamia College at Lahore, had resigned his post, and "is about to proceed to Cabool in obedience to the summon of His Majesty the Amir." Habib Allah had evidently found the man to lead his educational reform program, and he chose an Indian Muslim familiar with the Kabul court for the job.

By early December 1906, Dr. Ghani had submitted detailed plans to improve the Habibiye, beginning with a suitable building and increasing the number of available teachers. Ghani also recommended establishing an advanced commercial training school, for which more teachers would be recruited from India, and setting up scholarships for qualifying students. That Ghani had the full support of the amir is evidenced by the report of a 50,000 rupees annual grant marked for the institution and sanctioned by Habib Allah himself. As a further sign of the amir's confidence in the Indian physician and school administrator, Habib Allah officially appointed Dr. Ghani as Afghanistan's director of public instruction.[106]

Apart from appointing an Indian Muslim to spearhead his most important educational initiative, Habib Allah cultivated more direct ties with Afghanistan's eastern neighbor. In late 1906, a year after signing a friendship treaty with British India, the Afghan amir made plans to complete a grand tour of India in order to make his own study of educational and economic institutions in that land. Seeking models for educational reform in particular, it is in this context that Habib Allah embarked on a sixty-four-day trip to British India, the only foreign country he visited as amir.

Habib Allah's Tour of India

In the late fall of 1906, Amir Habib Allah (Figure 2.1) commenced a journey across the Durand Line to British India. That the amir looked to India for educational models to implement in his own kingdom is confirmed by the itinerary and objectives of Habib Allah's travels within India.[107] Documents from the Indian National Archives on the amir's trip through the subcontinent indicate that the Afghan monarch was most interested in surveying the land's educational institutions, particularly those of higher learning for Indian Muslims. Habib Allah's focus on colleges and universities, followed by factories and other industrial sites, appears to have been driven by the imperative of striking a balance in Afghanistan between preserving the Islamic cultural heritage of Afghans and meeting the needs of the modern industrial age through improved education and technology. In this way, by examining the institutions where Indian Muslims studied and taught in British India, Habib Allah sought to acquire a model for modern learning that was sensitive to the religious and cultural context of his subjects.

FIGURE 2.1. Amir Habib Allah Khan (r. 1901–1919). Universal History Archive / Universal Images Collection / Getty Images.

One of the amir's first meetings in India was with Himayat-i Islam, a Muslim philanthropic association of Peshawar. According to British accounts, when the association solicited him for a donation, the amir encouraged them but offered no funds, stating that he was entrusted with spending his money on educating Afghan orphans and children first.[108] On January 21, 1907, the amir arrived at Delhi, the former and last Mughal capital. Almost immediately upon arrival, he and his entourage traveled to visit the Red Fort, Qutb Minar, and the tombs of revered sufi saint Nizam al-Din Awliya' and Mughal emperor Humayun. The amir spent the day of January 23 at Ajmer with a small group, where he visited the famous shrine of another sufi saint, Shaykh Muʿin al-Din Chishti (Gharib Nawaz), in addition to a Jain temple, a number of railway workshops, and Mayo College—a British academy for Indian princes. He returned by train to Delhi in the evening.[109]

The next day Habib Allah toured a number of flour and cotton mills and a biscuit factory. As the following day was the Muslim holiday of *ʿĪd al-Aẓḥā*, he attended morning prayers at the local *ʿīdgāh* mosque, where word quickly spread of his presence. The Delhi crowds' interest in Habib Allah was reminiscent of the Ottoman envoy Ahmed Hulusi's arrival at Bombay three decades earlier: "Immense crowds of Mussulmans from all parts of the country were present," British informants reported. Over one hundred goats were sacrificed, but out of respect to Hindu custom, not cows.[110] As with the Ottoman mission to Kabul nearly three decades earlier, of particular interest to the authorities was whether the amir's name would be read in the khutba during Friday prayers, an action that would indicate greater Islamic claims to sovereignty, independence, and allegiance. This idea was so threatening to British officials that they issued strict orders to monitor whose name was read in the sermon.[111]

Completing his tour of Delhi, Habib Allah proceeded to Aligarh, where he visited the Muhammadan Anglo-Oriental College, founded by Muslim modernist intellectual Sir Sayyid Ahmad Khan (1817–1898).[112] Habib Allah first inspected the condition of campus buildings, which his British hosts stated had "delighted" the amir. After performing prayers at the main campus mosque, he attended classes on political economy, English, and theology, during which he even quizzed some of the students. On Habib Allah's assessment of the training at Aligarh, British accounts reported, "He had found the students perfect in religious knowledge and he exhorted them after having acquired religious knowledge by all means to learn as much western knowledge as possible."[113]

The amir and his entourage then proceeded to a large campus auditorium, where he was honored by the college trustees, and where he formally addressed the greater college community. According to transcripts of the speech housed in the Indian National Archives, Habib Allah had only admiring remarks for the college at Aligarh. He began by expressing praise for the excellent physical state of the campus buildings and boarding house and their upkeep. But the amir reserved the bulk of his acclaim for the quality of Aligarh's teachers and students, especially their success in synthesizing modern sciences with the principles of their faith: "I had heard from some people that the boys of the said College were not right in their belief of the tenets of Islam, but, in my presence and with my own tongue, I have myself examined the boys regarding some of the important principles of Islam and the dogmas about the offering of the Prayers and the Keeping of the Fasts," the amir was reported to have said in his remarks. "They have replied to all my questions rightly according to the belief of the Musalmans," the amir noted, further emphasizing they should be "at liberty to begin learning the sciences of Europe and then there is no harm in it."[114]

Habib Allah concluded his speech to rowdy applause from the audience. Adding to the enthusiasm, the amir promised to gift an annual endowment of six thousand Indian rupees in charitable contributions to the Muslim college in perpetuity, with an immediate cash present of twenty thousand rupees to the college.[115] He also alluded to himself having started a similar college in Kabul, words that were transcribed verbatim by British informants present. He had the following strong words for those opposed to modern education in Muslim lands:

> Let anyone who nevertheless still honestly thinks that religion and education are mutually antagonistic, and that religion must decline where education flourishes, come to this College as I have come, and see for himself as I have seen what education is doing for the religious beliefs of the rising generation . . . I stand here as the advocate of Western learning. So far from thinking it an evil, I have founded in Afghanistan a College called the Habibia College, after my own name, where European education is to be given as far as possible on European lines.[116]

Habib Allah's remarks were once again enthusiastically received. He also expressed gratitude to British authorities for allowing him to visit the college and meet with students.[117] In this way the amir's visit to Aligarh underscores the importance he placed on education, but also and just as significantly, where he was looking for models. The fact the amir did not visit—or was not permitted to visit—the Dar al-ʿUlum madrasa at Deoband, the preeminent seminary roughly two hours by train from Delhi, speaks to where he was not looking, as well.[118] It also appears to demonstrate that the British authorities were apprehensive about the kinds of Indian institutions the amir was forging stronger relations with. Habib Allah was known to make financial contributions to the Dar al-ʿUlum, where many Afghan ulema studied, but his relations with Deobandi ulema would be strained when the latter responded enthusiastically to the Ottoman government's declaration of jihad against the British after entering World War I.

For the time being, however, what the amir found in India exceeded his expectations. Beyond the spectacular receptions afforded to him by Raj officialdom, the amir was particularly allured by British India's technological innovations and bureaucratic organization, as well as its military-industrial prowess. But Habib Allah appears to have been especially impressed by the educational and professional advancements of India's Muslims, including those who had studied in hybrid-styled colleges like the Muhammadan Anglo-Oriental College at Aligarh, taken up jobs in the Raj's bureaucracy, and even served in the Indian imperial army.[119]

Habib Allah's tour was also not a one-way journey; it increased opportunities for Muslim organizations in India to build stronger ties with Afghanistan's amir. The first Indians to be employed in the amir's service were translators and court historians, physicians, teachers, and school administrators, filling positions in the first modern state hospital built in Afghanistan, and most of all, the Habibiye College. On the other hand, the tour was an opportunity for the government of India to impress on Habib Allah the benefits of British patronage at a time when Kabul was emerging from international isolation. Much to the satisfaction of British officials, the amir's visit to the thriving Muslim college at Aligarh proved to be a boon to their cause. While displaying no lack of reverence for a sovereign Muslim ruler visiting their college, the representatives of Aligarh were also unalloyed in their status as British subjects, providing living examples of the benefits of British rule as they saw it.

Still, underlying the entire visit were tensions between the coreligionist sentiments of Indian Muslims for a foreign Muslim monarch and their status as British subjects. Illustrative is a passage from an address dedicated to Habib Allah by a spokesman for the college trustees. The latter had the following carefully worded remarks in praise of the Afghan amir and British Crown, in tandem:

> [T]o us, the Indian Mussulmans, Your Majesty possesses an additional interest and fascination as the friend and ally of the British Government, which, at the present day, commands the allegiance of more Mussulman subjects than any other sovereign in the world. We, therefore, rejoice that cordial relations subsisting between Your Majesty's Government and that of His Gracious Majesty the King Emperor of India, is increasing day by day and we sincerely hope and trust that the present visit of Your Majesty may serve to knit the two Governments still more closely together, to the lasting good of Your Majesty's people and of the people of India.[120]

Couching their address in a language of friendship between the two states, the trustees of the Muhammadan Anglo-Oriental College carefully balanced their reverence for a foreign Muslim sovereign with an attempt to allay the concerns of British officials monitoring the spread of "Pan-Islamic" activity. Seeking to make a positive impression on the Afghan monarch of the conditions of Muslims under British rule, Raj officials preparing Habib Allah's itinerary through India made a slight gamble that appears to have paid off. What better way to extol the benefits of British rule than from the words of Indian Muslim subjects? The amir's Aligarh tour also revealed that in as much as Habib Allah had specific objectives in mind in his Indian tour, British officials had their own, too.

As a fitting conclusion to an extravagant tour, the amir's hosts prepared one more lavish reception—this time in the great Mughal city of Agra, home to the world-famous Taj Mahal. In a dazzling array of lights, local officials had the city adorned with incandescent lamps, beginning with the railroad tracks leading to the train station where Habib Allah arrived, and continuing to the bridges, overpasses, and state buildings across the historic town. Records of internal correspondence between Raj officials before Habib Allah's arrival in the city in late January 1907 reveal the purchase of ten thousand lamps, including fifty Vauxhall lights at twenty rupees each, a hundred dozen Chinese lanterns, and five thousand other kinds of illumination.[121] For his British hosts, it was a chance to showcase the Raj's industrial power, administrative organization, and technological progress. With no expenses spared, Raj officials sought to ensure that Afghan amir would be overawed by his British patrons. Commenting on the positive effects of the amir's visit, officials from the Indian Foreign Department concluded the entire operation was a success:

> The visit to India has brought home to the Amir how far removed his country is from the ladder of true progress, and what expenditure and system are required for keeping well-trained troops and for properly administering the country. The strength and greatness of the British Government have, moreover, been thoroughly impressed on his mind as will appear from the fact that after the review at Agra he openly declared before his counselors in his tent after seeing the British troops it could be said of the troops of Afghanistan they did not deserve to be called trained troops.[122]

Self-serving as these comments were, they do reflect a certain reality of the amir's tour: Habib Allah returned to Afghanistan with enhanced notions not only of British power and technological progress but also of the achievements of some Muslims under British rule.[123] What is more, judging from subsequent developments in Afghanistan, the tour seems to have impressed on the amir the benefits of British patronage, even while it limited the potential dangers of Afghan irredentism and Pan-Islamic sentiment arising from the amir's presence on Indian soil. Raj authorities managed the tour successfully so as to avoid repeating the mistakes of the 1877 Turkish mission to Kabul, when Indian authorities were caught unawares of pro-Ottoman sentiment.

At the same time, British officials monitoring events in Afghanistan at this time knew enough not to be complacent about the extent of their rapport with the amir. Just as Habib Allah returned from his sixty-four-day journey in India, the returned exile of Damascus Mahmud Tarzi was already welcoming a corps of Ottoman officers and bureaucrats in the Afghan capital. What is more, they soon learned that the Turks in Kabul were bringing some of the same benefits that the British claimed to monopolize in India.

Transient Turks, Partitioned Pashtuns, and Other Bordercrossers in Kabul

We have explored the outsized contributions of a relatively small number of Ottoman subjects who traveled to Afghanistan to serve as advisors to Habib Allah's government in a range of professional capacities. Despite a warm welcome and a good deal of fanfare surrounding their arrival in Kabul, by late 1908 some of the Ottoman migrants to Kabul were contemplating an early return home.

In some cases, individuals who had been in Afghanistan for hardly a few months were already planning their return to Istanbul.

Given the landmark Young Turk Revolution of late July 1908, the earlier than expected return of Ottoman subjects from Afghanistan does not appear to be a sign of disaffection. As even the British agent at Kabul noted about the departees, "The improvements and developments in the Turkish Government are attracting them."[124] Unsurprisingly, it was mostly Young Turks of the anti-Hamidian orientation who jumped at the opportunity to return home following the mutiny of Ottoman army units in the Balkans and subsequent restoration of the Ottoman constitution and parliament.

Meanwhile, Habib Allah, seemingly disturbed by the rumors of an impending Ottoman flight, summoned his Turkish staff to ask why they were leaving and to inquire whether he might influence them to stay by increasing their pay.[125] The amir's overtures reveal the significance he attached to the Ottoman community in his domain. He soon learned, however, that there was no uniform reason or attitude behind the early return of Ottoman subjects in Kabul, though he did encounter some disgruntlement. For some, it was a matter of pay; for others, the poor conditions of their accommodation; for others yet, dissatisfaction with the terms or conditions of their employment. Other evidence points to the mostly fluid nature of this transnational community that could not be held to long-term commitments in the country (with some notable exceptions).[126] This was most obvious with the outbreak of the 1908 revolution in Turkey, which in the case of several prominent Ottomans in Kabul like Ali Fehmi Bey and Mehmed Fazlı Effendi, was reason enough to cut their stay short in Afghanistan. The unexpected opportunity to return home likely proved too tempting to resist, especially given several of the Ottomans in Kabul had been living in exile from Hamidian repression to begin with.

Other cases of Turks departing Afghanistan and returning to Ottoman lands present a different set of reasons. At least one Ottoman subject became seriously ill, as Porte records describing his departure from Kabul and prolonged treatment in Istanbul's Haydarpaşa hospital indicate.[127] Some signaled a desire to stay if these conditions were remedied; others, perhaps for ideological reasons or simply out of homesickness, were bent on returning to Ottoman domains irrespective of the benefits of staying in Kabul. Given the dramatic events that had taken place back home in their absence, and the political nature of their exile, a considerable number if not most of the returning Ottoman exiles likely fall into this category.

Still, for some of the Turks in Kabul the watershed events in the Ottoman Empire were insufficient to dislodge them from their newfound employment in Kabul. Among the latter was Mahmud Sami, who displayed no intention of leaving Afghanistan. As we will see later, contrary to premature British assessments that Turkish influence in Kabul was one the wane, Ottoman inroads into Afghanistan not only continued but expanded through World War I and into the early 1920s.

The degree of unanimity among Ottoman and Indian Pan-Islamic activists in Kabul must also not be overstated. Disagreements emerged between members of different groups of Muslim foreigners in Afghanistan, in particular between Turks and Indians, over policy decisions and directions of reform. British Indian records describe a growing rift between the different factions in the Kabul court. For example, a secret Foreign Department file from February 1909 reveals how the British sought out, but indeed also found, tensions between Turks and Indian Muslim expatriates in Kabul to exploit. The report, discussing information supplied by the British agent at Kabul in reply to questions put by the Intelligence Branch regarding affairs in Afghanistan, reveal how some British officials were indeed looking for such fault lines between Turks and Indian Muslims.[128]

If rivalries between the Ottomans and Indians in Kabul were brewing under the surface of their collaborative projects, the British had less to worry about than some of the Raj's more incendiary reports on Pan-Islamic "fanatics" gathering in Kabul warned. British reports also suggest that far from Kabul's being a Pan-Islamic utopia, Turks and Indians alike brought their own cultural, professional, and political associations with them, associations that could not be separated from the forms of expertise they offered to the Kabul court. While sharing a common religion in Islam, even the latter was subject to different interpretations and perspectives, as well as methods and priorities for pursuing goals and imparting advice by the Ottoman and Indian members of Habib Allah's court. Sometimes, Turks were preferred over Indians for reasons of political association. For example, Turkish journalist Mehmed Fazlı was once reported to have said that "the Moslem representative of the Indian Government at Kabul is distrusted by the Afghans where a Turk is trusted."[129]

Watchful for brewing tensions between Turks, Afghans, and Indian Muslims in Kabul, British agents continued to report on growing strains, especially between select Ottoman and Afghan officers, from as early as 1909 until the eve of World War I. Such observations included those made in 1910 by a British informant on the alleged decline of Ottoman Pan-Islamic activity in Kabul; and in the mounting rivalry between Afghan general Nadir Khan and the Ottoman officers in particular. "Turkish officers at Kabul had not succeeded in exercising any great influence in the Durbar, or with the public," states the report, though this is likely an exaggeration.[130] At times, such communications sought to explain Nadir Khan's preference for Indian Muslim military instructors over the Turks. "The Afghan military officers were jealous of them," commented the above report on Ottoman officers in the amir's service, "and the city people would not communicate freely with them owing to their western manners."[131]

While "Western manners" were purportedly a source of division and tension according to some British intelligence sources, another report, dispatched to Delhi from the British Indian Frontier Branch in 1911, cites some of the Turks' own frustrations with conditions of their employment. As the diary of the British agent at Kabul reported on March 12, 1911:

> The Turk employés of the Afghan Government are apparently not satisfied with their lot here. They complain of inadequacy of pay and no promotion. Three of them—Yakub Beg, Jalaluddin Beg, and Asif Beg, who joined in 1909—recently returned to their country being disgusted of the inactive life they were leading here, as no work was given them. Mahmud Sami finds General Muhammad Nadir Khan a rival too formidable to match and may have also gone away but for the Muin-al-Saltanat who takes up his cause. Abbas Beg, the Drill Instructor, openly complains of the treatment he receives. Hasan Hilmi, an old man and past work, is the only one who has assumed an air of dignified quiet.[132]

The above passage gives us a glimpse into some of the more contentious circumstances surrounding the Ottoman officer corps in Kabul. Notably, the reporter brings up Nadir Khan as a "formidable" rival within the Afghan military establishment.

It is also important to recognize at this juncture that not all Ottoman subjects were even accepted into Afghanistan to begin with. For example, a routine log from the North-West Frontier Province colonial office dated April 9, 1910, reports, "Elhadj Elseid Hassan Tahsin Baba Bektachi of Constantinople, who is said to have been formerly a Colonel in the Turkish Army, arrived at Peshawar on 6th April 1910, *en route* to Kabul."[133] The following entry, corresponding to April 23, 1910, updates the log by noting that Habib Allah had rejected the said Ottoman subject's request to enter Afghan territory. The dejected applicant, according to the same source, subsequently departed Peshawar and returned to Istanbul.[134] In this manner, it cannot be said that an unrestricted corridor of access existed between Istanbul and Kabul at this time, whether for Ottoman officers or lay subjects seeking employment. As the above source indicates, first of all, it was necessary for the said individual to receive permission from the Afghan amir for entry into Afghanistan. Second, such petitions could be denied, as was the case with this particular Ottoman subject.

Other reports, again from British Indian archives, describe Ottoman Turks who had planned to migrate to Afghanistan but ultimately did not reach their destination owing to insufficient funds or other logistical roadblocks. In one extreme case, a disgruntled Ottoman subject went so far as to file a lawsuit in a British court against Habib Allah under these very circumstances. A secret Foreign Department file from April 1910 reports of a letter from the amir about a claim brought against the Afghan government by a certain Süleyman Midhat, a Turkish electrical engineer. The amir of Afghanistan, in his response of March 23 of the same year, rejected the claim that pay was due to Midhat, noting that he never even came to Afghanistan in the first place: "It is not the rule of any Government that a person should be given a salary without being engaged or doing any service," the amir curtly replied.[135] The story was likely to be far more complicated than this, and thus far we have not heard Midhat's side of the story. What we can glean from this incident, however, is that plans did not always unfold smoothly for Ottoman subjects seeking employment in Afghanistan. "No doubt," said the British ambassador, "Suleiman Midhat has not been well treated."[136]

Meanwhile, in India British officials were likely pleased to learn of such disputes within the "Pan-Islamic" community in Kabul. Some commented on the advantages offered by increasing discord between the Turks and Afghans: "The more Turks who are treated in this shabby manner," one official optimistically noted on reviewing said Süleyman Midhat's case, "the less likely will others be to volunteer for service in Afghanistan."[137] In this fashion, British intelligence reports on Afghan palace politics during the reign of Habib Allah provide glimpses of a brewing rivalry between the Ottoman and Indian actors in the country, the two major foreign Muslim currents in the Kabul court.[138]

Kabul on the Eve of the Great War

This chapter has trained its gaze on a pair of foreign Muslim communities gathering in the Kabul court during the reign of Habib Allah—Ottoman Turks from the west and Indian Muslims from the east. But it should not be forgotten that throughout this period another group of itinerants continued to shuttle in and out of the country's frontier in much greater numbers: Afghans themselves. During the "Iron Amirate" of ʿAbd al-Rahman, Afghans continued to study and teach at Muslim institutions of learning in India, including at the Dar al-ʿUlum in Deoband. In addition to Afghan exiles such as General Nadir Khan and the Musahiban family returning from British India, other less prominent Afghans who had studied in India also returned to serve in Kabul and in provincial governors' courts. ʿAli Ahmad Khan, who was said to be a favored protégé of Prince Nasr Allah Khan, was educated at Murree, India. To this more well-known group must be added bordercrossers of unknown or obscure lineage, such as Nur Ahmad Khan, who is described in British intelligence records as an "Indian *mawlawi*" (a teacher of Islamic theology, ethics, or law). The latter received a bachelor's degree from Aligarh and subsequently found employment in the Habibiye, but it is hardly clear if he was an Indian Pakhtun, an Afghan expat returning from study abroad, or another kind of "Indo-Afghan" with one foot in each country.[139] What we can be sure of is that the aforementioned individuals fall into the important category of Afghans and Indians who returned to or arrived in Afghanistan at this time, while being connected to three Indian Muslims institutions in particular: the Dar al-ʿUlum madrasa at Deoband, the Muhammadan Anglo-Oriental College at Aligarh, and Islamia College in Lahore. Each of these institutions also trained Afghan-born students, who returned to Afghanistan with varying levels of expertise following their studies, including in the highly sought-after professions of law, administration, and education.

When it comes to Indian influence in Afghanistan during Habib Allah's reign, it is also important to look beyond the Kabul court and remember the ongoing, everyday social and economic linkages embodied in Afghan and Indian merchants, students, and pilgrims, but also political activists, militants, and criminal or smuggling networks in the frontier zones between Jalalabad and Peshawar, and between Kandahar and Quetta, in particular. British foreign, political, and frontier department records contain reams of dossiers about the problems posed by Afghan tribes—especially but not exclusively Pashtuns and Baluchis—on both sides of the Durand Line. Raj communications with Habib Allah complain of the incessant danger of raids and "intrigues" launched by fugitives seeking refuge one side of the border for crimes committed on the other side, including the notorious Haji ʿAbd al-Raziq of Waziristan.[140] The latter's alleged subversive activities were underscored by the fact that India and Afghanistan probably shared the world's most porous border, thinly dividing longstanding ties of kinship, religion, and trade that connected families, tribes, and mercantile networks across both states.

We have focused on the activities and influence of Ottoman and Indian expatriates in Afghanistan, but this is not to suggest that the amir exclusively looked either to British India or to the Ottoman Empire. There were other potential models, too. "[I]n devising plans for the amelioration of the condition of his country and in making changes in the administration," noted one British informant in 1907, for example, "the Amir keeps constantly before his mind the example of Japan."[141] It is also possible that Young Afghan and Muslim modernist publications in Kabul like Mahmud Tarzi's *Siraj al-Akhbar*—which praised administrative and technological progress in industrialized countries of the East and global South more broadly—had a latent impact on the amir, in spite of his repression of their constitutionalist activities. Even closer to home, and in almost any historical period, it would be odd to discuss the role of foreign influences in Afghanistan without considering the glaring case of the country's immediate neighbor to the east, Iran. Sharing a common language in Persian, and even sharing earlier Safavid and Afsharid Iranian rule in Khorasan, Herat, and Kandahar, much more remains to be learned about the extent and nature of ties between the Tehran and Kabul courts at this time. But expectations do not always yield historical evidence, of which there is surprisingly little to show for Iranian participation in Habib Allah's state-building efforts. Some may presume that sectarian differences played a "natural" role in preventing episodes of substantial Iranian-Afghan collaboration or Qajar-Muhammadzai entente at this time. Afghans, and especially Pashtuns, were overwhelmingly Sunni, in contrast to Shiʿi-majority Iran. More important, Habib Allah's father, ʿAbd al-Rahman, notoriously persecuted the Shiʿi Hazaras of central Afghanistan, and Afghan accounts of prior Safavid and Afsharid rule over Kandahar and Herat are hardly sympathetic. Still, it is more likely that political differences—such as lingering Afghan (and of course, British) suspicion of Russian influence in the Qajar court, or earlier Perso-Afghan contestations and clashes in Sistan, for example—were dispositive in obstructing stronger ties between the Persianate sovereigns. At the end of the day, in spite of Habib Allah's respect for industrialized countries of the East like Japan, and despite Afghanistan's geographic and cultural proximity to Iran, no two states provided the actual personnel and professional networks to Afghanistan at this time as did the Ottoman Empire and British India.[142]

Inspired by what he had seen in India and disappointed by the state of affairs in his own realm, Habib Allah embarked on a series of revamped reform projects that included new power plants, textile factories, roads and government buildings (especially in Kabul, Paghman, and Jalalabad), a government printing press and translation bureau, a new postal system, and the country's first public health administration. Beyond new infrastructure, Habib Allah expanded the basic administrative, educational, and military institution-building programs launched by his father. Afghanistan was divided into six administrative provinces: Kabul, Kandahar, Herat, Farah, Afghan Turkistan, and Badakhshan. Habib Allah personally delegated governors responsible for the administration of each. In 1907 he appointed a vice-regent who reported directly to him. Provincial governors held administrative and judicial powers. However, judgments issuing death sentences were still required to pass through the amir. After administration, Habib Allah also set about organizing the army, continuing a program his father, ʿAbd al-Rahman, had initiated. In all of these reforms, Ottoman and Indian subjects played a significant role.

Most prominent of the amir's reforms were the Harbiye and Habibiye, staffed primarily by Ottoman and Indian Muslim teachers respectively. Kabul's Harbiye was modeled on similar institutions established in the Ottoman Empire during the Hamidian era, and, fittingly, an Ottoman Arab colonel of Baghdad was the driving force behind this Ottoman "transplant" in Afghanistan. On the civilian education side, after considerable improvements in recruiting teachers and organizing its curriculum in the years to follow at the amir's behest, largely under the directorship of the Indian physician Dr. Abdul Ghani Khan, the Habibiye eventually met Habib Allah's goal of providing homegrown administrative cadres for the government. A foreign visitor to the school at the height of World War I observed that the all-male student body received instruction in an impressive range of languages, including Persian, Pashto, Urdu, Turkish, and English. The campus library served as Afghanistan's first public library. Among the college's first teachers, the majority were Indian Muslims or Afghans educated in India, who thereby established an educational system that from the beginning followed the British Indian model of education. After World War I, however, Turkish teachers began arriving in Afghanistan in greater numbers, bringing a hybrid late Ottoman-French model that was later reported to have predominated during Aman Allah's reign.[143]

Pioneering as these institutions were, behind the scenes there were indications Habib Allah was becoming a victim of his own success at the Habibiye.

Among the unintended consequences of Habibiye's growth was that it became a breeding ground for Young Afghan and constitutionalist dissent. Even Dr. Abdul Ghani, the Punjabi migrant to Kabul personally appointed by Habib Allah as the school's director, was accused of coordinating opposition against the amir.[144] Still, historiographical emphasis on the antimonarchical and revolutionary liberalism of some of the Young Afghans and constitutionalists in Kabul has overlooked the fact that most Ottomans and Indians in Kabul worked in the amir's service, absolute monarch though he was.

We began this chapter with Habib Allah's succession to the "Iron Amir" ʿAbd al-Rahman, the smoothest transition of power in Afghanistan's history. Embedded in this transition is also a story of Muslim dynasts establishing the legitimacy of their hereditary line within a bounded territory while claiming to rule in the name of Islam and the Afghan nation. Though Habib Allah proudly articulated a vision of governance committed to upholding the shariʿa, and conscientiously recruited Muslim experts to staff a variety of administrative and military positions, his state-building project was not a campaign for greater territorial conquest or an attempt to establish a caliphate. To the contrary, Habib Allah reduced tensions with the British and upheld treaties delimiting Afghan territory. As with his father, Habib Allah continued to recognize Abdülhamid II's claims to the office of the caliphate, and, after the Second Ottoman Constitutional revolution, the Young Turk-appointed Mehmed V Reşad (r. 1909–1918). At the same time, for Habib Allah the notion of being a just king spoke not to representative or parliamentary politics but to traditional, paternalistic notions of Muslim monarchy and social contract theory over a delimited territory. That is to say, in exchange for obedience from his subjects, the amir swore to preserve Afghanistan's autonomy, strengthen Afghanistan's defenses against foreign aggression, respect religious authorities, personally administer justice if and when necessary, and abide by the limits of the shariʿa. He was reluctant to consider any dramatic changes to the political system of his amirate beyond that, and if Habib Allah's actions toward the Young Afghans reveal anything, it is that he feared the constitutional revolutions that transpired in Persia and Turkey at this time more than he supported them.

Most Ottomans who came to Afghanistan during the Habib Allah era arrived after the Anglo-Russian Convention of 1907, which coincided with the amir's intensified desire for international recognition and autonomy. By 1908, in contrast to earlier reports of isolated travelers from the Ottoman domains to Afghanistan, the British Agency at Kabul was describing a "community" of

Turks in Kabul.[145] Here, Habib Allah asserted the semisovereignty of his amirate by tiptoeing around British treaties that stipulated no independent foreign relations with outside powers. By recruiting individual Turkish and Arab experts from the Ottoman Empire, as well as from Indian Muslim educational institutions, the amir was able to launch a series of administrative, military, educational, and infrastructure projects intended to strengthen the Afghan state. As a result, the amir was able to push a gradualist reform program amid a host of competing tensions: fulfilling the domestic demands of *Islāmīyat*, or upholding "Islamic-ness" in a Muslim-majority country, and meeting international standards of "civilization" expected of free states, all the while abiding by formal treaty obligations with the British.

From the Ottoman Empire to Qajar Iran, the legitimacy of Muslim kingship as an ideology of governance became more challenging in an era of secret societies and increasingly assertive publics. With Young Turks and Young Afghans in Kabul, Afghanistan was no exception. But by the eve of World War I, unlike his counterparts in the Ottoman Turkish and Qajar Persian domains, Habib Allah had successfully contained dissident activity against his absolutist rule. As we turn to the tumultuous events of World War I and the impact that war had on the amir's reign, as well as on the "interislamic" connections between the Ottoman Empire, Afghanistan, and India, we have already seen how spaces for exchange and debate within a framework of upholding the shariʿa and a politically conservative model of Muslim kingship was emerging in Afghanistan under ʿAbd al-Rahman and Habib Allah. Of course, several other profoundly transformative events in the broader regional and global context relevant to our story took place, from the Persian and Russian constitutional revolutions in 1905–1906 (and in the Ottoman Empire in 1908), to Japan's military victory over Russia in 1905.[146] The former constitutional developments unleashed a wave of nationalistic enthusiasm for more participatory governance and pressured Habib Allah to reform his absolutist rule into a constitutional monarchy. Japan's military victory over Russia did inspire Habib Allah to join forces with Young Afghans to build a more robust military and thwart European colonial expansion, but he obdurately resisted substantial constitutional reform.[147]

The individualized nature of Ottoman and Indian migration to Afghanistan at this time was a loophole in the complicated legal status of Afghanistan as a self-governing British protectorate. Agreements signed by ʿAbd al-Rahman and Habib Allah prevented Kabul from conducting independent foreign relations, but, following its 1877 mission to Kabul, the Ottoman government increasingly saw it within their prerogative to conduct free relations with fellow Muslim monarchs and their subjects, even when the latter were vassals of the British Crown—on paper, at least. That the Ottomans ignored the Raj's absolute control over Afghanistan's foreign affairs is evident in the British Foreign Office's internal deliberations. A late nineteenth-century memorandum from Sir William White, ambassador at Constantinople, to the prime minister in London, "British Protection to Afghan Subjects in Turkey," for example, reveals how the highest echelons of Britain's empire brisked for confrontation with the Ottomans in regard to Afghans—ever a mobile and elusive group. As White correctly predicted in his 1890 communiqué to Lord Salisbury, Abdülhamid II was eager to strike back at European capitulations concerning the protections of Christians in the Ottoman domains and would likely respond in kind with his own version of Muslim protégés—in the British Empire:

> Under the present Sultan, the Ottoman authorities have made it a point to dispute to the utmost the foreign nationality of Mussalmans domiciled in Turkey; they have persistently denied to France the protection of Muhammadan natives of Algeria residing here, and the representations of the French Embassy have hitherto proved unavailable to secure the right of protection. Our own rights as regards Indian Mussalmans have also occasionally been disputed, though ostensibly for other reasons, and we must therefore be prepared for opposition regarding Afghans.[148]

And oppose they did. Beginning in the last quarter of the nineteenth century, the Hamidian government forcefully campaigned for its own extraterritorial privileges—not by overpowering military or economic might but through a series of legal and diplomatic protests the Porte lodged with the British Crown concerning Afghans and Indian Muslims.[149] As the Raj's legal department insisted on its dominion over subjects it ruled directly, like Indian Muslims, as well as its vassal states like Afghanistan, the Porte responded in kind with its own novel juridical interpretations, reminding all parties concerned that Afghans were under the religious authority of the Ottoman sultan and caliph of Islam, not the British Crown.[150]

Such jurisdictional tussles spiraled into the 1900s and in spite of the 1908–1909 regime change in Istanbul, Anglo-Ottoman contestations over Afghans continued through the Second Constitutional Era and Committee for Union and Progress rule. At the heart of these disputes was not simply an imperial contest over citizenship papers, property rights, and international prestige, but a more subtle rivalry over the loyalties and bodies of human beings who did not easily fall into either Ottoman or British imperial frameworks of subjecthood and sovereignty.[151] Ultimately, this Anglo-Ottoman "cold war" over Afghans would culminate in a struggle to control Afghanistan itself, when a devastating war engulfed both empires in the summer and autumn of 1914.

THREE

Exit Great Game, Enter Great War

Afghanistan and the Ottoman Empire during World War I

ON APRIL 2, 1914, a South African real estate agent of Indian descent by the name of Habib Motan composed a letter to the Ottoman Imperial Consulate in Johannesburg. Motan stated he had received a communiqué from a trusted associate in Afghanistan, a certain notable by the name of Shaykh ʿAbd al-Qadir al-Hanafi al-Qadiri, who claimed he was able to muster the support of five hundred thousand warriors in support of an Ottoman annexation of Afghanistan. "He writes to me," wrote Motan in a synopsis of al-Qadiri's letter dispatched through Indian couriers, "that the chiefs and olimas of his country, on account of the troubles amongst them and having no strong flag over them desire from their heart to be under the glorious flag of the Ottoman Empire to show their devotion, attachment, and sincerity to their Caliph, Commander of the Believers." According to ʿAbd al-Qadir, Afghanistan was ripe for the arrival of an Ottoman delegation that could help incorporate the landlocked territory into a stronger alliance, if not unification, with the Sublime Porte.[1] It did not take long before Motan's letter was in the hands of the grand vizier himself, Said Halim Pasha, in Istanbul. In transnational correspondence involving at least five languages and three continents, the exchanges between Motan, Shaykh ʿAbd al-Qadir, and Halim Pasha illustrate the extent of Indo-Ottoman connections on the eve of Ottoman entry into World War I.

Were the Afghan shaykh's estimates accurate? Was the letter genuine, and did a "Shaykh 'Abd al-Qadir al-Hanafi al-Qadiri" even exist? Or was the letter a British ruse to test the Porte's commitment to respect London's sphere of influence in Afghanistan? We may never know the full extent of the letter's authenticity, or its actual impact at the Porte. The Ottoman reply to the letter, addressed to Motan and composed in French, expressed gratitude and enthusiasm on paper but was ultimately noncommittal. Although Motan's letter does not seem to have produced an immediate reaction at the Porte, it was read and kept in mind for future projects. That Afghanistan was on the Ottoman government's radar in the early stages of World War I is confirmed by a Porte memorandum of December 5, 1914. Hardly a month after the Sublime Porte's entry into the conflict on the side of the Central Powers, an Ottoman foreign ministry memorandum described the locations of Afghan military forces, noting their proximity to the border with Peshawar and the Punjab. The document also described the state of Afghanistan's postal services, sure to be relevant for a jointly communicated surprise attack on British forces from Afghanistan.[2] As British intelligence in the frontier zone themselves discovered as early as 1909, Istanbul had already devised a regular means of communication with agents in Kabul via local couriers and the amir's postmaster at Peshawar and Karachi, right under the watch of Raj officials.[3]

It was also not lost on officials at the Sublime Porte in the late spring of 1914 that there was a groundswell of support for the Ottomans in Afghanistan, and Motan's letter was nothing new in that regard. Many recalled the memorable statement attributed to the amir of Afghanistan in 1907, in words read before one of the first sessions of parliament after the Young Turk revolution of 1908: "Afghanistan is the Ottoman Empire's younger brother and right arm in the struggles of the East!" With these bold words Amir Habib Allah Khan had received the first Ottoman delegation to arrive in his court. Not to be outdone, the response of the Turkish delegation was no less sanguine at the time: "All Ottomans are nourished by sincere concern and warm feelings for Afghanistan," proclaimed Ali Fehmi Bey, the designated spokesman for the group. "It is this sincere feeling and love which propelled us to work in union with our Afghan brothers, and to make this Islamic land a second home for us helpless servants," the Turkish official had proceeded to explain in his introductory address to the Kabul court.[4]

The above exchange took place in 1907, however, a year of relative calm and accord between major European powers, including Britain, France, Russia, and the Ottoman Empire. The same year witnessed the Second Hague Conference, a historic agreement furthering international protocols on the laws of war and peaceful resolution of conflicts. Even more remarkable, on August 31, 1907, bitter imperial rivals London and St. Petersburg signed a landmark entente in the Anglo-Russian Convention of 1907, seemingly putting to rest over a century of imperial competition between the British and Russian empires in Persia, Afghanistan, and Tibet. Significant as that agreement was for temporarily allaying Anglo-Russian rivalry in Asia, that it was concluded without the amir's approval incensed Habib Allah (and his Qajar Iranian counterpart, who was also not party to the agreement's stipulations concerning Persia). This disappointment moved Habib Allah to accelerate his state-building program by turning to the Ottoman Empire for experts and other forms of assistance. From the early 1900s to the eve of World War I, Ottoman experts traveled to Kabul to work in a variety of professional fields, strengthening political ties between the two Muslim-majority states in the process.

Significant as the 1907 convention was for temporarily allaying Anglo-Russian rivalry in Asia, what replaced the Great Game in Asia over the next decade would far exceed anything either power had seen in terms of cost to life, limb, and property. Between midsummer and autumn of 1914, a tinderbox assortment of military alliances stretching from Sarajevo to St. Petersburg and Berlin to Baghdad cast all the major powers of Europe—including Ottoman Turkey—into a global war of catastrophic proportions.

On August 1, the officially neutral Sublime Porte was poised for a fateful decision concerning its position in the Great War, internally fraught as Ottoman officials were as to which alliance was in Turkey's best interest. A day earlier, Tsar Nicholas II of Russia had ordered his forces to prepare for war with Germany as the latter brandished its mechanized army toward its eastern borders. On August 2, Ottoman Minister of War İsmail Enver Pasha (1881–1922) signed a secret defensive pact with the German ambassador in Istanbul, in effect committing the Sublime Porte to entering the Great War on the side of the kaiser. Though Enver's overtures to Berlin were staunchly opposed by several key Ottoman leaders—including the Ottoman Prime Minister Said Halim, who preferred neutrality and was outraged at Enver's overstepping his authority—ultimately it was the war minister and de facto commander of the Ottoman armed forces who succeeded in convincing powerful Committee for Union and Progress (CUP) party insiders to side with Germany. Chief among Enver's allies were Ottoman Minister of the Navy Ahmed Cemal Pasha (1872–1922) and

Minister of the Interior Mehmed Talat Pasha (1874–1921), forming the unionist triumvirate that would shape Ottoman policy by diktat for the duration of the war.[5]

On October 27 the Sublime Porte officially entered World War I. Bolstered by a fatwa from the sheikh ül-Islam, Sultan Mehmed Reşad declared a jihad against Britain and its allies, and with it the Ottoman Empire's formal entry into the Great War.[6] If ever there was an opportunity for the Afghan amir to prove his fealty to the Ottoman sultanate, that time had come.

FROM THE TIME Ottoman Turks began arriving in Kabul in the early 1900s to the outbreak of World War I in the summer of 1914, domestic affairs within Afghanistan and the Ottoman Empire had taken a dramatic turn. After three decades in power, in July 1908 Abdülhamid II was overthrown by a constitutional revolution that installed a titular caliph in the palace, reinstating the Ottoman Constitution of 1876 and paving the way for parliamentary elections. These elections energized political parties in major cities of the empire, cities that included a broad swath of Turks, Arabs, and Christian and Jewish minorities, who formed or newly revived political parties along religious, ethnic, and linguistic lines.[7] The Young Turk revolution and Second Ottoman Constitutional Era proved to be short-lived, however. In 1913, disgruntled with continued Ottoman territorial losses and fragmentation within the empire, an elite cadre of officers in the influential CUP launched a successful coup d'état, installing the unionist triumvirate of Enver, Cemal, and Talat Pashas. Formally upholding the Ottoman constitutional monarchy, in practice the three pashas exercised virtually supreme power over all major decisions impacting the empire's domestic and foreign policies, including one of colossal proportions beginning in the late summer of 1914.[8]

While the Young Turk constitutional revolution was under way in the Ottoman domains in 1908–1909, in Afghanistan Habib Allah was cracking down on an alleged Young Afghan conspiracy to overthrow his own absolutist rule and replace it with a constitutional monarchy. By the end of 1909, with several of the accused executed—and many more imprisoned, including one of Habib Allah's closest advisors and the Indian director of the Habibiye college, Dr. Abdul Ghani Khan—the Afghan amir had thwarted any apparent threats to his rule, real or imagined.[9] Before long, a sense of normalcy seemed to return to the Kabul court.

This, too, proved to be misleading. When a motorcade assassination in the Balkans and its aftermath spiraled out of control, leading to the outbreak of World War I, Habib Allah found himself caught between two opposing forces more powerful than he could manage: on the one hand, the Ottoman sultan and caliph of the world's Muslims; on the other, the British Raj, Afghanistan's patron state since the 1893 Durand Agreement. Even though Habib Allah had earlier declared formal neutrality, it was uncertain how he and the Afghans would respond to a war that joined the historic nemeses of Britain and Russia against the Ottoman Empire—with the Kabul court caught in between.

Initially Habib Allah played his cards agilely, gesturing friendship to both Ottoman and British envoys and preserving Afghanistan's neutrality.[10] Matters soon became more grave for Habib Allah, however, when successive waves of Indian revolutionaries began congregating in Kabul to organize support for the Ottoman jihad. The arrival of these revolutionaries led to a wave of Pan-Islamic fervor in Afghanistan, and even a provisional Indian nationalist government based in Kabul. Meanwhile, both British and Russian agents stationed in Afghanistan and the Indo-Afghan frontier began to suspect Kabul was rapidly becoming a conduit for an explosive combination of antiroyalist rebels, pro-Ottoman Pan-Islamic activists, and Bolshevik revolutionaries from North Africa to Japan. As a complicated system of alliances had turned Europe upside down, the strategic juncture of the Pamir, Karakoram, and Hindu Kush mountain ranges remained, in the words of British explorer Thomas Edward Gordon "the roof of the world"—with Afghanistan poised on top of it.[11]

Less than a decade after Habib Allah had welcomed returning Afghan exiles and foreign advisors to his kingdom, especially from the Ottoman Empire and British India, Kabul would become a pivotal meeting ground for disparate Pan-Islamic networks active during World War I. Among the latter were Ottoman military officers, Afghan nationalists, and Deobandi clerics from India, resulting in visions for a Pan-Islamic entente far more ambitious than those provoked by the 1857 Indian Rebellion or Sultan Abdülhamid II in earlier decades. The most dramatic expression of Pan-Islamic convergence in Afghanistan during World War I took place in the fall of 1915, when an Ottoman-German mission from the west and the Indian Muslim Silk Letters revolutionary plot from the east sought to join forces in the Afghan capital and organize a combined invasion of India. At the heart of both groups' plans was a shared goal of convincing Habib Allah to join the Central Powers, invade India, and oust the British from the subcontinent.

Because he saw only utopian visions that offered few material advantages or relief for Afghanistan's domestic problems, and because he was still observing his status as a protectorate of the British Empire, Habib Allah balked at these invitations. While the joint Ottoman-German mission and the Silk Letters conspiracy have been extensively treated by World War I scholars, especially military historians, what has not been given adequate attention are the deeper roots and lasting legacies of this mission for Afghanistan and its relations with the Ottoman Empire and British India.

Ottoman Pan-Islamism before the Great War

Sublime Porte records in the decade leading to World War I document a number of high-profile exchanges between Ottomans, Afghans, and Indian Muslims.[12] Following in the path of Afghan exiles returning to Kabul from the Ottoman Empire and India at the turn of the century, these Ottoman and Indian subjects were attracted to travel to Afghanistan by Habib Allah's cautiously liberalizing policies. For Ottoman travelers to Afghanistan at this time like Ali Fehmi, Mahmud Sami, and Dr. İzzet, the principal route to Kabul was still through India. As Russia tightly controlled much of Afghanistan's northern borders, as well as the eastern frontier with Iran, this meant passing through British ports of entry, usually at Bombay, before crossing overland through the Indian hinterland to Kabul via Peshawar and the Khyber Pass (see Map 2).

Still, Ottoman statecraft concerning Afghanistan in the early twentieth century refused to cede the strategic and internally autonomous territory to British suzerainty or consider it a carte blanche for British dominance. Symbolizing the close association Afghanistan retained in the Sublime Porte's imagination of a greater Turkistan region in Central Asia are Ottoman maps of the period. In spite of Afghan and Ottoman territories not being contiguous, Ottoman cartographers often presented Afghanistan within an orbit of Turkic Central Asia, with only the western extremities of India shown. One example is a new and more detailed map of Afghanistan in Ottoman Turkish dating to 1914 or 1915. The map includes Iran, Afghanistan, and Baluchistan as separate countries—and the only countries included in map's title—while hardly a sliver of the British Raj is visible (see Figure 3.1).[13] The latter speaks to a distinct reading of regional imperial frameworks—the early twentieth-century version of area

MAP 2. The Ottoman Empire, Afghanistan, and British India, early 1914

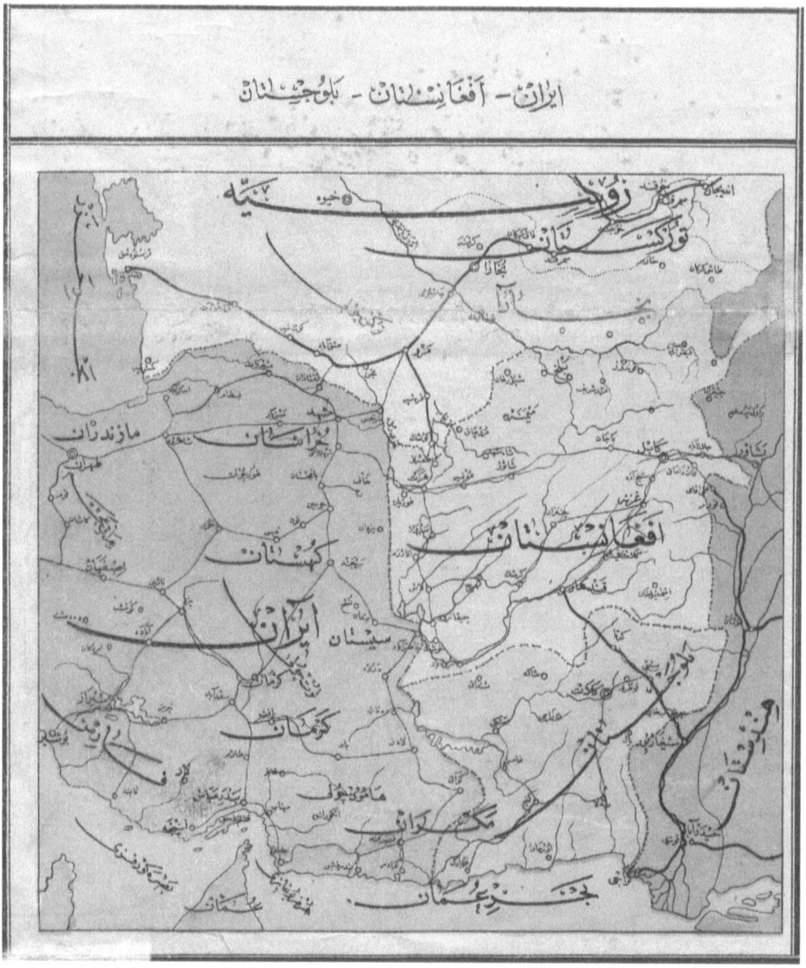

FIGURE 3.1. Ottoman map of Iran, Afghanistan, and Baluchistan, 1914/1915. Prime Ministry Ottoman Archives, Istanbul, Turkey (HRT.0118).

studies—and the association of Afghanistan with its western and northern neighbors to the exclusion of British India.

Raj officials were not nearly as receptive to such alternative readings of Afghanistan in the regional balance of power and imperial imagination. In contrast to Ottoman maps gazing on Kabul from the west, British Indian cartographers in Calcutta, Simla, Delhi, and other locales east of the Durand Line emphasized the unitary territorial integrity of the subcontinent under British rule, and as a result tended to distance Afghanistan from its northern and western neighbors on maps to accentuate the amirate's falling within a British zone of influence.

There was, of course, much more than a mapmaking contest at play here. During Habib Allah's reign, the British continued to monitor (and document) signs of perceived Pan-Islamic activity between Ottoman subjects, Indian Muslims, and Afghans. But they were not the only ones watching crossborder traffic shuttling in and out of Afghanistan in the early 1900s. A 1904 memorandum from Abdülhamid II's foreign intelligence bureau for India and Afghanistan, for example, reported on the arrival in Afghanistan, purportedly for trade, of British delegations.[14] Transcontinental reports from Kabul to Istanbul such as these demonstrated that the Porte had significantly enhanced its intelligence gathering in Afghanistan from the prior decade. Ottoman foreign ministry records from the early 1900s to the eve of World War I indicate the sultan's agents abroad continued to collect information on the conditions of Muslim populations in the British Empire and tsarist Russia, the two states who would end up being the Porte's chief adversaries in the Great War.

Ottoman foreign ministry records for the period also indicate the Porte strove to keep abreast of Muslim sentiment in India and Afghanistan, as reflected in repositories of articles collected from foreign newspapers on stirrings of Muslim unrest in India, Afghanistan, and Turkic Central Asia.[15] By highlighting the increasing frequency of Indo-Ottoman delegations and secret missions in both directions, these documents partly vindicate British concerns that such activities were not simply isolated incidents of the Hamidian regime's agents but rather a nexus of grassroots and institutions relations cultivated between Ottomans and Indian Muslims since Ahmed Hulusi's arrival in Bombay over a quarter century earlier. They also highlight how both the Ottoman and British empires were anxious to link their domains to populations and markets at the strategic gateway to India and Central Asia.

The growth of popular linkages to the Ottoman Empire from the late nineteenth century on is amply displayed in the role of public fundraising campaigns for pro-Ottoman causes in India and Afghanistan. The primary vehicle for Indian Muslim and Afghan participation in raising funds for Ottoman relief causes at this time was the Ottoman Red Crescent Society (Hilal-i Ahmer). The society was founded in 1868 as an affiliate of the International Conference of National Aid Societies for the Nursing of the War Wounded of 1867 (later, the International Committee for the Red Cross). It had its roots in multilateral relief efforts launched during the Crimean War (1853–1856), and grew liberally over the course of subsequent international conflicts involving the Ottoman Empire, from the Russo-Ottoman War (1877–1878) to the Balkan Wars (1912–1913). During World War I, the Red Crescent Society was a major vehicle for coordinating collaborative Ottoman humanitarian and fundraising projects with Muslims (and indeed, many non-Muslims) across the region.

Such contributions indicate that for many Indian Muslims and Afghans, pro-Ottoman stances were not simply sentimental displays of religious solidarity, but were institutionalized through concrete exchanges of financial support. Reams of receipts in the Red Crescent Society's archive in Ankara attest to hundreds of fundraiser and donor meetings in India's major cities, including Delhi and Calcutta, as well as in Afghanistan and Indian Muslim diaspora communities, from the first decade of the twentieth century until the dissolution of the empire.[16]

Still, Pan-Islam's role as an asset of Ottoman foreign policy at this time must not be overstated. As a political force, Pan-Islamic networks in Asia were still too diffuse, still bereft of a lightning-rod cause—such as an existential threat to the Ottoman Empire and caliphate—to constitute a direct threat to British rule in India or Russian domination in Turkistan. This would begin to change, however, during a succession of punishing wars in the early 1910s.

Catalyzing Crises: The Libyan and Balkan Wars, 1911–1913

In September 1911, Italy invaded the Ottoman province of Tripolitania, renaming the latter *Libia* after the ancient Latin name for northwest Africa. The annexation by a second-tier colonial power of territory the Ottomans had held since the sixteenth century sent shockwaves throughout the empire, and Muslim populaces under British rule from Egypt to India protested. Beyond letters and petitions, Muslims of major Indian cities like Calcutta organized public demonstrations and protests in support of the Ottomans, constituting some of the earliest displays of mass Muslim politics under British rule in the twentieth century.[17] Others chose to express their outrage in ink. An October 1911 petition by Muhammad Ali Khan Kazilbash, president of the Lahore Musulmans Association, to the British foreign secretary in London, beseeched their "beloved Emperor" and "greatest musulman monarch" to exercise his "transcendent British influence" and "thwart [the] unprovoked aggression of Italy." Couching his appeal in a language of entreaty and loyalty, an Indian Muslim barrister,

Mirayab Khan, similarly wrote the British foreign minister decrying Italy's invasion and occupation of Tripolitania, describing it as an unjust act of aggression "condemned by Musalmans who pray King's immediate intervention."[18]

Such pro-Ottoman activities were not forgotten by the Porte, and were given special attention by Turkish consular staff in the subcontinent. A 1913 memorandum from the Ottoman foreign ministry, for example, acknowledges the role of the Calcutta-based *al-Hilal* magazine in "protecting the nobility and honor of Islam." Here, there was little doubt the periodical's defense of the Ottoman Empire was being recognized as much as its efforts to thwart missionary attacks on the religion.[19]

Meanwhile, British officials continued to monitor the movements and activities of Ottoman subjects traveling between India and Afghanistan. Records from the India Office and the British Indian Foreign Department provide evidence of increasing contacts between the Ottoman authorities in Istanbul, Damascus, and Baghdad and Indian Muslim subjects, as well as the Afghan government in Kabul. Even more, they spoke to British misgivings about such contacts. A January 1912 memorandum from the British minister at Constantinople, Sir E. Grey Bart, revealed the Crown's growing unease over crossborder movements that exploited Pan-Islamic sentiments from Afghanistan to Libya to the benefit of the Ottoman government:

> [O]n the subject of the state of feeling prevailing in Afghanistan with regard to the Turco-Italian war, it may be of interest to you to know that reports have recently reached me from a secret native source here . . . that certain quarters in Constantinople, presumable Young Turkish, are sending emissaries to Afghanistan with a view to making trouble among the Afridi and Rukzai tribes, with the support, if possible, of the Amir . . . The object is said to be to induce England in this way to take up a favourable attitude towards Turkey in her present difficulties.[20]

British officials relied on unnamed and obscure sources for intelligence, so taken in isolation any single report does not present prima facie evidence of purported Pan-Islamic activity, but it does reveal British apprehensions. Taken as a whole, the hundreds of similar reports penned during the war by the India Office and government of India are unlikely to have all been fabricated. Other documents speak to the different kinds of material support Afghan and Indian Muslims offered the Ottomans. Among them were financial donations for the relief of wounded Ottoman soldiers and subjects, which continued and apparently increased during the Libyan and Balkan conflicts.[21]

Most alarming to British officials, however, was evidence that Indian Muslim and Afghan opposition to Italy's aggression in Ottoman territory was not limited to the discursive or financial field. In June 1912, a British Indian intelligence memorandum reported that a contingent of Afghan warriors had traveled to the Ottoman domains in order to help repel Italy's invasion of Tripolitania.[22] Even in cases where the volunteers' militancy was not directed against the British, but a rival colonial power in Africa, the rapid and covert movement of armed Afghans shuttling between the British and Ottoman empires was a source of concern for British administrators.

This was especially the case with Indian and Afghan volunteers who traveled to the North African war front to join Turkish lines. While the Sublime Porte did not represent an enemy state to the British Empire at this time, Pan-Islamic militancy constituted a red line for British officials, especially those already suspicious of foreign intrigue on the Afghan frontier. It was the possibility of such formations spiraling out of control that seems to have especially troubled British officials, from Constantinople to Calcutta.[23] Reports of Afghan and Indian volunteers continued to surface in the heat of the Libyan and Balkan wars. On October 19, 1912, British Vice-Consul Hough at Jaffa wrote to British Consul McGregor at Jerusalem concerning seventy-three Afghans having left for Libya as volunteers for the Ottoman war: "These Afghans are largely of British Indian nationality," the British vice-consul noted, "but only a small proportion of them are registered in this Vice-Consulate." Even more disturbing to the official was that at least one of the Afghans, Muhammad Jan, had originally been carrying British papers, but had become "an Ottoman subject just before leaving."[24]

With the onset of the Italo-Ottoman war in Libya (1911–1912) and the Balkan Crisis, British fears of Turkish activity in India and Afghanistan were reaching unprecedented levels. Amid escalating Muslim resentment over what was seen as London's acquiescence vis-à-vis the Italian invasion of Tripoli, the war in Libya witnessed an increasing number of Indian Muslims and Afghans volunteering for the Ottoman war effort. With the increased dangers came new opportunities for the Ottomans, then, including an enhanced ability to tap into Muslim disgruntlement in Asia and launch increasingly radical political projects under the banner of Pan-Islamic unity and support for the caliphate. The Libyan conflict had also generated some of the first instances of Ottoman guerrilla warfare using irregular Arab auxiliaries against Italian forces, including units led by Enver and Mustafa Kemal Pashas themselves, in a strategy both military leaders would later use in their Central Asian and Anatolian campaigns respectively.

Disconcerting as these developments were for British colonial administrations in Asia and Africa, fears of Afghan and Indian subjects constituting an external pool of Ottoman reserves in the heart of Britain's most valuable colony would only intensify. Soon, London and Calcutta faced a far greater problem than scattered Indian and Afghan volunteers attempting to travel under the British radar to Ottoman war fronts. Escalating tensions between the Ottomans and European powers during the Balkan Wars (1912–1913) represented a new chapter in regional Pan-Islamic politics, especially in India and Afghanistan, but they would pale in comparison to the calamities and dilemmas of World War I. Unlike the Libyan and Balkan conflicts, the scourge of war had now officially pitted the Ottoman Empire against the British Empire, with Afghans and Indian Muslims caught in between.

Between Caliph and Crown: Indian Muslims during the Great War

There is little evidence to suggest that Indian Muslims, from the outset, viewed Britain's entry into World War I negatively. To the contrary, London's declaration of war witnessed a general outpouring of pro-Crown sentiment among India's urban populations, including several outspoken Indian Muslim *anjumans*.[25] Early enthusiasm on the part of many Indian Muslims contrasted with the government of India's initial fears of a potential increase in subversive activities directed against the Raj.

Indians across regions and religions, Muslims included, provided far more than moral support to the Crown during the war, including a ready source of men, rations, and supplies for an imperial army in a global conflict. The Indian army fought in every major theater of combat operations during World War I—Europe, Africa, and the Middle East. Among the ranks were Hindus, Sikhs, and Muslims, with no small number being drawn from the so-called martial races of Pathans, Baluchis, and Punjabis. In all, roughly one million Indian soldiers and laborers served in these regions, with the Indian government and princely states supplying large amounts of foodstuffs, cash, and ammunition to the British war effort. Official figures suggest that nearly sixty-five thousand

Indian soldiers were killed and at least as many wounded in combat operations.[26]

Several Indian Muslim anjumans were also anxious to proclaim unflinching loyalty to the Crown when Britain entered the war. Take, for example, a November 1914 declaration of the Muhammadans of Ajmer, a local anjuman based in the city of India's most renowned sufi saint, Shaykh Muʿin al-Din Chishti (1141–1236). Seeking to allay government concerns, the association was at pains to express its untarnished allegiance to the British Indian government, issuing the following resolution:

> This meeting of the Muhammadans of Ajmer as subjects of His Majesty the King Emperor dutifully assures His Excellency the viceroy that the outbreak of the war would not make the slightest difference in the proved loyalty of the Muhammadans of this place and the Musalmans of Ajmer who have spent their lives and their forefathers before them under the benign shadow of the British Government would remain as faithful as they have been hitherto.[27]

The Ajmer anjuman was certainly not alone in issuing such strongly worded pro-British statements. Similar resolutions and town-hall meetings asserting the faithfulness of Indian Muslims as British subjects occurred throughout India, especially between late 1914 and early 1915.[28] Not to be outdone, at the November 6, 1914, general meeting of the Muslim Literary Union at Shimoga, a certain Abdul Zahir lectured in Urdu to the theme of "War and Blessings of British Rule in India." Describing His Majesty's rule as "a reign of peace, tranquility and religious liberty," Zahir contrasted the Crown's tolerance with earlier reigns of "terror" by foreign invaders, singling out the Mongol chieftain Hulagu Khan (1218–1265) and Afsharid Persian king Nadir Shah (1698–1747) in particular for censure. Lamenting the Mongol invasion of Khorasan and the eighteenth-century Iranian king's pillage of Delhi, Zahir characterized British authority in the subcontinent as benign, noting that in spite of a dreadful conflagration raging in Europe, "the Peace of India is least disturbed and the brunt of War is little felt," all being the result "of the able British rule in India."[29] Others chose to express their devotion in poetry. On November 7, 1914, Abdul Jalil Fiassi infused the pro-British atmosphere at a meeting of the Mussulman Community of Closepet (Shamserabad / Ramanagara) with a few choice lines from Tennyson:

> Self-reverence, self-knowledge, self-control,
> These three alone lead life to sovereign power.
> Yet not for power (power of herself
> Would come uncall'd for) but to live by law,
> Acting the law we live by without fear;
> And, because right is right, to follow right
> Were wisdom in the scorn of consequence.[30]

Resolutions and declarations of fealty such as that of the aforesaid Muhammadan associations at Ajmer, Shimoga, and Closepet assumed particular significance in light of fifth-column suspicions cast upon Indian Muslims during the war. For British colonial administrators from Cairo to Calcutta, the Pan-Islamic Question could not have been more marked when the Sublime Porte issued a proclamation of seismic proportions on November 14, 1914. Bolstered by a fatwa from Ottoman sheikh ül-Islam Hayri Effendi, Sultan Mehmed V Reşad declared a martial jihad against Britain and its allies, and with it the Ottoman Empire's formal entry into the Great War. Soon afterwards the proclamation was translated into Arabic and dispatched to scores of Muslim-majority locales across Asia and Africa, including India and Afghanistan (see Figure 3.2).[31]

As an initially secular nationalist conflict and interimperial tussle in Europe assumed new religious hues, British apprehensions concerning its Muslim subjects escalated to virtual paranoia, while stoking new anxieties for ordinary Indian Muslims themselves. As subjects of the British Empire's most populous and wealthiest colony, and representing the largest Muslim subject population in the world (numbering some seventy million), Indian Muslims found themselves at the crossroads of a new imperial struggle between Istanbul and London, now with heavier stakes than ever before.[32] To be sure, as a heterogeneous constellation of communities dispersed throughout the subcontinent, there was no monolithic Indian Muslim attitude with regard to questions of loyalty and allegiance to the British Crown or Ottoman sultan-caliph—during the Great War, or at any other time. But such nuances were often lost on a British colonial administration at war.

The loyalist declarations of several local Muslim anjumans notwithstanding, the British Raj was more aware than anyone that it was now going to war with the Ottoman caliph and sultan of the greatest Muslim power in the world, all the while governing the world's largest Muslim population in history. Just as some Indian Muslim anjumans were declaring their devotion to the British Crown,

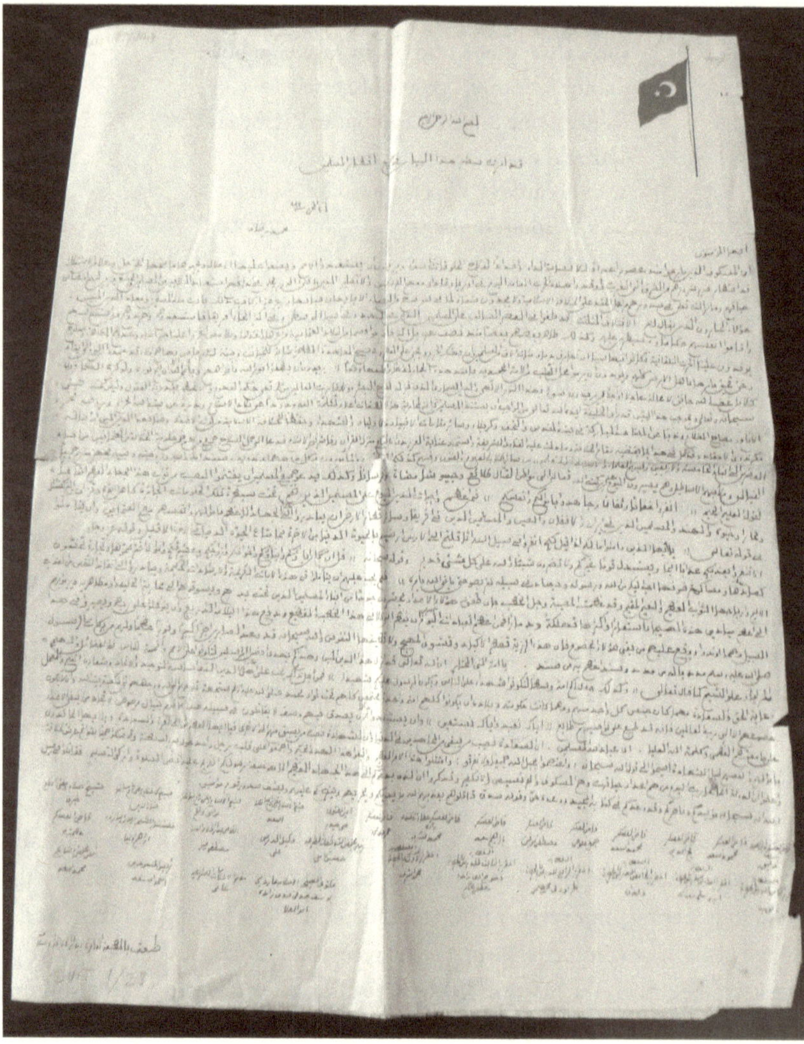

FIGURE 3.2. Ottoman World War I proclamation sent to Muslims of Africa, Asia, and Europe; Istanbul, November 23, 1914. Prime Ministry Ottoman Archives, Istanbul, Turkey (I.DUIT 1/28).

others had materially supported the Ottomans since the Russo-Ottoman War of 1877.[33] Beyond the caliphate question was the foreboding prospect of quelling an explosion of domestic unrest should British forces break through Ottoman lines and officially occupy Islam's holiest cities—in Hejaz, Jerusalem, and Iraq—as many Muslims across the region and irrespective of sect feared. From Egypt to India, as the stakes of public opinion among the British Empire's Muslim subjects only grew in importance, many British officials realized such sentiments could only be ignored at their peril.

For these reasons in May of 1915 the British Indian War Department took it upon themselves to draft an official statement for the viceroy to make in special regard to His Majesty's Indian Muslim subjects. "A Proclamation Issued Respecting the Holy Places of Arabia Including the Holy Shrines of Mesopotamia and the Port of Jeddah" included the following carefully worded assurances intended for Muslims across the British Empire, but especially India:

> PUBLIC ANNOUNCEMENT. In view of the outbreak of war between Great Britain and Turkey, which to the regret of Great Britain has been brought about by the ill-advised, unprovoked and deliberate action of the Ottoman Government, His Excellency the Viceroy is authorised by His Majesty's Government to make the following public announcement in regard to the Holy Places of Arabia including the Holy Shrines of Mesopotamia and the port of Jeddah, in order that there may be no misunderstanding on the part of His Majesty's most loyal Moslem subjects as to the attitude of His Majesty's Government in this war in which no question of a religious character is involved. These Holy Places and Jeddah will be immune from attack or molestation by the British Navy and Military Forces so long as there is no interference with pilgrims from India to the Holy Places and Shrines in question. At the request of His Majesty's Government the Governments of France and Russia have been given them similar assurances.[34]

The above announcement was translated into Urdu and prepared for distribution across Indian cities and towns known to have large Muslim populations. In sum, it is not surprising that British authorities in India felt the need to respond to growing malaise among their Muslim population during World War I, especially after the Ottomans entered the conflict and pitched battles between the Porte and Crown's forces were underway. It is also not surprising that the British Empire exploited—indeed, actively cultivated—proclamations as that of the aforesaid Muslim associations in India to shore up the Crown's authority among potentially conflicted populations. For propaganda purposes, copies of the Indian Muslim loyalist resolutions were reprinted by British authorities, translated into regional vernaculars, and then advertised in the newspapers of major cities with significant Muslim concentrations, including Agra, Allahabad,

Bombay, Calcutta, Delhi, Kanpur, Lahore, Lucknow, and Madras.[35] As Indian Muslim and Afghan loyalty became increasingly important, however, London realized this was not enough. With the aid of seasoned Raj officials in India, the British Empire sought to enhance its strategy vis-à-vis its global Muslim subjects by amplifying the voices of Muslim princes and rulers who had sided with the British Crown.

Britain and Its Muslim Princely States

Keen to prevent the spread of pro-Ottoman sentiment and activism in Indian territory, some British officials believed a more proactive campaign was needed than soliciting ad hoc pledges of loyalty from Muslim anjumans. Sir Stuart Mitford Fraser (1864–1963), British resident at Hyderabad during World War I, knew the danger of Muslim rulers of semiautonomous Indian princely states such as the Nizam of Hyderabad or Begum of Bhopal throwing in their lot or even expressing sympathy with the Ottomans. Bearing this in mind, Fraser proposed preemptive measures to court Muslim princely rulers to the British cause. He offered the following advice on utilizing the most prominent Muslim princely state and strategic asset the Indian government had at its disposal, the *Nizam al-Mulk* of Hyderabad:

> [T]he Nizam should at once publicly and in unmistakable terms declare that single-eyed loyalty to the British Government, to the exclusion of all further sympathy with the Sultan, is the paramount duty of every Muhammadan in India. And I have no doubt that His Highness would act upon the Resident's suggestion that he should stand forth as the leader and spokesman of Muhammadan India in the matter.[36]

Sir Fraser was not alone in his proposal; in the months that followed, the Indian government's wartime correspondence with Muslim maharajas revealed the Raj had embraced the strategy. It sought to capitalize on its strategic relations with the rulers of Muslim princely states by soliciting declarations of loyalty that were then publicized across the subcontinent. Declassified British records from World War I reveal high-level correspondence between Raj officials and Muslim maharajas, nawabs, and other semiautonomous notables, with the goal of encouraging pro-British sentiment among India's Muslim populations. Among them were the Nizam of Hyderabad and Begum of Bhopal, two of the most prominent and respected Muslim princely states in the Indian subcontinent. One particularly revealing dossier, "Declarations of Loyalty by the Leading Musalman Princes in India on the Outbreak of War with Turkey," reveals the extent to which Muslim maharajas and the British Indian government collaborated in curbing pro-Ottoman support on the subcontinent.[37] The dossier also reveals that, as a preemptive measure, said contacts commenced before the Ottomans had formally entered the war.

In some cases, British officials even drafted the loyalty proclamations themselves. Not content with leaving the job to the Nizam himself, the British resident at Hyderabad described in an internal memorandum to Calcutta the benefit of composing the princely state ruler's statement for him, thereby ensuring the Nizam's endorsement would have the greatest effect:

> [I]t would be well if we were ready with a draft of what the Nizam should say, to telegraph to the Viceroy, in case Turkey declared war, since the message would have to be very carefully worded, as from a religious Muhammadan and respecter of the Sultan, who rallied his fellow religionists to the side of the King, not only as the benefactor of all his Indian subjects, but as the Sovereign whom the Koran itself requires all true followers of Islam to support. The Sultan would not be fighting for any religious cause, nor in defence of his country, for the allies had already agreed to respect his territory, but Turkey would be going out of her way to side with the tyrant Germany whose brutality to the weak and harmless, like poor Belgium, had aroused the hatred of the whole civilized world.[38]

Manufactured as the results could be in some instances, the efforts of officials such as the British resident at Hyderabad yielded dividends. Attesting to this are the stacks of Muslim "loyalty declarations" from across India in British Raj archives. Whether expressed in private letters, town-hall resolutions, or formal proclamations issued by princely state rulers favorably disposed to British victory in the Great War, during the course of the war the Indian government received declarations from Ajmer, Anekal, Bangalore, Baroda, Bharatpur, Bhopal, Bikaner, Challakere, Channagiri, Chitradurga, Davanagere, Honnali, Hosadurga, Hyderabad, Indore, Jaipur, Jhalawar, Karauli, Kashmir, Kotah, and Mysore.[39]

A closer examination of these declarations of loyalty also reveals a geographic dimension to collective Indian Muslim expressions of pro-British loyalty, however. A disproportionate number of such declarations hailed from the central Indian provinces and from the southern coast, with particularly strong representation from the states of Karnataka, Rajasthan, and Gujarat. Declarations by prominent Indian Muslim leaders and associations of Greater Delhi and the northern Indian province of Uttar Pradesh (UP), however, are noticeably lacking. As the last bastion of Mughal sovereignty and home to some of the most active Muslim anjumans in India, UP also boasted India's leading Muslim educational and political institutions, including the Dar al-ʿUlum seminary at Deoband, the Muhammadan Anglo-Oriental College at Aligarh, and later, the Central Khilafat Committee at Lucknow. None of these institutions appears to have authored declarations akin to those by the local associations and princely states described earlier.[40] What is more, as the war progressed, India's northern provinces became a hotbed of Muslim support for the Ottomans, displayed through varied means of rhetorical and material assistance. Premised on the religiopolitical ideal of protecting the caliphate, public awareness campaigns by Ottoman Pan-Islamists such as Amir Shakib Arslan (1869–1946), the Druze leader of Lebanon, were matched by the equally determined activities of Indian Muslim scholars and revolutionary activists Mahmud al-Hasan (1851–1920), Muhammad Mian Mansoor Ansari (1884–1946), ʿUbayd Allah Sindhi (1872–1944), Mohammad Barakatullah (1854–1927), and Mohamed Ali Jauhar (1878–1931), among many others, who were pivotal in gathering support for the Ottoman war effort in India.[41]

A closer consultation of British Indian archival sources, then, reveals a more complex picture than a simplistic binary of loyalty and rebellion would allow for. Just as Raj authorities paraded declarations by Indian Muslims asserting complete loyalty to the British Crown, and even condemning the Porte for allying with Germany, other Indian Muslim alliances began to mobilize in more assertive ways to express fealty to the Ottoman sultan-caliph in Istanbul, including offering financial and material support. Among the latter, the most radical and ambitious of all took shape when Ottoman and German agents—in coordination with a cadre of Indian Muslim revolutionaries in UP, Punjab, and the Afghan frontier—organized a secret mission to Habib Allah's court in the summer of 1915.

The Ottoman-German Mission to Afghanistan

Compared to its public relations campaign with the Indian Muslim princely states during World War I, the British Raj was not nearly as successful in courting the public endorsement of one particularly prominent Muslim ruler nominally under British suzerainty: the amir of Afghanistan. Though British officials, including the resident at Kabul, repeatedly asked Habib Allah to clarify his position on the British war effort in the hope of securing an endorsement from him similar to that received from the Indian Muslim princely states, he preferred an official position of neutrality, and they were unable to acquire it.[42]

As British officials knew, Afghanistan was a protectorate of the Raj and not a princely state. The amir in Kabul hence retained complete sovereignty over his kingdom's internal affairs, though not its foreign relations, making his wartime position and relationship to Britain more complex but also relatively stronger than the Indian princes'. British officials also knew that Afghanistan's ties to the Sublime Porte had been warming ever since Mahmud Tarzi's return to Kabul from Damascus, and the amir's subsequent decision to employ Ottoman subjects as his advisors for a host of state-building projects. Among these projects was the training of a national army. That several Turks remained in the Afghan capital for this project even after the outbreak of the war was especially disconcerting to the British agent at Kabul and his superiors in Delhi and London.

This was not a case of Raj officials succumbing to paranoia. As evidenced in the Ottoman foreign ministry memorandum of December 1914, Ottoman agents in Central Asia were already researching the size, strength, and location of Afghan military forces, and were especially gauging their proximity to the border with British India. The report also described the state of Afghanistan's postal services, information that was just as critical to a potential attack on India launched from Afghanistan.[43] The timing of this report is not accidental, but indicates that the Ottomans were contemplating, from the earliest stage of the conflict, the Indo-Afghan frontier as a theater of war. As noted earlier, for the decade leading to 1914, the Porte was already taking stock of Muslim public opinion in India—via newspapers, anjuman activity, and charitable donations to the Ottoman Red Crescent Society—all information that could help the Porte assess the strength of its assets in Britain's biggest and most valuable colony.

To capitalize on this potentially game-changing source of Ottoman support at the height of World War I, in the summer of 1915 the Sublime Porte and Berlin launched a daring expedition to officially neutral Afghanistan. The mission's objective was to deliver a secret call to arms to the amir of Afghanistan from the Ottoman sultan and German kaiser. In a powerful alliance between Berlin, Istanbul, and Kabul, all three states would combine forces in a surprise attack on British India, where they would be welcomed as liberators by a population in revolt, or so the plan envisioned.

World War I historians would be hard-pressed to find a more ambitious and potentially table-turning mission. If successful, the mission to Afghanistan would open an entirely new front against Britain, and by extension Russia, in one strike. Only Afghanistan, after all, formed a soft underbelly of the Porte's two main nemeses in the war. Opening a new battle front in South or Central Asia would achieve a series of strategic objectives for the Ottomans, bogging down Allied forces far from the main theater of war in the eastern Mediterranean, adding tens of thousands of Afghan and Indian auxiliaries to the armies of the Central Powers, disrupting the military and economic supply routes of London's most populous and most valuable colony to the rest of Britain's empire, and relieving besieged Ottoman forces in eastern Anatolia and Mesopotamia. Most ambitious of all, should the aforesaid aims of the mission be met and the combined Central Powers defeat the Indian army, the Ottoman Empire would have in effect created a contiguous land bridge from Istanbul to Delhi, as British forces in Persia and Iraq would in all likelihood be diverted to a life-or-death struggle for the British Empire in India.[44] By the same logic, should the tsar's army be diverted eastward from its pitched battles with Ottoman forces in Anatolia to Central Asia, inflaming the Turkic and Muslim-majority regions of Bukhara and Fergana Valley in support of the sultan, the results would be calamitous for St. Petersburg's control of the steppe.

Tantalizing as these strategic goals were for the Porte and Berlin, a crucial piece of the operation has not been addressed: What would Afghanistan get out of the deal? Coreligionist sentiments and popular support for the Ottoman sultan-caliph aside, by turning the tide of the war in the Central Powers' favor, a successful German-Ottoman-Afghan alliance in Asia could deal a catastrophic defeat against Kabul's two greatest threats and perpetrators of Great Game imperialism in Afghanistan—the British and Russians—in one blow. With these grand objectives in mind, in the summer of 1915 the delegation set out for the Afghan capital.

As if the 1915 Ottoman-German mission was not ambitious enough in its goals, standing in the way of the covert expedition were some formidable logistical obstacles. Just to reach Kabul and deliver the invitation to Habib Allah, Ottoman and German emissaries had to pass undetected through enemy lines in Iran—the least fortified route to Afghanistan, yet still occupied by Russia in the north and Britain in the southeast. To evade surveillance and capture in enemy-controlled Persia, the expedition was divided into German and Turkish contingents, each contingent often further splitting into even smaller parties.

Relative to other episodes of Afghan history in the early twentieth century, the 1915 mission to Kabul has been the subject of considerable scholarly attention, particularly of the military history genre.[45] The expedition was indeed significant to the country's modern history for a number of reasons, including Germany's first diplomatic contact with Kabul. It therefore dealt another setback to British attempts to maintain a monopoly over Afghan foreign relations. The mission to Kabul is most commonly remembered in Western historiography as the Niedermayer-Hentig Expedition—so named after Oskar von Niedermayer and Werner Otto von Hentig, the German army officers who led the contingent from Berlin.[46] This designation is emblematic of scholarship on the binational mission to Afghanistan, scholarship that has tended to characterize the Turks as passive secondary actors, in effect tagging along with their German organizers to provide the operation with a veneer of Muslim credentials. Overlooking decades of earlier contact and exchange among Ottomans, Afghans, and Indians—from the Porte's first diplomatic mission to Kabul in 1877 through the Hamidian and Young Turk eras—the overarching narrative has been one of the Turks being duped into a German-engineered jihad.

More broadly, until recently, World War I historians have tended to present Turkish participation in the Great War either as a gradual culmination of burgeoning German influence in the Ottoman army—seen in the hiring of German military trainers and the building of the Berlin–Baghdad railway during the Hamidian period, for example—or as the kaiser's unbridled manipulation of Turkey's unionist leadership in the months leading to war. According to both British and German sources, a handful of German wartime officers—General Liman von Sanders (head of the German military mission to the Ottoman Empire), Rear Admiral Wilhelm Souchon (commander of the Ottoman Navy), and Vice Admiral Guido von Usedom (inspector general of the Ottoman Coastal Defense)—were the lead actors in a drama in which the Porte played only a supporting role.[47]

Restoring agency to Ottoman officers and their Muslim allies in Asia before and during the war, recent scholarship by historians utilizing Turkish and Arabic sources presents a more complex picture of Istanbul and Berlin's alliance than Eurocentric frameworks often admit.[48] Similarly, a closer examination of declassified records from Ottoman, Indian, and Afghan archives sheds light on the varied roles played by Porte officials, as well as by Indian Muslim revolutionaries and their Afghan interlocutors, not only in organizing the expedition to Kabul but also in laying the foundation for a continuation and transformation of Indo-Ottoman Pan-Islamism in Afghanistan well after the armistice was signed.

From the beginning, Ottoman sources reveal a picture that is more complex than a one-dimensional perspective of the mission to Afghanistan would allow. Starting with the name, a more fitting designation would be the Kazım-Niedermayer expedition—highlighting the Turkish role in the mission by remembering both the primary Ottoman and German commanders, Kazım Bey and Oskar von Niedermayer respectively, who led it. Real-time correspondence from Porte officials in Istanbul to Ottoman officers en route to Kabul also reveals substantial internal differences between the Turks and the Germans during the mission. Early German decisions to recruit their own Muslim agents for the mission were not in unison or even coordination with the Porte, some Ottoman officers complained.

For example, in the late autumn and early winter of 1914, the German government had already initiated efforts to recruit prominent officers for a mission to Afghanistan, including independently contacting key figures in the CUP's military and civil branches. Their first choice for the selection was the commander and former governor of Basra, Süleyman Şefik Pasha, along with the Ottoman parliamentary representative from Aydın, Abdullah Effendi.[49] In spite of Şefik Pasha's glowing military record, Ottoman internal records reveal some unease among Porte officials whether he was the best choice for leading the Turkish contingent, apparently out of concerns for his physical health. As it happened, Şefik returned from his mission to Afghanistan in September 1915 early, weeks before the Ottoman delegation even reached Kabul.[50] Subsequent Ottoman archival records reveal Şefik Paşa's condition worsening, compelling him to travel to Vienna and Berlin for medical treatment.[51] Incidents such as these reflected frustration among Ottoman officialdom that their German counterparts were overly aggressive and domineering in their early efforts to organize the mission. Based on Ottoman reservations with Şefik Pasha's appointment from the earliest stages, it also appears the German officers' mission went over the heads of the relevant Ottoman authorities in making important decisions. This issue would surface frequently between the Porte and Berlin during their fateful World War I alliance.

Partially owing to such differences, but also for strategic purposes, the mission split along national lines, with German and Ottoman contingents taking separate routes through Mesopotamia and Iran, culminating with an intended rendezvous in Kabul.[52] The Turkish party eventually chose the able Ottoman naval commander Hüseyin Rauf Bey (1881–1964) to head its expedition, though for tactical reasons he had to be replaced by Mehmed Kazım Bey while the

Turkish contingent was passing through Iran. Ottoman records also disclose that the Porte footed the bill for their own delegation to Kabul, including individual stipends and salaries for its members.[53] As mentioned, the German party was led by Werner Otto von Hentig (1886–1984), a diplomatic officer stationed in Iran, and Captain Oskar von Niedermayer (1885–1948), a multilingual Islamicist and intelligence officer for the German army. They were joined by Wilhelm "Wassmuss of Persia" (1880–1931), who was both Berlin's ambassador to Shiraz and also a seasoned master spy—a German counterpart to Britain's T. E. Lawrence.

As both parties proceeded through eastern Syria to enemy-controlled territory in Iran via Aleppo and Baghdad, there were also several shifts in personnel.[54] After Hüseyin Rauf Bey was sidelined by combat in western Iran, Kazım Bey took over as head of the Ottoman contingent, with Turkish diplomat Mehmed Ubeydullah İzmirli Effendi and officer Nedim Bey also playing leading roles. In another notable development revealed by Porte sources, according to a letter from the Ottoman consulate in Kirmanshah, the delegation was soon joined by Indian Muslims who were serving in British consulates in Persia but had crossed sides to join the Turks.[55] In total the Ottoman contingent numbered about twenty-five persons; Captain Niedermeyer's German group comprised roughly the same number.[56]

From the outset, it was obvious that intricate tactical and logistical considerations would be involved should the delegation reach the geostrategically central Afghanistan, nestled as it was between occupied Iran, Russian-controlled Central Asia, and British India. In order to reach Kabul, surrounded as it was by British and Russian enemy lines, it was decided Persia provided the most direct route and the least resistance. Still, for the Ottomans and Germans this was a journey fraught with peril. Iran remained an Anglo-Russian sphere of influence, was a key supply chain for the triple entente, and was occupied by both British and Russian imperial armies. As such, an elaborate array of schemes was designed for the strategic objective of evading British and Russian surveillance across the Iranian plateau and vast desert basin of eastern Persia. This included at least three separate Ottoman contingents, each departing from different starting points—led by Ubeydullah İzmirli Effendi, Nedim Bey, and Rauf Bey, respectively. By splitting forces into multiple smaller units, the mission aimed to evade detection and maximize the chances of at least one contingent's making it to Kabul.[57]

The strategy appears to have paid off. By early July, British agents in India and Persia had discovered the broad contours of the mission and made plans to intercept it. Soon thereafter London authorized the British secretary of state for India to counteract German activities in Persia by tracking and engaging the delegation and preventing both Germans and Ottomans from entering Afghanistan.[58] Yet, Ottoman archives describe the successful movement of Turkish and German contingents through Ottoman-controlled Syria and Mesopotamia before adopting separate paths through enemy-controlled Iran, so far undetected.[59] They also reveal the concocting of an elaborate, and ultimately successful, ruse: at least one of the three Turkish contingents—the party led by Ubeydullah İzmirli—served as a decoy, misleading British authorities in Persia as to the whereabouts of the German contingent, which proceeded toward the Iranian-Afghan border uncaptured.[60] In spite of a tumultuous early start, disagreements with their Turkish counterparts, and various shifts in personnel en route, the kaiser's delegation reached Kabul in August 1915, roughly five weeks after the first contingents had departed. As for the "real" Ottoman contingent, their entry into Afghanistan was delayed because they were engaged by the enemy near Kirmanshah. As a result, the Turks reached Kabul on October 7, 1915, after a daring dash through Iran's eastern provinces.[61]

According to most accounts, both delegations were warmly received by Habib Allah in the Afghan capital.[62] Hayri Bey, an Ottoman captain and military instructor in Kabul training the Afghan troops, gathered the Turks living in Kabul to give the arriving delegation a rousing military salute and parade. With the aim of persuading Habib Allah to enter the war on their side, the Turks brought gifts of gold, an ornamental sword, a strikingly calligraphed copy of the Qur'an, and a ceremonial banner; the German contingent presented weapons and gold.[63] An Ottoman general security directorate dossier from February 1915 contains a letter drafted in Arabic by the prominent Qaderi shaykh of Baghdad Sayyid ʿAbd al-Rahman Effendi—a relative of the Kabul Harbiye instructor Mahmud Sami—and addressed to the amir of Afghanistan. After cordial fraternal salutations to the amir, the letter introduced the Ottoman officers and their purpose in traveling to Kabul at this perilous time.[64] Extolling the mission "for the glory of Islam and elevating God's religion," the letter also indicates that Shaykh ʿAbd al-Rahman had the personal endorsement of Ottoman Fourth Army commander and Minister of the Navy Cemal Pasha and the Ottoman caliph, Sultan Mehmed V Reşad. With the hand delivery of this letter to Habib Allah in his Kabul darbar, the expedition had met the first and fundamental aim of the mission.

Still, complex and multifaceted as the mission was, the aforesaid activities by agents of the sultan and kaiser constituted only half of the story of a wider plot to bog down the British and Russian empires in Asia. The full scope of the 1915 mission to Afghanistan surfaces in light of the fact that as Turkish and German agents were busy latticing enemy lines in Persia en route to Kabul, a collateral plot was unfolding in Afghanistan's eastern borders, a plot that had similar goals but a very different set of orchestrators.

Enter Hindustani Revolutionaries: The 1915 Silk Letters Conspiracy

As Ottoman and German secret agents approached Kabul from the west, passing undetected through the Iranian plateau, another covert operation was already fomenting within India and Afghanistan. The plot entailed coordinating an armed insurrection against British rule in India, akin to the 1857 Sepoy Rebellion, beginning with the Pashtun tribes of Waziristan and broader Indo-Afghan frontier before spreading to the subcontinent at large. As with the Kazım-Niedermayer expedition from the west, the conspiracy's leaders in India sent emissaries to Kabul to persuade Habib Allah to heed the Ottoman sultan-caliph's call to arms and attack the British in India. To coordinate their respective plans across Indian, Afghan, and Ottoman territories, clandestine letters were stitched into silk handkerchiefs concealed in the baggage of travelers. Unbeknownst to British port authorities, Indian couriers were thus able to shuttle between the frontier and Kabul, and as far as Baghdad, Hejaz, and Istanbul, with valuable communications for Ottoman, German, and Afghan counterparts to further the plot.[65]

The origins of the Silk Letters conspiracy—as the mission was later described—originated with a group of primarily Muslim scholars and activists operating out of India's northern UP province but with robust links to local agents in the Punjab, the tribal belt of the northwest frontier, and Afghanistan itself. At the movement's helm was the preeminent Indian Muslim scholar of the Dar al-ʿUlum seminary at Deoband, Shaykh al-Hind Mahmud al-Hasan.[66] Also notable among the movement's ranks was Raja Mahendra Pratap (1886–1979), a Marxist revolutionary and Hindu graduate of Aligarh Muslim University, whose presence in the movement signaled broader support among a burgeoning independence movement that crossed communal lines.[67]

Initial plans for the subterfuge were assembled in the spring of 1915, just months after the Ottoman Empire officially entered the war. Over the course of the autumn of 1915 and into the spring of 1916, Hasan instructed two of his closest students at Deoband, 'Ubayd Allah Sindhi and Mian Mansur Ansari, to travel to Kabul and the tribal frontier respectively to prepare the ground for the mission, including by soliciting fighters and arms. In the meantime, Hasan departed to Mecca to rendezvous with Galib Pasha, Ottoman governor of Hejaz, reaching the holy city on October 9, 1915. To lead armed insurrections against the British forces, frontier militiamen Haji Sahib Turangzai (1858–1937) and Mawlawi Sayf al-Rahman (1859–1949) were appointed field commanders with an operational base at Bajaur, near the Indo-Afghan border, just east of the heavily forested Kunar valley in Afghanistan.[68]

Ansari's orders were to mobilize the predominantly Pashtun populations in the North-West Frontier Province and tribal zone for a war with the British. As for Sindhi, a Sikh convert and graduate of the madrasa at Deoband, he was to be joined in Kabul by the revolutionary activists Mohammad Barakatullah and Raja Mahendra Pratap to promote in Afghanistan both the Ottoman war effort and the Free Hindustan independence movement. During the war, Sindhi became the locus of communications conveying messages between participants of the revolutionary plot in India and Afghanistan, but also the Ottoman and German domains, including the radical Indian Independence Committee in Berlin (Das Indische Unabhängigkeitskomitee) and broader Hindu-German Conspiracy (1914–1917).[69] When all three men united in Kabul later that year, on December 1, 1915, they declared the first Provisional Government of India as a government in exile of Free Hindustan, with Pratab as president, Barakatullah as prime minister, and 'Ubayd Allah as home minister.

In the interim, Shaykh Mahmud al-Hasan's efforts to coordinate with the Ottomans and Germans were bearing fruit; in Mecca he obtained a signed declaration from the Ottoman governor, Galib Pasha, in support of the plan. Messages of support were also obtained from Kaiser Wilhelm II, Ottoman war minister Enver Pasha, and the deposed khedive of Egypt, Abbas II Hilmi, all endorsing the mission to Kabul and urging the amir to seize the opportunity of a lifetime and move against the British in India.[70] Meanwhile, Indian Muslim volunteers for the Ottoman war effort were already crossing the Durand Line into Afghanistan in hopes of joining an Afghan declaration of war against the British.

According to British intelligence sources in the frontier, the most dangerous of the Hindustani revolutionaries comprised the so-called Intriguers of Waziristan, a coalition of anti-British activists and their tribal confederates based in the North-West Frontier Province (NWFP), Waziristan, and surrounding tribal zone but with linkages to Punjab and northern India. Among them were the Bajauri party, led by 'Abd al-Rahman of Kotki, and the Swat party, headed by Mawlawi Fazl Muhammad, his brother Muhammad Ayub of Battal, 'Abd al-Rahman Mehtarjao of Chitral, 'Abd al-Sattar of Teri, and 'Abd al-'Aziz of Saidu. Most dangerous of all in the eyes of Raj officials, however, was the Indian Military party (Jam'iyat-i 'Askari-yi Hind), a bitterly anti-British crossborder militia led by Mawlawi Fazl Rabbi, Ghulam Muhammad 'Aziz, a former Muslim cavalry officer in the Indian army named Rukn al-Din, and Kemal al-Din, an Adamkhel Afridi Pashtun.[71]

In contrast to some of the more notorious Hindustani insurgents described above, not all of the participants in the Silk Letters conspiracy had a history of belligerence against the British or were monitored by Raj authorities for their militant activities per se. Among the latter was a fourth-year student of Lahore Government College and devoted pupil of 'Ubayd Allah Sindhi named Zafer Hasan, also known as Zafar Hasan "Muhajir" and Zafar Hasan "Aybek" in Indian and Turkish chronicles of the movement, respectively.[72] Hailing from the Karnal district of Punjab, Hasan would make several trips to Afghanistan over the course of his lifetime, beginning as a British subject in self-imposed exile during World War I. Later, Zafer Hasan would adopt the Turkish surname "Aybek" and become a citizen of the Turkish republic following his emigration to Anatolia in the early 1920s.

Zafer Hasan Aybek (1895–1989) was one of the earliest Hindustani revolutionaries to emigrate to Afghanistan at the height of the Great War, reaching the capital in February 1915 in the company of his teacher, 'Ubayd Allah Sindhi. During his first sojourn in Kabul he served as secretary to the radical government in exile, the Provisional Government of India, led by Raja Pratap and Mohammad Barakatullah.[73] Complementing his work in support of Indian independence and the Ottoman war effort from Afghanistan, Hasan left a remarkable record of his activities in Kabul during the war. Published in Urdu, Hasan's *Ap Biti* (Autobiography) includes a personal narrative of his sojourn in Afghanistan during World War I, and is one of the richest firsthand accounts of the Silk Letters conspiracy by an actual participant as it unfolded. The work also provides a sociological window into early twentieth-century Afghanistan, including the author's observations on the pace of governmental reforms and infrastructure projects in the capital, as well as more conventional notes on the geographic and ethnic makeup of the country from the perspective of an Indian Muslim in Kabul.[74] Hasan's memoir therefore remains an invaluable source of information not only about the Indian revolutionary movement and experience during World War I but also about Afghanistan during Habib Allah's reign.

On arriving in Kabul, Hasan estimated the city population to be seventy-eight thousand, which he increased to a hundred and fifty thousand when including all of the surrounding small settlements and villages on the outskirts of the city. The travel narrative includes a thick description of the city's layout and its most important and frequented sites, and several vivid depictions of public street and market scenes, alleyways, and housing arrangements. Embedded in Hasan's narrative are his own reactions as a Punjabi Muslim migrant living in Kabul during the Great War. These include observations which seem to have surprised Hasan, but also a problematic tendency to resort to British-Orientalist stereotypes of the Pashtuns as "noble savages" par excellence.[75]

Above all, however, Hasan took supreme interest in the state of Afghanistan's military forces, economic resources, and public schooling—issues that must have weighed heavily on the minds of the Indian revolutionaries as they entered Kabul at the height of World War I. They were also the same issues being examined in London and the Porte. In his comments on the state of the Afghan army, Hasan cited discontent about conscription policies being applied in a discriminatory and unfair manner. He noted protests by those who alleged the king's policies privileged the wealthy, as tribes and clans closely related to the amir's family—the Muhammadzais, the Sadozais, the Mangals, and the Jidrans—were exempt from conscription.[76]

Hasan appears to have been most disappointed by the state of education in the country. "[E]ducation and learning was not that widespread," he lamented, noting that "there was not a single school of the modern kind," save a handful of academies in the capital for the children of elites. As for the common masses, "People were taught according to the old methods of reading the Qur'an in the mosques."[77] Sufficient for a basic level education and literacy, Hasan noted, this left the role of training government bureaucrats to an ad hoc system of tutors whereby only the fortunate few entered the king's service after extraordinary effort or relations to the palace. As a sign of positive developments, Hasan initially spoke highly of Habib Allah's plans to establish a modern education system in the country—most of all with the Habibiye, which the author emphasized was built with the assistance of Indian teachers and administrators Dr. Abdul

Ghani, his brother Chiragh al-Din, and Mawlawi Husayn Khan Alighari. In the same breath, however, the author lamented how these very talented individuals and their Young Afghan compatriots had been accused of conspiring to overthrow Habib Allah and summarily imprisoned. Some were even executed after speedy trials.[78]

As for the purpose of his time in Kabul and the geostrategic stakes of the Silk Letters operation, Zafer Hasan was unambiguous about Afghanistan's pivotal role in the Free Hindustan independence movement: "In order for India to achieve freedom, it was necessary that Afghanistan join the war against the British," he declared. By convincing Habib Allah to attack India, the Afghans could open a third front and cause the British forces to be divided yet again. Raj troops destined for the European or Middle Eastern fronts would have to remain in India, allowing German and Ottoman forces to more easily press the war against Russia. In the end, Hasan proclaimed with no lack of nostalgia, Afghanistan and India could together win their freedom from the British.[79]

Early on it did not appear that Hasan's projections were so farfetched. Rather than dismissing the revolutionary Indian delegation when they arrived in his court, Habib Allah granted them an audience and, for a while, a good deal of room to carry out their activities unharrassed. After settling in Kabul, Hasan and his compatriots met with the Tarzi family, as well as with crown princes ʿInayat Allah and Aman Allah, and eventually with the amir himself. Some of these meetings proved to be fruitful to the Indian revolutionaries' cause, especially, as we shall subsequently see, their dealings with Prince Aman Allah. For now, however, Habib Allah was king and absolute monarch of the Afghans, and the opinion of other courtiers, no matter how influential, did not decide Kabul's policy in the war. Ultimately, Hasan was disappointed with his encounter with the amir. Habib Allah did not reject the mission's plans outright, and was apparently undecided, but the young student's high hopes soon turned into a sobering mistrust: "Amir Habib Allah Khan was a friend of the British and he took a salary from them," Hasan wrote in his memoir. "To convince a person like this to enter the war against the British was virtually impossible," he later concluded. "Even just his listening to our ideas was a concession."[80]

Yet, the Hindustani revolutionaries refused to give up on their mission. Sindhi, Barakatullah, and Pratap continued to lobby the Afghan court to their side, scoring some important victories. Sardar Nasr Allah, the king's brother, was especially enthusiastic about the prospects of defeating the British on their own turf, bolstered by an unstoppable alliance between Afghan warriors renowned for bravery, and Ottoman and German armies advancing behind them. As mentioned, he was joined by the young prince and Habib Allah's youngest son, Aman Allah, whose Turcophile and anti-British attitudes were well known, pupil of Ottoman teachers at Kabul's Harbiye as he was. In an enduring spirit of Pan-Islamic vision and a seemingly boundless notion of possibilities, the Indian revolutionaries and their allies in the Kabul court persisted in articulating a political platform for a post-British India. Not content with limiting their actions to mere militancy, Sindhi, the scholar of Deoband, himself proposed to the amir a binational political transition of breathtaking scope:

> If Afghan soldiers attack the British and liberate India from their sovereignty, an Afghan prince could be a constitutional monarch sitting on the throne of Delhi. With the Amir's approval, this prince would be Aman Allah Khan. Moreover, with the formation of a constitutional monarchy in Afghanistan, a framework for unity between India and Afghanistan could be established.[81]

In light of the sheer ambition and radical nature of calls such as these, it is unsurprising that for some in the officially neutral Kabul court, the goals of both the Ottoman-German mission and the Indian Silk Letters conspiracy were simply so farfetched as to appear outlandish. A more considered historical perspective, however, might appreciate the possibilities early twentieth-century transnationals such as Sindhi, Barakatullah, Pratap, and Hasan were proposing—and actively pursuing—during an exceptionally fluid period in the history of the wider region. After all, thousands of miles away and at exactly the same time, British and French officials were trading drafts for a new map of the Middle East that would redraw borders and create new sovereigns in even more radical ways.[82]

A Quiet and Fateful Decision

When the Ottoman Empire formally announced it was entering World War I on the side of the Central Powers, Habib Allah found himself still afloat, but he was standing on two drifting boats. On one side was the Ottoman sultan and caliph of the world's Muslims; on the other, the British Raj, Afghanistan's patron since the 1893 Durand Agreement. Initially, the amir performed the role skillfully, assuring both the Ottomans and the British of his support. Although he refused to commit troops to either power, and to provide Afghan territory for the passage of either side's troops, to the chagrin of the Foreign Office in London the Afghan amir never produced a declaration of loyalty akin to that of the Indian Muslim princely states. When it became clear that the amir was unwilling to join forces with the Ottomans, maintaining official neutrality for the duration of the war, both sides came to see his posturing as double-dealing.

Habib Allah's situation became more precarious as a volatile mix of Ottoman and German officers, Free Hindustan rebels, and crossborder Pashtuns congregated in his capital and made their case to sympathetic ears in his court. What is more, everyone knew the decision to enter Afghanistan into the Great War rested with one man. By the spring of 1916, the Turks and Germans in Kabul realized that they would not be able to persuade the Afghan amir to join the war. Sympathetic to the party's aims and wishing his coreligionists well, ultimately Habib Allah refused the invitation to join the Ottoman sultanate's jihad against either of Afghanistan's historic rivals, Russia or British India. As for policy makers in London and St. Petersburg, it appeared that the Great War had in effect trumped the Great Game, and the Anglo-Russian alliance held for the time being. It is also notable that throughout the war the amir continued to receive annual subsidies from the Raj in line with obligations in the Anglo-Afghan Agreement of 1905.[83]

Habib Allah's decision to maintain Afghanistan's neutrality during World War I reflected his diplomatic balancing skills, but also his aversion to the radical politics of the Young Afghans. Whether in domestic or foreign affairs, Habib Allah preferred a gradualist approach. Kabul's neutrality throughout the war reflected the amir's tactful combination of delay tactics, bet-hedging, and diplomatic posturing as he navigated the political minefield of maintaining cordial relations with both the Ottoman Empire and British Raj. Declassified wartime correspondence from Istanbul, Delhi, and London reveals some of Habib Allah's diplomatic acrobatics. As a testament to his skilled posturing, Habib Allah succeeded in keeping both Ottoman and British parties at bay, just as both sent representatives to his court. On the one hand, Ottoman participation in the mission reveals a mistaken belief that if Turkish and German emissaries could reach Kabul and, better yet, Central Power armies position themselves on the Afghan frontier, the amir would declare war against the British in India. Had the amir's pro-British inclinations or even permanent neutrality been a foregone conclusion, the Porte would not have spared so much expense and time in launching such a dangerous mission.

On the other hand, British sources reveal that Habib Allah's government supplied information of his interviews with Turkish and German agents to the Raj.[84] The latter likely played an important role in his court securing continued British subsidies for the duration of the war, though the Ottoman and German parties may not have known it. The amir's pretexts and affectations aside, one bottom line did become abundantly clear to the pro-Ottoman parties congregating in Kabul: Afghanistan under Habib Allah never officially declared war against any state or committed government troops to any foreign combat for the duration of World War I.

More than delay tactics and doublespeak, Habib Allah employed a calculated rhetorical strategy of defining what constituted a legally sanctioned jihad according to the shariʿa. In particular, he conditioned the proclamation of a valid martial jihad on the approval of the local Muslim political authority—namely, himself. When the amir learned of anti-British activities breaking out among the frontier tribes, for example, he issued directives reminding his people that even war and combat were strictly controlled by Islamic law and discussed at length in classical treatises, a position that was certainly accurate but which he employed for his own purposes. "Jihad requires the approval of the king and people of authority," he warned, citing the Qur'anic verses 4:59 on *ū'lil-'amr,* or "those with authority among you." Habib Allah also stressed that should an appropriate occasion arise for religiously sanctioned combat, he would be the first to declare such a jihad and personally direct it.[85] In the meantime, however, he sternly warned than an improperly declared and executed jihad would be an irreversible mistake with both worldly and eternal consequences. Explaining the role of the *ū'lil-'amr,* Habib Allah argued that "without them entering the war against the British would be a war for worldly purposes and would not be considered a jihad, and those who fight and die in such a war cannot attain the lofty station of martyrdom."[86]

Ottoman and Indian revolutionary activity in Afghanistan notwithstanding, it appears the amir's exhortations had some effect. For the duration of the war, there were no significant clashes between frontier tribes and British forces along the Durand Line. The crossborder Pan-Islamic menace many Raj officials had feared did not materialize. As the India Office wrote as late as 1917, Ottoman emissaries to the Indo-Afghan frontier were unsuccessful in stirring Pashtun tribes to rise up against the British.[87] For many villages, nomadic communities, and other frontier folk on both sides of the Durand Line, it seems, the Great War was simply not theirs to fight.

Meanwhile in Kabul, the amir still had to respond formally to an Ottoman and German delegation anxiously awaiting his reply. When it became clear that the amir was unwilling to commit forces to the Ottoman cause, the war party attempted to at least secure the right of passage for Ottoman and German forces to enter India via Afghan territory. The amir also refused these requests. Bereft of their raison d'être in Kabul, members of the Ottoman and German war parties eventually departed for home. Their allies from Istanbul and Berlin having left empty-handed, so it seemed, the Indian volunteers also saw little reason to remain in the Afghan capital. For some of the Hindustani revolutionaries, Sindhi included, it was time to build more direct links between the Porte and Indian Muslims—without the Afghans as intermediaries, that is. Crossing back into India, however, Sindhi and his companions were arrested by British authorities tipped off by the Punjab branch of the Criminal Investigation Department (CID), the Indian government's secret police. On confiscating his belongings, the officers discovered a cache of secret letters woven into silk handkerchiefs.[88] It was not long before the entire Silk Letters conspiracy was unraveled, resulting in the arrest of over two hundred Indian scholars and activists from across the subcontinent.[89] Unsurprisingly, some of the Indian revolutionaries, Zafer Hasan included, suspected the amir, or those around him, of disclosing their plot to the British. As disclosed in his memoir, Hasan believed that this more than anything had resulted in his mentor's arrest.[90]

The crackdown culminated in Shaykh Mahmud al-Hasan's apprehension by British authorities in Hejaz, together with the latter's accompanying supporters, including the Indian ulema Husayn Ahmad Madani, Wahid Ahmad Fayzabadi, ʿAziz Gul, and Hakim Saʿid Nusrat Husayn. On February 21, 1917, following their transport to Cairo, Shaykh al-Hind and his companions were interned in Malta for three years and four months. After countrywide petitions and protests, Mahmud al-Hasan was finally released in June 1920. He died four months later, and was buried in the cemetery adjoining the Dar al-ʿUlum seminary at Deoband, where he had originally studied and taught to wide acclaim.

Amir Habib Allah, Pan-Islam, and the Burdens of Neutrality

By the time Victorian author Rudyard Kipling popularized the term "Great Game" among English-reading audiences in his widely read novel *Kim* (1901), the British and Russian empires had been locked in over a century of geopolitical rivalry in Afghanistan. As the southern city of Kandahar had been a battleground between the early modern Mughal and Safavid empires, so Kabul became a contested space for imperial machinations, but of a very different kind. Beginning with the East India Company's dramatic expansion from Bengal to Peshawar in the late eighteenth century, and the Russian Empire's southward campaign into the Turkic Muslim khanates of Central Asia at roughly the same time, Britain and Russia had been embroiled in a bitter contest over Afghanistan. But between 1907 and the summer of 1914, as London and St. Petersburg faced a common enemy in Germany and Turkey, the Anglo-Russian Great Game rivalry transformed into a Great War alliance.

Dramatic as this political shake-up was, there were several signs of continuity as the world headed into the Great War, including in Central Asia, where the British and Russians had been bitter adversaries for over a century. One source of this continuity was that Afghanistan remained pivotal in the contests between world powers, including those between the Ottoman and British empires. Another was the continued vitality of the Ottoman Empire, even as it staggered through a controversial and internally fraught decision to enter World War I on the side of the Central Powers. As a reflection of the latter, in 1915 the Central Powers, along with local agents, concocted an elaborate plot of its own for Afghanistan, and possibly the most ambitious operation of the war. The 1915 Ottoman-German expedition to Kabul was in fact a synthesis of two separately coordinated secret missions. The first, the Kazım-Niedermayer expedition to Kabul, originated in the Ottoman Empire. The second, hitherto known in South Asian history as the Silk Letters conspiracy, generated along Afghanistan's volatile eastern border with ties to radical Free Hindustan activists in the Punjab and Greater Delhi. Fused by the lightning bolt of World War I, both projects pursued the shared goal of overthrowing British rule in India and based their operations in Kabul.

Like the Sublime Porte's first mission to Afghanistan, in 1877, the purpose of the 1915 expedition to Kabul was to convince an Afghan amir to open a Central Asian war front against a bitter foe threatening the Ottomans. These parallels notwithstanding, several key differences are worth noting. Instead of Raj officials facilitating an Ottoman mission to Kabul, as in 1877, in 1915 they were hunting one down. In 1877, the Ottoman delegation received British backing so the Afghans could attack Russia; in 1915, German officials were backing the Ottoman mission so the Afghans could attack the British.[91] But most glaring of all, in contrast to the first Turkish mission to Kabul, Indian Muslims played a far more substantial role in the Porte's World War I mission to Afghanistan. Half of the Central Powers' war aims in Asia, after all, entailed joining forces with an insurrection already brewing in India via Afghanistan. Utilizing contacts in Kabul as well as in Baghdad, Istanbul, and Hejaz, Indian revolutionaries based at the Dar al-ʿUlum seminary and their local affiliates in the Punjab and NWFP played a key role in the ambitious scheme. Sufi orders with strong grassroots support in Iraq, Afghanistan, and India, especially the Naqshabandi and Qaderi tariqas, were instrumental in galvanizing support for the Ottomans even before the delegation arrived.[92] Cemal Pasha's attempt to procure a letter from the Baghdad Naqib Sayyid ʿAbd al-Rahman Effendi through Hüseyin Rauf Bey, which the latter was to deliver to Habib Allah with the exhortation to join the Ottoman jihad, is instructive.[93] Even the April 1914 letter of a South African attorney of Indian descent in Johannesburg put Afghanistan on the map of Porte officials gazing eastward, in that case months before the Ottoman Empire's entry into the Great War. Together, this expansive range of networks connecting people and institutions from Istanbul to Greater Delhi—via Kabul—demonstrated the dramatic strengthening of ties between influential Ottomans, Afghans, and Indian Muslims from the Russo-Ottoman War of 1877 to World War I. It also showed how Afghanistan continued to be seen as a lucky pebble that could be leveraged to dislodge the mighty boulders of empire.

Yet, the second Ottoman mission to Afghanistan was not the Pan-Islamic triumph its organizers so daringly sought. Though the joint Turco-German expedition succeeded in one of its objectives—to reach Kabul—it failed to convince the amir either to join the war or to raise an insurrection within India. The caliph's grandiose Afghan army, and new Central Asian war front, never materialized. In the meantime, Habib Allah's ambivalence and vacillations played to Britain's favor, not the Sublime Porte's. By opting for neutrality, Habib Allah had in effect kept Afghanistan out of the theater of combat. This allowed the War Department in London to concentrate the Indian army's attention on Mesopotamia rather than bog it down in yet another eastern front and in the mountainous Indo-Afghan frontier at that, which could well have proved disastrous for the Raj's survival in the war—and possibly its survival in India, too.

So disappointing to Porte officials was Habib Allah's reluctance to join the jihad that it appears to have even created some misgivings about the activities of Afghan subjects in the Ottoman domains. Perhaps the Turks were wary of Afghanistan's ambivalent political stance in World War I. Ottoman sources tell us that the Porte's intelligence agencies monitored Afghans shuttling in and out of Ottoman territory during the war, precisely when Kabul's official neutrality cast doubts on Afghans in the realm. In February 1917, for example, provincial Ottoman authorities followed the movements of an Afghan prince through the Anatolian interior and Syrian cities of Aleppo and Adana.[94] An Ottoman general security directorate record from 1918 reports the arrival and departure of Afghans to a well-known sufi lodge in Üsküdar—by itself nothing extraordinary given the long-standing travel routes and tariqa networks connecting Central Asia and Istanbul. But Porte authorities displayed a keen interest in the activities of Ghulam Rasul Khan, a cousin of Habib Allah's, who resided at the lodge.[95] In the same year Ottoman intelligence reported the movement of three Afghans from the Istanbul lodge to Konya, only after the group secured permission to make the journey.[96] Furthermore, like any other subjects, Afghans were not strangers to the wrong side of the law during the CUP's emergency rule. As an Ottoman foreign ministry memorandum reported in June 1918, Afghans could be found among the prisoners of the Bursa garrison.[97]

The aforesaid instances of Ottoman surveillance of Afghans convey a more sobering view of the Porte's relationship to itinerant Afghans, including those found traveling within the sultan's domains. It should also not surprise; after all, a considerable number of Indian Muslims served in the British army, including Pashtuns from India's northwest frontier with Afghanistan; added to this suspicious lot (in Ottoman eyes) was a legion of British informants, as aforementioned documents from the India Office Records, including the Indian government's frontier department and CID units confirm. In contrast to the more idealized notions of Pan-Islamic euphoria that splashed the front pages of many a Turkish, Arabic, Persian, and Urdu newspaper from Constantinople to Calcutta during the Great War, the latter reports offer a more complex portrait of how Muslim subjects from diverse geographic, ethnic, and political backgrounds negotiated the contours of their interactions with the Ottoman and British Empires vis-à-vis Afghanistan in practice.

As for Habib Allah and his jittery advisors in the Kabul court, it was not until January 1916 that the Afghan monarch made the most lucent declaration yet of his intentions to maintain Afghanistan's neutrality. By the time the winter snows melted and summer approached, most visiting Turks and Germans had departed the city.[98] Ultimately, Habib Allah's decision to remain neutral was interpreted as a betrayal of the close links the Porte had nurtured with Afghans since the first Ottoman mission to Kabul in the 1870s through the first decade of his own reign.

As for Indian revolutionaries like Mohammad Barakatullah, Raja Mahendra Pratap, and ʿUbayd Allah Sindhi, they departed Afghanistan frustrated and disappointed, taking their radical agenda with them to locales as diverse as Berlin, Moscow, Tokyo, and San Francisco as they struggled to regroup and rekindle their efforts. Although they, too, had failed to persuade the Afghan amir to cast his lot with the Sublime Porte and secure Afghanistan's independence, the relationships and networks they had built in Kabul did not wither with Ottoman defeat. Some of the Indian and Ottoman migrants to Afghanistan during the Habib Allah era even chose to stay in Kabul in service to the Afghan government well after the war was over, a topic to which we will return in Chapter 4.[99]

For now, so disgusted were the staunchly Turcophile Afghans with the amir's wartime policy—including Mahmud Tarzi and Habib Allah's own son, Prince Aman Allah Khan—that a rift formed between the amir and these powerful insiders within the Kabul court. The amir was especially disparaged for lacking commitment to the caliphate in the Ottomans' darkest hour, leading Tarzi to abandon his editorship of *Siraj al-Akhbar* in protest.[100] Just as pro-Ottoman sentiment was rising in the major cities of India and Afghanistan, enhanced by cheaper steamship and railroad travel and improved technologies of print and communication, Habib Allah's decision to decline the Ottoman invitation produced waves of discontent in Kabul, on the Indo-Afghan frontier, and across swaths of the Indian subcontinent.

From Habib Allah's perspective, however, matters were far more complex than ideology could make room for. For him, angering the British risked forfeiting valuable subsidies promised to his court since 1905, a legacy of earlier Anglo-Afghan agreements under his father. As with Amir Shir ʿAli, Habib Allah also feared the nightmare scenario of being at odds with both of its historic Great Game rivals, the British and Russians, poised as they were with garrisons in all four cardinal directions of Afghanistan's borders. At the same time, Habib Allah doubted if the distant Ottomans and Germans—neither whom even shared a border with Afghanistan—could sufficiently support Afghanistan should either British or Russian forces invade.

Finally, Habib Allah's wartime policy represented a philosophical and strategic difference of opinion with the Turcophiles in his court. Contrary to the Young Afghans and constitutionalists' approach of seizing independence, Habib Allah opted for an accommodationist approach that sought to appease his British overlords, with the aim of negotiating full independence after the war. The latter would also represent the approaches of later monarchs such as the Hashemites in Hejaz and, later, the mandatory states of Iraq and Jordan, as well as the Wafd party in Egypt. Indeed, one might argue that the amir was in his own eyes signaling Afghanistan's independence when he welcomed the Ottoman and German delegations to his court at a time when Kabul was prohibited from conducting its own foreign relations per treaty obligations with the British. In this view, Afghanistan was already acting as a de facto independent power and as an already globalized nation-state.

Even so, Habib Allah's rejection of the Ottoman call to arms had profound consequences within Afghanistan, including in the corridors of power at Kabul. The amir's underhanded style of diplomacy, particularly his double-dealing with the Ottomans and accommodationist approach toward the British, were especially loathsome to the Young Afghans in the Kabul court, including members of the royal family. Although he successfully navigated the political minefield of Afghan neutrality during World War I, Habib Allah's unpopularity had all but paralyzed his internal administration. Most dangerous of all, his brother Nasr Allah, his son Aman Allah, and a number of Afghan notables in the Kabul court grew estranged from him, and his prestige fell significantly, including among some of his closest advisors.

At the same time, British fears about pro-Ottoman schemes in Afghanistan may not have been so farfetched. Declassified British wartime correspondence reveals the substantial threat the combined Ottoman-German and Indo-Afghan operations presented to the British Empire in Asia. In a telegram to the Secretary to the Government of India in the Foreign and Political Department, Delhi, on November 4, 1915, the British Consul at Sistan, Persia, wrote:

> If Baluch Sardars join us and Afghanistan remains neutral our position here would be secure until Germans and Turks arrive in force, but if jehad is taken up at once by the Afghans we should, I think, have to make as quickly as possible for British territory hardly waiting for the contingent at Birjand who perhaps would do better to go to Meshed and join the Russians.[101]

The urgent tone of this message underscores the seriousness with which British officials viewed the movement of Turks and Germans in Iran, Afghanistan, and the Indo-Afghan tribal zone. This document shows what a tremendous threat the mere idea of Afghanistan joining the Central Powers against Britain was to the Crown, and especially to the British Raj. Revealingly, declassified records from the British Indian Foreign and Political Department archives also divulge secret negotiations between Habib Allah and the British at the height of World War I. In a telegram to the British secretary of state for India in London on Christmas Eve, 1915, the viceroy in Delhi reported the positive signs of collaboration received from Habib Allah:

> The Amir's conversation, as described by the British Agent at Kabul, is regarded by us as satisfactory, and the somewhat grasping attitude adopted by him in regard to the subsidy, which was not unexpected, would appear to indicate confidence in our stability and to afford us, at the same time, a further political lever in Afghanistan.[102]

Documents such as this confirm suspicions that the amir was double-dealing with the Ottomans while engaging in underhand negotiations with the Raj. They also display British relief that the amir was pursuing a measured and judicious response to the combined intrigues of Ottoman, German, and Indian agents and their provocateurs in his court.

Habib Allah knew the risks he was taking and steep price he was paying for British loyalty, distasteful as it was to a growing mass of pro-Ottoman forces gathering in Afghanistan. When the war was over, he intended on reminding the British of his sacrifices, hoping to achieve the unprecedented prize of absolute independence. On February 2, 1919, over three years since he had declared Afghanistan's neutrality, Habib Allah pressed British officials to pay their debts by recognizing Afghanistan's full independence, including its right to control its foreign affairs. It appears to have been his most forceful request for an independent Afghanistan. He was to be disappointed. Citing the perils of revolution in Russia, and their fear of Bolshevism's spreading to Afghanistan, the British rejected his request and insisted on controlling Afghanistan's foreign relations.[103]

It would be difficult to capture the sense of exasperation, indeed betrayal, the amir must have experienced at that moment. He was certainly not the only aspiring Muslim sovereign in the region to have been let down by British wartime promises, but this was unquestionably an unwelcome setback for him. Further complicating matters for the amir was that public opinion in Kabul and other major cities seemed to be growing against him, if not in the street, then in the shadows of his own court. Many influential Afghans had doubted the path taken by Habib Allah during the war. Now, the amir's declining prestige was unbridled, reflecting anger and frustration on the part of many Afghans who witnessed their own Muslim ruler curry favor with the British while failing to aid their Ottoman brethren, the standard-bearers of the caliphate, in their darkest hour. In the end, the amir's unpopular policy caught up to him. In the twilight hours of February 19, 1919, following a day of hunting outside Jalalabad, he was found murdered in his tent, shot dead by an unidentified assailant.[104]

Burgeoning pro-Ottoman influence in the Kabul court, rising anti-British sentiment in India, and Habib Allah's murder dramatically altered the geopolitical landscape in Afghanistan, on the Indo-Afghan frontier, and across the wider region. Here, the historiographical tendency to render the Turco-German mission to Kabul as a complete failure elides the long-term consequences of bringing Ottoman, Afghan, and Indian Muslim networks in closer contact than ever before.[105] The Ottoman subjects who stayed in Kabul were eventually instrumental in building the strongest Turco-Afghan entente yet. It is this group of Ottomans and Indians, along with new arrivals after the war, who would have an even more lasting impact on Afghanistan's modern history—and in ways beyond the battlefield. The tensions between the Ottomans and British in Asia proved too much for one amir to manage, culminating in Habib Allah's assassination, but they also enabled a group of staunchly pro-Turkish and Muslim modernist Afghans to seize power in Kabul and steer Afghanistan toward a new horizon.

FOUR

Converging Crescents

Turco-Afghan Entente and an Indian Exodus to Kabul

ON FEBRUARY 20, 1919, when news reached Kabul that Amir Habib Allah had been assassinated, members of the city's foreign community feared for their safety. Zafer Hasan, the Indian revolutionary of Punjab who had migrated to Kabul during World War I, was less concerned with the possibility of mob violence than a more frightening prospect: the late amir had not appointed a successor, and with multiple contenders at large, a struggle for the Muhammadzai throne was imminent. What is more, whoever the victor, the incumbent would be expected to hunt down and mete out justice to the amir's killers. Hasan predicted in his diary that in the aftermath of a power struggle in the royal family, the need to find a culprit—and here he meant any culprit—to bolster the incumbent's succession would surely result in foreigners such as himself being rounded up, imprisoned, and promptly executed.[1]

Hasan was correct about the internecine struggle. Within twenty-four hours of Habib Allah's death, the late amir's brother, Nasr Allah Khan, who had been accompanying the king on his hunting trip, raced to Jalalabad with a band of supporters and declared his accession to the throne. Nasr Allah bolstered his claim to the throne with a declaration of allegiance by Habib Allah's son, ʿInayat Allah Khan. Meanwhile in the capital, another of Habib Allah's sons, Aman

Allah Khan—the governor of Kabul and custodian of the kingdom's central arsenal and military command—also declared himself king. By February 28, 1919, exploiting his strategic advantages and announcing he was increasing the pay of the army, Aman Allah succeeded in imprisoning many of Nasr Allah's supporters and gaining the loyalty of the military. Hardly ten days after his father's assassination, and with his key rivals for the throne in prison, Aman Allah proclaimed himself the new and undisputed amir of Afghanistan.[2]

In the days and weeks to follow a sense of calm and normalcy gradually returned to Kabul. For all except Nasr Allah and his dwindling group of supporters, a collective sigh of relief presided over the Afghan capital, but especially within the foreign community, where fear and trepidation were soon replaced by upbeat spirits, and even joy.[3] For radical Indian Muslim expatriates like Zafer Hasan, after all, it soon became clear that Aman Allah was not just a new amir on the Afghan throne but an independent Muslim king committed to the anticolonial struggle, with a particularly vehement antipathy for the British. As for the Ottomans in Kabul, Aman Allah represented a staunch ally of the Porte, a Turcophile with robust connections to the Young Turks since his childhood days as a student at the Kabul Harbiye. Far from fleeing for their lives, both Turks and Indians in Kabul began to rejoice in finding a seemingly ideal ruler who could implement radical visions of revolution and reform in a simultaneously Afghan nationalist and Pan-Islamic context.

AMAN ALLAH, THIRD son of Habib Allah and grandson of the "Iron Amir" ʿAbd al-Rahman, was born on June 1, 1892, in Paghman, a hill station just west of Kabul. Aman Allah's mother, ʿUlya Hazrat Siraj al-Khawatin, was widely considered Habib Allah's favorite and most influential wife and the most powerful woman in the kingdom.[4] A formidable figure by all accounts, ʿUlya Hazarat's commanding stature in the Kabul court played a decisive role in positioning Aman Allah for several key posts in Habib Allah's cabinet. By the time the latter embarked on his fateful hunting trip in February 1919, Aman Allah commanded the governorate of Kabul and the central arsenal, and had the loyalty of officers in the Afghan armed forces.

As a youth, Aman Allah attended the Harbiye military academy at Kabul, the very institution that the Ottoman colonel of Baghdad Mahmud Sami Bey had helped establish in the early years of Habib Allah's reign.[5] Having forged strong pro-Ottoman ties with his Turkish instructors at the Harbiye, Aman Allah's ideological identification with the Young Turks from a young and impressionable age would only increase in subsequent years. Defying his father's official stance of neutrality during World War I, Aman Allah joined the pro-Ottoman faction in the Kabul court by supporting the sultan-caliph's call for a jihad against the British. Underscoring the prince's Ottoman links was Aman Allah's marriage in 1916 to Syrian-born Suraya Tarzi, the daughter of the returning Afghan notable of Damascus, Mahmud Tarzi, and his Syrian wife, Asma Rasmiya.[6] When Aman Allah ascended to the Afghan throne in 1919, the pro-Turkish parties in Kabul had finally found their man to forge closer ties between Anatolia and Afghanistan.

Having defeated all rivals for the throne, including his powerful and more experienced uncle, Nasr Allah, Aman Allah did not rest on his laurels. Within days of his coronation the young monarch pledged to address two urgent matters facing the country without the slightest delay: first, to avenge his father's murder, and second, to seize Afghanistan's independence from the British. Regarding his first promise, the watchman on duty the night of Habib Allah's assassination, Captain Sayyid ʿAli Riza, was found guilty of conspiracy and promptly hanged.[7] As for his other promise, the amir informed his subjects that Afghanistan's independence from Britain was on the horizon and had never been closer.[8]

The Third Anglo-Afghan War

When Aman Allah ascended the Kabul throne in February 1919, Afghanistan was not a fully sovereign nation. Per earlier Anglo-Afghan agreements signed by amirs Muhammad Yaʿqub, ʿAbd al-Rahman, and Habib Allah, including the Treaty of Gandamak (1879), the Durand Agreement (1893), and the Anglo-Afghan Agreement (1905) respectively, Great Britain retained control over the country's foreign affairs, rendering it a British protectorate. These agreements prohibited the construction of Afghan embassies or consulates abroad and, according to the strictest British interpretations, even subjected the amir's foreign correspondence to the Raj's supervision. The 1893 Durand Agreement was an especially deep source of resentment for Afghans, especially Pashtun and Baluch irredentists, because it divided roughly half of the world's Pashtun population, and the historic lands they inhabited, from Afghanistan proper. Adding insult to injury was the amir's ceding of the historic Afghan cities of Peshawar and Quetta to British India.

Setting out to reverse these humiliations, Aman Allah focused his earliest policies on securing the state's absolute and unqualified sovereignty. On March 3, 1919, Aman Allah dispatched a letter to Lord Chelmsford, viceroy and governor-general of India. To the alarm of the viceroy, Aman Allah not only announced his accession to the Afghan throne but also proclaimed his nation's equal status with Great Britain:

> [L]et this remain known to that friend that our independent and free Government of Afghanistan considers itself ready and prepared, at every time and session, to conclude, with due regard to every consideration for the requirements of friendship and the like, such agreements and treaties with the mighty Government of England as may be useful and serviceable, in the way of commercial gains and advantages, to our Government and yours.[9]

Hardly two weeks in power, the twenty-six-year-old Aman Allah had demonstrated he knew how to pick a fight—with the greatest military power on earth. Given there were already treaties on the books governing relations between His Majesty's empire and the amirate, Aman Allah's letter could have only meant one thing to British authorities in Delhi and London. With one week passing and the amir still having received no reply, Aman Allah opted to express his intentions even more clearly and remove any doubt of his country's complete and absolute independence from Britain. On March 11, 1919, he issued another proclamation, this time addressed to his own people. The announcement was nevertheless forwarded to the British Indian government to send an even bolder message.

> O nation with a sense of honour! O brave army! While my great nation was putting the crown of the kingdom on my head, I declared to you with a loud voice that I would accept the crown and throne, only on the condition that you should all co-operate with me in my thoughts and ideas . . . [The first being] that the Government of Afghanistan should be internally and externally independent and free, that is to say, that all rights of Government, that are possessed by other independent Powers of the world, should be possessed in their entirety by Afghanistan.[10]

Seeing only pretentiousness and effrontery, London refused to indulge the amir's bravado. With no sign of reconciliation in the diplomatic field, it was not long before Afghan and British forces clashed in battle, with the Indian army invading Afghanistan for the third time in less than a century. By early May, the Third Anglo-Afghan War had officially begun. As Afghan troops led by Generals Nadir Khan and Salih Muhammad Khan squared off with Indian army units near Jalalabad and Kandahar, Pashtun tribal levies harassed British troops on both sides of the Durand Line. While Royal Air Force bombardiers launched punishing air strikes—some of the first in history—and inflicted heavy damage on Afghan troops, the guerrilla tactics of Pashtun tribal levies in the mountainous and forested borderlands were also wearing Indian forces thin. These guerrilla tactics played a critical role in bringing both sides to the negotiating table after a war of attrition that lasted barely three months.[11]

Although the Third Anglo-Afghan War concluded in a stalemate on the battlefield, in light of the massively disproportionate military strength and organization of the British forces vis-à-vis the Afghans, unsurprisingly Aman Allah claimed a resounding political victory when landmark peace negotiations were announced to take place in Rawalpindi, India, in August 1919. Put in regional and indeed global perspective, the Afghans' triumph was accentuated by the fact that it came at a time when Allied European armies and colonial administrations were occupying much of Asia, Africa, and the Middle East—including former lands of the Ottoman Empire. Few could know this better than Aman Allah Khan himself, who reveled in the fact that not only Afghans were celebrating his victory.

Peace Talks amid the Shooting: The Rawalpindi and Mussoorie Accords

Aman Allah's decision to unilaterally declare Afghanistan's independence was no doubt significant. As significant was selecting an envoy to represent the country as an independent state in landmark negotiations with the British at Rawalpindi. Preparing for the August 1919 peace talks, Aman Allah chose the eminent Afghan intellectual, former Ottoman bureaucrat of Damascus, and his father-in-law, Mahmud Tarzi, to represent Afghanistan abroad as the country's first minister of foreign affairs. Joining Tarzi was another notable figure in Kabul's Young Afghan community—the recently freed political prisoner and Indian Muslim migrant to Kabul, Dr. Abdul Ghani Khan, who joined the Afghans as a lead negotiator. On the British side, London chose as their chief representative the seasoned diplomat, administrator, and future High Commissioner of Iraq, Sir Henry Dobbs (1871–1934).

Convinced they were the stronger party, from the beginning Dobbs and his team established a noncommittal tone, stating that a bilateral agreement between "friends" would not be forthcoming until certain stringent conditions were met by the amir.[12] After several tense exchanges and anxiety-ridden days, a preliminary agreement was reached, but this agreement was far from a comprehensive reconciliation; it failed even to secure a cease-fire. A diplomatic milestone though it was, British officials had no illusions that the agreement at Rawalpindi would stop the shooting. For the remaining months of 1919 and through early 1920, sporadic skirmishes between the Indian army and tribal levies loyal to the amir continued on both sides of the Durand Line. On the pitched battles that continued well after the accord was signed, both the governments of India and Afghanistan knew that the agreement at Rawalpindi was marred by too many fundamental disagreements and impasses to constitute a lasting peace. As an internal memorandum of the Indian Foreign and Political Department noted soon after the accord, Raj officials were hardly optimistic.

> [T]he Government of India will not believe that the peace recently signed at Rawalpindi means the end of the Afghan trouble. All the conspirators are still at large, full of an immense capacity for evil, and behind them are the very busy figures of Enver Pasha and the Bolsheviks, who have joined hands in one of the ugliest facts known to history. The recent troubles on the Frontier may be only wavering gusts compared to the storm that is to come.[13]

As alluded to by the British officer's comments above, time was not on the side of the British Empire's already exhausted and overstretched forces. Still licking their wounds from the devastating losses of World War I—where Indian forces had participated in several costly battles in Mesopotamia—there was little appetite to carry an aggressive war into Afghanistan as they evaded potshots and crossborder raids on their own frontier. Undeterred, Pashtun tribesmen continued to launch attacks on British forces through 1920. One anxious officer from the British legation in Kabul described an "orgy of successful raiding" carried out by the amir's tribal proxies on British personnel and property on Indian soil. From 1919 to 1920 alone, the British legation reported 611 raids on British forces, with 690 British subjects killed or wounded, and 463 kidnapped.[14] In the meantime, with the new amir's support Afghan foreign minister Mahmud

Tarzi launched a vigorous shuttle diplomacy campaign, dispatching missions to the Soviet Union and a number of European capitals to bolster Afghanistan's diplomatic recognition abroad and thereby strengthen Kabul's bargaining position with London.[15]

By the spring of 1920, it had become evident that neither the British nor the Afghans could vanquish their opponent. In spite of superior British firepower, supplies, and numbers, the Afghans possessed greater command of the terrain, stronger links to local populations on both sides of the Durand Line, and the ability to engage in targeted guerrilla attacks against a more cumbersome imperial army. The latter ultimately wore down Indian forces on the frontier and eroded political will in London for another long war. The inability of the Raj's army to crush insurrection on the frontier ultimately brought the British back to the bargaining table in April 1920, when a second round of peace talks was held in the northern Indian hill station of Mussoorie. Sensing imminent triumph, the following words of General Nadir Khan, commander of Afghan forces and tribal levies on the frontier, must have especially stung British negotiators as they prepared for another grueling round of talks with the Afghans. Taunting the British ambassador in Kabul, Nadir remarked:

> You expected that within six months the Bolsheviks would have been smashed, Ireland pacified, the Indian troubles settled, and Turkey finally partitioned. You thought that after six months you would be in a much stronger position towards us, and would be able to impose your will on us. The opposite of all this has occurred. Every one of these difficulties has increased; and you are in a much weaker position towards us than if you had made an immediate and final treaty with us at Rawalpindi.[16]

As with the earlier impasse at Rawalpindi nine months earlier, one of the most contentious issues at the Mussoorie negotiations was the problem of crossborder raids by Afghan tribes. Refusing to speak of much else, British negotiators accused the amir of instigating Pashtun militias on both sides of the Durand Line to attack British installations, harass British personnel, abscond with their property, and, wherever possible, revolt against British authority in general. From 1920 to 1921 the British legation at Kabul reported 391 raids against British forces in the frontier, including 310 killed or wounded, and 56 kidnapped, still a remarkably high number of casualties for the world's greatest military power and after a formal armistice at that.[17] Though a reduction from the previous year, the high number of attacks against British targets was simply unacceptable for the government of India. Unfazed, the Afghan negotiating team upheld their commitment to maintaining law and order on the frontier, and as stated in Clause II of the draft treaty, agreed "to prevent on the said frontier, *to the best of its ability,* every kind of action which may tend to stir up strife and raids among frontier tribes or cause general excitement against the British Government."[18] Implied within this clause, however, was a denial that the amir was responsible for the actions of Indian subjects. This was no doubt a tongue-in-cheek stance, especially since both parties knew fully well that the amir still held widespread influence—and possibly ambitions—over the predominantly Pashtun northwest frontier of India and the ancient Afghan city of Peshawar.

Debilitating crossborder raids and Pashtun irredentism were not the only stumbling blocks in the negotiations at Mussoorie, however. British officials also expressed discomfort with Aman Allah's outspoken criticism of British policy in the Near East and India, especially the Allied partition and occupation of Ottoman territories. Closer to home, Raj officials were nervous about an independent Muslim king on their western flank vigorously backing the Indian Muslim Khilafat movement and making common cause with broader coalitions of Indian independence campaigns, including Gandhi's Noncooperation movement. Added to British concerns were Afghanistan's warming relations with Soviet Russia and, within the amirate itself, Britain's loss of jurisdiction over British subjects accused of crimes in a fully sovereign Afghanistan.

But as Tarzi, Dobbs, and their respective negotiating teams met again in late fall of 1921, it became apparent that the root issue plaguing Anglo-Afghan relations was the ambiguous state of Kabul's relationship with the British Crown. For the Afghans, nothing less than London's recognition of Afghanistan's absolute and unqualified independence was acceptable. This was the Afghans' clear demand from the very first meeting at Rawalpindi, where Afghan foreign minister Mahmud Tarzi forthrightly stated, "The British Government, the old friend of Afghanistan, should make plain its intentions with regard to the freedom and complete independence of Afghanistan, on the analogy of the freedom and independence of other nations."[19]

As negotiations again stalled and both sides dug in on their respective positions, Mahmud Tarzi's shuttle diplomacy was bearing fruit. As if to make up for nearly half a century of international isolation, in the spring and summer of 1921 Afghan diplomats visited Berlin (March), Rome (May), Paris (June), and Washington, D.C. (July).[20] All state visits resulted in bilateral treaties of recognition and friendship, with the exception of the United States, which offered a friendly letter from President Warren G. Harding, a formal diplomatic treaty not ensuing until the next decade.[21] By all accounts the amir's diplomatic investments had paid off. With bilateral treaties of recognition also signed with Eastern powers in Moscow (February 28), Ankara (March 1), and Tehran (June 22), the writing was on the wall for Britain's protectorate over Afghanistan and control over its foreign affairs. Later that autumn, the Afghans finally secured what they had set out to achieve: a complete recognition of their independence from Britain in the Anglo-Afghan Treaty of November 22, 1921. At the bottom of the agreement were the joint signatures of lead negotiators Mahmud Tarzi and Henry Dobbs.[22]

Although the 1921 Anglo-Afghan Treaty was a landmark in the eyes of many Afghans and for significant portions of the greater Islamicate world, in fact Aman Allah Khan's victory began two years earlier with the Rawalpindi Agreement of August 19, 1919. The latter date continues to be Afghanistan's official independence holiday. For many Muslim observers beyond the Afghan domains, in particular the burgeoning nationalist movements in Anatolia and India, Afghanistan's August 1919 independence marked the victory of an Asian, Eastern, and Muslim state against the world's premier imperial power. At a time when colonial armies and administrations outnumbered free and independent states in Africa and Asia, this was a remarkable political victory celebrated from Sivas to Bombay.[23]

What did Afghanistan's being one of the world's only independent and fully sovereign "Islamic states" mean for Afghans and for Muslims in other parts of the Islamicate world? Was the new Afghanistan to be a haven for oppressed Muslims, a laboratory for Islamist state making, or an ethnic nation-state along the lines of secular territorial nationalism in other parts of the region and world? By the time the Afghans negotiated their absolute independence with Britain in late November 1921, these questions were very much still unanswered. The way that Afghans—and a group of Turkish and Indian Muslims joining them—eventually answered these questions is tied to a host of political developments brewing in Afghanistan, India, and what remained of the Ottoman Empire during the pivotal years of 1919 to 1923. It was during this period that the legal, constitutional, and administrative foundations of the newly independent state of Afghanistan were laid, precisely as the once mighty Ottoman Empire staggered from its losses and was reconstituted into a host of European mandates and ethnic nation-states.

From National Independence to a Pan-Islamic Court

Although Aman Allah never claimed to be more than the successor to his father's throne and king of a free Afghanistan, from the beginning his drive for independence was embedded in complex—and at times contradictory—notions of Afghan nationalism, Pashtun irredentism, Pan-Islamism, Pan-Asianism, and other forms of extraterritorial influence. While earlier Ottoman and Indian missions to Kabul had failed to convince Afghan amirs to attack their regional enemies—be it Russia or British India—Aman Allah had done so without the Turks or Indians even asking. It certainly looked like Turkish and Indian Muslims with Pan-Islamic agendas had finally found their man on the Kabul throne. Notions of leveraging Afghanistan for greater regional purposes were amplified after Aman Allah secured the amirate's independence from Britain, making him one of the world's only completely independent Muslim monarchs, leading one of the only completely independent Muslim-majority states. From Indian migrants, or *muhājirs,* to the last Ottomans, Aman Allah's Afghanistan lured a motley crew of Muslim migrants to the island of Islamic sovereignty that the country seemed to represent.

What followed were two very different kinds of migrations to Afghanistan from two opposite directions. The first was a small movement from the west of former Committee for Union and Progress (CUP) officers and exiles from an Ottoman Empire in disarray. They included a high-profile group of Ottoman Turkish officials fleeing Allied-occupied Istanbul. The second was a much larger exodus from the east made up of Muslims from British India. In an uncanny foreshadowing of the trauma and dislocations of partition a quarter century later, an estimated sixty thousand Indian Muslims, mostly poor farmers from Sindh, Punjab, and NWFP, crossed into Afghanistan in the Hijrat movement (1920–1921), one of the most remarkable migrations in modern South Asian history. When added to the small but influential group of Indian Muslims who journeyed to Kabul during the Great War, some of the more elite Indo-Afghans became powerful members of Aman Allah's court, joining a coterie of ex-Ottoman officials in the amir's service.

Early on, then, in some significant ways the image of the nation-state that held in Afghanistan's royal court was far from uniform, and even displayed some cosmopolitan and non-ethnocentric features. Though still a Muhammadzai Pashtun aristocracy at its core, several key members of the amir's court were in fact not even Afghans. One of the participating negotiators for Afghanistan's independence, Dr. Abdul Ghani Khan Punjabi (1864–1945), was an Indian

Muslim who was also a leading voice in educational and administrative matters of both Habib Allah and Aman Allah's reigns. Other prominent examples include Osman Bedri Bey (1881–1923), an Ottoman lawyer whom Aman Allah appointed director of the country's first constitutional commission, and Cemal Pasha (1872–1922), the CUP exile and former Ottoman naval commander who was entrusted with modernizing the Afghan military, and about whom we will have more to say shortly. Aman Allah was also keen to employ Turkish, Egyptian, and Indian Muslim instructors in his schools, but refused to play sectarian politics, shoring up relations with Iran and the Hazara Shiʿi minority in Afghanistan, including the scholar and court historian Fayz Muhammad Katib (1862/3–1931).[24] Aman Allah also deftly exploited relations with Moscow and Germany to bolster Afghanistan's international prestige while sending a signal to the British and French that their actions in the Near East were being watched. At the same time, as early as the fall of 1919, Aman Allah was also supporting Basmachi guerillas contesting Bolshevik expansion in Central Asia, reflecting a broadly consistent support for anti-imperial struggles on Afghanistan's northern frontier, even though it antagonized his newfound Soviet friends.[25]

Such vastly divergent causes were able to coexist and even combine in powerful ways during the campaign for Afghan independence, but in the years that followed, Aman Allah and his advisors faced difficult decisions about the structure and domestic policies of the state he was building, as well as its foreign policy. Among the latter dilemmas were the definitions and limits of Afghan citizenship; the degrees to which he was willing to compromise a modernizing, liberalizing agenda with diverse segments of Afghan society; the sources of Afghan law, including tensions between decentralized, customary approaches that allotted a commanding influence to Afghan ulema and local chieftains, versus more positivist conceptions of law accruing from the sovereignty of the state; Aman Allah's support for the Indian independence movement and his own extraterritorial influence among Indian Muslims; and not to be forgotten, Afghanistan's relationship with the caliphate. Over the course of Aman Allah's decade in power, however, his position toward questions of citizenship matured as the Afghan government opted for a conception of nationhood that was more territorially bound and ethnocentric than a Pan-Islamic caliphate, Bolshevist-Muslim alliance, or other form of ideological politics. Ultimately, like his father and grandfather, Aman Allah had to accept that his state-building campaign was not a campaign for an expansive Pashtun empire or Islamic caliphate but an internal struggle for sovereignty and legitimacy over a bounded territory geographically located between British India, Soviet Russia, and Iran. The campaign reflected a goal to make Afghanistan a fully fledged participant, not a pariah, of a new state system that proposed self-determination for ethnic nations within defined territories rather than imperial or overly ideological notions of statehood.

Such consequences of Afghan political pragmatism were, however, far from an inevitable outcome when Aman Allah proclaimed his nation's unqualified independence in the spring of 1919. From the beginning of the Third Anglo-Afghan War to the spring of 1923, when the country ratified its first constitution and the bulk of over seventy *niẓāmnāmih* codes promulgated by Aman Allah, the reformist amir's court was fraught with internal rivalries and tensions. Some of these tensions were residual from the Habib Allah era and World War I; others sprung from the newfound opportunities and challenges of independence and state building; others still, from the fact that Aman Allah's advisors encompassed a cosmopolitan group of modern Muslims as diverse as Afghan ulema, Pashtun notables of the powerful Muhammadzai clan, and Indian and Ottoman officials recruited from Lahore to Istanbul.

Beyond ethnic and geographic differences, and though they were not known to use such terms themselves, one could also describe the formation of radical, conservative, and moderate factions in Aman Allah's court. The radicals, led by Mahmud Tarzi, comprised bureaucrats, journalists, and other liberalist intelligentsia, with ties to the Young Afghans and constitutionalist politics of the early Habib Allah era. This group enjoyed the closest rapport with the amir. They also included other constitutionalists (*mashrūṭih-khwāhān*) such as Mir Sayyid Qasim, former editor of *Aman-i Afghan,* and ʿAbd al-Hadi Dawi, a colleague of Mahmud Tarzi who had been imprisoned by Habib Allah for an alleged plot on the amir's life and later freed by Aman Allah and appointed to prominent posts in the latter's government. Politically the radicals had internal divisions as well—some, like Dawi, preferred a traditional but more progressive constitutional monarchy; others, like ʿAbd al-Rahman Ludin, opted for a more revolutionary idea: a republic. Both groups were staunchly pro-Turkish and embraced Pan-Islamism as a springboard for anticolonial politics rather than out of religious piety per se. They were also vehemently anti-British.[26]

The conservative faction was led by Aman Allah's uncle and brother of the late amir, Prince Nasr Allah Khan. This was a party dominated by Afghan ulema. Although they shared a deep reverence for the sultanate-caliphate in Istanbul and lamented Habib Allah's failure to respond to the Ottoman jihad during World War I, they were otherwise uneasy about many centralist measures espoused by Turkish officers in Kabul, the liberalism of the Young Afghans and, later, the threat of Kemalist-styled secularism seeping into Afghanistan from the top down.

Finally, relative to the other two factions, a moderate faction emerged around General Nadir Khan, the British-trained commander of the Afghan army under Aman Allah. This faction supported Aman Allah's war for independence, Afghanistan's unqualified sovereignty, and gradual measures of political and military reform to strengthen the Afghan state, but it was distinguished by its strong ties to southern and eastern Pashtun confederations on both sides of the Durand Line. As a result, Nadir resisted several of the Turkish-styled military reforms that stressed hierarchy, homogeneity, and uniformizing discipline, which clashed with more decentralized modes of military organization traditionally upheld in the country. The general was especially wary of supporting policies that could undo Kabul's relations with provincial tribes, ties that he had worked hard to stitch together during his tenure as commander of the Afghan armed forces before and leading up to the Third Anglo-Afghan War.[27]

One of the most remarkable aspects of the amir's cosmopolitan cabinet in the early years of his reign was that they achieved a great deal in spite of their differences: negotiating the country's independence from the greatest imperial power in the world, writing the country's first constitution and scores of supplemental legal and administrative codes, building the first national Afghan army, and establishing ministries of education and public health, and a host of other state institutions.[28] Afghanistan's early successes as a newly independent state were forged through the crucible of a king and his courtiers negotiating their differences and cooperating in a series of constructive projects and institution building, with concerted attention to projects in law, education, civilian administration, and the military. In order to understand how these different Afghan factions within the amir's court fit together while incorporating influential members of the late Ottoman and Indian community in Kabul, it is necessary to place Aman Allah's ascendance and the Afghan war of independence within a broader context of developments occurring in Turkey and British India.

"The Storm That Is to Come": Ankara and Kabul in Revolutionary Contact

On November 2, 1918, less than seventy-two hours after the Ottoman government had conceded defeat in the Great War at the Armistice of Mudros, a band of top CUP officials boarded a German warship anchored off the Sublime Porte at Istanbul.[29] Fleeing imminent arrest and a new government under Allied occupation, by the second week of November the entire wartime leadership of the CUP regime had scattered across eastern Europe and Asia, absconding to such locales as Berlin, Geneva, and Moscow. Others plotted attempts to return to power in Anatolia and engaged in ambitious pan-Turkic and Pan-Islamic projects that took them as far as Bukhara and Afghanistan.[30] Most of them were never to see Istanbul again.

On May 5, 1919, as Aman Allah was leading Afghan forces against the British Indian Army, the legal advisory board of the Ottoman government in Istanbul renewed arrest warrants for Talat, Enver, and Cemal Pashas for alleged war crimes. Two months later Cemal, Enver, and Talat were sentenced to death in absentia by the Ottoman government in occupied Istanbul.[31] Meanwhile further east in Anatolia, the CUP leadership's flight had left a vacuum that was already being filled. Six days before the May 5 indictment of the top CUP leadership by the Ottoman legal advisory board, Ottoman brigadier general Mustafa Kemal Pasha was assigned to be inspector of the Ottoman Ninth Army troops. Officially, Kemal was tasked with disbanding the remaining Turkish forces in the countryside, but this was a role he exploited to quite opposite ends.[32] Though he was not the only contestant for power in an extremely fluid Turkish political landscape, Kemal quickly emerged in the forefront of an independence movement that would contest not only Ottoman disarmament but also the partition of Anatolia itself. On May 16, Kemal and a carefully selected crew of supporting officers from the remnant Ottoman army departed Istanbul aboard the SS *Bandirma*. Their arrival at the Black Sea coastal town of Samsun three days later signaled the launch of a Turkish war of independence. As the Allies proceeded with partition plans for the Ottoman lands, including Anatolia, for Kemal and his supporters World War I had never ended.

By September 13, a fledgling nationalist congress met in the eastern Anatolian town of Sivas, where the vision and goals of a Turkish national movement were formulated. On January 28, 1920, the resistance movement led by Kemal adopted an official statement of aims known as the National Pact (*Misak-i Milli*), a manifesto for the war of independence that followed. Three months later, as British and French forces occupied Istanbul, a fledgling parliament for a Turkish republic calling itself the Grand National Assembly of Turkey (Türkiye Büyük Millet Meclisi, or TBMM) opened its first session in Ankara. Ten days later, the body declared Kemal the official head of a new Turkish state and official representative of the Turkish people in Anatolia. This declaration not only challenged the Allied partition of Anatolia but further discredited the lingering Ottoman government in Istanbul.[33]

Less than two years after Ottoman defeat in World War I, Kemal had succeeded in reorienting the Turkish political landscape away from Istanbul and the House of Osman to his leadership and a new capital in Ankara. By consolidating his authority over the Turkish national movement, Kemal had also effectively sidelined his greatest rivals to power—the former unionist leadership and Enver and Cemal in particular, although the latter pair continued to support the resistance from outside Anatolia. As subsequent events would reveal, former Ottoman Fourth Army commander and naval minister Cemal Pasha in particular would bolster ties between the new Turkish government and Afghanistan.[34]

Among the first foreign policy decisions of the nascent Ankara government was to dispatch emissaries to Baku, Azerbaijan, and Kabul, Afghanistan. Along with the Soviet Union, Azerbaijan and Afghanistan were the first countries in the world to recognize the Ankara-based government as the official representative of Turkey.[35] The significance of Ankara and Kabul strengthening ties when both countries were fighting wars of independence against European powers—especially Britain—can hardly be overstated. In one of his most famous speeches of the independence struggle, in the northeastern city of Erzerum in late July 1919, the similarities between two predominantly Muslim peoples waging wars of independence against the British was not lost on the late Ottoman general: "The army of Afghanistan is battling against British policies aimed at the annihilation of their nation," Kemal remarked, praising the Afghans' struggle for liberation under Aman Allah's leadership.[36] In his comments on the wars of independence under way in both countries, the Turkish leader went so far as to draw parallels between the participation of border-crossing Pashtuns in guerrilla attacks on British installations, and his own campaign to recruit Ottoman government officials and lay Turks to join the nationalist resistance in Anatolia: "[T]he border tribes whom the British expected to receive support from," Kemal was enthused to point out, "have sided with Afghanistan and this is why the British soldiers were compelled to withdraw as the newspapers are admitting."[37]

That Kemal and Aman Allah took great interest in each other's national struggles was also reported by British intelligence exchanges records from 1919 to 1920. For example, the commanding general officer of the British army of the Black Sea in Constantinople wrote to the Indian army commander in chief in Delhi concerning Afghans planning to attend the nationalist conference at Sivas in

September 1919.[38] The presence of Afghans at the historic Sivas national congress is also confirmed by firsthand accounts in archival records of the Institute for the History of the Turkish Revolution at Ankara University.[39] Other evidence indicates the presence of Afghan liaisons in other Turkish cities, including within the sultan's palace in Istanbul, where an Afghan national was reported to be working as a librarian "as a cloak for political activities."[40]

Most of all, the greatest demonstration of an emerging Turco-Afghan entente was the direct correspondence between Kemal's government and Aman Allah's. A trove of letters and telegrams in Ankara state archives attests to Kemal's continual requests for information about conditions in Afghanistan between 1919 and 1923.[41] Here, the Ankara-based government relied on two emissaries in particular: the former Ottoman navy and Fourth Army commander Cemal Pasha, and an Indo-Turkish military officer of Pashtun Waziri origin, Abdurrahman Samdani Peşaveri (1886–1925). Better known as Peşaverli Abdurrahman Bey in late Ottoman and early Republican parlance, the latter was personally chosen by Kemal to be his personal letter-bearer to Aman Allah. An Indian Pashtun of Peshawar, NWFP, Abdurrahman migrated to Anatolia to serve as a medic for the Turks in the Balkan Wars, and subsequently enlisted for Ottoman military service during World War I.[42] Described as "a well-known Indian revolutionary" in some of the earliest records of the Turkish republic, in spite of his foreign origins the Pashtun Turk ascended the ranks of the new Turkish army with prodigious success. Abdurrahman Bey eventually earned Kemal's confidence for his special knowledge of Iran, Eastern Turkistan, and the Indo-Afghan frontier.[43]

On August 18, 1920, hardly a week after the Treaty of Sèvres had partitioned the former Ottoman territories of Anatolia among the victors of World War I, the transitional Turkish parliament in Ankara further strengthened relations with Afghanistan by appointing its first official envoy to Kabul. Its choice was Abdurrahman Peşaveri, who served as Ankara's special envoy to Kabul until June 1922, when the Turkish republic announced its first fully fledged ambassador to Afghanistan and chargé d'affaires in Kabul.[44]

Representing a transitional Turkish government competing for recognition with the Ottoman government in Istanbul, Peşaveri had his work cut out. Passing from Erzerum to Moscow, he arrived in Aman Allah's court in the summer of 1921, carrying a letter from Kemal to the amir.[45] Kemal hailed the solidarity between Turks and Afghans in their joint struggle against the British: "[E]ver since the start of their wars with Britain, Afghanistan and Turkey share a common enemy."[46] Promising unity of action against common foes, the letter would begin a lifelong friendship between Kemal and Aman Allah.

Aman Allah's correspondence with Kemal in the same period reflected similar sentiments. In a letter from the Afghan amir that was read aloud to the Turkish parliament in Ankara, Aman Allah described his elation at the arrival of the Turkish envoy in Kabul and his high hopes for the future of Turco-Afghan ties: "Turkey shares the ties of an Islamic spirit with Afghanistan which can never erode. Turkish officers from time to time come here and provide their services to Afghanistan. Together, for the love of God, let us work towards our main goal: for the people of Islam to increase in unity."[47]

The formation of a Turco-Afghan entente in the early 1920s owed its beginnings to more than fraternal sentiments, however. As a rare sovereign Muslim-majority state amid European colonial powers, Afghanistan provided the nationalist movement in Anatolia with needed recognition as the official government of Turkey at a time when an Ottoman government and titular sultan-caliph were still based in Istanbul. Following a surge of correspondence and emissary exchanges in the months leading up to Afghanistan's independence in 1919 and continuing through Turkey's war of independence, an alliance between the two governments was formalized in another historic agreement, in spring 1921.

Turco-Afghan Entente Made Official

On March 1, 1921, representatives of the Turkish nationalist movement in Anatolia and of the amirate of Afghanistan met in Moscow to establish official diplomatic relations.[48] Recognizing the bonds of Islam and anti-imperialism between "two brother states, nations, and governments of the East," the Turco-Afghan Alliance Agreement promised mutual support and partnership between Turkey and Afghanistan in times of "happiness or misfortune."[49] In this formal pact Ankara officially recognized Afghanistan's independence; in return, Kabul acknowledged Kemal as the leader of a nationalist resistance in Turkey and the TBMM in Ankara as the sole legitimate representative of the Turkish nation. The agreement also stipulated that both parties must consult each other before concluding agreements with foreign adversaries of either state. It was also significant for the role of Moscow serving as hosts for the pact.[50]

Standard diplomatic protocols followed, but with an air of fraternity and comradeship. Plans were announced for the construction of an Afghan embassy in Ankara—one of the first foreign legations to be built in the city and new capital of Turkey.[51] Less than two months later, on June 10, 1921, the Afghan embassy celebrated its official opening with a gathering attended by Kemal, leading members of the Ankara national parliament, and Soviet diplomats.[52] During the ceremony Kemal raised the Afghan flag over the embassy, after which Kabul's first official ambassador to Ankara, Sultan Ahmad Khan, delivered words of gratitude and praise for the strengthening of ties between the two countries: "The Afghan nation's dream of sending an ambassadorial commission to Turkey, whom the Afghan nation has abiding respect for, is guided by, and considers a leader for itself, has finally come true . . . The acceptance of our ambassadorial commission, by Turkey's Grand National Assembly and its President makes us proud."[53] Not to be outdone in fraternal sentiments, the Afghan ambassador was joined by effusive comments from Kemal. The president and leader of the Turkish national movement had the following to say in response:

> As in Afghanistan, in Turkey our hearts beat together in brotherhood. For some reasons these ties were prevented from taking a concrete form. Until recently official relations were not able to be established. Thankfully, during this Anatolian independence struggle we have succeeded in doing so. The arrival of your commission is a source of pride for all of us. The joint efforts of Turkey and Afghanistan, working hand in hand, are critical to maintaining a balance in the political world.[54]

Beyond mutual political recognition and friendship, the first official treaty between the Turkish nationalist movement and Afghanistan contained several other notable clauses of a concrete and institutionalized nature. According to Article 7, Turkey promised military and educational training to Afghanistan, including the sending of officers and teachers for terms of at least five years, after which Kabul could request continuation. Kemal also informed the Afghan amir that joining the diplomatic mission would be a group of Turkish military officers to help advise the new Afghan government.[55] Such measures were in continuity and in addition to the Ottoman officers already serving the Afghan government in Kabul, including constitutional advisor and lawyer Osman Bedri Bey and military instructors Mahmud Sami and Ziya Bey, among others. Some of the latter assisted Afghan linguists in producing Ottoman Turkish lan-

FIGURE 4.1. "The Girl Writes," from *Kitab-i Alifba-yi Turki* (The ABCs of Ottoman Turkish), a lesson book for Afghan children, Kabul, 1920/1921. Afghanistan Digital Library, Kabul/New York (adl10302).

guage and grammar books for Afghan school children, replete with side-by-side Dari and Pashto translations (see Figure 4.1), while some Ottoman officers authored their own Persian grammar guides, probably for use by the Turks in Kabul.[56]

Afghanistan would become among the first countries to which Turkey would send successive delegations of officers and teachers in the early years of the republic. Although preceding the official establishment of the Turkish republic by over two years, the Turco-Afghan Alliance Agreement established a unity of aims and series of exchanges that would define relations between the two countries for decades to come.[57]

Although the agreement was a watershed, the strengthened relations between Turks and Afghans represented not so much the dawn of a new era of Turco-Afghan cooperation as a maturation of bonds that had been established earlier and cultivated in a more ad hoc fashion during the late Ottoman era. Nothing symbolized this more than the presence of Ottoman officials in Kabul who had arrived in Afghanistan before the war, including Colonel Mahmud Sami, as well as a band of former Porte officials fleeing prosecution by the Allies or occupied Ottoman government in Istanbul.[58] Among them was the former CUP triumvirate member and Ottoman army and naval commander during World War I, Cemal Pasha.

The Last Ottomans: Cemal Pasha and Enver Pasha in Central Asia

On October 27, 1920, two years after fleeing Istanbul following the Ottoman Empire's defeat in World War I, the former Ottoman naval minister, army commander, and CUP triumvirate member Cemal Pasha crossed into Afghanistan.[59] During the war Cemal had overseen the Syria, Palestine, and Sinai fronts, where he earned a reputation for ruthless diktats and the sobriquet of *al-Saffah* (Bloodspiller) for his harsh repression of Arabist dissidents in Damascus in particular. Most notoriously, evidence to date indicates Cemal played a leading role in the deportations and massacres of Ottoman Armenians during World War I, casting a long shadow over the life and activities of this controversial and seemingly ubiquitous figure of the empire's last days.[60]

Cemal is much less known for his activities in Afghanistan after the armistice. Along with Mahmud Sami, who had been active in Kabul since the late Hamidian era, it was Cemal and his assistant commander Ziya Bey who made a concerted effort to reorient the conscription and training of Afghan armed forces according to Ottoman or "Sultani" style.[61] For an Afghan amir who already exhibited Turcophile attitudes and was eager to reorganize his army along modern, conscription- and infantry-based lines, the former Ottoman military leader's arrival in Kabul could not have come at a more propitious time. Before long Cemal was appointed by Aman Allah as general inspector for the new Afghan army with these goals in mind.

In accordance with Aman Allah's expressed wish, Cemal established a new model regiment known as the *Kıta-i Numune* in Ottoman Turkish, including a proposal for new training methods, drill patterns, and even uniforms based on the last Ottoman army in history.[62] With the goal of acquiring the necessary supplies, manpower, and technical expertise, Cemal sent Mustafa Kemal a letter informing him of the amir's need for more officers, stating that salaries in gold, expenses, and comforts would be paid by Aman Allah himself.[63] Here, the history behind Cemal's assignment in Kabul had as much to do with Anatolian developments as it did with Aman Allah's state-building goals. Following his November 1918 flight from Istanbul, Cemal arrived in Germany, but he and other unionists struggled to regroup. During his stay in Europe, Cemal was invited by Aman Allah to come to Afghanistan, where his services could be duly employed. Aman Allah's letter made an impression, for Cemal departed soon thereafter for Afghanistan via Russia.[64]

While in Russia, Cemal met with Soviet leaders in Moscow, furthering discussions for a new system of alliances in the east. After informing them of his intentions to form a combined Turco-Afghan-Soviet pact against the British in India, Cemal obtained permission from Moscow to travel to Afghanistan via Turkistan and Herat in the summer of 1920.[65] His mission struck a familiar chord: to make contact with Afghan and Indian revolutionaries in order to incite an insurrection within India. "Islam's lucky star is about to be born in the East," Cemal confidently declared, describing independent Afghanistan under the young and staunchly pro-Turkish Aman Allah. In June of the same year, still in Moscow, Cemal wrote to Kemal suggesting the idea of sending a military delegation to Afghanistan. It was a subject he would reiterate in continual letters to Ankara through the summer and autumn of 1920, and especially after his arrival in Kabul in late October.[66]

On December 21, 1920, following successive appeals by Cemal to the Anatolian nationalist leadership to send Turkish officers to Kabul, Mustafa Kemal instructed Turkish national minister of defense Fevzi Çakmak Pasha to organize a special military delegation to Kabul. It seems that after some initial hesitations, Cemal's arguments for the pivotal role Afghanistan could play for the Turkish resistance had won over Kemal: "As a strong army in Central Asia is very important to protecting Anatolia," Kemal is reported to have noted in his instructions to the delegation, "it will be a means of bogging down the British in India far from Anatolia."[67]

Although pleased with the positive response from Ankara, Cemal was beset by a range of obstacles facing his mission in Kabul. In addition to the need for more officers, among the logistical challenges he faced was a lack of supplies to train and arm an efficient Afghan military. Realizing these were not forthcoming from Anatolia or Afghanistan, Cemal set his sights on persuading Russia and Germany to provide the needed supplies, weapons, and capital. He also hoped to attract the interest of capital-rich investors in Europe to secure Afghanistan's economic development.[68] With these goals in mind, Cemal departed Kabul for Moscow in early September 1921.[69]

Cemal's subsequent letters from Russia to Mustafa Kemal and Aman Allah demonstrate the continued primacy with which he held Afghanistan, and its pivotal role in regional geopolitics.[70] Correspondence between Cemal and leaders of the resistance in Anatolia also make it clear that the former CUP triumvirate member had much more in mind than training Afghan cadets. Rather, Cemal sought to transform Afghanistan into a launching ground for wider Asian ambitions in the battle against their chief nemesis, the British: "The insurrection must be nurtured here," wrote Cemal in another letter to Ankara. "In all the face of the earth, it is impossible to find a suitable place to launch a revolution in India other than Afghanistan."[71] Convinced he was at the center rather than on the periphery of a new phase in Turkey's war of independence, Cemal proposed three successive projects for Afghanistan's "revolutionary modernization," focusing on enhancing the economic, infrastructural, and military strength of the state. The first stage involved establishing a national bank in Afghanistan to attract and manage the capital needed for the large-scale projects to come; the second, building a railroad between Kabul and the northeastern city of Mazar-i Sharif, near the border with Russian Turkistan; and the third, attracting investors to exploit minerals and precious metals in Afghanistan. With these goals in mind, on November 12, 1921, while he traveled through Soviet Central Asia, Cemal wrote Kemal stating his intention to travel to Germany to procure funds and supplies before returning to Kabul. Two days later, Cemal also wrote Aman Allah informing him of the same.[72]

Kemal's reported conviction in Cemal's Afghan mission notwithstanding, in practice the Ankara government was slow to follow up. In spite of repeated requests from Cemal through the summer, autumn, and winter of 1921, the promised delegation had still not arrived.[73] Yet all other indications were that Kemal continued to encourage and believe in Cemal's activities in Kabul. On New Year's Day, 1922, as the Turkish army prepared for a major assault in Anatolia, Kemal reassured Cemal of his confidence in the Kabul mission: "Your service in Afghanistan will be beneficial to the Turkish nation and homeland."[74] The letter did not, however, provide a concrete response to Cemal's request for more officers or information on their anticipated arrival.

As Cemal waited for the promised delegation of officers and supplies to arrive in Kabul, conditions in Central Asia remained fluid. Just north of Afghanistan a major shift was underway in relations between the CUP exiles Enver and Cemal and the Soviet leadership in Moscow. Following an initial rapprochement with Russia's revolutionary government after the latter's withdrawal from World War I, and the safe passage Moscow provided to several CUP exiles in the years immediately after the armistice, by the summer of 1922 both Cemal and Enver had grown increasingly estranged from the Soviets. According to Zafer Hasan Aybek's memoir, by then the Russians had already retracted the promises of assistance they had made to the Afghans in light of Enver's support of anti-Soviet Basmachi rebels in Bukhara.[75]

Two major developments were at the root of the newfound bad blood. First, in the Russo-Turkish Treaty of February 1921, Moscow had formally recognized Kemal as the official leader of a new Turkish government in Ankara, further marginalizing the former CUP officials in Turkish internal politics. Second, the Red Army's conquest of Bukhara in 1920, part of a larger annexation of Turkistan (Central Asia), struck an all-too familiar pattern to the former Ottoman commander Cemal. The latter had made the fateful decision of joining forces with his former unionist triumvirate leader Enver—who had since been galvanizing pan-Turkic resistance in Soviet Central Asia—in stirring anti-Russian resistance among the predominantly Turkic Muslim Basmachis from Afghanistan's northern border to Samarqand. On July 21, 1922, while traveling between the Caucuses and Turkistan, Cemal was shot and killed by three assassins avenging the massacres of Armenians during World War I. Two weeks later, on August 4, 1922, Enver was killed in battle against the Red Army outside Dushanbe.[76]

Afghan and British sources offer contradictory accounts of the public response in Afghanistan to the demise of both Ottoman leaders.[77] On October 2, 1922, Aman Allah's government declared a countrywide day of mourning for both Cemal and Enver. The official *Aman-i Afghan* newspaper of Kabul dedicated whole sections of its autumn 1922 issues to the life and death of Cemal, as well as to the growing Turkish community in the capital. On October 7, 1922, the *Aman-i Afghan* published photographs of Enver and several Ottoman officers accompanying him while on an expedition in Turkistan. The same issue contained a discussion of Cemal's death, culminating with a eulogy. A related section on Turco-Afghan ties concluded on more optimistic tones, displaying a photograph of Afghanistan Independence Day celebrations in Ankara, underscoring that the ties between Turkey and Afghanistan were alive and well.[78]

According to India Office intelligence reports from October, however, even after the Afghan government's attempts to memorialize the late CUP officials, shops in Kabul remained open as usual, with no signs of public unrest—to say nothing of provincial towns and villages outside of the capital.[79] The conflicting accounts of Cemal Pasha's memory in Afghanistan also reflects an ambivalence about his legacy in Kabul. On the one hand, the *Kıta-i Numune* (model regiment) Cemal established during his tenure as chief instructor of the Afghan armed forces continued to be upheld by the amir as the blueprint for his new Afghan army. In accordance with the Friendship Agreement signed between Turkey and Afghanistan in March 1921, beginning in the summer of 1922 officers from Turkey were sent to Kabul to train Afghan soldiers, with select higher-rank Afghan officers to be sent to Turkey for advanced training.[80] In this way some of the most important projects launched under the aegis of Cemal during his short stay in Afghanistan continued beyond his death.

On the other hand, the enforcement of Cemal's new model regiment stoked old tensions between those favoring "Sultani"-style training, as Ottoman drilling practices were known, and those favoring more familiar British models espoused by Afghan officers trained in India, such as Nadir Khan. In an internal communiqué between British intelligence agencies in India and Afghanistan that autumn, the British representative at Kabul went so far as to state, "Jemal Pasha's scheme of army reorganization appears to have been definitely discarded, and shortly afterwards his new formation, the 'Qita Namuna', was disbanded."[81]

As seen in the correspondence between Cemal and Kemal, however, the strategic objective of stationing Turkish officers in Kabul had as much if not more to do with regional political goals as it did with a single-minded training of Afghan officers and soldiers. Some of the Turkish officers stationed in Kabul used the Afghan capital as a base to monitor British activity in India, as one of the last Ottoman archival records on Afghanistan illustrates.[82] As a personal rival to Kemal's political ascendance, Cemal was also a complicated representative of the Turkish republic, to say the least. As a former Ottoman triumvirate member accustomed to being at the apex of command structures and issuing orders to subordinates, Cemal did not always see eye to eye with members of Aman Allah's government either, including officials in the foreign ministry.[83] Still, the impact of Cemal's arrival in Afghanistan outlived him in several other ways relevant to the amir's state-building efforts. Some of the pasha's unionist associates who accompanied him in exile to Afghanistan would go on to make lasting contributions to Afghanistan in the civil and administrative realm; chief among them was the former Istanbul attorney and governor of Aleppo, Osman Bedri Bey (1881–1923), about whom we will have more to say later.

Far from dying with him, Turco-Afghan ties seem to have only strengthened in the months after Cemal's death, lending credence to the theory that Cemal Pasha—an old-party unionist leader and polarizing figure with a tattered reputation—was not the best representative of a new Turkish republic led by his own rival for power, Mustafa Kemal Pasha. One of the most visible signs of the resilience of Turco-Afghan ties at this time was Ankara's readiness to upgrade its diplomatic presence in Afghanistan to a fully fledged embassy. In October 1922, just weeks after the day of national mourning observed in Afghanistan for Cemal and Enver Pashas, the parliament of the nascent Turkish republic announced its first official ambassador and chargé d'affaires in Kabul.

Fahreddin Pasha and Republican Pan-Islam

Turkey's first official ambassador to Afghanistan was also an Ottoman officer and veteran of World War I. General Ömer Fahreddin Pasha (1868–1948) was the commander and governor of Medina during the Hejazi revolt (1916–1919), a venerated role for which he earned the honorific title "Tiger of the Desert" (*Çöl Kaplanı*).[84] Following his two-year internment by the British as a prisoner of war on the island of Malta, Fahreddin returned to Anatolia to fight in the war of independence under Kemal, leading units against French and Greek armies. In selecting a celebrated war hero who had defended the hallowed city of Medina against a British-supported siege, there are echoes of Abdülhamid II's decision to appoint the late Ottoman scholar Ahmed Hulusi as the Porte's first official envoy to Kabul in 1877. Though the Defender of Medina (as Fahreddin Pasha was also known) was not a scholar by any stretch, both Hulusi and Fahreddin were selected as emissaries to Afghanistan not for their extensive diplomatic experience—of which they both apparently had little—but for their impeccable "Pan-Islamic" credentials.[85]

Fahreddin's tenure as Ankara's representative in Kabul (1922–1926) coincided with Turkey's transition from a multiethnic empire to a secular republic. It also followed Abdurrahman Peşaveri's inaugural post as the Anatolian resistance's special representative to Kabul (1920–1922) and Cemal's tenure as lead trainer of the new Afghan army (1920–1921). In spite of the landmark shifts occurring in Anatolia during this time, there was a surprising amount of continuity with regard to the Turkish ambassador's job description. Fahreddin's primary duties in Kabul involved establishing a permanent diplomatic corps in Kabul and furthering Ankara's military and educational assistance in Afghanistan in line with the 1921 Turco-Afghan Alliance Agreement.[86] In this way Fahreddin continued where Peşaveri and Cemal had left off, dispatching intelligence on Central Asia and India to Ankara and facilitating the arrival of Turkish officers, teachers, doctors, and other professionals for short-term service in the Afghan government's military or civilian branches. Fahri Pasha, as he was more commonly known in Turkish and British sources, continued to represent Turkey in Pan-Islamic causes, including the collection of donations from Afghans and Indian Muslims for the war of independence in Anatolia. The latter was a foundational pillar of the Central Khilafat Committee (CKC) and broader Indian Khilafat movement.[87]

No doubt boosted by his sterling reputation, it did not take the Turkish ambassador long to make an impression in his new surroundings. British minister at Kabul Sir Richard Roy Machonachie (1885–1962) described Fahreddin's arrival in the capital as having a catalyzing effect on the Turkish expatriate community, and his influence on the amir profound: "The most prominent figure in Kabul at the moment is Fakhri Pasha," Machonachie noted in the summer of 1922, adding that the decorated war hero was "in the Amir's closest confidence, and with his arrival Turkish influence has attained its zenith."[88] Along with his secretarial staff, government records from Ankara indicate the new republic's first ambassador to Afghanistan was joined by a Turkish doctor and courier.[89] British sources were also keen to note that a former Indian Muslim subject in the British army, Surkha "Abbas Effendi," who had deserted to Ottoman lines during battle in Mesopotamia, accompanied the Turkish ambassador. Abbas Effendi was employed as a linguist at the Turkish embassy and also served as a cavalry instructor at the Kabul Harbiye.[90]

Although Fahreddin's arrival in Kabul signaled that Turco-Afghan bilateral relations had matured, some observers claimed to identify cracks beneath the seemingly rock-solid entente. Fahreddin was able to forge robust connections with Indian Muslims mobilizing in support of the Ottoman caliphate and Turkish war of independence, but some hinted that his influence with the amir may not have been so stalwart after all. On November 17, 1922, hardly a month after Fahreddin's arrival in Kabul, the British minister at Kabul telegrammed the British secretary of state for foreign affairs in London: "There are indications that Fakhri Pasha's personal popularity with the Amir is on the wane." The report goes so far as to claim that the former Turkish special envoy to Kabul, Abdurrahman Peşaveri, had already departed for Herat en route to

Anatolia, where "he intends to report to Kemal that Fakhri's mission to Kabul has failed."[91] Unsurprisingly, such observations often came from those who were most eager to see Turkish failure: the British in Kabul.

This is not to suggest descriptions offered by British states were always off the mark. According to Machonachie, the same British minister at Kabul who had described Fahreddin's soaring popularity upon his arrival in Afghanistan, real geographic, strategic, and even ideological obstacles impeded a Turco-Afghan alliance from realizing its goals in the long term. As the British minister penned in a secret memorandum to the secretary of state for foreign affairs in London on the subject of bilateral ties between Turkey and Afghanistan, such obstacles were initially obscured due to the highly charged and euphoric atmosphere created by both nations fighting simultaneous wars of independence against a common foe. But it was only a matter of time, Machonachie opined, before more deep-seated structural cleavages manifested in the relationship: "There is no historical or geographical connection between the two countries," the British minister emphasized, "while the Pan-Turanian programme must necessarily entail the absorption of Afghan Turkistan in the Turkish dominions, and is therefore a direct threat to the integrity of Afghanistan."[92]

Emphasizing the noncontiguous geographical realities of the two countries, but also lingering Greater Turan ambitions embedded in some of the more extreme iterations of Turkish nationalism, Machonachie was not oblivious to the bonds of religious solidarity and anticolonial struggle shared between Turks and Afghans. But what the British minister sought to highlight—and encourage, we can surmise—was a sense that the Turco-Afghan entente was a fleeting moment, born out of emotion and particular historical circumstances, rather than an abiding alliance. When faced with the harsh realities of each state's unique geostrategic interests, divergence was inevitable, and it was only a matter of time before the two countries found themselves at odds. The ebb and flow of Turco-Iranian relations, Machonachie was keen to analogize, was also obscured by a similarly short-term rapprochement at the time and taught them just as much: "Persia with the imminent menace of Turkish aggression in Azerbaijan before her eyes, has already realized the danger involved in this movement, masquerading as it does in Pan-Islamic guise, and if a Turkish conquest of Azerbaijan becomes an accomplished fact, it is possible that Afghanistan may take the warning to heart."[93]

Machonachie likely overstated the extent of Turkish republican ambitions in Central Asia—there is little evidence, for example, to suggest Kemal seriously intended to resume the same anti-Soviet campaigns that Enver and Cemal had launched in Bukhara and Turkistan before their deaths. The British minister's dismissal of Turkish ties to Afghanistan was not entirely accurate either, whether considering the Timurid, Safavid, and Mughal periods of rule when Afghan territory was incorporated into Turkic empires, or more significantly, late Ottoman histories of exchange as illustrated earlier. But in a foresighted assessment of subterranean cracks that very much were under the surface of Ankara and Kabul's alliance in the early 1920s, Machonachie noted the critical role of the Ottoman caliphate as the root of Pan-Islamic ties between the Turks and Afghans, but also its potential Achilles' heel: "[W]ere the Angora Government to carry out their alleged design of reducing the Sultan to the status of a puppet Caliph without a vestige of temporal power," predicted Machonachie, "the alliance might be severely tested by the resentment which such a policy would arouse among orthodox Afghans."[94] As events would show after the Turkish republic's abolition of the Ottoman sultanate in 1922, and caliphate in 1924, Machonachie's prediction turned out to be remarkably accurate in this respect.

Other British predictions—to say nothing of desires—of an impending collapse in Turco-Afghan relations focused on essentializing notions of an inherent cultural divide between Turks and Afghans, especially between their respective military officers: "[T]he manners of the Angora Turk are not ingratiating," noted one British official writing from Kabul in August 1922, "and the Afghan officers of the old school do not conceal their jealousy of the Turkish instructors who are displacing them."[95] There was likely some truth to these claims. In the early 1900s, Mahmud Sami arrived in Kabul to head the premier military training academy in the country just as the Indian-born and educated Nadir Khan was rising through the ranks of Habib Allah's Afghan army. Beyond the rivalry between these two powerful actors in particular, British agents in Kabul saw ample potential discord to exploit between the Ottoman-trained and British-trained Afghan officers during Habib Allah's reign.

It is all the more likely such tensions were exacerbated during the Aman Allah period, not least when the early appointment of another outsider with a much more blistering reputation for authoritarianism, Cemal Pasha, was appointed to completely overhaul the Afghan armed forces. For all these reasons, British officials in Kabul were not just observing and hoping for a wrench in the Turco-Afghan alliance, but planning on future internal discord: "The present *rapprochement* between Angora and Afghanistan appears then rather to be due to a political accident than to rest on a natural and permanent bond of union," Machonachie concluded in a tone of optimism. "When the lack of common secular interests has become apparent, the religious tie may be found inadequate to hold the two countries together."[96]

Notwithstanding the real potential for divisive rivalries within the Kabul court, the years 1919 to 1923 of Aman Allah's reign were ultimately defined not by personal discord between individual officers, nor even by the personal friendship of the two seemingly larger-than-life figures of Kemal and Aman Allah, but by a bigger and more complex story of two nations fighting concurrent wars of independence amid the collapse of the Ottoman Empire. The formation of a historic alliance promising mutual friendship and assistance was not simply a fleeting moment, nor even a marriage of convenience, but one that enriched the possibilities of Aman Allah's state-building project in Afghanistan. Contrary to British predictions, it is also a relationship that continues in many respects to this day.

Still, it is nevertheless true that Turco-Afghan ties in the 1920s, or any other period, were historically contingent and a constant work in progress. As subsequent events would reveal, the Turco-Afghan entente after World War I was neither a project of establishing a singular Pan-Islamic caliphate nor a Pan-Turanian empire, but an exercise in bilateral relations between two states committed to territorial nationalism and the ethnic nation-state model. It is worth recalling in this regard Mustafa Kemal's strict instructions to the first Turkish officers to arrive in Kabul during the reign of Aman Allah: "This commission must not in any form take part in political struggles; you are to engage in strictly military duties, and you will find yourself becoming extraordinarily dear to the Afghan, Turkistani, and Bukharan people and soldiers."[97]

His Pan-Islamic credentials notwithstanding, Fahreddin's assignment as Turkish chargé d'affaires in Afghanistan was no less clearly defined, although it was considerably more complex than the work of Turkish military trainers. As with any other foreign legation, the ambassador's duties and that of the republic's new diplomatic corps in Afghanistan included attending to the growing Turkish community's needs in Kabul and preserving good relations with the Afghan government. But by late 1923 into early 1924, Fahreddin was also tasked with maintaining the delicate balance of upholding Turkey's prestige among Muslims worldwide as defenders of the faith and house of the caliphate, just as these distinctions were being eroded in the new republic itself. What is more, Fahreddin's tenure as ambassador to Afghanistan coincided with Turkey negotiating new and improved postbellum relations with Britain.[98] Such were the tensions and nuances built into Turkish and Afghan states in flux during the contentious, tumultuous, and uncertain years of the 1920s.[99]

Crucial as their joint wars of independence were to the making of a Turco-Afghan treaty and entente, to limit the story of Aman Allah's foreign policy to that would miss a crucial third leg of the triangular relations driving Afghan Pan-Islamism at this time. As both Turkey and Afghanistan turned an important page in their relations with London by renegotiating treaties that promised cooperation and possibly even friendship with Britain, Indian Muslim migrants—the third leg of the Pan-Islamic triangle in Kabul—were not nearly as disposed to reconcile with the British and put aside differences with their colonial overseers.

Playing with Fire: Amir Aman Allah and the Indian Muhājirs

Beginning in July 1920, processions of Muslim migrants hailing primarily from the Indian provinces of NWFP, Punjab, and Sindh and numbering several thousand packed their belongings, sold their properties, and began a westward journey in the summer heat to Afghanistan. Unlike the cataclysmic events of partition roughly a quarter century later, these emigrants were relocating not to a newly imagined nation for Indian Muslims to be named Pakistan but to the geographically closest state ruled by an independent Muslim sovereign: Afghanistan. During one memorable crossing on the morning of August 14, 1920, an estimated seven thousand migrants departed from the Indian border town of Landi Kotal through the winding mountain slopes leading to the border with Afghanistan. Before long, the Khyber Pass was clogged with caravans of farmers and nomads, tending their animals and pushing bullock carts with their life's possessions on board.[100] Singing and chanting to themes of divine deliverance, prophetically inspired migration, and a promised land for all, when the Indian migrants confronted a meager Afghan border guard of fifty men attempting to blockade the road, it was the latter who yielded.[101]

As reflected in the spirited group of migrants above, there is little doubt the passage of tens of thousands of Muslims from British India to Afghanistan in 1920–1921 was partly inspired by the Prophet of Islam's migration, or Hijra (Urdu: Hijrat), from Mecca to Medina in 622 CE. It would be mistaken, however, to characterize the Indian Hijrat to Afghanistan as an antiquated, backward-looking movement. Seen through the lens of its primary sponsor, Aman Allah Khan, this remarkable exodus of people had much more to do with modern notions of anticolonial struggle, Afghan state building, and Muslim modernism in power than it did with resurrecting medieval notions of a so-called Abode of War and Abode of Islam.[102] Historians trying to understand the movement must, after all, address the following question: What drove tens of thousands of British Indian subjects to abandon their ancestral homes and migrate to Afghanistan at this time?[103]

Studies of mass migrations often involve a consideration of push and pull factors. According to one historian of the movement, the invitations of Aman Allah were an important pull factor. By gambling on the "excited state of mind" of Indian Muslims in the charged atmosphere of Ottoman defeat in World War I and burgeoning Khilafat movement across the subcontinent, Aman Allah sought to capitalize on his own visions for a Greater Afghanistan, including a possible recapture of Pashtun ancestral lands in the frontier. In at least one speech in the spring preceding the Hijrat movement, Aman Allah welcomed any Muslims, and even Hindus, who sought to make a new home in the free Afghan domains.[104] Aman Allah also attended the historic All-India Khilafat Conference at Bombay in February 1920, where the Indian independence activist brothers Mohamed Ali and Shaukat Ali were reported to be the first to receive the amir.[105] In this sense, Aman Allah's assurances to the Indian Khilafatists must be considered as a substantial impetus for those considering a move to Afghanistan.[106]

Amir Aman Allah (Figure 4.2) did not travel to India again for the same purpose, but he continued to voice his support for the Khilafatists—and to invite them to Afghanistan—through speeches and letters dispatched via diplomatic representatives in India, Europe, and the Middle East.[107] During the Anglo-Afghan peace negotiations at Mussoorie, the Afghan delegation was reported to have encouraged migration to Afghanistan even while it deliberated with the British. When Aman Allah's foreign minister, Mahmud Tarzi, arrived in the northwestern Indian town in April 1920 for the historic peace conference, he was reported to have delivered a rousing speech after Friday prayers at the local mosque, repeating earlier promises by the amir to Indian migrants that they would be welcomed in Afghanistan. Similar promises were made at the Khilafat Workers Conference at Delhi on April 18–19, 1920.[108]

To pit all responsibility for the Indian Hijrat on the overtures of Aman Allah, however, obscures Indian Muslim agency in the migration, as well as more longstanding relationships connecting India and Afghanistan well before Aman Allah's reign. Indian Muslims had served in the courts of Afghan amirs for even longer than their Ottoman Turkish counterparts in Kabul, and mercantile networks

FIGURE 4.2. Amir Aman Allah Khan (r. 1919–1929) (*far right*), in supplication with a visiting delegation. ullstein bild/Getty Images.

and sufi tariqas had for centuries linked markets and populations of the subcontinent to Central Asia via Afghanistan.[109] Among the Indian professionals who had traveled to Afghanistan before the Hijrat were doctors, teachers, and translators serving in the highest echelons of government and best schools of the country since at least the ʿAbd al-Rahman era. The founder of the great Mughal Empire, Babur (1483–1530), had established his first capital in Kabul, where he remains buried until this day.[110] Subsequent Mughal emperors extended their rule over Kandahar and the tribal frontier between Jalalabad and Swat, albeit for a limited time and amid relentless Pashtun insurrection and Safavid contestation.

Still, several unprecedented dimensions of the Indian Hijrat to Afghanistan in the early 1920s distinguished this mass exodus from earlier episodes of Indian contact with and migration to Afghanistan. These include the sheer numbers of the migrants over a short period of time, and the broader regional implications and radical politics of the movement. Emerging at the same time as the Turkish war of independence and following Aman Allah's successful campaign for independence, the Indian Hijrat movement to Afghanistan witnessed the migration of a conservatively estimated sixty thousand muhājirs to Jalalabad, Kabul, and portions of northern Afghanistan, including the surrounding environs of Kunduz and Balkh.[111] The men, women, and children at the heart of this remarkable migration were a diverse assortment of British Indian subjects who, having previously been domiciled on the eastern side of the Durand Line, crossed into Afghanistan beginning in the summer of 1920. According to the British legation at Kabul, the migrants could be divided into four main strands of Indian subjects: Khilafatist agitators and revolutionaries intent on overthrowing British rule in India; economic migrants, including poor, landless peasants from the Punjab and Sindh; British-side Pashtuns with long-standing ties to Afghanistan granted land in the amir's domains; and deserters from the Raj's frontier militias.[112]

The Hijrat movement was far from being a homogeneous group driven by a singular desire to live under a modern-day Dar al-Islam; the assortment of individuals and families represented a convergence of interests ranging from the short-term and pragmatic to the visionary and radical. Among them was a spillover effect of the broader Khilafat movement, particularly the protests of Indian Muslims against an Allied partition of the Ottoman Empire—including the British occupation of Istanbul, Palestine, and Mesopotamia—by voting with their feet. The latter no doubt intersected with the militant motivations of more radical political activists who sought to oust the British from India, vis-à-vis the aid of the Afghans and their unequivocally independent Muslim sovereign in Kabul, Aman Allah. For others, it seems, the Hijrat provided an opportunity for economic advancement, acquiring land, and escaping the oppressive circumstances of semifeudal overlords in India, be they Muslim or not. For still others, the Hijrat movement reflected the ideological urgency with which some Muslims called their coreligionists to live under the rule of shariʿa in a modern Islamic state.

Linked both to a nascent Indian independence movement in British India and to a struggle to save the Ottoman lands from European partition and occupation, the Indian Hijrat to Afghanistan was an early testing ground for the fluid ideals of citizenship Aman Allah had promoted in the early months of his reign, in an atmosphere that was simultaneously Pan-Islamic and Afghan nationalist. Still, the question remains: Was Aman Allah's exhortation to the Indian muhājirs limited to short-term objectives of realpolitik; that is to say, to enhancing Kabul's bargaining position in negotiations with the British? At least one historian has argued just as much: "Their motive in encouraging hijrat was to embarrass the British and thereby to strengthen their own bargaining position at the Mussoorie talks," argues Naeem Qureshi, concluding the gesture was never intended to be serious.[113] There is some evidence in British records to support this view. As remarked in a handwritten note by lead British negotiator Sir Henry Dobbs in the margins of the 1921 Anglo-Afghan Treaty, beyond the official Afghan support for the Indian revolutionaries in Afghanistan lay a more flexible position: "The Afghan delegation pointed out that anyone had a right of asylum in a Moslem country." The minister proceeded to add, however, that the Afghans made an additional message clear to him: "If our material interest were involved, and substantial friendship shown to us, we might perhaps be willing to waive some of these moral scruples."[114]

Sir Dobbs's marginal notes, still visible on the original copy of the 1921 Anglo-Afghan Treaty housed in the India Office records archive in London, call into question the amir's commitment to the Pan-Islamic dimensions of the Hijrat. While the British foreign minister's comments present only one side of the picture, further evidence of Kabul's double-speak on the Hijrat lay in the fact that, in practice, the Afghan authorities were hardly prepared for a full-scale migration. Though some resettlement programs were hastily assembled, in a matter of months after large numbers of Indians began arriving in Kabul the lack of governmental preparation was readily apparent. This was most evident in the contrast migrants experienced between the amir's promises and the paltry arrangements to fulfill them.

Beginning with auspicious promises, Afghan consulates in India circulated a royal *niẓāmnāmih* devoted to the subject of the Indian muhājirs. According to the proclamation, a revised version of which was published in 1923 (see Figure 4.3), each migrant was to receive six to eight *jaribs* of land upon entering the exalted domains, as well as access to interest-free loans (which were payable after three years and could be broken into installments), and other modest start-up provisions free of charge.[115] Moreover, per earlier statements by the amir and his foreign minister Mahmud Tarzi in India, the migrants were entitled to the same rights as Afghan citizens; in effect, legally speaking, they were to become Afghans.[116] Beyond official firmans to this effect, a number of warm receptions afforded to migrants in the Punjab and India's northwest frontier by Hijrat committees suggested they would be enthusiastically received in Afghanistan.[117]

The Indian muhājirs, many of whom had left land and property behind, were soon to be disappointed. By July 1920, British intelligence reported no less than

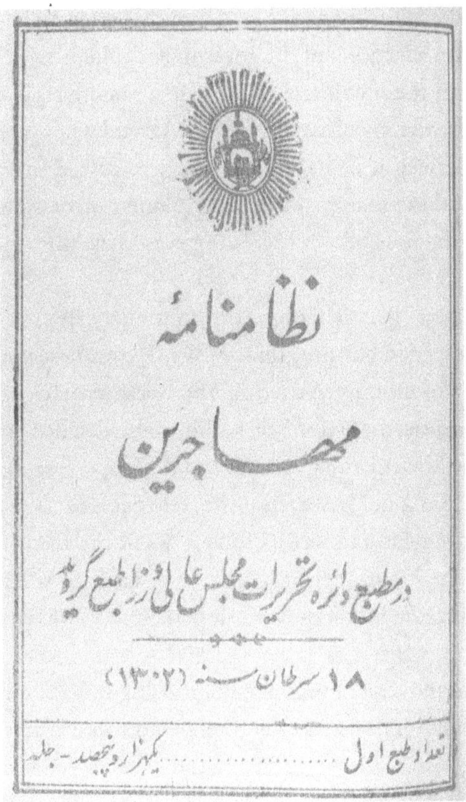

نظامنامه

مهاجرین

در مطبع دائره تحریرات مجلس عالی وزراء طبع گردید

۱۸ سرطان سنه (۱۳۰۲)

تعداد طبع اول .... یکهزار و پنجصد - جلد

FIGURE 4.3.
Nizamnamih-'i Muhajirin (Law Concerning Migrants), Kabul, 1923. Afghanistan Digital Library, Kabul / New York (adl0104).

eighteen thousand persons had left their homes in India for Afghanistan.[118] One month later, seven to eight thousand migrants were reported to be pouring into Afghanistan per week.[119] The numbers soon so overwhelmed the Afghan authorities that when the number of migrants reached thirty thousand, Aman Allah issued a moratorium on the Hijrat, urging that no more Indians be granted entry.[120] The amir's pleas notwithstanding, the migrants continued to make their way to Afghanistan, several following alternative routes to the crossing at the Khyber Pass. According to some estimates, by August as many as forty thousand muhājirs were in the country, the majority languishing in Kabul in makeshift accommodations as they awaited information, and provisions, from the government.[121]

The migrants did not find the promised land they had hoped for. Indian muhājirs were ordered to be temporarily relocated north to the Panjshir Valley or to the northwest region of Afghan Turkistan for two months, after which they would be permanently settled in a location of the government's choosing.[122] The idea of tilling land or serving in the provincial military in a remote region of the country was not welcomed by the majority of muhājirs; several who were already conscripted into military service at Jalalabad had since convinced their fellow migrants of just as much. Making matters worse, then came a succession of postponement orders, delaying the possibility of realizing even these already unsatisfactory plans.

Addressing his subjects at the next ʿId celebration, the amir also expressed frustration at the failure of the resettlement program.[123] While a number of Pashtun migrants from Peshawar eventually settled in the northern city of Kunduz, and Sindhis in the northeastern environs of Balkh, some decided to proceed further west or north to the Soviet Union, Anatolia, and Europe, leaving Afghanistan behind. Most of the muhājirs, however, ultimately decided to return to India: "By August the movement had lost its force," noted the British legation at Kabul in 1920, "and the emigrants began drifting back to their homes."[124] As hastily as it had begun, the Hijrat movement had rapidly come to an unglamorous end.

The collapse of the Indian Hijrat movement was an embarrassing setback for Aman Allah, Afghan representatives in India, and their interlocutors in the subcontinent. It provided a sobering lesson in the limits of radical Pan-Islamic projects for both Afghans and Indian Muslims. For the Afghans, it demonstrated the difficult choices, and priorities, their newly independent country faced and the economic constraints of what being a free Islamic state in the 1920s could mean. For Aman Allah himself it provided a prickling lesson in the limits of Pan-Islamic rhetoric and sentiment when not backed by concrete institutional support and planning. It also led him to the more pragmatic position of supporting the Khilafat movement in India rhetorically and diplomatically, which could strengthen Afghanistan's position in the region and shore up his popularity abroad, without the associated costs of opening the country's borders and extending citizenship to any Muslims willing to migrate.[125] In this way, Aman Allah could satisfy the Janus-faced nature of a Pan-Islamic discourse that aimed to bolster Aman Allah's legitimacy before his own subjects and to boost the international prestige of Afghanistan in a greater "Muslim world" under siege by European colonial powers.[126]

The end of the Indian migration and resettlement of muhājirs in Afghanistan did not spell the end for Pan-Islamic causes in either country. To the contrary, in the months and years that followed, both Afghan and Indian Pan-

Islamism evolved, albeit in different ways. In Afghanistan, as mentioned, Aman Allah adopted a more focused and realist policy of Pan-Islamism that limited itself to the diplomatic and rhetorical fields, but continued to employ Indian and Turkish professionals domestically in a variety of legal, educational, infrastructure, and military projects of state building. As for India, what had earlier during World War I been a covert mission of a relatively small number of agents operating out of UP, Punjab, and the Indo-Afghan frontier, and then a large-scale but still regionally contained Hijrat migration, now mushroomed into an even more popular mass movement known as the Khilafat movement. While firmly anchored in India, the history of the Khilafat movement of 1919–1924 and its relationship to Afghan politics under the early reign of Aman Allah owes its stimulus to events in the greater Middle East immediately following Ottoman defeat in World War I.

Hindustani Crescent: The Indian Khilafat Movement and Afghanistan

On August 10, 1920, the Allied powers signed an agreement at Sèvres, France, partitioning the Ottoman Empire into more than ten new states, internationalized territories, or European "zones of influence"—the harshest terms imposed on any of the Central powers (see Map 3). Two unexpected outcomes, however, emerged from the European accord at Sèvres. First, the Allies considerably underestimated the resistance Turkish nationalist forces, who were as wearied and bloodied as their opponents in the Great War, were willing to put up against the partition of Anatolia. Second, what the signatories also did not anticipate were the vociferous waves of discontent that erupted in distant India in response to the treaty's terms, particularly coming from the subcontinent's Muslims, but also supported by a broader swath of Indian independence activists including the Indian National Congress under Mahatma Gandhi's endorsement.

Incensed by reports of London's double dealing against Turkey during the war, and apparent encouragement to Greek offensives in western Anatolia after it, scores of Indian Muslim organizations mobilized in protest of the partition of Ottoman territory. Many cited pledges made by British prime minister Lloyd George during the war concerning respect for the territorial integrity of the Ottoman domains—or those made by the Indian viceroy as described in Chapter 3. More cynical parties cited a pattern of British duplicity since the Libyan and Balkan Wars of 1911–1913, where London stood by as other European

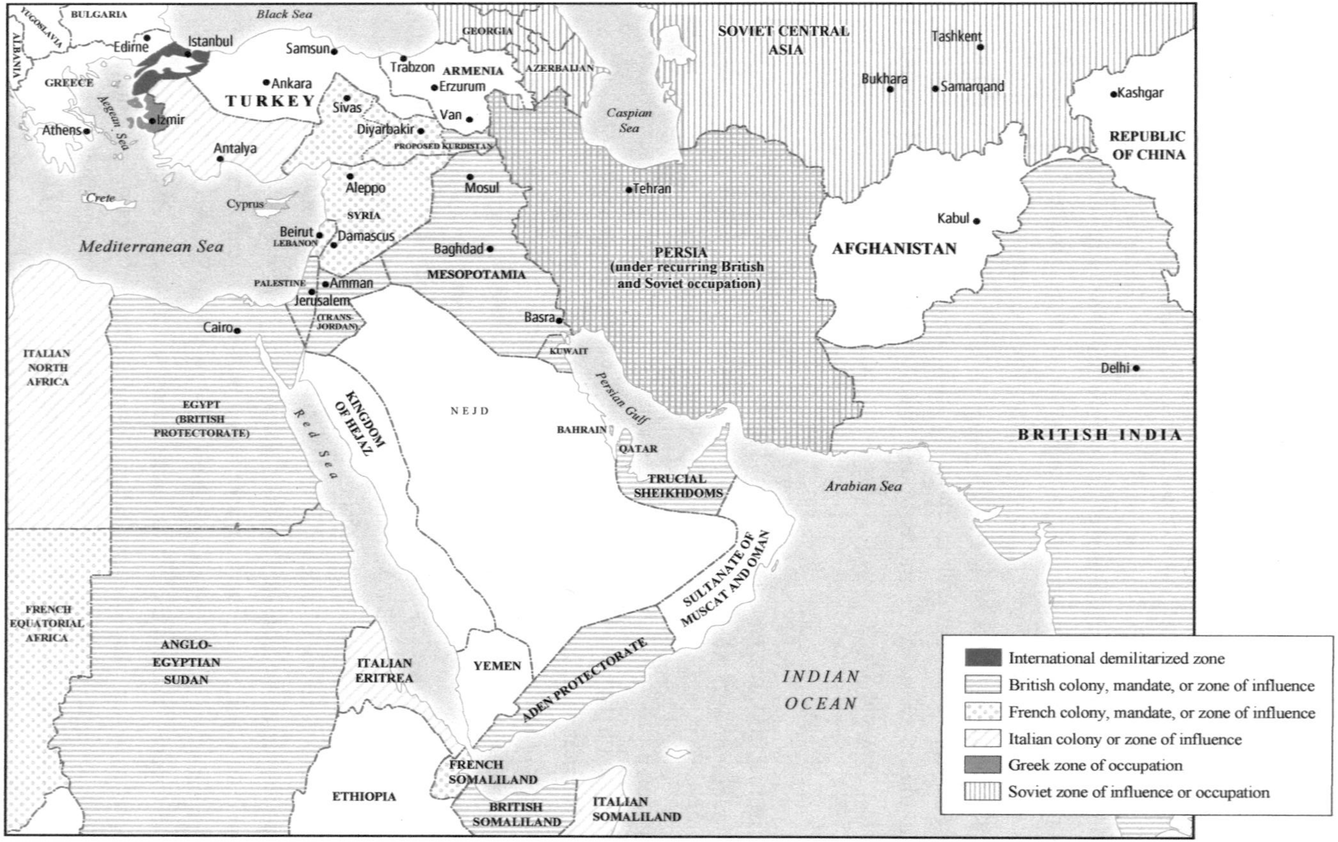

MAP 3. The Middle East as proposed by the Treaty of Sèvres and League of Nations mandates (with surrounding areas), 1920

powers annexed territory ruled by the Ottomans for centuries. As the British chargé d'affaires in Kabul, Sir Richard Machonachie, observed in a dispatch from India, "Seldom if ever can Great Britain's reputation for fair play and good faith have stood lower, in Indian estimation, that it did at this time."[127]

The Indian Khilafat movement (1919–1924) represented a convergence of a broad spectrum of Indian Muslims—but also influential Afghans and sympathetic Hindus, Parsis, and Sikhs—coalescing in opposition to the Allied partition of the Ottoman Empire. The roots of the campaign lay in a widespread malaise over the fate of Turkey following its defeat in World War I. Eventually the movement took a more focused shape under the All-India Khilafat Committee based out of Lucknow under the leadership of prominent Indian Muslim intellectuals and activists including the Oxford-educated Mohamed Ali Jauhar (1878–1931), his brother Shaukat Ali (1873–1939), Mushir Hussain Kidwai (1878–1937), Hakim Ajmal Khan (1868–1927), and Mukhtar Ahmad Ansari (1880–1936), as well leading Indian ulema Abul Kalam Azad (1888–1958) and Sayyid Ata' Allah Shah Bukhari (1892–1961), among others. A remarkable generation by all accounts, all of the former would play influential albeit sometimes opposing roles in the subsequent stages of the Indian and Pakistan independence movements while continuing to support the late Ottoman and Turkish causes.[128]

As a reflection of its internal diversity, the Khilafat movement employed a range of tactics that cannot be boiled down to a single modus operandi. Between 1919 and 1924 the movement incorporated protests in major Indian cities; letter-writing and editorial campaigns in Indian and British newspapers; fundraising campaigns in Indian mosques, schools, and community centers for the Anatolian resistance; actual migrations out of India, including the Hijrat and cases of Indian Muslims volunteering for the Turkish national resistance; as well high-level lobbying by Indian Muslim delegations dispatched to London. As the movement assumed anti-British imperial dimensions in general, it incorporated Hindu supporters and organizations in its ranks, most famously Mahatma Gandhi and the Indian National Congress, which threw its support behind the Khilafatists vis-à-vis its own simultaneous Noncooperation movement. In return, the recently founded Jam'iyat-i 'Ulama'-i Hind (Association of Indian Islamic Scholars) issued a fatwa endorsing Gandhi's Noncooperation movement and joint struggle with the congress in June 1920.[129] The Khilafat movement also encompassed the pro-Turkish diplomacy of Afghan delegates giving special prominence to the question of the Ottoman caliphate and Turkish territorial integrity in their own peace talks with the British at Rawalpindi, Mussoorie, and

Kabul from 1919 to 1921.[130] While critics of the movement saw the Khilafatist coalition as a marriage of convenience, others saw inspiration for Hindu-Muslim unity in India, a critical pillar of the Noncooperation and Indian independence movement led by the congress; others still, saw the roots of Muslim separatism in South Asia and a foundation for the Islamic state of Pakistan.[131] As for the not insignificant role of the Afghans, the Khilafat movement provided a vibrant anticolonial movement on Kabul's doorstep, further promoting Aman Allah's stature abroad and bolstering his legitimacy at home as a freedom-fighting *ghazi* king concerned for the plight of Muslims everywhere. It also allowed Aman Allah—even after the embarrassment of the Hijrat debacle—to continue to extend his influence across the Durand Line and the some seventy million Muslim subjects of the British Raj.

In spite of significant regional, class, and religious diversity within the Khilafatists' ranks, the common thread tying this amalgam of disparate groups into political alliance was an ardent plea to prevent the Ottoman caliphate's domains from partition by non-Muslim powers, including the new system of European colonial mandates. Here, in a jointly religious and political vernacular, the most consistent protest voiced by Khilafatist spokespersons such as the spirited journalists Mohamed Ali Jauhar and Shaukat Ali was the safeguarding of the holy sites of Hejaz, Jerusalem, and Mesopotamia (Iraq), but also the Ottoman caliph's religiopolitical jurisdiction over these Muslim-majority lands. Granted audience with the highest offices of government in Europe, including a private meeting with Lloyd George at 10 Downing Street, the Ali brothers boldly argued Muslims were obliged by their faith to support the caliphate. Couched in a language of loyalty, but also stern advice, Indian Khilafatists thereby carefully maneuvered around the sensitive topic of their allegiance to the British Crown by describing in strictly religious terms the Muslims' prerogative of protecting the Ottoman domains. At the same time, in a veiled threat to British colonial officialdom, the Ali brothers did not shy away from describing the potentially explosive consequences should the Crown fail to uphold its promises of a just resolution to Ottoman territorial questions in the aftermath of the Great War. It was in His Majesty's best interest, they emphasized, that any such resolution must take into account the very real factor of Muslim opinion in India—advice that also applied to the large Muslim populations of Egypt, South Africa, Malaya, and other British imperial domains.[132]

The Ali brothers were the most vocal and visible spokesmen of the Khilafat movement, helping establish the All-India Khilafat Committee headquarters in

Lucknow (later renamed the Central Khilafat Committee, or CKC), and traveling to London to meet senior British officials. But they were not the only ones. Other delegates working on behalf of the movement traveled to Anatolia to meet with Kemal and representatives of the nationalist government in Ankara, including the CKC's general secretary—referred to as Mirza Bey in some of the earliest records of the Turkish republic.[133] Others circulated fatwas supportive of the movement from India's most prominent ulema, and across sectarian lines. Most prominent in this regard was the work of Mawlana ʿAbd al-Bari of Firangi Mahal (1878–1926), who sought to unite and strengthen the voice of Indian Muslims in support of the Ottoman caliphate by procuring fatwas from multiple ulema on the CKC's behalf. These juridical opinions claimed to empower the Khilafat movement with the prestige of *ʿijmaʿ*, or Islamic scholarly consensus, underscoring the obligation of Indian Muslim support for the Ottoman caliphate and Turkish national resistance in Anatolia.[134] The collective fatwa held that Ottoman claims to the caliphate were legitimate irrespective of their non-Arab, non-Qurayshi descent, that it was incumbent on all Muslims to come to the aid of another Muslim country under attack, and that the Arabian Peninsula must be free from non-Muslim domination, including illegitimate proxies even though they be Muslims. The last point was a clear rebuke of the Hashemite dynastic claims of Sharif Husayn (1854–1931), leader of the Hejazi revolt against the Ottomans during World War I, but also his sons Faysal I (1883–1933) and ʿAbd Allah I (1882–1951), the kings of Iraq and Jordan, respectively.[135] In all, some sixty-six ulema affixed their signatures to the fatwa. The authority of the Khilafatists had never been clearer.[136]

Facing an onslaught of Indian Muslim protest from the streets of Bombay to 10 Downing Street, the response of British officials from Delhi to London was to mollify the Khilafatists by assuring the Crown would "fully respect" Muslim sentiments in Palestine and Iraq, where the British had recently established mandatory rule under the auspices of the League of Nations. As for Hejaz, the British government was quick to point out that an independent Muslim ruler of Qurayshi Arab lineage, Sharif Husayn, was in command of the Haramayn, not the British. Moreover, resorting to scholarly authorities of their own, the British Indian government also attempted to secure fatwas in support of their own position vis-à-vis the Ottoman caliphate. A pamphlet commissioned by the British Indian foreign department, for example, provides a case in point. Entitled *Facts about the Khalifate,* the work is a translation from an original manuscript by a certain Moulana Faizul Karim, with claims of being "authenticated by the principal Pirs and Ulemas of Sind." Printed in Karachi and discussed in a memorandum by the Raj's central intelligence department in July 1919, the pamphlet proceeds to undermine Ottoman claims to the caliphate, citing the opinions of some classical jurists that the caliph must hail from al-Quraysh, the tribe of the Prophet and his closest companions. With an underlying tone of political realism, the pamphlet concludes with a self-serving warning: "Be it remembered that the greatest monuments of the Prophet are the two Holy Places, and whosoever is their keeper has greater right to the Khalifate than his rivals."[137] These were points that the Indian Khilafatists—including Afghan allies in their ranks—hardly took seriously.[138] Referring indirectly to Sharif Husayn's kingdom of Hejaz—and by extension, subsequent Hashemite Iraq and Transjordan—as "British-manufactured sultans," the Indian CKC and Aman Allah continued to throw their weight behind the Ottoman caliph in Istanbul, with an understanding this went hand in hand with supporting the Turkish war of independence based in Anatolia under Kemal's leadership.[139]

As for Aman Allah and his newly independent Afghan government in particular, three main objectives overlapped with that of the Khilafatists. First, there was the shared goal of defending the territorial integrity of the Ottoman Empire, and later, supporting the Turkish national resistance in Anatolia.[140] Second, by sponsoring Pan-Islamic causes with strong Indian dimensions such as the Khilafat and Hijrat movements, Aman Allah was able to tap into reservoirs of Muslim political support outside of his own country. Here, the Afghan monarch's extraterritorial influence reinforced his stature as a rare independent Muslim sovereign, filling a vacuum left by the collapse of the Ottoman Empire—so much so that he was even considered as a potential candidate for the caliphate itself.[141] Pan-Islamic recognition also bolstered Afghanistan's international status among European and neighboring powers as a player to be reckoned with in regional and even global politics. Closer to home, and as important, the amir's support for Pan-Islamic causes abroad shored up his own domestic credentials as a just and righteous Afghan king. Finally, by expanding his sphere of influence into India's northwestern frontier in particular, where as many Pashtuns lived under British rule as within Afghanistan itself, Aman Allah could use Khilafat, Hijrat, and crossborder Pashtun agitation as bargaining chips against the British. Seeking to carve further territorial, legal, and commercial rights in India, that is precisely what his negotiating team did at peace talks in Rawalpindi, Mussoorie, and Kabul.

As a closer examination of Kabul's evolving policies during the 1920s reveals, however, while the Afghan government's interests in the Hijrat and Khilafat movements overlapped in some instances with that of their Indian Muslim allies, eventually they began to diverge along territorial nationalist lines. While this was no doubt a crushing blow to the muhājirs and those espousing more radical notions of annexation or a new transnational Pax Islamica, to others it demonstrated a maturation on the part of the Afghan leadership, struggling as it was to establish the first entirely free Muslim-majority nation-state after the fall of the Ottoman Empire.

Pan-Islam and the Islamic Nation-State

Far from the dust settling, the official armistice that ended Ottoman participation in World War I ushered in a new phase of war for Anatolia, and even opened a new chapter of conflict between Indian Muslim Khilafatists and the British Raj. Meanwhile in Afghanistan, during the volatile years between 1919 and 1923, the making of a multinational corps of Ottomans, Indians, and Afghans in Kabul had its roots in the remarkable convergence of a post-Armistice Turkey and Afghanistan fighting simultaneous wars of independence, and the Indian Khilafat movement emerging in full steam. As with previous episodes of Indo-Afghan-Ottoman activity, the focal point of this tripartite nexus was again Kabul, but with very different results.

With Aman Allah securing independence from Britain following the Third Anglo-Afghan War in the summer of 1919, Afghanistan became one of the only fully independent and sovereign Muslim-majority states in the world. What followed were two very different migrations to Afghanistan from opposite directions: an Ottoman Empire in shambles from the west, and British India from the east. The former included a high-profile group of Ottoman Turkish officials fleeing Allied-occupied Istanbul; the latter constituting one of the most remarkable migrations in South Asian history. In a foreshadowing of the trauma and dislocations of partition a quarter century later, an estimated sixty thousand Indian Muslims, mostly poor farmers from the Punjab, Sindh, and NWFP, migrated to Afghanistan in the Hijrat movement of 1920–1921. Meanwhile, a more exclusive group of Indian migrants had already become influential members of Aman Allah's court, joining a coterie of former Ottoman officials in the amir's service.

Upon his ascent to power, Aman Allah initially supported Muslim insurgencies against the British in the east and south and against the Soviet Red Army to the north, speaking to his uncompromisingly Pan-Islamic foreign policy in

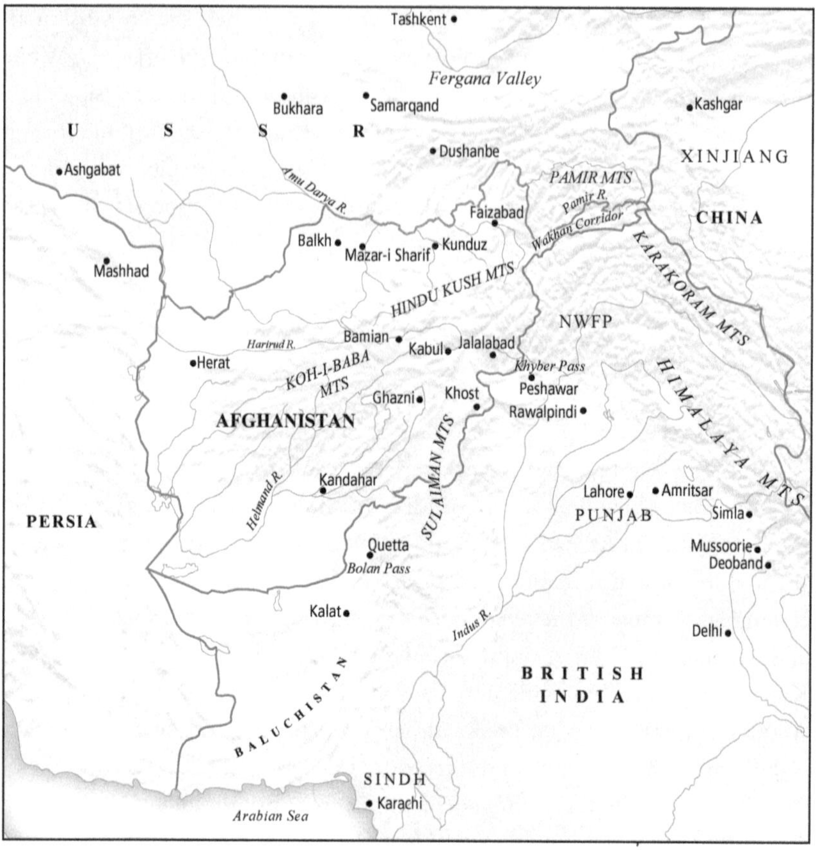

MAP 4. Afghanistan and its neighbors, 1923

the early months and years of his decade-long reign.[142] As the leader of a sovereign and territorially defined nation-state (Map 4), however—and not an expansive Muslim empire like the Ottomans or Mughals, or Hotakis and Durranis for that matter—Aman Allah found himself caught between more narrow conceptions of national interests and the ambitious calls of competing Pan-Islamic causes. While his early support for the Muslim Basmachi rebels in Turkistan also derived from the vacuum created by the dissolution of the tsarist Russian Empire and Bukharan amirate, for example, his northern policy soon collided with Soviet expansionism in Turkistan, until he was forced to abandon the cause. Eventually, the Afghan monarch was compelled to curb his own expansionist fervor and abandoned support for the Basmachis in order to stabilize his northern border and focus on securing gains from the British to the east and south.

The collapse of the Hijrat movement spelled the end neither of the Khilafat movement nor of Aman Allah's Pan-Islamism. But it was a chastening episode for Aman Allah and the Khilafatist leadership alike, not to mention a poignantly tragic plight for the muhājirs. It provided a sobering lesson in the limits of Pan-Islamism for Afghans and Indian Muslims operating in different stages and contexts of national independence movements. For the former, it demonstrated the priorities Afghanistan faced as a newly independent country and the limitations of being a free "Islamic state" in the 1920s. Over the course of his reign, facing economic scarcity and conflicting priorities with his erstwhile Muslim allies, Aman Allah increasingly opted for territorially limited nationalism over universal caliphatism. For Indian Muslims, many realized after the debacle of the Hijrat that they would have to carry their own weight in India under British rule and no longer entertain fanciful dreams of escaping to Afghanistan as a new promised land. But as late as 1923, Afghanistan still featured prominently in the imagination of many Indian freedom fighters, an island of Islamic sovereignty in a sea of European colonization across Asia and Africa. This allowed Aman Allah to continue to employ the Khilafat movement, the crossborder "Pathan question," and any remaining Indian Muslim muhājirs as bargaining chips in negotiations with the British.

From the dispatch and return of envoys between Anatolia, Afghanistan, and India during the Russo-Ottoman War (1877–1878) to public speeches made by Turkish, Afghan, and Indian Muslim nationalist leaders after World War I, a shared sense of Pan-Islamic struggle at different stages emerges in all three national independence movements. There is now a robust scholarship on the history of independence struggles in Turkey, India, and Afghanistan after the Great War, but they are largely nationalist portraits framed in isolation.[143] Missing are the collaborations—but also tensions—between the national movements, evident when we examine the convergence of all three in Afghanistan during Aman Allah's reign, especially between 1919 and 1923.

Still, a major facet of the history of modern Pan-Islamism between Turkey, India, and Afghanistan—and a goal of this book—continues to dangle before us. As mentioned earlier, the historiography of modern Muslim transnationalism has devoted considerable attention to militants, radical ideologues, and other confrontational figures—for predictable reasons, given the spectacular episodes of Pan-Islamic entente during and immediately after World War I. There was, however, something else remarkable about several of the Muslims who migrated to Afghanistan from Turkey and India following the ascent of Aman Allah: they contributed to an unprecedented integration of Islamic legal and administrative expertise into a modern nation-state. Fused by a struggle for legality and diplomacy rather than war, it is to this long-forgotten jihad of Muslim jurists in Afghanistan that we now turn.

FIVE

Legalizing Afghanistan

Islamic Legal Modernism and the Making of the 1923 Constitution

IN THE SPRING OF 1919, a newly crowned amir in Afghanistan led a motley crew of irregular troops and tribal levies against the British Raj's imperial army. Stunningly, the smaller and less organized party prevailed. Although the Third Anglo-Afghan War lasted scarcely three months and resulted in a military stalemate, the negotiations that followed heralded a historic political victory for the Afghans. By declaring his amirate to be an unconditionally free and independent state, the twenty-six-year-old Amir Aman Allah Khan defied Afghanistan's status as a British protectorate, a legal relic of the Second Anglo-Afghan War (1878–1880). Although Aman Allah's assertiveness was met with one of the first sustained aerial bombardments in history, by Britain's Royal Air Force, ultimately it was London that yielded by recognizing Afghanistan's independence in the Treaty of Rawalpindi (August 8, 1919). Soon thereafter Kabul signed bilateral treaties with countries across Europe, Asia, and the Middle East.

Having secured Afghanistan's sovereignty abroad, Aman Allah turned his attention inward, launching a determined state-building program aimed at centralizing governance in a constitutional monarchy. Within a year of his coronation he had recruited an elite team of Afghan, Ottoman Turkish, and Indian Muslim jurists to whom he assigned a single mandate: in his own words, to establish a "rule of law" in the country.[1] By 1923, the king's commission had promulgated scores of original statutes collectively titled the Nizamnamihha-yi Amaniyyih (Aman Allah Codes) in Dari and Pashto. The expansive campaign comprised civil and criminal law codes, judges' manuals, and a broad range of government-issued texts, including school syllabi and training exercises for cadets in a newly reorganized Afghan army. The reforms mandated universal primary education, including the opening of public schools for girls and teachers' colleges for preparing instructors of both sexes.[2] An ensuing penal code outlawed animal cruelty, detailing the required conditions of chickens in bazaars, banning animal fights, and prohibiting the overloading of livestock.[3] The most famous text of all, however, was the Qanun-i Asasi (Basic Code) of 1923, the country's first written constitution.

Outward resemblances to international development and reconstruction policies generated for Afghanistan in more recent years have led many observers, including some scholars, to describe Aman Allah's reign (1919–1929) in nostalgic terms. The young monarch was "progressive," "charming," and a "champion of modernization ahead of his time"; as a "revolutionary king," Aman Allah pushed for women's empowerment, minority rights, and an overall "secularization" of Afghan law, among other initiatives of "a Western flavor."[4] What these readings often elide, however, is the monarch's resolve that Afghanistan's constitutional reforms spring from within Islamic legal, religious, and ethical traditions, or the shariʿa.[5] As enshrined in Articles 4, 16, and 21 of the 1923 Constitution, the king and his courts were to "rule in accordance with the principles enunciated in the shariʿa."[6]

The abundant references to upholding shariʿa in Aman Allah's reforms may come as a surprise to those accustomed to associating the Afghan king with his more famous contemporaries, Mustafa Kemal Atatürk (1881–1938) of Turkey and Riza Shah Pahlavi (1878–1944) of Iran. In light of the amir's friendship with both leaders—warm receptions he received in Ankara and Tehran are commonly cited as evidence in this regard—it is often assumed that Aman Allah simply emulated his Turkish and Iranian counterparts, in effect completing a triad of Middle Eastern "westernizing, secularizing reformists" at the time.[7] Such framings give short shrift to modern Afghan legal history and Aman Allah's distinctive style of rule, especially during the pivotal years of 1919–1923, when the juridical foundations of a fully sovereign Afghanistan were laid. In contrast to Kemalist Turkey in particular, Amani Afghanistan's model of reform stressed continuity rather than rupture with the predominant Hanafi jurisprudential traditions of the country, and negotiation with the Afghan ulema establishment rather than confrontation. These traits also distinguish Aman Allah and his jurists from the founders of the modern *salafiyya* movement, Jamal al-Din "al-Afghani" (d. 1897), Muhammad ʿAbduh (d. 1905), and Rashid Rida (d. 1935), as well as their intellectual and political heirs in the twentieth and twenty-first centuries. Forsaking adherence to one school of law, "Salafis" continue to attract the lion's share of scholarly attention when it comes to Islamic modernism—in its legal dimensions, or any other domain.

A historical rebrushing of Aman Allah and his policy makers as Islamic legal modernists hinges on questions that have received insufficient attention. Does the role of Islamic law in Afghanistan's founding national charter transcend mere claims to be based on the shariʿa? Is there evidence of constructive conversations, debates, and collaborations between diverse strands of Muslim legal thought in the production of Afghanistan's Nizamnamihha-yi Amaniyyih? Far from simulating Europe or Kemalism, or another variety of diffusionist legal change, Afghanistan's Aman Allah Codes should be considered one of the twentieth century's first episodes of Islamic legal modernism in power, defined as a statist project by Muslim jurists to promulgate a uniform body of national laws via the codification of Islamic jurisprudence (*fiqh*). A hallmark of Islamic legal modernism is a deliberate resistance to "transplanting" European legal codes to Muslim-majority societies, instead opting for a synthesis of the Islamic jurisprudential heritage with the requirements of modern statehood, legality, and governance.[8] As a case in point, the architects of the Aman Allah Codes relied on the Hanafi madhab—the predominant school of Islamic law in the Ottoman Empire, India, and greater Central Asia—for the substantive legal rulings that they codified into Afghanistan's first corpus of nation-state law. In so doing, Aman Allah's lawgivers reflected jurisprudential continuity and innovation simultaneously. That scholars of modern Islamic legal history have overlooked Afghanistan's Nizamnamihha-yi Amaniyyih is surprising in light of its being the most ambitious—and arguably successful—codification of Hanafi *fiqh* since the Ottoman Mecelle (Civil Code).

This argument is grounded in a discussion of two features of the Nizamnamihha-yi Amaniyyih codification project in particular: the sources of its substantive law, and a social biography of its drafters. First, we will examine specific instances of canonical Hanafi works cited in the single most important text of the Aman Allah Codes after the Constitution itself—*Tamassuk al-Quzat al-Amaniyyih* (1921–1922) (Handbook for Aman Allah's Judges).[9] The handbook was a comprehensive primer on Afghanistan's criminal laws intended for judicial personnel across the country. The government printed two thousand copies to be distributed to and implemented in every criminal court of first instance (*maḥkamih-i ibitidāʾi*) and higher appellate court (*maḥkamih-i marāfiʿ-i jazāʾ*) in the country. Designed as a user-friendly handbook, *Tamassuk al-Quzat* was the chief instrument in Aman Allah's plan to establish a judicial grid for the country. Apart from the Basic Code, it is also the only statute that focuses on substantive law—including definitions of crimes and stipulation of punishments—rather than on more mundane procedural or municipal matters subsumed within the Islamic legal category of administrative law / public policy, or *siyāsa sharʿiyya*. For these reasons the handbook acted as a companion text to the 1923 Constitution, and as the amir's implementation of the "rule by shariʿa" clauses in Articles 4, 7, 16, 21, and 72 in particular.

As for the source of its rulings, the handbook is unequivocal in its reliance on canonical texts and authors of the Hanafi school of Islamic jurisprudence, from the *Hidaya* (Guidance) of medieval Transoxian jurist al-Marghinani (d. 1197) to *Radd al-Muhtar* (Answer to the Perplexed) of the late Ottoman mufti of Damascus, Ibn ʿAbidin (d. 1836). Given the existence of an alternative path—translating French, Belgian, Swiss, or German codes, as was done in neighboring Muslim-majority countries, for example—the actual legal content of the Aman Allah Codes serves as a reminder that building a state judiciary involves profoundly political choices.

Framing legislative policies as Islamic legal modernism in power also requires information about the authors themselves.[10] Among the "framers" of Afghanistan's first constitution were Afghan ulema trained in Deobandi madrasas, radical members of the Young Afghan republican movement, an Indian Muslim physician, and an Ottoman Turkish lawyer who was appointed to the very helm of the drafting commission. Apart from their common religion, the only characteristics tying the authors of Afghanistan's first constitution together were that they hailed from highly literate professional classes and had graduated from educational institutions in Afghanistan, India, or the Ottoman Empire. The section concludes with biographical snapshots of five leading, but very different, contributors to Afghanistan's Nizamnamihha-yi Amaniyyih. Subsumed within this treatment of the Aman Allah Codes, therefore, is a recognition of the diversity of Muslim thought and politics undergirding Islamic legal modernism in Afghanistan at this time.

This is not to suggest there was ideological uniformity between the Muslims of Aman Allah's court—far from it. Nor is this an account of a puritanical, insular, or monolithic Islam or "Muslim world view" in Afghanistan framed in juxtaposition to an equally imagined West. There is an account of ideological fault lines here—not between believers and nonbelievers, but among Muslim rulers, their advisors, and those they ruled, as they each promoted competing interpretations of the shariʿa in Afghanistan. Far from a simplistic binary dividing religionists and secularizers, Aman Allah refused to grant his opponents the discursive advantage, crafting a "rule of shariʿa" campaign of his own to counter more locally produced versions in the Indo-Afghan frontier especially.

The Nizamnamihha-yi Amaniyyih (Aman Allah Codes): Features and Sources

Far from a stand-alone text, the Nizamnamihha-yi Amaniyyih includes Afghanistan's first national constitution, also known as the Basic Code or Fundamental Law in Persian and Pashto, in addition to more than seventy separately bound statutes, courtroom manuals, and administrative regulations covering a broad range of civil, criminal, and military matters.[11] The supplementary texts introduce foundational pillars of modern bureaucracy, including the organization of ministries and municipalities, the collection of revenue and regulation of state employees, a standard system of measurements, the registration of marriages and children, as well as identity cards and passports for the increased legibility of subjects in and outside the country.[12] Together, the topics covered in the Aman Allah Codes are vast in scope, signaling the most ambitious attempt by any governing regime in Afghanistan to extend a single writ of authority and uniform law to the country as a whole up to that point in time.

As mentioned, the most prominent text promulgated during Aman Allah's reign was the Basic Code of 1923 (Figure 5.1). The document was ratified before a Loya Jirga assembly on April 9, 1923, and most scholars consider it the country's first constitution. Ludwig Adamec, for example, described the text as a bill of rights for Afghans and the "first written document dealing [with] the prerogatives of the ruler and the rights of the ruled."[13] The charter served as a blueprint for organizing the state's financial, political, and military organs, including limits on the authority of central, provincial, and municipal governments. It sowed the

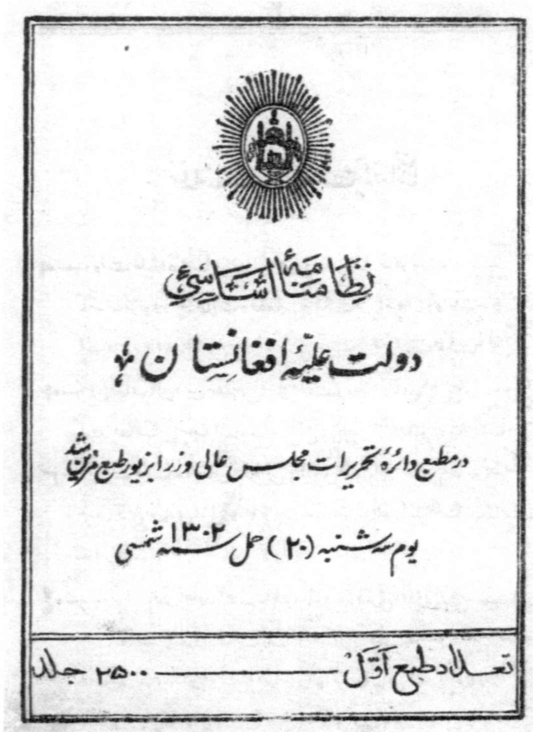

نظامنامهٔ اساسی

دولت علیهٔ افغانستان

در مطبع دائرهٔ تحریرات مجلس عالی وزرا بزیور طبع مزین شد

یوم سه شنبه (۲۰) حمل سنه ۱۳۰۲ شمسی

تعداد طبع اول ـــــــــ ۲۵۰۰ جلد

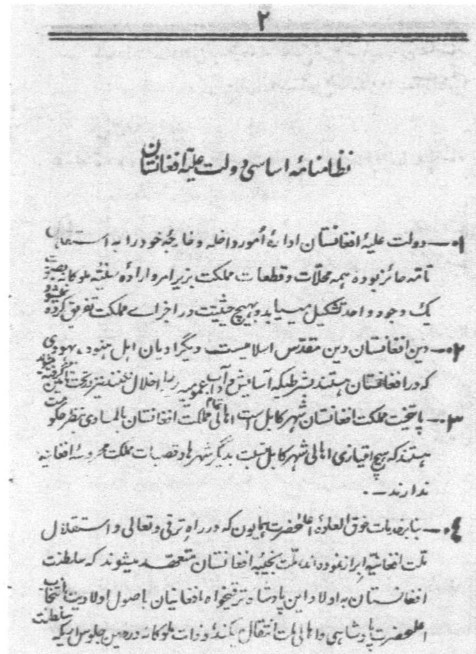

۲

نظامنامهٔ اساسی دولت علیهٔ افغانستان

FIGURE 5.1. Afghanistan's first constitution, Kabul, April 9, 1923. *Left to right:* cover and opening articles. Afghanistan Digital Library, Kabul / New York (adl0076).

seeds for a national parliament by establishing a state council (Shura-yi Dawlat), half of whose members were to be "identified and appointed by the people."[14] The formation of a vertically integrated network of law courts headed by a supreme court (Diwan-i ʿAli) in Kabul with a mandate for judicial review also speaks to a nascent separation of powers.[15] Notably, the document's common name (Qanun-i Asasi) is identical to that of the Ottoman Constitution of 1876 (Kanun-ı Esasi) and the Iranian Constitution of 1906.[16]

The Afghan Constitution of 1923: Organization and Content

Containing seventy-three articles, Afghanistan's Basic Code or Constitution of 1923 can be divided into three thematic sections: first, the king's duties and powers; second, the cabinet's duties and powers; and third, the fundamental rights of citizens. At the heart of the first section is Article 4. In exchange for allegiance to the king and to the royal succession of his male line, the king pledges to protect the independence of the country and "to rule in accordance with the principles enunciated in the shariʿa and in this Constitution." In pursuit of the aforesaid duties, the king's powers are divided into four branches—executive, legislative, judicial, and military—each being defined in Article 7. The king's executive powers comprise the appointment, dismissal, and transfer of government ministers, including the prime minister. His legislative powers comprise the promulgation, ratification, and preservation of public laws (*qānūn*) and the "laws of the shariʿa," while his judicial powers include the pardoning and commuting of punishments. His military powers include declaring war, serving as commander in chief of the armed forces, issuing and enforcing military regulations, and signing treaties. Notably, Article 7 also reserves a pair of ceremonial distinctions for the king: his mention in Friday prayers throughout Afghanistan, and the minting of coins in his name. Both were hallmarks of Muslim dynasties and have been attributed to the early caliphs of Islam. The 1923 Constitution represents one of the first historical instances of both practices being nationalized and constitutionalized in a modern, territorially defined state.

The duties and powers of the cabinet (Articles 25–49) include those pertaining to state ministers, members of provincial councils, and even some municipal officials. In general, the cabinet is responsible for executing the king's laws and the laws of the shariʿa. Regulations concerning this generic mandate, however, are detailed in separate *niẓāmnāmihs* governing each ministry—highlighting the interdependent relationship between the Basic Code and over seventy other Aman Allah Codes (a theme we will return to later).

As for the fundamental rights of citizens, the Basic Code does not contain a separate section devoted to this theme in one place; rather, relevant provisions are dispersed throughout the text. Article 8, for example, states categorically that "all persons residing in the Kingdom of Afghanistan" were Afghan nationals, thereby shelving chauvinistic approaches to "Afghan-ness" and Pashtun ethnocentrism in favor of territorial nationalism and citizenship. The latter article was especially important to incorporating the significant numbers of non-Pashtuns in the country, including Tajiks, Uzbeks, Baluchis, Persian-speakers hailing from Iran, and Indian migrants from the Punjab, as well as Hindu, Jewish, and Sikh minorities, assuring them they had an equal role in the country's future. Article 10, Afghanistan's due process clause, declares the personal freedoms of all citizens to be guaranteed. Article 16, an equal protection clause, describes all subjects of Afghanistan to have "equal rights and duties to the country in accordance with the shari'a and the laws of the state."[17]

The Supremacy of Afghan State Courts

Among the remarkable aspects of Afghanistan's 1923 Constitution is that it was written, published, and distributed in the first place. Committing to paper the fundamental laws of the state in a bound leaflet containing seventy-three articles and twenty-four pages, the Basic Code performs the modern constitutional function of "announcing the law."[18] It is important to remember, however, that in a majority-illiterate society such as Afghanistan, state officials—judges, administrators, and other government elites—rather than ordinary citizens were the primary consumers of the text. The written character of the charter therefore speaks more to a centralizing and legal positivist impetus on the part of Aman Allah's government than to a liberalist ideology per se.[19] Specifically, the Constitution of 1923 and supplemental Aman Allah Codes formed part of Kabul's goal of consolidating the myriad provincial, non-state-sponsored "customary" legal systems operating de facto across Afghanistan into a more legible judicial grid.[20]

Perhaps no other article of Afghanistan's 1923 Constitution provides a glimpse of the politics of centralization at play behind the charter than Article 55, which categorically states "no special court to hear and adjudicate a special case or issue may be established outside the framework of the regular judiciary." Similarly,

Articles 33–34 and 56–57 stipulate that Afghanistan's new judicial system would operate under a central legal authority represented by a supreme court, the members of which would be appointed by the amir himself. Here it must be emphasized that drafting constitutions and codifying laws need not signify liberal-participatory politics as much as the politics of centralization in modern administrative states. In this sense, by "fixing" legal outcomes via constitutions and codes, the Afghan government shared in global processes of modern state formation, but used a language and genealogy of its own.

Sources of Afghan State Law

The handful of scholarly works on Afghanistan's modern legal and constitutional history suggest that Aman Allah relied on Western, especially French, advisors and legal codes in building a newly independent state centered in Kabul.[21] Such accounts reflect diffusionist models of historical change in which European legal cultures and colonial practices were exported to a passive Asia, Africa, and Latin America through the forces of imperial administration. Applying this model to Afghanistan is curious, however, not least because the 1923 Constitution and scores of *niẓāmnāmih* codes promulgated alongside it declare unambiguously their rootedness in the shariʿa. This is also true of some other countries in the region that drew heavily on modern European legal codes. One way of reconciling this discrepancy is to consider such language merely as Islamic window dressing, endowing state legislation with the desired cultural legitimacy in Muslim-majority societies. This perspective assumes, however, that references to the shariʿa in the Aman Allah Codes are merely "feigning religion," providing a thin veneer to an essentially secular-liberal text of Western inspiration. Meanwhile, a fundamental question remains unanswered: From where did the architects of the Aman Allah Codes derive their laws in substance? Nearly a century after the reformist king's first *niẓāmnāmihs* were published in Kabul, historians have yet to satisfactorily answer this question.

A partial explanation for this surprising lacuna is that no records of the drafting commission appear to have been found. However, this dearth of records does not preclude us from scrutinizing the codes themselves. From in-text references and allusions we can glean the kinds of sources on which the commission members drew in producing these remarkably understudied legal texts. It is not uncommon for the last line of a *niẓāmnāmih* code, followed by the king or chief justice's signature, to state, "The provisions of this code are in conformity with the rulings of the Sacred Shariʿa according to the Hanafi school following strong chains of transmission."[22] More than empty claims, a close examination of the foremost law book of Aman Allah's reign after the Basic Code—a manual on criminal law compiled by Aman Allah's chief jurist—indicates a firm anchoring in the Hanafi madhab.

A Constitutional Companion: The Handbook for Afghan Judges

Completed roughly a year before the Basic Code, *Tamassuk al-Quzat al-Amaniyyih* (1921–1922) (Handbook for Aman Allah's Judges), is a comprehensive primer on criminal law compiled by the amir's chief jurist, Mawlawi ʿAbd al-Wasiʿ Qandahari, of whom we will have more to say in the next section. As is evident from the work's breadth and scope—comprising two volumes of fourteen chapters each and a total of 1,113 articles—the handbook was intended to be a "one-stop" reference for Afghan judges presiding over criminal cases in the newly created network of state courts. While the Aman Allah Codes are replete with statements that say legislation is in conformity with the shariʿa according to the Hanafi school, *Tamassuk al-Quzat* is unique in being the only text to cite the jurisprudential sources for virtually all its articles. Of the 1,113 rules in the handbook, 1,082 provide an explicit jurisprudential source (see for example Figure 5.2). Without fail, every reference cites a canonical work of Hanafi *fiqh* (Table 1). These works include over two dozen of the most well-known juristic treatises, glosses, and commentaries, which would be familiar to any advanced law student of the Hanafi school. Notably, references to European sources of law are entirely absent from the Aman Allah Codes.[23]

Skeptics might note that a single code, even an extremely significant one, does not establish beyond doubt that all of Aman Allah's codes drew only from Islamic, much less Hanafi, legal sources.[24] Yet to downplay *Tamassuk al-Quzat* as exceptional or unrepresentative of the Aman Allah Codes as a whole misses a crucial point. Apart from the Basic Code, the handbook, and the 1920 Marriage Code discouraging polygamy and child marriage,[25] the *niẓāmnāmihs* contain administrative regulations of a procedural nature rather than restatements of substantive law. Addressing such issues as the organization of government ministries, tax collection, national holidays, grazing zones, the standardization of measurements, identity cards and conscription, and spending caps on wedding parties, the vast majority of the Aman Allah Codes belong to the Islamic legal-

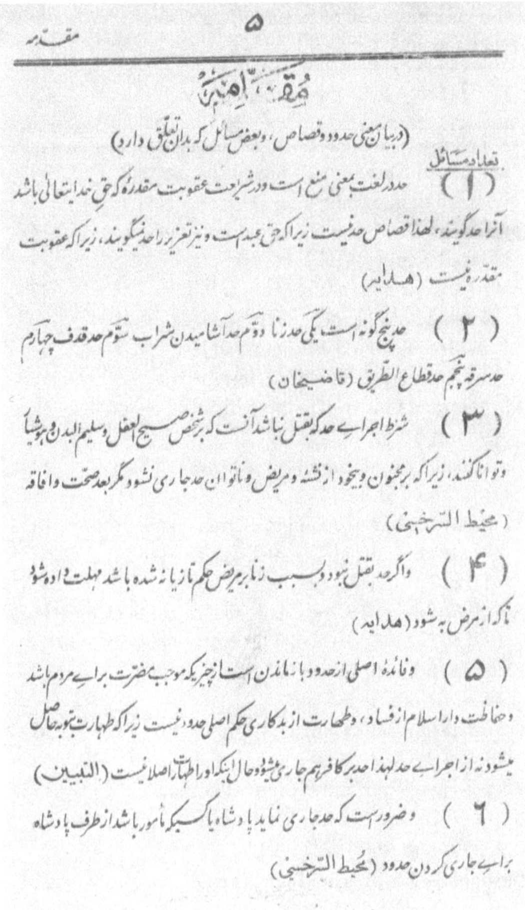

FIGURE 5.2. *Tamassuk al-Quzat al-Amaniyyih* (Handbook for Aman Allah's Judges), Kabul, 1921/1922. Sample page. Afghanistan Digital Library, Kabul/New York (adl0317).

administrative genre of *siyāsa sharʿiyya* (public policy–related ordinances). Meanwhile, the handbook is the only *niẓāmnāmih* to articulate the substantive criminal laws of Afghanistan to be applied in state courts, making it the country's first national criminal law code.[26] There is no equivalent civil law code for Afghanistan in this period.[27] While it hardly seems necessary to describe ordinances on measurement or zoning as reflecting Western or Islamic legal traditions, the same cannot be said for substantive law such as a criminal law code.

My argument does not reject wholesale the concept of legal borrowing—or rather, adaptation—but it does seek to highlight how the Nizamnamihha-yi Amaniyyih bears a more complex genealogy than has conventionally been assumed by the extant literature on Afghanistan. As one of the twentieth century's first

Table 1 References to works of the Hanafi school of Islamic jurisprudence in *Tamassuk al-Quzat al-Amaniyyih* (1921 / 1922)

Title	Author / Compiler	No. of references
Al-Muhit	Razi al-Din Muhammad bin Muhamamad al-Hanafi al-Sarakhsi (d. 1149)	195
Al-Hidaya	Burhan al-Din ʿAli bin Abi Bakr al-Marghinani (d. 1197)	124
Fatawa Qazi Khan	Fakhr al-Din Hasan bin Mansur bin Mahmud al-Uzjandi (d. 1195)	83
Al-Kafi	Al-Hakim al-Shahid Muhammad bin Muhammad al-Hanafi (d. 945)	69
Al-Mabsut	Muhammad bin Ahmad bin Abi Sahl al-Sarakhsi (d. 1097)	59
Al-Dhakira al-Burhaniyya	Burhan al-Din Mahmud bin Ahmad al-Bukhari (d. 1219)	49
Fatawa Zahiriyya	Muhammad bin Ahmad bin ʿUmar al-Hanafi Zahir al-Din al-Bukhari (d. 1222)	48
Al-Siraj al-Wahhaj	Abu Bakr bin ʿAli al-Haddadi al-ʿAbbadi (d. 1397 / 1398)	35
Khazanat al-Muftiyin	Al-Husayn bin Muhammad al-Samiqani al-Hanafi (d. 1339)	32
Minah al-Ghaffar	Shams al-Din Muhammad al-Timurtashi (d. 1595)	26
Fatawa Hammadiyya (1825)	Abu al-Fath Rukn bin Husam al-Nakuri	23
Fath al-Qadir	Muhammad bin ʿAbd al-Wahid bin al-Humam (d. 1459 / 1460)	22
Muhit al-Burhani	Burhan al-Din Mahmud bin Ahmad al-Bukhari (d. 1219)	21
Mukhtasar al-Quduri	Abu al-Husayn Ahmad bin Muhammad al-Quduri al-Baghdadi (d. 1037)	21
Tabyin al-Haqaʾiq	Fakhr al-Din ʿUthman bin ʿAli al-Zaylaʿi (d. 1342 / 1343)	19
Al-Ashbah wa-l-Nazahir	Zayn al-Din Ibrahim bin Nujaym (d. 1563)	18
Fatawa ʿAtabiyya	Zayn al-Din Ahmad bin Muhammad bin ʿUmar al-ʿAttabi al-Bukhari (d. 1190)	18
Khulasa al-Fatawa	Tahir bin Ahmad Iftikhar al-Din al-Bukhari (d. 1147 / 1148)	18
Fatawa-yi ʿAlamgiri (1675)	Shah Aurangzeb ʿAlamgir; Nizam Burhanpuri	17
Fatawa Sirajiyya	Siraj al-Din ʿUmar bin Ishaq al-Hindi (d. 1372)	14

Title	Author / Compiler	No. of references
Al-Bahr al-Ra'iq	Abu Hanifa al-Thani Zayn al-Din bin Ibrahim bin Nujaym al-Misri (d. 1562 / 1563)	13
Al-Jawhara al-Nayyira	Abu Bakr bin 'Ali al-Haddadi al-'Abbadi (d. 1397 / 1398)	12
Fatawa Tatarkhaniyya	'Alim bin 'Ala' al-Dihlawi al-Hanafi (d. 1384 / 1385)	11
Al-Nahr al-Fa'iq	Siraj al-Din 'Umar bin Ibrahim bin Nujaym al-Misri (d. 1596 / 1597)	8
Jami' al-Rumuz	Shams al-Din Muhammad al-Quhistani (d. 1543)	7
Ikhtiyar Sharh al-Mukhtar	'Abd Allah bin Mahmud bin Mawdud al-Mosuli al-Hanafi (d. 1284 / 1285)	7
Al-Nihaya	Husam al-Din Husayn bin 'Ali al-Sighnaqi (d. 1311)	6
Radd al-Muhtar	Muhammad Amin bin 'Abidin (d. 1836)	6

Source: ADL-0317 (Muhammad 'Abd al-Wasi' Qandahari, *Tamassuk al-Quzat al-Amaniyyih* [Kabul: Dar al-Saltanih, 1300j / 1921–1922]).

examples of Islamic legal modernism in power, the Afghan Constitution of 1923 and supplemental codes displayed a remarkably adaptable approach to shari'a-based legislation, drawing from canonical works of the Hanafi school of *fiqh*, but also on modern notions of political sovereignty, territorial nationalism, and the general will as embodied in a national constitution and a bounded legal code.[28] The latter signified a creative endeavor by Muslim jurists to develop a theory of the modern nation-state governed by shari'a, blurring conventionally dichotomized understandings of Afghan society at this time.

Still, by themselves, the legal sources cited in the Nizamnamihha-yi Amaniyyih corpus do not provide us with a clear picture of Islamic legal modernism in action in Kabul during this era. This picture only emerges through an examination of the sociolegal history behind the Aman Allah Codes, particularly the individuals who actually wrote them.

The Framers of Afghanistan's 1923 Constitution

Historical scholarship on Afghan constitutionalism (*mashrūṭiyat*) has focused not on the legal reforms of Aman Allah but on the revolutionary politics of an underground network that emerged in the capital prior to his rule. The Young Afghans (Jawanan-i Afghan), as discussed in Chapter 2, was a secret society of intelligentsia with anti-imperial and parliamentary leanings who coalesced during the reign of Aman Allah's father, the absolutist monarch Amir Habib Allah Khan (r. 1901–1919). Branding themselves constitutionalists (*mashrūṭih-khwāhān*), and resembling parallel movements in Turkey and Iran, the Young Afghans comprised a loose association of disgruntled bureaucrats, liberal clerics, radical courtiers, and a handful of military officers united by the twin demands of a more representative government and complete independence from Britain.[29] Important as this movement was in generating momentum for parliamentary politics, as well as Pan-Islamic and Pan-Asian sentiments in Afghanistan, the attention devoted to it has caused it to overshadow the committee of jurists who actually wrote Afghanistan's first constitution and supplemental codes after the country gained independence in 1919.

The most significant exception is the Afghan historian ʿAziz al-Din Popalzai's magnum opus, *Dar al-Qazaʾ dar Afghanistan* (The Judiciary of Afghanistan), published in Kabul on the heels of the Soviet withdrawal from the country.[30] Based on rare government records from the early twentieth century, many of which are lost or destroyed, or have disappeared, Popalzai's work provides the most exhaustive list of jurists who participated in lawmaking projects in Afghanistan after World War I. According to Popalzai, within months of Aman Allah's ascent to the Kabul throne, the amir personally organized a Codification of Laws Commission (Mahfil-i Wazʿ-i Qawanin, hereafter CLC) to promulgate a comprehensive body of laws for the newly independent state.[31] The CLC comprised distinguished Afghan scholars and civil servants, who were joined by a coterie of Muslim professionals recruited from Ottoman and British Indian domains.

While the CLC was established with a singular purpose—to lay the judicial foundations for a newly independent Afghan state—the internal dynamics of its formation and final roster were complex. Structurally, the commission was bicameral, comprising two separate but complementary divisions. Each division represented distinct classes of legal experts. The first, named here as the Islamic Scholars' Division, comprised leading Afghan clerics selected from the High Religious Council (Hayʾat-i Tamiz) in Kabul, the most prominent association of ulema in the country.[32] The Islamic Scholars' Division performed a supervisory function by ensuring that all drafts submitted to the king for ratification were "in conformity with the laws of shariʿa," a condition later enshrined in Article 72 of the 1923 Constitution. In effect, the Islamic Scholars' Division exercised a

Table 2 Members of Afghanistan's Codification of Laws Commission (Mahfil-i Waz'-i Qawanin), 1919–1923

Name	Occupation	Nationality
A. Islamic Scholars' Division		
'Abd al-Wasi' Qandahari	Justice, Supreme Court; Chief Mufti	Afghan
'Abd al-Shukur Khan	Justice, Supreme Court	Afghan
Sayf al-Rahman	Military Court Judge	Indian (Pakhtun)
'Abd al-Hamid Khan	Judge, High Provincial Civil Court	Afghan
'Abd al-Rahman Begtuti	Judge, High Provincial Criminal Court	Afghan
Muhammad Amin Khan	Judge, Civil Court of First Instance	Afghan
'Abd al-Jalil Khan	Judge, Criminal Court of First Instance	Afghan
'Abd al-Rashid Khan	Judge, Court of Bail and Collaterals	Afghan
B. Administrative Division		
Muhammad Ibrahim Khan	Governor; Minister of Justice	Afghan
Osman Bedri Bey	Public Prosecutor; Police Chief; Governor	Ottoman (Turk)
Nayk Muhammad Khan	(unknown)	Afghan
Fath Muhammad Khan	(unknown)	Afghan
Jum'a Khan	(unknown)	Afghan
Habib Allah Khan	Public Prosecutor	Afghan
Abdul Ghani Khan	Physician; College Administrator	Indian
Najaf 'Ali Khan	College Instructor	Indian
'Abd al-Rahman Ludin	Mayor; Customs Minister; Ambassador	Afghan
Muhammad Qasim Khan	(unknown)	Afghan
Amir Muhammad Khan	(unknown)	Afghan

Sources: BOA-DH.SAİDd 110/493 (1298h Z 29/1881 11 21); BOA-EV.VKF 4/12 (1313h Z 29/1896 06 11); BOA-İ.AZN 72/1325Ca-28 (1325h Ca 15/1907 06 26); IOR-R/12/LIB/107 (1928), 19; IOR-R/12/197 (1930), 6–9; *WWA* (1920), 47, 129, 178; *WWA* (1930), 60, 205; 'Aziz al-Din Wakili Popalzai, *Dar al-Qaza' dar Afghanistan: Az Awayil-i 'Ahd-i Islam ta 'Ahd-i Jumhuriyat* (Kabul: Markaz-i Tahqiqat-i 'Ulum-i Islami, 1369j/1990–1991), 518–519; Mir Ghulam Muhammad Ghubar, *Afghanistan dar Masir-i Tarikh* (Qum: Payam-i Muhajir, 1359j/1980–1981); 717–719; Mas'ud Puhanyar, *Zuhur-i Mashrutiyat wa Qurbaniyan-i Istibdad dar Afghanistan* (Peshawar: Saba Kitabkhanih, 1375j/1996–1997), 54, 98–110, 244–249; 'Abd al-Hay Habibi, *Junbish-i Mashrutiyat dar Afghanistan* (Kabul: Ihsani, 1346j/1967–1968), 52–55, 276–277; Sayyid Sa'd al-Din Hashimi, *Nukhustin Kitab darbarih-'i Junbish-i Mashrutih-khwahi dar Afghanistan* (Kabul: Shura-yi Farhangi-yi Afghanistan, 2008), 274–276.

form of judicial prereview over all legislation to be promulgated with Aman Allah's seal. Notably, with the exception of one Indian Pashtun, all members of this division were Afghan nationals.[33]

By contrast, the second branch of the CLC—here named the Administrative Division—comprised a body of technocrats with diverse backgrounds (Table 2). Though most were Afghan bureaucrats, others were professionals recruited from the Ottoman Empire and British India, some of whom had been appointed to leading roles on the commission. In nationality and profession these members embodied Aman Allah's vision of a dynamic and cosmopolitan commission that would bring both a familiarity with Islamic jurisprudence of the Hanafi order and administrative expertise in a centralized, bureaucratic state such as British India or Ottoman Turkey. The strategy delivered. For the vast majority of Nizamnamihha-yi Amaniyyih codes, the Administrative Division drafted the laws before they were submitted to the Islamic Scholars' Division for review. In this way, the reformist king's legislative agenda placed a premium on synthesizing different registers of legal expertise, namely the interpretive *fiqh* tradition of the Hanafi school with modern bureaucratic practice. This synthesis was crucial to establishing a national legal system that not only resolved local disputes between private parties but also engineered "macrolegal" policies shaping the social and economic life of the country as a whole.

While Table 2 identifies verified authors of Afghanistan's 1923 Constitution and Aman Allah Codes by name, we have not as yet considered the personal backgrounds, professional histories, and associated networks of learning and expertise that they brought to the committee's work. This inquiry leads not only to Afghanistan but also, as we will see, to India and the Ottoman Empire. The following section offers brief profiles of five of the most prominent members of the CLC—representing Afghan, Ottoman Turkish, and British Indian nationalities.

Mawlawi Muhammad ʿAbd Al-Wasiʿ Qandahari (1873–1929)

Born in the southeastern city of Kandahar, Muhammad ʿAbd al-Wasiʿ Akhundzadih was the son and protégé of the distinguished nineteenth-century Islamic scholar of Afghanistan, Mawlawi ʿAbd al-Raʿuf Akhundzadih. The latter was chancellor of Afghanistan's most prestigious seminary, the Madrasih-ʾi Shahi of Kabul; founder and editor-in-chief of one of Afghanistan's first national newspapers, *Siraj al-Akhbar* (The Lamp of the News); and, according to some historians, the chief *ʿālim* in Habib Allah's royal court.[34] After completing a personalized course of study, mainly from his father, ʿAbd al-Wasiʿ emerged as an influential *mawlawi* (a term used for specialists of Islamic law in Afghanistan and India) in his own right. He authored books in Arabic, Persian, and Pashto in a range of Islamic sciences, including grammar, theology (*ilāhiyyat*), Qurʾanic exegesis (*tafsīr*), jurisprudence (*fiqh*), and political theory (*ḥukūmat*).[35] He was also politically engaged, participating in constitutionalist agitation against the absolutist policies of Habib Allah, including via sermons from the pulpit of

Kabul's central Pul-i Khishti mosque.[36] Representing a liberal and reformist strain of ulema within the capital, 'Abd al-Wasi' was eventually imprisoned, but not executed, for his dissident activities.[37]

After Habib Allah's assassination in 1919, Amir Aman Allah appointed 'Abd al-Wasi' to the preeminent judicial post in the country, Qazi al-Quzat, or chief mufti of Afghanistan. Aman Allah's choice of 'Abd al-Wasi' for the role reflected his esteem for the scholar's erudition as well as for his political leanings. For the same reasons, we may presume, he appointed 'Abd al-Wasi' to Afghanistan's first supreme court and to the Islamic Scholars' Division of the CLC. Over and above the aforesaid duties, Aman Allah charged 'Abd al-Wasi' with drafting a comprehensive criminal law manual for implementation in the new state courts. The result was the aforementioned judge's handbook, *Tamassuk al-Quzat al-Amaniyyih.*

'Abd al-Wasi''s weighty influence on the CLC is also apparent in the Aman Allah Codes themselves; several *niẓāmnāmihs* conclude with the seal of the amir, followed by one other title and signature: "Servant of the Scholars, 'Abd al-Wasi' Qandahari."[38] In addition to serving on the lawmaking commission, 'Abd al-Wasi' helped establish a school of law (*maktab-i qużāt*) and a school of administration (*maktab-i ḥukkām*) in Kabul, where he served as a professor of Islamic jurisprudence.[39]

Osman Bedri Bey (1881–1923)

Born and raised in Istanbul, Osman Bedri Bey was a graduate of the Ottoman Empire's most prestigious high school and law school, the Mekteb-i Mülkiye Şahane and the Mekteb-i Hukuk Şahane respectively.[40] The son of a civil servant in the Porte's military pension bureau, Bedri's remarkable career trajectory reflected the middle-class beginnings and social mobility of late Ottoman bureaucrats and officers who burst through the glass ceiling of the Hamidian era to climb to the uppermost echelons of the new Ottoman command structure after the Young Turk Revolution of 1908.[41] According to his profile in the *Siccil-i Umumi,* a central registry of the Porte's civil servants, the trained lawyer swiftly scaled the ranks of Istanbul's Nizamiye court system, beginning with his assignment to a local court of first instance in September 1911. In April 1912 he was appointed public prosecutor for the lucrative Beyoğlu district.[42] Bedri's loyalty to the Committee for Union and Progress (CUP) government during his time as police chief was amply rewarded. By the time of the Ottoman Empire's entry into World War I, in November 1914, Bedri had reached the apex of the Porte's civil administration, being appointed as police commissioner for Istanbul. Two years later he was promoted to the governorship of Aleppo province in Syria.[43] The range of activities described in Ottoman records from the war period reflect an additional aspect of Bedri's professional history: his coordination of large infrastructure projects with multinationals (in this case, Germans and Austro-Hungarians), an aptitude he would later put to use under very different circumstances in Afghanistan.

A close confidante of the CUP's top leadership, Bedri's meteoric rise to late Ottoman imperium was not to last, however. As a prominent official in the CUP wartime government, Bedri soon found himself on the occupied Ottoman government's list of most wanted fugitives.[44] On November 1, 1918, the eve of the Allied occupation, Bedri and a band of CUP officials fled Istanbul, never to return. After a whirlwind trail of exile through Germany and Russia, Bedri journeyed to Kabul in 1920 on the heels of a more notorious fugitive, the Ottoman naval minister, Fourth Army commander, and CUP triumvirate member, Cemal Pasha. Cemal had arrived in Afghanistan only months earlier seeking to establish a new base of operations in geostrategic Central Asia. Cemal's plan was embraced by the staunchly Turcophile Aman Allah, who entrusted Cemal with training a new Afghan army.[45] By all accounts Aman Allah was equally pleased when the Ottoman attorney and Istanbul police chief Bedri arrived in his court, for the amir appointed him director of the country's first ever constitutional commission.[46]

Dr. Abdul Ghani Khan Punjabi (1864–1945)

Born in 1864 in the provincial town of Jalalpur Jattan, Punjab, Abdul Ghani Khan was the son of an Islamic scholar of local repute, Dosand Khan. Abdul Ghani completed his preliminary studies in the Punjab with distinction, earning a seat in the prestigious Mohammedan Anglo-Oriental College at Aligarh.[47] Soon thereafter he accepted a scholarship to further his education in England. Abdul Ghani's arrival in London in 1885 coincided with an official state visit by Prince Nasr Allah Khan, the son of Amir ʿAbd al-Rahman (r. 1880–1901). After meeting the Indian youth, Nasr Allah is reported to have been so impressed that he offered to sponsor Abdul Ghani through his studies at the University of Cambridge, where he subsequently enrolled to study medicine.[48] In 1890, Dr. Ghani (as Afghan sources refer to him thereafter) emigrated to Kabul, where he assumed an advisory role in the court of ʿAbd al-Rahman. It was a short appointment, however. British intelligence sources indicate that by the late 1890s Abdul Ghani had returned to India to serve as principal of Islamia College in Lahore, a position he held for three years.[49] Still, he did not sever his relations with Afghanistan; while in Lahore, he maintained contacts with influential persons in Kabul, including serving as personal news-writer to the Muhammadzai court.[50]

Following ʿAbd al-Rahman's death and the coronation of his eldest son, Habib Allah, Abdul Ghani returned to Afghanistan. The new amir appointed him to an array of significant posts: chief medical officer, director of public instruction, and principal of the newly established Habibiye college in Kabul. Ostensibly in the amir's service, Abdul Ghani would eventually become known for his founding of an underground constitutionalist society, Sirr-i Milli (National Secret). By 1909, the Indian doctor's associations with the Young Afghans had attracted the amir's suspicions. Along with a number of followers, Abdul Ghani was arrested and imprisoned for allegedly conspiring to assassinate the amir and establish a constitutional government in his place. Habib Allah's murder in February 1919, and Aman Allah's subsequent ascent, led to Abdul Ghani's official pardon and release.[51]

What followed was another meteoric rise in the Kabul court, beginning with Abdul Ghani's appointment to the reformist king's privy council. The then British consul in Kabul, Sir Richard Machonachie, writes that Abdul Ghani became "one of Aman Allah's closest advisors," unsurprisingly, given the latter's Young Afghan associations as a prince.[52] Aman Allah appointed Abdul Ghani to several high-profile positions related to domestic and foreign affairs, including in the delegation representing Afghanistan at the Rawalpindi peace talks with the British in August 1919, his Indian background notwithstanding. A month later, Abdul Ghani was appointed director of public instruction, while also serving on the commission that drafted the Afghan Constitution of 1923.[53]

Muhammad Ibrahim Khan Barakzai (d. 1929)

Hailing from the powerful Barakzai clan whose patriarchs had ruled Afghanistan since 1826, Muhammad Ibrahim Khan descended from a distinguished line of government officials. His father, Muhammad Sarwar Khan Barakzai, was a former governor of Herat. Ibrahim was also the brother of ʿUlya Hazrat, a wife of Habib Allah, making him Aman Allah's maternal uncle. During Habib Allah's reign, Ibrahim served as Prince Nasr Allah's chief of logistics (*farāshbāshī*).[54] Judging by the frequency of his signature at the end of several Aman Allah Codes, he was one of the most prominent members on the lawmaking commission.

Ibrahim's service in Aman Allah's court began in March 1919, hardly a month after Aman Allah had ascended the Afghan throne, when the new amir appointed him minister of justice. The young monarch only weeks earlier had dispatched his uncle to the strategic eastern frontier post of Jalalabad to proclaim his accession to the throne following Habib Allah's assassination in February 1919. Later that year he was transferred to the Kabul governorate to be appointed *muʿīn al-ṣalṭanat* (aide-de-camp), one of the most influential advisors in the amir's cabinet.[55] The seasoned governor also served briefly in the northwestern city of Mazar-i Sharif and, finally, in Herat, where he served as an administrator until his death in 1929.[56] In addition to the royal family connections and political clout he brought to the *niẓāmnāmih* codification project, Ibrahim's appointment to the constitutional commission speaks to the amir's vision for a lawmaking body with extensive administrative experience, as opposed to ecclesiastical knowledge alone. As is evident in the qualifications of other commission members profiled here, he was not alone in this respect.

ʿAbd al-Rahman Ludin (d. 1929)

Another versatile administrator in the ranks of Aman Allah's constitutional commission, but of a very different political stripe, was the public servant, diplomat, and journalist extraordinaire, ʿAbd al-Rahman Ludin. Beginning with his staunchly constitutionalist and anti-absolutist politics during Habib Allah's reign, Ludin published fiery articles in Mahmud Tarzi's Muslim modernist periodical *Siraj al-Akhbar,* where he argued that Habib Allah's lofty speeches hailing a new era of progress failed to materialize in practice because of the amir's obeisance to the British abroad, combined with his own stifling autocracy at home. Ludin also shared both the Young Afghans' and conservatives' biting critique of Habib Allah's neutrality during World War I. He described the amir's wavering as a betrayal of their coreligionists and the Ottoman caliphate in their darkest hour, and he blamed Habib Allah for swindling Afghanistan's best chance at independence from the British.[57]

As with his Young Afghan comrade Abdul Ghani, Ludin was accused of participating in a plot to assassinate Habib Allah and subsequently imprisoned.[58] Also like Abdul Ghani, Ludin was released by order of Aman Allah, who rewarded the former political prisoner with a prominent role in his cabinet. In addition to serving on the committee that ratified many of the Aman Allah Codes in the early 1920s, Ludin held a number of posts in Aman Allah's government, including serving as Afghanistan's official envoy to Soviet Bukhara, as mayor of Qandahar, and as director of customs (*raʾīs-i gumruk*) in Kabul.[59] Over the course of his versatile career, Ludin also established a reputation as one of Afghanistan's most admired poets.[60]

Such was Ludin's commitment to constitutionalist ideals that even after Aman Allah's accession to the throne, the accomplished bard did not even spare his emancipator from reproach. In spite of his appointment to prominent positions in Aman Allah's government—including to the committee to draft the country's first constitution—Ludin denounced policies that empowered the executive at the expense of building more representative institutions of governance. For these reasons, he has been described as belonging to a radical wing of the Young Afghans, the Jumhuriyat-khwahan (Republicans), a faction within the liberalist camp of Aman Allah's cabinet that especially opposed absolutism and abuse of office in any form.[61]

Beyond his own principled stance vis-à-vis executive power, Ludin's positions reveal an important ideological split in the CLC: one faction promoted a strong royal executive; another sought to build more robustly representative institutions. The former viewed law, including constitutions, as a tool to empower the ruler and extend the central government's writ of authority over the entirety of the country; for Afghan republicans like Ludin, constitutions were a necessary means to restraining rulers and protecting the citizenry's inviolable rights. For the republicans, as with the Ottoman and Persian constitutions of earlier decades, the Afghan constitution was supposed to represent a genuine attempt by Muslim jurists to theorize the role of the modern state *under* Islamic law; that is, by imposing *limits* on the head of state's powers. Here, the more liberalist architects of the Aman Allah Codes like Ludin sought to create a single, supreme legal document to adjudicate over all Afghans, removing the possibility of the powerful exempting themselves from the rules that governed the common man and woman. This, in effect, represented the quintessentially "constitutional" aspects of the Basic Code to radical Young Afghans like Ludin. Still, in light of the 1923 Constitution's provisions favoring a powerful executive, and its sidestepping the formal establishment of an Afghan parliament, it is evident that Ludin's avant-garde positions were not adopted in the end—at least at this particular juncture of Afghan history.[62]

Hanafism, Salafism, and Islamic Legal Modernism

The portraits above describe five of the most prominent members of Afghanistan's first constitutional commission. Table 2 provides the names of additional contributors confirmed to have participated in the CLC's work, none of whom were European nationals.[63] Nationally, all members were Afghan, Indian, or Ottoman; confessionally, all were reputed Sunni Muslims of the Hanafi order.[64] Put together, the aforesaid features of the lawmaking commission reflect the premium Aman Allah placed on recruiting experts who were familiar with Muslim cultures (in a broad sense and including varying approaches to Islamic law), were trained in respected educational institutions, and wielded professional experience in a modern bureaucratic setting. The monarch likely saw such a versatile combination of personnel as crucial to formulating state codes that resolved not only disputes between private citizens but also more broad-ranging administrative matters involving public policy for the new Afghan state. At the same time, as highlighted in the above profiles, the members of the CLC were not uniform in background or outlook. Some managed multiple appointments, indicating not only their professional versatility but also the fluidity of Kabul's transition during Aman Allah's reign from older, patrimonial styles of governance to a newer, more bureaucratically oriented politics of expertise.[65]

In light of the distinguishing features of the Nizamnamihha-yi Amaniyyih project, it is worthy to consider the judicial reform project's importance to the study of Islamic modernism, which is often inaccurately conflated with modernist Salafism.[66] To begin with, Aman Allah's law commission was not comprised of Salafi iconoclasts who challenged *taqlid* or the monopoly of any one Sunni school of law; to the contrary, his jurists worked squarely and unapologetically within the Hanafi school. In other words, although he opposed transplanting European civil law to Afghanistan, the reformist king shunned puritanical campaigns to find an "original" or "authentic" Islam of the seventh and eighth centuries, stripped of the voluminous commentary and gloss literature of the historical Sunni madhabs. Judging from the texts they produced, neither did Aman Allah's jurists endorse a skeptical approach to classical conceptions of jurisprudence by calling for a new methodology to interpret Islamic theology, exegesis, or law.[67] Nor did they seek a renovation (or "reformation") of Islamic thought based on European Enlightenment principles, as did the liberal reformers Sir Sayyid Ahmad Khan (d. 1898), Chiragh ʿAli (d. 1895), and Muhammad Iqbal (d. 1938) of India. Rather, the authors of the Nizamnamihha-yi Amaniyyih—at least half of whom were Afghan clerics—worked to extend the living precepts of the Hanafi school of law to the new challenges of modern governance in a fully sovereign Afghanistan, one of the first Muslim-majority nation-states in the world. So far scholarly literature on Islamic modernism, with its focus on the iconoclastic *salafiyya* generation and their global interlocutors during the prior century and a half, has overlooked an important arena, episode, and cast of actors. In spite of the undoubtedly profound impact of thinkers such as Muhammad 'Abduh and Rashid Rida, few modernists of the Salafi persuasion ever wielded political power or implemented state policies in the way Aman Allah and his Hanafi jurists did in Afghanistan.

To be sure, Afghan fealty to the Hanafi school notwithstanding, that the Nizamnamihha-yi Amaniyyih represented a modern approach to shari'a and the historically decentralized interpretive *fiqh* literature cannot be disputed. In it, a sacred law tradition was instrumentalized to fulfill the prerogatives of sovereign power—accumulating capital, defining property relations, settling disputes and maintaining civil order, and supervising officials, subjects, and markets. That Aman Allah's legal codes were bound to unleash havoc on local and historically decentralized modes of dispute resolution in Afghanistan must also be acknowledged. As critical legal scholars attentive to the ruptures of colonialism and modernization campaigns in Islamic countries have emphasized, the idea of codifying shari'a has raised alarm for many Muslims—and not just of the secular-liberal persuasion, as some might presume. As Wael Hallaq, Talal Asad, and Iza Hussin have shown, nineteenth-century colonial officials from North Africa to India to the Malay Archipelago engineered a slew of "Muhammadan" digests and codes, often working in tandem with Orientalist scholars and local elites. Far from preserving Islamic legal heritage, colonially generated texts such as the Anglo-Muhammadan Law and Droit musulman algérien produced an even bolder invention—"Sharia Law." The latter is a modern construct that, paradoxically, constricted the scope of Islamic jurisprudence to family and personal status law, all the while dismantling a broader constellation of institutions, social norms, and juristic vocabularies associated with shari'a as a means of centralizing rule over Muslims. Bolstered and accelerated by the modern disciplinary technologies of surveillance, bureaucracy, government schools, and incarceration, the net results were nothing short of devastating: grassroots *fiqh* praxis replaced by the singular code; the *'ālim,* by the magistrate; the madrasa, by the civil law school; and communal pressure, by the prison.[68]

The above factors may lead some to conclude that Aman Allah's reforms were intended to produce the same paradoxical result: a dismantling of the shari'a. In the latter view, the shari'a could never be confined to codes, constitutions, or statutory law without losing its soul—an impossible state, so to speak.[69] The modern nation-state—with its monopoly on violence and evisceration of traditional forms of knowledge transmission, mediation, and arbitration—becomes a culprit external to the shariʿa, irrespective of how many Islamic codes or rule-by-shariʿa clauses a Muslim government might produce.

Such views imagine a premodern mold for Islamic law, whereby only the most superficial vestiges of the shariʿa survive the ruptures of colonialism and twentieth-century modernization campaigns. This is certainly a tempting and, for some countries and Islamist movements, convincing assessment. When applied here, however, the framework wears thin. It cannot be said, for example, that Aman Allah dismantled the shariʿa as a capitulation to colonial masters, as it was he who had led Afghanistan to become an entirely independent and sovereign state. Nor was the reformist amir engaging in European or Kemalist mimicry by stockpiling the government's legislation with French legal codes. Rather, one of the most overlooked though essential dimensions of the Nizamnamihha-yi Amaniyyih was the attempt to synthesize Afghanistan's predominantly Hanafi jurisprudential traditions with a project of modern statecraft. From this perspective, the 1923 Constitution, and the Aman Allah Codes more broadly, constituted a bold experiment: an attempt by Muslim jurists to develop an Islamic legal theory of the modern nation-state in a noncolonial context through a process that cannot be dismissed as unwarranted innovation, capitulation, or misrepresentation.[70] To dismiss it as such would be to ignore the very real struggles of a group of Afghan, Turkish, and Indian jurists to render the modern state *part* of the moral community of Muslims—that is to say, *under* Islamic law and ethics, a conceptual and aspirational framework we may aptly term Islamic statecraft. As declared in the 1923 Constitution itself, "The process of codifying laws [*tanẓīm-i niẓāmāt*] is to be implemented in light of the actual conditions of the people [*maʿlūmāt-i ahālī*] and the exigencies of the time [*maqtażīyāt-i zamān*], with particular and careful attention to the rulings of shariʿa [*makhṣūṣan aḥkām-i sharʿiyyih bi-naẓar-i diqat gariftih mi-shawad*]" (Article 72). In light of the substantial strides Aman Allah made toward advancing Islamic legal modernism as an operative framework for the newly independent Afghan state—by way of laws and lawmakers—constitutional language such as Article 72 can hardly be dismissed as the vacuous rhetoric of an aspiring politician.

As for the long-term legacies it bequeathed to Afghanistan, Aman Allah's 1923 Constitution laid the foundations for all of Afghanistan's subsequent twentieth-century constitutions (1931, 1964, 1977, and 1990)—save a pair ratified under

Soviet occupation by Kabul's communist regime (1980 and 1987).[71] Of more recent note, it provided a historical model for Afghanistan's latest national charter, adopted on January 4, 2004.

Constituting Afghanistan

As the dust from World War I settled and copious ink was spilled over the future of the Ottoman lands, in 1919 a newly crowned king, Aman Allah Khan (1892–1960), was laying the foundations for a grand state-building program of his own. He had, only months earlier, led Afghanistan to independence from Britain, establishing the first completely sovereign Muslim-majority state after the fall of the Ottomans. Within three years Afghanistan had ratified its first constitution, supplemented by over seventy statutes eponymously titled the Aman Allah Codes after its royal patron. Meanwhile in the Ottoman heartland of Anatolia, a Turkish war of resistance and national remaking was gaining steam under the leadership of former Ottoman general Mustafa Kemal (1881–1938), with whom Aman Allah would correspond and whom he would later famously meet in Ankara in 1928. While it would be several years before the full extent of Atatürk's radical campaign to remake Turkey into a secular republic was manifest, in 1923 Afghanistan already stood apart as a virtual island of Islamic sovereignty in a region torn apart by the Great War, Ottoman collapse, and the expansion of European colonial rule.

Zooming in on the legal and constitutional topography of that island of sovereignty reveals, however, not an insular backwater or no-man's-land but a remarkably well-connected, even cosmopolitan Afghanistan, interweaved as it was with at least three vibrant reform movements of the late nineteenth- to early twentieth-century greater Islamicate world: Young Turk (and prior, Young Ottoman) reformism in the late Ottoman Empire; Indian Muslim religious revivalism under the British Raj; and the constitutional activism of a highly politicized group of literati in Kabul known as the Young Afghans. Historical scholarship predominantly in Turkish, English, and Persian exploring the origins and thought of these movements has offered largely nationalist portraits of these developments in Turkey, India, and Afghanistan respectively.[72] Missing are the collaborations—and tensions—between Ottoman, Indian, and Afghan actors at this time, and how the formation of an Indo-Ottoman network in Kabul shaped a constitutional order in the newly independent state of Afghanistan.

Ultimately, it was that nexus of "interislamic" juridical activity that legalized Afghanistan, so to speak, as the first sovereign Muslim-majority nation-state after the fall of the Ottoman Empire.

There are other reasons explaining this scholarly lacuna than the blinders of area studies or ethnic nationalism. Historical scholarship on Islam and modern state building has tended to concentrate on a handful of cases: in the nineteenth century, on the late Ottoman Empire, Mehmed Ali and Khedival Egypt, and Qajar Persia; in the twentieth century, on Egypt, Saudi Arabia, Indonesia, Pakistan, and revolutionary Iran. Similarly, scholarship on Islamic modernism has tended to focus on the Arab world, the Indian subcontinent, and the Malay Archipelago, as well as on Turkey and Iran—again predictably so, as these are the largest and most populous Muslim polities in the modern world. Yet Afghanistan, the first Muslim-majority country to gain independence after the collapse of the Ottoman Empire following World War I, was a virtual laboratory for building an Islamic state under the reformist king Aman Allah. The tendency to give short shrift to Afghan legal history has resulted in important opportunities missed not only for better understanding Afghanistan but also, because of some of the country's distinguishing characteristics in the greater Islamicate world, for studying modern Islamic law at large.

Afghanistan was an important player for the growth of Islamic legal modernism in the twentieth century, decades before the establishment of its better-studied peers. The Pan-Islamic legal circuits at work in the Aman Allah Codes should help jettison once and for all diffusionist models of literature that presume a tutorial role for European legal culture, supposedly exported to darker continents through the forces of colonial administration. Having cast off the legal vestiges of British imperium after the Third Anglo-Afghan War, Aman Allah's next achievement was to launch a state-building program that capitalized on juridical resources within the country, including prominent Afghan ulema and professionals who emigrated from India and the Ottoman Empire to Afghanistan following the latter's independence. The international makeup of Aman Allah's lawmaking commission also demonstrates that Afghanistan's transition to a nation-state was complex and staggered, and not insular or chauvinistic; the reformist king was more interested in legal and administrative expertise—within Islamic frameworks—than in national identification or geographical origins.

To focus on Aman Allah's accomplishments in the early years of his decade-long reign and ignore the later years, however, would be to overlook critical historical developments that took place outside of the Kabul court. Behind the legalese of the Aman Allah Codes, an intensifying political battle was brewing over what it meant in practice to be a free and independent Islamic state. At one level, the codes pitted the king's reformist elite against powerful tribal confederations wary of Kabul encroaching on their autonomy, with each side employing Islamic discourses to promote its view of the good society. Even more lethal to Aman Allah's campaign, beginning in 1924 fresh divisions emerged between pro-Kemalist and pro-Khilafat members of Aman Allah's court, in no small part caused by ruptures in Turkey and its transformation into a secular republic seen to have abandoned the caliphate (and, presumably, the shariʿa). Though thousands of miles away, many Afghan and Indian Muslim participants in the resolutely pro-Ottoman Khilafat movement (1919–1924) were dismayed by developments in Ankara, which provoked anxiety over whether Aman Allah would follow suit.[73] Without an operational bureaucracy, police, or army to enforce his laws, or a unified cabinet to amend them, Aman Allah's government collapsed as a conflagration of rebellions converged on Kabul, deposing the king in 1929.[74] No Afghan government would impose reforms of so broad a scale until the decade of Soviet occupation following the communist coup d'état of April 1978.

While histories of Afghanistan during the Aman Allah era have largely focused on the second half of the reformist king's decade in power, dwelling on his overthrow at the hands of the violent revolts of 1929 falls too easily into conventional tropes of Afghanistan as the world's failed state par excellence. What has often gone unnoticed is that while some of the original provisions of the Basic Code were later amended in the face of violent revolts in the southern and eastern provinces of the country, structurally the 1923 Constitution established a model for future Afghan constitutions.[75] Aman Allah's constitution was extensively copied in the 1931 Constitution passed and implemented by his Musahiban successors, Nadir Shah (r. 1929–1933) and Zahir Shah (r. 1933–1973), though no mention of the original constitution was made in the document or, indeed, in Afghan historiography for decades to come. By designing new kinds of governmental institutions, including a wide-ranging bureaucracy with a multitiered cabinet, subordinate ministries, and centralized network of courts applying uniform legal codes, Aman Allah laid the foundations for a "rule of law" in the country. As political scientist and former US envoy to Afghanistan Leon Poullada (1913–1987) once summarized, "even if Aman Allah had done nothing else, the juridical base he provided for Afghanistan was of considerable importance since it gave the country the skeleton of the government it was eventually to develop. In this sense the 1923 Constitution was unquestionably a landmark document."[76]

Despite such praise, nearly a century after the promulgation of Afghanistan's first constitution and supplemental Aman Allah Codes, their origins have hitherto been obscure. In particular, the role of Islamic jurisprudence and schools of law, as well as the authors' roles in the production of the codes, have largely been overlooked or ignored. Taking the criminal law manual *Tamassuk al-Quzat* as a case in point, we can see that while the jurists who crafted the Aman Allah Codes adhered to canonical texts of the Hanafi school of *fiqh* for deriving substantive legal rules, the structure and aesthetic layout of the Nizamnamihha-yi Amaniyyih resembled modern legal codes such as the Ottoman Mecelle. The latter's influence is evident in the organization of every *niẓāmnāmih* into distinct issue-oriented sections, each containing vertically enumerated articles followed by a brief statement of the rule. Simply put, this was the most robust attempt to engineer a comprehensive *fiqh* code for an entire field of substantive law since the Mecelle.

So, Aman Allah may have been a "progressive," a "reformist," and even a "revolutionary king," but Afghanistan under his rule should also be described as one of the first Islamic state projects of the twentieth century. The only other fully sovereign Muslim states in the region—Kemalist Turkey, Pahlavi Iran, Hashemite Hejaz, Northern Yemen, and Oman—formally marginalized the shariʿa as a source of law, imported European codes to constitute the new state's laws, or cannot be said to have developed a comprehensive body of statutory law reflecting an Islamic theory of the nation-state in a substantial way. Far from seeing the shariʿa as dead after colonialism, and its custodians as passive spectators of their own marginalization, the jurists of Aman Allah's Afghanistan were skilled agents who struggled—and negotiated—to carve a space of autochthonous legal production that has largely gone unnoticed. Here, it must be emphasized, the architects of the Nizamnamihha-yi Amaniyyih pursued their goals by engaging the challenges of modern state building from within the Hanafi legal tradition, not from outside it.

This approach was certainly not exclusive to Afghanistan's Aman Allah Codes, or to the modern era for that matter. As legal scholars Sherman Jackson, Baber Johansen, and Mohammad Fadel have shown, medieval Hanafi and Maliki jurists developed moral theories of the state not only to legitimate individual sultans but also to cultivate mutual dependency between rulers and the ruled in ways that limited and not just legitimated governments.[77] Similarly, as scholars of the early modern Ottoman Empire have warned, it is important to recognize an equally suspect counterpart to Orientalist images of Islamic decline: that of apolitical jurists "keeping the law pure from the interventions of the political authority until the European colonialists got there."[78] Though opting for romanticism over demonization, and useful for distinguishing a sophisticated scholarly tradition from the policies of many "Islamic states" today, such frameworks preserve essentialist binaries that presume the incommensurability of shariʿa and modernity.

Situated in historical context it is unsurprising that Islamic legal modernism emerged at a transitional moment worldwide, as loosely governed empires and patrimonial regimes from the eighteenth and early nineteenth centuries were replaced by highly centralized, bureaucratic, and territorially bound regimes in the twentieth century. The nation-state, in the Middle East as elsewhere, brought new legal discourses of constitutionalism and citizenship, but also disciplinary tools such as the judge's manual and code.[79] As in the late Ottoman Empire, Egypt, and Malay Archipelago, among other locales, Islamic legal modernism in Afghanistan was neither landlocked nor an island to itself but shared in regional strategies of statecraft and governance. But it should also not be forgotten that Afghanistan, remarkably cosmopolitan for a so-called Forbidden Kingdom, produced novel contributions on its own terms.

SIX

Turkish Tremors, Afghan Aftershocks

Anatolia and Afghanistan after the Ottomans

ON THE BALMY summer afternoon of August 19, 1919, Amir Aman Allah Khan of Afghanistan was likely basking in his glory. Presiding over the nation's first independence day celebration, in Paghman, a resort town west of Kabul, the twenty-seven-year-old monarch had just confronted the greatest empire in history and emerged victorious. Beyond solidifying his seat on the Muhammadzai throne, Aman Allah's triumph catapulted Afghanistan to global preeminence as one of the only free and fully sovereign Islamic states in the world. As throngs of Afghans across ethnic and regional divides gathered in the hilltop gardens and meadows near Aman Allah's birthplace to celebrate God, king, and country, one could not be blamed for concluding he was the most beloved Afghan ruler in history.

Aman Allah's fame was not limited to the borders of his landlocked country. In neighboring India and as far as Anatolia, Muslims hailed the amir as Ghazi Aman Allah, a triumphant warrior king who had defeated the British for the glory of Islam as the once magnificent Ottoman Empire staggered from its defeat in the Great War. The renowned Indian poet-philosopher Muhammad Iqbal presented his 1923 work *Payam-i Mashriq* (Message from the East) to Aman Allah, itself a response to the German poet Goethe's *West–östlicher Divan.*

Similarly, in one of his odes to the Afghan monarch, Iranian bard Vahid Dastgardi lavished praise on Aman Allah as a champion of independence and unity, and as a just Muslim king.[1]

Aman Allah's popularity across the greater Islamicate world was no doubt reinforced by the exceptional status of his kingdom as an entirely free and independent state at a time of widespread colonization across Asia and Africa. As Allied armies and administrations occupied Greater Syria, North Africa, and soon Istanbul itself, Persia remained divided between British and Russian spheres of influence. Meanwhile, the British Empire continued to rule over its century-old colonial possessions in India, and nearly a half century in Egypt, now a full-fledged protectorate of the Crown. Among Muslim-majority states in the region, Aman Allah's Afghanistan truly stood apart as an island of Islamic sovereignty. Attesting to his preeminent standing in Pan-Islamic circles, it was not long before rumors circulated of the Afghan amir becoming caliph, acceding to the office from the virtually defunct House of Osman. Though he ultimately declined to be considered for the office, Aman Allah continued to be recognized as one of the last remaining sovereign Muslim rulers, governing his territory free from European suzerainty and enjoying the widespread support of his people.

That was 1919. The same could not be said, however, five years into Aman Allah's reign. In a stunning political reversal, by 1924 Aman Allah faced the first of two major revolts in his ten-year reign. The first uprising erupted from the eastern border town of Khost in March that year, in a rebellion of predominantly Mangal Pashtuns. Aman Allah's government was barely able to quell the revolt, and only after offering weighty concessions to rival clans and tribes, and some influential ulema who did not serve on the CLC, by scaling back some of his more controversial reforms. Among the latter were *niẓāmnāmihs* imposing new family and education laws—the schooling of girls and training of female teachers, the state registration of marriages (including a minimum age), and restrictions on polygamy, for example—all of which were challenged by the Khost rebels and their sympathizers early on.[2] Difficult as these concessions were for Aman Allah to make, the resulting conciliation temporarily bolstered the government's besieged forces with a powerful confederation of Pashtun tribes and ulema who had hitherto been concerned over the direction of the amir's internal policies. Aman Allah's compromises enabled Kabul to reassert its national authority, isolate the Khost rebels, and finally suppress the revolt in January 1925.[3]

The second rebellion ended much less favorably for Aman Allah. In autumn 1928, a pair of nearly simultaneous provincial uprisings in the north and southeast shook the country and further weakened Aman Allah's already tenuous grip on power. From the north, a Kuhistani brigand named Habib Allah Kalakani (1891–1929), backed by a coalition of predominantly Tajik forces, declared himself the leader of a revolution against Aman Allah. From the restive southeastern Pashtun belt, Shinwari confederates also declared Aman Allah's claim to the throne illegitimate, and made their way for the capital. Kalakani's forces reached Kabul first, capturing the main fortress, arsenal, and palace, forcing Aman Allah to flee southward to Kandahar. The embattled king hoped to rally supporters for a return march on the capital. Aman Allah was outdone, however, by the ferocity of the revolts and abandoned by his court advisors, and the early weeks of 1929 marked the beginning of the end for his reign. On the night of January 14, 1929, Aman Allah accepted defeat and relinquished his throne to his older brother, ʿInayat Allah Khan, who himself abdicated three days later in favor of Kalakani.[4] Meanwhile, in one of the most stunning reversals in the country's modern political history, the dethroned king and once lionized ghazi who had championed Afghanistan's independence quietly crossed over the Durand Line into British Indian territory, never to see his beloved country again.[5]

LIKE A DARK cloud lingering over the Kabul palace, the meteoric rise and fall of Aman Allah (r. 1919–1929) cast a shadow over Afghan royal politics for decades. No other monarch in Afghan history soared to such popular heights, only to fall to such depths of scorn, in so short a time.[6] Wary of repeating his missteps, subsequent Afghan rulers were keen to remember the legacy of Aman Allah's reign. The interregnum of Kalakani—Aman Allah's ouster and the only non-Pashtun ruler in Afghanistan's history—lasted barely nine months before Kalakani was defeated and executed by forces loyal to General Nadir Khan (1883–1933), who had returned to Afghanistan to make his own claim on the throne. On October 16, 1929, the latter was crowned Nadir Shah and head of the new Musahiban dynasty in Kabul. Under the Musahibans (1929–1973), Afghanistan's last royal family, the next four decades would be marked by cautious gradualism and conservative development policies, until the rise of republican and Marxist-inspired parties in the 1970s and, most radically, the communist coup d'état in 1978, half a century after Aman Allah's dethronement.

The memory of Aman Allah has also captivated the attention of many a historian since. Relative to other eras in pre-1979 Afghanistan, the revolts that toppled the reformist king have been the subject of a sizable scholarly literature.[7]

Excepting Senzil Nawid's outstanding study of the Amani era, scholars by and large seem to have been interested more in Aman Allah's dramatic overthrow from provincial uprisings than in the considerable administrative and constitutional legacy he built for the country during the first half of his reign. Meanwhile, historical work on Afghanistan during the Amani era continues to frame the period as one of Manichean conflict between progressive modernity and stagnant traditions. Here, the modern is read as "secular and westernized" Afghans, epitomized in Aman Allah himself as the progressive, avant-garde modernizer; while antiquated mullahs and bellicose tribes fall into the stagnant, regressive category of the traditional. Insular and xenophobic, violently fearful of change, and ever prone to irrationality and recalcitrance, timeless Pashtun "tribals" become the explain-all factor of tumult and rebellion in Afghan politics.

For centuries European writers—and to be sure, several Afghans, Indians, and Turks, as noted—have spilled ink about Pashtuns to the tune of the "noble savage" theme. Essentialist, reductionist, and prejudiced as it is, to apply this framework to the Amani era and dramatic overthrow of the reformist king would in that sense not be new. But the unraveling of Aman Allah's government did not take place in a Pashtun frontier vacuum, supposedly cut off from the outside world. We have seen how the reigns of the late Muhammadzai amirs ʿAbd al-Rahman, Habib Allah, and Aman Allah—and the making of Afghanistan's modern legal and constitutional foundations under their leadership—were interlaced with social and educational networks, political movements, and migrations of persons in and out of the country, especially to and from the Ottoman Empire and British India. In the same vein, the discrediting of Aman Allah's government was not a result of purely internal factors alone, but was also shaped by events taking place far from Afghanistan.

Turks, Afghans, and the Dissolution of the Ottoman Empire

On November 1, 1922, the Turkish Grand National Assembly in Ankara abolished the office of the sultanate, bringing to an end 631 years of rule by the House of Osman and sealing the dissolution of an empire that once spanned three continents. The radical decision to abolish the Ottoman sultanate—the last great imperial Muslim power in world history—sent shockwaves throughout the region and beyond, including Afghanistan. Members of Aman Allah's cabinet could not help but watch developments in Ankara with circumspection and concern, and probably some confusion. Having ratified their landmark friendship treaty with the Turkish national government in March 1921, the Afghans respected the Turkish parliament's right to govern their own affairs, but the Pan-Islamic institution of the caliphate—the successor to the Prophet for Sunni Muslims worldwide—was unique.

Notwithstanding some raised eyebrows, Afghan officials had their own priorities to worry about, and the fate of the House of Osman was but one rope in a series of ties binding Ankara and Kabul in anticolonial struggle. Meanwhile, Turco-Afghan ties appeared to only grow stronger, especially at the official level. On December 28, 1922, British intelligence in the Indian frontier city of Peshawar reported two of the Afghan amir's couriers passing through town. Their destination: the Afghan legation at Ankara. Even with the sultanate gone, a hallowed legacy of the Ottoman dynasty remained in Istanbul. Abdülmecid II (r. 1922–1924), the titular monarch and successor to the last Ottoman sultan, Mehmed VI (r. 1918–1922), continued to be recognized in and outside the Turkish republic as the caliph of Muslims. Even as far as Afghanistan, the new caliph had been officially acknowledged, with Aman Allah sending Ankara a congratulatory message, delivered by the aforesaid pair of couriers observed passing through Peshawar.[8] As the British legation observed in Kabul in July 1923, the Friday sermon in Kabul's main mosques was read in caliph Abdülmecid II's name, attracting the attention of the British minister Sir Humphrys and his counterparts in Delhi and London. "By the ratification of the Treaty with Angora," Humphrys noted, "and the use of Abdul Majid's name in the *khutba*—the only prayer offered for the Caliph in this country—the Afghan Government have publicly endorsed the appointment made by the Angoran Government."[9] Abdülmecid II would be the last Ottoman caliph to bear the distinction of having his name read in the Friday sermon—in Afghanistan, or anywhere else.

The Afghan government's recognition of Abdülmecid II as the new caliph went hand in hand with an arguably even more important acknowledgment at the time: that the national parliament in Ankara was the official representative and sovereign government of Turkey. With rather ironic undertones, that recognition further closed the door on a return to politics by the House of Osman in Istanbul. Friday sermons in Kabul acknowledging the new caliph made Afghanistan among the first Muslim-majority states to recognize Ankara's decision.[10] The already warm ties between Aman Allah and Mustafa Kemal were further reinforced by subsequent actions to strengthen bilateral relations between the two countries taken by both leaders. On March 27, 1923, the Afghan government bestowed honorary medals on Kemal and his close associates Fevzi Çakmak and İsmet İnönü, celebrating their leadership in Turkey's successful war of independence.[11]

Still, as doubts and questions emerged over the future of the caliphate in a new Turkish republic, an international Muslim conference was proposed to discuss the institution, in Ankara. Reports in the Afghan and Indian press hinted at rumors that Aman Allah was planning to attend Ankara's anticipated Islamic Congress to discuss the question of the caliphate. In the words of British intelligence scouting the congress, the purpose of the forum was "to discuss the formation of a league of Moslem nations and the future of the khilafat."[12] With regard to said rumors of the Afghans' attendance, it appears Aman Allah initially planned to attend, but later respectfully offered his regrets. On May 18, 1923, Simla-based newspaper *The Statesman* proclaimed just as much to the headline, "Islamic Congress in Angora, Amir Not to Participate." As the article explained, "It is stated in a well-informed quarter that His Majesty has no such intention his time being too fully occupied with effecting improvements in the administration of his country and with furthering its advancement in the paths of civilization."[13] With the country's first constitution having been promulgated only a month earlier, on April 9, 1923, and with various other reform projects underway, the amir's absence may have been understandable. But given this was the first Pan-Islamic conference held on the question of the Ottoman caliphate, and as one of the premier candidates for the office, the Afghan amir's absence was noted, and was likely to have been consequential.

Meanwhile in Anatolia, decisive victories by the Turkish resistance catapulted Kemal's nationalist forces to prominence and a place at the negotiating table with the victors of World War I. With it came an opportunity to reverse Ottoman losses in the Great War—but not nearly all of them. On July 24, 1923, officials representing Kemal's nationalist government in Ankara met with representatives of Britain, France, Greece, Italy, Romania, and Japan in Lausanne, Switzerland. Their goal: to sign a peace agreement putting an end to the array of conflicts dividing the Turks and Allies from the onset of World War I, with a focus on the Anatolian peninsula and surrounding territories. The agreement annulled the partition of Anatolia dictated by the Treaty of Sèvres (1920), thereby concluding a four-year Turkish war of independence. Among the terms was a reincorporation of nearly all of Anatolia, Istanbul, and eastern Thrace until Edirne into the new Republic of Turkey, which was to enjoy total sovereignty within its new borders (see Map 5). In return, the Turkish republic abandoned

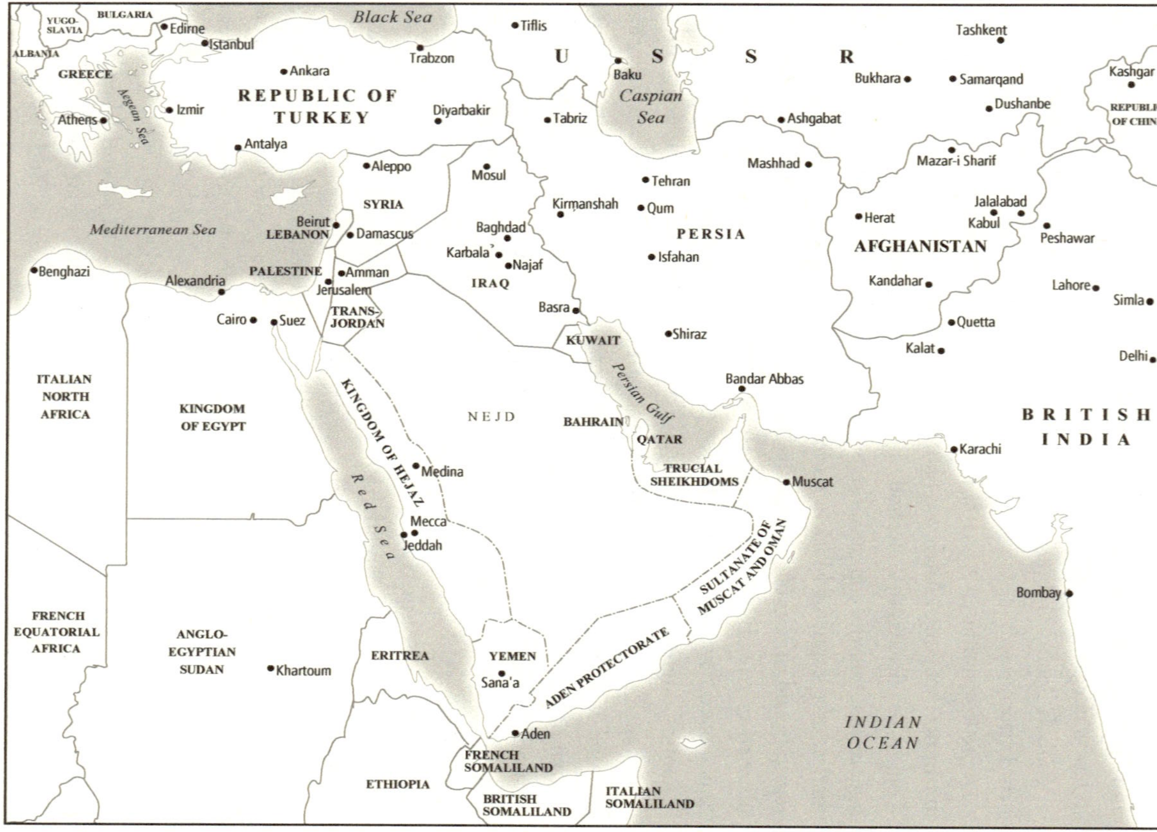

MAP 5. The greater Middle East after the Treaty of Lausanne, 1923

claims to former Ottoman territories of Greater Syria, Mesopotamia, and the Arabian Peninsula, while settling borders with the neighboring states of Greece, Bulgaria, and Armenia. The treaty also officially established the Ankara-based Republic of Turkey as the successor state to an officially defunct Ottoman Empire.

Hours after the signing of the agreement, Afghanistan's ambassador in Ankara, Sultan Ahmad Khan, dispatched a telegraph to Mustafa Kemal in Izmir congratulating the Turkish people on behalf of Aman Allah and the Afghan nation. The communication made Afghanistan one of the first Muslim-majority states to recognize the Lausanne Agreement.[14] So momentous was the agreement at Lausanne that both Ankara and Kabul deemed it in their interest to negotiate a new treaty between the Turkish republic and Afghanistan, superseding the Turco-Afghan Agreement of March 1921. An August 1923 memorandum, one of the last documents attributed to an Ottoman foreign ministry in Istanbul, revealed plans to dispatch Turkish representative Şevket Bey to Kabul to negotiate a new treaty.[15]

On October 29, 1923, the Turkish government in Ankara officially proclaimed the establishment of the Republic of Turkey under the leadership of its first president, Mustafa Kemal "Atatürk" (Father of the Turks). Shortly thereafter, Sultan Ahmad Khan shared a congratulatory note with the republic's minister of foreign affairs celebrating a new chapter in Turkish history.[16] Wishing the new state "all success on the path to progress and development," he also declared Turkey would continue to be a model for Muslim nations, including Afghanistan: "This Turkish-born Republic is the star of the earth, illuminating all the Islamic countries," he stated in no uncertain terms.[17]

Back in Afghanistan, however, it appears the ambassador had spoken too soon. Turkey's decision to abolish the caliphate in spring 1924 sent shockwaves through the Afghan populace, especially in major cities, and the Kabul government alike. On the commotion the Ankara's decision created in Afghanistan, the British minister in Kabul, Sir Richard Machonachie, observed that the Turkish government was "severely criticized" in Kabul for the former's action concerning the caliphate.[18] Of all the controversial proclamations the Kemalist republic would go on to make over the next decade, the elimination of the transnational, Pan-Islamic institution of the caliphate was at the top of the list. As the distinguished Afghan historian Senzil Nawid relates, "[T]he most important contributing factor to the decline of pan-Islamism was Kamal Atatürk's abolition of the caliphate in 1924. The news of the repudiation of the caliphate became known in Kabul in early March of that year, shortly before the outbreak of the Khost Rebellion, and created outrage among the ulama and other supporters of the caliphate in Afghanistan."[19]

In response to the Turkish parliament's decision, public petitions were drawn up and circulated around the Afghan capital in protest; some went so far as to call for an immediate downgrading of Turco-Afghan ties. The trauma and shock—and no other words could be more appropriate—in response to the Türkiye Büyük Millet Meclisi's (TBMM) decision were so severe in Afghanistan that Turco-Afghan relations were nearly derailed, even moving the staunchly Turcophile Aman Allah to condemn the decision. The latter went so far as to publish an article in Kabul's government-sponsored newspaper, *Aman-i Afghan,* to this effect.[20] Describing a "most marked" deterioration in bilateral ties between the two countries, Machonachie identified the TBMM's decision as the single biggest cause of a "decline in Turkish prestige and influence in Kabul," he noted later that spring. "The main reasons for it," the British minister opined on the first major Turco-Afghan row in the history of the two young states, "are probably to be found in the abolition of the Caliphate by Mustapha Kemal."[21]

Meanwhile within Turkey itself the decision to abolish the caliphate was only one act—albeit an enormously symbolic one—among a constellation of new laws passed by the Turkish parliament under Kemal's direction. From 1923 until his death in 1938, Mustafa Kemal led his nascent republic through a top-down revolution of social, cultural, and political upheaval with a clear goal: to transform Turkey from a multiethnic caliph-sultanate spanning three continents to a secular republic and nation-state based in Anatolia. Soon after the TBMM's elimination of the caliphate, remaining members of the royal Ottoman dynasty were expelled from the country.[22] Ottoman-era madrasas and sufi lodges, including those housing pilgrims from Central Asia, India, and Afghanistan in Istanbul, were shut down and banned. The Ministry of Religious Affairs and multiple privately administered charitable endowments, or *waqfs,* shared the same fate as their operations were absorbed by the new state's bureaucracy in Ankara. In the juridical realm, the shari'a courts (*Şeriat mahkemeleri*), and the office of the mufti, were replaced by the Turkish republic's adoption of the Swiss civil legal code, the Italian penal code, and a new commercial code largely imitating German and Italian models.[23] Before long a flood of secularizing legislation targeting Turkish dress, language, education, and cultural mores began to impact the everyday lives of Turkish citizens, especially but not limited to urban locales, or the country's majority Sunni Muslim and Turkish-speaking populations for that matter.[24] Saturday replaced Friday as the start of the official weekend; the Gregorian solar calendar replaced the Islamic (Hijri) lunar calendar; most sweeping of all, the Latin script replaced the Arabic script, combined with efforts to purge Turkish from its extensive Persian and Arabic loanwords. Mehmed Seyyid Çelebizade (1873–1925), a law professor and former Committee for Union and Progress deputy, played a critical role in advising Kemal on these overlapping social, cultural, and legal aspects of the new secular republic. The goal: to reorder government institutions and completely remake Turkish public life such that "religious" affairs would never again interfere in matters of the public and state.[25]

So powerful was the agitation in Kabul against the Turkish decision over the fate of the caliphate that even Afghan officials who only months earlier had congratulated the Turks on their independence felt the pressure of an entente at risk of collapse. While Aman Allah's foreign ministry officials did not favor downgrading ties with Ankara, they did favor a newly worded agreement. In particular they raised the need to amend Article 3 of the 1921 Turco-Afghan Friendship Treaty, which had proudly acknowledged Turkish religious leadership as the upholder of the Caliphate for centuries.[26] The controversial clause of the treaty between two Muslim-majority countries was not only subsequently amended, but an entirely new agreement had to be redrafted and negotiated between Afghanistan and the Republic of Turkey, with a final accord not approved until 1928.[27] These developments reflected the heaviness with which Afghan officials received the TBMM's decision, and the consternation it caused even among the staunchest Turcophiles in the Kabul court.

On a broader scale, Afghan domestic opposition against several of Aman Allah's Turkish-inspired measures—especially new modes of conscription, military training, and codification of laws—were amplified by Ankara's controversial decision concerning the caliphate. As the British minister in Kabul further noted, such a combined outpouring of anger against the elimination of the caliphate and Aman Allah's legislation often resulted in extreme anti-Turkish statements as, "The provisions of the Nizam Nama or Fundamental Code which had been drafted by Bedri Bey were first misrepresented, and then denounced as the work of a nation which had deposed the Caliph and turned its back on Islam."[28] In this way, controversial decisions made in Ankara but impacting the broader Islamicate world, including Afghanistan, played into the hands of Aman Allah's opposition, who were bent on challenging the Afghan king's radical, reformist agenda and now had momentum in their favor.

That the wave of anti-Turkish feeling unleashed in the 1924 Khost Rebellion came just weeks after the Ankara government's expulsion of the last caliph,

Abdülmecid II, appears to be instructive rather than coincidental. The timing of the revolt and the clear anti-Turkish undertones in the rebels' discourse against Aman Allah—including an inaccurate conflation of Kemalist republicanism and secularism with the Nizamnamihha-yi Amaniyyih reforms—once again reflected an explosive convergence of local and foreign-inspired factors. Far from "just another flare-up" of supposed Pashtun insularity and provincialism, that Aman Allah's strong relations with the Turks had now become a liability—such that the reformist king had to distance himself from the TBMM's decision on the caliphate—displayed the lingering connections between distant Anatolia and Afghanistan, albeit not in the way Aman Allah and Kemal had intended for either of their countries. Furthermore, even as Aman Allah finally put down the rebellion that nearly ended his reign in 1924, it was not lost on the king's more cautious advisors that certain powerful elements and vested interests in the countryside opposed to his centralizing plans were beginning to win the rhetorical battle for Afghanistan's future, and for what a free and independent Islamic state should mean.

The End of the Khilafat Movement

Even more than the shockwaves felt in Afghanistan, Ankara's decision to abolish the Ottoman caliphate had a devastating impact on Pan-Islamic campaigning in India. Bereft of their raison d'être, most baffled of all was the hitherto staunchly pro-Turkish Khilafat movement. British officials described the impact on the movement as no less than "paralysing."[29] Having launched an international campaign to save the Ottoman caliphate from European aggression, supporters of the Khilafat movement were left aghast by the Turkish government's decision as their activities came to a sudden and unexpected halt. Like a rug being pulled from beneath them, the bewildered Khilafatists in India and Afghanistan were powerless to press their case before the major world powers concerning the fate of the Ottoman caliph when Turkey itself—and not London, Paris, or any other colonial power—had disavowed the House of Osman once and for all. At the same time, developments in Hejaz had also knocked the wind out of the movement. With Sharif Husayn sent into exile and Ibn Saud establishing a lackluster tribal dominion in his place, Indian Muslim leaders struggled to find the charismatic and prestigious caliph they sought. With the Khilafat movement in tatters, these events no doubt strengthened the British hand in Asia, "shattering" Aman Allah's Pan-Islamic card in the process.[30]

With the writing on the wall for the international campaign to defend the caliphate, the events of 1924 commenced an "inward" turn in Afghan and Indian politics as Aman Allah and Muslim revolutionaries within India increasingly turned their attention to domestic and local concerns. The result was a noticeable decline in the pace and intensity of Pan-Islamic projects linking the Indian, Afghan, and Turkish publics, as domestic agendas came to take precedence over the more radical and grandiose visions of Pan-Islamic unity that had been entertained during World War I and its immediate aftermath. The shock of these events for many Muslims of India and Afghanistan notwithstanding, it could be argued that for Indian Muslims the Khilafat movement was always driven by a short-term fusion of differentiated interests rather than by a monolithic, uniform bloc of Muslim political will or fraternal sentiments. The single thread uniting these complex, multifaceted interests was the shared desire to protect the territorial integrity of the Ottoman caliphate, and to protest the creation of mandates by the Allies in Syria, Palestine, and Iraq, or by "British-manufactured sultans" in Hejaz. With Turkey's signing of the Lausanne Treaty, and its abolition of the caliphate a year later, the Turks themselves had accepted just as much. Bereft of its lightning-rod cause, Indian Khilafatism did not so much disappear as withdraw and reconstitute itself into a fledgling nationalist movement of a different kind. From the mid-1920s on, former Khilafatist agencies and members continued to mobilize pan-Indian networks of awareness, fundraising, and resistance, but for the more geographically local goal of representing the communal interests of India's Muslims.[31] As Machonachie noted even from Afghanistan,

> The abolition of the Caliphate had a paralysing effect . . . upon the Khilafat agitation . . . With the defeat of [Sharif Husayn's] son Ali by Ibn Saud, and the election of the latter as King of the Hedjaz in January 1926, this weapon too was removed; and the Indian Moslem leaders, humbled by the earlier cavalier treatment accorded by Ibn Saud to their representatives, thereafter tended more and more to devote themselves to domestic problems, and to their own communal interests.[32]

Over time, however, as the Kabul court distilled its own vision of national interests, the Afghan government signed agreements with foreign states and initiated policies within that were increasingly opposed to the Pan-Islamic goals of the Indian *muhājirs,* and of the Khilafatists more broadly. The eclipse of the Khilafat movement accelerated Kabul's turn to Afghan territorial nationalism—and plain realpolitik—over and above any competing ideological causes such as Pan-Islamism, Pan-Asianism, or even Pashtun irredentism. As the head of state of Afghanistan—and of nowhere and no one else, he was reminded—Aman Allah faced difficult sacrifices in order to shore up the foundations of his increasingly unsteady hold on power.

The latter was perhaps most evident in the scaling back of several of Aman Allah's more radical liberalizing provisions in the 1923 Constitution and associated Nizamnamihha-yi Amaniyyih reforms following a national Loya Jirga held at Paghman in July 1924.[33] According to British informants present at the assembly, among Aman Allah's concessions were reducing exemption fees for conscription, with the option of offering a substitute conscript; restricting female education to girls under twelve years of age; and annulling controversial *niẓāmnāmihs* concerning marriage and family law, including new restrictions on polygamy.[34] Said revisions were imposed on the amir at the behest of a powerful group of Afghan ulema associated with the Deobandi school in India. The latter deemed a number of provisions of the Aman Allah Codes to be in contravention of shariʿa—their interpretation of it, that is—in particular, those provisions targeting women, marriage, and the family. This reversal of events underscored the victory of the more socially and politically conservative segments of Afghan society allied to the Deobandi movement in northern India, NWFP, and the Indo-Afghan frontier more broadly, over the pro-Turkish elements in the Kabul court.[35] It is in this light that Aman Allah had earlier attempted to ban Afghans from studying at the influential seminary at Deoband.[36]

Between 1924 and 1929, however, the triumph of Deobandi Indian influence over Kemalist Turkish influence in Afghanistan was sealed when prominent Afghan ulema of the Deobandi persuasion—with the support of the succeeding Afghan king, Nadir Shah (r. 1929–1933)—established a national association of religious scholars, the Jamʿiyat-i ʿUlama'-i Afghanistan. The latter was akin to the identically named association established by Deobandi scholars across India a decade earlier, the Jamʿiyat-i ʿUlama'-i Hind.[37] Ironically, it was members of the latter organization of ulema that earlier played an instrumental role in galvanizing India-wide support for Aman Allah and his war of independence from the British, and in supporting the Turkish resistance in Anatolia under Mustafa Kemal's leadership underway at the same time.

It is important to note that while many of Aman Allah's controversial reforms were rescinded, and there were certain amendments to the Basic Code, structurally the Qanun-i Asasi and several other *niẓāmnāmihs* remained the foundation for future Afghan constitutions and legislation. While symbolically repudiating the controversial provisions, it was upon these foundations established by Aman Allah and his Indo-Ottoman-Afghan codification committee that subsequent Afghan governments operated, even if they refused to admit it. Such long-term contributions were likely not in the mind of the reformist king from the turbulent spring of 1924 until the quashing of the Mangal revolt in January 1925, however. The constitutional amendments he enacted at the Loya Jirga at Paghman represented Aman Allah's compromise with a greater Afghan ulema establishment, who in return for the amir's withdrawal of controversial reforms, renewed their support for him and endorsed his government's campaign against the Mangal rebels of Khost. After a whirlwind series of events that began with Afghan celebrations of Turkey's independence in 1923 and ended with protests against the Turkish parliament in 1924, Aman Allah had managed to stave off a rebellion and remained the undisputed king of Afghanistan. But for the amir's foes and friends alike, it had also become obvious that the Pan-Islamic crest he had ridden to power had come to an inglorious end.

Shah Aman Allah from (De)tour to Deposal

The Khost Rebellion taught Aman Allah and his court that laws on paper did not automatically translate into substantive change in Afghanistan. Dynamic and skilled as his lawmaking commission was, it was no match for the long-standing social realities of tribal sovereignty, fiercely defended local autonomy, and the authority of actual power holders on the ground, especially beyond Kabul. After 1924, instead of limiting his reforms to formal laws, Aman Allah enhanced his centralization tool kit through a series of government plans aimed at establishing a new administrative grid for the country. He divided the country into five provinces: Kabul, Kandahar, Afghan Turkestan, Herat, and Badakhshan, each supervised by a governor. Each province was further divided into districts which were to be administered by government-paid judges and magistrates. In this way, Aman Allah continued the territorial division of federal administration launched by his grandfather the Iron Amir, while also maintaining ʿAbd al-Rahman's practice of serving as the last court of appeal, reserving one day of the week for hearing personal cases of individual subjects.[38] In this way, after the Khost Rebellion Aman Allah increasingly shifted from strictly legal to administrative reforms, designed to build up a centralized bureaucracy that would organize and rationalize the regulatory state in practice.

After a cooling off period of roughly a year, in which the king recalled some of his more radical reforms—in particular, those related to conscription, taxation, family law, and women's rights—by early 1926 Aman Allah was kindling the fires of another state-building campaign, but this time of a noticeably different ilk. Hardly two years after the rebellion in Khost had almost toppled his rule, Aman Allah discarded his older title *amir* for the more secular Persianate term for king, *pādishāh.* Less than a year later, Shah Aman Allah made the consequential decision to complete a tour of Europe, and thereby became the first Afghan ruler to leave the Asian continent and travel further than the neighboring countries of India, Iran, and Bukhara.

Seeking to acquire the latest technologies for modernizing his country and to put Afghanistan "on the map" with industrial nations, Aman Allah's international tour began in December 1927, setting out from the Indian seaport of Karachi for Rome, via Cairo. Accompanied by Queen Suraya and their children, in what soon became a spectacle in Western newspapers, the Afghan king proceeded over seven months to visit Egypt, Italy, France, Switzerland, Germany, Belgium, Britain, Poland, the Soviet Union, and Turkey, receiving red carpet receptions at virtually every stop. Over the course of the tour Aman Allah met with an array of fellow monarchs and heads of state, including King Fuad I in Cairo; King Victor-Emmanuel III of Italy, joined by his prime minister, Benito Mussolini, in Rome; Pope Pius XI in the Vatican City; President Gaston Doumergue of France in Paris; King Albert I and Queen Elisabeth of Belgium in Brussels; President Paul von Hindenburg of Germany in Berlin; King George V and Queen May of Great Britain, who hosted the royal family at Buckingham Palace; Polish president Ignacy Mościcki in Warsaw; and Soviet president Mikhail Kalinin, joined by senior chiefs of the Soviet Red Army, in Moscow. Aman Allah concluded his regional circuit in neighboring Turkey and Iran, where he was warmly welcomed by Kemal in Ankara and Riza Shah Pahlavi in Tehran, before returning to Kabul by automobile in July 1928.[39]

Western media outlets from Bombay to New York took a keen interest in Aman Allah's European tour. Representative in this respect was the weekly coverage of the Afghan royal family's travels and activities from the *Times* of London to the *New York Times.* Publishing articles headlined to the tunes of

"Absolute Monarch of Untamed Asian Hill People Prepares to Modernize His Ancient and Turbulent Land" and "Picturesque and Martial King Aman Allah Greatly Impresses the Italian Crowds," the US newspaper of record's Orientalizing depictions of the Afghan monarch as an enlightened despot were not in short supply.[40] At the same time, Aman Allah seemed to revel in the attention, and was not shy to exploit the spotlight cast on his nation to his advantage. Helping to soften images of Aman Allah's "martial" grandeur and Afghanistan as a forbidden kingdom was a charm offensive by Queen Suraya, whose glamour became a sensation in Europe and the United States, with leading newspapers doting on her and the royal Afghan princesses.[41] Photographs of the queen and her daughters partially unveiled and sporting respectable Parisian fashions in public attracted admiration in Europe but generated a scandal when they were mysteriously leaked in Afghanistan.[42]

Though Aman Allah's grand seven-month tour to Europe was denounced by his critics as an extravagant and wasteful expense on an already strained budget, and exposed the monarch to even more fierce rhetorical attacks and scandal-mongering at home, the reformist king did return to Kabul with some substantive results. He had signed nine new treaties with European states, in addition to revising those already existing with Turkey, Iran, and the Soviet Union. Of all the countries he had visited and the leaders he had strengthened bonds with, however, Kemalist Turkey appears to have stood out.[43] To the dismay of a mounting opposition at home, Aman Allah was preparing a radical new campaign of reforms of even greater ambition for Afghanistan, but one that did not share the nuances and Islamic legal modernist dimensions of the first half of his reign, when the majority of the Nizamnamihha-yi Amaniyyih Codes were produced.

At yet another Loya Jirga assembly, held at Paghman in early autumn 1928, only weeks after his return, Aman Allah announced the goal of writing a new series of codes. According to a British informant present, the purpose of these laws was to formalize a "separation of Church and State" in Afghanistan.[44] Before long Aman Allah introduced a series of edicts aimed even more squarely at implementing social and cultural programs of a radical ultra-secularist ilk. Most controversial were those impacting everyday practices, including dress code, education, and women's rights. One order required Western dress and hats and banned traditional Afghan headgear. The sartorial edicts for men were coupled with an encouragement to urban women to partially unveil, a practice announced to have been implemented in practice by the queen herself.[45] As if the resemblance to Kemalist laws promoting westernization and European-styled secularization in Turkey was not strong enough, the question of promulgating a civil law code for Afghanistan on the lines of the Swiss-based 1926 Turkish Civil Code was also introduced, though this was ultimately withdrawn by the government.[46] Aman Allah also established a new political party, Firqih-ʾi Istiqlal wa Tajaddud (Independence and Modernity Party), one of whose goals was to remove the impact of "superstitious and heretical beliefs" popular in society.[47]

Though hardly implemented outside Kabul, these measures sent a chill throughout the country. The measures also sent a clear message that, contrary to his more moderate early years, which might be described as Islamic legal modernism in power, Aman Allah was unapologetically shifting directions along lines more reminiscent of contemporaneous Kemalist and Pahlavi reforms underway in Turkey and Iran.[48] The resemblance to Kemal and what had transpired in Turkey was not lost on the Afghan ulema present. The timing was also noticeable: Aman Allah's reinvigorated campaign came on the heels of his return from Turkey, where news of the Afghan ruler's admiration for Kemal was hardly a secret. Photographs of Aman Allah with Kemal in Ankara, and the aforementioned images of an unveiled Queen Suraya, said just as much. Even before Aman Allah's grand European tour, however, the British minister at Kabul observed the persistence of Turkish influence in the Kabul court in the years following the 1924 Khost Rebellion:

> Despite the strong anti-Turkish feelings that emerged during the rebellion and were expressed during the Loya-Jerga of 1924, Aman Allah now strengthened diplomatic and political ties with Kamalist Turkey, doing just the opposite of what the ulama had wished. The years 1926 and 1927 witnessed a dramatic rise in Turkish influence in Kabul as evidenced by a large influx of Turkish advisors, educators, and administrative personnel . . . Afghan religious leaders began to suspect that Aman Allah was following the path of Ataturk, who had abolished the caliphate and secularized the Turkish state.[49]

Contrary to the more sensational theories of Aman Allah's fall from power, fears of resurgent Turkish influence in the Kabul court appear to be founded on the reformist king's actual policies (not on the role of Queen Suraya's sartorial choices, as sometimes emphasized in Afghan historiography and public memory). In May 1926, Nebil Batı Bey replaced the Ottoman war hero Ömer

Fahreddin Pasha as Ankara's ambassador to Afghanistan and Turkish chargé d'affaires in Kabul, a position he held until June 1928.[50] In his inaugural speech in Kabul, the new Turkish ambassador described a renewed relationship between the two countries. For the remainder of Aman Allah's rule, Nebil's tenure oversaw the appointment of Turks to several high positions in the Afghan government, including in the State Council, Ministry of Foreign Affairs, and Ministry of Finance.[51] Mehmed Cevad Bey, a close associate and related to Kemal by marriage, became a prominent legal advisor in Afghanistan's foreign ministry.[52]

Hence, two years after the Anatolian government's unpopular decision to abolish the caliphate, Turkey continued to play a role in the development of Afghanistan's governmental, military, and educational institutions—even as influential voices in the country chafed from Aman Allah's realignment with Ankara. Together with the ongoing work of former Ottoman subjects in Kabul like Mahmud Sami, republican Turks came to Afghanistan as teachers, physicians, and military officers through the mid to late 1920s to open schools, provide medical and public health services, and assist in the training of a national army.[53] For example, in 1926 a Turkish Ministry of Foreign Affairs report on Afghanistan—incidentally, still housed in the Ottoman central archives in Istanbul as opposed to the Republican archives in Ankara—discussed Turkey's sending a delegation of physicians to Kabul to initiate various projects in public health.[54] In the same year, İsmail Hakkı Bey led a military unit of Turkish officers to Afghanistan, with a supplemental foreign ministry memorandum discussing the expenses made in preparation for the mission.[55] As late as autumn 1928, a delegation of Turkish advisors was scheduled to arrive in Kabul to advise and assist in various governmental initiatives.[56]

As should be clear by now, this was not the same Kabul court, nor the same Afghanistan, as existed during the first half of Aman Allah's reign. Cemal Pasha, appointed to build a new Afghan army, and Osman Bedri Bey, director of the country's first constitutional commission, were dead.[57] The Ottoman Empire and the caliphate were defunct, reducing the prestige of the Turks in the eyes of many Afghans. Mawlawi 'Abd al Wasi' Qandahari and other liberal ulema who had contributed to the Aman Allah Codes had been discredited, demoted, or entirely removed from office, replaced by conservative clerics with ties to the Indian madrasa at Deoband.[58] At the same time, the collapse of the Hijrat movement and broader Khilafat movement in India resulted in fewer Indian technocrats serving in Aman Allah's government, further reducing his court's Pan-Islamic appeal. Most of all, Aman Allah himself was only a fraction as popular as when he had ridden a nationwide wave of euphoria following his successful war of independence against Britain in the summer of 1919, having only narrowly defeated an uprising on Afghan soil in 1924.

When it became evident that the monarch's new reforms were even more radical than the first round, with ample external resemblances to the Kemalist revolution in Turkey, those opposed to Aman Allah's second round of liberalizing reforms did not stand idly by. In autumn 1928, still only weeks after his return from Europe, a conflagration of revolts erupted in the north and southeast of the country, challenging the king's already tenuous hold on power. By the beginning of 1929, exactly a decade after his dramatic political victory over the British Raj with the aid of tribesmen who now opposed him, Aman Allah was forced to flee to Kandahar. Regrouping in Afghanistan's first capital and the heartland of the southern Pashtuns, the beleaguered king attempted a comeback by courting influential ulema and tribes in exchange for a promise to annul (again) his controversial laws. In early January 1929, humbling negotiations with the Shinwari rebels forced him to cancel the vast majority of his reforms and administrative measures. In one particularly desperate concession, Aman Allah assented to the formation of a council of fifty notables to be chosen from among respected religious luminaries and tribal chiefs, and promised to abide by their advice and interpretations of the shariʿa. What is more, the council would hold veto power over any legislation passed by his government—an extraordinary concession for a monarch to make, but for the staunchest elements of the southern and eastern opposition it proved to be too little, too late.[59] Two weeks later, Aman Allah was no longer king, or even residing in the country he had helped win independence for.

Aman Allah's Fall: From Reforms to Revolts, Revisited

Scholars of Afghanistan's modern history have differed as to the root causes of the uprisings against Aman Allah in 1924 and 1928–1929. Afghanistan's preeminent historian from the twentieth century, Mir Ghulam Muhammad Ghubar (1897–1978), was the first scholar to give serious attention to the Amani era. In his magnum opus, *Afghanistan dar Masir-i Tarikh* (Afghanistan in the Course of History), published in 1967 and banned in Afghanistan soon after, Ghubar argued British covert activities were to blame for the revolutionary king's fall from power.[60] Vartan Gregorian, in his pioneering 1969 work on the late

Muhammadzai dynasty, stressed Aman Allah's lack of a strong financial base and centralized army to implement the ambitious state-building program, factors we shall return to.[61] Former US envoy to Afghanistan and political scientist Leon Poullada, in the first major Western academic work dealing exclusively with the Amani era, focused on a dramatic clash between "a tradition-encrusted society, dominated by flinty and xenophobic codes of tribal politics, and an idealistic, uncompromising modernizer."[62] Several historiographical contributions notwithstanding, here the intricacy of this period of Afghan history is too often captured through the Manichean lens of "tribal separatism and bellicosity" and some projected analyses of Aman Allah's psychology and character flaws. Finally, after a near two-decade lull in scholarly production on the era, in 1999 Afghan-American historian Senzil Nawid published the most rigorous study devoted to the Amani period in any language. Utilizing rare private manuscripts and government archives in Dari and Pashto, Nawid cited souring state-ulema relations and the determined opposition of religiously inspired resistance to the reforms as the key factors in Aman Allah's fall from grace.[63]

While much of the historiography on the Amani era focuses on an inherent clash between progressive reformers and regressive traditionalism, a closer examination of evidence points less to cultural divides than to contingent historical factors dealing with power, property, and privilege. Declassified British intelligence cables from Kabul and the Indo-Afghan frontier—some of the only available records of firsthand observers during the revolts—suggested that the unrest stemmed from a variety of social, economic, and political tensions. Among the most commonly cited were discontent over new policies of conscription, taxation, government schooling, edicts impacting women in Afghan society, and dress codes. The British minister at Kabul especially identified as sources of unrest the new *hasht-nafari* ("every eighth man") conscription lottery, controversial provisions of the Basic Code, and the introduction of girls' schools. To the above factors, Machonachie adds financial exhaustion, internal disunion, the disrepute of the Afghan army, the deterioration of the bureaucracy, and the stymying of "moral and educational progress" from the closing of schools.[64]

Even after Aman Allah's Kemalist "turn," the Afghan monarch's measures generated complex responses that cannot be boiled down into a simplistic binary of submission or rebellion. As Robert D. McChesney has noted, "Although he asserted the underlying authority of the Shariah for this legislation, the ordinances presented in this legislation were seen by many as actually contravening the spirit of the Shariah and removing much legal authority from the hands of

Muslim judges, the *qazis*."[65] Some of the most problematic and contested decrees in this regard were those governing marriage and family law, particularly the *niẓāmnāmihs* discouraging, though not prohibiting, polygamy. Related measures included the required registration and minimum age for marriage, as well as new limits on dowries.[66] While it is tempting to read the controversy surrounding these particular reforms as a cultural clash between a "progressive" Aman Allah and "traditional" provincial tribes, it is important to contextualize the power politics surrounding these new laws. Largely imposed by Kabul without regard for the social and cultural sensibilities of local populations that had historically governed their affairs unharassed, issues such as the status of women and children in Afghan law were politicized into symbolic, linchpin issues for a broader opposition to Aman Allah's state-building program and Kabul's unprecedented interference in provincial life. Conversely, for the reformist king these issues were simply too important, and virtually nonnegotiable, to be sacrificed to the caprices of vested interests hiding behind a cloak of cultural relativism, tradition, or essentialized notions of the shariʿa. Therein lie the roots of an intractable conflict in Afghanistan's history—not between progressives and reactionaries, or liberators and misogynists, but between the center and the periphery, between the centralization of power and wealth in Kabul and the autonomy of communities living outside of the capital's reach. Even the ongoing and ever-consequential struggle between competing interpretations of Islamic orthodoxy in Afghanistan must be viewed in light of these broader political and economic contestations.

For other observers, like the security establishment of the British Raj watching the Afghan government fall apart, questions of finding the right balance between center and periphery, or the nuances of Islamic legal discourse, were largely academic. To them, Aman Allah's reign was doomed by one fatal flaw above all: his failure to develop a robust, disciplined, and loyal military. His extensive spending on legal, educational, and social reforms was as short-sighted as it was ineffectual, leaving little room to recruit, train, and equip an army that ultimately performed poorly against more experienced tribesmen on the battlefield.[67] "[T]he insurrection [could not] have become the real menace it undoubtedly has been, if the Afghan army had not been reduced far below the margin of safety, and its interests neglected," the British agent at Kabul Sir Richard Machonachie noted.[68] "The Afghan soldier is miserably housed, badly paid and treated as a menial servant, even by the clerks in the Government offices," he added, assessing the king's forces after five years in power.[69] In light of these fundamental maladies facing the Afghan army (and nascent police force), Aman Allah would likely struggle to uphold his laws if forced to do so.

British Raj officials' realpolitik notions of "might is right" aside, it would be inaccurate to conclude that Aman Allah did not try to build his military forces. Seeking to build a professional army of national rather than ethnic or tribal composition, in 1926 Aman Allah ordered that a mandatory system of conscription be imposed. This was followed by a lowering of the draft age to seventeen, and an increase in the term of service from two years to three.[70] Attempting to do away with privileges and exemptions of military service to powerful southeastern tribes, Aman Allah introduced a new universal conscription policy based on a lottery—every eighth eligible male was to be drafted, hence the term *hasht-nafari*, or "eighth person."

There is an additional irony to British criticisms of Aman Allah's military-building strategy: it was the amir's new conscription policies themselves that helped stir insurrection against his government. In a classic catch-22 paradox, Aman Allah's *hasht-nafari* scheme led to a profound falling out with provincial tribes accustomed to combat but unaccustomed to being centrally managed by Kabul. Soon potential recruits became rebels, further decimating the fighting strength of government armed forces and broadening the opposition against Aman Allah. Aman Allah's insistence on the universal equality of royal subjects and his rescinding long-standing exemptions from army service for powerful Pashtun confederations—especially the Mangals, Zadrans, and Ahmadzais, as well as the royal Barakzais of Kandahar, all of whom had previously been exempt—angered those who regarded themselves as natural warriors and resented being forced to learn new military skills from Turkish officers and advisors. A related law mandating the use of national passports was perceived as a restriction on Pashtun tribesmen's movement across the border and thus contributed to growing discontent.[71] By encouraging the forces of separatism and insurrection they were designed to control, Aman Allah's military reforms backfired.

There were also broader effects of the *hasht-nafari* law on the general, non-drafted population. Aman Allah's declared goals and the lack of capacity to implement them also prompted a certain domino effect—the failure of one reform led to the failure of another. For example, compulsory military service meant increased taxes to cover the expenses of the enlarged army. This was reported to have led to extreme levels of graft and corruption as local governors exploited the absence of accurate census data in applying the conscription law.[72] Furthermore, even though the law intended to reduce tribal privileges and promote universal equality, government officials often exempted the sons of influential or rich families, instead recruiting among families who could not afford to bribe them or among those with whom they had feuds. This corruption generated more discontent in an already disgruntled rural peasantry and tribally governed public.[73] Finally, the controversial prohibition on sufi *pir-murid* relationships for soldiers revealed a desire to create a unified, disciplined armed force loyal only to the central government and without alternative identities, foreign influences, or non-state-centric ideological orientations. "Your spiritual leader must be your rifle," Aman Allah was reported to have emphasized in explaining the order to a group of conscripts in October 1928.[74]

Not helping the Afghan king's cause were rumors—and for some, real experiences—concerning whom the national army would be used against. Given Aman Allah's government had signed peace treaties with all of Afghanistan's historical nemeses—Soviet Russia to the north, British India to the south and east, and Iran to the west—it was not lost on many Afghans that a strong, centralized army at the king's disposal would be a tool for quashing internal dissent rather than for defending the country from foreign enemies.[75] Aman Allah's grandfather, the "Iron Amir" 'Abd al-Rahman Khan, was a clear precedent in this regard. As Leon Poullada aptly summarized, "The fact that the allegedly beneficent moves of the central government were usually supported by military force reinforced the tribesman's paranoiac conviction that no good was intended toward him, else why the need for force or threat of force?"[76]

For the many Pashtun tribal confederations, particularly in the south and east, the idea of a state army drafting their young and able-bodied men to fight relatives was unacceptable. It was not long before soldiers displayed reluctance to fight more experienced tribes at best, and defected to their relatives' side in more extreme cases. Closely monitoring Aman Allah's moves in this regard was the British Raj, Afghanistan's former patron state: "Afghan regular army is untrained, miserably paid and equipped, and unable, even if willing, to stand up against tribesmen," wrote Sir Francis Humphrys, the British agent at Kabul, in mid-December 1928.[77] As a previously localized uprising against Aman Allah began gaining ground, another British intelligence official made a prediction that would turn out to be fairly accurate: "Military service against their fellow countrymen is most distasteful to the Afghans, and, in my opinion, Amir will have to make concessions to the Mullahs in order to avoid serious danger of the disaffection spreading."[78]

Other evidence points to a crushing fiscal crisis that pulled the plug on most if not all of Aman Allah's ambitious programs. Having forfeited the annual British subsidies that his grandfather and father had received, Aman Allah struggled to find new sources of revenue to pay for the large projects he commissioned, including the construction of new government buildings, gardens, cement factories, and roads; the purchase of more advanced military weapons; and paying a larger army.[79] Furthermore, as Vartan Gregorian has observed in one of the only economic surveys of the era, Aman Allah simply did not have the resources or revenue to enact a large-scale land reform program that could have earned him the rural peasantry's support. As the king fixated on largely urban problems, and specifically Kabul, Afghan farmers faced a variety of new taxes to underwrite the cost of Aman Allah's reforms, many of which were of questionable value to them.[80] A shortage of cash in the country impacted trade negatively, and the exchange value of the Afghan rupee remained low. In light of the ambitious and wide-ranging reforms proposed by Aman Allah's government, in less than five years of rule he faced a financial crisis.[81]

There is little evidence to suggest that Aman Allah was blind to the economic drain of his reforms, however. As early as 1920 Aman Allah's government had promulgated *niẓāmnāmihs* increasing land and livestock taxes, the collection of tax arrears, going so far as to require their collection in cash. New regulations concerning the sale of state lands and government property were issued in 1920 and 1923 respectively.[82] Yet, as late as August 28, 1928, Aman Allah remained troubled by the state of his government's finances. At the Loya Jirga held at Paghman that year, the last he would ever preside over as king, Aman Allah introduced the following fiscal reforms: an increase in taxes on landed property to augment the revenue for industrial works, education, and the army; the introduction of a national bank; and the issue of currency notes.[83] To cover the cost of building and training a new army, Aman Allah asked for the imposition of a new poll tax. The latter was to be levied on every male over fifteen, amounting to between three to five rupees, while government officials were to pay a month's salary.[84]

On October 2, 1928, less than two months after the announcement of the tax increase, violent antigovernment demonstrations broke out in Kabul. Although these demonstrations were quickly suppressed by the Afghan army, another armed insurrection began in early November, this time in the rural eastern provinces, where the Shinwari tribe met Aman Allah's tax collectors and army recruiting officers with gunfire. The Shinwaris were subsequently joined in revolt by the Muhmand, Khugiani, Jadran, and Jaji tribal confederations.[85] The uprising came at a time when the peasants' economic position had deteriorated severely, primarily because of increased taxes but also because the taxes had to be paid in cash. As Gregorian notes in his economic history of the Amani decade, in the nine years Aman Allah was on the throne, taxes on horses and donkeys rose 400–500 percent; the tax on land increased three to four times; the tax on short-horned cattle quadrupled (from seven puls to thirty); and the tax on long-horned cattle tripled (from twenty puls to sixty). The requirement that taxes be paid in cash not only led to bureaucratic abuses but also increased the indebtedness of many peasants, who reportedly were forced to rely heavily on moneylenders. Even after crops failed in 1925, the government failed to ease the peasants' tax burden.[86] In 1928 about 30 percent of Aman Allah's revenue was derived from land tax. Roland Wild, an English journalist who visited Kabul in 1928 and author of the social biography *Amanullah: Ex-King of Afghanistan* (1933), offered the following sobering description of the country's finances and broader social conditions:

> Since the tussle with the British, increased pressure had been brought to bear on the landowners. Their taxes were steadily mounting . . . The tax-gatherers were more pressing than ever they had been in the past. Hardly a month went by but they came with news of a new valuation. There were new taxes on houses, and new demands made on weddings and funerals and village ceremonies. There seemed to be more taxation officers than tax-payers. Gradually the peasant began to know the other side of the "reform." . . . There was a new education tax, and an added tax for building. There was a tax to pay for the war, and tax merely labeled "development." . . . The peasant paid, and when he could not, suffered the annexation of his land in the cruel winter.[87]

Discontent at increased taxation was not limited to rural areas. The government had also taxed the urban population heavily, with increases in the duties on exports and imports hitting the merchant class especially hard. On paper, customs duties ranged from 100 percent on luxury items to 15–40 percent on useful or necessary items, but in practice the duties were much higher, ranging more often from 20 percent to 200 percent, with internal trade subject to a 5 percent tax. This lack of awareness concerning the price and value of industrial goods brought in to the country led to poor economic decisions, Gregorian argues, further alienating the mercantile class.[88] In yet another demonstration of the domino effect of Aman Allah's reforms, the failure of the government's new tax regime opened a Pandora's box because the king's officers could not pursue a campaign against corruption when he was barely able to pay them, let alone pay more junior government employees. Additionally, some observers criticized Aman Allah's tendency to focus on the trappings of modern cities and "civilizational progress" at the expense of more systematic institutions to build economic independence. "Perhaps one of his greatest failings," concludes Gregorian, "was that instead of concentrating on the economic development of the country, he dissipated his efforts and resources by introducing mere symbols of progress: thus, he purchased phonographs and microphones, built bandstands and hotels, opened a café and a movie house, issued passports, and insisted on the adoption of Western dress."[89]

Aman Allah's downfall was no doubt a result of a perfect storm—but scholars of political economy like Gregorian stress above all his lack of a sound financial base, and the failure to build a strong centralized army, police, and bureaucracy to implement his reforms. Put another way, such institutional weaknesses and lopsidedness reflected the absence of a cohesive state-building vision and plan. Though Aman Allah could not be faulted for lacking ambition, the king's initiatives were so wide-ranging that few of them ever took root within Afghan society, as limited resources and energies were spread thin. Like a house of cards, failure in some areas prevented success in others. It was not long before the combined weight of taxation and administrative abuses encouraged brigandage amid already weakened socioeconomic conditions in the countryside, including in the Kohistan region just north of Kabul.[90] It is from the latter region that Habib Allah Kalakani—also known as *Bacha-i Saqao* (son of a water-carrier) and the "bandit king" in Afghan historiography—led a successful insurrection against Aman Allah in the fall of 1928, resulting in the first and only non-Pashtun monarch in Afghanistan's history.

Like conscription and taxation, the idea of universal education also presented a host of political challenges because it threatened local communities' control over their social and economic affairs, and not just fears of cultural "indoctrination." At the August 29, 1928, Loya Jirga, Aman Allah announced the compulsory education of both sexes to be a fundamental goal of his reforms.[91] The scope of Aman Allah's campaign was breathtaking. It included the free and mandatory education of all children—boys and girls—between the ages of six and eleven, throughout Afghanistan. The king also prided his efforts to send

Afghan students abroad. "Turkey is educating, free of charge, the 100 boys and the fifteen girls to whom I and the Queen have just bidden farewell in your presence," Aman Allah declared to an official audience in mid-autumn of 1928. "Italy will educate twenty-five boys," he added, "and promises of help in education have been received from other countries."[92] Aman Allah also announced the launch of secondary education programs, with French and German schools to be opened in Kandahar and Herat, and a new Turkish school in Kabul.[93] Students were to wear uniforms in public, salute in European fashion, and speak in the primary language of their instructors, be they French or German. In addition to opening new schools, Aman Allah announced plans to establish public libraries, reflecting his broader goal of promoting a national culture of learning and scholarship, and recalling earlier eras when cities like Balkh and Herat were the pride of the region in the study of theology, law, physical sciences, or the arts. Reflecting his commitment to raising a new generation of Afghans, education was to be the second largest expense of the national budget.[94] In addition to these calls for expanded primary schools, Aman Allah also established a medley of professional schools for instruction in Kabul, including faculties of civil law, agriculture, nursing and first aid, carpentry and masonry, and music and art, as well as a nascent police academy.[95]

Intertwined with Aman Allah's educational reforms was a broader campaign to more equitably define gender roles and improve the status of women as he saw it. At the August–September 1928 Loya Jirga, for example, Aman Allah announced the abolition of purdah, the legal imposition of monogamy, in addition to the aforementioned laws requiring the compulsory education of both sexes.[96] With regard to Aman Allah's avowal of monogamy, the king invited attention to the fact that he himself, his brother ʿInayat Allah, and the regent, had only one wife each, also noting that they had between them twenty-eight children.[97] Beyond formal laws and his own family life, Aman Allah spoke at length about the plight of the Afghan woman under what he described as stagnant, backward traditions. British intelligence records reported the following passage from a speech given by Aman Allah at the 1928 Loya Jirga:

> Religion does not require women to veil their hands, feet and faces, or enjoin any special type of veil . . . Women should now discard the old *purdah* (*burqa*), and either go unveiled or wear modest garments and a light veil. Outside Kabul, the decision of the whole matter must rest with the individual. But tribal custom must not impose itself on the free will of the individual.[98]

Underscoring these points, as Aman Allah was again confident to point out, was the example of his own wife, Queen Suraya. The queen had customarily worn a light, transparent facial veil in public, and continued to do so for the duration of Aman Allah's speech. But on this occasion she removed her veil, to applause from the audience, in the hope other women would follow her example. The king was not in favor of forced unveiling, however; nor did he abandon the minimalist standards of dress code for men and women as held by other schools of Islamic law, including a woman covering her hair, for example. Rather, as he expounded in a subsequent speech, the monarch seems to have been mostly driven by ideals of individualization and the "privatization" of religion—manifested by a particular emphasis on personalized choice, balanced by the requirements of public order and law. Once again, these views surfaced in the sensitive issue of the women's full veil in comments made by the king at the conclusion of the Jirga:

> As regards the vexed question of *purdah*, His Majesty said: "I leave the question of *purdah*; that is to say, if any person sees any advantage in being unveiled, she may remove her veil; if anyone is in favour of being veiled, she many remain veiled. Should I order all females to be veiled, a large number of my subjects, nomads and villagers, will find it very difficult to observe the order. Should I, on the other hand, order *purdah* to be abolished, I will have to face a great opposition against an ancient custom in cities like Kabul and Kandahar. I will therefore follow the injunctions of the Islamic code and punish those who expose the parts of the body which it is ordained therein should be kept covered."[99]

As much as Aman Allah tried to package his reforms in the language of Islamic modernism in his speeches, they were interpreted as a challenge to the authority of many ulema and local power holders who held a different view. The king was consequently branded as unorthodox, stirring up foment, particularly among several Pashtun tribes in the south and east of the country. By the first major revolt in 1924, there were signs Aman Allah, the warrior king who had won Afghanistan's independence, had lost the discursive ground within his own dominion. But following his return from Europe in early 1928, he enacted a reformist program that was so iconoclastic and jarring that even his liberal advisors were expressing reservations.[100] By late 1928 Aman Allah had squandered virtually all the social capital he had so painstakingly earned after his political victory in 1919.

That educational reforms—a cornerstone of the reformist amir's state-building agenda—played a major role in the opposition to Aman Allah can be seen in the concessions Aman Allah was forced to make, both after the 1924 Khost and 1928 Shinwari Rebellions. British records note the following rebel demands following the Shinwari truce in 1928: "Among terms demanded by Shinwaris are recall of 15 Afghan girl students recently sent to Turkey and cancellation of orders about female education, wearing European dress and abolition of veil."[101] A note written by a British intelligence officer in the margins of a December 1928 article on Afghanistan from the *Times* states, "The Shinwaris not only object to the taking out of certificates of nationality, but to the abolition of the purdah and to the education scheme, particularly the King's insistence that a proportion of students should go to Europe."[102]

National conscription; tax-based public spending; universal education; women's empowerment—auspicious as these programs sounded to outside observers and a coterie of advisors in the Kabul court, there is also little question they were read very differently by other actors in the country. Common to these interlaced agendas of the reformist king, after all, was an attempt to reassert central government authority across the country, rein in local autonomy in the provinces, and limit the de facto sovereignty of Afghan tribes. "Behind the tribal administration usually came the school teacher and the tax collector," Poullada aptly noted in 1973, alluding to the power struggle at play in Aman Allah's reforms and the revolts against them.[103] In this way, the center-periphery conflict may help us understand that the reforms were dismally received partly because they were often delivered at the end of a bayonet and hinted at further interference from a regulatory state. That is to say, military service, taxation, education, and new family laws became weapons—and unquestionably symbols of sovereignty—to empower the central government at the expense of provincial communities, particularly in the southern and eastern Pashtun belt. In this way, conscripts, crops, schools, and women's bodies became the virtual battlegrounds over which a larger political war was being waged in the country.

Afghanistan beyond Rulers and Rebels

Few questions have vexed historians of early twentieth-century Afghanistan more than the dramatic collapse of Aman Allah's government from the last months of 1928 to January 1929.[104] From preeminent historians writing from within the country, such as Fayz Muhammad Katib (1862/3–1931) and Mir Ghulam Muhammad Ghubar (1897–1978), to monographs of Western academics like Leon Poullada (1913–1987), Vartan Gregorian, and the groundbreaking work of Afghan-American historian Senzil Nawid, a diverse group of scholars have contributed their insights to explaining the rise and fall of the "revolutionary king." Although these works are rigorously researched and stress different historical factors in their analyses, a common dialectic runs through each of them: a virtual Manichean conflict between progressive modernity and stagnant tradition. Westernized bureaucrats and advisors fall into the dynamic, progressive category of modernizers, while mullahs and tribal leaders violently opposed to change fall into the stagnant, regressive category of the tradition-bound. Beyond a narrative tendency toward modernization theory teleology, civilizing missions, and other linear models of progress, framing the revolts against Aman Allah in this way has four major problems.

The first concerns our empirical knowledge of the actual participants in the revolts against Aman Allah's government. Extant evidence, including internal correspondence of the British Raj's intelligence agencies in Afghanistan and India's northwest frontier from the beginning of the uprising to Aman Allah's deposal, challenges the notion of a countrywide rebellion against the reformist king. The latter sources—including documents in the National Archives of India, India Office Records, and the 2002-released compendium *Afghanistan Strategic Intelligence British Records* (Volume 1: 1919–1928)—constitute some of the only available written records of the revolts by firsthand witnesses, but still mostly secondary and tertiary sources, during the tumultuous months of late 1928 to early 1929. According to these sources, the pattern that emerges is not a populist grassroots revolution taking hold across the country, nor a polarized country divided between pro- and anti-Aman Allah forces, but a more complex picture. Large parts of the country, including many urban ulema as well as prominent Afghan tribal confederations, did not rebel against Aman Allah's government for the duration of his reign, but neither did they necessarily rally to his aid. Focusing on a supposedly inherent cultural conflict between Western modernizers and traditional actors, or between urban and rural, overlooks that the Khost and Shinwari Rebellions were largely localized revolts limited to select portions of eastern and southern regions of Afghanistan. As Nazif Shahrani and Sana Haroon have shown, whole swaths of the country did not rise against Aman Allah in either revolt.[105] Similarly, as Poullada observes, both revolts began in the largely autonomous, tribally governed regions of the country;

urban areas generally did not revolt, remaining loyal to Aman Allah's central government. Also, the factional divisions between Kalakani's northern forces (which eventually besieged Kabul and overthrew Aman Allah) and the various eastern and southern Pashtun tribes who allied with Nadir Khan must not be overlooked. These are noteworthy details that speak to the social, political, and ideological diversity of Afghanistan, and should caution us from making generalizations about the characters of the rebellions against Aman Allah.

British Indian records from Kabul and the Indo-Afghan frontier corroborate the localized nature of the uprisings. Both in 1924 and the crucial months of November 1928 to January 1929, British intelligence on Afghanistan report that significant parts of the country were calm during the revolts, even in the often restive east. "Apart from the Southern Province the outward state of Afghanistan has been comparatively peaceful during the last five months," one British intelligence weekly wire reported during the Khost Rebellion of 1924.[106] Furthermore, several reports corroborate how not all confederacies rose up against Aman Allah; many supported him, and for just as many reasons. As the chief commissioner of India's North-West Frontier Province wrote on the king's speech at the Paghman Loya Jirga in the summer of 1924, "It may be expected that this address and the prospect of loot will appeal to large numbers of the tribesmen who will, at least, welcome the opportunity of obtaining an Afghan Government rifle."[107]

Hence Aman Allah actually succeeded in enlisting Pashtun tribal levies in a military campaign against the Mangals and other parties involved in the Khost Rebellion.[108] As for the 1928 Shinwari Rebellion that eventually overthrew Aman Allah, during the course of which the British legation moved to Jalalabad, the legation reported on December 3, 1928, that "only a few Khugianis had joined the rebels, and all other tribes were still loyal [to Aman Allah]."[109] Other declassified records of British correspondence during the revolt indicate it was far from being an organized, let alone a united, countrywide uprising.[110]

A second problem in conventional treatment of the uprisings deals with an oversimplification of the reformist king's court. Had the root of Aman Allah's downfall been a dichotomous conflict between progressive modernizers and regressive traditionalists, the reformist king would not have suffered from so much internal fragmentation in his own court. Factional dissent was already stirring in the palace itself, among his closest advisors, and this was far more serious than public critique. Members of the radical branch of Aman Allah's court, such as 'Abd al-Rahman Ludin, openly criticized the amir's new policies for displaying signs of authoritarianism. At the same time, Aman Allah's increasingly unilateral decisions alienated other advisors as well, eventually leading to the departure of capable officials who had been in the amir's highest confidence and had taken part in some of the most important decisions of the early 1920s, including General Nadir Khan, Muhammad Wali Khan, and the influential Musahiban family. The latter carried a great deal of influence in the Afghan army, especially among officers, who increasingly chafed under the clout of civilian officials like Mahmud Tarzi, as well as the Turkish officers and technocrats in Aman Allah's court. What is more, an even graver sign of schism in the royal court was foreshadowed with Mahmud Tarzi's appointment as ambassador to France in July 1922—ostensibly for health reasons, but a distancing that contrasted sharply with the closeness Tarzi enjoyed with his protégé and son-in-law Aman Allah since the latter was a prince. This fragmentation in the Afghan court led to Aman Allah's increasing isolation. By 1928, following the monarch's return from Europe, even liberal members of his government were organizing, or tendering resignations, to oppose his increasingly unilateral decisions.[111]

In his bid to build a modern, centralized army, Aman Allah enlisted Turkish military training support, but this alienated officers in the king's armed forces and tribal chieftains, who sided with the leadership of the Indian-born, British-educated general Nadir Khan. The latter argued that the attitudes and policies promoted by the Turkish advisors did not accord with the requirements of Afghanistan's tribal society, which Nadir Khan believed the officers from Istanbul were disinclined to respect. The anti-Turkish camp further urged Aman Allah that it was imprudent to reject loyal, qualified, and senior officers merely on the basis of efficiency on paper. Here, even the once cherished idea of employing Turkish Muslim officers (as opposed to non-Muslim Europeans, for example)—an idea promoted by Tarzi and a distinguishing hallmark of several of Aman Allah's earlier reforms—seems to have backfired on the king. Nadir was not opposed to military reform or to the building of a modern Afghan national army. Rather, he strongly favored the idea, but clashed with Aman Allah and the pro-Turkish Afghans over the methods for achieving it—particularly where "tribal sensibilities" were concerned. What is more, it did not alleviate tensions when the general emphasized his perspective to Aman Allah in a less than subtle way: by reminding the king that he owed his throne to the army.[112]

Not helping the king's cause was the fact that former close advisors had started to see their patron—who by now had been in power for nearly a decade—as increasingly autocratic. The latter emerged as a consistent theme in the reports of British informants embedded in the Kabul court, especially following the king's return from Europe and the lead-up to the Shinwari Rebellion.[113] In the end, Aman Allah even turned away from the advice of his personal mentor and father-in-law, Mahmud Tarzi, who urged the king to surround himself with a strong army, as Kemal had done in Turkey, before unleashing so many radical reforms on the populace. In this manner, Aman Allah grew into an increasingly isolated leader who alienated both his one-time liberalizing allies and the purported targets of his reforms. This was a weakness that even the British foreign minister repeatedly warned the king about. On November 24, 1928, Humphrys had a long audience with Aman Allah concerning the Shinwari Rebellion. "In the frankest possible manner," Humphrys later penned in a debriefing on the meeting with British intelligence in India, "I dwelt on the folly of alienating the sympathy of all classes of his subjects simultaneously, and I told His majesty that priests, merchants, agriculturalists and soldiers were seething with discontent at new reforms, increased taxation and forced contributions."[114]

Even Aman Allah's liberalist allies in the capital harbored frustration over the direction their king was taking. The latter included former members of the underground Young Afghan movement during Habib Allah's absolutist reign, who were already upset with the lack of sufficient checks on the king's executive authority in the Basic Code, but were adamantly opposed to further entrenchment of executive power.[115] After all, Aman Allah retained certain relics of his father's and grandfather's authoritarian rule, including exercising the supreme powers of commander in chief (Article 7) and reserving the last court of appeal to himself (Article 13), but in the latter years of his reign he expanded his powers even further with new supplemental legislation. Instead of relying on the independent judgment of the ulema, or representative institutions such as a parliament and local councils, to legislate, adjudicate, or mediate disputes, the king's new penal code of 1927, for example, consolidated even greater power in the king's hands through a heavy employment of juristic devices that favored executive discretion and policy-making powers, like *taʿzīr*, *qānūn*, and *siyāsa sharʿiyyih*.[116] The result was new limitations on public expression and censorship, while several clauses in the penal code effectively extended the range of crimes that could be prosecuted by the state, including Articles 33–45. The vaguely worded Article 54, for example, criminalized publications and speeches inciting "public unrest."[117]

Meanwhile, a growing number of the liberal elites in Kabul and the king's erstwhile supporters were troubled that Aman Allah was single-handedly appointing the ministers of justice, education, commerce, finance, and public security, all of whom were responsible only to him, with little to no oversight structure in place.[118] By opting for personal loyalty over ability, one British official opined, Aman Allah had chosen a prime minister, cabinet, and indeed entire government composed of "mediocre sycophants."[119] Exacerbating the situation was that there was no effective Afghan parliament to dilute the centralization of power. For many veterans of the Young Afghan constitutional movement, these were not the hallmarks of a constitutional monarchy but of a regime seeking to maintain control over recalcitrant populations. Even Aman Allah's former chief mufti and head scholar of the High Religious Council (Hay'at-i Tamiz), Mawlawi ʿAbd al-Wasiʿ Qandahari, as early as 1926 expressed disagreement with the king's increasingly authoritarian direction.[120] As for members of the republican wing of Aman Allah's former cabinet, including ʿAbd al-Rahman Ludin who had also contributed to the drafting of the 1923 Basic Code, the latest round of supplemental *niẓāmnāmihs* were not signals of progress, but instruments to concentrate power in the hands of the king.[121] And so quietly, over time, the fiery Young Afghans lost confidence in their champion.

The frustration of elites was insignificant, however, compared to more popular discontent over the common man's tax burdens and such issues as conscription and controversial social reforms. Considering the estrangement of Afghans across so many different political persuasions, economic and ethnic backgrounds, and regional affiliations, the chances for Aman Allah's ambitious reforms to survive became increasingly thin. This is reinforced by the fact that support for Aman Allah's social reforms were already limited to the royal court, divided as it was. "The King and his reforms receive but little support outside the Court circle," British agents revealed in correspondence with their superiors in India on September 21, 1928.[122] By alienating so many groups at the same time, including some of his closest advisors, and by failing to rally a stable base of supporters to administer his reformist agenda, Aman Allah's political survival was soon at risk. Lacking the support of a robust urban class, intelligentsia, or prosperous peasantry, before long even his small coterie of court advisors saw no choice but to abandon him.[123]

The reformist-versus-rebel binary so common in literature on Afghanistan suffers from a third consequential problem. While much of the literature argues a somewhat monolithic "religious establishment" led the campaign to oust Aman Allah because of his "anti-Islamic, westernizing" reforms, this dualistic narrative fails to account for the heterogeneity and complexity of forces Aman Allah marshaled for his social and legal reforms. In particular, it ignores the pivotal role of a diverse cast of ulema, bureaucrats, and jurists from a broad spectrum of Islamic ideological backgrounds who supported (and in some cases even drafted) the 1923 Constitution and associated Nizamnamihha-yi Amaniyyih Codes, as shown in Chapter 5. In framing the era as a romantic conflict between a progressive Western modernizer and stagnant tribal-religious traditions, works on the Amani era have instead promoted a stark modern-traditional binary, eliding the discursive nature of Islamic law and the crucial role of a dynamic, transnational team of Muslim scholars and politicians in producing the codes. Such episodes of cooperation challenge us to discard a singularized, secular-liberal model of modernity in Afghanistan that either succeeds or fails based on its proximity to Euro-American instantiations of the rule of law, or to an equally imagined traditional society.

Finally, by framing Aman Allah's reforms as suffering from a problem of method—rather than as an inherently violent extension of the state's central authority and social engineering from the top down—works on the Amani era perpetuate a flawed vision of centralized governance as the only path to progress in Afghanistan. This is akin to saying that if only better methods were used, then the traditionally recalcitrant members of Afghan society (read: tribes and mullahs) would have been guided to the light of modern progress, or have faced the cudgel if they did not. Taken to its logical conclusion, such a vision would have unleashed a devastating scourge of violence on smaller, local communities in Afghanistan, something many were willing to resist, as subsequent events showed. There is sufficient reason to question, in other words, the presumption that a highly centralized state—taxing, disciplining, and surveilling subjects—would naturally be the best thing for Afghans outside Kabul or other major cities of Afghanistan. Historically speaking, such provincial regions have hardly seen the benefits of a strengthened relationship with Kabul, to say nothing of the enormous violence accompanying top-down state-building and collectivization programs from Mehmed Ali's Egypt and Pahlavi Iran to communist Russia and China, among other examples.[124]

The impact and significance of the 1928–1929 rebellion notwithstanding, a major undercurrent of this book has been to shift historiographical attention away from the chronic violence and tumult that has come to characterize Afghanistan's political history for the past four decades, but less so in the first half of the twentieth century when examined on the whole. Focusing on Aman Allah's overthrow in 1929 at the hands of violent tribal revolts that shook portions of southeastern Afghanistan falls too easily into conventional framings of the country as the world's failed state par excellence. What these commonplace and uncritical perspectives ignore is that Aman Allah's reforms actually laid the foundation for one of the most stable Islamic states of the twentieth century: Afghanistan under the subsequent Musahiban dynasty (1929–1973). Though the Musahiban dynasty may have been loath to recognize it, its policy of nonalignment in the Cold War built on the country's unqualified independence achieved under Aman Allah's leadership, opening the doors to relations with European, Asian, and Middle Eastern countries as relations among equals.

But that is not all. Internally, Aman Allah expanded his father's modern schools and founded new ones. He supported Afghans to study abroad, improved communications and infrastructure, and—aided by his wife, Queen Suraya—vigorously campaigned for the education and empowerment of women and protection of minorities. He launched archaeological and preservation initiatives to appreciate and showcase the country's now world-renowned ancient heritage. Signifying the dawn of a new era, Aman Allah replaced the former British protectorate's old flag—which the King criticized as resembling the Jolly Roger—with a new flag of three colors, selected in his own words with the following symbolism in mind:

> Black, in token of the dark days before independence was won.
> Red, for the blood of the martyrs who won freedom.
> Green, for hope and progress.

As a final touch, Aman Allah made what proved to be another long-lasting choice as the central inset of Afghanistan's national flag and government seal: a rising sun over sheaves of ripening corn.[125] In sum, and in more than aesthetic ways, Aman Allah sowed the seeds for future policies and reforms under subsequent Afghan monarchs and governments.[126]

In retrospect, Aman Allah's most important achievement, apart from Afghan independence, also came during the early years of his reign. That was his assembly of a skilled council of Muslim scholars, bureaucrats, and administrators between 1919 and 1923, who synthesized their diverse expertise and experience toward a constructive result: Afghanistan's first constitution and over seventy supplemental codes spanning a range of social, political, and economic affairs. Just as the Third Anglo-Afghan War of 1919 produced Afghanistan's unqualified independence from without, Aman Allah's legal advisors and legislation laid the juridical foundations for the country to become a constitutional monarchy and nation-state within. Afghanistan's Nizamnamihha-yi Amaniyyih was far from a flawless legislative campaign, and its memory as a success story can certainly be contested. But given these accomplishments in law and statecraft—at a time of rapid expansion by European colonial powers in the greater Islamicate world—even Aman Allah's overthrow cannot erase a sense of achievement marking those years leading to the spring of 1923.

Aman Allah's policies in the second half of his reign did not share the same nuances and characteristics of Islamic legal modernism as did those from the first half of his reign, nor did they enjoy the same longevity in Afghanistan. However, the collapse of a remarkable Indo-Ottoman-Afghan juridical nexus in Kabul was the result neither of insular Afghan politics nor of outside factors dictating the country's fate but a convergence of more complex factors. This included Aman Allah's own missteps as much as developments outside the king's control, such as the landmark abolition of the Ottoman sultanate and caliphate thousands of miles away in Anatolia, which could hardly have come at a worse time for the amir.

Reflecting on the historical arc of the dramatic rise and fall of Aman Allah, then, it is nevertheless difficult to escape a sense of tragedy surrounding the era and the person, but also surrounding the closest people to him: among them, his mentor and father-in-law, Mahmud Tarzi. After spending the tender years of his youth in Ottoman Baghdad, Istanbul, and Damascus as an Afghan exile, in the early 1900s Mahmud Tarzi returned to Kabul and spent the prime of his career serving his country of birth, Afghanistan. Establishing a landmark Muslim modernist journal, leading the country's negotiations for independence, and serving as Afghanistan's first foreign minister, Tarzi would eventually return to Istanbul in the wake of Aman Allah's downfall. Disheartened at the state of affairs in his homeland, Mahmud Tarzi devoted his last years to family, poetry, and reflection; he passed away quietly in Istanbul in 1933. He was buried in one of Turkey's most venerated religious sites: the historic Eyüp Sultan cemetery of Istanbul, celebrated for its mausoleum of the revered companion of the Prophet, Abu Ayub al-Ansari (576–674). Tarzi's grave rests in a tranquil meadow overlooking Istanbul's Bosporus, at the literal meeting point of the European and Asian continents, and metaphoric intersection "where East meets West."

Beyond that unmistakable imagery, there is, perhaps, something fitting to Afghanistan's most famous twentieth-century intellectual resting alongside some of the Ottoman Empire's most illustrious scholars and jurists, among whom is Mehmed Ebussuud Effendi (1490–1574), the eminent sheikh ül-Islam and compiler of *kanunnames* during the reign of Sultan Süleiman "the Lawgiver" (r. 1520–1566). It is precisely Ebussuud and Süleiman who—through the administrative device of *kanunnames* and *nizamnames*—reorganized, remade, and reconstituted the Ottoman Empire's juridical field from an eclectic patchwork of heterogeneous principalities and fiefdoms into a more cohesive and centralized legal framework in the early modern period. Four centuries later, this is precisely what Aman Allah and the Istanbul lawyer Osman Bedri Bey sought to do in Afghanistan under the banner of building an Islamic rule of law, a modern state-building project that Tarzi encouraged and facilitated via his long-standing connections with Ottoman officials in Damascus, Aleppo, Baghdad, and Istanbul. It was in the latter locales, after all, where Tarzi's cosmopolitan education took root, and to which he owed much of his inspiration for the remainder of his remarkable career.

As for the champion of Afghan independence and revolutionary king himself, one of the last references to Aman Allah in Turkish government archives dates to April 29, 1935. The former amir was found in Mecca, Hejaz, in the newly formed state of Saudi Arabia, performing the rites of the hajj.[127] Only a few years after his dethronement, some queried whether the former monarch still had designs on power. Others saw a personal act of devotion and piety. Still others saw the poignant scene of a former king who had defied the British Empire, bolstered Pan-Islamic alliances, and won the hearts of Muslims from Anatolia to Afghanistan circumambulating the Kaʿba—not as a ruler, nor as a rebel, but as an ordinary pilgrim confessing his impoverishment before the Sublime.

Conclusion

ON JANUARY 4, 2004, a provisional government in Kabul known as the Afghan Transitional Administration ratified a constitution. As a successor state to the Taliban Amirate (1996–2001), the UN-endorsed authority was tasked with a Herculean array of responsibilities, including: coordinating the resettlement of six million refugees, preparing free and fair elections for a multiethnic society torn apart by two decades of civil war, and managing a multibillion dollar reconstruction program with donors as diverse as the European Union, the United States, China, India, Iran, and Saudi Arabia—all the while battling domestic and foreign insurgents intent on overthrowing the government.[1] With the promulgation of the 2004 Constitution, one less burden was lifted off the interim authority's shoulders, paving the way for the establishment of the internationally recognized Islamic Republic of Afghanistan. Afghanistan's 2004 Constitution has been praised by world leaders and scholars as a "historic achievement," a "model for the Islamic world," and a process by which "there is no winner or loser—everbody has won."[2] Other officials experienced with the challenges of postconflict state-building struck a more cautious tone, including UN Special Envoy to Afghanistan Lakhdar Brahimi. Speaking in Kabul after the approval of the constitution, the veteran Algerian diplomat forthrightly warned, "There is no rule of law in this country yet."[3]

While the 2004 Constitution remains a source of both celebration and controversy in and outside Afghanistan, most observers continue to assume that it was the country's first. This is, perhaps, not so surprising. After four decades of chronic civil war in the country, fueled by the machinations of neighboring and world powers, Afghans are rarely thought to be able to stand on both feet and shape their own historical destiny. Like so many of the country's citizens literally rendered invalid by land mines and mortars, by jet fighters and drones, or by suicide bombings and IEDs, Afghans are either victims or self-destructive aggressors, with the result they simply occupy the margins of someone else's narrative; their only literary genre: tragedy. The aim of this book was to fill an acute gap in historical knowledge about modern law, statecraft, and diplomacy in Afghanistan that would lead one to fall into such hollow assumptions about this pivotal country's past and its people. From Afghanistan's first national maps and law codes in the 1880s and 1890s, to its first modern colleges and hospitals in the 1900s and 1910s, to the promulgation of the country's first constitution in 1923, Afghans were anything but latecomers to modern legality and state-building in the Islamicate world. What is more, the transnational Muslim circuits of expertise at work in the legal, administrative, and diplomatic projects during this period challenge diffusionist models of literature, models that presume a tutorial role for European legal culture exported to the colonized world through the forces of imperial administrations.

Afghanistan Has a Legal History (and Much More)

This book has focused on how three Afghan monarchs over five decades galvanized a highly capable group of Muslim scholars and administrators from the Ottoman Empire, British India, and Afghanistan for a series of Pan-Islamic campaigns. Those campaigns were launched from an ideally situated haven for crossborder activities—Kabul—but they were not of the stereotypical militant stripe with which the world has become accustomed to associating Afghans and foreign migrants to their country in recent decades. Rather, this was a story of the first Muslim-majority nation-state to gain independence and constitutionalize Islamic law within internationally recognized borders after the fall of the Ottoman Empire: Afghanistan.

Among the persistent themes of our subject were the legal and jurisprudential dimensions of Pan-Islamic networks, what has sometimes been called juridical Pan-Islam. By focusing on the juridical connections made between influential

Muslims of the late Ottoman Empire, Afghanistan, and British India, the work locates an important corridor for exchanges and debates on what modern Islamic law and constitutionalism, as well as statecraft and diplomacy, can mean.

There are certainly undercurrents of religious, moral, and cultural conflicts at work in our subject; but this is not an account of a puritanical, insular, or monolithic Islam framed in juxtaposition against an equally imagined West; nor is the plot scheme read as "secular, progressive modernizers" versus "religious, tribal fanatics." There is a role for ideological fault lines here—not between believers and nonbelievers but between Muslim rulers and the Muslims they ruled, each promoting their own interpretation of the shariʿa. Refusing to cede "the discursive high ground," to cite a manifest parallel with Brinkley Messick's history of the Ottoman tussle with Yemeni highlanders, the Muhammadzai amirs also mobilized "a shariʿa politics of their own" to counter more locally tailored versions in the Indo-Afghan frontier and southeastern regions of Afghanistan in particular.[4] By enlisting the support of Ottoman and Indian bureaucrats, but also of leading Afghan jurists from Kabul and Kandahar, the Muhammadzai monarchs espoused a complex and dynamic approach to the intersection of law, religion, and governance at the turn of the twentieth century, an approach that might best be described as Islamic legal modernism. As Amirs ʿAbd al-Rahman, Habib Allah, and Aman Allah—each in their own way—sought to propel top-down political, administrative, and even social change in Afghanistan through law, a closer examination of their actual legislation and the jurists who authored that legislation reveals a sustained attempt to craft a modern state within the interpretive traditions of shariʿa *and* international norms of legality.

By unearthing a deeper history of scholarly and administrative exchanges linking Ottoman Turkey, British India, and Afghanistan since the Sublime Porte's first mission to Kabul in 1877, this book has highlighted the appeal of multiple modernist legal interpretations and political governance models exchanged within an interislamic region during the era of imperial globalization. Attention to models of good governance and legal reform within a particular region—in this case between Istanbul and Kabul, and between Kabul and Delhi—invites us to rethink our notions of modernization and westernization centered on Eurocentric experiences and epistemes.

There is, of course, more than a conventional legal history at play here. This was a story of legal texts, but also geopolitics and new technologies; it was also a story of steamers and trains, new postal services and telegraph lines, as well as better printing and bookbinding. This was a story of imperialism and the racialization of Muslims, where European powers denigrated and scorned the oriental despotism of the Sick Man of Europe (read: late Ottoman Empire) and the Forbidden Kingdom (read: Afghanistan) at the same time. But it was also an account of how Ottomans, Afghans, and Indian Muslims contested, internalized, and sometimes even reasserted such caricatures themselves. By focusing on Afghanistan, the book highlights the development of new and expanded regional currents between Muslims of different imperial, national, and transnational entities within a paradigm of modern, juridical Pan-Islam. Rather than treating the country in a landlocked vacuum, this was also a book about the making of a modern Balkans-to-Bengal complex, an ink triangle that connected Istanbul, Kabul, and greater Delhi, among other locales, in increased contact, collaboration, and exchange. It explains how just at the time of Eurocentric globalization and scramble for African and Asiatic colonies, the ties between the Ottoman Empire, Afghanistan, and the Muslims of British India were growing stronger than ever before.

Whether in the nineteenth, twentieth, or twenty-first centuries, a Google Earth view of Kabul would find the potential for Afghanistan to be an ideal conduit through which an assortment of radical political coalitions could take shape—and did take shape. In 1877, the Ottomans dispatched their first official envoy to Kabul in the hope of goading the Afghan amir to declare war on Russia and open a devastating new front in Turkic Central Asia against the Porte's chief nemesis. In 1915, in one of the most ambitious missions of the Great War, Berlin and Istanbul succeeded in sending a secret delegation of officers to Kabul through enemy territory in Persia, but they failed to convince Habib Allah to join the Central Powers and invade India, in what could have opened a decisive new front against Britain's global empire. Four years later, catapulted to regional prominence by Aman Allah's successful drive for independence from Britain, Afghanistan after World War I presented a strategic nexus for diverse political agendas, including Pan-Islamism, Pan-Turkism, and the Indian Khilafat and Noncooperation movements, as well as Bolshevik and Pan-Asian activists seeking opportunities for expansion. It would not be the last time Afghanistan was eyed for broader regional and global ambitions by outside actors, as attested to by the not-so-cold war policies of Moscow and Washington in the 1980s, Islamabad and New Delhi in the 1990s, or the United States and a host of other powers, again, in the 2000s. Most recently, if the attempts by the terrorist network and rogue statelet otherwise known as ISIS to enhance its Islamist credentials by vying with Taliban insurgents are any indication, Afghanistan will continue to play a pivotal role in regional agendas for some time to come.

But we need not wait or rely on the future behavior of world powers and extremist groups to teach us what history has already shown to be true about Afghanistan on more than one occasion. In 1925, a Norwegian philologist named Dr. Georg Morgenstierne decided to travel to Kabul to see for himself the fanfare the reformist king and his advisors were making in the country and across the region—not as pariahs, but as pioneers in the fields of Islamic law and statecraft. Visiting Kabul at the midpoint of Aman Allah Khan's decade-long reign, the scholar from Norway recognized the accomplishments, but also the ambiguities and challenges, facing the country at the time. Having arrived on the heels of the 1923 Constitution and the 1924 Khost uprising, Morgenstierne was cautiously optimistic but in the end uncertain about the direction the country would take in subsequent years and decades. In an article he penned in the summer of 1925 entitled "Afghanistan and World Politics," Dr. Morgenstierne wielded enough historical background and foresight to make one remarkably accurate prediction about the country's future, however. "One thing in any case is certain," he stressed, "Afghanistan will for a long time keep her place as one of the most important pieces on the political chessboard of the world."[5]

Islamic State, or Islamic Nation-States?

This book centered Afghanistan as an important player and precedent in the rise of Islamic legal modernism in the twentieth century, decades before the establishment of its better-studied peers, including the Islamic republics of Pakistan (1947) and Iran (1979), the Arab republics of Egypt (1953) and Algeria (1962), or the conservative Arab monarchies of Saudi Arabia (1932), Jordan (1946), and Morocco (1956). It is true that Afghan intellectuals did not produce seismic theoretical treatises on Islamic modernism, philosophy, or the reconstruction of legal thought akin to those of Muhammad ʿAbduh and Rashid Rida in Egypt, Said Nursi Bediüzzaman in Turkey, Muhammad Iqbal in India, or ayatollahs Murtaza Motaharri and Muhammad Husayn Tabatabaʾi in Iran, for example. But even before Afghanistan's complete independence in 1919, the Muhammadzai amirs and their advisors in Kabul promulgated actual legislation and policies for internal governance while commanding the reins of government in their hands—a virtual laboratory for Islamic state-building, in other words—while Islamist movements from Algeria to Iran were in their embryonic stages as an oppositional politics, still far from wielding legislative authority in their societies.

One of the most striking features of the successive reigns of Amirs 'Abd al-Rahman Khan (1880–1901), Habib Allah Khan (1901–1919), and Aman Allah Khan (1919–1929) was they each represented sustained enterprises to synthesize Afghanistan's predominantly Islamic jurisprudential traditions with a project of modern state-building that was in tune with the nascent international system as they knew it. With the help of Afghan clerics, but also Ottoman and Indian bureaucrats, the legislation they drafted and implemented signaled a bold experiment: an attempt by Muslim jurists to develop an Islamic legal theory of the modern nation-state in a noncolonial context, through a process that cannot be dismissed as European imitation on the one hand, or playing footloose and fancy-free with the shari'a on the other.[6] To presume so would be to ignore the very real struggles of Afghan, Turkish, and Indian Muslim jurists to render the modern state and its administrators subject to the greater moral community—that is to say, under Islam's rule of law. The Muhammadzai monarchy's campaign for independence and internal governance, therefore, presents us with one of the first Islamic nation-state projects of the modern era. Afghanistan's Constitution of 1923 represented a culminating episode and achievement of Islamic legal modernism in that sense. It also laid the foundations for all subsequent Afghan constitutions of the twentieth century (1931, 1964, 1977, and 1990)—save a pair ratified under Soviet occupation by Kabul's communist regime in the 1980s.[7] Of more recent note, it provided a model for Afghanistan's latest national charter, adopted on January 4, 2004.

Situated in historical context, Islamic legal modernism emerged not against but in conversation with social and political developments across the region and globe, as more loosely governed empires and patrimonial regimes of the eighteenth to nineteenth centuries were replaced by highly centralized administrative nation-states of the twentieth. The nation-state, in the Middle East as elsewhere, brought new discourses, including constitutionalism, citizenship, and the laws of nations, but also disciplinary technologies such as codification of law, government schools, and the prison. What may come as a surprise even to Middle East and South Asia scholars is that over a century earlier, Afghanistan was a leading contributor in this field. These features demonstrate that Islamic legal history in Afghanistan was not insulated from regional or global developments such as the rise of the administrative state but evolved in tandem with them. By the time of its independence in 1919, Afghanistan was pursuing these goals not in isolation from neighboring Muslim populaces and the international community at large but in coordination with them, sharing in processes of centralization but also making novel contributions—and even leading—on its own terms. At the same time, this unique style of Islamic law, statecraft, and diplomacy contrasts with later post-Ottoman governments in the region that relied on French, Belgian, Austrian, or German advisors for judicial reform and state-building expertise, even as Habib Allah and Aman Allah made references to the Turks and Indian Muslims as "brothers and guides" in charting alternative paths to modernization.[8]

Hopes and Fears, Histories and Futures

From the winding cliffs of the Khyber Pass to the shores of the Mediterranean, for over a millennium Muslims crisscrossed regions we today call the Middle East, Central Asia, and the Indian Ocean in pursuit of trade, learning, and pilgrimage, and often all three purposes combined. For the time being, academic and public discourse on Muslim migrants continues to dwell on more disquieting themes. Tides of refugees; trafficking of narcotics, weapons, and other contraband; militant "jihadis"—specter-like, these fears have pervaded European writings about Muslims crossing borders from the Durand Line in 1915 to the Schengen Area in 2015; from Turkey's accession to the European Union, and Britain's exit from it. In this charged atmosphere of crisis, Pan-Islamism continues to be represented as an inherently threatening force with a singular goal: world domination, a totalitarian implementation of "Sharia Law," and political unification under a restored caliphate. Privileging themes of confrontation and extremism, such militaristic narratives thrive on a dichotomy between a "Muslim World" versus a "Judeo-Christian West," a constructed binary that still dominates multiple Islamist ideologies today, as well as their fellow adherents of civilizational clash in the secular-liberal West.

Such emphases on conflict and confrontation with the West have long overshadowed more subtle internal processes and connections linking modern, mobile Muslim populations across geographic and political boundaries. Through travel, correspondence, and periodical subscriptions, Muslim scholars, students, and journalists shuttled between Asian, African, and European territories at increasing speed and frequency, from the advent of locomotives and steamships to the first automobiles and airplanes. Focusing on Muslim jurists and other literate elites who traveled to Kabul between the last quarter of the nineteenth century and the first quarter of the twentieth, this book has shown Afghanistan as a crucial site for the study of transnational Muslim networks pushing "Pan-Islamic" agendas, but of a very different kind: establishing rule of law, homegrown state-building, and constructive diplomatic ties with the rest of the world.

If Afghanistan from the 1980s on has become equated with an international conduit for drugs, sectarianism, and terrorism, *Afghanistan Rising* has told a story of no less global proportions, but of a very different nature. More than a temporary escape from the morass of ongoing conflicts in the Middle East, South Asia, and within Afghanistan itself today, there are yet other reasons to take the history of Islamic legal modernism in the country seriously. The people and places at the heart of this book provide real, lived examples of a diverse group of Muslims engaged in modern state-building and international diplomacy, challenged as they were by the obstacles and the vested interests of powerful forces lining up against them. The latter included the imperial armies of colonial powers from without, and domestic insurgencies contesting state centralization campaigns from within. For the legal historian as much as the military historian, then, there is much to be appreciated about this era of modern Afghan history.

Beyond the achievements embodied in Afghanistan's survival as a self-governing amirate from the reign of ʿAbd al-Rahman Khan in the 1880s to an independent state under Aman Allah Khan in the 1920s, our subject also imparts lessons on the importance of history for enhancing our understanding of Islamic law in the modern world, and for fostering more pluralistic and participatory modes of governance in our world today. As one contemporary scholar of Islamic law recently emphasized, historicism can provide valuable opportunities to explore how modern Muslims committed to positive social transformation navigated challenges "to defend the Islamic tradition against hostile hegemonic western discourses while at the same time maintaining a posture of internal criticism in order to achieve the political goal of a more just and egalitarian society."[9] For many Muslim-majority societies, as well as Muslim minorities, across the world at this time, it is difficult to imagine a more vital project than that.

The future of Islamic legal history, then, in Afghanistan and practically anywhere else, is intertwined with profoundly political stakes. On the one hand, for scholars of shariʿa to reject projects like the Ottoman Mecelle and Ottoman Constitution of 1876, the Persian Constitution of 1906, or Afghanistan's 1923 Constitution and Aman Allah Codes as capitulations to modernity and failing the "Islamic" test is to perpetuate hyperbolized notions of a frozen, ossified legal tradition; the shariʿa, nothing more than artifact of the premodern world. On the other hand, for secular-liberal thinkers and jurists to not take such legal and constitutional experiences seriously is to slam the door shut on instructive dialogues and conversations about what law and the pursuit of justice means in a pluralistic world. As legal scholar Mohammad Fadel has justly noted, both narratives thrive on an overly pessimistic outlook when it comes to the survival, and adaptability, of Muslim jurists and the Islamic legal tradition in the modern world. With no choice but to submit to the stamp of colonial modernity as a fait accompli, Muslims are rendered "powerless" to access the moral and legal precepts of their tradition, and must simply accept the brave new world "in a permanent state of loss." The political stakes of such an approach are truly bleak: Muslims committed to a real and not just reverential place for Islamic law today must presumably choose between violent rage or passive despair.[10]

Beyond the hopeless futures such ominous perspectives forecast, ahistorical or dismissive approaches to Islamic legal modernism also fail to appreciate the human agency behind innovative, hybrid works in this genre of modern law, of which the Aman Allah Codes are not the only example. More than just texts, the role of madrasa-trained jurists turned *ʿālim*-administrators and constitutionalists—including Ahmed Cevdet Pasha (1822–1895) in the late Ottoman Empire, Sayyid Muhammad Tabataba'i (1842–1920) in the Iranian Constitutional Revolution, or Mawlawi 'Abd al-Wasiʿ Qandahari (1873–1929) in Amani Afghanistan, for example—speak to the dynamism of ulema as a heterogeneous class of legal actors conventionally assumed to be the region's most reactionary or politically conservative.[11] Put another way, the latter class of ulema become especially important for seeing modern Muslim jurists as embodying a resilient, living, and evolving tradition rather than agents of Western imperialism, stagnant reactionaries, or apologists for oppressive regimes.[12]

Far from seeing the shariʿa as dead after colonialism, and its custodians as passive spectators of their own marginalization, this book has presented Muslim jurists and administrators as skilled agents who struggled—and negotiated—to carve a space of autochthonous legal production that has gone unnoticed. The story of Afghanistan here is of a Muslim dynasty establishing the legitimacy of its hereditary line while claiming to rule in the name of Islam and the territory of a nation. The Muhammadzai dynasty and supporting political elites read the global situation and developed a notion of modern kingship accordingly. Of course, the legitimacy of Muslim kings became more challenging in an era of Young Afghans and Young Turks, yet the 1923 Constitution illustrated a case when older notions of monarchy could be synthesized with new notions of legality, legitimacy, and sovereignty. In light of the fact that all of the 2011 Arab Spring uprisings were in republics—with the exceptional sectarian case of

Bahrain—the resiliency of the model of Muslim kingship has drawn attention to historians, lawyers, and political scientists alike. Today, these debates are filtered through the extremist ideologies of the so-called Islamic State on the one hand, and latent Orientalism on the other—but history teaches us it need not be either way. Focusing on the historical experience of Muslim kingship in the case of Kabul under the Muhammadzai amirs, this book has told a transnational story of legal modernity through the Afghan prism. In so doing, it has offered a new interpretation against the conventional "Western modernity versus traditional Islam" binary, suggesting a model of modernity that was not necessarily Eurocentric, while blurring our usual dichotomized understandings of Afghan society.

This is not to romanticize the achievements, or lament the lost possibilities, of Afghan modernity in earlier times, including under the reformist king Aman Allah Khan. There is much that contemporary sensibilities could find problematic in the policies of the governing regimes described in this book, be it the insufficient protection (or empowerment) of Afghan women, the status of minorities, or raw authoritarianism and the modern state's violence, to name a few enduring ills that are clearly still with us worldwide. That is to say nothing of the locally tailored civilizing missions embedded in the Muhammadzai state-building campaigns, themselves drawing on attitudes of British or even Ottoman Orientalisms brought by Indian and Turkish expatriates in the Afghan domains.[13]

As many a lawyer and judge would recognize, however, the earthly struggles for justice at the heart of any legal tradition are riddled with imperfection, creating new challenges for new generations whose work is never finished. A historian might add that agents of those struggles are more empowered with the knowledge and understanding (and better yet, appreciation) of a society's legal heritage than without. Though clearly a top-down attempt at social engineering through law, among other shortcomings, the lasting contribution of the state-building campaigns of Afghanistan's late Muhammadzai amirs must be acknowledged. They reflected a perceptive attempt to circumvent the widening gulf between Islamic and secular, a dualism whose roots were being laid in several predominantly Muslim countries at roughly the same time, and have been fiercely contested ever since.

MANY YEARS AGO, when friends or colleagues asked what I thought were Kabul's most iconic sites, I invariably responded with Dar al-Aman, an abandoned palace on the western outskirts of the city. Translating as the Abode of

Safety, this haunting, liberally photographed, and neoclassically designed edifice sits atop a dry knoll, not far from rolling foothills where Afghan royalty once picnicked and hunted. Originally constructed in the early 1920s under the aegis of Aman Allah's spirited modernization campaign, the gutted building now stands solitary and ghostlike, hollowed out from decades of war, neglect, and looting. The total devastation of a celebrated national monument once hailed as the seat of a future parliament has become a tragic symbol for all that Afghans have endured in their recent history. From political false starts to the broken promises of leaders, and from manipulation by superpowers to the machinations of neighbors, above all Kabul's Abode of Safety symbolizes tragically, if not mockingly, abandonment by the international community.

Today, however, I no longer give that answer. It is not because plans in recent years to reconstruct the palace have erased the painful memories of Afghans, or rendered them moot—they have not. It is not because the promised funding for these plans has largely failed to materialize. It is also not due to the presence of more pleasant gardens and parks, restaurants and cafés, or the stunning combination of urban and natural landscapes beyond the old city walls. Rather, it is because the ruins at Dar al-Aman are not nearly representative of the multiple layers of Afghanistan's modern history strewn across its capital. Aman Allah's palace, poignant and photogenic as it is, simply cannot do justice to the broader story of Afghanistan's modern history.

When asked the same question now, I point to a pair of lesser known buildings from the late nineteenth and early twentieth centuries. If not nearly as dramatic, they stand in respectable condition at the heart of Kabul's modest downtown sprawl, and impart a remarkable symbolism and history of their own. The first, Shah Do Shamshira Mosque (Figure C1), straddles the Darya-i Kabul, a mere trickle of a river that can rise in summer months following melting snows. Like Dar al-Aman, Shah Do Shamshira was built during the early reign of Aman Allah, at the peak of Ottoman influence in Kabul. With its distinctive cube-shaped foundation, half-moon arches, and six-windowed façades fashioned in neobaroque style, this two-storied mosque bears an unmistakable resemblance to Istanbul's iconic Ortaköy Mosque on the Bosporus (Figure C2). A testament to late Ottoman influence in Kabul and a surviving relic of that remarkable era, no other mosque in Afghanistan looks quite the same.

A brisk twenty-minute walk away is a site of invaluable importance to any student of Afghan history: the Arshif-i Milli, or National Archives of Afghanistan (Figure C3). Located in Bagh-i Charm Gari (Tanners' Garden) district of

FIGURE C1. Shah Do Shamshira Mosque, Kabul, Afghanistan. Author photograph.

FIGURE C2. Ortaköy Mosque, Istanbul, Turkey. Photograph by Jung Hsuan / Shutterstock.

FIGURE C3. National Archives, Kabul, Afghanistan. Author photograph.

downtown Kabul, this structure houses centuries of government documents, collectors' relics, and other memorabilia, from ancient Kufic calligraphy to the family photos of Afghan kings and presidents. Originally constructed in 1892 by Amir 'Abd al-Rahman, it was specifically designed to suit the tastes of his eldest son and heir, Habib Allah, who admired the architectural style of British Indian cantonments. The building's aesthetic features hence instilled the Raj's historic influence in the Kabul court at a time when Britain was the only foreign power allowed to have official diplomatic relations with the amir.

And yet, emblematic of Afghanistan in general, the building itself betrays a rich and more varied history than meets the eye. Its Victorian influences notwithstanding, starting in the early 1900s the site was used for Afghanistan's Mekteb-i Harbiye, the Ottoman-designed and administered royal military academy in Kabul. It was here that the Arab colonel of Baghdad, El-Seyyid Mahmud Sami Bey, served as the school's director and principal instructor, training cadets from the Muhammadzai royal family, including the teenaged prince Aman Allah Khan. While the building fell into disrepair during the subsequent Musahiban dynasty, following restorations in the 1970s the Afghan government decided to move its archival material to the refurbished site. Remarkably, this rather unassuming building in downtown Kabul survived the three ensuing decades of foreign occupation and civil war largely intact. Its holdings, while diminished, remain rich and of immense value. Some visitors have described the archive's condition as miraculous.[14] Others have worked diligently to rescue its treasures from further deterioration.[15] Still others were overcome by the promise and responsibility to write new histories of Afghanistan—and just maybe, of the world.

And in that are glad tidings for the broken-hearted: not all may be lost in even the hardest of times.

ABBREVIATIONS

ARCHIVES

ADL	Afghanistan Digital Library, Kabul, Afghanistan; New York, USA; and http://afghanistandl.nyu.edu
BCA	Başbakanlık Cumhuriyet Arşivi, Ankara, Turkey
BOA	Başbakanlık Osmanlı Arşivi, Istanbul, Turkey
IOR	India Office Records, London, UK
NAI	National Archives of India, New Delhi, India
TİTE	Türk İnkılap Tarih Enstitüsü Arşivi, Ankara, Turkey
TKA	Türk Kızılayı Arşivi, Ankara, Turkey

ORGANIZATIONS, PUBLICATIONS, AND REGIONS

ASIBR	*Afghanistan Strategic Intelligence British Records*
CID	Criminal Investigation Department
CKC	Central Khilafat Committee
CLC	Codification of Laws Committee

CSSAAME	*Comparative Studies of South Asia, Africa, and the Middle East*
CUP	Committee for Union and Progress
FATA	Federally Administered Tribal Areas
IJMES	*International Journal of Middle East Studies*
JOTSA	*Journal of the Ottoman and Turkish Studies Association*
JPS	*Journal of Persianate Studies*
JRCAS	*Journal of the Royal Central Asian Society*
NWFP	North-West Frontier Province
TBMM	Türkiye Büyük Millet Meclisi
UP	Uttar Pradesh
WWA	*Who's Who in Afghanistan*

CALENDAR SYSTEMS

h	Hijri
r	Ottoman Rumi
j	Persian Jalali

HIJRI MONTHS IN OTTOMAN TURKISH / ARABIC

M	Muharrem / Muḥarram
S	Safer / Ṣafar
Ra	Rebiülevvel / Rabīʿ al-Awwal
R	Rebiülahir / Rabīʿ al-Ākhir
Ca	Cemaziyelevvel / Jumādā al-Ūlā
C	Cemaziyelahir / Jumādā al-Ākhira
B	Recep / Rajab
Ş	Şaban / Shaʿbān
N	Ramazan / Ramaḍān
L	Şevval / Shawwāl
Za	Zilkade / Dhū al-Qaʿda
Z	Zilhicce / Dhū al-Ḥijja

NOTES

INTRODUCTION

1. Ostrom's original letter and a copy of Sir Acheson's forwarded response are held in the Indian National Archives in New Delhi. NAI-Foreign-Political / Frontier / 1929 / 217-F.

2. For a rare exception by a distinguished scholar of Afghanistan and Islamic law, see Mohammad Hashim Kamali, *Law in Afghanistan: A Study of the Constitutions, Matrimonial Law and the Judiciary* (Leiden: Brill, 1985).

3. Sultan Mohammad Khan, *The Constitution and Laws of Afghanistan* (London: John Murray, 1900), vii.

4. See for example Leon B. Poullada, *Reform and Rebellion in Afghanistan: King Aman Allah's Failure to Modernize a Tribal Society* (Ithaca, NY: Cornell University Press, 1973), 93.

5. Robert Hager, *Forward of Laws of Afghanistan* (Kabul, 1354J / 1975), iv.

6. On the history and politics of area studies as a scholarly paradigm, especially in regard to studies of the Middle East in the United States and Europe, see Osamah F. Khalil, *America's Dream Palace: Middle East Expertise and the Rise of the National Security State* (Cambridge, MA: Harvard University Press, 2016); Zachary Lockman, *Contending Visions of the Middle East: The History and Politics of Orientalism* (New York: Cambridge University Press, 2004). On South / Southeast Asia, see Willem van

Schendel, "Geographies of Knowing, Geographies of Ignorance: Jumping Scale in Southeast Asia," *Environment and Planning D: Society and Space* 20, no. 6 (2002): 647–668. For new directions and challenges to conventional area studies, see Dina Rizk Khoury and Dane Kennedy, "Comparing Empires: The Ottoman Domains and the British Raj in the Long Nineteenth Century," *CSSAAME* 27, no. 2 (2007): 233–244; C. A. Bayly, "Distorted Development: The Ottoman Empire and British India, circa 1780–1916," *CSSAAME* 27, no. 2 (2007): 332–344; Nile Green, "Rethinking the 'Middle East' after the Oceanic Turn," *CSSAAME* 34, no. 3 (2014): 556–564; Michael Chris Low, "Empire and the Hajj: Pilgrims, Plagues, and Pan-Islam under British Surveillance, 1865–1908," *IJMES* 40, no. 2 (2008): 269–290.

7. Poullada, *Reform and Rebellion in Afghanistan*, 99–104; Vartan Gregorian, *The Emergence of Modern Afghanistan, 1880–1946* (Stanford, CA: Stanford University Press, 1969), 239–249; Amin Saikal, *Modern Afghanistan: A History of Struggle and Survival* (New York: I. B. Tauris, 2006), 74–77; Articles 274, 277, and 279, ADL-0526 (*Nizamnamih-ʾi Jaza-yi ʿUmumi* [Kabul: Matbaʿ-ʾi Daʾirih-ʾi Tahrirat-i Majlis-i ʿAli-yi Wuzara, 1304J / 1925]).

8. Milan L. Hauner, "Afghanistan between the Great Powers, 1938–1945," *IJMES* 14, no. 4 (1982): 481.

9. See for example Turan Kayaoğlu, *Legal Imperialism: Sovereignty and Extraterritoriality in Japan, the Ottoman Empire, and China* (Cambridge, UK: Cambridge University Press, 2010); Lâle Can, "The Protection Question: Central Asians and Extraterritoriality in the Late Ottoman Empire," *IJMES* 48, no. 4 (2016): 679–699; Julia Stephen, "An Uncertain Inheritance: The Imperial Travels of Legal Migrants, from British India to Ottoman Iraq," *Law and History Review* 32, no. 4 (2014): 749–772; Mary Dewhurst Lewis, "Geographies of Power: The Tunisian Civic Order, Jurisdictional Politics, and Imperial Rivalry in the Mediterranean, 1881–1935," *Journal of Modern History* 80, no. 4 (2008): 791–830. Emergent scholarship in this direction not dealt with here concerns religious minorities and how they navigated both Ottomanism and European extraterritoriality in increasingly complex ways. See for example Michelle Campos, *Ottoman Brothers: Muslims, Christians, and Jews in Early Twentieth Century Palestine* (Stanford, CA: Stanford University Press, 2010); Julia Cohen, *Becoming Ottoman: Sephardi Jews and Imperial Citizenship in the Modern Era* (New York: Oxford University Press, 2014); Sarah Abrevaya Stein, *Extraterritorial Dreams: European Citizenship, Sephardi Jews, and the Ottoman Twentieth Century* (Chicago: University of Chicago Press, 2016).

10. The Hanafi madhab, or school of Islamic jurisprudence, was the predominant interpretive tradition of Islamic law adopted by the public administrations of the Ottoman Empire, Mughal India, and Bukharan khanates, among other Muslim jurisdictions from the medieval to early modern eras. It has since survived as the largest school of Islamic law observed in the Sunni-Islamicate world, including Turkey, India, Pakistan, Afghanistan, and the Central Asian republics. On the illustrious founder

of the Hanafi school, Abu Hanifa al-Nuʿman bin Thabit bin Zuta (702–772), see Asma Afsaruddin, *The First Muslims: History and Memory* (Oxford: Oneworld, 2008), 34–44, 96–102, 137–149. On the evolution of the Hanafi legal doctrine and practice during the later Mamluk and Ottoman eras, including the intertwinement of the school with the Ottoman state in particular, see Baber Johansen, *The Islamic Law on Land Tax and Rent: The Peasants' Loss of Property Rights as Interpreted in the Hanafite Legal Literature of the Mamluk and Ottoman Periods* (New York: Croom Helm, 1988); Guy Burak, *The Second Formation of Islamic Law: The Hanafi School in the Early Modern Ottoman Empire* (Cambridge, UK: Cambridge University Press, 2015). On the continuing influence of the Hanafi school, its scholastic modes of argumentation, and its jurisprudence in modern Islamicate South Asia, see Muhammad Qasim Zaman, *The Ulama in Contemporary Islam: Custodians of Change* (Princeton, NJ: Princeton University Press, 2002).

11. This tendency has extended to treatments of Afghan state building in later eras as well, including the Cold War, where U.S. and Soviet advisors are represented as the main drivers of technical assistance and development programs in the country. See for example Paul Robinson and Jay Dixon, "Soviet Development Theory and Economic and Technical Assistance to Afghanistan, 1954–1991," *Historian* 73, no. 3 (2010): 599–623; Nick Culather, "Damming Afghanistan: Modernization in a Buffer State," *Journal of American History* 89, no. 2 (2002): 512–537.

12. See for example Suraiya Faroqhi, *Pilgrims and Sultans: The Hajj under the Ottomans, 1517–1683* (London: I. B. Tauris, 2014); Nile Green, "Blessed Men and Tribal Politics: Notes on Political Culture in the Indo-Afghan World," *Journal of the Economic and Social History of the Orient* 49, no. 3 (2006): 344–360; Butrus Abu-Manneh, "The Naqshbandiyya-Mujaddidiyya in the Ottoman Lands in the Early Nineteenth Century," *Die Welt des Islams* 22, no. 1 (1984): 1–36; Thierry Zarcone, *Sufi Pilgrims from Central Asia and India in Jerusalem* (Kyoto: Research Center for Islamic Area Studies, 2009).

13. For a fuller exploration of this argument in a broader global context, see Cemil Aydin, *The Idea of the Muslim World: A Global Intellectual History* (Cambridge, MA: Harvard University Press, 2017).

14. On the Balkans-to-Bengal concept, and its methodological problems when employed ahistorically, see Shahab Ahmed, *What Is Islam? The Importance of Being Islamic* (Princeton, NJ: Princeton University Press, 2016), 33–81.

15. Laura Nader, *The Life of the Law: Anthropological Projects* (Berkeley: University of California Press, 2005), 16–17, 44–51, and 168–211; Pierre Bourdieu (trans. Richard Terdiman), "The Force of Law: Toward a Sociology of the Juridical Field," *Hastings Law Journal* 38, no. 5 (1987): 805–853. On the politics of law and legal education in Afghanistan during subsequent communist rule, see M. G. Weinbaum, "Legal Elites in Afghan Society," *IJMES* 12, no. 1 (1980): 39–57.

16. Christopher Tomlins, "The Many Legalities of Colonization: A Manifesto of Destiny for Early American Legal History," in *The Many Legalities of Early America*,

ed. Christopher L. Tomlins and Bruce H. Mann (Chapel Hill: University of North Carolina Press, 2001), 4.

17. On the beginnings and evolution of this legal-administrative apparatus in British India and its legacies in Pakistan, see Benjamin D. Hopkins, "The Frontier Crimes Regulation and Frontier Governmentality," *Journal of Asian Studies* 74, no. 2 (2015): 369–389.

18. Tomlins, "The Many Legalities of Colonization," 14. For additional British projects of imperial codification in the subcontinent, including other "tribal" or "frontier" zones, see Elizabeth Kolsky, "Codification and the Rule of Colonial Difference: Criminal Procedure in British India," *Law and History Review* 23, no. 3 (2005): 631–683; Jörg Fisch, *Cheap Lives and Dear Limbs: The British Transformation of the Bengal Criminal Law 1769–1817* (Wiesbaden: Franz Steiner Verlag, 1983); Sandra B. Freitag, "Crime in the Social Order of Colonial North India," *Modern Asian Studies* 25, no. 2 (1991): 227–261; Radhika Singha, "'Providential' Circumstances: The Thuggee Campaign of the 1830s and Legal Innovation," *Modern Asian Studies* 27, no. 1 (1993): 83–146. On Anglo-Islamic legal codifications in India, and contestation by local legal actors, see Scott Alan Kugle, "Blamed and Renamed: The Recasting of Islamic Jurisprudence in Colonial South Asia," *Modern Asian Studies* 35, no. 2 (2002): 257–313 and Mitra Sharafi, "The Semi-Autonomous Judge in Colonial India: Chivalric Imperialism Meets Anglo-Islamic Dower and Divorce Law," *Indian Economic & Social History Review* 46, no. 1 (2009): 57–81.

19. Hopkins, "The Frontier Crimes Regulation," 369–389.

20. Annelise Riles, *The Network Inside Out* (Ann Arbor: University of Michigan Press, 2004).

21. For outstanding recent works in this genre, see for example Nader Sohrabi, *Revolution and Constitutionalism in the Ottoman Empire and Iran* (New York: Cambridge University Press, 2014); Iza R. Hussin, *The Politics of Islamic Law: Local Elites, Colonial Authority, and the Making of the Muslim State* (Chicago: University of Chicago Press, 2016).

22. For exceptional studies based on Afghanistan's national laws from the mid-twentieth to twenty-first centuries, see Nadjma Yassari and Mohammad Hamid Saboory, "Sharia and National Law in Afghanistan," in *Sharia Incorporated: A Comparative Overview of the Legal Systems of Twelve Muslim Countries in Past and Present*, ed. Jan Michiel Otto (Amsterdam: Leiden University Press, 2010), 273–318; Martin Lau, "An Introduction to Afghanistan's Legal System," *Yearbook of Islamic and Middle Eastern Law* 8, no. 1 (2001–2002): 27–44; G. Vafai, *Afghanistan: A Country Law Study* (Washington, DC: Library of Congress, 1988); Kamali, *Law in Afghanistan*.

23. See for example Mohammed Ayoob, *The Many Faces of Political Islam: Religion and Politics in the Muslim World* (Ann Arbor: University of Michigan Press, 2007); Shadi Hamid, *Islamic Exceptionalism: How the Struggle over Islam Is Reshaping the World* (New York: St. Martin's, 2016). It is important to recognize the dangers of

geo-religious constructs such as a "Muslim World" or "Islamic World," including the elision of internal heterogeneity among Muslims; the essentializing of religion and downplaying of other kinds of identities and social processes in the histories of these regions; and the marginalization of non-Muslim minorities in these territories (or Muslim minorities in Europe and the Americas, for that matter). For similar reasons the notions of a "Judeo-Christian World," "Hindu World," "Confucian World," etc., are equally suspect and should be employed with similar caution. In opting for the more fluid and historically contingent term *Islamicate world,* this book adapts Marshall Hodgson's notion of "Islamicate" to refer to lands in which Muslims have been politically dominant or culturally ascendant since at least the fifteenth century CE; it should not be taken as a fixed territory or indication of religious orthodoxy. See Marshall G. S. Hodgson, *The Venture of Islam: Conscience and History in a World Civilization* (Chicago: University of Chicago Press, 1958), 57–60, 95.

24. On the long-standing influence of Deobandi scholars in Afghanistan and the Indo-Afghan borderlands, including their complicated relationship with Afghan amirs, see Sana Haroon, "Religious Revival across the Durand Line," in *Under the Drones: Modern Lives in the Afghanistan-Pakistan Borderlands,* ed. Shahzad Bashir and Robert D. Crews (Cambridge, MA: Harvard University Press, 2012), 45–59, and more broadly, Haroon, *Frontier of Faith: Islam in the Indo-Afghan Borderland* (New York: Columbia University Press, 2007). In this center-province dialectic are parallels with centralizing Muslim governments and more locally tailored brands of Islam elsewhere, as in Ottoman Yemen and Mesopotamia, for example. See Brinkley Messick, *The Calligraphic State: Textual Domination and History in a Muslim Society* (Berkeley: University of California Press, 1993); Selim Deringil, *The Well-Protected Domains: Ideology and the Legitimation of Power in the Ottoman Empire, 1876–1909* (New York: I. B. Tauris, 1999); Dina Rizk Khoury, *State and Provincial Society in the Ottoman Empire: Mosul, 1540–1834* (New York: Cambridge University Press, 2002).

25. On the long shadow these thinkers have cast on the study of Muslim modernism across generations of Islamicists, see Albert Hourani, *Arabic Thought in the Liberal Age, 1798–1839* (New York: Oxford University Press, 1962); Malcolm H. Kerr, *Islamic Reform: The Political and Legal Theories of Muhammad ʿAbduh and Rashid Rida* (Princeton, NJ: Princeton University Press, 1966); Malika Zeghal, "Religion and Politics in Egypt: The Ulema of al-Azhar, Radical Islam, and the State," *IJMES* 31, no. 3 (1999): 371–399; Samira Haj, *Reconfiguring Islamic Tradition: Reform, Rationality, and Modernity* (Stanford, CA: Stanford University Press, 2008); Henri Lauziere, *The Making of Salafism: Islamic Reform in the Twentieth Century* (New York: Columbia University Press, 2015).

26. Hence this book departs from most studies on Islamic legal modernism and political Islam by focusing on a qualitatively different genre of Muslim thinkers than those represented by ʿAbduh, Rida, or other modern Salafists. On modern Salafists' juristic eclecticism and generally anti-taqlīd approaches to the law (also known as

takhayyur and *talfiq*), see Haj, *Reconfiguring Islamic Tradition,* 142–143, 150. For a more detailed treatment of the emergence of *takhayyur* and *talfiq* within and beyond the four Sunni schools of law, see Ahmed Fekry Ibrahim, *Pragmatism in Islamic Law: A Social and Intellectual History* (Syracuse, NY: Syracuse University Press, 2015).

27. Mansoor Moaddel, *Islamic Modernism, Nationalism, and Fundamentalism: Episode and Discourse* (Chicago: University of Chicago Press, 2005), 2.

28. For an in-depth treatment of these themes in the late Ottoman Empire and Qajar Iran, see Sohrabi, *Revolution and Constitutionalism.*

29. On the arc of Afghan historiography after four decades of chronic conflict, see Amin Tarzi, "The Maturation of Afghan Historiography," *IJMES* 45, no. 1 (2013): 129–131.

30. For notable exceptions in this regard, see Hasan Kawun Kakar, *Government and Society in Afghanistan: The Reign of Amir ʿAbd al-Rahman Khan* (Austin: University of Texas Press, 2011); Robert D. McChesney, *Waqf in Central Asia: 400 Years in the History of a Muslim Shrine, 1480–1889* (Princeton, NJ: Princeton University Press, 1991); Ashraf Ghani, "Islam and State-Building in a Tribal Society: Afghanistan 1880–1901," *Modern Asian Studies* 12, no. 2 (1978): 269–284; Christina Noelle, *State and Tribe in Ninetieth-Century Afghanistan: The Reign of Amir Dost Muhammad Khan, 1826–1863* (London: Curzon, 1997); Amin Tarzi, "The Judicial State: Evolution and Centralization of the Courts in Afghanistan, 1883–1896" (PhD diss., Department of Middle East Studies, New York University, 2003). On the centrality of Afghanistan to broader imperial, economic, and cultural histories from early modern to contemporary times, see Robert D. Crews, *Afghan Modern: History of a Global Nation* (Cambridge, MA: Harvard University Press, 2015).

31. See for example Ludwig W. Adamec, *Afghanistan, 1900–1923* (Berkeley: University of California Press, 1967); Thomas L. Hughes, "The German Mission to Afghanistan, 1915–1916," *German Studies Review* 25, no. 3 (2002): 447–476.

32. See for example Poullada, *Reform and Rebellion in Afghanistan;* Gregorian, *The Emergence of Modern Afghanistan*; Rhea Talley Stewart, *Fire in Afghanistan, 1914–1929: Faith, Hope, and the British Empire* (Garden City, NY: Doubleday, 1973); or even earlier, Roland Wild, *Aman Allah: Ex-King of Afghanistan* (London: Hurst & Blackett, 1932); and Ikbal Ali Shah, *The Tragedy of Amanullah* (London: Alexander-Ouseley, 1933). A notable exception is Senzil Nawid's unmatched work on the Amani period, based on a meticulous study of Afghan government records and private papers in Pashto and Dari. Nawid, *Religious Response to Social Change in Afghanistan, 1919–29: King Aman-Allah and the Afghan Ulama* (Costa Mesa, CA: Mazda, 1999).

33. I am grateful to Cemil Aydin for his keen observations on Asian and African parallels in this regard.

34. Noah Feldman, "Why Sharia?" *New York Times Magazine,* March 16, 2008. ("For many Muslims today, living in corrupt autocracies, the call for Shariah is not a call for sexism, obscurantism or savage punishment but for an Islamic version of what

the West considers its most prized principle of political justice: the rule of law.") For his expanded argument on this theme, see Feldman, *The Fall and Rise of the Islamic State* (Princeton, NJ: Princeton University Press, 2008).

35. Talal Asad, *Formations of the Secular: Christianity, Islam, Modernity* (Stanford, CA: Stanford University Press, 2003), 205–256. On MacIntyre's original use of "tradition" in this sense, see Alasdair MacIntyre, *Whose Justice? Which Rationality?* (Notre Dame, IN: University of Notre Dame Press, 1988), 12. For a lucid and sensitive approach to the shariʿa as a discursive tradition and "a framework of inquiry rather than a set of unchanging doctrines or culturally specific mandates," see Hāj, *Reconfiguring Islamic Tradition*, 4–5. On the early evolution of Islamic law, with attention to historical and interpretive contingency, see Lena Salaymeh, *The Beginnings of Islamic Law: Late Antique Islamicate Legal Traditions* (Cambridge, UK: Cambridge University Press, 2016); Intisar Rabb, *Doubt in Islamic Law: A History of Legal Maxims, Interpretation, and Islamic Criminal Law* (New York: Cambridge University Press, 2015); Wael B. Hallaq, *Authority, Continuity, and Change in Islamic Law* (Cambridge, UK: Cambridge University Press, 2001); Baber Johansen, *Contingency in a Sacred Law: Legal and Ethical Norms in the Muslim Fiqh* (Leiden: Brill, 1999); Sherman A. Jackson, *Islamic Law and the State: The Constitutional Jurisprudence of Shihab al-Din al Qarafi* (Leiden: Brill, 1996).

36. For these reasons Islamic law is hardly a satisfactory translation for shariʿa. Signifying a much broader constellation of socioreligious norms, institutions, and practices, including devotional acts of worship and ethics, the shariʿa cannot be reduced to Western notions of law, in other words binding rules enforced by state authority, nor purely private morality or piety alone. On the shariʿa as a "total discourse" of institutions and practices see Messick, *The Calligraphic State*, 3; as "etiquette, styles of argumentation, and modes of transmitting knowledge," see Zaman, *The Ulama in Contemporary Islam*, 6. Furthermore, similar to the words "justice," "virtue," or even "truth" itself in the English language, the shariʿa is an abstract and aspirational concept—signifying God's guidance to Muslims for a wholesome and contented life in this world and the next—which can never be the monopoly of a single jurist or even group of people. The more praxis-oriented Arabic term *fiqh* (literally, "insight" or "understanding"), on the other hand, connotes a qualified Muslim legist's best attempt to *interpret what the shariʿa is* for an applied situation based on a reasoned analysis of the Qurʾan, Prophetic example, and associated methodologies of interpretation. It is the latter process that results in "Islamic law," "Islamic jurisprudence," or "the Islamic legal tradition" as we know it.

37. See for example Sherman A. Jackson, "Shariʿah, Democracy, and the Modern Nation-State: Some Reflections on Islam, Popular Rule, and Pluralism," *Fordham International Law Journal* 27, no. 1 (2003): 88–107; Khaled Abou El Fadl, *The Authoritative and the Authoritarian in Islamic Discourses: A Contemporary Case Study* (Austin, TX: Dar Taiba, 1997). The nonbinding and advisorial nature of Islamic juristic opinions, or fatwas, may come as a surprise to readers accustomed to associating the

word, and shari'a more broadly, with the authoritarian implementation of clerical diktats. Here, it is important to distinguish the shari'a as a holistic sociolegal world on the one hand, from another technical concept of great importance in this study, *sīyāsa shar'iyya* (shari'a-compliant public policy). The latter signals the de facto power of Muslim political authorities to produce legislative enactments of an administrative nature known as *qānūn/qawānīn* (Arabic), *kanunnames* (Ottoman Turkish), or *niẓāmnāmihs* (Persian), translating as "codes," "regulations," or "ordinances." Akin to modern notions of administrative law and executive orders in secular-liberal states, per the doctrine of *sīyāsa shar'iyya,* the regulations of a Muslim ruler carry the weight of enforceable law—barring sufficient opposition from the legists, that is. For a further elaboration of this concept amid scholarly advances in the field, see Amr Shalakany, "Islamic Legal Histories," *Berkeley Journal of Middle Eastern and Islamic Law* 1, no. 1 (2008): 16–24, 59–82.

38. For an overview of the historical development of Islam's schools of law, see Wael B. Hallaq, *Shari'a: Theory, Practice, Transformations* (New York: Cambridge University Press, 2009); Ahmed El Shamsy, *The Canonization of Islamic Law: A Social and Intellectual History* (New York: Cambridge University Press, 2013); Afsaruddin, *The First Muslims.* For an innovative approach to the period highlighting parallels and divergences between the formation of the early Islamic and Jewish legal traditions with case studies, see Salaymeh, *The Beginnings of Islamic Law,* 21–42, 105–135, and 163–196.

39. By employing the phrase "Islamic law and statecraft," this book focuses its inquiry on how said Muslims engaged questions of jurisprudence, public law and administration, and international relations in a modern Muslim-majority nation-state setting by creatively accessing rather than jettisoning their religio-legal heritage. The latter distinguishes our focus from other parallel inquiries relevant to the study of modern Islam not covered here, such as how Muslims have approached questions of theology, mysticism, or even language and literature in the modern world. It should be remembered, after all, that Islamic jurisprudence (*fiqh*) constitutes only one strand amid an amalgam of other arts and sciences subsumed within the history of Islam, including theology, mysticism, grammar, astronomy, botany, and medicine, for example. For one academic scholar's magnum opus dedicated to this theme, as well as notions of orthodoxy and heterodoxy in Islam, see Ahmed, *What Is Islam?.* Ahmed's trenchant critique of dogmatic, ahistorical, and essentialist deployments of the term notwithstanding, this work enlists "Islamic" to describe the self-identifying and aspirational character of policies launched by Afghan, Ottoman, and Indian Muslim actors at the heart of this story. In the end, to dispense with this modifying adjective would misrepresent the pronounced emphasis the latter placed on describing their struggles in exactly that way.

40. Saba Mahmood, *Politics of Piety: The Islamic Revival and the Feminist Subject* (Princeton, NJ: Princeton University Press), xi.

41. Wael B. Hallaq, *The Impossible State: Islam, Politics, and Modernity's Moral Predicament* (New York: Columbia University Press, 2014); Abdullahi Ahmed

An-Na'im, *Islam and the Secular State: Negotiating the Future of Shari'a* (Cambridge, MA: Harvard University Press, 2010). Shared between these thoughtful works is their incisive treatment of the modern political violence, *a la* Foucault, anywhere in the world. Here, the modern state's disciplinary technologies of registration, codification, surveillance, and prisons, and overall epistemic violence unleashed on pluralistic world views and ways of being, constituted an irreversible historical rupture for shari'a-based societies. For Hallaq and An-Naim, shari'a praxis was always driven by the epistemic authority of the jurists, and not the violent arm of the state, hence rendering modern projects for an "Islamic state" to be fatally flawed from the outset. I deal more closely with these important arguments as they pertain to our subject in Chapter 5 and the Conclusion.

42. See for example Jerry Brotton, *The Sultan and the Queen: The Untold Story of Elizabeth and Islam* (New York: Viking, 2016); David Motadel, ed., *Islam and the European Empires* (Oxford: Oxford University Press, 2014).

43. Dilip Parameshwar Gaonkar, ed., *Alternative Modernities* (Durham, NC: Duke University Press, 2001), 18.

44. For similar themes in a later period, see Susan Gunasti, "The Late Ottoman Ulema's Constitutionalism," *Islamic Law and Society* 23, no. 1–2 (2016): 89–119.

45. Alan M. Guenther, "Hanafi Fiqh in Mughal India: The Fatawa-yi 'Alamgiri," in *India's Islamic Traditions, 711–1750*, ed. Richard M. Eaton (New Delhi: Oxford University Press, 2003).

46. Schacht famously argued that as a case of "jurists' law," the shari'a (or *fiqh*, rather) was confined to the realm of the theoretical exercises, while rulers and their courtiers developed the legal fiction of *siyāsa*, or public policy, to carry out the day-to-day administration of empire. Joseph Schacht, *An Introduction to Islamic Law* (Oxford: Clarendon, 1964), 70–71, 104. For Schacht and other adherents to the Shari'a-Siyāsa divide, a fundamental gulf existed between doctrine and practice in Islam. Through *siyāsa*, Muslim rulers and their governors could bypass this chasm by endorsing administrative edicts—known as *qānūn*, *kanunnames*, or *niẓāmnāmihs*—which fulfilled the prerogatives of sovereign power even if ostensibly contravening the rulings of the Qur'an, sunna, or scholarly consensus. Hence the notion of an unbridgeable gulf between two worlds of Islamic law: Shari'a in theory, *siyāsa* in practice. Ibid., 104. A related thesis also proposed by Schacht held that the so-called doors of *ijtihād*, or innovative legal argumentation in Islam, were shut by the beginning of the tenth century. Ibid., 70–71. Schacht's aforesaid theses have been heavily critiqued by subsequent generations of Islamicists, including Wael Hallaq. See for example Wael B. Hallaq, "From Fatwas to Furu': Growth and Change in Islamic Substantive Law," *Islamic Law and Society* 1, no. 1 (1994): 29–65; Hallaq, *Authority, Continuity, and Change in Islamic Law*. On this subject Schacht nevertheless accurately noted that for Muslim jurists administrative codes such as Mamluk or Ottoman *qānūn* represented the furthest distance from the divine and divinely inspired sources of Islam, the Qur'an

and sunna, and the greatest proximity to human intervention in the domain of law-making. They are hence the most subject to being overturned or disregarded by subsequent generations of Muslim rulers, scholars, or communities at large, who may not wish to be held captive to time-bound articulations of the law.

47. On the enduring role of Ottoman ulema in republican Turkey, see Amit Bein, *Ottoman Ulema, Turkish Republic: Agents of Change and Guardians of Tradition* (Stanford, CA: Stanford University Press, 2011). Similarly, recent work on the first Pahlavi era has eroded historiographical orthodoxy on Riza Shah and the Iranian Shiʿi clerical establishment. See for example Janet Afary, "Foundations for Religious Reform in the First Pahlavi Era," *Iran Nameh* 30, no. 3 (2015): XLVI–LXXXVII. On South Asian ulema, see Zaman, *The Ulama in Contemporary Islam.*

48. Huricihan İslamoğlu, ed., *Constituting Modernity: Private Property in the East and West* (New York: I. B. Tauris, 2004); Ariel Salzman, "An Ancien Régime Revisited: 'Privatization' and Political Economy in the Eighteenth-Century Ottoman Empire," *Politics and Society* 21, no. 4 (1993): 393–423; James C. Scott, *Seeing Like a State: How Certain Schemes to Improve the Human Condition Have Failed* (New Haven, CT: Yale University Press, 1999); Michel Foucault, *Discipline and Punish: The Birth of the Prison* (New York: Vintage, 1995).

49. On premodern theories of Muslim kingship, including the synthesis of Timurid and other Turco-Mongolian models of sovereignty within an Islamic framework, see A. Azfar Moin, *The Millenial Sovereign: Sacred Kingship and Sainthood in Islam* (New York: Columbia University Press, 2014) and Aziz Al-Azmeh, *Muslim Kingship: Power and Sacred in Muslim, Christian, and Pagan Politics* (New York: I. B. Tauris, 2001). On medieval theories of the caliphate and the imamate and their evolution in modern times, see Hugh Kennedy, *Caliphate: The History of an Idea* (New York: Basic Books, 2016); Mona Hassan, *Longing for the Lost Caliphate: A Transregional History* (Princeton, NJ: Princeton University Press, 2016).

1. AN OTTOMAN SCHOLAR IN VICTORIAN KABUL

1. BOA-Y.A.HUS 159 / 14 (1294h Ş 01 / 1877 08 10); BOA-İ.HR 276 / 16873 (1295h C 05 / 1878 06 06); NAI-Foreign / Secret / Mar.1878 / 70–145. Ahmed Hamdi Effendi, a journalist and member of the delegation, has also left us with glimpses of the arrival at Bombay in his travel memoir, *Hindistan, Swat ve Afghanistan Seyahatnamesi* (Istanbul: Mahmud Bey Matbaası, 1882 / 83), 11–12. See also Azmi Özcan, *Pan-Islamism: Indian Muslims, the Ottomans and Britain, 1877–1924* (Leiden: Brill, 1997), 86; Dwight Lee, "A Turkish Mission to Afghanistan, 1877," *Journal of Modern History* 13, no. 3 (1941): 349; M. Cavid Baysun, "Şirvanizade Ahmed Hulusi Efendi'nin Efganistan Elçiliğine Aid Vesikalar," *Tarih Dergisi (Istanbul Üniversitesi Edebiyat Fakültesi)* IV (1952): 147–158.

2. Mehmet Saray, *Türk-Afgan Münasebetleri* (Istanbul: Veli Yayınları, 1984), 17.

3. Hamdi, *Hindistan, Swat ve Afghanistan Seyahatnamesi,* 11–12.

4. BOA-Y.A.HUS 159/14; BOA-İ.HR 276/16873; NAI-Foreign/Secret/Mar.1878/70–145; Özcan, *Pan-Islamism,* 86; Lee, "A Turkish Mission," 349.

5. Various theories have been put forward as to the coining and earliest usage of the term. See for example Dwight E. Lee, "The Origins of Pan-Islamism," *American Historical Review* 47, no. 2 (1942): 280; Özcan, *Pan-Islamism,* 24; M. Naeem Qureshi, *Pan-Islam in British Indian Politics* (Leiden: Brill, 1999), 9. Common between them is the notion of European coinage in the late nineteenth century. While the term could be roughly rendered into phrases found in Arabic, Persian, and Ottoman Turkish literature of the era, approximating "Islamic Unity" or "Union of Muslim Peoples," "Pan-Islamic" or "Pan-Islamism" were absorbed into these languages as loanwords, e.g. "*pān-islāmī*" in Persian and "*Pan-İslamizm*" in Turkish.

6. Özcan, *Pan-Islamism,* 24.

7. As Adeeb Khalid and Cemil Aydin have shown, to focus exclusively on Pan-Islamism misses the latter's intersection with multiple anticolonial ideologies that emerged in the late nineteenth to early twentieth centuries including Pan-Turkism and Pan-Arabism, Pan-Asianism, and Bolshevism, all of which overlapped with Pan-Islamism in complex ways from the late Ottoman period to decolonization after World War II. Cemil Aydin, *The Politics of Anti-Westernism in Asia: Visions of World Order in Pan-Islamic and Pan-Asian Thought* (New York: Columbia University Press, 2007); Adeeb Khalid, *The Politics of Muslim Cultural Reform: Jadidism in Central Asia* (Berkeley: University of California Press, 1998).

8. Jacob M. Landau, *The Politics of Pan-Islam: Ideology and Organization* (Oxford: Clarendon, 1994); Malcolm Kerr, *Islamic Reform: The Political and Legal Theories of Muhammad ʿAbduh and Rashid Rida* (Berkeley: University of California Press, 1966); Qureshi, *Pan-Islam.*

9. On the Ottoman-Afghan war of 1726, a still largely unknown event, see Laurence Lockhart, *The Fall of the Safavi Dynasty and the Afghan Occupation of Persia* (Cambridge, UK: Cambridge University Press, 1958), 282–293; Dina Rizk Khoury, *State and Provincial Society in the Ottoman Empire: Mosul, 1540–1834* (New York: Cambridge University Press, 2002), 56, 64, 161–162.

10. Özcan, *Pan-Islamism,* ix-1; Naimur Rahman Farooqi, *Mughal-Ottoman Relations: A Study of Political and Diplomatic Relations between Mughal India and the Ottoman Empire, 1556–1748* (Delhi: Idarih-i Adabiyat Delli, 2009), 10–15; Farooqi, "Moguls, Ottomans, and Pilgrims: Protecting the Routes to Mecca in the Sixteenth and Seventeenth Centuries," *International History Review* 10, no. 2 (1988): 198–220.

11. On the Sublime Porte's foreign relations in the early modern period, see Suraiya Faroqhi, *The Ottoman Empire and the World around It* (New York: I. B. Tauris, 2004). Historically, the terms Turk, Afghan, and Hindustani were far from fixed or airtight categories. Filtered by myriad social factors including language, religion, trade, region,

and period, the meaning of these terms varied according to speaker and listener; more often, they conveyed a loose sense of geographic and linguistic association rather than fixed ethnicity or nationhood. Bruce Lawrence and David Gilmartin, eds., *Beyond Turk and Hindu: Rethinking Religious Identities in Islamicate South Asia* (Gainesville: University of Florida Press, 2000), 4; D. P. Singhal, *India and Afghanistan: A Study in Diplomatic Relations* (New Delhi: South Asian Publishers, 1963), 1. For the largely interchangeable terms of Afghans, Pashtuns, Pathans, and Rohillas before the nineteenth century, see Jos. J. L. Gommans, *The Rise of the Indo-Afghan Empire, 1710–1780* (Leiden: Brill, 1995), 9–12; Barbara Metcalf, *Islamic Reform in British India: Deoband, 1860–1900* (Princeton, NJ: Princeton University Press, 1982), 298; and Louis Dupree, *Afghanistan* (Princeton, NJ: Princeton University Press, 1973), 321. This book employs the terms "Indian Muslim" and "Muslims of India" primarily as geographical referents; they should not be taken to connote a static or homogeneous people, obscuring the profound regional and linguistic diversity of the Indian subcontinent. On Indian Muslims as a modern legal and political category, see Ayesha Jalal, *Self and Sovereignty: Individual and Community in South Asian Islam since 1850* (New York: Routledge, 2000), 139–186.

12. On Ottoman-Portuguese maritime rivalry in the Indian Ocean, and the ramifications for Indo-Ottoman relations in the fifteenth and sixteenth centuries, see Giancarlo Casale, *The Ottoman Age of Exploration* (Oxford: Oxford University Press, 2010), 205; Özcan, *Pan-Islamism,* 4–5; Farooqi, *Mughal-Ottoman Relations,* 21–22, 152; Farooqi, "Moguls, Ottomans, and Pilgrims," 198–220.

13. Naimur Rahman Farooqi, "Six Ottoman Documents on Mughal-Ottoman Relations during the Reign of Akbar," *Journal of Islamic Studies* 7, no. 1 (1996): 32–48; Farooqi, "Moguls, Ottomans, and Pilgrims," 198–220; Özcan, *Pan-Islamism,* 4–5.

14. According to Azmi Özcan, the delay in substantial contact stemmed from a legacy of animosity dating to Timurlane's devastating attack on the Ottomans at the Battle of Ankara in 1402, where Ottoman Sultan Bayezid I was taken captive and imprisoned by Timurid forces. With Babur and the Mughals being descendants of the Timurids, there was possibly little desire for contact on either side. Özcan, *Pan-Islamism,* 6. This theory is challenged, however, by evidence demonstrating amiable relations between the Ottomans and Mughals from as early as the fifteenth century. Farooqi states that several Ottoman Turks were enlisted in the service of the first emperor and founder of the Mughal dynasty, Babur (r. 1526–1530) and his son Humayun (r. 1530–1540; 1555–1556), among them a chief artillery officer, his two assistants, and a physician, all of whom are reported to have personally served the founding Mughal rulers with distinction. Farooqi, *Mughal-Ottoman Relations,* 11–13.

15. Özcan also hints that the Ottomans first regarded Mughal ascendance in India with some suspicion in light of the Porte's alliance with Gujarati kings who were then at war with Mughal emperor Humayun. Alongside these accounts is the remarkable travel memoir of Ottoman shipwreck survivor-turned-envoy Seydi Ali Reis

(1498–1563), whose vessel crashed along the south Indian coast in the mid-sixteenth century. It appears Reis's dramatic escape after nearly drowning at sea was enough to thaw diplomatic ice in the Mughal court, where the Ottoman naval officer was eventually hosted by Humayun in royal darbar. Seydi Ali Reis, *The Travels and Adventures of the Turkish Admiral Sidi Ali Reïs in India, Afghanistan, Central Asia, and Persia, during the Years 1553–1556,* trans. Arminius Vambery (Lahore: al-Buruni, 1975), 21–63.

16. For a late nineteenth-century dossier from the central Ottoman archives grouping together Moroccan, Uzbek, Indian, and Afghan mendicants in the sultan's domains, see BOA-ŞD 2276 / 41 (1315h B 11 / 1897 12 05). Most documents about Afghans in the Ottoman Empire concern communities in Istanbul, Hejaz, Palestine, and Mesopotamia. See for example BOA-ZB 443 / 102 (1316r 05 28 / 1900 08 10); BOA-A.MKT.UM 79 / 12 (1267h Z 20 / 1851 10 14); BOA-C.HR 66 / 3255 (1252h Ra 03 / 1836 06 18). On Afghan lodges in Istanbul, see BOA-A.MKT.MVL 97 / 73 (1274h L 05 / 1858 05 19); BOA-Y.PRK.AZJ 47 / 25 (1320h Z 29 / 1903 03 28); BOA-Y.MTV 254 / 114 (1321h 01 17 / 1904 01 05); BOA-ZB 608 / 57 (1323h / 1905–1906); BOA-BEO 2787 / 208952 (1324h M 25 / 1906 03 21). On Afghans in Jerusalem, see DH.MKT 1358 / 9 (1303h Za 1 / 1886 08 01), and in more depth, Thierry Zarcone, *Sufi Pilgrims from Central Asia and India in Jerusalem* (Kyoto: Center for Islamic Studies at Kyoto University, 2009). Other Ottoman records from the late nineteenth and early twentieth centuries contain instances of the Porte corresponding with (or reporting on) Afghan travelers, scholars, and pilgrims, especially in the Mesopotamian cities of Baghdad, Najaf, Mosul, and Kirkuk. For example, on Ottoman contacts with the family of a prominent Afghan scholar who died in Mosul, and the provision of a stipend of support to his family, see BOA-BEO 2047 / 153500 (1321h M 21 / 1903 04 19). On Afghans in Kirkuk and Baghdad, see BEO 471 / 35318 (1312h Ra 08 / 1894 09 08) and BEO 690 / 51712 (1313h R 19 / 1895 10 08).

17. Archaeologist Louis Dupree went so far as to conclude Paleaeolithic man probably lived in northern Afghanistan as early as 50,000 BC. Dupree, *Afghanistan,* xvii, 255–272.

18. According to Olaf Caroe and Louis Dupree, variations of the word "Afghan" originate in the third century CE, when Sassanian Persian sources reference the term "Abgan" in imperial chronicles. Since around this time, "Afghan" and "Pashtun" were practical synonyms used to describe Pashto-speaking nomads inhabiting the region between today's Iran, Central Asia, and India. Caroe dates the first reference to Afghans in a Muslim source to the tenth century. Olaf Caroe, *The Pathans, 550 B.C.–A.D. 1957* (New York: St. Martin's, 1958), 79–80, 112; Dupree, *Afghanistan,* xvii; Thomas Barfield, *Afghanistan: A Cultural and Political History* (Princeton, NJ: Princeton University Press, 2010), 24. In a popular but less reliable interpretation among some Persian speakers in Iran, Tajikistan, and Afghanistan itself, the term Afghan is believed to be a corruption of the Persian word "*afqān*," meaning "wild," "wailing," or "noisy." It goes without saying these notions tell us more about the long history of prejudicial

stereotypes projected onto Afghans by others than their alleged "characteristics" as a people.

19. It is hence a commonly repeated but inaccurate claim that Afghanistan, as a territory, has never been conquered or subjugated by a foreign power. To claim so would be to erase the eastern frontiers of various Greco-Macedonian, Persian, and Arab empires, among others. All of the latter invaded and conquered territory falling within today's Afghanistan, only to lose interest in holding it amid domestic rebellion. The result was dwindling foreign communities that were eventually absorbed into the local population. As Afghan-American novelist Tamim Ansary has appropriately put it, on many occasions the invaders simply "became Afghans." Ansary, *Games without Rules: The Often Interrupted History of Afghanistan* (New York: PublicAffairs, 2012), 4. The impact of these passing imperial ventures should not be underestimated, as they brought the territory stretching from the Fergana Valley to the Indian Ocean, and Khorasan to the Indian Gangetic Plateau, into broader regional contact with Hellenistic, Persian, and early Arab-Islamic influences.

20. For a concise overview of the ancient history of Afghans in India, see Gommans, *The Rise of the Indo-Afghan Empire.*

21. Metcalf, *Islamic Reform,* 33.

22. For an outstanding study on Ottoman-Afghan relations during this period see Hakeem Naim, "The Ottoman Empire and Afghanistan: A Record of Failure and Great Power Intrigue" (BA Robert and Colleen Haas Scholars Thesis, Department of Middle Eastern Studies, UC Berkeley, 2010). I am grateful to Naim for sharing his work with me and the many fruitful exchanges we have had on this topic. On the failed Ottoman-Suri attack on Safavid Iran, see Farooqi, *Mughal-Ottoman Relations,* 146–147; Naim, "The Ottoman Empire and Afghanistan," 9–10.

23. For the earliest examples known to the author, see BOA-D.BŞM.d 40946 (1137h M 24 / 1724 10 13); BOA-C.DH 127–6634 (1141h Za 28 / 1729 06 25); BOA-C.HR 67–3313 (1157h Ra 12 / 1744 04 25). There is a considerable gap from these early Ottoman records on Afghans to the next group of documents several decades later, dating to 1790, 1804, and 1836. BOA-A.DVN.DVE 191 (1205h / 1790–1791); BOA-C.HR 92 / 3777C (1218h Z 08 / 1804 03 20) and BOA-C.HR 66 / 3255 (1252h Ra 03 / 1836 06 18).

24. Shah Mahmoud Hanifi, *Connecting Histories in Afghanistan: Market Relations and State Formation on a Colonial Frontier* (Stanford, CA: Stanford University Press, 2011), 14–17. One of the oldest documents in the Prime Ministry Ottoman archives in Istanbul dealing with Afghans dates to 1724–1725. BOA-D.BŞM.d 40946 (1137H). A later use of the term "Afghanistan" dates to 1790–1791. BOA-A.DVN.DVE 191 (1205H). On the other hand, there are relatively more references to city-states and provinces of today's Afghanistan, including Kabul, Kandahar, Herat, Balkh, Jalalabad, and Badakhshan. See for example BOA-AE.SAMD.III 31 / 2920 (1115h Z 29 / 1704 05 04); BOA-C.HR 824 / 37402A (1230h Z 29 / 1815 12 02); BOA-C.HR 161 / 6721 (1215h R 06 / 1800 08 27); BOA-A.AMD 37 / 28 (1268h C 29 / 1852 04 20); BOA-C.ML

521 / 21292 (1259h S 29 / 1843 03 31); BOA-C.HR 5 / 160 (1150h Z 29 / 1738 04 19); BOA-C. HR 1 / 6 (1231h M 30 / 1816 01 01); BOA/A.MKT.NZD 364 / 91 (1278h S 25 / 1861 09 01); BOA-A.MKT.UM 508 / 96 (1278h R 16 / 1861 10 21). As late as the 1890s Ottoman records also refer to "Afghan tribes" (*Afgan kabileleri*); inhabiting the provinces of Russian Turkistan and Bukhara. BOA-Y.PRK.TKM 26 / 7 (1310h M 10 / 1892 08 04). Beyond official Porte records, one of the most important works produced by Ottoman cartographers in the early modern period, *Kitab-ı Cihannüma* (1732), depicts three major political formations intersecting in the region of today's Afghanistan: India (*Hind/Hindustan*), Iran (*Iran/Acemistan*), and Transoxiana (*Mavarannahr*). Although the atlas labels Kabul and Kandahar as well as Ghazni, Herat, Ghor, Balkh, and Badakhshan—all Afghan cities or provinces today—a separately demarcated "Afghanistan" is not found. See Katip Çelebi and İbrahim Müteferrika, *Kitab-ı Cihannüma li-Katib Çelebi* (Istanbul: Dar al-Tiba'at al-'Amira, 1145h/1732). Similarly, a subsequent Ottoman atlas from the early nineteenth century, *Cedid Atlas Tercümesi* (1803), fails to demarcate a separate Afghanistan between the Asian territories of Khorasan, India, Tibet, and Turkistan, although it also marks prominent Afghan cities within this region. See Mahmud Raif Efendi, *Cedid Atlas Tercümesi* (Istanbul: Tabhane-i Hümayun, 1218h/1803).

25. It is important to remember that with territorial-based ideas of nationalism and citizenship gaining ascendancy in the nineteenth and twentieth centuries, constructions of "Afghan-ness" legally evolved to incorporate the significant numbers of non-Pashtuns in the country, including Tajiks, Uzbeks, Baluchis, Persian-speakers hailing from Iran, and Indian migrants from the Punjab, as well as Hindu, Jewish, and Sikh minorities. At the same time, not until fixed Indo-Afghan borders were established in the late nineteenth century were Indian Pashtuns (that is, those residing on the eastern side of the Durand Line) juridically separated from their co-ethnics in Afghanistan. On this interminable issue and its implications beyond territory disputes, see Shah Mahmoud Hanifi, "Quandaries of the Afghan Nation," in *Under the Drones: Modern Lives in the Afghanistan-Pakistan Borderlands*, ed. Shahzad Bashir and Robert D. Crews (Cambridge, MA: Harvard University Press, 2012), 83–101.

26. Dupree, *Afghanistan*, 332–334; Mir Ghulam Muhammad Ghubar, *Afghanistan dar Masir-i Tarikh* (Qum: Payam-i Muhajir, 1980), 355. For a more critical account of this narrative and the role of Loya Jirgas in manufacturing purported national consensus in Afghanistan, see M. Jamil Hanifi, "Editing the Past: Colonial Production of Hegemony through the 'Loya Jerga' in Afghanistan," *Iranian Studies* 37, no. 2 (2004): 295–322.

27. Ahmad Shah's success followed the short-lived Afghan Hotaki dynasty established by Mir Wais Khan (1673–1715) in 1709. The latter's son Mahmud eventually captured and plundered Isfahan in 1722, bringing an end to over two centuries of Safavid rule in Iran. See Gommans, *The Rise of the Indo-Afghan Empire*; Lockhart, *The Fall of the Safavi Dynasty*; Willem M. Floor, *The Afghan Occupation of Safavid Persia,*

1721–1729 (Paris: Association pour l'Avancement des Études Iraniennes, 1998), 39–63. On the rapid growth and constriction of the Durrani Empire, see Barfield, *Afghanistan,* 97–99; Amin Saikal, *Modern Afghanistan: A History of Struggle and Survival* (New York: I. B. Tauris, 2006), 20–22.

28. Asghar H. Bilgrami, *Afghanistan and British India, 1793–1907: A Study in Foreign Relations* (New Delhi: Sterling, 1972), 19; Gommans, *The Rise of the Indo-Afghan Empire,* 49–56; Naim, "The Ottoman Empire and Afghanistan," 17–18.

29. Gommans, *The Rise of the Indo-Afghan Empire,* 46–51; Naim, "The Ottoman Empire and Afghanistan," 17–18. On Ottoman use of the caliphate in the early modern period (challenging arguments that the office was resuscitated by Abdülhamid II in the nineteenth century), see Casale, *The Ottoman Age of Exploration,* 206; Özcan, *Pan-Islamism,* ix–1.

30. For a concise overview of Ahmad Shah Durrani's remarkable achievements in this regard, see ibid., 47–66.

31. Dupree, *Afghanistan,* 339. As Gommans notes, the gift of the cloak was not merely a pietistic gesture, but carried with it great political significance: the perceived transfer of regional Muslim leadership from Bukhara to Kandahar. Gommans, *The Rise of the Indo-Afghan Empire,* 65–66.

32. Istanbul's Pan-Islamic credentials soared when the Ottomans assumed custodianship of the holy sites of Jerusalem and Hejaz in 1517 following Selim I's defeat of the Mamluks, itself on the heels of a major victory over the Safavids at the Battle of Chaldiran three years earlier. After Ottoman supremacy in Mesopotamia was sealed in the Treaty of Zuhab (1639), establishing Ottoman sovereignty over Shiʿi pilgrimage sites in Najaf and Karbala', the Ottomans enjoyed the preeminent position of administering Islam's holiest sites until the collapse of the empire after World War I.

33. On the rise of Mir Wais Khan Hotak, the Afghan dynasty he established, and early Ottoman-Hotaki relations, see Ghubar, *Afghanistan,* 319; Lockhart, *The Fall of the Safavi Dynasty,* 86–88; Gommans, *The Rise of the Indo-Afghan Empire,* 46; Naim, "The Ottoman Empire and Afghanistan," 10–15.

34. Nonruling elements, such as traders and scholars, also benefited from the pilgrimage's largesse, including contact with wider mercantile circuits and educational networks in and beyond Ottoman Hejaz. A central Ottoman archives record from 1815, for example, describes a young Afghan scholar traveling to the Ottoman domains with the intention to perform hajj, but also visit Egypt and Istanbul, where he was hosted by the Ottoman sheikh ül-Islam. BOA-C.HR 679 / 33104 (1230h Z 29 / 1815 12 02). It should also be noted that Indian and Afghan pilgrims in the Ottoman lands were never limited to the hajj season nor to Hejaz, but included those performing the minor pilgrimage (*ʿumra*) as well as visitations of saintly tombs (*zīyārat*) year round. The latter attracted substantial numbers of Indian Muslims to travel and emigrate to Syria, Mesopotamia, and Egypt, and for Indian Shiʿa in particular, to the hallowed shrine cities of Iraq. For an 1882 British report on the large community of Indian subjects residing in Najaf and Karbala', for example, see NAI-Foreign / GNL / B / Apr.1882 / 14.

35. Rudyard Kipling, *Kim* (London: Penguin, 1994); Arthur Conan Doyle, *A Study in Scarlet* (New York: Penguin, 2001). For a robust corrective to long-standing reliance on the Great Game paradigm in conventional histories of Afghanistan, see B. D. Hopkins, *The Making of Modern Afghanistan* (London: Palgrave Macmillan, 2008).

36. Naim, "The Ottoman Empire and Afghanistan," 19.

37. Milan L. Hauner, "Afghanistan between the Great Powers, 1938–1945," *IJMES* 14, no. 4 (1982): 481.

38. Özcan, *Pan-Islamism,* 112. On Ottoman diplomacy in India before British rule, see Farooqi, *Mughal-Ottoman Relations.*

39. A large number of these reports are declassified letters and telegrams from the Ottoman ambassador in Tehran. For a pair of documents from 1862 discussing Ottoman interest in skirmishes between Iran and Afghanistan over the contested province of Herat, see BOA-İ.HR 195 / 11056 (1279h Ra 19 / 1862 09 14) and BOA-İ.HR 195 / 11088 (1279h R 11 / 1862 10 06). The following year Ottoman correspondence discusses the death of Afghan amir Dost Muhammad Khan. BOA-İ.HR 201 / 11443 (1280h M 13 / 1863 06 30). For additional documents illustrating a burgeoning Ottoman interest in Afghan internal affairs during the second half of the nineteenth century, see (in chronological order) BOA-İ.HR 257 / 15381 (1289h L 13 / 1872 12 14); BOA-İ.HR 259 / 15477 (1290h S 21 / 1873 04 20); BOA-Y.PRK.HR 1 / 16 (1293h Z 15 / 1877 01 01); BOA-İ.HR 273 / 16494–01 (1294h M 14 / 1877 01 29); BOA-HR.SYS 4 / 40 (1878 12 13); BOA-Y.PRK.TKM 10 / 62 (1304h L 24 / 1887 07 16); BOA-HR.HMŞ.İŞO 173 / 20 (1307h Ra 06 / 1889 10 31); BOA-Y.PRK.PT 9 / 99 (1312h S 10 / 1894 08 13). This is not to suggest the Sublime Porte did not have access to or interest in Central Asian affairs before the late nineteenth century. See for example Kemal H. Karpat, "Yakub Bey's Relations with the Ottoman Sultans: A Reinterpretation," *Cahiers du monde russe et soviétique* 32, no. 1 (1991): 17–32. Whereas in earlier decades the Porte relied on local agents and intermediaries such as the aforesaid Yakub Bey in eastern China and Central Asia, by the time of Yakub Bey's death in 1877 and for the remainder of the empire, the Porte demonstrated an enhanced ability to conduct reconnaissance, espionage, and official diplomatic missions under the aegis of its own government officials.

40. NAI-Foreign / Secret / Apr.1878 / 163–164.

41. NAI-Foreign / Secret / Nov.1881 / 86. According to British intelligence reports, among the leading members in this organization were Khuda Bakhsh and Sayyid Amir ʿAli, who would play leading roles in the Khilafat movement after World War I. As Özcan has shown, Ottoman foreign ministry records for the period also provide several examples of private correspondence between Porte officials and Indian anjumans. Özcan, *Pan-Islamism,* 69–70, 96–97.

42. On long-standing Ottoman-Asian links between the Naqshabandi, Qaderi, and Mevlevi sufi orders in particular, see Lâle Can, "Connecting People: A Central Asian Sufi Network in Turn-of-the-Century Istanbul," *Modern Asian Studies* 46, no. 2 (2012): 373–401; Nile Green, "Blessed Men and Tribal Politics: Notes on Political Culture in the Indo-Afghan World," *Journal of the Economic and Social History of the*

Orient 49, no. 3 (2006): 344–360; Butrus Abu-Manneh, "The Naqshbandiyya-Mujaddidiyya in the Ottoman Lands in the Early Nineteenth Century," *Die Welt des Islams* 22, no. 1 (1984): 1–36; Dina Le Gall, *A Culture of Sufism: Naqshbandis in the Ottoman World, 1450–1700* (Albany: State University of New York Press, 2005); Karpat, "Yakub Bey's Relations with the Ottoman Sultans." Similar to the aforesaid fatwa by the Naqibs of Baghdad in support of the Ottoman war against Russia in 1877, in subsequent conflicts the Porte turned to its Sanusi and Qaderi linkages in battling French and Italian forces in North Africa, and as we shall see, once more in Afghanistan during World War I. On the latter theme and Ottoman imperial competition in Africa, see Mostafa Minawi, *The Ottoman Scramble for Africa: Empire and Diplomacy in the Sahara and the Hijaz* (Stanford, CA: Stanford University Press, 2016).

43. BOA-Y.PRK.HR 1/16 (1293h Z 15/1877 01 01).

44. Ibid.

45. BOA-Y.A.HUS 159/14. This letter was probably delivered to Ottoman envoy Ahmed Hulusi Effendi during his travels in India while he journeyed to or returned from Kabul.

46. Among the most salient sites in this regard were the Uzbek, Afghan, and Indian *tekkes,* or dervish lodges, of Üsküdar. Of these, we know most about the Uzbek tekke, which is also the best preserved. Originally established by Bukharan Naqshabandi pilgrims in 1752, probably on the site where they pitched their tents, the Uzbek lodge famously hosted Central Asian pilgrims en route to the hajj, and later, refugees from the Russo-Ottoman War (1877–1878). Hülya Küçük, *The Role of the Bektāshis in Turkey's National Struggle* (Boston, MA: Brill, 2002), 102–104; Dina Le Gall, *A Culture of Sufism,* 31. For Porte records on the Afghan tekke in Üsküdar, see BOA-Y.PRK.AZJ 47/25 (1320h Z 29/1903 02 27); BOA-Y.MTV 254/114 (1321h L 17/1904 01 05); BOA-ZB 608/57 (1323h/1905–1906); BOA-BEO 2787/208952 (1324h M 25/1906 03 21).

47. Emblematic of the Porte's long-standing relations with the Nizam was Ottoman patronage of Osmania University, Hyderabad. See BOA-BEO 1182/88583 (1316h R 05/1898 08 23). On the role of Ottoman educational models at the Muslim College at Aligarh, see Syed Tanvir Wasti, "Sir Syed Ahmad and the Turks," *Middle Eastern Studies* 46, no. 4 (2010): 529–542.

48. For earlier but unsustained diplomatic contacts with Muslims of southern India in the context of maritime rivalry with the Portuguese in the Indian Ocean, see Casale, *The Ottoman Age of Exploration* and Özcan, *Pan-Islamism,* 4–5.

49. During the last two decades of the nineteenth century, Abdülhamid II grew increasingly adept at employing Pan-Islamic rhetoric for diplomatic gains, a strategy adopted by his Young Turk successors in the Libyan and Balkan conflicts through World War I as well. Even before Abdülhamid II's ascendance to the sultanate, however, Ottoman efforts to "strike back" at the European Capitulations played a critical role in domestic reform policies as diverse as the Tanzimat edicts and the Young Ottoman constitutionalist movement. The latter underscored how Porte officials

were not spectators to European economic and political ascendance in the region. On the early modern and internal roots of Ottoman state centralization campaigns well before the nineteenth-century Tanzimat reforms—including the role of interelite competition, managing banditry, and class struggle rather than a reactionary attempt to strengthen the empire amid European encroachment—see Rifa'at 'Ali Abou-El-Haj, *Formation of the Modern State: The Ottoman Empire Sixteenth to Eighteenth Centuries* (New York: State University of New York Press, 1991); Karen Barkey, *Bandits and Bureaucrats: The Ottoman Route to State Centralization* (Ithaca, NY: Cornell University Press, 1994); Martha Mundy and Richard Suamarez Smith, *Governing Property, Making the Modern State: Law, Administration, and Production in Ottoman Syria* (London: I. B. Tauris, 2007); and Elizabeth Thompson, *Justice Interrupted: The Struggle for Constitutional Government in the Middle East* (Cambridge, MA: Harvard University Press, 2013), 13–36.

50. Lâle Can and Michael Christopher Low, "The 'Subjects' of Ottoman International Law," *JOTSA* 3, no. 2 (2016), 223–234, 227. See also Adeeb Khalid, "Pan-Islamism in Practice: The Rhetoric of Muslim Unity and Its Uses," in *Late Ottoman Society: The Intellectual Legacy*, ed. Elisabeth Özdalga (London: RoutledgeCurzon, 2005), 201–224.

51. Abdülhamid II's Pan-Islamic policies grew even more entrenched after the devastating losses of the 1877–1878 Russo-Ottoman War. Following an onslaught of brutal wars with Russia and Austria-Hungary that included ethnic cleansing of religious minorities in the border regions of the Balkans, the Caucasus, and eastern Anatolia, the flight of Christian refugees and arrival of Muslim refugees altered the religious composition of the Ottoman state by substantially increasing the percentage of Muslims in the empire. That Abdülhamid II reoriented the Porte's domestic and foreign policy following these demographic shifts of the late nineteenth century to reflect the empire's more "Muslim" or "Islamic" character has been well documented by historians. On the massive demographic transformations of the late nineteenth- to early twentieth-century Ottoman Empire and their relationship to the Hamidian administration's policies, see Selim Deringil, *The Well-Protected Domains: Ideology and the Legitimation of Power in the Ottoman Empire, 1876–1909* (New York: I. B. Tauris, 1999).

52. NAI-Foreign / Secret / Mar.1878 / 208–209. Abdülhamid II's choice of an Islamic scholar was in continuity with older, premodern norms for Muslim envoys, however, who were often distinguished religious personalities, especially when sent to other Muslim domains. Before the Ottoman conquest of Egypt, for example, the Mamluks were known to send ulema to Istanbul as envoys, where they were received in high esteem. See for example Meir Hatina, *Ulama, Politics, and the Public Sphere Ulama: An Egyptian Perspective* (Salt Lake City: University of Utah Press, 2010), 24; Muhammad As-Saffar, *Disorienting Encounters: Travels of a Moroccan Scholar in France in 1845–1846,* ed. Susan Gilson Miller (Berkeley: University of California Press, 1992), 12.

53. British and Ottoman sources offer conflicting interpretations as to the first Ottoman envoy to Kabul. British Raj intelligence records in the 1870s circulated rumors of secret envoys and messengers shuttling between Istanbul and Kabul during the reign of Shir 'Ali Khan (r. 1863–1879). A cache of Indian archival documents from the mid-1870s, for example, establish the presence of a suspected Ottoman double agent in Kabul by the name of Shaikh Süleyman years before Hulusi's arrival in the autumn of 1877. NAI-Foreign / Secret / Jul.1875 / 193–196; NAI-Foreign / Secret / Mar.1879 / 38–4; NAI-Foreign / Secret / Dec.1878 / 72–97. For a detailed consideration of this episode, see Azmi Özcan, "Şeyh Süleyman Efendi Bir Double Agent mi idi?" *Tarih ve Toplum* 17 (1992): 100–121. As for the financial costs of the 1877–1878 expedition, Indian archival records indicate that the Ottoman consulate in Bombay footed the mission's expenses. NAI-Foreign / Secret / Mar.1878 / 213.

54. Mehmed Süreyya, *Sicill-i Osmani, I. Cild* (Istanbul: Matbaa-i Amire, 1890), 307. Ahmed Hulusi's venerated lineage was also noted by British colonel Herbert Disbrowe of the Bombay Staff Corps. In his report of October 29, 1877, which includes a rare transcript of his conversation with the Ottoman envoy, Hulusi described his father's highly regarded status as "a Cazi and a Syud," which "entitled me to respect and added to my influence." NAI-Foreign / Secret / Mar.1878 / 207.

55. Hulusi Yavuz, "Ahmed Hulusi Efendi," in *Türkiye Diyanet Vakfı İslam Ansiklopedisi* (Istanbul: TDV İslam Araştırmaları Merkezi, 2013); Mehmet Ali Beyhan, "Şirvanizade Mehmed Rüşdü Paşa," in *Türkiye Diyanet Vakfı İslam Ansiklopedisi.*

56. NAI-Foreign / Secret / Mar.1878 / 6–63. Two weeks later the British ambassador at Constantinople, Sir A. H. Layard, described Hulusi as "a high dignity amongst the Ulemah, and one commanding influence with Mahometans." Ibid.

57. Süreyya, *Sicill-i Osmani,* 307; BOA-A.MKT.DV 14 / 26 (1265h C 28 / 1849 05 21). See also Ebül'ula Mardin, *Medeni Hukuk Cephesinden Ahmed Cevdet Paşa* (Istanbul: T. C. Mardin Valiliği, 2011), 202–203; Ahmed Şimşirgil and Ekrem Buğra Ekinci, *Ahmed Cevdet Paşa ve Mecelle* (Istanbul: Adem Eğitim Kültür ve Sosyal Hizmetler Derneği İktisadi İşletmesi, 2008), 53; Yusuf Hikmet Bayur, *Hindistan Tarihi, III. Cilt* (Ankara: Türk Tarih Kurumu, 1950), 438. In addition to his judicial duties, Hulusi continued to engage in supplementary scholarly activities, including private teaching. A Porte record from 1867, for example, refers to his service as a tutor for two women, likely from one of Istanbul's elite families, if not the Ottoman palace itself. BOA-MVL 545 / 36 (1284h Ca 11 / 1867 09 10).

58. BOA-İ.DH 566 / 39435 (1284h Ca 13 / 1867 09 12).

59. For Hulusi's participation on the Mecelle commission, see Şimşirgil and Ekinci, *Ahmed Cevdet Paşa,* 53; Ekrem B. Ekinci, "Hukuk Tarihimizin Abide Eseri: Mecelle," *Tarih ve Medeniyet* 38 (1997): 54–56; Mardin, *Medeni Hukuk Cephesinden,* 202–203; Hulusi Yavuz, "Mecelle'nin Tedvini ve Cevdet Paşa'nın Hizmetleri" (paper, Ahmed Cevdet Paşa Semineri, İ.Ü. Edebiyat Fakültesi Basımevi, Istanbul, May 27–28, 1985), 72–73.

60. This is particularly the case in Muslim communities and states predominantly adhering to the Hanafi school of law, including India, Pakistan, Afghanistan, Turkey, and the Central Asian republics, but also in elite scholastic environments such as al-Azhar University in Cairo, where Islamic legal pluralism is the norm rather than the exception. In spite of several novel features, the Mecelle did not emerge from an Ottoman juristic vacuum. From the mid-nineteenth century until the end of the empire, the Ottoman state promulgated a host of codes intended to homogenize Ottoman law and streamline the empire's administration. Most prominent among these codes were the Ottoman Land Code (1858), a Code of Commercial Procedure (1861), and the Code of Provincial Administration (1864); but in total they comprised scores of *nizamnames* and *kanunnames* across the fields of constitutional and administrative law, public and private law, penal law and procedure, as well as financial and international law. For an overview of late Ottoman codes, see Ahmet Akgündüz, ed., *İslam ve Osmanlı Hukuku Külliyatı* (Istanbul: Osmanlı Araştırmaları Vakfı, 2011). The latter are distinguished from earlier sultanic decrees and Hanafi fatwa compilations, such as the *kanunnames* of Süleiman I, *Multaq al-Abhur,* and the late Mughal empire's *Fatawa-yi 'Alamgiri*, by their streamlined presentation of numbered rules of law, without discussion of scholastic differences or other glosses.

61. Mardin, *Medeni Hukuk Cephesinden,* 53; Şimşirgil and Ekinci, *Ahmed Cevdet Paşa,* 53, 57. Sample records illustrating Hulusi's service on the Mecelle drafting commission, including documents affixed with his personal seal, are found in BOA-İ.DUİT 91/37 (1293h Ş 13/1876 09 03); BOA-İ.DUİT 91/40 (1296h Ca 20/1879 05 12); BOA-İ.DUİT 91/52 (1293h S 06/1876 03 03). For a particularly striking copy of the *Book on Admissions* (*İkrar*), embellished with golden-trimmed borders and Hulusi's seal affixed to the cover sheet, see BOA-İ.DUİT 91/30 (1288h Z 24/1872 03 05). For honors recognizing his service on the Mecelle commission, see BOA-A.MKT.MHM 447/11 (1289h Z 08/1873 02 06); BOA-A.MKT.MHM 447/46 (1289h Z 17/1873 02 15). Identical matches of Hulusi's seals in the Mecelle papers and the 1877–1878 mission to Afghanistan can be seen in BOA-İ.HR 276/16873 (1295h C 05/1878 06 06) and BOA-İ.HR 335/21534 (1295h C 21/1878 06 22).

62. Hulusi's voyage from Istanbul to Kabul and back in 1877–1878 has been the subject of modest scholarly attention. A handful of works have touched on the geopolitical dimensions of the Ottoman expedition to Kabul in the context of the Russo-Ottoman War of 1877–1878 and British machinations to check tsarist expansion in Central Asia; in other words, Great Game imperial rivalries. A fixation on geopolitics has resulted in a lack of consideration for other kinds of impact accruing from the mission, however. See Lee, "A Turkish Mission"; Baysun, "Şirvanizade Ahmed Hulusi Efendi"; Mehmet Saray, *Afganistan ve Türkler* (Istanbul: İstanbul Üniversitesi Edebiyat Fakültesi Basımevi, 1987), 60–63; Özcan, *Pan-Islamism,* 81–86. For dual British perspectives on the mission—split between the British Indian government in

Calcutta and Simla, and the India Office in London—see NAI-Foreign / Secret / Mar.1878 / 208–209; NAI-Foreign / Secret / Mar.1878 / 70–145; NAI-Foreign / Secret / Mar.1878 / 191–201; Trevor Chichele Plowden, *Precis of the Principal Correspondence &c. Showing the Policy and Relations of the British Government toward Afghanistan, April 1872–May 1879* (Calcutta: Foreign Department Press, 1879). For Ottoman perspectives on the journey and mission to Afghanistan, including Hulusi's conversation with Khedive Ismail in Alexandria, a description of the clamorous reception at Bombay, and the anticipated meeting with Shir ʿAli, see BOA-Y.A.HUS 159 / 14; BOA-İ.HR 276 / 16873; BOA-İ.HR 335 / 21534. The latter include correspondence between Hulusi and the Porte, mostly dispatched via Peshawar and Bombay. One historian contends ʿAbd al-Rahman dispatched envoys to Abdülhamid II earlier, "but little came out of it." Landau, *The Politics of Pan-Islam,* 44, citing Arminius Vambery, *Western Culture in Eastern Lands* (London, 1906), 353.

63. BOA-Y.A.HUS 159 / 14; BOA-İ.HR 276 / 16873; NAI-Foreign /Secret / Mar.1878 / 70–145.

64. BOA-Y.A.HUS 159 / 14; BOA-İ.HR 276 / 16873, and NAI-Foreign / Secret / Mar.1878 / 70–145. For an eyewitness account of the delegation's arrival at Bombay by one of the Ottoman delegates, see Ahmed Hamdi, *Hindistan,* 11–12. See also descriptions in Saray, *Türk-Afgan Münasebetleri,* 17; Özcan, *Pan-Islamism,* 86; and Lee, "A Turkish Mission," 349.

65. NAI-Foreign / Secret / Mar.1878 / 6–63.

66. NAI-Foreign / Secret / Mar.1878 / 207.

67. NAI-Foreign / Secret / Mar.1878 / 70–145; NAI-Foreign / Secret / Mar.1878 / 191–201.

68. NAI-Foreign / Secret / Mar.1878 / 207.

69. Indeed Hulusi reported no obstacles in the occasionally treacherous journey from Peshawar to Jalalabad: "The Khyberees acknowledge the Ameer's authority and paid me every respect in the press." NAI-Foreign / Secret / Mar.1878 / 207.

70. NAI-Foreign / Secret / Sept.1878 / 48–49. According to Colonel Disbrowe, Hulusi returned from Kabul bearing three letters for the Ottoman government, in his own words, "one to the Sultan, one to the Sadr-e Azim, and one to the Shaykh ool Islam. The three letters were all sealed and their contents were not made known to me." NAI-Foreign / Secret / Mar.1878 / 207. See also Baysun, "Şirvanizade Ahmed Hulusi Efendi," 156–158.

71. Ottoman accounts of the encounter between Hulusi and Shir ʿAli are found in BOA-İ.HR 276 / 16873 and BOA-İ.HR 335 / 21534. See also Saray, *Afganistan ve Türkler,* 61–63. For a purported transcript of some of the conversations between the envoy and the amir, see NAI-Foreign / Secret / Mar.1878 / 208–209. Because these reports are not corroborated by other sources, however, it is difficult to ascertain their accuracy. They were often generated from the memory of informants present in the Kabul court, quite possibly long after the actual events had transpired.

72. This is a sharp contrast from the virtual house arrest of most Western visitors to the so-called Forbidden Kingdom of Kabul. See for example the memoir of Joseph Harlan, the first American in Afghanistan and a closely watched visitor to the court of Amir Dost Muhammad Khan in 1838. Ben Macintyre, *The Man Who Would Be King: The First American in Afghanistan* (New York: Farrar, Strous, and Giroux, 2004). Transcending the Victorian era and English-speaking world, when Berlin dispatched a delegation of officers to Kabul during World War I, one of the leaders of the German expedition described Afghanistan as *Verschlossene Land*, or the Closed Country. Werner Otto von Hentig, *Meine Diplomatenfahrt ins Verschlossene Land* (Berlin: Ullstein, 1918). For similar impressions by European travelers even during the reign of Aman Allah Khan, see Roland Wild, *Aman Allah: Ex-King of Afghanistan* (London: Hurst & Blackett, 1932).

73. A similar question arises with regard to the watershed Ottoman *Kanun-ı Esasi* of 1876 for that matter, arguably the first modern constitution in the Islamicate world. It was adopted just months before Hulusi's departure from Istanbul. As a liberalizing measure established to constrict the authority of the sultan, however, it is likely that a discussion of Ottoman constitutionalism would not have been as favorable to Shir ʿAli as the codification of Hanafi *fiqh*. The latter, by contrast, was likely to have been interpreted as a potential centralizing measure that could empower rather than weaken the authority of the amir's writ, especially over the Afghan ulema and provinces.

74. On the legal codification projects launched by ʿAbd al-Rahman during his two-decade reign, see Hasan Kawun Kakar, *Government and Society in Afghanistan: The Reign of Amir ʿAbd al-Rahman Khan* (Austin: University of Texas Press, 2011); Ashraf Ghani, "Islam and State-Building in a Tribal Society: Afghanistan 1880–1901," *Modern Asian Studies* 12, no. 2 (1978): 269–284; and Ghani, "Disputes in a Court of Sharia, Kunar Valley, Afghanistan: 1895–1890," *IJMES* 15, no. 3 (1983): 353–367. For evidence of external influence from Qajar Iran in Central Asian, Russian, and Afghan archives, see Amin Tarzi, "The Judicial State: Evolution and Centralization of the Courts in Afghanistan, 1883–1896" (PhD diss., Department of Middle East Studies, New York University, 2003), 277, 328–330.

75. On the inter-imperial roots of Anglo-Afghan wars in the nineteenth century, see Saikal, *Modern Afghanistan*, 25–35; Robert D. Crews, *Afghan Modern: The History of a Global Nation* (Cambridge, MA: Harvard University Press, 2015), 58–68. On the convergence of internal dynastic struggles and Great Game competition in the First Anglo-Afghan War in particular, see William Dalrymple, *Return of a King: The Battle for Afghanistan, 1839–1842* (New York: Knopf, 2013).

76. For a succinct overview of ʿAbd al-Rahman's internal state-building campaign, see Kakar, *Government and Society*, 238–246; Barfield, *Afghanistan*, 139–140, 174–175; Saikal, *Modern Afghanistan*, 33–34; Dupree, *Afghanistan*, 406–407. Louis Dupree famously dubbed the Iron Amir's centralization campaign as "internal imperialism,"

a series of wars to crush tribal recalcitrants and incorporate them into a new centralized state system. Dupree, *Afghanistan,* xix.

77. See for example Kakar, *Government and Society;* Ghani, "Islam and State-Building"; Saikal, *Modern Afghanistan,* 35; Barfield, *Afghanistan,* 151, 159.

78. On earlier Afghan rulers in the nineteenth century, including the founding of the Barakzai-Muhammadzai dynasty and first Muhammadzai amirs, see Christina Noelle, *State and Tribe in Nineteenth-Century Afghanistan: The Reign of Amir Dost Muhammad Khan, 1826–1863* (London: Curzon, 1997); Asta Olesen, *Islam and Politics in Afghanistan* (Richmond, UK: Curzon, 1995); Barfield, *Afghanistan,* 111–129. Robert McChesney's work remains the best historical account of Afghan *waqfs* (Islamic trusts and endowments), with a focus on the country's northwestern region of Turkistan. Robert D. McChesney, *Waqf in Central Asia: 400 Years in the History of a Muslim Shrine, 1480–1889* (Princeton, NJ: Princeton University Press, 1991).

79. Mountstuart Elphinstone, *An Account of the Kingdom of Cabul and Its Dependencies in Persia, Tartary, and India* (London: Richard Bentley, 1839), 138. See also Noelle, *State and Tribe,* 469–475.

80. Notable exceptions are Noelle's work on Dost Muhammad Khan, and Shah Mahmoud Hanifi's broader transborder economic history of nineteenth-century Afghanistan. Hanifi's work in particular has expanded the historical gaze beyond the confines of Afghan courts and colonial regimes into the vibrant social and economic world of crossborder merchants, currency exchangers, and lending networks across the Indo-Afghan frontier. Hanifi, *Connecting Histories.* See also Shah Mahmoud Hanifi, "Impoverishing a Colonial Frontier: Cash, Credit, and Debt in Nineteenth-Century Afghanistan," *Iranian Studies* 37, no. 2 (2004): 199–218.

81. Saikal, *Modern Afghanistan,* 36–37. On the enduring role of the Durand Line in Afghan nationalism and state making, as well as in Pashtun irredentism, see Hanifi, "Quandaries of the Afghan Nation."

82. The tendency to extol ʿAbd al-Rahman's accomplishments, including internationally recognized boundaries and maps, as well as a more regular taxation and conscription base, marginalizes the extreme violence with which he achieved these goals. The brutality of the Iron Amir's repression is a consistent theme in academic works on the autocrat's two-decade reign. Of particular note is the Iron Amir's persecution of Shiʿi Hazaras and other minorities in Afghanistan, though he hardly spared recalcitrants among his own Pashtun ethnic group from torture, forced displacement, and execution. For a summary of atrocities in this regard, see Barfield, *Afghanistan,* 146–158 and Saikal, *Modern Afghanistan,* 36–39.

83. Tarzi, "The Judicial State," 103.

84. David B. Edwards, *Heroes of the Age: Moral Faultlines on the Afghan Frontier* (Berkeley: University of California Press, 1996), 79–84.

85. Tarzi, "The Judicial State," 126–127. See also Barfield, *Afghanistan,* 43–53.

86. Among the new features of Ottoman maps was better coverage for the remote and mountainous areas along Afghanistan's borders with Turkistan, China, and India's NWFP, including Badakhshan, Swat, Bajaur Agency, Chitral, and the Wakhan corridor. See for example BOA-Y.PRK.TKM 26 / 7 (1310h M 10 / 1892 08 03).

87. On the shariʿa courts of ʿAbd al-Rahman, the groundbreaking studies of Ashraf Ghani (1978; 1983) and Amin Tarzi (2003) remain the best accounts, including their use of scarce unpublished sources from the period. Ghani's work bears the distinction of being the first and only to access late nineteenth-century provincial court records in Afghanistan, offering a rare and highly-textured glimpse into ʿAbd al-Rahman's centralization campaign in local praxis. Ghani, "Islam and State-Building," 269–284, and Ghani, "Disputes in a Court of Sharia," 353–367. Amin Tarzi's dissertation deftly utilizes Russian, Uzbek, and Afghan archival records from the 1880s and 1890s, including correspondence between local administrators in Khost and Kuhdaman provinces, to provide a detailed blueprint of ʿAbd al-Rahman's internal conquest of Afghanistan, beginning with his exile in Central Asia. Tarzi, "The Judicial State." Both scholars argue that a key (and overlooked) pillar of ʿAbd al-Rahman's state-building campaign were a series of legal-administrative codes and state courts through which the amir introduced greater center-province integration and legibility of government institutions within a framework of upholding the shariʿa.

88. ADL-0129 (Ahmad Jan Khan Alakozai, *Asas al-Quzat* [Kabul: Matbaʿ-ʾi Dar al-Saltanih, 1303h / 1885–1886]). For a subsequent edition, see ADL-0603 (Alakozai, *Asas al-Quzat* [Kabul: Matbaʿ-ʾi Dar al-Saltanih, 1311h / 1893–1894]).

89. For example, see Alakozai, *Asas al-Quzat,* 20, where following the statement of a rule, the article merely cites the famed Hanafi compendium from the late Mughal Empire, "*Kitab-i ʿAlamgiri*" (also known as the *Fatawa-yi ʿAlamgiri,* or *Fatawa Hindiyya* outside India) as the source of the rule. As for the social and political ramifications of bureaucratic functionaries replacing traditionally trained Hanafi jurists and jurisconsults, this would be another parallel with the Mecelle and other projects of codification in the late Ottoman Empire, as well as a number of colonial settings. On the social and professional impact of codification, civil law schools, and the duality of "shariʿa" tribunals versus "secular" (Nizamiye) courts in the late Ottoman Empire, see Avi Rubin, *Ottoman Nizamiye Courts: Law and Modernity* (New York: Palgrave Macmillan, 2011). For a succinct overview of European projects to codify Islamic law as a strategy of imperial rule, see Wael B. Hallaq, *An Introduction to Islamic Law* (New York: Cambridge University Press, 2009), 85–93, 110–114. On the codification of Islamic law in French Algeria and British India, see Alan Christelow, *Muslim Law Courts and the French Colonial State in Algeria* (Princeton, NJ: Princeton University Press, 1985); Bernard S. Cohn, "Law and the Colonial State in India," in *History and Power in the Study of Law: New Directions in Legal Anthropology,* ed. June Starr and Jane F. Collier (Ithaca, NY: Cornell University Press, 1989), 131–152.

90. ADL-0199 (Mir Muhammad ʿAzim Khan, *Sarrishtih-ʾi Islamiyyih-ʾi Rum* [Kabul: Dar al-Saltanih, 1304h / 1886–1887]).

91. For additional details on this text, including references to the Ottomans as a model of reform, see Tarzi, "The Judicial State," 150, 328.

92. ADL-0199, 2.

93. ADL-0203 (Gul Muhammad ʿAbd al-Subhan Muhammadzai, *Jang-i Rum wa Rus* [Kabul: Dar al-Saltanih, 1308h / 1890–1891]).

94. On the complex relations between the Afghan scholarly establishment and amirs in Kabul, including the formation of a state-sponsored clergy and associated institutions remotely akin to the Ottoman *ilmiye*, see Olivier Roy, *Islam and Resistance in Afghanistan* (New York: Cambridge University Press, 1986), 44–58; Senzil Nawid, "The State, the Clergy, and British Imperial Policy in Afghanistan during the Nineteenth and Early Twentieth Centuries," *IJMES* 29, no. 4 (1997): 581–605; Edwards, *Heroes of the Age*, 94–97, 102–103, 116–117. On transborder ties between Kabul's Madrasih-ʾi Shahi, other Afghan institutions of learning, and the Dar al-ʿUlum madrasa at Deoband where several Afghans studied, see Sana Haroon, "Religious Revival across the Durand Line, in *Under the Drones: Modern Lives in the Afghanistan-Pakistan Borderlands*, ed. Shahzad Bashir and Robert D. Crews (Cambridge, MA: Harvard University Press, 2012), 45–59.

95. It is also possible ʿAbd al-Rahman's vision for the Afghan ulema and shariʿa courts drew on earlier Ottoman models of a justice system—such as the transformative policies of Sultan Süleiman I "the Lawgiver" (r. 1520–1566) and sheikh ül-Islam Ebussuud Effendi (1490–1574)—but more evidence is needed to confirm this. On Ebussuud and the making of an early modern Ottoman scholarly establishment (*ilmiye*), see Colin Imber, *Ebu's-Su'ud: The Islamic Legal Tradition* (Stanford, CA: Stanford University Press, 1997).

96. On new Ottoman scouting reports, maps, and other reconnaissance from the region in this period, see n. 86. It is also noteworthy that the Porte's enhanced knowledge of Afghan frontiers coincided with their participation in arbitrations delineating borders with neighboring Persia in the late nineteenth and early twentieth centuries. See Firoozeh Kashani-Sabet, *Frontier Fictions: Shaping the Iranian Nation, 1804–1946* (Princeton, NJ: Princeton University Press, 1999), 24–30, 114; Benjamin D. Hopkins, "The Bounds of Identity: The Goldsmid Mission and the Delineation of the Perso-Afghan Border in the Nineteenth Century," *Journal of Global History* 2, no. 2 (2007): 233–254; and more generally, Sabri Ateş, *Ottoman-Iranian Borderlands: Making a Boundary, 1843–1914* (New York: Cambridge University Press, 2013).

97. NAI-Foreign / Frontier / B / Aug.1893 / 207–209.

98. NAI-Foreign / Secret / E / Feb.1883 / 211.

99. In another parallel between Abdülhamid II and ʿAbd al-Rahman, both sovereigns bestowed on the Victorian notable and British convert to Islam William

Henry Abdullah Quilliam (1856–1932) the honorific title of "Shaykh al-Islam of the British Isles," signifying their mutual desire to aid Muslim communities within Britain itself. On Quilliam, see Ron Geaves, *Islam in Victorian Britain: The Life and Times of Abdullah Quilliam* (Leicestershire, UK: Kube, 2010).

100. See for example Seema Alavi, *Muslim Cosmopolitanism in the Age of Empire* (Cambridge, MA: Harvard University Press, 2015).

101. For example, see NAI-Foreign / Frontier / A / Feb.1888 / 30–31, including a translation of ʿAbd al-Rahman's condemnation of Wahhabi doctrines.

102. For a succinct overview of the history and ideological underpinnings of the Wahhabi movement of central Arabia from the late eighteenth to early twentieth centuries, see Hamid Algar, *Wahhabism: A Critical Essay* (Oneonta, NY: Islamic Publications International, 2002).

103. ADL-0004 (Mulla Abu Bakr, Mir Muhammad Azim Khan, and ʿAbd al-Razaq Dihlawi, *Taqwim-al Din* [Kabul: Dar al-Saltanih, 1306h / 1888]). See also Tarzi, "The Judicial State," 328–329.

104. A translation of the proclamation can be found in NAI-Foreign / Frontier / A / Feb.1888 / 30–31. This was not the first instance of Afghan ulema denouncing Wahhabi ideas. The ADL catalogue contains an earlier anti-Wahhabi polemic from Afghanistan by a certain Mullah ʿAbd al-Rahman. Entitled *Risalih-ʾi Hujjih Quwiyih dar Ibtal-i ʿAqaʾid-i Wahhabiyyih,* the treatise is currently unavailable but is reported to have been published between 1871 and 1872.

105. Cevdet Pasha's original Ottoman Turkish text has been republished as *Faideli Bilgiler* (Istanbul: Hakikat Kitabevi, 2010). See chapter 6, "Vehabilik," 57–86.

106. For debates on the caliphate across different epochs and regions of Muslim history, see Mona Hassan, *Longing for the Lost Caliphate: A Transregional History* (Princeton, NJ: Princeton University Press, 2016).

107. NAI-Foreign / Secret / F / Oct.1896 / 166–186.

108. Ibid.

109. Although the Ottoman sultans enjoyed a privileged position in the eyes of many Afghan amirs, they certainly did not constitute the only or even principal Muslim sovereigns whom Afghan rulers historically engaged with in the region. From the fifteenth- and sixteenth-century Pashtun dynasties of the Lodi and Suri kingdoms in northern India to the foundation of a Pan-Afghan state in the eighteenth century, Afghan rulers corresponded with, warred against, and occasionally allied with rival Muslim principalities in India, Central Asia, and Iran. As far as the Qajar shahs of Iran are concerned—arguably the penultimate Muslim power in the late nineteenth century after the Ottomans—much more remains to be learned about the extent and nature of ties between the Tehran and Kabul courts at this time. The lack of scholarly work on Iranian influence in Afghan legal and administrative history is a particularly glaring lacuna in light of the significant state-building campaign of Amir Kabir (1807–1852), chief minister to Qajar king Nasir al-Din Shah (r. 1848–1896). In the latter's grand

centralization project, especially the attempted bureaucratization of the Iranian ulema, there are parallels both to ʿAbd al-Rahman's campaign and to Ottoman reforms from the transformative era of sheikh ül-Islam Ebussuud Effendi (1490–1574) to the Tanzimat. Nonetheless, in spite of Afghans and Iranians sharing a common administrative language and even political history in former Safavid and Afsharid Iranian rule over Khorasan, Herat, and Kandahar, one does not see the same vigorous interest, or state-supported patronage of literature, by ʿAbd al-Rahman in the Qajar rulers of Iran as one does in the Muhammadzai amirs vis-à-vis the Ottoman Empire.

110. Lâle Can, "The Protection Question: Central Asians and Extraterritoriality in the Late Ottoman Empire," *IJMES* 48, no. 4 (2016): 679–699; Faiz Ahmed, "Contested Subjects: Ottoman and British Jurisdictional Quarrels *in re* Indians and Afghans," *JOTSA* 3, no. 2 (2016): 325–346; Ahmed, "Istanbul and Kabul in Courtly Contact: The Question of Exchange between the Ottoman Empire and Afghanistan in the Late Nineteenth Century," *Journal of Ottoman Studies* 45 (2015): 265–296. Ottoman and British Indian intelligence records document scores of instances of Ottoman and Afghan subjects traveling to and from each other's territories in this period—to say nothing of the cases that went unmonitored. On the increase in Muslim travelers between the Ottoman and various Asian domains during the Hamidian period, see John Slight, *The British Empire and the Hajj, 1865–1956* (Cambridge, MA: Harvard University Press, 2015); Eileen Kane, *Russian Hajj: Empire and the Pilgrimage to Mecca* (Ithaca, NY: Cornell University Press, 2015); Nile Green and James L. Gelvin, eds., *Global Muslims in the Age of Steam and Print* (Berkeley: University of California Press, 2013).

111. Lee, "A Turkish Mission," 352.

112. Özcan, *Pan-Islamism,* 84; Lee, "A Turkish Mission," 335–356.

113. On the participation of Ottoman ulema in the compilation of the Mecelle, see Deringil, *The Well-Protected Domains,* 50–52; Hulusi Yavuz, "Ahmed Cevdet Paşa and the Ulema of His Time," *İslam Tetkikleri Enstitüsü Dergisi* 7, no. 3–4 (1979): 177–198; Hulusi Yavuz, "Events Leading to the Compilation of the First Ottoman Civil Code," *İslam Tetkikleri Enstitüsü Dergisi* 8, no. 1–4 (1984): 89–122. On the hybrid nature of late Ottoman education at this time, blurring a conventionally dichotomized understanding of late Ottoman society, see Benjamin C. Fortna, "Islamic Morality in Late Ottoman 'Secular' Schools," *IJMES* 32, no. 3 (2000): 369–393 and Amit Bein, "Politics, Military Conscription, and Religious Education in the Late Ottoman Empire," *IJMES* 38, no. 2 (2006): 283–301.

114. NAI-Foreign / Secret / May.1879 / 171–173.

115. Süreyya, *Sicill-i Osmani,* 307.

116. BOA-İ.DH 1118 / 87407 (1306h Ca 18 / 1889 01 20).

117. On Cevdet Pasha's training and professional history as a late Ottoman "transitional" who straddled both the late Ottoman *ilmiye* and bureaucracy, see Richard L.

Chambers, "The Education of a Nineteenth-Century Ottoman Alim, Ahmed Cevdet Pasha," *IJMES* 4, no. 4 (1973): 440–464, especially 440–446.

2. A DAMASCENE ROAD MEETS A PASSAGE TO INDIA

1. NAI-Foreign / Frontier / B / Oct.1908 / 192. According to a British informant present at the speech, Habib Allah impressed on his courtiers that he accepted their allegiance and would continue to "work in the interests of his people and country" as his late father had done.

2. Among the amir's mandates "of great responsibility," to quote a British informant in the Kabul court, were such familiar state centralization measures in the nineteenth-century Ottoman Empire as the replacement of older officials from established courtly families with a new bureaucratic class, a reorganization of government troops, and the reduction of pensions and allowances to provincial notables. NAI-Foreign / Frontier / B / Oct.1908 / 192.

3. NAI-Foreign / Secret / F / Jun.1908 / 146–199.

4. Ibid. See also NAI-Foreign / Sec / F / Mar.1909 / 44–49.

5. For decades the standard reference on the topic has been Mehmet Saray, *Afganistan ve Türkler* (Istanbul: İstanbul Üniversitesi Edebiyat Fakültesi Basımevi, 1987). There are, however, signs of advancement in the field. See for example Michael B. O'Sullivan, "'The Little Brother of the Ottoman State': Ottoman Technocrats in Kabul and Afghanistan's Development in the Ottoman Imagination, 1908–23," *Modern Asian Studies* 50, no. 6 (2016): 1846–1887; Faiz Ahmed, "Istanbul and Kabul in Courtly Contact: The Question of Exchange between the Ottoman Empire and Afghanistan in the Late Nineteenth Century," *Journal of Ottoman Studies* 45 (2015): 265–296; Faridullah Bezhan, "Pan-Islamism in Afghanistan in the Early Twentieth Century: From Political Discourse to Government Policy, 1906–22," *Islam and Christian-Muslim Relations* 25, no. 2 (2014): 193–210; Hakeem Naim, "The Ottoman Empire and Afghanistan: A Record of Failure and Great Power Intrigue" (BA Robert and Colleen Haas Scholars Thesis, Department of Middle Eastern Studies, UC Berkeley, 2010).

6. It is difficult to reliably determine the exact or even approximate number of Ottoman subjects in Afghanistan during the reign of Habib Allah. Partly to blame are the lack of rigorous recordkeeping of foreign visitors, emigrants, or other travelers by the Afghan government at this time—as far as we can tell from national archives, that is—or the lingering possibility such records have been lost or destroyed. But other historical factors also play a role behind this lacuna, including the transient—and especially during World War I, clandestine—nature of many Ottoman arrivals during this period. Most of all, the lack of an official Ottoman legation or embassy at this time—per treaty stipulations with Britain, Afghanistan was barred from hosting

foreign diplomatic sanctuaries on its soil—meant the Turks in Kabul did not have a single residence, compound, or repository to store official papers and correspondence with Istanbul, nor administer the functions of a conventional embassy or consulate for its citizens. Put together, this has resulted in the peculiar condition of British records on the Ottoman community in Kabul—including reports by agents and intelligence officers in Delhi, Calcutta, Peshawar, and Kabul itself—far exceeding those of the Ottoman government at this time. As for rough estimates on the number of Turkish expats in the country, British sources in the late 1900s and early 1910s vary widely—anywhere from a few dozen Ottoman subjects to nearly a hundred. In a September 1910 memorandum the official British agent at Kabul estimated the total number of Ottoman officers at the time in the country to be fifteen. In November 1912, however, the British Secretary of State for India cited an informant's report that the number of Turkish military instructors alone in Afghanistan "actually amounts to 80 officers," but then himself opined, "this is clearly an exaggeration." NAI-Foreign/Secret/F/May.1913/1–23. Combining available evidence from Afghan, British Indian, and Ottoman records, this chapter focuses more on the qualitative conclusions we can draw on this understudied foreign community in Afghanistan—including their most prominent members, contributions, and legacies—than the question of their precise numbers.

7. BOA-Y.PRK.BŞK 11/25 (1303h Z 29/1886 09 27). Indicating the Porte's high regard for the Tarzi family, Ottoman records detail these stipends as lasting well into the 1890s. The first reports in the central Ottoman archives on the official sponsorship of the Tarzi family are found in BOA-A.MKT.UM 565/25 (1278h Za 15/1862 05 14); BOA-BEO 459/34377 (1312h S 17/1894 08 19); BEO 488/36529 (1312h R 03/1894 10 02). Porte records describe Ghulam Muhammad Khan Tarzi with a range of notable titles: an Afghan prince ("*Afghanistan Sardarı*"), BOA-BEO 488/36529; an Afghan commander and relative of the amir of Afghanistan ("*Afgan ümera-yı askeriyesinden ve emirin akrabasından*"), BOA-BEO 2739/205415 (1323h Za 18/1906 01 13); a resident of Damascus originally of Kandahar ("*Şam'da mukim Kandeharlı*"), BOA-BEO 2420/181461 (1322h B 20/1904 09 30); and the Afghan-Ottoman notable in exile ("*Afghanistan serdarı olup Osmanlıya iltica edip*"), BOA-BEO 459/34391. Beyond descriptive titles, at least one Ottoman archive document indicates the Tarzi family patriarch received an official decoration from the government in Istanbul. BOA-Y.PRK.ASK 149/35 (1316h Za 23/1899 04 04).

8. In addition to the aforesaid documents, see also BOA-İ.DH 1154/90257 (1307h S 05/1889 09 30) and BOA-İ.DH 968/76510 (1303h S 06/1885 11 13). BOA-DH.MKT 1386/3 (1304h Ra 23/1886 12 19) and BOA-DH.MKT 1386/47 (1304h Ra 24/1886 12 20) mention the allotment of a portion of land in Damascus for the family patriarch, Ghulam Muhammad Khan, and his family. On their provision of travel funds to and from Damascus, see BOA-İ.DH 1011/79807 (1304h Ra 03/1886 11 29) and BOA-İ.DH 1278/100575 (1309h Za 12/1892 06 07). Ottoman records

indicate the family comprised thirty-five persons, servants and attendants likely included. BOA-MV 13 / 43 (1304h M 28 / 1886 10 26).

9. On Mahmud Tarzi's life and thought, see Nushin Arbabzadah, "Modernizing, Nationalizing, Internationalizing: How Mahmud Tarzi's Hybrid Identity Transformed Afghan Literature," in *Afghanistan in Ink: Literature between Diaspora and Nation,* ed. Nile Green and Nushin Arbabzadah (London: Hurst, 2013), 31–66; May Schinasi, *Afghanistan at the Beginning of the Twentieth Century* (Naples: Instituto Universitario Orientale, 1979); Louis Dupree, "Mahmud Tarzi: Forgotten Nationalist," *American Universities Field Series Report: South Asia Series* 8, no. 1 (1964): 21–42. For an autobiographical essay on Mahmud Tarzi's early years, see Mahmud Tarzi (Wahid Tarzi, trans. and ed.), "Reminiscences: A Short History of an Era (1869–1881)," *Afghanistan Forum: Occasional Paper* 36 (1998).

10. BOA-DH.MKT 1666 / 17 (1307h S 17 / 1889 10 12).

11. BOA-DH.MKT 2508 / 121 (1319h Ra 23 / 1901 07 10); BOA-DH.MKT 2501 / 27 (1319h Ra 03 / 1901 06 20); BOA-DH.MKT 2505 / 140 (1319h Ra 16 / 1901 07 03).

12. Dupree, "Mahmud Tarzi," 4.

13. Abidin Ünal et al., *Geçmişten Günümüze Türk-Afgan İlişkileri* (Ankara: Genelkurmay Askeri Tarih ve Stratejik Etüt Başkanlığı Yayınları Basimevi, 2009), 57. As Nikki Keddie has argued, Jamal al-Din's claims to Afghan Sunni ancestry are dubious, as he most likely hailed from an Iranian Shiʿi family of Asadabad. Nikki R. Keddie, *An Islamic Response to Imperialism: Political and Religious Writings of Sayyid Jamal ad-Din "al-Afghani"* (Berkeley: University of California Press, 1983).

14. On the ideology and politics of the Young Ottomans, see Şerif Mardin, *The Genesis of Young Ottoman Thought: A Study in the Modernization of Turkish Political Ideas* (Syracuse, NY: Syracuse University Press, 2000).

15. Dupree, "Mahmud Tarzi," 5. On the cosmopolitan milieu of turn-of-the-century Damascus, Aleppo, and Istanbul where the young Tarzi came of age, see Murat Gül, *The Emergence of Modern Istanbul: Transformation and Modernisation of a City* (London: Tauris, 2009), 54–58, 73, 84–88; and Keith David Watenpaugh, *Being Modern in the Middle East: Revolution, Nationalism, Colonialism, and the Arab Middle Class* (Princeton, NJ: Princeton University Press, 2006).

16. BOA-İ.TAL 11 / 1310C-052 (1310h C 15 / 1893 01 04); BOA-BEO 123 / 9216 (1310h Ca 28 / 1892 12 18).

17. Ashraf Ghani, "Literature as Politics: The Case of Mahmud Tarzi," *Afghanistan* 29, no. 3 (1976): 63–72.

18. Composed in Persian and bearing Habib Allah's seal, this elegant manuscript is embellished with golden trimmings and calligraphy. BOA-Y.A.HUS 467 / 1 (1321h Z 01 / 1904 02 17). On Tarzi's correspondences with the Sublime Porte concerning his potential return to Afghanistan, see also BOA-Y.PRK.AZJ 49 / 33 (1321h Z 29 / 1904 03 16); BOA-İ.HUS 121 / 1322B-077 (1322h B 19 / 1904 09 29).

19. BOA-İ.HUS 121 / 1322B-116 (1322h B 26 / 1904 10 06).

20. BOA-Y.MTV 254/64 (1321h L 11/1903 12 30); BOA-BEO 2420/181461 (1322h B 20/1904 09 30); BOA-DH.MKT 896/7 (1322h B 25/1904 10 05). The Porte responded favorably to Tarzi's plans, not only granting permission for the departure but also offering financial support for the journey and a letter of commendation. BOA-BEO 2232/167329 (1321h N 18/1903 12 07); BOA-BEO 2351/176275 (1322h R 01/1904 06 15); BOA-Y.PRK.ASK 192/19 (1320h/1902–1903). On Tarzi's arrival in Peshawar, see BOA-BEO 2420/181461 and BOA-DH.MKT 896/7. Similarly, the British Indian Foreign Department reported Tarzi "had arrived at Peshawar from Turkey, and left for Kabul on the 1st May." Notably, the British report alleged Tarzi was bearing a secret letter for the amir from the Ottoman sultan. NAI-Foreign/Secret/F/Nov.1902/23–28.

21. On Habib Allah's special interest in educational reforms from the early stages of his reign, see Yahia Baiza, *Education in Afghanistan: Developments, Influences and Legacies since 1901* (New York: Routledge, 2013), 47–53.

22. Government records from Istanbul indicate permission was duly granted by the Porte for Tarzi to return to Damascus with the aim of retrieving his family and resettling in Afghanistan. BOA-Y.MTV 254/64.

23. This is not entirely surprising in light of an outbreak of cholera in Afghanistan in 1902 that continued through 1903, precisely during Mahmud Tarzi's return to Syria. Ünal et al., *Geçmişten Günümüze,* 32.

24. A 1904 dossier from the Ottoman central archives addresses the activities of Mahmud Tarzi in Istanbul and his desire to return to Afghanistan with a corps of Ottoman experts. BOA-BEO 2338/175290 (1322h Ra 07/1904 05 23); BOA-BEO 2351/176275.

25. BOA-Y.A.HUS 470/14 (1322h M 18/1904 04 04). Mahmud Tarzi also received a generous travel stipend of 1,000 kuruş in preparation for his upcoming return to Afghanistan. This was in addition to what he was already receiving from the Porte. BOA-BEO 2739/205415; BOA-BEO 2748/206077 (1323h Za 28/1906 01 23); BOA-DH.MKT 1041/67 (1323h Za 19/1906 01 14).

26. BOA-BEO 2403/180192 (1322h C 24/1904 09 05).

27. On the Young Afghans, see Senzil K. Nawid, *Religious Response to Social Change in Afghanistan, 1919–29: King Aman-Allah and the Afghan Ulama* (Costa Mesa, CA: Mazda, 1999), 44–46, 146–147; Amin Saikal, *Modern Afghanistan: A History of Struggle and Survival* (New York: I. B. Tauris, 2006), 41–44, 48; Amin Tarzi, "Islam and Constitutionalism in Afghanistan," *JPS* 5, no. 2 (2012), 207–209; Wali Ahmadi, *Modern Persian Literature in Afghanistan: Anomalous Visions of History and Form* (London: Routlege, 2008), 20; Arbabzadah, "Modernizing, Nationalizing, Internationalizing," 31–66. On political developments in Habib Allah's reign (1901–1919) more broadly, see Schinasi, *Afghanistan;* Ludwig W. Adamec, *Afghanistan, 1900–1923* (Berkeley: University of California Press, 1967). For a relatively more advanced historiography in Persian, see ʿAbd al-Hay Habibi, *Junbish-i Mashrutiyat dar Afghanistan* (Kabul: Ihsani, 1346j/1967–1968), 34–47; Sayyid Saʿd al-Din Hashimi, *Nukhustin Kitab darbarih-ʾi Junbish-i*

Mashrutih-khwahi dar Afghanistan (Kabul: Shura-yi Farhangi-yi Afghanistan, 2008), 66–71; Mas'ud Puhanyar, *Zuhur-i Mashrutiyat wa Qurbaniyan-i Istibdad dar Afghanistan* (Peshawar: Saba Kitabkhanih, 1375j/1996–1997); Mir Ghulam Muhammad Ghubar, *Afghanistan dar Masir-i Tarikh* (Qum: Payam-i Muhajir, 1980), 716–721.

28. As Wali Ahmadi has observed, so prominent has Mahmud Tarzi factored in modern Afghan intellectual history that his legacy has tended to overshadow the contributions of other Young Afghan constitutionalists and literati, who have not received nearly as much scholarly attention. An example of the latter was the remarkable Afghan scholar, political activist, and ultimately constitutionalist martyr, Muhammad Sarwar Wasif (d. 1909). Ahmadi, *Modern Persian Literature,* 29–32.

29. Scholars of early twentieth-century Afghanistan have debated the number, cohesiveness, and exact names of constitutional movement(s) brewing in Kabul at this time, offering no less than six different names of organizations: the Jami'iyat-i Sirr-i Milli (National Secret), Jan-nisaran-i Islam (Islamic Loyalists), Mashrutih-khawahan (Constitutionalists), Ikhwan-i Afghan (Afghan Brothers), Anjuman-i Mu'alliman-i Hindi (Indian Teachers' Association), and most commonly, the Jawanan-i Afghan (Young Afghans). Beyond the question of numbers and designations, historians have also debated the ambiguous role of Indian physician and administrator Dr. Abdul Ghani in Young Afghan politics in particular. See for example Tarzi, "Islam and Constitutionalism," 208; Mir Muhammad Siddiq Farhang, *Afghanistan dar Panj Qarn-i Akhir* (Qum: Mu'assasih-'i Matbu'ati-yi Isma'iliyan, 1992), 2:464.

30. The predominant interpretation of scholars of the period, including Amin Tarzi, Amin Saikal, and Senzil Nawid, is that a radical secret organization by the name of Sirr-i Milli (National Secret) was first founded in Kabul with the goal of establishing constitutional rule in the country. After the plot on Habib Allah's life and the mass arrests of Afghans and Indians in Kabul associated with the Sirr-i Milli, the latter was followed by a more moderate but larger group led by Mahmud Tarzi known as the Young Afghans. On leading members of both movements, numbering between some 45 and 56 individuals according to Afghan chroniclers, see Habibi, *Junbish,* 258–299; Puhanyar, *Zuhur,* 45–47; Ghubar, *Afghanistan,* 719. As mentioned, there is considerable debate among historians concerning the cohesiveness of the Young Afghans, and the purportedly opposing roles of Dr. Abdul Ghani and Mahmud Tarzi in particular. Adamec's account represents the predominant view among historians of the era, considering Ghani to have been "a champion of political and social reform [who] attracted a circle of 'Young Afghans' who formed the clandestine organization, *Sirr-i Milli.*" Ludwig W. Adamec, *Historical Dictionary of Afghanistan* (Metuchen, NJ: Scarecrow, 1991), 7. See also Puhanyar, *Zuhur,* 98–100, 106–110; Hashimi, *Nukhustin Kitab,* 274–276; 'Aziz al-Din Wakili Popalzai, *Dar al-Qaza' dar Afghanistan: Az Awayil-i 'ahd-i Islam ta 'Ahd-i Jumhuriyat* (Kabul: Markaz-i Tahqiqat-i 'Ulum-i Islami, 1369j/1990–1991), 518. For an opposing account, see Tarzi, "Islam and Constitutionalism," 208. Notably, Abdul Ghani had two brothers—Najaf 'Ali, a schoolmaster at Rawalpindi, and Muhammad Chiragh

al-Din of Lahore—who joined their sibling as instructors at the Habibiye in Kabul. For brief biographies of Najaf ʿAli and Muhammad Chiragh al-Din and their political activities at the Habibiye where they taught, see Puhanyar, *Zuhur,* 98–100, 106–110; Hashimi, *Nukhustin Kitab,* 274–276; Popalzai, *Dar al-Qazaʾ*, 518. In spite of their Indian background, all three brothers played prominent roles in the Young Afghan constitutionalist movement. See also *WWA* (1920), 47; Ghubar, *Afghanistan,* 717–719.

31. On the history and readership of *Siraj al-Akhbar* under Tarzi's editorial leadership, see Schinasi, *Afghanistan*; Vartan Gregorian, "Mahmud Tarzi and the Saraj-al-Akhbar: Ideology of Nationalism and Modernism in Afghanistan, 1880–1946," *Middle East Journal* 21, no. 3 (1967): 345–368. For an early history of Afghan journalism by an early twentieth-century observer, see L. Bogdonov, "Notes on the Afghan Periodical Press," *Islamic Culture* (Hyderabad Deccan, India) 3, no. 1 (1929): 126–152.

32. *WWA* (1914), 56.

33. NAI-Foreign / Secret / F / Jan.1909 / 74–76.

34. Ibid.

35. Halil Bal, "Afganistan-Türkiye İlişkilerinin Başlıca Yönleri," in *Afganistan Üzerine Araştırmalar,* ed. Ali Ahmetbeyoğlu (Istanbul: Tarih ve Tabiat Vakfı Yayınları, 2001), 246.

36. On the Naqibs of Baghdad, see Gökhan Çetinsaya, *The Ottoman Administration of Iraq, 1890–1908* (New York: Routledge, 2006), 19–20. On the influence of the Qaderi order in Afghanistan, see Olivier Roy, *Islam and Resistance in Afghanistan* (New York: Cambridge University Press, 1986), 42. On the historical influence of Qaderi shaykhs in India, see Simon Digby, "The Sufi Shaikh as a Source of Authority in Medieval India," in *India's Islamic Traditions, 711–1750,* ed. Richard M. Eaton (New Delhi: Oxford University Press, 2003), 234–262.

37. NAI-Foreign / Secret / F / Sept.1909 / 1–3. This source also mentions Sayyid Hassan received a monthly honorable stipend of Rs. 1,000 in addition to a plot of land. See also NAI-Foreign / Secret / F / Oct.1907 / 152–159.

38. More commonly known as Imam Ghaws-i Aʿzam, or simply "Pir Sahib" in Afghanistan, Pakistan, and India, Shaykh ʿAbd al-Qadir Gilani is one of the foremost patron saints revered by Afghans, and among the preeminent sufi shaykhs of the Islamicate world.

39. NAI-Foreign / Frontier / B / Nov.1910 / 92–93.

40. Ibid.

41. Ibid; NAI-Foreign / Secret / F / Oct.1907 / 152–159.

42. O'Sullivan, "'The Little Brother'," 35; Schinasi, *Afghanistan,* 129–130.

43. There is some historiographical debate over Sami's role in founding the college, or simply serving as principal later in 1909. See for example Bal, "Afganistan-Türkiye," 246; O'Sullivan, "'The Little Brother'," 35; Schinasi, *Afghanistan,* 129–130. For Sami's publications in Afghanistan, see Appendix B.

44. On Ottoman Harbiyes more generally, see Benjamin C. Fortna, *Imperial Classroom: Islam, the State, and Education in the Late Ottoman Empire* (New York: Oxford University Press, 2002); Selçuk Akşin Somel, *The Modernization of Public Education in the Ottoman Empire* (Leiden: Brill, 2001). On the Mekteb-i ʿAnbar in Damascus, the most prestigious Ottoman academy in Syria during the Hamidian era, see Michael Provence, "Ottoman Modernity, Colonialism, and Insurgency in the Interwar Arab East," *IJMES* 43, no. 2 (2011): 205–225; Provence, *The Great Syrian Revolt and the Rise of Arab Nationalism* (Austin: University of Texas Press, 2005), 39–40. On the Imperial Tribal School (Mekteb-i Aşiret-i Hümayun) in Istanbul, founded in 1892, see T. C. Başbakanlık Osmanlı Arşivleri Genel Müdürlüğü, *Osmanlı Eğitiminde Modernleşme* (Istanbul: Osmanlı Arşivi Daire Başkanlığı, 2014), 209–211.

45. According to Yahia Baiza, Kabul's Harbiye was divided into two sections, upper and lower class. The upper class had two sections, Maktab-i Malikzagan-i Junubi and Sitara-yi Dawlat, indicating access was primarily limited to southern Pashtun tribal chieftains and the royal elite. Prince Aman Allah himself studied in the upper section. The lower sections of the military academy were named the Maktab-i ʿAskari Ardiliyan-i Huzur (The School of Soldier Servants) and Maktab-i ʿAskari Jadid al-Islam (The Military School of the Newly Converted to Islam). As the names indicate, the purpose of these divisions was to train ordinary soldiers to serve officers of the upper-class section. Baiza, *Education in Afghanistan*, 51. The practice of separating the children of tribal elites from more regular soldiers drawn from the countryside and urban locales was a practice similar to the Ottoman Imperial Tribal School, but it was also a structure that had long-term implications in Afghanistan. As Baiza astutely notes in this regard, "Although the establishment of the modern military school was an important step towards the development of a national army and modern education, the admittance of students from certain ethnic groups and provinces marked the beginning of ethnic discrimination and a policy that would divide ethnic groups in the country, thereby creating tensions between them." Ibid.

46. As British intelligence agents in Kabul further reported, "It is intended that Turkish element should be brought into the Afghan service gradually and in a limited measure so as to avoid jealousy of Afghan officials in Kabul, and should only be confined to training purposes." NAI-Foreign / Secret / F / Jan.1909 / 74–76.

47. Ünal et al., *Geçmişten Günümüze*, 32; Rahmanhoca İmamhocayev, "Afganistan ve Türkiye," *Atatürk Üniversitesi Türkiyat Araştırmaları Enstitüsü Dergisi* 8, no. 17 (2001): 264–265.

48. NAI-Foreign / Secret / F / Sept.1909 / 1–3.

49. Ibid.

50. Ibid.

51. NAI-Foreign / Secret / F / Feb.1910 / 5.

52. NAI-Foreign / Secret / F / Jun.1908 / 146–199.

53. BOA-HR.SYS 5 / 17 (1910 02 19). Among this group of "sultanis" were eight persons, including an engineer, a land surveyor, a physician and two medical assistants, an office bureaucrat, and a military expert. "All of them are the relatives or friends of Mahmud Sami, Effendi, through whom they have been summoned to Kabul," British agents in the Afghan capital observed. NAI-Foreign /Secret / Jan.1909 /74–76.

54. For original copies of Turkish textbooks in the Afghanistan National Archives during the Habib Allah and Amani eras, see ADL-0274 (Muhammad Nazif, *Sarf-i Turki* [Ottoman Turkish grammar, with commentary in Dari] [Kabul: Matba'-'i 'Inayat, 1336h / 1917–1918]); ADL-0275 (Muhammad Nazif, *Qira'at-i Zaban-i Turki* [Reading exercises in Ottoman Turkish] [Kabul: Matba'-'i 'Inayat, 1336h / 1917–1918]). For the Amani era, see ADL-0302 (Muhammad Nazif and Muhammad Sulayman Khan, *Kitab-i Alifba-yi Turki* [The ABCs of Ottoman Turkish] [Kabul: Matba'-'i Nizarat-i Ma'arif, 1299j / 1920–1921]).

55. BOA-ŞD 37 / 27 (1331h S 16 / 1913 01 24); BOA-ŞD 40 / 3 (1332h S 01 / 1913 12 29).

56. Ünal et al., *Geçmişten Günümüze,* 34.

57. On the ebbs and flows of Turkish influence in Afghan education, including during the late Ottoman and early republic era, see Mehmet Ali Dağpınar, "Afganistan'da Mülkiye," *Mülkiye* 26, no. 237 (2002): 175–182.

58. For Porte records on Ali Fehmi's service in Afghanistan, see BOA-MF.MKT 1138 / 61 (1327h Ş 01 / 1909 08 18) and BOA-BEO 3628 / 272077 (1327h Ş 17 / 1909 09 03). For British perspectives, see NAI-Foreign / Secret / F / Mar.1909 / 44–49 ("Mehmed Ali Fehmy, licencié de l'école, ancient sous-directeur de lycée, ancien professeur de droit criminal à l'école de Genève et plus tard à Philippopoli; ancient rédacteur en chef de l'*Ahali* et chargé, à Caboul, de la reorganisation des finances afghanes"). See also O'-Sullivan, " 'The Little Brother'," 2–3.

59. BOA-Y.A.HUS 517 / 16 (1325h Za 05 / 1907 12 11); BOA-Y.MTV 165 / 125 (1315h Ra 23 / 1897 08 21). Controversy and intrigue appears to have followed Ali Fehmi well after his service in Afghanistan. A Turkish foreign ministry memorandum from 1924 describes his death under unnatural circumstances and the apprehension of his suspected murderers. BOA-HR.İM 103 / 16 (1924 04 21).

60. NAI-Foreign / Secret / F / Jan.1909 / 74–76.

61. Author's translation. NAI-Foreign / Secret / F / Mar.1909 / 44–49.

62. Mehmed Fazlı, *Resimli Afgan Seyaheti* (Istanbul: Matbaa-i Ahmed İhsan, 1325h / 1907–1908). This work has been transliterated into republican Turkish under the title, Mehmed Fazlı, *Afganistan'da bir Jöntürk: Mısır Sürgününden Afgan Reformuna,* trans. Kenan Karabulut (Istanbul: Türkiye Bankası Kültür Yayınları, 2007).

63. NAI-Foreign / Frontier / B / Aug.1911 / 40–42. Similarly, the diary of the assistant surgeon Dasaundhi Khan, in charge of the British Agency dispensary at Kabul, reported in late May 1911 that "Doctor Munir Beg Khan Effendi, who had gone on furlough, has returned to Kabul and resumed his duties." Other British sources

described him as a capable physician who "knows the art of preparing medicines." NAI-Foreign / Secret / F / Jun.1908 / 146–199.

64. Bal, "Afganistan-Türkiye," 246.

65. NAI-Foreign / Frontier / B / May.1913 / 71–72.

66. *WWA* (1920), 72, 155.

67. NAI-Foreign / Secret / F / Feb.1904 / 247–249.

68. Ibid.

69. Bal, "Afganistan-Türkiye," 246; Ünal et al., *Geçmişten Günümüze,* 34. According to Bal, a portion of production went to meet the needs of the army, with the number of workers at these plants reaching five thousand by 1919. Bal, "Afganistan-Türkiye," 246–247.

70. NAI-Foreign / Secret / Jan.1909 / 74–76.

71. Ibid.

72. Ünal et al., *Geçmişten Günümüze,* 32; İmamhocayev, "Afganistan ve Türkiye," 264–265.

73. NAI-Foreign / Secret / Jan.1909 / 74–76.

74. Makdisi, "Ottoman Orientalism"; Brinkley Messick, *The Calligraphic State: Textual Domination and History in a Muslim Society* (Berkeley: University of California Press, 1993); Timothy Mitchell, *Rule of Experts: Egypt, Techno-Politics, Modernity* (Berkeley: University of California Press, 2002). For a discerning analysis of Ottoman experts in Kabul at this time, including a Turkish "civilizing mission" at play in their professional assistance to Afghanistan, see O'Sullivan, " 'The Little Brother'."

75. See for example Selim Deringil, *The Well-Protected Domains: Ideology and the Legitimation of Power in the Ottoman Empire, 1876–1909* (New York: I. B. Tauris, 1999); Fortna, *Imperial Classroom;* Christine Philliou, *Biography of an Empire: Governing Ottomans in an Age of Revolution* (Berkeley: University of California Press, 2010); Makdisi, "Ottoman Orientalism."

76. For an exploration of this theme in the context of colonial Africa, see Mostafa Minawi, *The Ottoman Scramble for Africa: Empire and Diplomacy in the Sahara and the Hijaz* (Stanford, CA: Stanford University Press, 2016).

77. In 1913, the Frontier Branch of the Foreign Department produced three reports for the month of May of that year documenting the individual names and professions of Ottoman Turks in Afghanistan up to that date. It is also one of our most complete lists available of Turks employed by Habib Allah before the convulsions of World War I. NAI-Foreign / Frontier / B / May.1913 / 71–72.

78. IOR-L / PS / 10 / 196 (P4327–3 / 11: Turco-Italian War: Moslem Representations) (1911), 148–149.

79. NAI-Foreign / Secret / F / Jun.1908 / 146–199. Unfortunately, I have been unable to identify the name of this Ottoman "barrister." That Ottoman lawyers were arriving in Kabul as early as 1908 might challenge the predominant historiographical narrative

that Ottoman juridical influence in Afghanistan began in the Aman Allah and Kemalist eras, but more evidence is needed.

80. NAI-Foreign / Secret / F / Jun.1908 / 146–199.

81. Ibid.

82. Ibid.

83. It is reported that said Turks traveled to Kabul after visiting Hyderabad (Deccan). Their purpose: to join other Turkish officials recently hired by the amir to oversee the training of the police and military forces. NAI-Foreign /Secret / F / Sept.1910 / 1–12.

84. NAI-Foreign / Secret / F / Oct.1907 / 152–159.

85. Ibid.

86. NAI-Foreign / Secret / Jan.1909 / 74–76.

87. On transborder ties between Kabul's Madrasih-'i Shahi and the Dar al-'Ulum seminary of Deoband, India, where several Afghan ulema and students enrolled beginning in the late nineteenth century, see Roy, *Islam and Resistance*, 58. On broader Afghan-Deobandi links in the nineteenth and early twentieth centuries, especially in the borderlands frontier, see also Sana Haroon, *Frontier of Faith: Islam in the Indo-Afghan Borderland* (New York: Columbia University Press, 2007), 98–104; Haroon, "Religious Revival across the Durand Line," in *Under the Drones: Modern Lives in the Afghanistan-Pakistan Borderlands*, ed. Shahzad Bashir and Robert D. Crews (Cambridge, MA: Harvard University Press, 2012), 45–59. On Indo-Afghan linkages at Deoband and Aligarh, see Nile Green, "The Trans-Border Traffic of Afghan Modernism: Afghanistan and the Indian 'Urdusphere,'" *Comparative Studies in Society and History* 53, no. 3 (2011): 479–508.

88. Scott C. Levi, *The Indian Diaspora in Central Asia and Its Trade, 1550–1900* (Leiden: Brill, 2002).

89. For a vivid history of the First Anglo-Afghan War based on Afghan and British sources, see William Dalrymple, *Return of a King: The Battle for Afghanistan, 1839–1942* (New York: Knopf, 2013).

90. Robert D. McChesney, *Kabul under Siege: Fayz Muhammad's Account of the 1929 Uprising* (Princeton: Markus Weiner, 1999), 11.

91. Green, "The Trans-Border Traffic of Afghan Modernism."

92. Ibid.

93. As Barbara Metcalf observed in her landmark study of the Dar al-'Ulum madrasa at Deoband, Afghans composed an important part of the students and even faculty from the earliest years of the institution. Barbara Metcalf, *Islamic Reform in British India: Deoband, 1860–1900* (Princeton, NJ: Princeton University Press, 1982), 107, 111, 135. On Afghans at the Muslim college in Aligarh, including student and faculty exchanges between Kabul and Aligarh, see Baiza, *Education in Afghanistan*, 53. On Indian students at Aligarh claiming Afghan descent, see David Lelyveld, *Aligarh's First Generation: Muslim Solidarity in British India* (New Delhi: Oxford University Press, 1996), 224.

94. Levi, *The Indian Diaspora in Central Asia.*

95. Thomas Barfield, *Afghanistan: A Cultural and Political History* (Princeton, NJ: Princeton University Press, 2010), 175.

96. Peter Tomsen, *The Wars of Afghanistan: Messianic Terrorism, Tribal Conflicts, and the Failures of Great Powers* (New York: PublicAffairs, 2013).

97. Nadir Khan and the Musahiban clan were not the only prominent Afghan exiles living in India, but they were among the most influential and powerful. For example, another instance of prominent Afghan exiles residing and working in India is General Parvez Shah Khan. Born in 1840 and the son of a certain Agha Sayyid Abbas, Parvez Shah Khan was an Afghan refugee residing at Lahore, and drew Rs. 350 monthly from the Indian government. British intelligence records document he had sixty-nine "followers," many of whom were also in the employment of the British Indian government, signifying his continuing geopolitical importance and activities while in India, but also his associations with the British government. NAI-Foreign / Frontier / A / Feb.1903 / 56–57.

98. Adamec, *Afghanistan,* 264–265.

99. Nadir Khan would later acquire great renown in the Third Anglo-Afghan War, or Afghan War of Independence, particularly in his ability to rally the Masud and Waziri tribes on the Indian side of the Durand Line to secure victory over the British at Thal, Waziristan in May 1919. This would earn him the venerated Nishan-i Almar (Order of the Sun) breast medal under Aman Allah, whom he succeeded as king in 1929.

100. On the leading role of Dr. Ghani in establishing the Habibiye, British Criminal Intelligence reported on November 21, 1906, that "Dr. Abdul Ghani will accompany the Amir and at Lahore will present his friends to the Amir. At Abdul Ghani's instigation the Amir has decided to establish a University at Kabul. This is considered as the best means of extending the Amir's influence over the Indian Muhammadans." NAI-Foreign / Secret / F / Jun.1907 / 34–52. See also Halil Toker, "Zafer Hasan Aybek ve Afganistan Anıları (1915–1922, 1933–36, 1937)," in Ali Ahmetbeyoğlu, ed., *Afganistan Üzerine Araştırmalar* (Istanbul: Tarih ve Tabiat Vakfı Yayınları, 2001), 156. For the official proclamation on the establishment of the Habibiye, see ADL-0467 (*Nizamnamih-ʾi Madrasih-ʾi Mubarakih-ʾi Habibiyyih-ʾi Dar al-Saltanih-ʾi Kabul* [Kabul: Matbaʿ-ʾi Hurufi-yi Dar al-Saltanih, 1332h / 1913–1914]).

101. According to ʿAbd al-Rahman's biographer, the Punjabi barrister and Cambridge law graduate Sultan Mohammad Khan, it was Amir ʿAbd al-Rahman who established a school at Kabul for the teaching of sciences "according to European methods." Khan, *The Life of Abdur Rahman, Amir of Afghanistan* (London: 1900). British sources largely dismiss these claims as exaggerated, however, as a 1906 article in the *Daily Telegraph* states: "Unfortunately, there is reason to believe that this roseate picture was absolutely over-coloured, and that the late Ameer, or his Secretary of State who compiled the autobiography was drawing a very long bow. Mr. Angus Hamilton, in his recent book

on Afghanistan declares that the education system of the country has made no advance whatever upon the native principle of oral teaching. 'There are no schools,' he says, 'or colleges under European supervision similar to those which exist in other Eastern countries, and the young is only trained to read Persian, to quote extensively from the Koran, to write, to shoot, and to read.'" NAI-Foreign / Frontier / B / Nov.1906 / 220–222. On the remarkable life and career of the Indian Muslim barrister Mir Munshi Sultan Mohammad Khan, father of celebrated Pakistani poet Fayz Ahmad Fayz, see Sarfraz Khan Noor Ul Amin, "Mir Munshi Aala Sultan Muhammad Khan and His Services to Afghanistan," *Central Asia Journal* 72 (2013): 17–35.

102. Ibid.

103. NAI-Foreign / Frontier / B / Sept.1906 / 141. Habib Allah's declared emphasis on expanding educational opportunities for all his subjects notwithstanding, it was not until the reign of his son Aman Allah Khan—and specifically, the tireless advocacy of his wife, Queen Suraya—that Afghan women were seen to be included in the promise of universal education. On the first major initiatives for girls' education in early twentieth-century Afghanistan, see Baiza, *Education in Afghanistan*, 75–80; Nawid, *Religious Response to Social Change*, 96, 126–127, 221–222.

104. NAI-Foreign / Frontier / B / Sept.1906 / 141.

105. Another British Indian frontier branch intelligence report of 1906 described Habib Allah's "wrathful" depiction of the "retrogression" of the college that he had founded only a few years earlier. NAI-Foreign / Frontier / B / Nov.1906 / 220–222. At the same time, Habib Allah was careful not to assume blame for the unsatisfactory state of affairs, deflecting responsibility to "the stubborn prejudices of the Afghan officials, of whom not two out of ten are fit for State service, if education is to be taken as the test." A more balanced assessment would find that the scarce educational and professional training opportunities for young Afghan students were likely the most pressing obstacle facing Habib Allah's envisioned reform program, rather than the imagined and stereotypical "Afghan's incurable suspiciousness of the foreigner, whether British or Russian, which the Ameer is trying to overcome." Ibid. For these reasons, Habib Allah was likely to agree with Lord Curzon's assessment and advice for young Muslims in India: "If I were a Mohamedan prince or a man of wealth," said Lord Curzon to the students of Aligarh College in 1901, "I would concentrate my attention on education, and on education alone." Ibid.

106. NAI-Foreign / Frontier / B / Jun.1907 / 226.

107. NAI-Foreign / Frontier / B / Nov.1906 / 220–222.

108. NAI-Foreign / Secret / F / Jun.1907 / 34–52; NAI-Foreign / Secret / F / Feb.1907 / 119–137; NAI-Foreign / Secret / F / Jun.1907 / 34–52. Notably, Habib Allah appears to have reversed this policy when subsequently endowing the Muslim college at Aligarh, and even the Dar al-ʿUlum seminary at Deoband. Metcalf, *Islamic Reform*, 112.

109. NAI-Foreign / Secret / F / Feb.1907 / 119–137.

110. Ibid.

111. NAI-Foreign / Secret / F / Jun.1907 / 34–52.

112. On the founder and early history of the Muhammadan Anglo-Oriental College at Aligarh, see Lelyveld, *Aligarh's First Generation.*

113. NAI-Foreign / Secret / F / Jun.1907 / 34–52.

114. NAI-Foreign / Frontier / B / Mar.1907 / 36.

115. A. C. Yate, "The Visit to India of the Amir Habibullah Khan, the Fourth Amir of the Barakzai Dynasty," *Imperial and Asiatic Quarterly Review and Oriental and Colonial Record* 24, no. 47 (January–April 1907): 29–37.

116. Ibid.

117. Ibid.

118. Alternatively, the amir might have sought to visit the seminary at Deoband, but British authorities did not allow him given the potentially threatening nature of such a visit, and amid the Raj's lingering suspicions the seminary harbored Pan-Islamic sentiments of the anti-British variety. Habib Allah's rapport with his British patrons notwithstanding, it is likely Raj authorities feared the consequences of strengthening Afghan-Deobandi ties beyond the robust levels they were already enjoying. This is more probable, given we also know that Habib Allah gifted an endowment to the Dar al-ʿUlum at Deoband, as Barbara Metcalf has noted, including the construction of one of the outer gates of the campus. Metcalf, *Islamic Reform,* 112–113.

119. On Indian Muslims serving in the Raj army, see Nile Green, *Islam and the Army in Colonial India: Sepoy Religion in the Service of Empire* (New York: Cambridge University Press, 2009).

120. NAI-Foreign / Secret / F / Jun.1907 / 34–52.

121. NAI-Foreign / Intl / B / Jun.1907 / 625–639.

122. Ibid.

123. It goes without saying that the amir's thoughts on less pleasant aspects of colonial rule in India do not surface in British records of the tour.

124. NAI-Foreign / Frontier / B / Dec.1908 / 62.

125. In early October 1908, the Kabul Agency also reported to the Indian Foreign Department, "His Majesty the Amir has enquired from the Turks whether they have really resolved to return to their country in any case, or whether they consider that they have not been well treated." NAI-Foreign / Frontier / B / Dec.1908 / 62.

126. For example, in late November 1908 the Kabul agent's diary observed an unusual number of Turks were returning to the Ottoman lands via Peshawar (and from there, usually Karachi or Bombay). The report subsequently predicted, "The other Turks will follow his example. They do not want to stay here." NAI-Foreign / Frontier / B / Dec.1908 / 62.

127. BOA-MF.MKT 1174 / 41 (1329h Ş 18 / 1911 08 13).

128. NAI-Foreign / Secret / F / Feb.1909 / 20–21.

129. NAI-Foreign / Secret / F / Sept.1910 / 1–12.

130. NAI-Foreign / Secret / F / May.1913 / 1–23.

131. Ibid. For additional British perspectives on underlying tensions between the Ottomans and Indians in Kabul, and how Foreign Department officials saw this as a welcome development, see NAI-Foreign / Secret / F / Feb.1909 / 20–21; NAI-Foreign / Secret / F / Sept.1910 / 1–12; NAI-Foreign / Secret / F / Mar.1910 / 4–7; NAI-Foreign / Frontier / B / Aug.1911 / 40–42.

132. NAI-Foreign / Frontier / B / Aug.1911 / 40–42.

133. NAI-Foreign / Secret / F / Sept.1910 / 1–12.

134. Ibid. Sure enough, several years later a report in the Turkish Red Crescent Society's archives reported that a Captain (Yüzbaşı) Hasan Tahsin had not only arrived in Kabul by 1921 but was appointed as an instructor in the Harbiye military academy where several other Ottoman officers were also employed. TKA-1361 / 72 (1340r Şubat 10 / 1925 02 23).

135. NAI-Foreign / Secret / F / Apr.1910 / 5–6.

136. A March 1910 secret Foreign Department file sheds more light on Süleyman Midhat's side of the story regarding his engagement by the Afghan government as an electrical engineer. According to Midhat, his contract with the Afghan government promised to pay for his travel expenses to Kabul. Midhat never received the said funds, he alleged, preventing him from making the journey to Afghanistan. Without Kabul's side of the story, it is unclear if this was a case of miscommunication, a failure to perform contractual obligations, or a change of mind on the Afghan amir's part to recruit Ottomans to his court. NAI-Foreign / Secret / F / Mar.1910 / 4–7.

137. Ibid.

138. Reporting by British informants in Kabul also reveal that the government of India knew of Habib Allah's officers attempts to recruit Ottoman experts, even when they entered via Russian and Iranian frontiers. Ibid.

139. *WWA* (1914), 17, 67.

140. For the extensive British paper trail on Haji ʿAbd al-Raziq, including the innumerable border raids he was alleged to have organized against the Raj's forces on both sides of the Durand Line, see IOR-L / PS / 10 / 1019 (1921–1924).

141. From a special report by Malik Khuda Bakhsh, Tiwana, British agent at Kabul, dated January 22, 1907. NAI-Foreign / Secret / F / Feb.1907 / 176–179.

142. On Afghan-Iranian contestations over Sistan and other territorial disputes between the neighboring states, see Firoozeh Kashani-Sabet, *Frontier Fictions: Shaping the Iranian Nation, 1804–1946* (Princeton, NJ: Princeton University Press, 1999), 30–33, 40. The relative lack of Iranian officers or advisors in Habib Allah's court notwithstanding, this does not negate the indirect influence of the Iranian constitutional revolution (1905–1911) in Afghanistan. Amin Tarzi, "Islam and Constitutionalism," 208; Touraj Atabaki, "Constitutionalists *Sans Frontières:* Iranian Constitutionalism and Its Asian Connections," in *Iran's Constitutional Revolution: Politics, Cultural Transformations and Transnational Connections,* ed. H. E. Chehabi and Vanessa Martin (London: I. B. Tauris, 2010), 341–355. One should also not discount the longstanding

scholastic and educational ties linking Afghan Shiʿa to *ḥawzas* and other Shiʿi institutions of learning in Mashhad, Qum, and the shrine cities of Iraq, among other locales in Iran and the Ottoman Empire.

143. Bal, "Afganistan-Türkiye," 246.

144. Partly owing to its secretive origins, and the fact few historical documents were left behind by its members, there is considerable debate among Afghan historians on the aims and makeup of the first constitutional movement, including Dr. Ghani's purported role. For wildly differing theories on the latter's part in the movement, including as a British agent to assassinate Habib Allah and Habib Allah's agent to spy on Afghan dissidents in jail, see Amin Tarzi, "Islam and Constitutionalism," 208, and Habibi, *Junbish*, 101–104.

145. NAI-Foreign / Secret / F / Aug.1908 / 203–209. British and Ottoman sources continued to document the arrival of Turks in Afghanistan through the early 1910s. See for example NAI-Foreign / Frontier / B / Aug.1911 / 40–42; BOA-DH.EUM.4.Şb 3 / 62 (1333h Za 10 / 1915 09 21).

146. On the inspirational role of Japan's military victory of Russia in 1905 in several Asian and Muslim-majority countries, including Afghanistan, see Cemil Aydin, "A Global Anti-Western Moment? The Russo-Japanese War, Decolonization, and Asian Modernity," in *Competing Visions of World Order: Global Moments and Movements, 1880s-1930s*, ed. Sebastien Conrad and Dominic Sachsenmaier (New York: Palgrave MacMillan, 2007), 213–236. On roughly coinciding constitutional revolutions in Turkey, Persia, and Russia, see Nader Sohrabi, *Revolution and Constitutionalism in the Ottoman Empire and Iran* (New York: Cambridge University Press, 2014); Fariba Zarinebaf, "From Istanbul to Tabriz: Modernity and Constitutionalism in the Ottoman Empire and Iran," *CSSAAME* 28, no. 1 (2008): 154–169.

147. Barfield, *Afghanistan*, 295.

148. IOR-L / PS / 20 / 42 (1914), 406.

149. For a sample case of jurisdictional clashes between the Ottoman and British governments involving Afghans in Turkey, see NAI-Foreign / Secret / F / Oct.1891 / 116–122. For a broader examination of Anglo-Ottoman legal tussles concerning both groups from the 1880s to the eve of the World War I, see Faiz Ahmed, "Contested Subjects: Ottoman and British Jurisdictional Quarrels *in re* Afghans and Indian Muslims," *JOTSA* 3, no. 2 (2016): 325–346.

150. Ottoman sources also provide a different perspective on Afghan travelers than most British sources would lead us to believe. Far from hapless subjects beholden to either London or Kabul, Porte records describe Afghans applying for Ottoman nationality (*Osmanlı tabiiyeti*) with the expectation that the sultan's protection, and not the British Crown's, extended to Afghans found in Ottoman territory. See for example BOA-HR.HMŞ.İŞO 173/20 (1307h Ra 6/1889 10 31); BOA-DH.SN.THR 47/94 (1332h S 6/1915 01 3); and more generally, Ahmed, "Contested Subjects," 343–345.

151. Ahmed, "Contested Subjects," 346. For sample cases of Anglo-Ottoman quarrels over Afghans and Indian Muslims (including Indian Pakhtuns, or "Pathans") from the early 1900s, see NAI-Foreign / Secret / F / May.1904 / 266–273; NAI-Foreign / Frontier / A / Feb.1903 / 56–57; NAI-Foreign / Frontier / A / Jan.1900 / 56–58; NAI-Foreign / External / A / Jul.1904 / 17–18. Jurisdictional contests between the British and Ottomans over the legal status of itinerant Afghans continued into subsequent decades, and as Lâle Can has shown, often drew in Bukharans and Russia as well. Lâle Can, "The Protection Question: Central Asians and Extraterritoriality in the Late Ottoman Empire," *IJMES* 48, no. 4 (2016): 679–699.

3. EXIT GREAT GAME, ENTER GREAT WAR

1. BOA-HR.SYS 5 / 20 (1914 05 26).
2. BOA-DH.EUM.2.Şb 3 / 10 (1333h M 17 / 1914 12 05).
3. The British agent in Kabul reported in 1909 on Turkish communications between the Porte and Ottoman subjects in Afghanistan: "They have arranged for their letters to be sent to them through Dost Muhammad Khan, the Amir's Agent at Karachi, who arranges for their despatch to Kabul through the Afghan Post Master at Peshawar." NAI-Foreign / Secret / F / Feb.1909 / 8.
4. My translation. Abidin Ünal et al., *Geçmişten Günümüze Türk-Afgan İlişkileri* (Ankara: Genelkurmay Askeri Tarih ve Stratejik Etüt Başkanlığı Yayınları Basimevi, 2009), 33.
5. The Ottoman Empire's entry into World War I was far from a foregone conclusion. Enver Pasha's August 1914 defense pact did not constitute a formal Ottoman declaration of war, and as late as mid-autumn of 1914 Porte officials remained divided on whether to join the fray—and on whose side. On the complicated events surrounding and leading up to Ottoman entry into World War I, see Mustafa Aksakal, *The Ottoman Road to War in 1914: The Ottoman Empire and the First World War* (New York: Cambridge University Press, 2010); M. Şükrü Hanioğlu, *A Brief History of the Late Ottoman Empire* (Princeton, NJ: Princeton University Press, 2008), 173–182.
6. On the roots and ramifications of Ottoman entry into World War I in the broader Islamicate world, see Erik-Jan Zürcher, *Jihad and Islam in World War I* (Leiden: Leiden University Press, 2016).
7. On the Ottoman Second Constitutional Era and descent to CUP triumvirate rule, see Hasan Kayalı, *Arabs and Young Turks: Ottomanism, Arabism, and Islamism in the Ottoman Empire, 1908–1918* (Berkeley: University of California Press, 1997) and Bedross Der Matossian, *Shattered Dreams: From Liberty to Violence in the Late Ottoman Empire* (Stanford, CA: Stanford University Press, 2014).
8. Hasan Kayalı has cast doubt on the triumvirate's supremacy, arguing that there were counterbalancing factions within the broader CUP leadership. Kayalı, *Arabs and Young Turks,* 195.

9. Senzil K. Nawid, *Religious Response to Social Change in Afghanistan, 1919–29: King Aman-Allah and the Afghan Ulama* (Costa Mesa, CA: Mazda, 1999), 37.

10. Amin Saikal, *Modern Afghanistan: A History of Struggle and Survival* (New York: I. B. Tauris, 2006), 52–53.

11. Thomas Edward Gordon, *The Roof of the World* (Edinburgh: Edmonston and Douglas, 1876).

12. An Ottoman foreign ministry document from 1906, for example, discusses the impending travels to Istanbul of an Indian Muslim, 'Abd Allah Suhrawardi "Effendi" of Calcutta, and the warm reception he was to receive from the Ottoman government. BOA-BEO 2955/221596 (1324h L 16/1906 12 03). The purpose of Suhrawardi's reception was to honor his service "in defense of Islamic rights and the Ottoman Caliphate" ("*hukuk-ı İslamiye ve hilafet-i Osmaniye müdafaa etmek üzere*") through a series of staunchly pro-Ottoman publications he published in India.

13. BOA-HRT.h 118 (1330r/1914–1915).

14. BOA-Y.A.HUS 481/150 (1322L N 29/1904 12 07).

15. See BOA-HR.SYS 5/19 (1912 06 14). This dossier includes a June 13, 1912, article from the *Times* submitted by Tevfik Bey, a correspondent in the Ottoman embassy at London, to Aasim Bey, the minister of foreign affairs in Istanbul. The article describes Habib Allah's unpopularity in Afghanistan, the outbreak of a rebellion in Khost province, and the activities of the Turks in Kabul. Unofficial Ottoman perspectives on Afghanistan can also be found in multiple articles of the Turkish-language Muslim modernist newspapers *Takvim-i Vekayi* and *Sebilürreşad* between 1908 and 1915 in particular, but also late Ottoman newspapers more generally. See for example "Afganistan bir seda," *Takvim-i Vekayi* 75/10 (1326h/1908–1909): 1; S. M. Tevfik, "Hayat-ı Akvam-ı İslamiye: Afganistan Müslümanları," *Sebilürreşad* 17/1999 (1912): 327–328; Tahir el-Mevlevi, "Tarih: Afganistan, Emir Abdurrahman Han," *Sebilürreşad* 25/207 (1912): 482–483; Afganizade, "Afganistan Herhalde İngiltere Aleyhine Kıyam Edecektir," *Sebilürreşad* 13/316 (1915): 28–29; "Afgan Emiri Hazretlerinden Gazi Mustafa Kemal Paşa Hazretlerine," *Hakmiyet-i Milliye*, 17 Şubat 1922, 1. Notably, Mahmud Tarzi, the Afghan journalist and editor of Kabul's *Siraj al-Akhbar*, also contributed to *Sebilürreşad*. See for example Mahmud Tarzi, "İdare-i Sıraci'l Ahbar-ı Afganiye," *Sebilürreşad* 11/275 (1914): 279.

16. My research uncovered over four hundred and fifty dossiers of Muslim contributions to the Ottoman Red Crescent Society from India and Afghanistan at the organization's central archive in Ankara. For an illustrative example, on a local fundraising campaign for the organization in Deoband, northern India, during the Balkans Wars, see TKA-21/63 (1913 04 19). The latter is also described by the Ottoman foreign ministry's translation office in BOA-HR.TO 544/48 (1913 03 12). For examples of fundraisers in Afghanistan for injured Ottoman soldiers and civilians, see TKA-99/87 (1328r Hazıran 17/1912 06 30). It was also not uncommon for Indian and Afghan donors to contribute together. See for example TKA-19/165 (1327r Şubat 25/1912 03 09). On Deoband's contributions to the Hilal-i Ahmer by its foremost

chronicler, see Sayyid Mahbub Rizwi, *History of the Dar al-Ulum Deoband* (Deoband: Idara-e Ihtemam Dar al-Ulum, 1980–1981), 1:180.

17. Azmi Özcan, *Pan-Islamism: Indian Muslims, the Ottomans and Britain, 1877–1924* (Leiden: Brill, 1997), 137–145; Jacob M. Landau, *The Politics of Pan-Islam: Ideology and Organization* (Oxford: Clarendon, 1994), 192–197. See also IOR-L / PS 10 / 196 (1911).

18. IOR-L / PS 10 / 196, 132–133.

19. BOA-HR.TO 543 / 105 (1913 01 26).

20. IOR-L / PS / 10 / 196, 148–149.

21. A June 1913 report housed in the Ottoman central archives notes with appreciation the donation of three hundred British pounds by the owner of the Lahore-based *Watan* magazine, a Punjabi Indian Muslim by the name of Muhammad Inshaullah. BOA-İ.MBH 12 / 1331 B-003 (1331h B 05 / 1913 06 10). We learn from another government source that this particular three hundred pounds was the fifteenth such installment dispatched by the magazine editor, equaling a staggering sum of seven thousand British pounds donated "for the relief of the wounded and refugees." BOA-Y.A.HUS 377 / 4 (1315h Ca 01 / 1897 09 27). Beyond these considerable financial contributions, the Punjabi Muslim of Lahore expressed his longing for even more personal attachment to the sultan. In one August 1897 letter, composed in Urdu and addressed to the Ottoman consul general in Karachi, after courtesies and salutations Muhammad Inshaullah "Effendi" proceeded to describe his four sons, their education and qualifications, and their aspiration to serve the Ottoman realm. On Inshaullah and his contributions to Sultan Abdülhamid's Hejaz railway project in particular, see Syed Tanvir Wasti, "Muhammad Inshaullah and the Hijaz Railway," *Middle Eastern Studies* 34, no. 2 (1998): 60–72.

22. This report clashed with prior intelligence shared by the British agent at Kabul in 1909, who concluded, "The Afghan public know nothing about the Balkan crisis and are quite ignorant of the state of affairs in Turkey." NAI-Foreign / Secret / F / Feb.1909 / 8. Given the rise of a Pan-Islamic press in Kabul, including periodicals like Mahmud Tarzi's *Siraj al-Akhbar,* this state of affairs could hardly hold for long. What is more, the British Agency in Kabul was well aware that the Ottomans in Afghanistan were themselves conveying information about events in Turkey to their Afghan counterparts: "The Turks in Kabul are, of course, in correspondence with their friends in Constantinople," the British agent also noted in 1909, adding that "they informed the Amir and Sardar Nasrulla Khan of whatever news they receive from Turkey." Ibid.

23. A declassified Foreign Department memorandum of April 1913, "Movements of the Afghan Volunteers for Service with Turkey during the Turko-Balkan War," suggests that these were not just paranoid misgivings. NAI-Foreign / External / B / Apr.1913 / 301–302.

24. NAI-Foreign / External / B / Apr.1913 / 301–302.

25. Özcan, *Pan-Islamism,* 160–170; M. Naeem Qureshi, *Pan-Islam in British Indian Politics* (Leiden: Brill, 1999), 1, 88, 447; Ayesha Jalal, *Self and Sovereignty: Indi-*

vidual and Community in South Asian Islam since 1850 (New York: Routledge, 2000), 192–193.

26. On the role of the Indian army in World War I, see David E. Omissi, *Indian Voices of the Great War: Soldiers' Letters, 1914–1918* (Basingstoke, UK: Macmillan, 1999). See also Philippa Levine, "Battle Colors: Race, Sex, and Colonial Soldiery in World War I," *Journal of Women's History* 9, no. 4 (1998): 104–130; Jeffrey Greenhut, "The Imperial Reserve: The Indian Corps on the Western Front, 1914–15," *Journal of Imperial and Commonwealth History* 12, no. 1 (1983): 54–73.

27. NAI-Foreign-Political / International / B / Apr.1915 / 259–305. Subsequently the Ajmer Association issued a second resolution lamenting Ottoman entry into the war: "Resolution II. This meeting of the Muhammadans of Ajmer expresses sorrow and anxiety at the news of the outbreak of war between Great Britain (which rules over the greatest number of Muhammadans in the world) and the Ottoman empire which has caused a regrettable estrangement between two Empires which were on terms of the greatest friendship for a long time past." Ibid.

28. In the neighboring city and provincial capital of Jaipur, Rajasthan, for example, British intelligence sources reported that on November 20, 1914, at approximately 4 p.m., "a crowded and representative meeting of the Muhammadans of Jaipur" was held in the Ramnivas gardens of Rajasthan province, where they gathered to express their "deep devotion and unflinching loyalty to the British Government." Ibid. Some Indian Muslim assemblies went so far as to condemn the Ottoman decision for not joining the side of Britain. At a public meeting of the Muhammadans of Bharatpur held in the town's central Jama Masjid on November 5, 1914, a certain "Moulvi" Muhammad Ashiaq Hasan Khan read out an Urdu communiqué at a "largely attended public gathering" at 4:30 p.m. The statement deplored Turkey's decision to join Germany and "her old enemy Austria" in the war. According to an informant present, the mawlawi proceeded to exclaim "the paramount duty of the Musalmans to rally to the British Government, the greatest Moslim power in the world, and to support it whole heartedly in the present situation, which has been rendered critical by the action of the Turks." Ibid.

29. NAI-Foreign-Political / International / B / Apr.1915 / 259–305.

30. Ibid. Quoting Tennyson's "Oenone" (1829).

31. Addressed to "all Muslim lands" (*jamīʿ aqṭār al-muslimīn*) the subsequently printed proclamation of Sultan Mehmed V Reşad specifies by name the following countries, peoples, and regions: Afghanistan, Africa, Austria, Bukhara, Central Asia, China, Crimea, Europe, Fezzan (Libya), Germany, Medina (*Ravza-i Mübareke*), India, Iran, Khive, Montenegro, Ottomans (*Osmanlılar*), and Turkistan. BOA-İ.DUİT 1 / 28 (1333h M 04 / 1914 11 23).

32. Hamid Enayat, *Modern Islamic Political Thought* (New York: I. B. Tauris, 2008), 58.

33. On the Ottoman government expressing its gratitude to the Muslim community of Hyderabad, India, for their support during the Russo-Ottoman war, for example, see BOA-HR.TO 126 / 76 (1877 05 16).

34. NAI-Foreign-Political / Secret / War / May.1915 / 453–487. Notably, the viceroy's statement was silent on the fate of Jerusalem, Palestine, and Greater Syria more broadly.

35. NAI-Foreign-Political / International / B / Apr.1915 / 259–305.

36. NAI-Foreign-Political / Secret / War / May.1915 / 453–487.

37. For example, in an internal memorandum from the British resident at Hyderabad in early September 1914, the latter revealed that Raj officials were already conversing with the Nizam's representative and chief minister, Salar Jung, on the position of the princely ruler should the Ottomans enter the war on the side of Germany.

> [T]he Nizam was, I knew, looked up to by Muhammadans both in the north and south of India, and, whatever the weight he carried, he must not lose this, the opportunity of his life. To Salar Jung himself there would fall the same chance of service as fell to this grandfather at the time of the Mutiny. With this he quite concurred, and said that he had used the 1857 precedent with the Nizam, who realized how much more claim the Delhi Emperor had on Hyderabad than the Sultan of Turkey. He also referred to the telegram which certain Muhammadans of Bengal have sent to the Sultan, advising him to maintain his neutrality; and he asked my opinion whether the Nizam should send a similar message.

NAI-Foreign-Political / Secret / International / Oct.1916 / 13–34.

38. Ibid.

39. Though personal gain and attempts to curry favor can certainly always motivate in such situations, it is at least as likely that Indian Muslim notables and associations such as the Ajmer Muhammadans adopted staunchly pro-British positions in order to secure their own community's interests—or survival—during the war. Under the same calculus, they may have also sought to better position themselves to influence British policy vis-à-vis the Ottoman Empire, especially in the holy lands of Hejaz, Jerusalem, and Mesopotamia.

40. Scattered instances of pan-Indian Muslim consciousness surfaced in the partition of Bengal in 1906, but the historical conditions leading to the emergence of "All-India" Muslim politics and institutions were not strongly rooted at this time. It would not be another two decades until pan-Indian organizations such as the Indian National Congress, Muslim League, Jamʿiyat-i ʿUlamaʾ-i Hind, and Jamʿiyat-i ʿUlamaʾ-i Islam eclipsed smaller and more localized associations of the late nineteenth and early twentieth centuries. Ayesha Jalal, *Self and Sovereignty: Individual and Community in South Asian Islam since 1850* (New York: Routledge, 2000), 212.

41. For an example of the Porte's acknowledging Indian Muslims in providing such "material and spiritual" support to the Ottomans at this time, see BOA-DH.KMS 63 / 53 (1332h R 02 / 1914 02 27).

42. Saikal, *Modern Afghanistan,* 52–53.

43. BOA-DH.EUM.2.Şb 3/10 (1333h M 17/1914 12 06).

44. Ludwig Adamec summarized the mission's overarching objectives as follows: "revolutionizing India, inducing Afghanistan to attack India, and securing Iran as a bridge from the Ottoman Empire to Afghanistan." Ludwig W. Adamec, *Afghanistan, 1900–1923* (Berkeley: University of California Press, 1967), 108–109.

45. See for example Thomas L. Hughes, "The German Mission to Afghanistan, 1915–1916," *German Studies Review* 25, no. 3 (2002): 447–476; F. J. Moberly, *Operations in Persia, 1914–1919* (London: HMSO, 1987), 116.

46. Von Hentig and Niedermayer both later published works on the mission to Afghanistan, including a richly illustrated memoir and travel log boasting some of the first aerial photographs of the country. Werner Otto von Hentig, *Meine Diplomatenfahrt ins verschlossene Land* (Berlin: Ullstein, 1918); von Hentig, *Mein Leben, eine Dienstreise* (Göttingen: Vandenhoeck & Ruprecht, 1962); Oskar von Niedermayer and Ernst Diez, eds., *Afghanistan* (Leipzig: Verlag Karl W. Hiersemann, 1924).

47. For a summary of German-centric sources and perspectives, see for example Hughes, "The German Mission," 447–451.

48. See for example Mustafa Aksakal, "Holy War Made in Germany? Ottoman Origins of the 1914 Jihad," *War in History* 18, no. 2 (2011): 184–199; Mostafa Minawi, *The Ottoman Scramble for Africa: Empire and Diplomacy in the Sahara and the Hijaz* (Stanford, CA: Stanford University Press, 2016); Kayalı, *Arabs and Young Turks.*

49. BOA-DH.EUM.KLU 5/18 (1333h M 10/1914 11 29).

50. BOA-DH.EUM.4.Şb 3/62 (1333h Za 10/1915 09 21).

51. BOA-DH.EUM.SSM 18/27 (1336h Ca 08/1918 02 20).

52. Porte correspondence reveals that significant differences emerged between the German and Turkish camps not long after they departed. In particular, after a dispute arose between the two groups while traveling between Mesopotamia and Iran, the German delegation returned to Aleppo. From then on the two delegations found it necessary to continue the mission separately, even though their overall strategic objectives in the mission overlapped. Ünal et al., *Geçmişten Günümüze,* 34. An Ottoman interior ministry communiqué reveals that just weeks after the expedition began a dispute arose between the German officers and the Ottoman commander Hüseyin Rauf Bey, who was leading the Turkish delegation. BOA-DH.ŞFR 465/6 (1331r 05 01/1915 07 14). Roughly a month later, a telegraph held in the Ottoman archives reports of Rauf Bey's delegation having reached Baghdad and entering the city's main Şirin fortress, but no mention of the Germans is made, suggesting they had taken another route. BOA-DH.ŞFR 467/66 (1331r 05 30/1915 08 12). Other interior ministry files from the period contain telegrams updating the Porte on the Turkish contingent's movements, including in Iran, where again the Germans are not mentioned as part of the expedition. BOA-DH.ŞFR 493/11 (1331r/1915).

53. BOA-DH.EUM.4Şb 4/7 (1334h M 09/1915 11 18).

54. BOA-İ.HB 166/1333h R-061 (1333h R 26/1915 03 13) indicates the delegation early on called on Captain Hayri Effendi's knowledge of the Afghan army due to his earlier experience in training the army cadets in Kabul. On the latter's activities in Afghanistan, see Adamec, *Afghanistan,* 88–89. In addition to the core mission members from Istanbul, Aleppo, and Baghdad, Ottoman records from 1915 indicate that the Turkish ambassador in Tehran, Asim Bey, dispatched a separate group of officers to rendezvous with the main delegation in Herat. BOA-HR.SYS 2337/11 (1915 02 28).

55. BOA-HR.SYS 2338/67 (1915 05 25). Ludwig Adamec mentions the mission was joined by a contingent of Afridi Pashtuns who had been freed from a prisoner-of-war camp. Adamec, *Afghanistan,* 108–109. As British intelligence from India reported through the 1920s, Indian Muslim desertions to Turkey continued into the Republican period. See for example the British file on a certain "Abbas Effendi, real name Surkha, son of Alam Sher of Shahpur." The latter absconded from his post as a consular guard at the British legation in Kirmanshah in 1925, and eventually adopted Turkish nationality. This event is reported by British sources in the 1930 edition of the Raj's secret manual for informants in Afghanistan, *Who's Who in Afghanistan* (*WWA*). Surkha later traveled to Afghanistan with a Turkish delegation and was appointed as a cavalry instructor at the Kabul Harbiye. *WWA* (1930), 1.

56. Ünal et al., *Geçmişten Günümüze,* 34.

57. Adamec, *Afghanistan,* 85.

58. Ibid.

59. For example, one party, led by Mehmed Ubeydullah, departed from his hometown of Izmir for Isfahan; Nedim Bey departed from Istanbul en route to Kirmanshah. BOA-DH.ŞFR 511/54 (1331r 12 16/1916 02 29); DH.ŞFR 512/107 (1331r Şu 28/1916 03 12); DH.ŞFR 61/54 (1334h R 15/1916 02 19); DH.ŞFR 63/398 (1334h B 10/1916 05 13). BOA-DH.ŞFR 48/278 (1333h S 18/1915 01 05). Mehmed Ubeydullah İzmirli, an accomplished Ottoman diplomat with a rather flamboyant personality, earlier served as the Sublime Porte's honorary consul in the United States, including as a special representative to the 1893 Chicago World's Fair. For his memoirs, see Ömer Hakan Özalp, ed., *Mehmed Ubeydullah Efendi'nin Malta, Afganistan, ve İran Hatıraları* (Istanbul: Dergah Yayınları, 2002); Ahmed Turan Alkan, ed., *Sıradışı Bir Jön Türk: Ubeydullah Efendi'nin Amerika Hatıraları* (Istanbul: İletişim Yayınları, 1989); and Ömer Hakan Özalp, ed., *Ulemadan Bir Jöntürk: Mehmed Ubeydullah Efendi* (Istanbul: Dergah Yayınları, 2005). Thanks to Hakeem Naim for bringing Ubeydullah İzmirli Effendi's writings to my attention. For a keen analysis of the latter's activities in Mesopotamia and Iran during World War I while purportedly en route to Afghanistan, see Naim, "The Ottoman Empire and Afghanistan: A Record of Failure and Great Power Intrigue" (BA Robert and Colleen Haas Scholars Thesis, Department of Middle Eastern Studies, UC Berkeley, 2010), 51–52.

60. Beyond misleading British forces in Persia, Ubeydullah İzmirli's role in the Porte's covert mission to Afghanistan included the important task of dispatching up-

dates and reconnaissance from his unit's journey to Kirmanshah. The latter included brief stops in Konya, Urfa, Adana, Aleppo, Mosul, Sulaymaniyah, and Baghdad, thereby providing the capital with updated information on the state of Ottoman territory in southern Anatolia, northern Syria, and Mesopotamia. BOA-DH.MTV 38/46 (1331r/1915); BOA-DH.ŞFR 474/80 (1331r 05 25/1915 08 07); BOA-DH.ŞFR 54A/57 (1333h N 08/1915 07 21); BOA-DH.ŞFR 54A/61 (1333h N 10/1915 07 23); BOA-DH.ŞFR 54A/365 (1333h N 29/1915 08 11); BOA-DH.ŞFR 51/229 (1333h Ca 22/1915 04 07); BOA-DH.ŞFR 510/72 (1331r 12 09/1916 02 22). When contrasted with other dossiers from the ministry on the 1915–1916 covert mission to Afghanistan, the former records present a curious development: Ubeydullah İzmirli's travel party was coordinated separately from two other Ottoman units led by Nedim and Rauf Beys—who were also destined for Kabul. BOA-DH.ŞFR 512/119 (1331r 12 29/1916 03 13); BOA-DH.ŞFR 61/54. As mentioned, Ubeydullah İzmirli's party departed for Isfahan, while the second Ottoman delegation, led by Nedim Bey, departed for Kirmanshah before returning to Istanbul. BOA-DH.ŞFR 511/54; BOA-DH.ŞFR 511/76 (1331r 12 17/1916 03 01); BOA-DH.ŞFR 512/91 (1331r 12 28/1916 03 12). Ubeydullah İzmirli was ultimately captured by British authorities in Tehran—which very well may have been intended. Ubeydullah İzmirli's status as a British prisoner-of-war in Persia are described in several dispatches to the Porte from the Ottoman embassy in Tehran through 1917 and 1918. BOA-HR.SYS 2340/56 (1917 11 3); BOA-HR.SYS 2340/60 (1917 11 10). Talat Pasha's attempts to secure his release are found in BOA-HR.SYS 2340/65 (1917 12 5); BOA-HR.SYS 2340/83 (1918 01 9); BOA-HR.SYS 2340/85 (1918 01 10); BOA-HR.SYS 2340/96 (1918 02 18); HR.SYS 2454/22 (1918 06 06); BOA-HR.SYS 2454/32 (1918 06 08).

61. Ünal et al., *Geçmişten Günümüze,* 34.

62. Adamec, *Afghanistan,* 88–89. Notably, the delegations were housed on the historic grounds of Bagh-i Baber hill, where the first Mughal emperor, Zahir al-Din Muhammad Babur (1483–1530), is buried. They were also provided with supplies at the Afghan government's expense. In spite of this hospitality, Adamec is less upbeat in his overall description of the mission, writing that it "was not at all the dignified affair which its members hoped it would be." Ibid., 89. See also Hughes, "The German Mission," 464–465.

63. Hughes, "The German Mission," 464–463; Ünal et al., *Geçmişten Günümüze,* 34.

64. BOA-DH.EUM.7.Şb 3/18 (1333h Ra 21/1915 02 06). The role of the Qaderi sufi order and Naqibs of Baghdad in particular as intermediaries between the Sublime Porte and Indian and Afghan Muslims was therefore in continuity with their earlier role played in the Russo-Ottoman War (1877–1878).

65. For Deobandi chroniclers' perspectives on these events, see Rizwi, *Dar al-Ulum Deoband,* 1:192, 2:135–149. For a broader overview of Indian revolutionary activity in Afghanistan leading up to and after World War I, see Lal Baha, "The Activities of the Mujahidin, 1900–1936," *Islamic Studies (Islamabad)* 18, no. 2 (1979): 97–168.

66. On Shaykh al-Hind Mahmud al-Hasan's life and legacy, see Barbara Metcalf, *Islamic Reform in British India: Deoband, 1860–1900* (Princeton, NJ: Princeton University Press, 1982), 92–120, 131–136, 157–168; S. P. Sen, ed., *Dictionary of National Biography* (Calcutta: Institute of Historical Studies, 1974), 3:12.

67. On Pratap's remarkable life and political career, see Vir Singh, ed., *The Life and Times of Raja Mahendra Pratap* (Delhi: Suraj Mal Memorial Education Society, 2005); Sen, *Dictionary of National Biography,* 3:10. For British intelligence on Pratap's background and global activities from Afghanistan to North America, see IOR-R / 12 / LIB / 107 (1928), 272–73.

68. Muhammad Miyan, *Silken Letters Movement: Accounts of 'Silken Handkerchief Letters Conspiracy Case' from British Records,* trans. Muhammad Qasmi (Delhi: Manak, 2012), 4, 44–60, 88–90, 100–105. For a concise overview of the movement from the perspective of another chronicler of the madrasa at Deoband, see also M. Burhanuddin Qasmi, *Recounting Untold History: Darul Uloom Deoband* (Mumbai: Markazul Maʿarif, 2001).

69. On Sindhi, see Sen, *Dictionary of National Biography,* 3:10; Ludwig W. Adamec, *Historical Dictionary of Afghanistan* (Metuchen, NJ: Scarecrow, 1991), 181; Zafer Hasan Aybek, "Ubayd-Allah Sindhi in Afghanistan," *Journal of the Regional Cultural Institute* 6 / 384 (1973): 129–136.

70. Özcan, *Pan-Islamism,* 160–170, 207; Adamec, *Afghanistan,* 83–85.

71. IOR-R / 12 / LIB / 107, 270.

72. Miyan, *Silken Letters Movement,* 135, 212.

73. *WWA* (1930), 255.

74. Zafer Hasan Aybek, *Ap Biti* (Lahore: Mansur Book House, 193?). Published posthumously in Pakistan, Zafer Hasan's memoirs have been the subject of an important study by Turkish scholar Halil Toker, who has also translated portions of the work into Turkish. Halil Toker, "Zafer Hasan Aybek ve Afganistan Anıları (1915–1922, 1933–36, 1937)," in *Afganistan Üzerine Araştırmalar,* ed. Ali Ahmetbeyoğlu (Istanbul: Tarih ve Tabiat Vakfı Yayınları, 2001), 149–176.

75. In describing one of the city squares, for example, Aybek was astonished at seeing so many prospering Hindu merchants. Ibid., 155–156. That the relative mildness of relations between Hindus and Muslims in a Muslim-majority country like Afghanistan appears to have surprised Aybek is likely owing to his preconceived notions and experiences of rising communalism in the Punjab. On essentializing stereotypes of Afghans, see Toker, "Zafer Hasan Aybek," 151–152.

76. Ibid., 152–153.

77. My translation. Ibid., 156.

78. Ibid. Hasan was shocked to learn that those convicted were to be executed by being blown from a cannon. Since the 1857 revolt, this form of punishment was a favorite of the British in reprisals against suspected rebels in India and the communities they lived in across northern India. On the brutality of British methods in quelling the rebellion, and for a good deal after, see William Dalrymple, *The Last Mughal: The*

Fall of a Dynasty, Delhi 1857 (New York: Vintage, 2008). Other suspects implicated in the plot against Habib Allah, including Dr. Abdul Ghani, were sentenced to life imprisonment.

79. My translation. Toker, "Zafer Hasan Aybek," 159.

80. My translation. Ibid., 159–160.

81. My translation. Ibid.

82. The most infamous example of Anglo-French schemes for the postbellum partition of the Ottoman Empire at this time is the Sykes-Picot Agreement (1916). But the conflicting promises made by British officials in the Husayn-MacMahon correspondence (1915–1916) and the Balfour Declaration (1917) should also be considered in this context.

83. Habib Allah's subsidies from the British Raj were in line with an Anglo-Afghan agreement of March 21, 1905, which in effect renewed Afghanistan's protectorate status as formulated in his father's earlier agreements with the British. Halil Bal, "Afganistan-Türkiye İlişkilerinin Başlıca Yönleri," in *Afganistan Üzerine Araştırmalar,* ed. Ali Ahmetbeyoğlu (Istanbul: Tarih ve Tabiat Vakfı Yayınları, 2001), 245.

84. Adamec, *Afghanistan,* 82–84; Toker, "Zafer Hasan Aybek," 160; Özcan, *Pan-Islamism,* 182; Hughes, "The German Mission," 471–472.

85. My translation. Toker, "Zafer Hasan Aybek," 160.

86. Ibid.

87. The British agent at Kabul, Sir Richard Roy Machonachie, reported Turkish emissaries being sent to the Kuki-Khels in Tirah, and the Kambar-Khels along the Indo-Afghan frontier, in 1917, but they failed to raise substantial support for the Ottoman war effort. IOR-R/12/LIB/107 (1928), 6.

88. Adamec, *Afghanistan,* 83–85.

89. Miyan, *Silken Letters Movement,* 7. For the names of the most prominent scholars and activists arrested by Raj officials for alleged involvement in the conspiracy, see 108–110.

90. Toker, "Zafer Hasan Aybek," 179–180.

91. There is some evidence suggesting Berlin early on pushed the idea, with the Porte initially responding with skepticism (perhaps from prior disappointment in this regard). Hughes, "The German Mission," 447–450. Adamec, for his part, presents a mixed picture of Enver Pasha's characteristic aggressiveness and Berlin's warming to the plan. Adamec, *Afghanistan,* 83–85. In any case it was not long before the Porte took an active role in organizing their own expedition to Kabul.

92. The Ottoman government's recognition of Naqshabandi and Qaderi notables rallying support for the caliph's jihad, including formal proclamations, is discussed in an exchange between the Porte and the Ottoman ambassador in Tehran. BOA-DH.EUM.7.Şb 2/54 (1333h S 03/1914 12 21). In addition to the Naqshabandi and Qaderi orders, Porte records also mention the Mevlevi order as a transnational connection between Afghans and Turks. BOA-DH.MKT 1985/91 (1310h M 17/1892 08 10); DH.MKT 2017/115 (1310h R 15/1892 11 05). Incidentally, the founder of the order and

world-renowned sufi saint of Konya, Mevlana Jalal al-Din Rumi (1207–1273), is believed to have been born and spent his early life in the area roughly triangulated between Balkh, Afghanistan; Dushanbe, Tajikistan; and Samarqand, Uzbekistan. Franklin Lewis, *Rumi—Past and Present, East and West: The Life, Teachings, and Poetry of Jalal al-Din Rumi* (Oxford: Oneworld, 2007), 647.

93. BOA-DH.EUM.7.Şb 3 / 18.

94. BOA-DH.ŞFR 72 / 177 (1335h R 15 / 1917 02 08); BOA-DH.ŞFR 72 / 230 (1335h R 20 / 1917 02 13).

95. BOA-DH.EUM.5.Şb 69 / 2 (1336h Z 09 / 1918 09 16).

96. BOA-DH.EUM.5.Şb 70 / 17 (1336h Z 24 / 1918 10 01).

97. BOA-HR.SYS 2230 / 50 (1918 06 02).

98. Nawid, *Religious Response*, 40.

99. Others stayed for the duration of the war, as one Ottoman archives document reveals about a certain Hüseyin Hanoğlu Sayyid İsmail. An Ottoman Turk from Izmir, the latter expressed a desire to return to his hometown after supporting the sultan's cause in Afghanistan "for religion and country." BOA-DH.EUM.5.Şb 56 / 36 (1336h C 07 / 1918 03 20). İsmail was granted permission to return to Izmir from Kabul in November 1918. BOA-DH.EUM.5.Şb 57 / 49 (1336h C 29 / 1918 04 11).

100. Saikal, *Modern Afghanistan*, 52, 54. As even the veteran British Indian diplomat and author Sir Percy Molesworth Sykes noted, Habib Allah's neutrality during the Great War aroused a "bitter feeling that Afghanistan had failed Islam in its hour of need." Percy Molesworth Sykes, *A History of Afghanistan* (London: MacMillan, 1940), 2:265.

101. NAI-Foreign-Political / Secret / War / May.1916 / 1–288.

102. Ibid.

103. Bal, "Afganistan-Türkiye," 249; Mehmet Saray, *Afganistan ve Türkler* (Istanbul: İstanbul Üniversitesi Edebiyat Fakültesi Basımevi, 1987), 88–90.

104. Bal, "Afganistan-Türkiye," 249; Saray, *Afganistan ve Türkler*, 88–90.

105. Even after the formal conclusion of hostilities, British agents stationed between the Mediterranean and the Indian Ocean continued to report signs of a lingering "Pan-Islamic intrigue" involving Turkish provocateurs. As late as October 8, 1919, the British consul general at Mashhad, Persia, reported that Kazım Bey, "a Turkish agent in Afghanistan," was spreading a message of economic boycott among Afghan merchants. According to the British consul, said Ottoman official was urging Afghans not to remit money to India, but instead to use Iranian banks based out of Mashhad in their place. NAI-Foreign-Political / Frontier / B / Nov.1919 / 50.

4. CONVERGING CRESCENTS

1. Halil Toker, "Zafer Hasan Aybek ve Afganistan Anıları (1915–1922, 1933–36, 1937)," in *Afganistan Üzerine Araştırmalar*, ed. Ali Ahmetbeyoğlu, 149–176 (Istanbul: Tarih ve Tabiat Vakfı Yayınları, 2001), 161–162.

2. On March 3, 1919, Aman Allah had his uncle Nasr Allah arrested and imprisoned in Kabul on charges of involvement in the late king's murder. Historians continue to debate whether the real assassin was ever found. What is certain is several would-be suspects were rounded up in the aftermath, including an Afghan captain in charge of the king's security detail the night of his assassination; most of them were then quickly tried and executed. Nasr Allah died roughly a year later in captivity. On the fluid aftermath surrounding Habib Allah's murder and subsequent trials and convictions, see Amin Saikal, *Modern Afghanistan: A History of Struggle and Survival* (New York: I. B. Tauris, 2006), 54–55, 262; Thomas Barfield, *Afghanistan: A Cultural and Political History* (Princeton, NJ: Princeton University Press, 2010), 179–180.

3. Toker, "Zafer Hasan Aybek," 161.

4. Saikal, *Modern Afghanistan,* 47–49; Senzil K. Nawid, *Religious Response to Social Change in Afghanistan, 1919–29: King Aman-Allah and the Afghan Ulama* (Costa Mesa, CA: Mazda, 1999), 44.

5. Halil Bal, "Afganistan-Türkiye İlişkilerinin Başlıca Yönleri," in *Afganistan Üzerine Araştırmalar,* ed. Ali Ahmetbeyoğlu, 243–276 (Istanbul: Tarih ve Tabiat Vakfı Yayınları, 2001), 246; Aliye Yılmaz, "Emanullah Han'ın Islahatları ve Atatürk," *Süleyman Demirel Üniversitesi Fen-Edebiyat Fakültesi Sosyal Bilimler Dergisi* 21 (2010): 156.

6. Nawid, *Religious Response,* 49; Saikal, *Modern Afghanistan,* 47–49.

7. The circumstances surrounding Habib Allah's murder remain shrouded in mystery, and theories abound over suspects. In light of the subsequent investigation and trial's speed, to say nothing of the charged and politicized environs in which they took place, the conviction and execution of Captain ʿAli Riza hardly closed the case.

8. Saikal, *Modern Afghanistan,* 60–61; Barfield, *Afghanistan,* 180–182.

9. IOR-R/12/LIB/107 (1928), 13.

10. Ibid.

11. The Third Anglo-Afghan War is the subject of a robust literature in English, not surprisingly of the military history genre. For two opposing but representative examples, see G. N. Molesworth, *Afghanistan 1919: An Account of Operations in the Third Afghan War* (New York: Asia Pub., 1962); S. A. Akhtar Kazmi, *Anglo-Afghan Tussle* (Islamabad: National Book Foundation, 1984). For a contemporaneous account in Ottoman Turkish, see *1919 Afgan-İngiliz Harbi* (Istanbul: Harbiye Umumiye/ Matbaa-i Askariye, 1341/1919–1920).

12. Among the conditions imposed for British "friendship" was a probationary period of six months during which the amir's actions would be subject to the Raj's approval. IOR-R/12/LIB/107, 33–34.

13. NAI-Foreign-Political/Secret/F/Nov.1920/1–582.

14. IOR-R/12/LIB/107, 48.

15. Bal, "Afganistan-Türkiye," 249–250; Mehmet Saray, *Afganistan ve Türkler* (Istanbul: Edebiyat Fakültesi Basımevi, 1987), 91. Before long the Afghans would eventually establish consulates in several European countries, beginning with Britain's chief European rivals: Germany, Russia, and France. Incidentally, a 1923 communiqué from

the Ottoman foreign ministry discusses financial activities of the Afghan consulate in Paris, including the establishment of bank accounts and loans made to Afghans and even Turks abroad, especially in Germany and France. BOA-HR.İM 93/41 (1923 12 27).

16. IOR-R/12/LIB/107, 33–34. Based on correspondence he would later make to the India Office, it seems the British minister at Kabul Sir Richard Machonachie at the time reluctantly agreed with Nadir Khan's cutting remarks. Machonachie had the following to say about the first six months of Aman Allah's reign:

> The Amir thus found his gamble justified. Not only has he, contrary to all expectation, emerged from the war with India without losing his throne, but he was also able to display an official acknowledgement of his independence, which enhanced his prestige and was of great value for propaganda. The war had shown him both his weakness and his strength. For, if his regular troops had been unable to stand against the Indian Army, he had discovered his ability to raise [in] the Frontier tribes a lever of which he was to make full use in subsequent negotiations.

IOR-R/12/LIB/107, 28.

17. Ibid., 48.

18. Emphasis added. IOR/R/12/LIB/8 (1921), 13, 79.

19. IOR-R/12/LIB/107, 37.

20. Ibid., 399–400.

21. Leon B. Poullada and Leila D. J. Poullada, *The Kingdom of Afghanistan and the United States, 1828–1973* (Lincoln, NE: Dageforde, 1995).

22. Bal, "Afganistan-Türkiye," 251. Original British copies of the agreement, with annotated notes in the margins by the British envoy, Sir Henry Dobbs, rests in the India Office records. The marginal notes provide a glimpse of British perspectives and priorities vis-à-vis peace talks with the Afghans, as well as how seriously they took the Afghans on points of tension and what they considered to be bluffs.

23. On the Pan-Islamic dimensions of Aman Allah's political victories of 1919–1921, including their commemoration and political significance for burgeoning nationalist movements in Turkey and India, see *1919 Afgan-İngiliz Harbi*; M. Şükrü Hanioğlu, *Atatürk: An Intellectual Biography* (Princeton, NJ: Princeton University Press, 2011), 120; Nawid, *Religious Response*, 62–67.

24. On the prolific scholarship of Fayz Muhammad Katib Hazara, a Shiʿi Afghan cleric and official court historian to the Kabul court during the Habib Allah and Aman Allah eras, see his recently translated magnum opus, *The History of Afghanistan: Fayẓ Muḥammad Kātib Hazārah's* Sirāj al-tawārīkh, 11 vols., trans. and ed. R. D. McChesney and M. M. Khorrami (Leiden: Brill, 2016).

25. Nawid, *Religious Response,* 69–71.

26. Nawid opts for a four-part division, further segmenting the liberals into moderate-liberal and radical-liberal camps. Nawid, *Religious Response,* 150–151.

27. The rift between Aman Allah and his top general, Nadir Khan, had many potential sources, but the role of the amir's military reforms appears to have been especially divisive. As Poullada notes, "Most of the Afghan army officers, who resented the superior air of the Turks, sided with Nadir Khan, while a number of Aman Allah's civilian officials backed Tarzi. The result was the formation of pro- and anti-Turkish factions and a serious schism in the Aman Allah cabinet which eventually resulted in the complete alienation of Nadir Khan and his influential Musahiban family." Leon B. Poullada, *Reform and Rebellion in Afghanistan: King Aman Allah's Failure to Modernize a Tribal Society* (Ithaca, NY: Cornell University Press, 1973), 116.

28. For a list of major personages in Aman Allah's cabinet not related to judicial reforms, see IOR-R/12/LIB/107, 7.

29. "Enver ve Cemal Paşaların Firarı," *Vakıt,* 28 M 1337h/November 3, 1918; "Eski hükümet erkanının firarı," *Vakıt,* 29 M 1337h/November 4, 1918. Both articles report that Talat, Enver, and Cemal Pashas as well as other prominent unionist officials, including Bahaeedin Şakir, Nazım, Azmi, and Bedri Beys, had also fled the country.

30. Erik J. Zürcher, *Turkey: A Modern History* (London: I. B. Tauris, 1997), 134.

31. Zeki Sarıhan, *Kurtuluş Savaşımız'da Türk-Afgan İlişkileri* (Istanbul: Kaynak, 2002), 67; Zürcher, *Turkey,* 134–135.

32. Zürcher, *Turkey,* 141–142, 147–152; Hanioğlu, *Atatürk,* 92–105.

33. IOR-R/12/LIB/107, 29.

34. Abidin Ünal et al., *Geçmişten Günümüze Türk-Afgan İlişkileri* (Ankara: Genelkurmay Askeri Tarih ve Stratejik Etüt Başkanlığı Yayınları Basimevi, 2009), 36.

35. Ibid., 39.

36. Sarıhan, *Kurtuluş,* 43–44; Ünal et al., *Geçmişten,* 39, 35.

37. Sarıhan, *Kurtuluş,* 43–44.

38. NAI-Foreign-Political/Secret/F/Nov.1920/1–582. Indian Muslims are also reported to have been present at the historic Turkish nationalist congress at Sivas. According to a January 28, 1920, telegram from the British commanding officer for the Black Sea to the commander in chief of India in Delhi, several prominent Indians, including the son of notorious anti-British fugitive of NWFP, ʿAbd al-Rabb, were spotted leaving Sivas for Afghanistan and India via Sulaymaniyah and Baghdad: "It is believed they are on a Pan-Islamic mission from Turkish Nationalists and may be accompanied by certain unknown Afghans, who were lately in touch with Nationalists." The memorandum also reported that more than eighty-five Indians previously posted at the British consular guard at Kirmanshah had deserted to Ottoman lines in 1915. Ibid.

39. See for example TİTE-2448/325/20 (1337h/1919).

40. British intelligence in Constantinople reported that a certain Wali Muhammad Khan, while serving as a librarian at the Ottoman palace, founded a secret Afghan

committee as the city was under Allied occupation. NAI-Foreign-Political / Secret / F / Nov.1920 / 1–582.

41. For a sample of such correspondence from the named archive, see TİTE-2538 / 333 / 6 (1920 08 13); TİTE-2539 / 324 / 30 (1920 12 11); TİTE-2574 / 326 / 30 (1921 07 26); TİTE-2594 / 326 / 21 (1921 10 05); TİTE-2599 / 326 / 20 (1921 10 17); TİTE-2607 / 326 / 11 (1921 11 14); TİTE-2612 / 326 / 12 (1921 12 12). For reprinted letters between Cemal and Kemal at this time, see the Autumn 1945 weekly "Tarihi Mektuplar" (Historic Letters) series in Istanbul's *Tanin* newspaper, including: "Cemal Paşanın Mustafa Kemal Paşa'ya yazdığı mektuplar," *Tanin,* 26 Ocak 1945, 1, 3; "Cemal Paşa M. Kemal Paşa'ya Afganistandaki Ankara mümessilinin değiştirilmesini teklif ediyor," *Tanin,* 3 Şubat 1945, 1, 7; "Cemal Paşa, Afgan Emiri hakkında dolaşan rivayetleri naklediyor," *Tanin,* 31 Ocak 1945, 1, 6.

42. On Abdurrahman Peşaveri's services to the Ottoman army in 1912–1913, see Syed Tanvir Wasti, "The Indian Red Crescent Mission to the Balkan Wars," *Middle Eastern Studies* 45, no. 3 (2009): 393–406. Peşaveri was not alone in this respect. Late Ottoman records report other examples of Afghans and Indian Muslims serving in Turkish nationalist forces during the latter's war of independence, including the revolutionary activist of Punjab and migrant to Kabul, Zafer Hasan Aybek. In another example, a declassified memorandum from the Ottoman foreign ministry of 1920 describes the activities of Elif Khan, an Afghan Harbiye graduate who was commissioned to the European front. BOA-HR.SYS 2464 / 28 (1920 08 19). Afghan contributions to the Turkish war of independence were also not limited to the battlefield. An Ottoman foreign ministry record of 1921, for example, notes a Persian-language article by the Afghan ambassador to Turkey condemning the Greek occupation of Turkish territory. The document states the article was published in an Istanbul magazine. BOA-HR.İM 59 / 31 (1921 12 31).

43. Bilal Şimşir, *Atatürk ve Afganistan* (Ankara: Avrasya Stratejik Araştırmalar Merkezi, 2002), 38–39. On Abdurrahman Peşaveri's Indo-Afghan origins and legacy in Turkey and South Asia, see A. S. Shahjahanpuri, *Ghazi Abdurrahman Peshawari Shaheed* (Karachi: North Western Hotel, 1979).

44. Şimşir, *Atatürk ve Afganistan,* 92. On the Ankara government's financial support to Abdurrahman Peşaveri's legation in Kabul, see BCA-30.18.1.1 / 3 / 31 / 3 / 114–4 (1921 07 29).

45. Ünal et al., *Geçmişten,* 39; Bal, "Afganistan-Türkiye," 256.

46. My translation. Bal, "Afganistan-Türkiye," 256–257. For the TBMM's official instructions to Abdurrahman Peşaveri and Kemal's letters to Aman Allah, see Bilal Şimşir, *Atatürk ve Yabancı Devlet Başkanları* (Ankara: Türk Tarik Kurumu, 1993), 1:5–7, 1:109, 1:111.

47. My translation. Bal, "Afganistan-Türkiye," 257. For original printed versions in Turkish periodicals, see *TBMM Zabıt Ceridesi* 16 (16 Şubat 1922): 282; *Hakimiyet-i Milliye* (17 Şubat 1922); *Tevhid-i Efkar* (18 Şubat 1922); *İkdam* (19 Şubat 1922); *Yeni*

Gün (17 Şubat 1922). After receiving Aman Allah's letter, the TBMM in Ankara followed suit with a written expression of thanks upon receiving the amir's cordial letter and message of solidarity. Bal, "Afganistan-Türkiye," 257.

48. For the official Dari version of the treaty, see ADL-0106 (*Sawad-i Mu'ahadih-'i Dawlatayn-i 'Aliyyatayn Afghanistan wa Turkiyih* [Kabul, 1301j Mizan 26/1922 10 19]). The original Turkish copy of the agreement signed in Moscow on March 1, 1921, rests in the Ottoman central archives in Istanbul. BOA-HSD.AFT 6/101 (1339h B 04/1921 03 14). Declassified records in the Turkish republic archives in Ankara describe the signing of the original agreement in Moscow, and subsequent events to ratify the treaty in both states. On July 21, 1921, the national congress in Ankara endorsed the treaty, bringing it into effect in Turkey. On October 22, 1922, Aman Allah approved the agreement in front of an official gathering at Kabul's 'Idgah mosque. BCA-30.18.1.1/3/29/11 (1921 07 03); BCA-30.10.0.0/257/731/2/435 (1922 11 22).

49. Preamble, ADL-0106.

50. The Turco-Afghan Alliance was intertwined with both countries signing a Soviet pact as well. Reaching Moscow on October 10, 1919, the Afghan delegation was warmly received by Soviet government. Only weeks earlier, the revolutionary Soviet regime had dispatched Michael Bravin as an envoy to Afghanistan, reaching Kabul on September 12, 1919. A succession of diplomatic exchanges and conferences between the Afghans and Soviets in each other's capitals over the next eighteen months would culminate in the signing of the February 28, 1921, Russo-Afghan Agreement. Soviet signatories were Georgy Vasilievich Chichérin and Lyov Mihailovich Karahan; the Afghan signatories, General Wali Khan, Mirza Muhammad Khan, and Ghulam Siddiq Khan. Out of a dozen principles framed by the agreement, the most important were: (1) The Soviet government agreed to assist Afghanistan in meeting its need of weapons, ammunition, and funds; (2) The Afghan and Soviet governments were in full agreement on the freedom and independence of all "Eastern nations"; (3) Both parties accepted the independence and freedom of Bukhara and Khiva, whatever might be the form of their government, in accordance with the wishes of their peoples; and (4) Afghan borderlands seized by Russia in the previous era (since 1885) would be returned to Afghanistan. Bal, "Afganistan-Türkiye," 250–251; Saray, *Afganistan ve Türkler,* 95. That the Ankara government took a deep interest in the Russo-Afghan agreement is evident in correspondence concerning the treaty's translation into Turkish. BCA-30.18.1.1/7/14/7/435–5 (1923 03 27). Letters exchanged between Cemal, Kemal, and Enver at the time also signify the great importance the Turkish national government gave to the agreement. See for example "Ruslar Afgan muahedenamesinden henüz haberdar olmadıklarını bildirdiler," *Tanin,* 4 İkinciteşrin 1944, 1, 3; "Rusların yeni Sefaret Başkatibi Rosenberg, Moskovada hükümetçe tastik edilmiş Rus-Afgan muahedesini Kabile getirdi," *Tanin,* 9 Ocak 1945, 1, 3; "Efgan Hariciye Nazırı muahede hakkında görüşmek üzere Rus sefirini davet edecekti," *Tanin,* 10 Ocak 1945, 1, 6; "Cemal Paşa'ya Efgan Emirine Rus muahedesini tastik etmesini

söylüyor," *Tanin,* 12 Ocak 1945, 1, 3. Similarly, Turkish newspapers also followed Kabul's relations with Afghanistan's other neighbors, Iran and India, just as closely. See for example "İran-Afganistan Muahedesi," *Yeni Kafkasya* 9 (1924): 12–13; "Iran ve Afganistan: iki İslam hükümet arasında münasebet"; *Yeni Gün,* 25 C 1340h / February 23, 1922; "Hind Hilafet Komitesinin Dört Kararı," *Hakmiyet-i Milli,* 15 L 1341h / May 31, 1923. On the Afghan mission to Paris, see "Afganistan'ın Paris sefireyle mülakat," *Tevhid-i Evkar,* 11 C 1340 / February 9, 1922.

51. Article 6, ADL-0106.

52. BCA-30.18.1.1 / 6 / 42 / 19 / 114–13 (1922 12 31). On April 25, 1921, in his capacity as head of the Turkish national movement, Kemal welcomed the establishment of the Afghan embassy in a letter to the newly appointed Afghan ambassador in Ankara. Ünal et al., *Geçmişten,* 41. A December 1922 document in the Turkish Republic archives describes Ahmad's energetic presence in Anatolia, citing his desire to tour the peninsula, especially the western coast and areas bordering Greece. BCA-30.10.0.0 / 131 / 936 / 7 / 114 (1922 12 22). The Ottoman newspaper *Hakmiyet-i Milli* also took an interest in the Afghan ambassador and his arrival in Ankara. See for example "Afgan sefiri," *Hakmiyet-i Milli,* N 22 1341h / May 8, 1923. Turkish press interest in visiting Afghan delegations was not new, of course. *Sebilürreşad,* the Istanbul journal established by the renowned Turkish poet and Muslim modernist thinker Mehmet Akif Ersoy (1873–1936), closely followed an earlier Afghan delegation's visit to Turkey, including a meeting with the Ottoman sultan-caliph, Reşad V. See for example Eşref Edib, "S. Reşat Heyetinin Afgan Sefirini Ziyareti," *Sebilürreşad* 19 / 478 (1921): 101–102; Mirza Ahmed Han, "Afgan Sefiri Hazretlerinin Mütalaat-ı Fazilaneleri," *Sebilürreşad* 19 / 487 (1921): 212. The Afghan ambassador to Ankara would later publish an article in the same periodical. See Sultan Ahmed, "Uhuvvet-i İslamiye: Afghanistan Sefiri Hz. nin Tebrikatı," *Sebilürreşad* 20 / 517 (1922): 274–275. For additional examples of publications on Afghanistan in the same journal, see Zeydan Effendi, "Afganistan'da Hareket-i İlmiye," *Sebilürreşad* 20 / 509 (1922): 172–174, about "scientific progress" being made in Afghanistan. A similar theme is presented in the Turkish journal of economics, "Afganistan'ın İktisadi Vaziyeti," *Türkiye İktisad Mecmuası* 14 (1923): 6–7.

53. My translation. Portions of speeches delivered on this occasion can be found in Ünal et al., *Geçmişten,* 43 and Şimşir, *Atatürk ve Afganistan,* 66–67.

54. My translation. Ünal et al., *Geçmişten,* 43. See also Şimşir, *Atatürk ve Afganistan,* 66–67; Sarıhan, *Kurtuluş,* 151.

55. Şimşir, *Atatürk ve Afganistan,* 68–78; Ünal et al., *Geçmişten,* 44–45.

56. See for example ADL-0302 (Muhammad Nazif, *Kitab-i Alifba-yi Turki* [Kabul: Nizarat-i Maʿarif, 1339h / 1920–1921]); ADL-0274 (Muhammad Nazif, *Sarf-i Turki* [Kabul: Matbaʿ-ʾi ʿInayat, 1336 / 1917]); ADL-0275 (Muhammad Nazif, *Qiraʾat-i Asar* [Kabul: Matbaʿ-ʾi ʿInayat, 1336 / 1917]); ADL-0602 (Mahmud Sami, *Mukhtasar magar Mukammal: Sarf wa Nahwi Farsi bih Tarz-i Jadid* [Kabul: Matbaʿ-ʾi Maktab-i Funun-i Harbiyyih, 1301 / 1922]).

57. Salim Cöhce, "Atatürk Döneminde Afganistan ile İlişkiler ve İngiltere," in *Afganistan Üzerine Araştırmalar,* ed. Ali Ahmetbeyoğlu (Istanbul: Tarih ve Tabiat Vakfı Yayınları, 2001), 135; Ünal et al., *Geçmişten,* 40. The 1921 Turco-Afghan Friendship Treaty therefore constituted one of Kemal's earliest achievements in the international diplomatic field for the nascent Turkish republic. The agreement was not free, however, from controversy. Article 3, which describes Turkey as "the seat of the Caliphate" and "a leader to be followed," would become a point of contention in Afghanistan after Turkey's abolition of the caliphate in 1924. The full article states, "The Sublime State of Afghanistan recognizes the leadership of Turkey, in light of having rendered distinguished services to Islam for centuries, and holding in her hand the standard of the Caliphate" (my translation).

58. In another example of Ottoman officers arriving in Kabul after World War I, Aman Allah wrote to Kemal that three Turkish officers who had been taken prisoner by the tsarist Russian army had entered Afghanistan via Bukhara after the armistice. Aman Allah stated that said officers—Ziya Bey, Rıfat Bey, and Hüseyin Cahit Effendi—had escaped Russian captivity and offered their services to the amir. Having accepted the Turks' offer, the amir proceeded to describe how pleased he was with their service. Aman Allah used the eventual return of said officers to Anatolia to deliver additional letters to Ankara. This time Aman Allah reiterated his desire for a larger and more robust Turkish commission to be sent to Afghanistan to help reorganize and train a new Afghan army. Şimşir, *Atatürk ve Afganistan,* 68–78; Ali Fuat Cebesoy, *Moskova Hatıraları* (Ankara: Kültür ve Turizm Bakalığı, 1982), 61–63; Şevket Süreyya Aydemir, *Makedonya'dan Orta Asya'ya Enver Paşa* (Istanbul: Remzi, 1985), 3:530–531; Zeki Velidi Togan, *Bugünkü Türk İli Türkistan ve Yakın Tarihi* (Istanbul: Enderun Yayınlari 1981), 2:424–429.

59. Ünal et al., *Geçmişten,* 36–37; Sarıhan, *Kurtuluş,* 77.

60. On Cemal's ignominious legacies during the Great War, including his summary executions of Arab dissidents in Syria and widely suspected role in the deportations and massacres of Ottoman Armenians, see Hasan Kayalı, *Arabs and Young Turks: Ottomanism, Arabism, and Islamism in the Ottoman Empire, 1908–1918* (Berkeley: University of California Press, 1997), 176–77, 192–196; Zürcher, *Turkey,* 114–117; and most critically, Taner Akçam, *The Young Turks' Crime against Humanity* (Princeton, NJ: Princeton University Press, 2013), and Ronald Gregory Suny, *"They Can Live in the Desert but Nowhere Else": A History of the Armenian Genocide* (Princeton, NJ: Princeton University Press, 2015).

61. For Ziya's Bey's twelve-week instruction booklet for Afghan military trainers, see ADL-0309 (*Prughram-i 12-Haftih bara-yi Taʿlim-i Tarbiyyih-ʾi Munfaridih* [Kabul?: 192?]). Originally composed in Ottoman Turkish, the work was translated into Dari by Muhammad Amin between 1920 and 1922.

62. Ünal et al., *Geçmişten,* 36–38.

63. The amir asked that the Ottoman officers front their own expenses until reaching Baku. The Afghan government was to cover all costs of the delegation's

remaining journey to Kabul, where they would be honored as distinguished public servants of the Afghan state. Ünal et al., *Geçmişten,* 37–38, Şimşir, *Atatürk ve Afganistan,* 44–45. For Cemal's letters to Kemal requesting officers, weapons, and supplies be sent to Afghanistan, see "Cemal Paşa, Afganistana on kişilik bir zabit heyetinin gönderilmesini istiyordu," *Tanin,* 27 Ocak 1945, 1, 6; "Cemal Paşa, Afganistana yeni bir zabit heyetinin daha gönderilmesini isliyor," *Tanin,* 2 Şubat 1945, 1, 3; "Cemal Paşa, Afganistana silah ve teçhizat gönderilmesinde ısrar ediyordu," *Tanin,* 6 Ocak 1945, 1, 6. On the triangular correspondence between Enver, Cemal, and Kemal during this period more generally, see Masayuki Yamauchi, *The Green Crescent under the Red Star: Enver Pasha in Soviet Russia, 1919–1922* (Tokyo: Institute for the Study of Languages and Cultures of Asia and Africa, 1991).

64. Toker, "Zafer Hasan Aybek," 169; Bal, "Afganistan-Türkiye," 252.

65. Cebesoy, *Moskova Hatıraları,* 61–63; Aydemir, *Makedonya'dan,* 3:530–531.

66. My translation. Ünal et al., *Geçmişten,* 36–37; Sarıhan, *Kurtuluş,* 77; Bal, "Afganistan-Türkiye," 252.

67. My translation. Cöhce, "Atatürk Döneminde Afganistan," 111–112; Ünal et al., *Geçmişten,* 37; Bal, "Afganistan-Türkiye," 253–254.

68. Ünal et al., *Geçmişten,* 38; Şimşir, *Atatürk ve Afganistan,* 53; Sarıhan, *Kurtuluş,* 92.

69. IOR-R/12/LIB/107, 45. Ünal et al., *Geçmişten,* 38; Şimşir, *Atatürk ve Afganistan,* 53; Sarıhan, *Kurtuluş,* 92. On Cemal's covert mission after leaving Kabul, including his use of a pseudonym while seeking entry to Europe from Russia, see TİTE-2605/326/17 (1921 10 10); TİTE-2607/326/11 (1921 10 14); TİTE-2612/326/12 (1921 12 12); TİTE-2599/326/20 (1921 10 17).

70. "Amanı Afgan Cemal Paşanın gelmesini pek manidar bir lisan ile ilan ediyor," *Tanin* 1, Şubat 1945, 1, 6; "Kabilde bulunan Türkler şerefine Hariciye Nezaretinde bir ziyafet tertip olunuyor," *Tanin,* 13 Ocak 1945, 1, 6. Cemal's emphasis on Afghanistan as a site of anticolonial struggle owed in large part to the country's proximity and complex relationship with British India. See for example "Cemal Paşa, Pamir yaylasından, ihtilal kıtaatı ile Hindistana akınlar yapmağı kararlaştırmıştı," *Tanin,* 3 Ocak 1945, 1, 6; "Efgan Emiri Cemal Pasanın ihtilal ve Hindistana taaruz projesini kabul ediyor," *Tanin,* 8 Ocak 1945, 1, 3; "Cemal Paşa, Hindistan ihtilalini kendine gaye edinmişti," *Tanin,* 30 Birincikanun 1944, 1, 6; "Cemal Paşa'ya göre Afganistan Hint ihtilaline nasıl yardım edebilir," *Tanin,* 15 Ocak 1945, 1, 3. Nearly three decades after Cemal's death, no less an observer than Zafer Hasan Aybek, the Indian revolutionary who migrated to Anatolia and adopted Turkish citizenship after World War I, published an article on the intertwining of Afghanistan and India in Cemal's revolutionary politics. Zafer Hasan Aybek, "Cemal Paşa; Afganistan'ın teşkilatanma ve Hindistan meseleleri," *Resimli Tarih Mecmuası* 7 (1950): 260–263.

71. Toker, "Zafer Hasan Aybek,",170; Saray, *Afganistan ve Türkler,* 111.

72. Bal, "Afganistan-Türkiye," 255.

73. Toker, "Zafer Hasan Aybek," 255; "Afganistan ve Cemal Paşa," *İkdam*, 18 Teşrinievvel 1922; Cebesoy, *Moskova Hatıraları*, 370–378; Saray, *Afganistan ve Türkler*, 104–110; Hülya Baykal, "Milli Mücadele Yıllarında Mustafa Kemal Paşa ile Cemal Paşa Arasındaki Yazışmalar," *Atatürk Araştırma Merkezi Dergesi* 5 (1989): 379–381; Ünal et al., *Geçmişten*, 38; Zeki Sarıhan, *Kurtuluş Savaşı Günlüğü, IV* (Ankara: Türk Tarih Kurumu, 1996), 147, 213. Likely frustrated at the slow response from Ankara, from this point on Cemal's letters reflect a closer engagement with his work in Afghanistan. "Cemal Paşa Efganistandaki mücadeleleri," *Tanin*, 7 Ocak 1945, 1, 6; "Cemal Paşa Afganistan'da iyi bir mevki kazanmış, ciddi ve esaslı bir surette çalışmaya başlamıştı," *Tanin*, 18 İkinciteşrin 1944, 1, 3; "Cemal Paşa Efganistan'da bir ordu ve bir devlet teşkiliyle meşgüldü," *Tanin*, 26 İkinciteşrin 1944, 1, 3; "Cemal Paşa Efganistan'da yapmak tasavvurunda olduğu işlerianlatıyor," *Tanin*, 25 Birincikanun 1944, 1, 3.

74. Ünal et al., *Geçmişten*, 38; Sarıhan, *Kurtuluş Savaşı*, 147, 213.

75. Aybek, "Cemal Paşa"; Bal, "Afganistan-Türkiye," 171. For the same reasons Cemal also dispatched letters to Enver seeking men and supplies to be directed to Kabul, even as the latter was occupied in a nascent campaign against the Soviets in Central Asia. "Enver Paşa Afganistan'a dışarından malzeme getirmenin imkansız olduğuna kaniydi." *Tanin*, 30 Birinciteşrin 1944, 1, 7; "Enver Paşa, Afganistan'da bulunan Cemal Paşa'ya teşkilat için rehber gönderiyor," *Tanin*, 5 İkinciteşrin 1944, 1, 6.

76. On the last stands of Cemal and Enver in Central Asia, see Toker, "Zafer Hasan Aybek," 255–256; Aydemir, *Makedonya'dan*, 3:641–647; Saray, *Afganistan ve Türkler*, 114; Ünal et al., *Geçmişten*, 39; Sarıhan, *Kurtuluş Savaşı*, 503. For his last attributed letter to the nationalist resistance in Anatolia, see "Cemal Paşanın yazdığı en son mektup," *Tanin*, 17 Ocak 1945, 1, 6. An August 12, 1922 memorandum describes the Ankara government granting permission for his burial in Turkey. BCA-30.10.0.0/204/392/17/245 (1922 08 12).

77. IOR-R/12/LIB/107, 119.

78. *Aman-i Afghan*, 15 Mizan 1301/October 7, 1922.

79. IOR-R/12/LIB/107, 119.

80. Ünal et al., *Geçmişten*, 39; Şimşir, *Atatürk ve Afganistan*, 357.

81. IOR-R/12/LIB/107, 119.

82. BOA-HR.İM 20/162 (1923 08 30).

83. As several of Cemal's letters illustrate, among their key differences of opinion were decisions over the kinds and pace of domestic reforms to be prioritized in Afghanistan. See for example "Cemal Paşa'ya Afgan Hariciye Nazırının siyasetini tenkit etmişti," *Tanin*, 11 Ocak 1945, 1, 6; "Cemal Paşanın Afgan Hariciye Nazırına yazdığı tezkere," *Tanin*, 14 Ocak 1945, 1, 6.

84. Fahreddin Pasha's exploits during Sharif Husayn's nearly three year siege of Medina from June 1916 to January 1919—among the longest in recorded history—are the subject of several works in Turkish. Among the deeds for which Fahreddin has been lionized as the last Ottoman commander of Medina was the weight he placed

on protecting the hallowed grounds of the Prophet's mosque and adjoining Jannat al-Baqiʿ cemetery, and his refusal to hand over the sacred city to Husayn's forces even after orders came from Istanbul commanding him to do so. Naci Kaşif Kiciman, *Medine Müdafaası: Hicaz bizden nasıl ayrıldı?* (Istanbul: Sebil Yayınları, 1971); Feridun Kandemir, *Medine Müdafaası: Peygamberimizin Gölgesinde Son Türkler* (Istanbul: Yağmur Yayınları, 2010); İsmail Bilgin, *Medine Müdafaası: Çöl Kaplanı Fahreddin Paşa* (Istanbul: Timas Yayınları, 2009). In English, see Elie Kedourie, *Islam in the Modern World* (London, 1980), 277–296; S. Tanvir Wasti, "The Defence of Medina, 1916–1919," *Middle Eastern Studies* 27, no. 4 (1991): 642–653; Martin Strohmeier, "Fakhri (Fahreddin) Paşa and the End of Ottoman Rule in Medina (1916–1919)," *Turkish Historical Review* 4, no. 2 (2013): 192–223. For an alternative view of the siege, see Alia El Bakri, "'Memories of the Beloved': Oral Histories from the 1916–19 Siege of Medina," *IJMES* 46, no. 4 (2014): 703–718. For a brief biography of the late Ottoman and early Republic official, see Süleyman Yatak, "Fahreddin Paşa," in *Türkiye Diyanet Vakfı İslam Ansiklopedisi* (Istanbul: TDV İslam Araştırmaları Merkezi, 2013). For his multiple decorations and honors from the Ottoman government, see BOA-İ.DUİT 151/38 (1334h N 16/1916 07 17); BOA-İ.DUİT 69/10 (1335 R 11/1917 02 04); BOA-İ.DUİT 154/4 (1335h Ca 12/1917 03 06); BOA-İ.DUİT 17/42 (1337h Ra 25/1918 12 29).

85. In this respect Fahreddin poses a stark contrast to Enver and Cemal, and a host of other top CUP officials accused of war crimes during World War I. Declassified British wartime intelligence records from London to Delhi—hardly places for flattering the Turks—indicate Fahreddin earned the respect, even admiration, of his wartime opponents. A secret handbook composed by the British Admiralty War Staff's Intelligence Division on the Ottoman leadership in 1916, for its part, described General Fahreddin as a "quiet, studious soldier," "Nationalist, but not Union and Progress," and even "a good man" with "moderate views." IOR-L/PS/20/C132 (1916), 17. Eight years later, the British minister in Kabul Sir Robert Machonachie would write in a letter to the secretary of state for foreign affairs in London that the newly formed Ankara government had made "an excellent selection" in appointing their former wartime adversary Fahreddin as the Turkish republic's first official ambassador to Afghanistan. The same letter describes Fahreddin as "the heroic defender of Medina." NAI-Foreign-Political/Secret/External/477(2)-X/1922–1923 (No. 6328 Ext.A). Still, by the end of Fahreddin's tenure as Turkish charge d'affairs in 1926, Machonachie could not spare the ambassador from censure, describing him as "an Anglophobe to the verge of mania." IOR-R/12/LIB/107, 119.

86. Symbolizing his role as a late Ottoman "transitional," official records of Fahreddin's ambassadorial service in Kabul are housed at Turkey's republican archives in Ankara, rather than the Ottoman central archives in Istanbul. On Fahreddin's official appointment as ambassador to Kabul, and Ankara's preparations for the mission's costs and daily allowances in Afghanistan, see BCA-30.18.1.1/3/34/4/107–4 (1921 10 27);

BCA-30.18.1.1 / 4 / 43 / 3 (1922 01 01); BCA-30.18.1.1 / 4 / 48 / 4 (1922 02 15); BCA-30.18.1.1 / 4 / 50 / 11 (1922 02 26); BCA-30.18.1.1 / 6 / 49 / 5 / 51–16 (1923 02 04).

87. A declassified memorandum from the North-West Frontier Province intelligence bureau of late January 1923, "Remittances to Angora by the Central Khilafat Committee, Bombay of Funds Collected in India for Ghazi Mustafa Kemal Pasha," presents us with one such example of republican "Pan-Islamism" in Kabul under the auspices of Fahreddin's embassy. The file includes a copy of Fahreddin's acknowledgment of Rs. 12,350 received from Indian Muslims. This donation was submitted to the Afghan consul at Bombay, on account of the "Angora Fund," an Indian Muslim fundraising campaign in support of the Ottoman caliphate and the Turkish war of independence. At the time, these were intertwined and inseparable goals to the CKC in India. In acknowledging receipt of the funds, Fahreddin congratulated and expressed appreciation to the Indian Muslims for "carrying on Jihad for centuries." The Turkish ambassador also added that he would promptly forward the money to Ankara, and furnish a receipt when the funds reached their intended destination in Turkey. NAI-Foreign-Political / Secret / External / 1923 / 669-X / 1–38.

88. IOR-R / 12 / LIB / 107, 119.

89. BCA-30.18.1.1 / 4 / 52 / 1 / 39–28 (1922 03 08). For rare images of Fahreddin's activities in Kabul, see Ömer Faruk Şerifoğlu, "Kabil'de Yangın Söndüren İki Türk: Medine Müdafii Fahreddin Paşa'nın Afganistan yılları," *Toplumsal Tarih* 16, no. 95 (2001): 6–8 and Ayşe Çavdar, "Türk Paşası Afganistan'da," *Atlas* 115 (2002): 138–150.

90. *WWA* (1930), 1.

91. NAI-Foreign-Political / Secret / External / 477(2)-X / 1922–1923 (No. 7277 Ext.A).

92. NAI-Foreign-Political / Secret / External / 477(2)-X / 1922–1923 (No. 6328 Ext.A).

93. Ibid.

94. Ibid.

95. Ibid.

96. Ibid.

97. My translation. Bal, "Afganistan-Türkiye,", 253–254.

98. As a sharp contrast from their World War I hostilities, by mid-1923 British and Turkish governments were resuming more regular exchanges and diplomatic ties in ways that began to resemble the prewar era. A pair of declassified records from the Ottoman foreign ministry in Istanbul dating to 1923—and hence some of the last ever produced by this office—provide telling examples. The first describes how the Turkish ministry of foreign affairs had taken the courtesy of asking the British consulate in Istanbul whether they had permission to send encrypted telegraphs, using the Eastern Telegraph Company—a British multinational communications services company—from Peshawar to their own Turkish representative in Kabul. BOA-BEO

HR.İM 86/11 (1923 10 15). Sir Nevile Henderson (1882–1942), interim British High Commissioner in Constantinople, responded that the Foreign Office had informed the Turkish minister that they saw no problem with the Eastern Telegraph Company transmitting the dispatches, provided the transmission charges for the mails in question were prepaid in Istanbul, not in Peshawar. Similarly, in the summer of 1923 the Turkish foreign ministry submitted a formal inquiry to British authorities in India as to whether the latter allow Fahreddin Pasha's family to disembark at Bombay en route to joining the Turkish chargé d'affaires in Kabul. British officials informed the Turkish ministry of foreign affairs in Ankara that Fahreddin's family would be allowed to disembark in safety at Bombay, provided they presented their passports to the British consulate general in Istanbul for visas before departing for India. BOA-HR.İM 77/74 (1923 07 05); BOA-HR.İM 80/2 (1923 08 05); BOA-HR.İM 81/52 (1923 08 22).

99. Emblematic of both change and continuity in Turco-Afghan ties during this period was a late 1924 memorandum from the Afghan embassy in Turkey to the Ankara government. The communiqué begins and ends with customary diplomatic respects and compliments to Turkish officials, but is devoid of the longstanding Islamic convention of offering salutations and prayers to the Ottoman sultan-caliph in Istanbul—an office that no longer existed by that time. BOA-HR.İM 119/6 (1924 10 01).

100. Gail Minault, *The Khilafat Movement: Religious Symbolism and Political Mobilization in India* (New York: Columbia University Press, 1982), 106–107.

101. Dietrich Reetz, *Hijrat: The Flight of the Faithful, a British File on the Exodus of Muslim Peasants from North India to Afghanistan in 1920* (Berlin: Arbeitshefte, 1995), 9.

102. The classical terms *Dar al-Harb* (lit., Abode of War) and *Dar al-Islam* (Abode of Islam, or Abode of Peace) have often been misconstrued to refer to perpetual war against non-Muslims on the one hand, and a utopian Islamic society on the other, neither of which bears resonance with the writings of classical jurists, particularly of the Hanafi and Shafi'i schools. Such Manichean views overlook the considerable debates between ulema over the necessary conditions for applying either term in practice. As some late Hanafi jurists maintained, if even a few ordinances of the shari'a were upheld by a government—any government, that is—lands under non-Muslim rule could still be considered *Dar al-Islam*. Similarly, according to the classical political theorist and Shafi'i jurist of Baghdad Abu al-Hasan al-Mawardi (972–1058), the ability to openly practice one's religion rendered a territory *Dar al-Islam*, not the demographics of the population or religious adherence of its rulers. Muhammad Qasim Zaman, *The Ulama in Contemporary Islam* (Princeton, NJ: Princeton University Press, 2002), 36. See also Khaled Abou El Fadl, "Islamic Law and Muslim Minorities: The Juristic Discourse on Muslim Minorities from the Second/Eighth to the Eleventh/Seventeenth Centuries," *Islamic Law and Society* 1, no. 2 (1994): 141–187; *Encyclopaedia Iranica* (1993), s.v. "Dar-al-Harb." In a shift from the classical consensus as articulated by al-Mawardi, beginning in the late eighteenth century some prominent ulema of the subcontinent, including hadith scholar Shah 'Abd al-'Aziz

Dihlavi (1746–1824), argued that India transformed to *Dar al-Harb* when the East India Company usurped the Mughal emperor's de facto administration of territory, replacing the supremacy of the shari'a with British rule. Barbara Metcalf, *Islamic Reform in British India: Deoband, 1860–1900* (Princeton, NJ: Princeton University Press, 1982), 50–52; M. Naeem Qureshi, *Pan-Islam in British Indian Politics* (Leiden: Brill, 1999), 17–18, 174–178. This remained a heavily contested position, however, for the duration of British rule in India. For ongoing scholarly debates on this issue through the Indian independence and Pakistan movement struggles, see Zaman, *The Ulama in Contemporary Islam,* 17–38, 87–110.

103. The 1920–1921 Hijrat movement was not the first example of Indian Muslim migration to Afghanistan in the modern era. As described in Fayz Muhammad's epic six-volume *Siraj al-Tawarikh,* and noted by Robert D. McChesney, a component of 'Abd al-Rahman's policies of ethnic cleansing and internal displacement was to colonize Hazara Shi'i lands and resettle them with ethnic Pashtun muhājirs from India's northwest frontier. See for example Fayz Muhammad Katib Hazarah, *The History of Afghanistan,* vol. 3, *The Reign of Amir 'Abd al-Rahmān Khān,* ed. and trans. R. D. McChesney and M. M. Khorrami (Leiden: Brill, 2012), 15–18 ("Events of 1310 / 1892–1893," 984–987, in original Persian manuscript).

104. Qureshi, *Pan-Islam,* 181.

105. Allah Bakhsh Yusufi, *Maulana Mohamed Ali Jauhar* (Karachi: Mohammad Ali Educational Society, 1980), 295–296.

106. Historian A. C. Niemeijer, author of a study on the muhājirs, writes that "They were stimulated by a declaration from the Amir of Afghanistan, who promised them an asylum in his country and every kind of help." A. C. Niemeijer, *The Khilafat Movement in India, 1919–1924* (Hague: Martinus Nihjoff, 1972).

107. In the absence of an all-Indian Muslim sovereign akin to the Mughal emperor, Aman Allah filled a political vacuum left by the dethronement and exile of the last Mughal emperor, Bahadur Shah II, in 1857. While Aman Allah's virtual wardenship may have been welcomed by some Indian Muslims, it was likely more disconcerting to the Khilafat movement's many Hindu supporters, stoking memories of Turkic and Afghan invasions in earlier centuries. Ibid.

108. Qureshi, *Pan-Islam,* 181–182.

109. Scott C. Levi, *The Indian Diaspora in Central Asia and Its Trade, 1550–1900* (Leiden: Brill, 2002).

110. Annemarie Schimmel, *The Empire of the Great Mughals: History, Art and Culture* (London: Reaktion, 2004). Hailing from the Fergana Valley, Babur and the Mughal dynasty he founded present a complicated example of "Indian" rule over Afghanistan in light of their Turkic origins. Similarly, our period of study focuses on Ottoman Turks, but we should not forget the profound impact of the earlier Timurid dynasty (1370–1507), a Turkic empire that ruled over much of today's eastern Afghanistan, including a splendid capital in Herat.

111. The exact number of migrants is debated by historians. Citing widely varying sources of the Afghan and British Indian governments, as well as the oral histories of the migrants themselves, estimates range from eighteen thousand to a hundred and twenty thousand to as high as two million. In two studies of the movement citing a variety of British government and Indian Muslim anjuman sources, Naeem Qureshi estimates a conservative but more reliable number of sixty thousand. Qureshi, *Pan-Islam,* 230–231; M. Naeem Qureshi, "The Ulama of British India and the Hijrat Movement of 1920," *Modern Asian Studies* 13, no. 1 (1979): 41–59. See also Reetz, *Hijrat,* 52–53.

112. IOR-R/12/LIB/107, 270.

113. Qureshi, *Pan-Islam,* 182.

114. IOR-R/12/LIB/107, 40.

115. Qureshi, *Pan-Islam,* 190–191. For the revised version of Kabul's policy on muhājirs, including provisions for homes and access to medical care, see ADL-0104 (*Nizamnamih-'i Muhajirin* [Kabul: Matba'-'i Da'irih-'i Tahrirat-i Majlis-i 'Ali-yi Wuzara, 1302j/1923]).

116. Qureshi, *Pan-Islam,* 190–191.

117. Ibid., 181–182, 190–191.

118. IOR-R/12/LIB/107, 31.

119. Qureshi, *Pan-Islam,* 190–191.

120. IOR-R/12/LIB/107, 31. See also, Minault, *The Khilafat Movement,* 106–107.

121. Qureshi, *Pan-Islam,* 190–191. As Qureshi notes, even these estimates were inaccurate, as many of the migrants traveled without the assistance of Hijrat committees in India or without notifying Afghan authorities altogether.

122. Qureshi, *Pan-Islam,* 190–191.

123. Ibid., 216.

124. IOR-R/12/LIB/107, 31; Ludwig W. Adamec, *Afghanistan, 1900–1923* (Berkeley: University of California Press, 1967), 110; Qureshi, *Pan-Islam,* 215.

125. Reetz, *Hijrat,* 32.

126. On the "Janus-faced" dimensions of Pan-Islamism more broadly, especially in the late Ottoman Empire, see Lâle Can and Michael Christopher Low, "The 'Subjects' of Ottoman International Law," *JOTSA* 3, no. 2 (2016): 223–234, 228.

127. IOR-R/12/LIB/107, 29.

128. For an illustrative series of social biographies on some of the leading Indian Khilafatists and their times, see Syed Tanvir Wasti, "The Political Aspirations of Indian Muslims and the Ottoman Nexus," *Middle Eastern Studies* 42, no. 5 (2006): 709–722; Wasti, "The Circles of Maulana Mohamed Ali," *Middle Eastern Studies* 38, no. 4 (2002): 51–62; Wasti, "Mushir Hosain Kidwai and the Ottoman Cause," *Middle Eastern Studies* 30, no. 2 (1994): 252–261.

129. The Jam'iyat-i 'Ulama'-i Hind held its first conference at Amritsar on December 28, 1919, presided over by 'Abd al-Bari of Firangi Mahal as the organization's first president. In addition to demanding the British release of Shaykh al-

Hind Mahmud al-Hasan (still interned at Malta) and Abul Kalam Azad, decisions to endorse the Noncooperation movement were launched during spring and summer 1920, including additional fatwas prohibiting Muslim patronage of British courts and government institutions. Qureshi, *Pan-Islam,* 133–135; Minault, *The Khilafat Movement,* footnote 59.

130. Qureshi, *Pan-Islam,* 7. In his survey history of Muslims in British India, Peter Hardy challenges the notion of uniformity of purpose among the leaders and rank-and-file participants of the Khilafat movement. "It would be wrong indeed," Hardy warns, "to believe that all Muslims who supported the Khilafat movement were imbued with the same ideas and purposes." Peter Hardy, *Partners in Freedom and True Muslims: The Political Thought of Some Muslim Scholars in British India, 1912–1947* (Westport, CT: Greenwood, 1971), 191. See also R. K. Sinha, *The Turkish Question: Mustafa Kemal and Mahatma Gandhi* (Delhi: Adam, 1994).

131. Minault, *The Khilafat Movement,* 208–212.

132. Qureshi, *Pan-Islam,* 146.

133. BCA-30.10.0.0 / 200 / 365 / 1 / 239 (1920 07 10); TİTE-2568 / 333 / 43 (1921 07 15).

134. Qureshi, *Pan-Islam,* 101. ʿAbd al-Bari procured the fatwa by following traditional methods of *istiftaʾ*, albeit with some additional twists. First, he submitted a request for scholarly opinion on the question of the Khilafat movement to a group of ten eminent Deobandi scholars constituting the Anjuman-i Muʿid al-Islam (Association for the Aid of Islam). The scholars comprised Shaykh al-Hind Mahmud al-Hasan, Sayyid Husayn Ahmad Madani, Ahmad Saʿid Dihlavi, Kifayat Allah Dihlavi, Muhammad Naʿim Ludhiyanvi, Ahmad ʿAli Lahori, Bashir Ahmad Bhatta, Sayyid Gul Badsha, Hifz al-Rahman Seoharvi, and ʿAbd al-Bari Firangi Mahali. Ibid.

135. Qureshi, *Pan-Islam,* 101.

136. Ibid., 101, 122. What is more, ʿAbd al-Bari's initiative established a model for the formation of the profoundly influential pan-Indian Muslim scholarly council, Jamʿiyat-i ʿUlamaʾ-i Hind. Founded in November 1919 at the genesis of the Khilafat and Noncooperation movements, the organization represented the reinvigorated political activism of ʿAbd al-Bari and other eminent Indian Islamic scholars, including Abul Kalam Azad, ʿAbd al-Majid Badaʾuni, Daʿud Ghaznavi, Shabbir Ahmad ʿUsmani, and Hifz al-Rahman. Hardy, *Partners in Freedom,* 31. Though stopping short of a "constitution" for the Indian Muslim community, in subsequent decades the organization would serve to galvanize and mobilize scores of Indian ulema to instrumentalize their scholarly authority and throw their weight behind the most pressing issues facing Muslims for the remainder of British rule in the subcontinent (and in the Republic of India until the present day). Ibid., 31–32. It also established a model for a subsequent Afghan scholars' association with similar aims. See for example the founding charter of the Jamʿiyat-i al-ʿUlamaʾ-i Afghanistan (Association of Islamic Scholars of Afghanistan), ADL-0659 (*Maramnamih wa Surat-i Tadwir-i Majlis-i Jamʿiyat-i al-ʿUlamaʾ-i Afghanistan* [Kabul: Matbaʿ-ʾi ʿUmumi, 1308j / 1929]).

137. NAI / Foreign-Political / External / Secret / B / May.1920 / 816–817.

138. On Afghan official views of Sharif Husayn's rebellion and claims to rule in Hejaz, note the scathing editorial articles in Kabul's *Aman-i Afghan* criticizing "British-manufactured sultans." For sample articles that caused particular concern to the British intelligence in this regard, see NAI-Foreign / External / A / 1923 / 477-X.

139. Meanwhile, Indian Muslim delegations to Anatolia signaled a growing recognition in the subcontinent of Mustafa Kemal as the de facto representative of the Turkish people, even as a diminished Ottoman caliph-sultan's government remained in occupied Istanbul. Other delegations, such as representatives of the Bombay Khilafat Committee, were careful to not interject themselves in the delicate internal politics within Turkey at the time, and decided to visit both Istanbul and Ankara in support of the movement. TİTE-2568 / 333 / 43 (1921 07 15).

140. An undated pamphlet authored by Aman Allah and found in the Ottoman central archives in Istanbul provides a telling example of the lengths Aman Allah's government went to defend the Turks following the debacle at Sèvres. Appearing to be a French translation of a speech given by Aman Allah in Afghanistan or India in 1920, and printed in Paris—presumably by the newly established Afghan embassy opened there—the four-page pamphlet was intended to demonstrate to European powers the robust global support for preserving the Ottoman caliphate, including from within Afghanistan. Aman Allah Khan, *S.M.R. l'Emir de l'Afghanistan et le Califat* (Paris: Imp. Lang. Blanchong et cie, 1920). BOA-HR.SYS 5 / 21 (n.d.).

141. Nawid, *Religious Response,* 62–67.

142. On Aman Allah's on-and-off relationship with the Bolsheviks and Soviet Russia, and the pivotal question of free Afghanistan's relationship with the Basmachi revolts, see Saikal, *Modern Afghanistan,* 66–72. On the politics of Muslim modernist reform and Basmachi resistance in Soviet Central Asia, including the roles of Enver and Cemal, see Adeeb Khalid, *The Politics of Muslim Cultural Reform: Jadidism in Central Asia* (Berkeley: University of California Press, 1998). For a broader history of previous Russian empires' relationships with their long-standing Muslim populations and the construction of a distinctive Russian Islam, see Robert D. Crews, *For Prophet and Tsar: Islam and Empire in Russia and Central Asia* (Cambridge, MA: Harvard University Press, 2009).

143. For English-language works on the Young Afghans, see Nawid, *Religious Response,* 44–46, 146–147; Saikal, *Modern Afghanistan,* 41–44, 48; and Amin Tarzi, "Islam and Constitutionalism in Afghanistan," *JPS* 5, no. 2 (2012): 205–243, 207–209. In Persian, see ʿAbd al-Hay Habibi, *Junbish-i Mashrutiyat dar Afghanistan* (Kabul: Ihsani, 1346j / 1967–1968); Sayyid Saʿd al-Din Hashimi, *Nukhustin Kitab darbarih-ʾi Junbish-i Mashrutih-khwahi dar Afghanistan* (Kabul: Shura-yi Farhangi-yi Afghanistan, 2008); Masʿud Puhanyar, *Zuhur-i Mashrutiyat wa Qurbaniyan-i Istibdad dar Afghanistan* (Peshawar: Saba Kitabkhanah, 1375j / 1996–1997); Mir Ghulam Muhammad Ghubar, *Afghanistan dar Masir-i Tarikh* (Qum: Payam-i Muhajir, 1980), 716–721; Mir

Muhammad Siddiq Farhang, *Afghanistan dar Panj Qarn-i Akhir* (Tehran: Kitab-khanih Milli Iran, 1380/2001–2002), 482–487. On Islamic revivalism and the Indian independence movement, see Ayesha Jalal, *Self and Sovereignty: Individual and Community in South Asian Islam since 1850* (New York: Routledge, 2000). On the early history of the Deobandi movement, see Metcalf, *Islamic Reform;* Muhammad ʿUbayd Allah al-Asʿadi Qasmi, *Dar al-ʿUlum Deoband* (Karachi: Fazl Rabi An-Nadwi, 2005); Sayyid Mahbub Rizvi, *History of the Dar al-Ulum Deoband* (Deoband: Idara-e Ihtemam Dar al-Ulum, 1980–1981); on the Aligarh movement, see David Lelyveld, *Aligarh's First Generation: Muslim Solidarity in British India* (New Delhi: Oxford University Press, 1996). On the Young Turk revolution, see Feroz Ahmad, *The Young Turks: The Committee of Union and Progress in Turkish Politics, 1908–1914* (Oxford: Clarendon, 1969); M. Şükrü Hanioğlu, *Preparation for a Revolution: The Young Turks, 1902–1908* (New York: Oxford University Press, 2001).

5. LEGALIZING AFGHANISTAN

1. Ludwig W. Adamec, *Afghanistan, 1900–1923* (Berkeley: University of California Press, 1967), 111. From Aman Allah's address to the nation on the occasion of *ʿĪd al-Fiṭr,* reprinted in Kabul's *Irshad-i Niswan* newspaper 1:12 (Hut 1302/March 1923) and cited in Senzil K. Nawid, *Religious Response to Social Change in Afghanistan, 1919–29: King Aman-Allah and the Afghan Ulama* (Costa Mesa, CA: Mazda, 1999), 72. See also Nazif Shahrani, "King Aman Allah of Afghanistan's Failed Nation-Building Project and Its Aftermath," *Iranian Studies* 38, no. 4 (2005): 661–675.

2. Leon B. Poullada, *Reform and Rebellion in Afghanistan: King Aman Allah's Failure to Modernize a Tribal Society* (Ithaca, NY: Cornell University Press, 1973), 99–104; Vartan Gregorian, *The Emergence of Modern Afghanistan, 1880–1946* (Stanford, CA: Stanford University Press, 1969), 239–243; Amin Saikal, *Modern Afghanistan: A History of Struggle and Survival* (New York: I. B. Tauris, 2006), 74–77.

3. Articles 274, 277, 279, ADL-0526 (*Nizamnamih-ʾi Jaza-yi ʿUmumi* [Kabul: Matbaʿ-ʾi Daʾirih-ʾi Tahrirat-i Majlis-i ʿAli-yi Wuzara, 1304j/1925]); Gregorian, *The Emergence of Modern Afghanistan,* 249.

4. See for example Poullada, *Reform and Rebellion in Afghanistan,* 93–94, 109; Gregorian, *The Emergence of Modern Afghanistan,* 273; and *Encyclopaedia Britannica Online,* s.v. "Aman Allah Khan," accessed May 16, 2017, https://global.britannica.com/biography/amanullah-khan; Micheline Centlivres-Demont, "Afghan Women in Peace, War, and Exile," in *Politics of Social Transformation in Afghanistan, Iran, and Pakistan,* ed. Myron Weiner and Ali Banuazizi (Syracuse, NY: Syracuse University Press, 1994), 333, 363. For popular media representations reflecting these themes from Afghanistan to the United States, see for example "A Glimpse Into the Life of King Amanullah Khan," *Tolo* (Kabul), August 19, 2015, www.tolonews.com/node/11068; and

Michael Hughes, "No Peace without Justice and Equality in Afghanistan," *Huffington Post,* November 1, 2010, www.huffingtonpost.com/michael-hughes/no-peace-without-justice_b_776810.html. On Aman Allah as a "revolutionary king" (*pādishāh-i inqilābī*) among other positive characterizations, see Mir Ghulam Muhammad Ghubar, *Afghanistan dar Masir-i Tarikh* (Qum: Payam-i Muhajir, 1980), 813; *Encyclopaedia Iranica,* vol. 6 (2011), s.v. "Constitutional History of Afghanistan."

5. This work defines the shariʿa as the entirety of laws, ethics, devotional practices, principles of jurisprudence, and associated methodologies of interpretation derived from or inspired by the Qur'an and Sunna. A derivative concept, *siyāsa sharʿiyya,* signals the de facto power of Muslim political authorities to produce legislative enactments of an administrative nature, known in Arabic as *qānūns* (Persian: *qānūnnāmihs/nizāmnāmihs;* Ottoman Turkish: *kanunnames/nizamnames*), translating as "codes," "regulations," or "ordinances." Per the doctrine of *siyāsa sharʿiyya,* the administrative regulations of a Muslim ruler carry the weight of enforceable law. As Mohammad Fadel has argued, drawing from the towering legists and founders of the Hanafi school Abu Yusuf Yaʿqub bin Ibrahim al-Ansari (d. 798) and Muhammad bin Hasan al-Shaybani (d. 805), early Hanafi jurists recognized that the ruler exercised discretionary administrative powers under the law as ruler, but not brute force. Mohammad Fadel, "A Tragedy of Politics or an Apolitical Tragedy?" *Journal of the American Oriental Society* 131, no. 1 (2011): 109–127, 117. See also notes 35–41 in the Introduction concerning this book's use of the terms "shariʿa," "Islamic law," and "Islamic state."

6. Articles 4, 7, 10, 13, 16, 21, 72, Qanun-i Asasi-yi Dawlat-i ʿAliyyih-ʾi Afghanistan (1923). Afghanistan's 1923 Constitution was published in both Dari and Pashto languages under the titles *Nizamnamih-ʾi Asasi-yi Dawlat-i ʿAliyyih-ʾi Afghanistan* and *Asasi Nizamnamih da Lur Dawlat da Afghanistan* respectively. Translating as "The Basic Code of the Exalted State of Afghanistan," the most common shorthand for the text is the Qanun-i Asasi, or Basic Code. My idiomatic translation of Afghanistan's 1923 Qanun-i Asasi as a "constitution" corresponds to *Black's Law Dictionary* usage as "The fundamental and organic law of a nation or state, establishing the conception, character, and organization of its government, as well as prescribing the extent of its sovereign power and the manner of its exercise." Bryan Garner, *Black's Law Dictionary* (St. Paul: West Publishing, 2001), 135. For an original copy of the Persian version, see ADL-0076 (*Nizamnamih-ʾi Asasi-yi Dawlat-i ʿAliyyih-ʾi Afghanistan* [Kabul: Matbaʿ-ʾi Daʾirih-ʾi Tahrirat-i Majlis-i ʿAli-yi Wuzara, 1302j/1923]). For the Pashto version, see ADL-0676 (*Asasi Nizamnamih Dalur Dawlat da Afghanistan* [Kabul: Matbaʿ-ʾi Daʾirih-ʾi Tahrirat-i Majlis-i ʿAli-yi Wuzara, 1302j/1923]).

7. See for example Louis Dupree, *Afghanistan* (Princeton, NJ: Princeton University Press, 1973), 451; Amin Saikal, "Kemalism: Its Influence on Iran and Afghanistan," *International Journal of Turkish Studies* 2, no. 2 (1982): 25–32; Ludwig W. Adamec, *Historical Dictionary of Afghanistan* (Metuchen, NJ: Scarecrow, 1991), 28; and Touraj Atabaki and Erik J. Zürcher, *Men of Order: Authoritarian Modernization under*

Atatürk and Riza Shah (London: I. B. Tauris, 2004), 225. We might also consider the "peripheral" status accorded to Afghanistan in the Middle East to be a contributing factor in such representations. After a handful of works on the Amani era published in the 1960s and 1970s, Aman Allah and his legacy seem to have been largely forgotten in the Western academy for the remaining decades of the twentieth century. The notable exception was Soviet historiography, which took an active interest in the reformist king, as Moscow was anxious to find historical precedent for its own radical reformist agenda in the USSR's occupation of Afghanistan. The result was to paint Aman Allah "red" and further distance the Muslim modernist monarch from discussions of Islamic modernism, legal or otherwise. For a representative Soviet history of Afghanistan from this era, see Urii Vladimirovich Gankovski, *A History of Afghanistan* (Moscow: Progress, 1982).

8. It should also be noted here that the codification of *fiqh* was not without debate, and remains controversial as a practice (or goal) among Islamic legists until this day. Some opponents have gone so far as to argue that codification violates the principles of the shariʿa, given the earliest caliphs and classical jurists expressed reservations about the idea of imposing a singular interpretation over matters in which there was a genuine difference of opinion among scholars. The latter argument, however, seems to collapse the substantial empirical differences from a premodern society in which the size, scope, and administrative mandates of governments were extremely limited compared to their modern bureaucratic counterparts. For examples of divergent views and ongoing polemics over the codification of Islamic law, see Wael B. Hallaq, *Shariʿa: Theory, Practice, Transformations* (New York: Cambridge University Press, 2009), 39; Abdullahi An-Naʿim, "Shariʿa and Positive Legislation: Is an Islamic State Possible or Viable?" *Yearbook of Islamic and Middle Eastern Law* 5 (1998): 29–42; Paul Robinson, "Codifying Shariʿa: International Norms, Legality and the Freedom to Invent New Forms," *Journal of Comparative Law* 2, no. 1 (2007): 1–53. It should also be noted that administrative laws, as opposed to substantive codifications of *fiqh*, represent the furthest distance from the founding, divine sources of Islam, and the greatest proximity to human intervention in the domain of lawmaking. They are hence the most subject to being overturned or disregarded by subsequent generations of Muslims, who may not wish to be held captive to time-bound articulations of the law.

9. ADL-0317 (Muhammad ʿAbd al-Wasiʿ Qandahari, *Tamassuk al-Quzat al-Amaniyyih* [Kabul: Matbaʿ-ʾi Sangi-yi Mashinkhanih, 1300j / 1921–1922]).

10. This also serves to distinguish Islamic legal modernism as the work of Muslim jurists on behalf of sovereign Muslim governments from colonial codes such as the Anglo-Muhammadan Law or Le Droit musulman algérien. For a succinct overview of European projects to codify Islamic law as a strategy of imperial rule from French North Africa to Dutch Indonesia, see Wael B. Hallaq, *An Introduction to Islamic Law* (New York: Cambridge University Press, 2009), 85–93, 110–114 and Aharon Layish, "Islamic Law in the Modern World: Nationalization, Islamization, Rein-

statement,' *Islamic Law and Society* 21, no. 3 (2014): 3. On the roots and evolution of "Muhammadan law" codifications and "shariʿa courts" in British India, see Bernard S. Cohn, *Colonialism and Its Forms of Knowledge: The British in India* (Princeton, NJ: Princeton University Press, 1996); in French Algeria, see Alan Christelow, *Muslim Law Courts and the French Colonial State in Algeria* (Princeton, NJ: Princeton University Press, 1985). For an incisive comparative treatment of this subject in Malaya, Egypt, and India, see Iza R. Hussin, *The Politics of Islamic Law: Local Elites, Colonial Authority and the Making of the Muslim State* (Chicago, IL: University of Chicago Press, 2016).

11. Images of original Aman Allah Codes, including the 1923 Constitution, can be found in the spectacular collections of the Afghanistan Digital Library, available at http://afghanistandl.nyu.edu/index.html. For a partial list of *niẓāmnāmihs* promulgated during Aman Allah's reign, see Poullada, *Reform and Rebellion in Afghanistan,* 99–103.

12. For sample codes regulating Afghan state officials, see ADL-0609 (*Kitabchih-ʾi Qanun-i Karguzari-yi Hukkam* [Kabul: Dar al-Saltanih, 1298j / 1919–1920]); ADL-0600 (*Kitabchih-i Dastur al-ʿAmal-i Mahsul-i Tujjaran* [Kabul: Dar al-Saltanih, 1298j / 1919–1920]); ADL-0064 (*Nizamnamih-ʾi Baladiyyih* [Kabul: Matbaʿ-ʾi Daʾirih-ʾi Tahrirat-i Majlis-i ʿAli-yi Wuzara, 1302j / 1924]); and ADL-0671 (*Nizamnamih-ʾi Usul-i Muhakamat-i Jazaʾiyyih-ʾi Maʾmurin* [Kabul: Matbaʿ-ʾi Shirkat-i Rafiq, 1305j / 1926]).

13. Adamec, *Historical Dictionary,* 58.

14. Article 41. Procedures for the election of State Council members as well as local officials are detailed in a separate code, Law of Basic Governmental Organization (Nizamnamih-ʾi Tashkilat-i Asasiyyih), also promulgated in 1923. ADL-0075 (*Nizamnamih-ʾi Tashkilat-i Asasiyyih* [Kabul: Matbaʿ-ʾi Daʾirih-ʾi Tahrirat-i Majlis-i ʿAli-yi Wuzara, 1302j / 1923]).

15. Articles 21, 33–34, 50–57.

16. On the influence in Afghanistan of the constitutional revolutions in Turkey and Iran, see Amin Tarzi, "Islam and Constitutionalism in Afghanistan," *JPS* 5, no. 2 (2012): 205–243; Nawid, *Religious Response,* 44–49; and Saikal, *Modern Afghanistan,* 41–49. On Iranian legal advisors in Afghanistan during the reign of Aman Allah, British intelligence sources recorded the arrival in 1923 of a certain ʿAli Akbar Khan Daftari, a notable of Tehran and nephew of a former Persian Foreign Minister. Daftari served as a legal consultant to the Afghan Foreign Ministry in the mid-1920s. NAI-Foreign-Political / 636-F / 1923 / 1-70. To the extent of my research, however, there is no evidence of Daftari or any other Persian subjects serving on the constitutional and codification of laws committee appointed by Aman Allah or by his chief legal officer, Mawlawi ʿAbd al-Wasiʿ Qandahari.

17. For an alternative perspective on the 1923 Constitution's prominent features, see Nighat Chishti, *Constitutional Development in Afghanistan* (Karachi: Royal Book Company, 1998), 22–23.

18. The procedural act of "announcing" the law to foreign and domestic subjects alike before inflicting state punishment is a hallmark of modern constitutional theory and "rule of law" ideology. See for example David Clark, "The Many Meanings of the Rule of Law," in *Law, Capitalism, and Power in Asia: The Rule of Law and Legal Institutions,* ed. Kanishka Jayasuriya (London: Routledge, 1999); Franz L. Neumann, *The Rule of Law under Siege: Selected Essays of Franz L. Neumann and Otto Kirchheimer* (Berkeley: University of California Press, 1996).

19. Just as the Young Ottomans and Young Afghans shared a grassroots expression of Islamic constitutionalism "from the ground up," so, too, did legislative programs in Amani Afghanistan and the late Ottoman Empire share the feature of top-down legal positivism. As Umut Özsu has noted in the latter context, legal positivism in centralizing Islamic states, as with in non-Islamic contexts, embodied a "theory that law is best understood as an outgrowth of state authority, not a reflection of some set of deep-seated moral principles that endow it with normative weight." Umut Özsu, "Ottoman International Law?" *JOTSA* 3, no. 2 (2016): 374. Needless to say, this was an extraordinarily controversial component to both late Ottoman and Afghan Muhammadzai codification projects, as they represented the state's usurpation of a role historically seen as the prerogative of the ulema, the authorized interpreters of the shariʿa. On the latter theme in Hamidian Turkey, see Noah Feldman, *The Fall and Rise of the Islamic State* (Princeton, NJ: Princeton University Press), 59–79.

20. On the politics and polemics of customary law in Afghanistan, see Faiz Ahmed, "Shariʿa, Custom, and Statutory Law: Comparing State Approaches to Islamic Jurisprudence, Tribal Autonomy, and Legal Development in Afghanistan and Pakistan," *Global Jurist* 7, no. 1 (2007): 1–56.

21. See for example Poullada, *Reform and Rebellion in Afghanistan,* 93–94 ("Aman Allah employed some French advisers in his legislative program"); Chishti, *Constitutional Development,* 21 ("Aman Allah Khan employed some French Advisors to help him in his legislative programme"); and Daniel Balland, "Afghanistan, Political History," *Encyclopaedia Iranica,* Online Edition, July 22, 2011, www.iranicaonline.org/articles/afghanistan-x-political-history ("With the aid of French and Turkish experts, more than seventy ordinances were published"). Although Gregorian mentions the founding of the binational archaeological mission Delegation Archeologique Française en Afghanistan in 1922, and the presence of five French teachers at Kabul's Lycée Istiqlal, no legal connections are made. Gregorian, *The Emergence of Modern Afghanistan,* 239. See also Nadjma Yassari and Mohammad Hamid Saboory, "Sharia and National Law in Afghanistan," in *Sharia Incorporated: A Comparative Overview of the Legal Systems of Twelve Muslim Countries in Past and Present,* ed. Jan Michiel Otto (Leiden: Leiden University Press, 2011), 273–318; G. Vafai, *Afghanistan: A Country Law Study* (Washington, DC: Library of Congress, 1988).

22. ADL-0061 (*Nizamnamih-ʾi Marasim-i Taʿziyadari,* 1303j / 1924), 2:7.

23. It is important to note that some *niẓāmnāmihs* bypass secondary Islamic legal sources to quote the Qur'an directly, as in Article 1 of the 1920 Marriage Code (citing 4:3 to restrict polygamy). ADL-0518 (*Nizamnamih-'i 'Arusi, Nikah, wa Khatnasuri* [Kabul: Matba'-'i Da'irih-'i Tahrirat-i Majlis-i 'Ali-yi Wuzara, 1302j / 1923]), 2.

24. For example, it is possible that the committee's work was divided among different classes of jurists within the lawmaking commission—some codes (or sections thereof) delegated to clerics working squarely within a Hanafi *fiqh* interpretive tradition, and others to courtiers and bureaucrats drawing from more mundane and eclectic sources, such as the administrative codes or municipal ordinances of other states.

25. ADL-0518.

26. As steadfast Weberians might note, Aman Allah's emphasis on codifying Afghanistan's criminal law first in the form of the *Tamassuk al-Quzat* reflects one of the modern state's distinguishing characteristics: a monopoly on the instruments of violence. As also seen in the attempts to build a single national army and police under Cemal Pasha and other Turkish advisors, Kabul's monopoly on force was a priority of Aman Allah's government and one of the purposes of legislating a criminal law code.

27. It is possible that Aman Allah had a similar vision in mind for a comprehensive Afghan civil law code or judge's handbook of civil law that, like the Ottoman Mecelle and the *Tamassuk al-Quzat al-Amaniyyih,* drew from Hanafi *fiqh* for its substantive law. One indication he was heading in that direction, and possibly the closest he got to it, was the December 1921 treatise authored by his top judicial official and chief mufti 'Abd al-Wasi' Qandahari on principles of Islamic jurisprudence, *Kulliyat wa Istillihat Fiqhiyya* (Maxims and Conventions in Islamic Jurisprudence). Published in Arabic, this thirty-six-page booklet was designed as an authoritative restatement of general principles (or maxims) for the application of Islamic law by Afghan judges. Though not a civil code in itself, it may well have been the first step, and an important juristic device, for a more ambitious "Islamic civil law" codification project. Given the short duration of Aman Allah's rule and preoccupation with revolts toward the second half of his reign, we may never know the full extent of his Islamic legal modernist agenda (or that of his chief legal advisor, Mawlawi 'Abd al-Wasi', who died in 1929). For an original copy of this work, see ADL-0319 (Muhammad 'Abd al-Wasi' Qandahari, *Kulliyat wa Istillihat Fiqhiyya* [Kabul: Dar al-Saltanih, 1300j / 1921]). On the role of maxims in Islamic law and legal history, see Intisar Rabb, *Doubt in Islamic Law: A History of Legal Maxims, Interpretation, and Islamic Criminal Law* (New York: Cambridge University Press, 2015).

28. The synthesis of national sovereignty, general will, and an emphatic commitment to upholding the shari'a is a notable parallel between the Ottoman (1876, 1908), Iranian (1906), and Afghan Constitutions. On the role of ulema and Muslim modernists in Young Ottoman and Young Turk constitutionalism, see Şerif Mardin, *The Genesis of Young Ottoman Thought: A Study in the Modernization of Turkish*

Political Ideas (Syracuse, NY: Syracuse University Press, 2000) and Susan Gunasti, "The Late Ottoman Ulema's Constitutionalism," *Islamic Law and Society* 23, no. 1-2 (2016): 89–119. For similar hybridity in Afghanistan's 1923 Constitution, see Articles 3–4, 41–42, and 72. For an argument on earlier episodes in the early modern Ottoman Empire, see Elizabeth F. Thompson, *Justice Interrupted: The Struggle for Constitutional Government in the Middle East* (Cambridge, MA: Harvard University Press, 2013), 13–36; and Hüseyin Yılmaz, "Containing Sultanic Authority: Constitutionalism in the Ottoman Empire before Modernity," *Journal of Ottoman Studies* 45 (2015): 231–264. On the Ottoman, Egyptian, and Iranian constitutional experiments in the early twentieth century more generally, and links between them, see Nader Sohrabi, *Revolution and Constitutionalism in the Ottoman Empire and Iran* (New York: Cambridge University Press, 2011); Fariba Zarinebaf, "From Istanbul to Tabriz: Modernity and Constitutionalism in the Ottoman Empire and Iran," *CSSAAME* 28, no. 1 (2008): 154–169; Mina E. Khalil, "Early Modern Constitutionalism in Egypt and Iran," *UCLA Journal of Islamic and Near Eastern Law* 15, no. 1 (2016): 33–54.

29. On the Young Afghan movement, see Nawid, *Religious Response,* 44–46, 146–147; and Saikal, *Modern Afghanistan,* 41–48. In Persian, see ʿAbd al-Hay Habibi, *Junbish-i Mashrutiyat dar Afghanistan* (Kabul: Ihsani, 1346j / 1967–1968); Masʿud Puhanyar, *Zuhur-i Mashrutiyat wa Qurbaniyan-i Istibdad dar Afghanistan* (Peshawar: Saba Kitabkhanah, 1375j / 1996–1997); Sayyid Saʿd al-Din Hashimi, *Nukhustin Kitab darbarih-ʾi Junbish-i Mashrutih-khwahi dar Afghanistan* (Kabul: Shura-yi Farhangi-yi Afghanistan, 2008).

30. ʿAziz al-Din Popalzai, *Dar al-Qazaʾ dar Afghanistan* (Kabul: Markaz-i Tahqiqat-i ʿUlum-i Islami, 1369j / 1990–1991).

31. Popalzai, *Dar al-Qazaʾ,* 518–519. The committee is also described in official records from Aman Allah's reign and in the historiography under the following roughly synonymous names: the Advisory Council (Majlis-i Shura / Hayʾat-i Shura), the Legislative Council (Mahfil-i Qanun), the Administrative Law Forum (Markaz-i Qanunguzari), and the National Council (Shura-yi Milli). Saikal, *Modern Afghanistan,* 73; Puhanyar, *Zuhur,* 245; Nawid, *Religious Response,* 79. While Popalzai bases his list on a rare manuscript of 1920, *Tarikh-i Qazaʾ dar Afghanistan,* I corroborated and added to his list by cross-checking it with declassified sources from Afghan, Ottoman, and British Indian archives.

32. The Islamic Scholars' Division was also known as the Mahfil-i Shura-yi ʿUlum (Islamic Sciences Council). Nawid, *Religious Response,* 79.

33. Comparable "repugnancy clauses" are employed in the national constitutions of Pakistan and the Islamic Republic of Iran. Pakistan's Federal Shariʿat Court and Iran's Council of Guardians are empowered to strike down legislation deemed to contravene the shariʿa. See Articles 227, 229, and 230, Constitution of the Islamic Republic of Pakistan (1973), accessed May 16, 2017, www.na.gov.pk/uploads/documents/1333523681_951.pdf; Articles 4, 72, 91–99, and 112, Constitution of the Islamic Re-

public of Iran (1989), in Firoozeh Papan-Matin, trans., "The Constitution of the Islamic Republic of Iran (1989 edition)," *Iranian Studies* 47, no. 1 (2014): 159–200. Unlike in Afghanistan, however, in Pakistan and Iran shariʿa tribunals review legislation after bills are ratified by their national parliaments, rather than before. On the Pakistani and Iranian constitutions, see Paula Newberg, *Judging the State: Courts and Constitutional Politics in Pakistan* (New York: Cambridge University Press, 2002), 25–31, 119–244; Saïd Arjomand, "Shariʿa and Constitution in Iran: A Historical Perspective," in *Shariʿa: Islamic Law in the Contemporary Context,* ed. Abbas Amanat and Frank Giffel (Stanford, CA: Stanford University Press, 2007), 156–164.

34. Puhanyar, *Zuhur,* 53; Nawid, *Religious Response,* 36–37. On the Madrasih-ʾi Shahi of Kabul, an institution that we still do not know much about, see Adamec, *Historical Dictionary,* 124. On the crossborder ties between Kabul's Madrasih-ʾi Shahi and the Dar al-ʿUlum Deoband, India, where a number of Afghan ulema and students were trained beginning in the late nineteenth century, see Olivier Roy, *Islam and Resistance in Afghanistan* (New York: Cambridge University Press, 1986), 58; Sana Haroon, "Religious Revival across the Durand Line," in *Under the Drones: Modern Lives in the Afghanistan-Pakistan Borderlands,* ed. Shahzad Bashir and Robert D. Crews (Cambridge, MA: Harvard University Press, 2012), 45–59.

35. Habibi, *Junbish,* 54–55. For samples of his publications in Persian, Arabic, and Pashto, respectively, see ADL-0318 (Muhammad ʿAbd al-Wasiʿ Qandahari, *ʿUnwan-i Asasi Diniyat dar Mazmun-i Taʿlimi Falsafih-i Islami Qurʾani wa Hikmat-i Yamani Imani* [Kabul: Dar al-Saltanih, 1300j / 1921]); ADL-0319; and ADL-0332 (Muhammad ʿAbd al-Wasiʿ Qandahari, *Yuzani Pashtu / Khas-i Afghani* [Kabul: Matbaʿ-ʾi Wizarat-i Jalilih-ʾi Maʿarif, 1301j / 1922–1923]).

36. Puhanyar, *Zuhur,* 53–75; Habibi, *Junbish,* 276–277.

37. Habibi, *Junbish,* 52. As Wali Ahmadi, Nushin Arbabzadah, and James Caron have shown, associates of the Kabul court read Muslim modernist periodicals in Persian not only from Iran but also from as far as Calcutta and Constantinople, such as *Habl al-Matin* and *Akhtar-i Istanbul.* Access to foreign news in a familiar vernacular enabled Afghan constitutionalists to closely follow revolutionary events in Iran and the Ottoman Empire between 1905 and 1909, and protests in British Bengal around the same time, while shaping a distinctive national literature and politics of their own. Wali Ahmadi, *Modern Persian Literature in Afghanistan: Anomalous Visions of History and Form* (New York: Routledge, 2008), 47–48; Nushin Arbabzadah, "Modernizing, Nationalizing, Internationalizing: How Mahmud Tarzi's Hybrid Identity Transformed Afghan Literature," in *Afghanistan in Ink: Literature between Diaspora and Nation,* ed. Nile Green and Nushin Arbabzadah (New York: Columbia University Press, 2013), 31–66; James M. Caron, "Cultural Histories of Pashtun Nationalism, Public Participation, and Social Inequality in Monarchic Afghanistan, 1905–1960" (PhD diss., Department of South Asia Studies, University of Pennsylvania, 2009), 26. Be-

yond these privileges, the more elite members of the Young Afghan movement often benefited from political protection not available to their less connected associates.

38. See for example ADL-0642 (*Nizamnamih-ʾi Jaza-yi ʿUmumi* [Kabul: Matbaʿ-ʾi Daʾirih-ʾi Tahrirat-i Majlis-i ʿAli-yi Wuzara, 1302j / 1923]).

39. Hashimi, *Nukhustin Kitab,* 276.

40. BOA-DH.SAİDd 110 / 493 (1298h Z 29 / 1881 11 21); BOA-İ.AZN 72 / 1325Ca-28 (1325h Ca 15 / 1907 06 26); BOA-EV.VKF 4 / 12 (1313h Z 29 / 1896 06 11).

41. On the middle-class roots of the CUP leadership, see Sohrabi, *Revolution and Constitutionalism;* M. Şükrü Hanioğlu, *Preparation for a Revolution: The Young Turks, 1902–1908* (New York: Oxford University Press, 2001); Hanioğlu, *The Young Turks in Opposition* (New York: Oxford University Press, 1995).

42. With roots in the Tanzimat reforms of the mid-nineteenth century, late Ottoman courts were split into two separate tracks: the Nizamiye courts, governed by civil codes and administered by graduates of Ottoman civil law schools; and "shariʿa courts," which were administered by traditionalist scholars of the Hanafi school of Islamic law, most of whom were graduates of Ottoman madrasas. The dualistic jurisdictional system allotted most civil matters to the Nizamiye courts, with family law and criminal matters falling under the jurisdiction of shariʿa courts. In practice, as Avi Rubin has shown, there was significant overlap in both judicial personnel and substantive law. On the rise of the late Ottoman Nizamiye (civil law) courts, where Bedri Bey served the majority of his posts in Istanbul, see Avi Rubin, *Ottoman Nizamiye Courts: Law and Modernity* (New York: Palgrave Macmillan, 2011).

43. BOA-DH.SAİDd 110 / 493. Additional information on Bedri's educational and professional history not found in the *Siccil-i Umumi* are in BOA-BEO 3087 / 231504 (1325h Ca 16 / 1907 06 27); BOA-İ.AZN 106 / 1330Ca-15 (1330h Ca 12 / 1912 04 30); BOA-İ.DUİT 39 / 55 (1334h B 09 / 1916 05 12); BOA-İ.DUİT 40 / 36 (1334h B 11 / 1916 05 14); BOA-İ.DUİT 40 / 39 (1336h Ra 05 / 1917 12 20); BOA-İ.AZN 72 / 1325Ca-28; BOA-DH.HMŞ 3 / 1–112 (1337h / 1918–1919).

44. It would be unconscionable to characterize Bedri's tenure as Istanbul's police chief during World War I simply as a succession of prestigious posts in the Ottoman CUP government. According to the memoir of Henry Morgenthau, US ambassador to Constantinople from 1913 to 1916, it was none other than the Istanbul's wartime police chief Osman Bedri Bey who implemented the Ottoman minister of interior Talat Pasha's infamous order for the mass arrests of Armenian notables in the capital on April 24, 1915. Henry Morgenthau, *Ambassador Morgenthau's Story* (New York: Doubleday Page, 1918). On Bedri's alleged role in the persecution of Armenian notables as police chief of Istanbul, see especially chapters 19–20 and 24. Ambassador Morgenthau's memoir has been the subject of controversy and attack by some historians. See for example Heath Lowry, *The Story behind Ambassador Morgenthau's Story* (Istanbul: Isis Press, 1990). Incidentally, only months before these mass arrests the US ambassador and Bedri joined

forces "in active accord" to investigate and duly shut down a number of clandestine human trafficking networks in the city. The *New York Times* attributed the successful operation to Morgenthau's efforts and the "vigorous administration of Bedri Bey." See "Curb White Slavery in Constantinople: Ambassador Morgenthau's Efforts Effectively Seconded by the Sultan's Police," *New York Times,* February 27, 1915. The veracity of Morgenthau's account aside, and the complexity of Bedri's tenure as police chief notwithstanding, the undeniable mass arrests of Armenian notables in Constantinople in April 1915 are now widely considered by historians to be the first stage of a broader process of forced deportation and ethnic cleansing of Ottoman Armenians during World War I. For additional sources on Bedri's suspected harassment and persecution of Armenians in Istanbul from the perspective of his victims, see Grigoris Balakian, *Armenian Golgotha: A Memoir of the Armenian Genocide, 1915–1918* (New York: Vintage, 2010), 33–35, 56–59, 322–326, 424–426, 442; Ronald Gregory Suny, *'They Can Live in the Desert but Nowhere Else': A History of the Armenian Genocide* (Princeton, NJ: Princeton University Press, 2015), 242, 334. On the postwar occupied Ottoman government's State Council (Şura-yı Devlet) judgment in absentia against Bedri and other senior unionist officials, see BOA-HR.HMŞ.İŞO 216/2 (1339h M 08/1920 09 22). It goes without saying that Bedri's associations with wartime atrocities against fellow Ottoman citizens would tarnish, with great irony, the legacy of his subsequent contributions to building a rule of law in Afghanistan.

45. On Cemal's mission to Kabul and Enver's related activities in neighboring Russian Turkistan, see Masayuki Yamauchi, *The Green Crescent under the Red Star: Enver Pasha in Soviet Russia, 1919–1922* (Tokyo: Institute for the Study of Languages and Cultures of Asia and Africa, 1991); Mehmet Saray, *Afganistan ve Türkler* (Istanbul: Edebiyat Fakültesi Basımevi, 1987); and Ayşe Çavdar, "Türk Paşası Afganistan'da," *Atlas* 115 (2002): 138–150.

46. According to most sources, Bedri held the most prominent rank on the committee, serving as director/president (*ra'īs*). There is some minor disagreement over his exact title, however. Popalzai, the only author to describe him in a deputy position, states that Bedri was "vice-president and member of this commission" (*nā'ib-i ra'īs wa ʿażū-yi īn mahfil*).

47. *WWA* (1920), 47; Hashimi, *Nukhustin Kitab,* 274. It is likely that Abdul Ghani acquired Persian and English here in addition to his native Urdu and Punjabi. On the survival of Persian learning in India into the late nineteenth and twentieth centuries (after a precipitous decline in the mid-nineteenth century), and the role of Urdu as a lingua franca for Afghans and Indian Muslims, see Francis Robinson, *The ʿUlama of Farangi Mahal* (Delhi: Permanent Black, 2001), 27–34; Barbara Metcalf, *Islamic Reform in British India: Deoband, 1860–1900* (Princeton, NJ: Princeton University Press, 1982), 73; Nile Green, "The Trans-Border Traffic of Afghan Modernism: Afghanistan and the Indian 'Urdusphere,'" *Comparative Studies in Society and History* 53, no. 3 (2011): 479–508.

48. Ghani is presumed to have completed a medical degree, given his subsequent post in Kabul as chief medical officer and both British and Afghan sources refer to him as "Doctor Abdul Ghani." Hashimi notes he was "successful in his exams" at Cambridge, though his graduation from medical school has not been definitively established. Hashimi, *Nukhustin Kitab,* 274–276; Adamec, *Historical Dictionary,* 7; *WWA* (1920), 47.

49. *WWA* (1920), 47.

50. Ibid., 47; Hashimi, *Nukhustin Kitab,* 274–276; Puhanyar, *Zuhur,* 98, 106–110.

51. Adamec, *Historical Dictionary,* 7; Hashimi, *Nukhustin Kitab,* 274–276; Puhanyar, *Zuhur,* 106–110.

52. IOR-R / 12 / LIB / 107 (1928), 19.

53. *WWA* (1920), 47; Puhanyar, *Zuhur,* 98, 106–110; Adamec, *Historical Dictionary,* 7. Publishing under the Anglicized spelling of his name "Abdul Ghani," he also authored two works on contemporary political economy: *A Review of the Political Situation in Central Asia* (Lahore: Aziz, 1921); and *The Punjab Industrial Labour* (Lahore: Punjab Co-operative Printing Press, 1929).

54. Curiously, Afghan sources are less revealing on this influential juridical actor of the Amani era, particularly with regard to his birth, education, and early career. Fortunately, I uncovered an obscure declassified British Indian intelligence file on Afghanistan containing reports on the activities of Muhammad Ibrahim Khan in Kabul during the 1920s. *WWA* (1920), 129. A Pashtun family anthology of the Barakzai clan discusses some of Muhammad Ibrahim Khan's various offices in the Aman Allah government. Mohammad Masoom Hotak, "Afghan Shahghasis," 2008, 36, accessed May 16, 2017, http://hotakonline.com/uploads/Kitaboona/Afghan.Shahghasis.pdf.

55. *WWA* (1920), 129. According to British intelligence records, Aman Allah dispatched Muhammad Ibrahim Khan to Jalalabad to command troops in Pusht-i Rud and Farah but was later recalled to Kabul for unstated reasons to assume the aide-de-camp position.

56. IOR-R / 12 / 197 (1930), 6.

57. For examples of his fiery poetry along these lines with outstanding translations, see Ahmadi, *Modern Persian Literature in Afghanistan,* 33–34.

58. Ibid., 153. On accusations of Ludin's role in the plot, still unproved, see "Taj Mohammad Paghmani's memoriam," *Kabul Times,* August 3, 1978, 2; "Reminiscences of a Staunch Revolutionary," *Kabul Times,* August 7, 1978, 2–4.

59. Puhanyar, *Zuhur,* 244–249.

60. Ahmadi, *Modern Persian Literature in Afghanistan,* 33–35.

61. Ibid. On Ludin's membership in a radical republican wing of Aman Allah's court, see IOR / R / 12 / 197, 9. I am grateful to Monir and Sara Ludin for sharing insightful oral histories on their ancestor in this regard.

62. Arts. 4, 7, 27–29, and 41, Qanun-i Asasi-yi Dawlat-i ʿAliyyih-ʾi Afghanistan (1923).

63. On the life and career of another influential Indian member of the CLC, but of a very different scholastic and intellectual persuasion, see the portrait of the Indian Pakhtun scholar of Mathra, north of Peshawar, and the Deoband graduate Sayf al-Rahman (1859–1949) in Haroon, "Religious Revival," 46–53.

64. It does not appear that the CLC included any Shiʿa within its ranks. In light of Afghanistan's substantial Shiʿi minority, this is undoubtedly a structural weakness in the constitution-making process. Following the violent outbreak of rebellion in Khost province in 1924 against Aman Allah's reforms, a powerful group of clerics upped the ante by clamoring for a constitutional amendment naming the Hanafi school as the official madhab of Afghanistan. Their successful amendment at a 1924 Loya Jirga convened by Aman Allah served to check not only Shiʿi counterparts but also Salafis and other Sunni schools of law. For a critical account of the use of "National Loya Jirgas" to endorse statist and particularist (as opposed to genuinely representative) national agendas, see M. Jamil Hanifi, "Editing the Past: Colonial Production of Hegemony through the '*Loya Jerga*' in Afghanistan," *Iranian Studies* 37, no. 2 (2004): 295–322.

65. It is also important to remember that official titles in Afghanistan under Aman Allah's reign were still profoundly mediated by court, family, and personal politics. Among the amir's balancing acts in his reformist agenda was the need to mollify rivals in the royal family by appointing them to prominent positions—such that official titles for some relatives of the king did not always correspond to power in practice.

66. While not denying the profound impact of modern Salafi thinkers such as Muhammad ʿAbduh and Rashid Rida on the development of new religious and political ideologies based on Islam in the twentieth century, other strands of Islamic modernism—particularly among jurists and policy makers who opted to work within the four traditional schools of Sunni Islam—have been given insufficient attention. For a notable exception on the predominantly Hanafi ulema of modern South Asia, see Muhammad Qasim Zaman, *The Ulama in Contemporary Islam: Custodians of Change* (Princeton, NJ: Princeton University Press, 2002).

67. Mansoor Moaddel, *Islamic Modernism, Nationalism, and Fundamentalism: Episode and Discourse* (Chicago, IL: University of Chicago Press, 2005), 2.

68. The most incisive articulation of this argument is found in Hallaq, *Shariʿa,* especially 357–370. See also Cohn, *Colonialism,* 57–75; Talal Asad, *Formations of the Secular: Christianity, Islam, Modernity* (Stanford, CA: Stanford University Press, 2003), 205–256; and most recently, Hussin, *The Politics of Islamic Law.*

69. Wael B. Hallaq, *The Impossible State: Islam, Politics, and Modernity's Moral Predicament* (New York: Columbia University Press, 2014). See also Abdullahi Ahmed An-Naʿim, *Islam and the Secular State: Negotiating the Future of Shariʿa* (Cambridge, MA: Harvard University Press, 2010). For an argument on "dismantling" the shariʿa in the nineteenth and twentieth centuries generally, see Hallaq, *Shariʿa,* 357–370. For how it played out historically in late Ottoman, Qajar, and colonial periods as opposed to in postcolonial Muslim countries, see Hallaq, *Shariʿa,* 370–442 and 443–499 respectively.

70. One might ask whether it was significant that the composition of Aman Allah's law commission was entirely Muslim in a predominantly Muslim country such as Afghanistan. It would not be remarkable for an English law commission of the period to be significantly Anglican, and an Italian one to be significantly Catholic, for example. In contrast to the aforesaid examples, however, the significance of an all-Muslim confessional makeup in Afghanistan contradicts historiographical claims (or presumptions) that European advisors wrote the Nizamnamihha-yi Amaniyyih. In other words, that Aman Allah's law commission comprised Afghans, Turks, and Indian Muslims underscores that it was not European legal advisors who codified Afghanistan's laws (a practice followed to varying degrees in other Muslim states at the time). In this way, the national composition of Aman Allah's lawmaking commission underscored his approach to lawmaking as a matter of intense national pride whereby the free, independent, and Islamic dimensions of the committee could not be compromised.

71. On subsequent Afghan constitutions, see Tarzi, "Islam and Constitutionalism," 214–238.

72. See note 143 in Chapter 4 for a list of major works in each genre.

73. For Afghan and Indo-Muslim responses to the Turkish Grand Assembly's abolition of the caliphate, see Nawid, *Religious Response,* 127–130; M. Naeem Qureshi, *Pan-Islam in British Indian Politics* (Leiden: Brill, 1999), 374–386; and Hamid Enayat, *Modern Islamic Political Thought* (New York: I. B. Tauris, 2008), 51–61.

74. The 1924 Khost Rebellion and 1928–1929 revolts that toppled Aman Allah's government have been the subject of far more scholarly attention than the early years of Aman Allah's reign. See note 32 in the Introduction.

75. On amendments to the most controversial *niẓāmnāmihs* passed at the 1924 Loya Jirga, and again in 1928–1929, see Nawid, *Religious Response,* 106–113, 168–169.

76. Poullada, *Reform and Rebellion in Afghanistan,* 92–93.

77. Fadel, "A Tragedy of Politics?," 109–127; Sherman A. Jackson, *Islamic Law and the State: The Constitutional Jurisprudence of Shihab al-Din al-Qarafi* (Leiden: Brill, 1996); Baber Johansen, *Contingency in a Sacred Law: Legal and Ethical Norms in the Muslim Fiqh* (Leiden: Brill, 1999); Baber Johansen, *The Islamic Law on Land Tax and Rent: The Peasants' Loss of Property Rights as Interpreted in the Hanafite Legal Literature of the Mamluk and Ottoman Periods* (New York: Croom Helm, 1988). See also Baki Tezcan, *The Second Ottoman Empire: Political and Social Transformation in the Early Modern World* (New York: Cambridge University Press, 2010).

78. Guy Burak, *The Second Formation of Islamic Law: The Hanafi School in the Early Modern Ottoman Empire* (Cambridge, UK: Cambridge University Press, 2015), quote from Baki Tezcan on back cover.

79. For comparisons with nineteenth-century codification projects in a non-Islamicate but anticolonial context, see Matthew Minow, "The Power of Codification in Latin America: Simon Bolivar and the Code Napoleon," *Tulane Journal of International and Comparative Law* 8 (2000): 83–116.

6. TURKISH TREMORS, AFGHAN AFTERSHOCKS

1. Senzil K. Nawid, *Religious Response to Social Change in Afghanistan, 1919–29: King Aman-Allah and the Afghan Ulama* (Costa Mesa, CA: Mazda, 1999), 67; Nile Green, "The Trans-Border Traffic of Afghan Modernism: Afghanistan and the Indian 'Urdusphere,'" *Comparative Studies in Society and History* 53, no. 3 (2011): 505.

2. IOR-R/12/LIB/107 (1928), 137. See also Nawid, *Religious Response*, 95–96, 109–110.

3. Leon B. Poullada, *Reform and Rebellion in Afghanistan: King Aman Allah's Failure to Modernize a Tribal Society* (Ithaca, NY: Cornell University Press, 1973), 94–96, 117–118; Amin Saikal, *Modern Afghanistan: A History of Struggle and Survival* (New York: I. B. Tauris, 2006), 80–83; Nawid, *Religious Response,* 84–85, 189–190.

4. "Aman Allah Abdicates from Afghan Throne; Flees by Plane, Leaving Brother to Rule," *New York Times,* January 15, 1929; "Aman Allah Abandons Fight to Regain Throne; Afghan King and Queen Seek Refuge in Europe," *New York Times,* May 25, 1929; "Aman Allah Reaches Bombay on Flight: Mullahs and People's Objections to Westernization Cost Him Throne, Deposed King Says," *New York Times,* May 28, 1929. See also Nawid, *Religious Response,* 167–170; Saikal, *Modern Afghanistan,* 87–90.

5. Averse to reside in British territory—Aman Allah and his supporters would ever hold London responsible for his overthrow—the deposed monarch boarded a ship in Bombay for Italy, the same country that had granted asylum to the last Ottoman sultan, Mehmed VI, seven years earlier. Aman Allah spent the last three decades of his life in modest exile, first in Rome, and later, Switzerland. On April 25, 1960, the sixty-seven-year-old former amir and king of Afghanistan passed away in Zurich. His coffin was brought into Afghanistan, and he was buried next to his late father and former amir, Habib Allah, in Jalalabad.

6. Until the late 1960s and 1970s, Aman Allah and his legacy seem to have been largely forgotten—or censured—in discussions of Afghan national law and legal history. Indeed, as Leon Poullada noted in 1973, even copies of Aman Allah's 1923 Constitution were difficult to find until they were fortuitously discovered in a Kabul booksellers' bazaar decades after their promulgation. Poullada, *Reform and Rebellion in Afghanistan,* 93.

7. See for example Poullada, *Reform and Rebellion in Afghanistan;* Vartan Gregorian, *The Emergence of Modern Afghanistan, 1880–1946* (Stanford, CA: Stanford University Press, 1969); Rhea Talley Stewart, *Fire in Afghanistan, 1914–1929: Faith, Hope, and the British Empire* (Garden City, NY: Doubleday, 1973). Senzil Nawid's 1999 work, *Religious Response to Social Change in Afghanistan, 1919–29,* remains the best and most thoroughly-researched study of the Amani era in any language.

8. NAI-Foreign-Political/Secret/External/477(2)-X/1922–1923 (No. 210 Ext.A).

9. IOR-R/12/LIB/107, 262.

10. M. Şükrü Hanioğlu, *Atatürk: An Intellectual Biography* (Princeton, NJ: Princeton University Press, 2011), 120.

11. BCA-30.18.1.1 / 7 / 13 / 19 / 235–21 (1923 03 27); Nusret Baycan, *Atatürk'ün Nişan ve Madalyaları* (Ankara: Genelkurmay Başkanlığı, 1986), 117.

12. NAI-Foreign-Political / Secret / External / 477(2)-X / 1922–1923 (No. 865-X).

13. Ibid. Similarly, a telegram from the British minister at Kabul to the secretary of state for foreign affairs in London, dated May 5, 1923, states, "Amir told me that his attention was absorbed by administrative reforms and that it was impossible for him to leave Afghanistan. He told me definitely that he would not attend Congress at Angora." NAI-Foreign-Political / Secret / External / 477(2)-X / 1922–1923 (No. 662–X).

14. Abidin Ünal et al., *Geçmişten Günümüze Türk-Afgan İlişkileri* (Ankara: Genelkurmay Askeri Tarih ve Stratejik Etüt Başkanlığı Yayınları Basimevi, 2009), 52.

15. BOA-HR.İM 48 / 90 (1923 08 29).

16. Bilal Şimşir, *Doğu'nun Kahramanı Atatürk* (Ankara: Bilgi Yayınevi, 1999), 228–229.

17. Ünal et al., *Geçmişten Günümüze,* 52, 53; Bilal Şimşir, *Atatürk ve Afganistan* (Ankara: Avrasya Stratejik Araştırmalar Merkezi, 2002), 128, 229.

18. IOR-R / 12 / LIB / 107, 169–170.

19. Nawid, *Religious Response,* 127.

20. Nawid, *Religious Response,* 127; Poullada, *Reform and Rebellion in Afghanistan,* 67.

21. IOR-R / 12 / LIB / 107, 169–170.

22. For debates on the abolition of the sultanate and the caliphate within the Turkish National Assembly and beyond, see Hamid Enayat, *Modern Islamic Political Thought* (New York: I. B. Tauris, 2008), 54–56. See also Hanioğlu, *Atatürk,* 135–152; Mona Hassan, *Longing for the Lost Caliphate: A Transregional History* (Princeton, NJ: Princeton University Press, 2016), 218–252.

23. Erik J. Zürcher, *Turkey: A Modern History* (London: I. B. Tauris, 1997), 166–177. For a more complex portrait of these reforms, including the role of late Ottoman ulema in the construction of the Turkish republic's new juridical field, see Amit Bein, *Ottoman Ulema, Turkish Republic: Agents of Change and Guardians of Tradition* (Stanford, CA: Stanford University Press, 2011).

24. Hale Yilmaz, *Becoming Turkish: Nationalist Reforms and Cultural Negotiations in Early Republican Turkey, 1923–1945* (Syracuse, NY: Syracuse University Press, 2013). For a critical assessment of the Kemalist revolution from the perspective of religious and ethnic minorities, see Kabir Tambar, *The Reckoning of Pluralism: Political Belonging and the Demands of History in Turkey* (Stanford, CA: Stanford University Press, 2014).

25. For Mehmed Seyyid's legal and political thought on the subject of the caliphate, see *Hilafetin Mahiyet-i Şer'iyyesi* (Ankara: TBMM Matbaası, 1924), an influential public speech delivered to the TBMM on the matter. See also Hanioğlu, *Atatürk,* 150–152; Hassan, *Longing for the Lost Caliphate,* 220–225. As Talal Asad has argued, creating a "secular public" was premised on first creating the "religious private," a discursive and institutional transformation shared with colonial and postcolonial regimes across the region, including but not limited to Egypt. Talal Asad,

Formations of the Secular: Christianity, Islam, Modernity (Stanford, CA: Stanford University Press, 2003).

26. IOR-R/12/LIB/107, 169–170. See note 57 in Chapter 4 for a translation of Article 3's controversial provisions. An alternative rendering of the key Turkish phrase "*hilafet dünyası elinde tutan Türkiye'nin bu alanda lider olduğunu*," could also read: "Holding the standard of the Caliphate in her hand, Turkey is a leader to be followed in this domain." For the original Ottoman Turkish version of the 1921 Turco-Afghan agreement, see BOA-HSD.AFT 6/101 (1339h B 04/1921). For the official Dari version, see ADL-0106 (*Sawad-i Muʿahadih-ʾi Dawlatayn-i ʿAliyyatayn Afghanistan wa Turkiyih* [Kabul, 1301j Mizan 26/1922 10 19]).

27. For original copies of the 1928 Turco-Afghan treaty in Persian, see ADL-0694 (*Qarardad-i ʿIrfani-yi bayn-i Dawlat-i Shahi-yi Afghanistan wa Hukumat-i Jumhuriyyih-ʾi Turkiyih* [Kabul: Matbaʿ-ʾi Wizarat-i Maʿarif, 1928]); ADL-0700 (*Muʿahadih-ʾi Widadiyyih wa Taʾminiyyih bayn-i Hukumat-i Shahi-yi Afghanistan wa Hukumat-i Jumhuriyyih-ʾi Turkiyih* [Kabul: Matbaʿ-ʾi Shirkat-i Rafiq, 1307j/1928]). For official Turkish correspondence on the agreement, currently housed in republican archives in Ankara, see BCA-30.18.1.1/29/46/20 (1928 07 22). Notably, the fourth resolution of the July 1924 Loya Jirga called for a complete review of the relationship with Turkey, not just a rewording of particular articles.

28. IOR-R/12/LIB/107, 169–170.

29. Ibid., 130.

30. Poullada, *Reform and Rebellion in Afghanistan,* 67.

31. On the long-term impact of the Khilafat movement in the Indian independence movement, and Pakistan movement, see Gail Minault, *The Khilafat Movement: Religious Symbolism and Political Mobilization in India* (New York: Columbia University Press, 1982); Ayesha Jalal, *Self and Sovereignty: Individual and Community in South Asian Islam since 1850* (New York: Routledge, 2000), 187–247. Still, even the disillusioned and disappointed Indian revolutionaries made their way back to Kabul; for some, even multiple times. Among the latter was Zafar Hasan Aybek, the Indian migrant to Kabul during World War I, who had since migrated to Anatolia and adopted Turkish nationality. According to British agents in Kabul he was teaching at the Kabul Harbiye military academy as late as 1926 while also serving as a translator and secretary to General Nadir Khan. *WWA* (1930), 255. He later published a Turkish-English dictionary on military terminology, and a pair of articles on his former mentor ʿUbayd Allah Sindhi's activities in Afghanistan, and the history of an Indian sufi lodge in Istanbul, respectively. Zafer Hasan Aybek, *Söyleyişli İngilizce-Türkçe Askeri ve Teknik Sözlük* (Istanbul: Askeri Basımevi, 1948); Aybek, "Ubayd-Allah Sindhi in Afghanistan," *Journal of the Regional Cultural Institute* 6, no. 3–4 (1973): 129–136; Aybek, "Hindiler Tekkesi," *Hayat Tarih Mecmuası* 7 (1977): 96. According to an April 1937 document in the Turkish republican archives, Lieutenant Zafer Hasan returned to Kabul to represent the Ankara government as a military instructor for the Afghan army during the reign of Muhammad Zahir Shah (r. 1933–1973). BCA-30.18.1.2/73/30/5/112–192/2 (1937 04 14).

32. IOR-R/12/LIB/107, 130.

33. Nawid, *Religious Response,* 106–113; Poullada, *Reform and Rebellion in Afghanistan,* 98; Gregorian, *The Emergence of Modern Afghanistan,* 262. For a copy of the Loya Jirga's resolutions, see ADL-0012 (Burhan al-Din Kushkaki, *Ruydad-i Loya Jirgih-i Dar al-Saltanih* [Kabul: Dar al-Saltanih, 1303j/1924]). On Aman Allah's use of the Loya Jirga as an instrument to approve legislation drafted by his jurists, rather than a popular assembly or parliament as such, see Thomas Barfield, *Afghanistan: A Cultural and Political History* (Princeton, NJ: Princeton University Press, 2010), 295; M. Jamil Hanifi, "Editing the Past: Colonial Production of Hegemony through the '*Loya Jerga*' in Afghanistan," *Iranian Studies* 37, no. 2 (2004): 295–322. At the same time, given the staunch opposition many of the participants in the 1924 Loya Jirga waged against many of Aman Allah's reforms, including several that were ultimately repealed or amended against his desires, the institution cannot be deemed a mere rubber stamp for his policies either.

34. IOR-R/12/LIB/107, 137.

35. On the early history of the Dar al-ʿUlum madrasa at Deoband in India, see Barbara Metcalf, *Islamic Reform in British India: Deoband, 1860–1900* (Princeton, NJ: Princeton University Press, 1982). On the subsequent growth of the Deobandi movement in India and Afghanistan, see Sana Haroon, *Frontier of Faith: Islam in the Indo-Afghan Borderland* (New York: Columbia University Press, 2007); Olivier Roy, *Islam and Resistance in Afghanistan* (New York: Cambridge University Press, 1986); Muhammad Qasim Zaman, *The Ulama in Contemporary Islam* (Princeton, NJ: Princeton University Press, 2002).

36. Poullada, *Reform and Rebellion in Afghanistan,* 261.

37. For the proclamation of aims of Afghan scholars' association, see ADL-0659 (*Maramnamih wa Surat-i Tadwir-i Majlis-i Jamʿiyat-i al-ʿUlamaʾ-i Afghanistan* [Kabul: Matbaʿ-ʾi ʿUmumi, 1308j/1929]).

38. Gregorian, *The Emergence of Modern Afghanistan,* 248.

39. On Aman Allah's visit to Turkey and meeting with Kemal, see Ömer Erden, *Mustafa Kemal Atatürk Döneminde Türkiye'yi Ziyaret Eden Devlet Başkanları* (Ankara: Atatürk Araştırma Merkezi, 2006), 117–176.

40. The *New York Times* provided week-by-week coverage of Aman Allah's tour. See for example "Absolute Monarch of Untamed Asian Hill People Prepares to Modernize His Ancient And Turbulent Land," *New York Times,* October 16, 1927; "Afghan Rulers Welcomed to Rome: Picturesque and Martial King Aman Allah Greatly Impresses the Italian Crowds," *New York Times,* January 9, 1928; "Afghan King to Study German Industries: Aman Allah on His Visit Hopes to Get Ideas for Electrification of His Country," *New York Times,* February 8, 1928. For coverage in the *Times* of London, see "From Bombay with King Aman Allah," *Times* of London, January 6, 1928, 15; "Afghan King at Oxford," *Times* of London, March 24, 1928, 14; "Afghan King at Sandhurst," *Times* of London, March 26, 1928, 9; "Afghan King's Gift to London Poor," *Times* of London, March 27, 1928, 16.

41. See for example "Afghan Rulers Welcomed to Rome: Queen's Beauty Admired, She and Her Daughters Appear in Public Unveiled and Dressed in Latest Paris Fashions," *New York Times,* January 9, 1928.

42. Nawid, *Religious Response,* 153; Poullada, *Reform and Rebellion in Afghanistan,* 129–130.

43. İsmail Akbaş, "Afgan Kralı Emanullah Han'ın Türkiye Gezisi," *Çağdaş Türkiye Tarihi Araştırmaları Dergisi* 7, no. 16–17 (2008): 311–333.

44. A. L. P. Burdett, *Afghanistan Strategic Intelligence: British Records 1919–1970* (Slough, UK: Archive Editions Limited, 2002) (hereafter *ASIBR*), 1:902–903.

45. Saikal, *Modern Afghanistan,* 86–87; Gregorian, *The Emergence of Modern Afghanistan,* 260–261; Nawid, *Religious Response,* 140–143.

46. *ASIBR,* 1:918–919.

47. Nazif Shahrani, "King Aman Allah of Afghanistan's Failed Nation-Building Project and Its Aftermath," *Iranian Studies* 38, no. 4 (2005): 671, citations omitted.

48. It is possible that an emphasis on these later developments contributed to many scholars largely misreading Aman Allah's early years in power. This included a commonplace tendency to project Kemalist or Pahlavi imitation backwards on the Aman Allah Codes, the majority of which were drafted between 1919 and 1923 and well before his tour of Europe.

49. IOR-R / 12 / LIB / 107, 132.

50. Şimşir, *Atatürk ve Afganistan,* 92.

51. A foreign ministry memorandum from 1926, for example, mentions the dispatch of Turkish advisors Nusret Bey and Kemal Atıf Bey to Afghanistan. BOA-HR.İM 255 / 24 (1926 10 31).

52. IOR-R / 12 / LIB / 107, 132.

53. On continued Turkish assistance through the second half of Aman Allah's reign, see Özlem Korkmaz, "Afganistan'a Türk Yardımı (1920–1960)," in *Afganistan Üzerine Araştırmalar,* ed. Ali Ahmetbeyoğlu (Istanbul: Tarih ve Tabiat Vakfı Yayınları, 2001), 205–224; and Saikal, *Modern Afghanistan,* 65.

54. BOA-HR.İM 205 / 33 (1926 10 30).

55. BOA-HR.İM 254 / 125 (1926 10 11); IOR-R / 12 / LIB / 107, 163; Masayuki Yamauchi, *The Green Crescent under the Red Star: Enver Pasha in Soviet Russia, 1919–1922* (Tokyo: Institute for the Study of Languages and Cultures of Asia and Africa, 1991), 374.

56. In October 1928 a Turkish foreign ministry memorandum discussed preparations being made and travel documents issued for the delegation's travel to Afghanistan. BOA-HR.İM 24 / 73 (1928 10 31). A year later, a pair of Turkish documents written in the new Latin script, though still housed in the Prime Ministry Ottoman archives in Istanbul, discusses the mission of Turkish legal advisor Mehmed Cevad Bey to Afghanistan. BOA-HR.İM 229 / 74 (1929 02 05). See also his earlier Afghan activities described in BOA-HR.İM 255 / 91 (1926 12 29). With the outbreak of revolts and Aman

Allah's government unraveling at the seams, needless to say the Turkish commission was unable to fulfill its purpose. Turkey's development aid would not fully resume until the arrival of the republic's next ambassador to Kabul, the historian and diplomat Yusuf Hikmet Bayur (1891–1980), who served as Ankara's chargé d'affaires in Kabul until August 1931. Şimşir, *Atatürk ve Afganistan,* 92.

57. On the mysterious circumstances surrounding Bedri's death, one month after the ratification of the constitution he directed, see IOR-L/PS/11/233/, P1730/1923 (No. 1730/23) (1923); BOA-HR.İM 96/2 (1924 01 28); BOA-HR.İM 119/66 (1924 10 07); BOA-HR.İM 120/97 (1924 10 20). Bedri's will and other arrangements regarding his estate are contained in BOA-HR.İM 115/14 (1924 08 31), with a transcribed copy notarized by the Turkish republic's Ministry of Foreign Affairs available in BOA-HR. İM 133/35 (1925 02 21); BOA-138/44 (1925 04 07); BOA-HR.İM 174/18 (1926 01 28); BOA-HR.İM 133/35 (1925 02 21); and BOA-HR.İM 155/25 (1925 08 19). For additional details and theories surrounding Bedri's death in Kabul, see Ali Fuat Cebesoy, *Moskova Hatıraları* (Ankara: Kültür ve Turizm Bakalığı, 1982), 61–63.

58. Even more revealing, the ulema representing those opposing Aman Allah's most controversial reforms were now heading many of the new legislative committees—a juridical coup d'état that left 'Abd al-Wasi' Qandahari in prison, and his most bitter opponents (Mawlawis Ibrahim Kamawi, Mawlawi 'Abd al-Ghafur, and other mostly Deobandi ulema from both the Afghan and Indian sides of the Durand Line) amending and drafting new codes. Apart from Nawid's work, insufficient scholarly attention has been paid to the juridical transformations unleashed by the rebellion, particularly the intense negotiations that took place at the 1924 Loya Jirga, where the *niẓāmnāmihs* were fiercely debated. Aman Allah eventually rescinded several of the most controversial laws in order to shore up his popular support. Ultimately taking the fall was Mawlawi 'Abd al-Wasi', Aman Allah's chief mufti and promulgator of the Aman Allah Codes, who was blamed and even arrested for approving laws contrary to the shari'a. Nawid, *Religious Response,* 111.

59. Gregorian, *The Emergence of Modern Afghanistan,* 264–265.

60. In a representative passage from his discussion on Aman Allah's downfall, Ghubar describes the British as having complete mastery over Afghan internal affairs, stating "the enemy, whatever it desired to do, easily implanted it in the minds of soldiers and common person alike." My translation. Mir Ghulam Muhammad Ghubar, *Afghanistan dar Masir-i Tarikh* (Qum: Payam-i Muhajir, 1980), 823. Without access to British or Indian government archives, however, Ghubar's argument relied on emphasizing British geostrategic interests in maintaining a weak Afghan government in Kabul, speculating this led to British involvement in the revolts that eventually toppled the reformist king. It is also clearly an overstatement of British capacity in the country. In a similar vein, Rhea Stewart attributes Aman Allah's overthrow to British intrigue based on circumstantial evidence, but no concrete proof, of the Raj's support for anti-Aman Allah forces in the frontier. Stewart, *Fire in Afghanistan.*

61. Gregorian, *The Emergence of Modern Afghanistan,* 272.

62. Poullada, *Reform and Rebellion in Afghanistan,* 58–59.

63. Nawid, *Religious Response.* See also Nawid, "The State, the Clergy, and British Imperial Policy in Afghanistan during the Nineteenth and Early Twentieth Centuries," *IJMES* 29, no. 4 (1997): 581–605.

64. IOR-R/12/LIB/107, 138.

65. Robert D. McChesney, *Kabul under Siege: Fayz Muhammad's Account of the 1929 Uprising* (Princeton, NJ: Markus Weiner, 1999), 12–13.

66. ADL-0518 (*Nizamnamih-'i 'Arusi, Nikah, wa Khatnasuri* [Kabul: Matba'-'i Da'irih-'i Tahrirat-i Majlis-i 'Ali-yi Wuzara, 1302j/1923]).

67. Gregorian, *The Emergence of Modern Afghanistan,* 273.

68. IOR-R/12/LIB/107, 337. Five years into Aman Allah's reign, British intelligence records provided a dismal prognosis of army's state: "It is evident that King Amanullah has never taken sufficient interest in his troops, and has done nothing to establish that feeling of personal loyalty which would be of particular value in his case." *ASIBR,* 1:914.

69. IOR-R/12/LIB/107, 337. See also *ASIBR,* 1:914–916.

70. Gregorian, *The Emergence of Modern Afghanistan,* 260.

71. Shahrani, "King Aman Allah," 669.

72. Gregorian, *The Emergence of Modern Afghanistan,* 268–273.

73. Ibid.

74. *ASIBR,* 1:912. See also Nawid, *Religious Response,* 145–146.

75. For important regional precedents in this regard, and contrasting with Aman Allah's inability to build a national army, see Touraj Atabaki and Erik J. Zürcher, *Men of Order: Authoritarian Modernization under Atatürk and Reza Shah* (London: I. B. Tauris, 2004); Khaled Fahmy, *All the Pasha's Men: Mehmed Ali, His Army, and the Making of Modern Egypt* (New York: Cambridge University Press, 1997).

76. Poullada, *Reform and Rebellion in Afghanistan,* 33–34.

77. *ASIBR,* 1:945. The apathy of army soldiers was widely demonstrated during Kalakani's sacking of Kabul, when government troops were virtually nowhere to be seen. The king was left to rely on his bodyguard, top army chiefs, and a band of tribal levies for the defense of the capital and ultimately his own life. *ASIBR,* 2:4–5.

78. *ASIBR,* 1:564.

79. Shahrani, "King Aman Allah," 669, citations omitted.

80. Gregorian, *The Emergence of Modern Afghanistan,* 270.

81. *ASIBR,* 1:914.

82. Shahrani, "King Aman Allah," 669, citations omitted.

83. *ASIBR,* 1:902–903.

84. Gregorian, *The Emergence of Modern Afghanistan,* 260.

85. Ibid., 264.

86. Ibid., 270.

87. Roland Wild, *Amanullah: Ex-King of Afghanistan* (Quetta, Pakistan: Nisa Traders, 1978), 68–69; see also Gregorian, *The Emergence of Modern Afghanistan,* 270–271.

88. Ibid., 272.

89. Ibid., 273–274.

90. Ibid.

91. *ASIBR,* 1:902–903.

92. Ibid., 908.

93. Gregorian, *The Emergence of Modern Afghanistan,* 260. On October 5, 1928, the king addressed an official gathering at Kabul for eleven hours on his general education policy, which included the compulsory wearing of European dress and coeducation in Kabul from the ages of six to eleven. *ASIBR,* 1:928.

94. *ASIBR,* 1:908–910.

95. Ibid., 913.

96. Ibid., 902–903.

97. Ibid., 633.

98. Ibid., 910.

99. Ibid., 923. On the applause at Queen Suraya's earlier removal of her facial veil, see Ibid., 910.

100. According to Senzil Nawid and 'Abd al-Hayy Habibi, some of the leading Young Afghan liberals within Aman Allah's court who expressed discomfort with the amir's decisions on social and cultural affairs included the editor of the government newspaper *Amani-i Afghan,* 'Abd al-Hadi Dawi, and the radical republican 'Abd al-Rahman Ludin. Both, for example, staunchly opposed the king's policies on women's unveiling on the grounds that "the unveiling of women in the capital would produce negative repercussions in the country and would provide ample opportunity for the British to foment another popular uprising against the government." Nawid, *Religious Response,* 151; 'Abd al-Hayy Habibi, *Junbish-i Mashrutiyat dar Afghanistan* (Kabul: Ihsani, 1346j / 1967–1968), 191.

101. *ASIBR,* 1:932.

102. Ibid., 936–937.

103. Poullada, *Reform and Rebellion in Afghanistan,* 33–34.

104. On the "reactive violence" of peasantries as a "perennial theme in discussions of the countryside," see Timothy Mitchell, *Rule of Experts: Egypt, Techno-Politics, Modernity* (Berkeley: University of California Press, 2002), 14. Discussing rural Egypt from the state-building campaign of Mehmed Ali to USAID development projects a century later, Mitchell's observations aptly relate to the historiography of modern Afghanistan where scholars have largely been focused on explaining the dramatic collapse of Aman Allah's government more than on the juridical foundations and legacies built during his decade-long reign.

105. Shahrani, "King Aman Allah," 661–675. On the role of Wazirs, Mahsuds, Muhmands, and Afridis in supporting Aman Allah against the Mangals and Ahmadzai Ghilzais, see Haroon, *Frontier of Faith,* 117–124. For a broader historical and ethnographic treatment of the Indo-Afghan frontier from British India's NWFP to Pakistan's Khyber Pakhtunkhwa, see Benjamin D. Hopkins and Magnus Marsden, *Fragments of the Afghan Frontier* (New York: Columbia University Press, 2012).

106. *ASIBR,* 1:653.

107. Ibid., 614.

108. Ibid., 603–609.

109. Ibid., 933.

110. For one British officer's insistence on the ad hoc and localized character of the revolts, including the rebellion's "lack of generalship and of any central organization," see *ASIBR,* 1:599.

111. Nawid, *Religious Response,* 88–89, 148–151; Poullada, *Reform and Rebellion in Afghanistan,* 116.

112. Poullada, *Reform and Rebellion in Afghanistan,* 116–117.

113. *ASIBR,* 1:916.

114. Ibid., 929–930.

115. Nawid, *Religious Response,* 149–151. On the reported disenchantment of several Young Afghan republicans with the amir, including ʿAbd al-Rahman Ludin, see IOR/R/12/197 (1930), 9.

116. Gregorian, *The Emergence of Modern Afghanistan,* 249–250. It should also be noted that Article 15 of the 1923 Constitution already sought to exclude a range of educational activities from the direct control of the ulema. For the 1927 penal code, see ADL-0537 (*Nizamnamih-ʾi Jaza-yi ʿUmumi* [Kabul: Matbaʿ-ʾi Riyasat-i Shirkat-i Rafiiq, 1306j/1927]).

117. ADL-0537.

118. Gregorian, *The Emergence of Modern Afghanistan,* 252. Nawid, *Religious Response,* 149–151.

119. *ASIBR,* 1:916.

120. By this time, as mentioned, ʿAbd Al-Wasiʿ had been removed from his position as chief mufti and from the high council. Nawid, *Religious Response,* 152.

121. Ibid., 150.

122. *ASIBR,* 1:916.

123. Gregorian, *The Emergence of Modern Afghanistan,* 263–269; Poullada, *Reform and Rebellion in Afghanistan,* 58–59. Not all of Aman Allah's former supporters were able to escape in time, and some were even accused of siding with the king's challenger, Kalakani. Among them was the Ottoman colonel of Baghdad, Mahmud Sami, whose prolific career in Kabul came to an abrupt end when he was arrested and executed by Nadir Shah's government in 1930 for allegedly supporting Kalakani during the latter's capture of Kabul.

124. See for example James C. Scott, *Seeing Like a State: How Certain Schemes to Improve the Human Condition Have Failed* (New Haven, CT: Yale University Press, 1999); Atabaki and Zürcher, *Men of Order;* Fahmy, *All the Pasha's Men.*

125. From British minister at Kabul Sir Francis Humphrys's summary of the king's speech in Kabul in October 1928. *ASIBR,* 1:909.

126. Gregorian, *The Emergence of Modern Afghanistan,* 273–274.

127. BCA-30.10.0.0 / 258 / 733 / 13 / 435 (1935 04 29).

CONCLUSION

1. "The Afghan Transitional Administration: Prospects and Perils," International Crisis Group, Kabul / Brussels, July 30, 2002, https://www.crisisgroup.org/asia/south-asia/afghanistan/afghan-transitional-administration-prospects-and-perils.

2. Quotes from former UN Secretary General Kofi Annan, Professor Noah Feldman of Harvard Law School, and former Afghan President Hamid Karzai respectively. "Afghan Charter Wins World Praise," *BBC News,* January 5, 2004, http://news.bbc.co.uk/2/hi/south_asia/3367847.stm; Noah Feldman, "A New Democracy, Enshrined in Faith," *New York Times,* November 13, 2003.

3. Roland Flamini, "Afghans Write Constitution Version," *Washington Times,* January 10, 2004, www.washtimes.com/world/20040109-085157-1139r.htm. See also Amin Tarzi, "Islam and Constitutionalism in Afghanistan," *JPS* 5, no. 2 (2012): 238–241; Faiz Ahmed, "Judicial Reform in Afghanistan: A Case Study in the New Criminal Procedure Code," *Hastings International and Comparative Law Review* 29, no. 1 (2005): 93–134.

4. Brinkley Messick, *The Calligraphic State: Textual Domination and History in a Muslim Society* (Berkeley: University of California Press, 1993), 50.

5. NAI-Foreign-Political / 636-F / 1923 / 1–70.

6. Sherman A. Jackson, review of *Shari'a: Theory, Practice, Transformations,* by Wael B. Hallaq, *Journal of the American Academy of Religion* 82, no. 1 (2014): 259–264.

7. On subsequent Afghan constitutions, see Tarzi, "Islam and Constitutionalism," 214–238.

8. While this phrase is drawn from Aman Allah's speech in Istanbul on May 19, 1928, hailing the fraternal ties between Afghanistan and Turkey, similar expressions are found in speeches of Habib Allah and Aman Allah in regard to Ottoman Turks and Indian Muslims, as discussed in earlier chapters. Leon B. Poullada, *Reform and Rebellion in Afghanistan: King Aman Allah's Failure to Modernize a Tribal Society* (Ithaca, NY: Cornell University Press, 1973), 258.

9. Mohammad Fadel, "Is Historicism a Viable Strategy for Islamic Law Reform?" *Islamic Law and Society* 18, no. 2 (2011): 137. See also Sa'diyya Shaikh, "Transforming

Feminisms: Islam, Women and Gender Justice," in *Progressive Muslims on Justice, Gender, and Pluralism*, ed. Omid Safi, 147–162 (Oxford: Oneworld Publications, 2003).

10. Mohammad Fadel, "A Tragedy of Politics or an Apolitical Tragedy?" *Journal of the American Oriental Society* 131, no. 1 (2011): 115, 127.

11. On the enduring role of Turkish ulema in late Ottoman and Republican Turkey, see Amit Bein, *Ottoman Ulema, Turkish Republic: Agents of Change and Guardians of Tradition* (Stanford, CA: Stanford University Press, 2011); Susan Gunasti, "The Late Ottoman Ulema's Constitutionalism," *Islamic Law and Society* 23, no. 1–2 (2016): 89–119. Similarly, recent work on the first Pahlavi era has eroded historiographical orthodoxy on Riza Shah and the Shiʿi clerical establishment. See for example Janet Afary, "Foundations for Religious Reform in the First Pahlavi Era," *Iran Nameh* 30, no. 3 (2015): XLVI–LXXXVII. Comparable arguments might be awaiting to complicate conventional treatments of Kemal's complex relationship with Islam, or even Turkey's adoption of European codes. See for example M. Şükrü Hanioğlu, *Atatürk: An Intellectual Biography* (Princeton, NJ: Princeton University Press, 2011), 102–113, 145; Ruth Miller, "The Ottoman and Islamic Substratum of Turkey's Swiss Civil Code," *Journal of Islamic Studies* 11, no. 3 (2000): 335–361.

12. In the same genre as the Aman Allah Codes, therefore, are the Mecelle and the Ottoman Constitution of 1876, as well as the legal manuals and codes of Egyptian jurists Muhammad Qadri Pasha (1821–1888) and ʿAbd al-Razzaq al-Sanhuri (1895–1971). See for example Samy Ayoub, "The *Mecelle,* Sharia, and the Ottoman State: Fashioning and Refashioning of Islamic Law in the Nineteenth and Twentieth Centuries," *JOTSA* 2, no. 1 (2015): 121–146; Amr Shalakany, "Between Identity and Redistribution: Sanhuri, Genealogy and the Will to Islamise," *Islamic Law and Society* 8, no. 1 (2001): 201–244; Nabil Saleh, "Civil Codes of Arab Countries: The Sanhuri Codes," *Arab Law Quarterly* 8, no. 2 (1993): 161–167.

13. In accounts of Ottoman modernization of the nineteenth century, for example, one finds an unmistakable civilizing mission in the Porte's policies toward such subaltern groups as the Kurds of eastern Anatolia, and Arab tribes of Iraq and Yemen. As Selim Deringil emphasizes in his study of the Hamidian era, the latter groups were known to be described by Ottoman officials as "in a state of nomadism and savagery," and were to be "gradually brought into the fold of civilization." Selim Deringil, *The Well-Protected Domains: Ideology and the Legitimation of Power in the Ottoman Empire, 1876–1909* (New York: I. B. Tauris, 1999), 41–42. For other examples from the Ottoman administration of the empire's Arabic-speaking provinces in Syria, Mesopotamia, and Yemen, see Ussama Makdisi, "Ottoman Orientalism," *American Historical Review* 107, no. 3 (2002): 768–796; and Reşat Kasaba, *A Moveable Empire: Ottoman Nomads, Migrants, and Refugees* (Seattle: University of Washington Press, 2009). Accounts by Deringil, Makdisi, and Kasaba of the Ottoman imperial center's view of provincial tribes and nomadic populations shares parallels

with that of the Afghan government of Aman Allah Khan in particular, where the latter was known to gaze on frontier regions of southern and eastern Afghanistan with similar hues. On July 15, 1925, for example, the amir described his successful war against the Khost rebels as "a war between enlightenment and ignorance." Following his triumph at Khost, the amir went so far as to erect a public monument commemorating the "victory of the knowledge over ignorance." The monument still stands in one of the downtown Kabul's roundabouts today. *ASIBR,* 1:651.

14. For one prominent Indian author's trip to the site and his pertinent reflections, see Amitav Ghosh, "Kabul, National Archives of Afghanistan," February 27, 2012, http://amitavghosh.com/blog/?p=2481.

15. For an outstanding example, see the pioneering work of the Afghanistan Digital Library Project at New York University, http://afghanistandl.nyu.edu.

APPENDIX A

Genealogy of Afghan Monarchs, 18th–20th Centuries

Genealogy of Afghan Monarchs, 18th–20th centuries

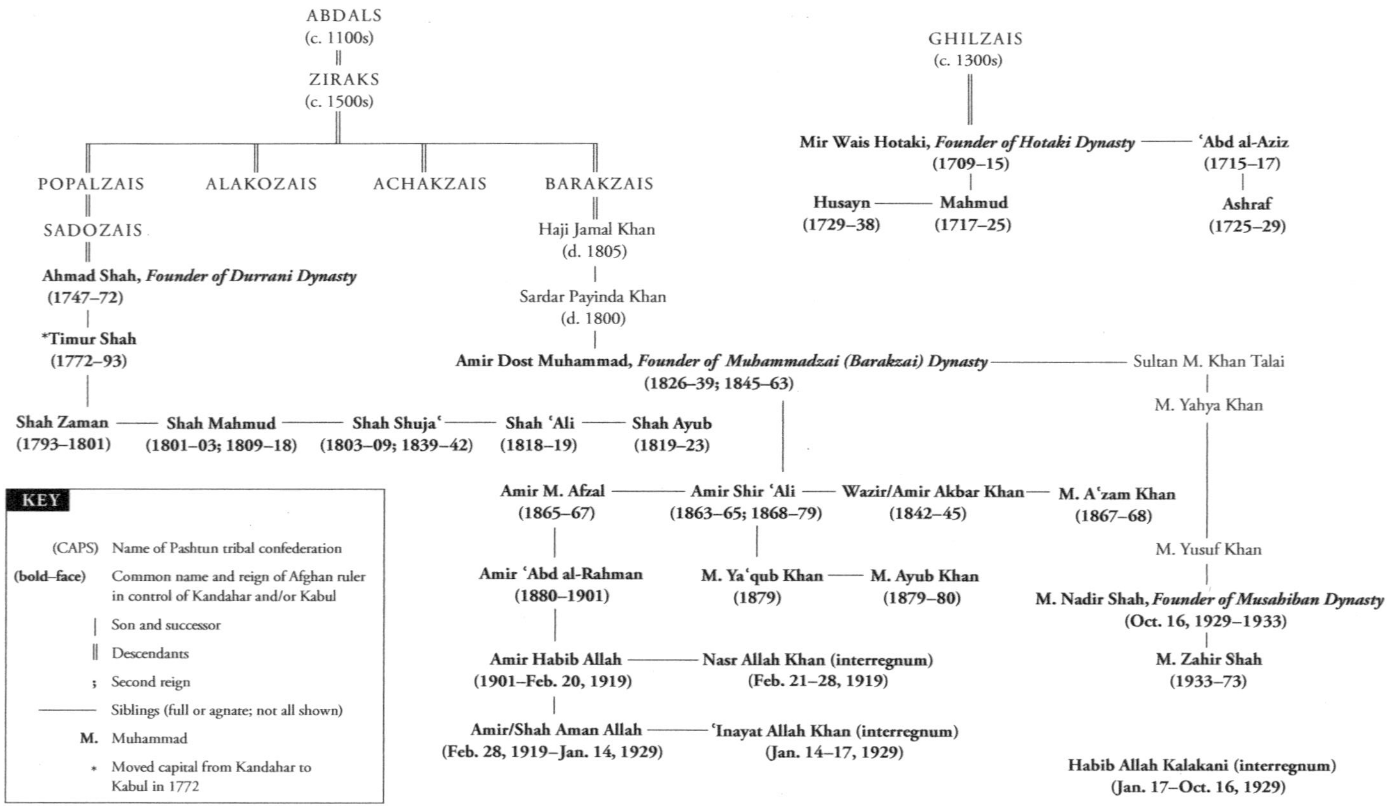

APPENDIX B

Ottoman Publications on Afghanistan (1871–1923)

Title	Author	Published	Language
Afgan Tarihi (Afghan History)	(anon.)	Istanbul, 1871/1872	Turkish
Hindistan, Svat, ve Afganistan Seyahatnamesi (A Travel Book through India, Swat, and Afghanistan)	Ahmed Hamdi Effendi	Istanbul, 1882/1883	Turkish
Tarihçe-i Afganistan (A History of Afghanistan)	El-Seyyid Mehmed Tahir	Istanbul, 1898/1899	Turkish
Afganistan: Küçük Seyahatlar (Afghanistan: Brief Travels)	(anon.)	Istanbul, 1903/1904	Turkish
Resimli Afgan Seyaheti (An Afghan Journey, with Illustrations)	Mehmed Fazlı Effendi	Istanbul, 1907/1908	Turkish
Multiple articles in *Sebilürreşad* newspaper	Tahir el-Mevlevi; S. M. Tevfik; Afganizade; et. al.	Istanbul, 1908–1923	Turkish
Multiple articles in *Takvim-i Vekayi*, *İkdam*, *Şura-yı Ümmet*, *Tanin*, *Vakıt*, *Hayat*, and *Tevhid-i Efkar* magazines and newspapers	(multiple and anon.)	Istanbul, 1908–(1923)	Turkish
Tabkh-i Taʿam bara-yi Maktab-i Funun-i Ḥarbiyyih (Culinary Manual for Harbiye College)	El-Seyyid Mahmud Sami	Kabul, 1918/1919	Persian
Jughrafiyyih-i ʿUmumi-yi Ibtidaʾi bara-yi Shagirdan-i Makatib-i Rushdiyyih-ʾi ʿAskariyyih-ʾi Afghanistan (Beginning Geography for Students of the Military High Schools of Afghanistan)	El-Seyyid Mahmud Sami	Kabul, 1919	Persian
Taʿlimnamih-ʾi Mukhabarih bi-wasitih-ʾi Flamih yaʿni Bayraq (Communications Field Manual, using Flags)	El-Seyyid Mahmud Sami	Kabul, 1919	Persian
Multiple articles in *Hakmiyet-i Milliye* newspaper	(multiple and anon.)	Ankara, 1920–(1923)	Turkish
Bahs-i Akhpur az Taʿlimnamih-ʾi Piyadih (Infantry Field Manual)	El-Seyyid Maḥmud Sami	Kabul, 1920	Persian

Prughram-i ʿIlm-i Hisab bara-yi Shagirdan-i Makatib-i ʿAskariyyih (Arithmetic Course for Students of the Military Schools)	El-Seyyid Mahmud Sami	Kabul, 1920	Persian
Masaʾil dar Bab-i Taʿlim wa Tarbiyyih-ʾi Akhpuri-yi Munfarid (Exercises in Military Education and Training)	El-Seyyid Mahmud Sami	Kabul, 1921	Persian
Miqyasat-i Jadidih (New Handbook on Weights and Measurements)	El-Seyyid Mahmud Sami	Kabul, 1921	Persian
Prughram-i 12-Haftih bara-yi Taʿlim-i Tarbiyyih-ʾi Munfaridih (12-week Manual of Military Instruction and Training)	Ziya Bey (Muhammad Amin, trans.)	Kabul, c. 1920–1922	Turkish, Persian
Amsilih dar Bab-i Qumandihha (Examples from the Field of Command)	El-Seyyid Mahmud Sami	Kabul, 1921/1922	Persian
Mukhtasar magar Mukammal: Sarf wa Nahwi Farsi bih Tarz-i Jadid (Concise but Complete: Modern Persian Grammar and Syntax)	El-Seyyid Mahmud Sami	Kabul, 1922	Persian
Prughram-i Durus-i Fann-i Andakht (Artillery Training Manual)	El-Seyyid Mahmud Sami	Kabul, 1922	Persian
1919 Afgan-İngiliz Harbi (The 1919 Anglo-Afghan War)	(anon.)	Istanbul, 1922/1923	Turkish
Jughrafiya-i ʿAskari (Military Geography)	El-Seyyid Mahmud Sami	Kabul, 1923	Persian
Khadamat-i Safariyyih (On Military Service)	El-Seyyid Mahmud Sami	Kabul, 1923	Persian
Khulasih-i Bahs-i Bayt-i Nizam az Kutub-i ʿAskariyyih-ʾi ʿUsmaniyyih (Primer on Ottoman Military Regulations and Practice)	El-Seyyid Mahmud Sami	Kabul, 1923	Persian
Mukhtasarha-yi Taʿlimnamih-ʾi Suwari (Cavalry Instruction Manual, Abridged)	El-Seyyid Mahmud Sami; Hasan Tahsin	Kabul, 1923	Persian
Prughram-i Nazariyat-i Taʿlim (Theory and Principles of Education)	El-Seyyid Mahmud Sami	Kabul, 1923	Persian
Taʿbiyah (Tactics Manual)	El-Seyyid Mahmud Sami	Kabul, 1923	Persian

APPENDIX C

British Publications on Afghanistan (1839–1933)

Title	Author	Published	Language
An Account of the Kingdom of Cabul and Its Dependencies in Persia, Tartary, and India	Mountstuart Elphinstone	London, 1839	English
Précis of the Principal Correspondence &c. Showing the Policy and Relations of the British Government toward Afghanistan	Trevor Chichele Plowden	Calcutta, 1879 (Confidential)	English
Notes on Afghanistan and Part of Baluchistan	Henry George Raverty	London, 1888	English
Biographical Accounts of Chiefs, Sardars, and Others of Afghanistan	Government of India	Calcutta, 1888 (Confidential)	English
"Progress in Afghanistan," *The Imperial and Asiatic Quarterly Review and Oriental And Colonial Records*	John Alfred Gray	Woking, 1894	English
At the Court of the Amir: A Narrative	John Alfred Gray	London, 1895	English
The Ameer Abdur Rahman	Stephen Wheeler	New York, 1895	English
Multiple issues of *Routes in Afghanistan*	Army Head Quarters, Government of India	Simla / Calcutta, 1907–1923 (Confidential)	English
Under the Absolute Amir	Frank A. Martin	London, 1907	English
"The Visit to India of the Amir Habibullah Khan, the Fourth Amir of the Barakzai Dynasty," *Imperial and Asiatic Quarterly Review and Oriental and Colonial Record*	A.C. Yate	Woking, 1907	English
A Dictionary of the Pathan Tribes on the North-West Frontier of India	Army Head Quarters, Government of India	Calcutta, 1910	English, Pashto
Final Report on Afghanistan	Foreign Department, Government of India	Simla, 1910, 1914 (Secret)	English

Multiple issues of *Summary of Events in Afghanistan*	General Staff, Government of India	Delhi, 1922–1930 (Confidential)	English
Multiple issues of *Gazetteer of Afghanistan*	General Staff, Government of India	Calcutta / Simla, 1908–1917 (Secret)	English
Précis on Afghan Affairs	C. J. Windham	Calcutta, 1914 (Confidential)	English
Multiple issues of *Who's Who in Afghanistan*	General Staff, Government of India	Simla / Delhi, 1914–1933 (Confidential)	English
Notes on Ghilzai and Powindah Tribes	Charles Edward Bruce	Peshawar, 1925 (Confidential)	English
Handbook of the Afghan Army	General Staff, Government of India	Delhi, 1927 (Confidential)	English
A Précis on Afghan Affairs	Richard Roy Machonachie	Simla, 1928 (Secret)	English
"Notes on the Afghan Periodical Press," *Islamic Culture*	L. Bogdanov	Hyderabad Deccan, 1929	English
Afghanistan: From Darius to Amanullah	George Fletcher MacMunn	London, 1929	English
Amanullah: Ex-King of Afghanistan	Roland Wild	London, 1932	English
Handbook of Kandahar Province	General Staff, Government of India	Simla, 1933 (Secret)	English

APPENDIX D

Indian Muslim Publications on Afghanistan (1900–1933)

Title	Author	Published	Language
The Constitution and Laws of Afghanistan	Sultan Mohammad Khan	London, 1900	English
Nayrang-i Afghan (Afghan Charm)	Sayyid Muhammad Husayn	Lucknow, 1904	Urdu
Afghanistan ki Tab'i Jughrafiya'i Tarikhi aur Tamaduni Halat (Afghanistan's Natural, Geographic, Historical, and Civil Conditions)	(anon.)	Lahore, 1909	Urdu
Multiple articles in *Zamindar*	Zafar 'Ali Khan (ed.)	Lahore, 1911–(1933)	Urdu
Multiple articles in *The Comrade*	Mohamed Ali Jauhar (ed.)	Calcutta / Delhi, 1911–1914, 1924–1926	English
Multiple articles in *Hamdard*	Mohamed Ali Jauhar (ed.)	Delhi, 1913–1914, 1924–1929	Urdu
Multiple articles in *Al-Hilal*	Abul Kalam Azad (ed.)	Calcutta, 1912–1914	Urdu
Multiple articles in *Al-Balagh*	Abul Kalam Azad (ed.)	Calcutta, 1915–1916	Urdu
"Afghanistan and the War," *The Near East*	Ikbal Ali Shah	London, 1918	English
"Afghanistan in 1919," *JRCAS*	Ikbal Ali Shah	London, 1920	English
A Review of the Political Situation in Central Asia	Abdul Ghani	Lahore, 1921	English
"The Federation of the Central Asian States under the Kabul Government," *JRCAS*	Ikbal Ali Shah	London, 1921	English
Tuhfih-'i Amaniyyih (The Amani Era)	Najaf 'Ali Khan	Lahore, 1924	Persian

Afghanistan of the Afghans	Ikbal Ali Shah	London, 1928	English
Westward to Mecca: A Journey of Adventure through Afghanistan, Bolshevik Asia, Persia, Iraq, and Hijaz to the Cradle of Islam	Ikbal Ali Shah	London, 1928	English
Siyahat-i Afghanistan Mushtamil bar Kawa'if-i Ta'limat (A Travel Book on Afghanistan, including Educational Conditions)	Haji Mir Shams al-Din	Lahore, 1929	Urdu
Ap Biti (Autobiography)	Zafer Hasan Aybek	Lahore, 193?	Urdu
"Afghanistan since the Revolution," *JRCAS*	Abdul Qadir Khan	London, 1930	English
The Tragedy of Amanullah	Ikbal Ali Shah	London, 1933	English

APPENDIX E

Afghan Works in Islamic Law and Statecraft (1885–1923)

Title	Author	Published	Language
Asas al-Quzat (Foundation of the Judiciary)	Ahmad Jan Khan Alakozai	Kabul, 1885/1886	Persian
Nasaʾih-ʾi Namchih (Advice for Governing)	Amir ʿAbd al-Rahman; ʿAbd al-Razzaq Dihlawi	Kabul, 1885/1886	Persian, Pashto
Risalih-ʾi Najiyih (Book of Salvation)	Qazi ʿAbd al-Rahman	Kabul, 1886/1887	Persian
Sarrishtih-ʾi Islamiyyih-ʾi Rum (The Islamic Administration of the Ottoman Empire)	Mir Muhammad ʿAzim Khan	Kabul, 1886/1887	Persian, Pashto
Kalimat Amir al-Bilad fi al-Targhib ila al-Jihad (Proclamation of the Amir concerning the Call to Jihad)	Amir ʿAbd al-Rahman; Mir Muhammad ʿAzim Khan	Kabul, 1886/1887	Persian
Taqwim al-Din (Almanac of Religion)	Mulla Abu Bakr; ʿAbd al-Razzaq Dihlawi; Mir Muhammad ʿAzim Khan	Kabul, 1888/1889	Persian
Kitab-i Jang-i Rum wa Rus (The Russo-Ottoman War)	Gul Muhammad Khan Muhammadzai	Kabul, 1890/1891	Persian
Kitab-i Qanun-i Afghanistan (The State Laws of Afghanistan)	Amir ʿAbd al-Rahman; Gul Muhammad Khan Muhammadzai	Kabul, n.d. (c. 1890–1900)	Persian
Kitabchih-ʾi Hukumati (Book of Government)	Ahmad Jan Khan Alakozai; Muhammad Jan	Kabul, 1891	Persian
Risalih-ʾi Mauʿizih (Treatise of Admonition)	Gul Muhammad Khan Muhammadzai	Kabul, 1892/1893	Persian, Pashto
Risalih-ʾi Nasayihnamih (Treatise of Advice)	Gul Muhammad Khan Muhammadzai	Kabul, 1893	Persian
Zikr-i Shah-i Islam (An Account of the King of Islam)	Haji Muhammad Khan	Delhi, 1906/1907	Persian, Urdu
Siraj al-Ahkam fi Muʿamalat al-Islam (The Light of Rulings in Islamic Law)	Mir ʿAli Jan Khan; ʿAbd al-Raziq Khan; Muhammad Sarwar Khan	Kabul, c. 1909–1917	Persian, Arabic

Tuhfat al-Amir fi Bayan-i Suluk al-Muluk wa-l-Tadbir (The Amir's Masterpiece in Kingship and Counsel)	Muhammad Taj al-Din Afghani	Lahore, 1910/1911	Persian, Arabic
ʿIlm wa Islamiyat (Sacred Knowledge and Islamic Studies)	Mahmud Tarzi; ʿAbd al-Raʾuf Qandahari	Kabul, 1912	Persian
ʿUmdat al-Faraʾiz (Essentials of Religion)	Nayk Muhammad	Kabul, 1915/1916	Persian
Itaʿat-i Ula al-Amr (Obeying Those in Authority)	ʿAbd al-Rabb; Salih Muhammad	Kabul, 1916	Persian, Pashto
Siraj-i Arkan-i al-Islam (The Light of the Pillars of Islam)	Haji ʿAbd al-Razzaq; ʿAbd al-Rabb	Kabul, 1916	Persian
Kitabchih-ʾi Qanun-i Karguzari-yi Hukkam (Book of Laws for Governors)	(anon.; compiled for Amir Aman Allah)	Kabul, 1919	Persian
S.M.R. l'Emir de l'Afghanistan et le Califat (His Highness the Amir of Afghanistan and the Caliphate)	Amir Aman Allah	Paris, n.d. (c. 1920)	French (translation of speech)
Tamassuk al-Quzat al-Amaniyyih (Handbook for Aman Allah's Judges)	Muhammad ʿAbd al-Wasiʿ Qandahari	Kabul, 1921/1922	Persian
Kulliyat wa Istillihat-i Fiqhiyyih (Maxims and Conventions in Islamic Jurisprudence)	Muhammad ʿAbd al-Wasiʿ Qandahari	Kabul, 1921	Arabic
Nizamnamih-ʾi Asasi-yi Dawlat-i ʿAliyyih-ʾi Afghanistan (The Basic Code of the Exalted State of Afghanistan)	Afghanistan CLC	Kabul, 1923	Persian, Pashto
Seventy-plus supplemental *niẓāmnāmihs* (laws, regulations, or ordinances) spanning civil, criminal, administrative, and municipal affairs including, *inter alia*, marriage and family law; commerce and agriculture; immigration, naturalization, and customs; identity cards and passports; education; taxation; conscription; and government employment	Afghanistan CLC	Kabul, 1919–(1928)	Persian, Pashto

ACKNOWLEDGMENTS

On the evening of June 28, 2011, nine persons armed with AK-47 Kalashnikov machine guns, hand grenades, and vests strapped with explosives stormed the hilltop Kabul Inter-Continental Hotel, one of Afghanistan's most iconic Cold War–era buildings still standing. The fact that I was not pre-identified as a target at the "Inter-Con" did not make the situation any less grave, nor would it have made a difference had I encountered the assailants face to face. Armed with a single wooden chair, I waited for hours in my fourth floor room in suspense as the attackers climbed stairwells and detonated explosions below me, and NATO helicopters fired missiles at them from above. As the floor and walls rocked with explosions, bullets sprayed the hallways, and fire, smoke, and ash filled the building I was trapped in, my chances for lasting the night were slim.

For reasons that remain unknown, however, I did. While this story is of the genre some readers and filmgoers look for when it comes to modern Afghanistan, I have mentioned it here for more personal reasons: other civilians were not so fortunate to tell it. This book is therefore first dedicated to the victims of that night's attack, to their families, and to all children who have endured the scourge of modern warfare—in Afghanistan, in "the region," or anywhere else in the human family.

While surviving that midsummer night in Kabul was a requirement for finishing this book, far more vital to writing it were the years of support of scholars, companions, and relatives across the globe. Their contributions ranged from the financial aid of universities and foundations to the timely advice of colleagues and friends to the unquantifiable and lifelong care of family, for which words can hardly do justice. If I succeeded in telling a different kind of story about Afghanistan, it is because of their help, while all faults and shortcomings remain my own.

The research and writing of this book were made possible by grants from the Social Science Research Council; the Andrew W. Mellon Foundation and Council on Library and Information Resources; the Council of American Overseas Research Centers; the American Institute of Afghanistan Studies; the American Research Institute in Turkey; the Public Interest Law Foundation at Hastings Law; Middle East Studies and the Watson Institute for Public and International Affairs at Brown University; and the Department of History, Center for Middle Eastern Studies, Institute of International Studies, and Center for the Study of Law and Society at the University of California, Berkeley.

An earlier version of Chapter 5 appeared as "In the Name of a Law: Islamic Legal Modernism and the Making of Afghanistan's 1923 Constitution," *International Journal of Middle East Studies* 48 (2016): 655–677. I am grateful to Cambridge University Press for allowing me to reprint it here, as well as to Jeffrey Culang, Akram Khater, and the anonymous readers for their comments on earlier drafts.

At Brown University, several colleagues in the History Department provided invaluable feedback and encouragement during final revisions. I remain obliged to Cynthia Brokaw, Vazira Zamindar, Rebecca Nedostup, Robert Self, Kerry Smith, and Mike Vorenberg for their diligent comments on the entire manuscript. Many thanks also go to participants at a number of conferences and workshops where draft sections were presented, including the Modalities of Modern Muslim Thought panel at the 2017 American Historical Association conference in Denver; the International Law, Sovereignty, and Subjecthood in the Ottoman Empire roundtable at the 2016 Middle East Studies Association conference in Boston, preceded by the 2014 Ottomans Abroad panel in New York; the Islamic Law and Empire conference at Harvard Law School in June 2015; the Early Modern Law in the Muslim World panel at the 2013 American Society of Legal History conference in Miami; the 2012 Social Science Research Council IDRF Workshop in Savannah; and smaller seminars organized at UC Berkeley, UCLA, Istanbul University, and the American Research Institute in Turkey. I am especially grateful to Palmira Brummett, Alan Mikhail, Osamah Khalil, Heather Ferguson, Lena Salaymeh, Malissa Taylor, Nile Green, Leyla Amzi-Erdoğdular, Lâle Can, Chris Low, Will Hanley, Daniella Sarnoff, Robert D. McChesney, Elaine Maisner, Boğaç Ergene, Samy Ayoub, Dina Rizk Khoury, Isa Blumi, Susan Gunasti, Naor Ben-Yehoyada, and Cihan Tuğal for their input at these meetings as discussants or participants, and for many of them still, their enduring advice at different stages of the project.

Cemil Aydin needs to be singled out for his exceptionally keen feedback on the entire manuscript, helping me distill its bigger arguments and contributions, which

I would not have seen otherwise. In the same vein Kerry Smith's indefatigable support and advice on publishing an academic monograph were critical and appreciated at so many stages. At Harvard University Press, I would like to thank my editor, Kathleen McDermott, as well as other members and associates of the professional staff, including Mihaela-Andreea Pacurar, Alexander Morgan, Brian Ostrander of Westchester Publishing Services, Daniel Sentance, and the anonymous readers—all of whom helped improve the entire manuscript. Isabelle Lewis designed five exceptionally difficult maps with exceptional precision and care—a true blend of art and science I am proud to adorn this book with. Not to be forgotten in calling this ship to port were my colleagues Mary Beth Bryson, Cherrie Guerzon, and Julissa Bautista in the History Department, Barbara Oberkoetter in the Middle East Studies program, as well as Joel Revill, Anne Windham, and Kevin McLaughlin in the Dean of Faculty Office at Brown University. Together they provided invaluable logistical support in bringing the book to completion, including myriad administrative tasks, a junior sabbatical, and an unforgettable semester of teaching relief to care for my newborn daughter.

At the opposite end of the timeline, a number of faculty and colleagues at the University of California's Hastings College of Law provided some of the earliest seeds, and timeliest encouragement, to advance my project in uncharted directions as a law student. They include Jo Carillo, George Bisharat, Naomi Roht-Arriaza, Ugo Mattei, Keith Wingate, Reuel Schiller, Evan Lee, Richard Boswell, Karen Musalo, Christina Itturralde, Radhika Rao, John Paul, Ahmed Ibrahim, Mustafa El-Farra, and Salman Alam. I am grateful to every one of them for their support from the earliest stages of this journey.

And then, of course, came the marathon in-between years. At the University of California, Berkeley, the lion's share of this project was completed in the Department of History under an extraordinary team of scholars: Beshara Doumani, Wali Ahmadi, Rebecca McLennan, and Laura Nader. I additionally benefited from the insights and advice of Hamid Algar, Huri İslamoğlu, Munis Faruqui, Baki Tezcan, Janaki Nair, Salim Tamari, Hakeem Naim, and Robert Chester, who read and commented on smaller parts of the work in progress. Also playing memorable roles in the hallways and courtyards of Dwinelle and Barrows Halls were Margaret Anderson, Nicholas Daum, Waldo Martin, David Yaghoubian, Louis Segal, Paula Fass, Robert Brentano, James Vernon, Prachi Deshpande, Thomas Metcalf, Barbara Metcalf, Yuma Totani, Ronald Takaki, Irum Sheikh, Kerwin Klein, Nora Barakat, Melanie Tanielian, Zoe Griffith, Murat Dağlı, Hilary Falb, Samantha Iyer, Nick Kardahji, Giuliana Perrone, Riyad Koya, Kevin Schwartz, Nazanin Shahrokni, Germán Vergara, Pablo Palomino, Mabel Lee, Barbara Hayashida, and Victor Rotenburg—each in their own way and in varying legs of the journey. Columba Muñoz provided timely assistance in the hallowed stacks of Berkeley's Moffitt-Gardner-Doe library complex, as did Adnan Malik and Shayee Khanaka in the South Asia and Middle East special collections, respectively. Beyond this sizeable historians' club, Saba Mahmood, Charles Hirschkind, Stefania Pandolfo, and Lawrence Cohen offered foundational and magnanimous support in a class of its own, sheltering at their inn a young shipwrecked traveler until sunnier skies returned. At Berkeley Law, Calvin Morrill and fellow participants in the first Empirical Legal Studies seminar helped push the project from ideas to ink. I am thankful for their feedback and counsel, pro bono as ever.

The following instructors, many of whom are scholar-poets in their own right, provided invaluable keys to new and inherited linguistic worlds, without which this book would have been a mere daydream: Emad Bakry, Noha Ridwan, Armando Vargas, Muhammad Siddiq, Sonia S'hiri, John Hayes, Yusuf ʿAbd al-Fattah, Ahmad ʿAjwa, Mona Kamel Hassan and all faculty at the Center for Arabic Study Abroad in Cairo, Jaleh Pirnazar, Ahmad Snobar, Faraz Khan, Aftab Ahmad, Ahtesham Ahmad and all faculty at the American Institute of Indian Studies in Lucknow, Ayla and Hamid Algar, Jason Vivrette, Kristin Dickerson, and Eda Ocak. Special gratitude belongs to Recep Çelik, a bona fide Ottoman gentleman, for unlocking the doors of *Osmanlıca*—the less perilous Turkish delight.

From Kabul to California's "Little Kabul" and back, this project would have been unimaginable without the kindness and bigheartedness of Zabiullah and Sara Asmatey and their family, especially Veda and Nemat, Asmat, Khawaja Arghistani, and most of all, Yalda Asmatey. This book is dedicated to them and their relatives for the care and respect they have always shown me.

In Kabul and New York, I also owe an unquantifiable debt to Natalie Rea, Karim Khurram, Mohamed Asem, and the entire staff of the International Legal Foundation's Legal Aid Afghanistan team. Together with many other courageous Afghan lawyers and judges from whom I learned so much in Kabul, they were an inspiration for this book, and much more. Justice Abdul Rasheed Rashid and his family provided especially needed camaraderie and reflection before, during, and thankfully, after a harrowing night. Not to be forgotten are the underappreciated employees of the Afghanistan National Archives in Kabul, an emblem of the city's resilience through decades of war. Not a pixel less of my abiding gratitude goes to Robert D. McChesney and the staff of the Afghanistan Digital Library at New York University, whose contributions were foundational to the research, writing, and illustrations in this book. In San Francisco, Mir Tamim Ansary's kindness and treasured gifts from his emphatically undigitized library were equally appreciated.

In the San Francisco Bay Area, New York and New Jersey, Washington D.C., and the aptly named city of Providence, I have been blessed with the support of a truly special group of colleagues and friends, some of whom would more aptly be called mentors. Ahsan Shaikh, Zaakir Yoonas, Basim Elkarra, Tarek Ghanem, Zaid Shakir, Tahir Anwar, Yahya Rhodus, Ebadur Rahman, Dustin Craun, Justin Benavidez, Armando Vargas, Adriana Valencia, Jed Kroncke, Matthew Ingalls, Munes Tomeh, Yasin Mohammad, Waleed Rashid, Abdul Rahman Jandali, Khaled Kadir, Faisal Ghori,

Akbar Rahel, Farid Yoonas, Rami Elkinawy, Hatem Bazian, Sherman Jackson, Farid Senzai, Najeeb Hasan, Fadia Rafeedie, Najeeb Khoury, Usama Mahmood, Zohaib Ghani, the Iqbals, Sheriffs, and Shibli-Sheriffs, Abdul Hamid and Shaheen Khan, Fiza Qureshi and Adil Haq, Parween and Asmat Qureshi, Abdul Basit Khan (and family), Saadia Yacoob (and family), Amin Venjara, Farah Sheriff, Gadeir Abbas, Issmat Atteereh, David Coolidge, Ikram ul-Haqq, Kazi Salahuddin, Nabeel Sheikh, Adrian Wood-Smith, Sara Ludin, Janet Cooper-Nelson, Françoise Hamlin, Naoko Shibusawa, Vazira Zamindar, Rebecca Nedostup, Mike Vorenberg, Cynthia Brokaw, Robert Self, Caroline Castiglione, Jonathan Conant, Doug Cope, Evelyn Hu-DeHart, Maud Mandel, Ken Sacks, Paris Chronakis, Tom and Sarah Gleason, Jo-Anne Hart, Bill and Susan Twaddell, Engin Akarlı, Jo Guldi, Lukas Rieppel, Daniel Rodriguez, Jeremy Mumford, Jennifer Johnson, Jenny Lambe, Amy Remensnyder, Ethan Pollock, Nancy Jacobs, Tara Nummedal, Lin Fisher, Joan Richards, Sarah Tobin, Stephen Mathis, Ian Straughn, Sherine Hamdy, Zareena Grewal, Hamada Hamid, Nancy Khalek, Elias Muhanna, Mayssun Succarie, Amal Sachedina, Anila Daulatzai, Elizabeth Williams, Zoe Griffith, Julia Gettle, Maariyah Lateef, Naeel Cajee, and Suvaid Yaseen all provided brotherly and sisterly spirits during challenging times—at home and abroad—with a formidable combination of sharp minds and big hearts.

In Istanbul and Ankara, Tony Greenwood, Gülden Güneri, and Nancy Leinwand of the American Research Institute of Turkey, Ayşegül Komsuoğlu, Huri İslamoğlu, Selçuk Esenbel, Yakup Koyuncu, Recep Şentürk, Necmettin Kızılkaya, Mürteza Bedir, Owais Khan, Said Kaymakcı, Meral and Tansel Kaya, and old friends Savaş Serbest, Hayati Aktaş, İnan Bayramoğlu, and Yusuf Alkan provided gracious hospitality, logistical assistance, and ever-ready good cheer. Many thanks are due to the highly professional staff of Turkey's Ottoman, Republican, and Red Crescent Archives, especially Ayten Ardel, Önder Bayır, Esra Oğuztürk, Recep Can, Ülkü Doğan, Hande Uzun Külcü, and Mehtap Baykal Yeşilyurt, even as more urgent responsibilities occupied their schedules. In the same spirit the librarians of Türk Tarih Kurumu, Beyazıt Devlet Kütüphanesi, Boğaziçi University, and Ankara University's Faculties of Theology and Languages, History and Geography were exceedingly helpful in locating rare Ottoman material on Afghanistan in unexpected places. I am also grateful to Ömer Tarzi, Mahmut Tarzi, and Princess Zeynep Ertuğrul Osmanoğlu for the rich oral histories they shared, and for guiding me to the tranquil environs where their grandfather and other revered Ottoman Afghan ancestors were laid to rest.

In India and Pakistan, Justice Nadim Akhtar and family, Anwar Alam, Zafarul Islam, Ebrahim Moosa, Waris Mazhari, ʿAbd al-Qasim and ʿAbd al-Khaliq Madrasi and the deans of Dar al-ʿUlum Deoband, Farhan Zubairi, Najma Rizvi, David Boyk, Sean Chauhan, Ajlai Basu, the Centre for West Asian Studies at Jamia Millia Islamia, Elise Auerbach, Pernima Mehta, and the American Institute of Indian Studies provided generous hospitality and timely aid in securing permissions and other logistics. In "Londonistan," the Altaf and Rahim families and Parvez, Ammar, and Emad Akhtar provided good company and a home away from home during research sojourns in the UK. I am also grateful to all staff of the British Library and India Office Records in London, the National Archives of India in New Delhi, Maulana Azad Library at Aligarh Muslim University, Dar al-ʿUlum Karachi, and the High Court of Sindh for their professional assistance while working in their rich repositories.

East or west, this book could not have been realized without the engaged scholarship, conscientious mentorship, and abiding support of Beshara Doumani, Laura Nader, and Wali Ahmadi, who deserve to be thanked in more places than here. Words cannot describe the faithful pillars, and lighthouses, they have been over the years. Their lanterns were lit during many a dark and foggy night, which a wandering traveler can never forget.

In all of the aforesaid places and more, this journey would have been inconceivable without my greatest companions of all. If not always voluntarily, they weathered the fiercest storms of graduate school and early academic life in my tattered ship without setting foot on a university campus. Aftab and Nazli Ahmed, Khalid and Yasmeen Rauf, Ahmer, Sidra, Saeed, Maria, Mohsen, and Yuna; and the toughest for last, Saman and Enise—you were the most needed, and present, from journey's beginning to end. Beyond words, this book is dedicated to you.

INDEX

www.ingramcontent.com/pod-product-compliance
Lightning Source LLC
LaVergne TN
LVHW102013210926
848483LV00014B/447/J
* 9 7 8 0 6 7 4 9 7 1 9 4 3 *